SPECIAL PUBLICATION
of CARNEGIE MUSEUM OF NATURAL HISTORY

T. M.

SPECIES OF SPECIAL CONCERN
IN PENNSYLVANIA

compiled by
PENNSYLVANIA BIOLOGICAL SURVEY

edited by
HUGH H. GENOWAYS
Carnegie Museum of Natural History

FRED J. BRENNER
Grove City College

THIS SPECIAL PUBLICATION IS PUBLISHED
WITH SUPPORT FROM THE PENNSYLVANIA WILD
RESOURCE CONSERVATION FUND

NUMBER 11   PITTSBURGH, 1985

SPECIAL PUBLICATION OF CARNEGIE MUSEUM OF NATURAL HISTORY

Number 11, pages 1–430

Issued 25 January 1985

Price $30.00 a copy

ISBN 0-935868-11-9

Library of Congress number 84-73248

Financial support for this project was supplied by the following agencies and foundations:
    Carnegie Museum of Natural History
    Landfall Foundation
    Leonard S. Mudge Environmental Education Program, Carnegie Museum of Natural History
    Mid-Atlantic Region, National Audubon Society
    Pennsylvania Department of Environmental Resources
    Pennsylvania Fish Commission
    Pennsylvania Game Commission
    Pennsylvania Herpetological Survey, Carnegie Museum of Natural History
    Philadelphia Academy of Natural Sciences
    Rockwell Foundation

Maps used in text were prepared by Patricia E. Brenner, Grove City, PA

CARNEGIE MUSEUM OF NATURAL HISTORY, 4400 FORBES AVENUE
PITTSBURGH, PENNSYLVANIA 15213

PENNSYLVANIA BIOLOGICAL SURVEY

Coordinating Committee

John Ginaven . . . . Tyler Arboretum
Barbara Haas . . . . Ridley Creek State Park
Frank Haas . . . . Ridley Creek State Park
Robert Leberman . . . . Powdermill Nature Reserve
Alexander Nagy . . . . Hawk Mountain Sanctuary
David Pearson . . . . Pennsylvania State University
Phillip S. Street . . . . Chester Springs, PA
James G. Stull . . . . Waterford, PA
Jean H. Stull . . . . Waterford, PA
Merrill Wood . . . . Pennsylvania State University

Mammal Committee

Hugh H. Genoways, *Chairman* . . . . Carnegie Museum of Natural History
Kenneth Andersen . . . . Gannon University
Harry N. Cunningham . . . . Behrend Campus of Pennsylvania State University
Peter L. Dalby . . . . Clarion University
John E. Enders . . . . Keystone Junior College
John S. Hall . . . . Albright College
Gordon L. Kirkland, Jr. . . . . Shippensburg University
Joseph F. Merritt . . . . Powdermill Nature Reserve
Duane A. Schlitter . . . . Carnegie Museum of Natural History
Alan Woolf . . . . Southern Illinois University
David A. Zegers . . . . Millersville University

CONTENTS

EDITORS' FOREWORD

We feel very privileged to have been involved in the production of this book. The completion of this project has taken the ideas and work of many people throughout the Commonwealth and beyond. All of these individuals gave their time and efforts on a strictly voluntary basis, because they believed that an evaluation of the species of special concern was needed in Pennsylvania.

This book should not be viewed as a static conclusion to our efforts but as a dynamic beginning. This book is meant to be a blueprint for action in saving the most endangered and threatened portions of our flora and fauna. This action is the responsibility of several state agencies, professional scientists, and the general public of the Commonwealth. As will be pointed out in many places in this book, the lists of plants and animals will need to be updated on a regular basis. Professional scientists will be responsible for generating the necessary basic research information concerning the species on this list. The responsible government agencies must maintain these lists and formulate management plans that will improve the status of species on the lists and will eventually lead to their removal from the lists.

The general public can have a significant impact on the future of these species. They can demand and support the implementation of management plans that improve the status of these species of special concern. Citizens of the Commonwealth now have the opportunity to give direct financial contributions to programs concerning plants and nongame species of animals. With the passage of the Pennsylvania Wild Resource Conservation Act, these citizens can check off a portion or all of their state income tax return for support of these programs. This will be the first time that substantial funds will be available for the study and management of these plant and animal groups.

With the passage of time, the data in this book will become outdated; however, these data will always be the baseline against which future studies will be measured. This book represents the best estimation of the Pennsylvania Biological Survey of the status of the species of special concern in Pennsylvania as of 31 December 1982. The distributional and biological information available for each of the species have also been summarized. Each account includes citations to more extensive information concerning the species.

We would like to take this opportunity to thank several people who were very instrumental in assisting us in the preparation of the final manuscript for publication. Patricia E. Brenner translated our rough maps into the camera-ready copy that you see throughout this book. Marion A. Burgwin, Suzanne B. McLaren, and Jane A. Casne tenaciously sought out errors and inconsistencies in the materials that we were editing. Their efforts have significantly improved this book. Mary Ann Schmidt retyped many pages of the manuscript and made numerous telephone calls to coordinate our efforts and to gather final information for several of the accounts. The assistance of Stephen L. Williams on several aspects of this project has hastened the completion of the final manuscript. Finally, we wish again to thank all of the authors and editors who have worked on this book. Without their efforts, this book would not be a reality.

Hugh H. Genoways
Pittsburgh, PA

Fred J. Brenner
Grove City, PA

11 April 1983

INTRODUCTION
and
ENVIRONMENT

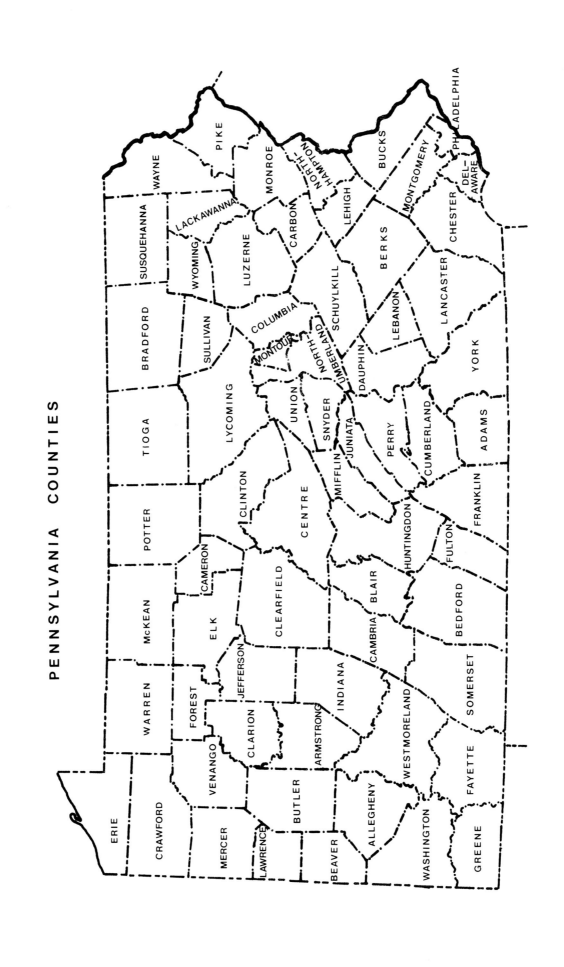

PENNSYLVANIA COUNTIES

INTRODUCTION

FRANK DUNSTAN—*National Audubon Society*

The Pennsylvania Biological Survey (PBS) was formed in early 1979 when representatives of the sponsoring organizations (National Audubon Society, Pennsylvania Game Commission, Pennsylvania Fish Commission, and Department of Environmental Resources) met to discuss the need for an organized, coordinated, and integrated biological inventory and assessment of the flora and fauna of the Commonwealth. It was decided that the first activity of the PBS was to determine which plant and animal species were in trouble within the state. Thus Phase 1 of Pennsylvania's Biological Survey, published here, determines the degree of threat to species, subspecies, and unique local populations of the native fauna and flora of the Commonwealth. *Species of Special Concern in Pennsylvania* deals with those plant and animal species whose continued existence in the Commonwealth is either threatened to a significant degree or which, because of biological factors or other causes, have a potential likelihood of becoming extirpated if present trends continue.

The species accounts included in this volume are not simply listing and categorizing species, but they include a description of the organism and its habitat requirements, geographic occurrence, population status, other aspects of its life history and ecology, and the documented threats to its existence. Authors have recommended actions that may stabilize the species by correcting factors influencing its decline. The value of this information in the decision-making process at the federal, state, local and private level is obvious. Unfortunately, we cannot guarantee that with the biological facts available, ecologically sound decisions will be made. What can be achieved, however, by this effort is the removal of ignorance with respect to Pennsylvania's fauna and flora that today characterizes many of the actions and decisions of our fellow citizens.

In 1979, when the need for a biological survey was discussed, it was recognized that we had little more than a concept. We had no financial support for field inventories or paid staff; therefore, if efforts to create a Pennsylvania Biological Survey were to succeed, we would have to utilize volunteers and limit our effort to existing and available resource information. Fortunately, Pennsylvania has a vast cadre of interested and knowledgeable professional biologists and amateur naturalists. It is these volunteers who contributed their time and knowledge so that *Species of Special Concern in Pennsylvania* could be published. We chose to pattern our endeavor after that of Florida, with some modification, hence many similarities occur in the format as well as in the definitions of the status categories.

Chairmen of the taxonomic committees were selected based on their expertise and willingness to contribute to the work. They, in turn, solicited members to participate in committee deliberations and species descriptions. Committee chairmen and representatives from sponsoring organizations formed the Coordinating Committee. The committee's initial presentation to the public was at a March 1981 conference hosted by Carnegie Museum of Natural History and sponsored by the Leonard S. Mudge Environmental Education Program. Approximately 250 participants attended the one day conference in Pittsburgh, thus demonstrating a sincere public interest in Pennsylvania's endangered and threatened species. The comments received at this meeting were included in the revised species accounts by the committees, thereby reflecting broader citizen participation. Although the status of a few species were debated, the group generally concurred with committee designations for the majority of the species.

The collective findings for the five classes of vertebrates, selected taxons of invertebrates, and vascular plants found within Pennsylvania are as follows: endangered, 36 species; threatened, 41 species; vulnerable, 85 species; status undetermined, 55 species; extirpated, 79 species; and extinct, 1 species.

It should be noted, however, that the status of each species was evaluated only with regard to its condition within the Commonwealth. Thus, a peripheral species whose range extends into Pennsylvania may be listed, even though the species may be abundant in other states. Although the use of political boundaries as a limit to define species status is an artifact, it nevertheless has potential value after the causal factor is identified. If the range of a species in Pennsylvania is limited because of natural reasons, it may not warrant concern; while on the other hand, if human activities are the cause of the limited range then action may be necessary.

These then, in the judgement of experts, are the species that deserve attention and action in order to stabilize or increase their populations thereby removing the threat to their existence. In the case of those species listed as endangered or threatened, immediate action must be undertaken if we are to maintain these organisms as a part of the Pennsylvania environment. While the degree of threat to vulnerable species is less than that of endangered or threatened species, in many cases management or other protective measures undertaken now will have a better chance of being successful and most likely, will be less costly to implement. The vulnerable category serves as a first warning to resource agencies and should be included with endangered and threatened species for targeting Wild Resource Fund monies. Species assigned to the status undetermined category clearly need a consorted effort to obtain additional information on their status. This category should serve as a priority list for field research and inventory.

In a broader sense, *Species of Special Concern in Pennsylvania* may serve to illustrate geographical portions of the state that are under the heaviest pressures from human activities. If a disproportionate number of species of special concern share similar geographic ranges, we may assume therefore, that this area is stressed. Consequently, we may be able to determine the exact factors associated with stressed habitats or plant-animal communities.

As the practical uses for *Species of Special Concern in Pennsylvania* are identified and consolidated actions are implemented to save species from extirpation or extinction, we must not forget that the PBS must be an ongoing process in order to be successful. There not only is a need to monitor our efforts to save these species but we must also update information on these species on a regular basis. Beyond monitoring endangered and threatened species we need to develop a system for monitoring and assessing all native plant and animal species within the Commonwealth. Only after this type of biotic information is available to us can we fully evaluate the impacts of human activities on the environment.

For Pennsylvania, an ongoing biological survey program may present political problems because three state agencies with separate jurisdictional responsibilities and powers are involved. Historically, little cooperation has occurred between these agencies perhaps because of the narrow limits they have previously imposed on themselves and parochial attitudes harbored by some of their staff. However, as they expand from their traditional user-oriented roles to encompass endangered and threatened species and nongame programs based on ecological principals, there exists ample opportunity for cooperation. The recently enacted Wild Resources Conservation Act serves not only as a mechanism to generate funds but also as the focal point for continuing and coordinating the Pennsylvania Biological Survey. Integration of the biotic information in one centralized location seems more logical than creation of three separate data banks. Because each of the agencies requires access to all the biological information (not just the information for which it has responsibility), cooperation would appear to be a necessity.

It is our recommendation that the Pennsylvania Biological Survey formally be continued by the renewable resource agencies. A data storage and retrieval system should be organized, perhaps under the Wild Resources Board, so that the biotic information can be integrated by the individual agencies that implement actions on behalf of organisms under their jurisdiction. If properly managed, the Pennsylvania Biological Survey will continue to be a unique blend of professional biologists and amateur naturalists contributing their time and knowledge to the continued existence of the native fauna and flora of Pennsylvania. — *(Current address) Sanctuary Department, National Audubon Society, West Cornwall Road, Sharon, CT 06069.*

Ralph W. Abele—*Pennsylvania Fish Commission*

Although the Pennsylvania Fish Commission has for many years been responsible for fish, frogs, tadpoles, and turtles, a series of statutory changes beginning in 1974 and culminating in the present Fish and Boat Code has given the Fish Commission jurisdiction for all fishes, amphibians, reptiles, and aquatic organisms found in the Commonwealth. Included among these are 16 species of fishes, amphibians, and reptiles currently listed as endangered or threatened by our agency or by the U.S. Fish and

Wildlife Service, and made a part of our regulations following recommendations from a Herpetology Advisory Committee and an Advisory Committee on Fishes. These committees also recommended another 36 species of fishes, amphibians, and reptiles for indeterminate status. Although not made a part of our regulations, this list of indeterminate species identifies those species most likely to become endangered or threatened.

Because there are about 250 species or subspecies of fishes, amphibians, and reptiles indigenous to Pennsylvania, the 52 endangered, threatened, or status-indeterminate species constitute about 20 percent of that number. While that percentage may seem small to some, we consider it much too high. Added to this figure are 24 other species, or about 10 percent of the total number, that no longer occur in the Commonwealth. Among these species are two fishes, the blue pike (*Stizostedion vitreum glaucum*) and longjaw cisco (*Coregonus alpenae*), both former inhabitants of the Great Lakes.

As a conservative estimate, there are perhaps 20,000 invertebrate species in Pennsylvania. The Fish Commission is responsible for the aquatic species, including those of the mollusks, crustaceans, and insects, among others. They are important to man as living barometers of environmental conditions, as food organisms, and as efficient performers of unique tasks required for the proper functioning of a healthy environment. We have often taken them for granted, or treated them with contempt. We need to monitor the status of these species because their well-being is inextricably tied to the well-being of man and other life forms.

The *extirpation* of any of our species from Pennsylvania, or the *extinction* of any of these from the face of the earth, may be considered by some to be the result of natural forces at work. But, in fact, the direct and indirect results of man's activities have been, and are, largely responsible for the growing number of species' extirpations and extinctions. Man's ignorance and greed concerning the relative importance and right to existence of other living things have impoverished his own existence, but that circumstance must, and can, be changed.

This publication will assist in dispelling our ignorance about those species of concern in Pennsylvania that require man's assistance if they are to survive. It will serve to identify those species which require priority expenditures of time and money, in order that their essential habitat and other needs may be protected and maintained, and their future status as secure members of the Commonwealth's flora and fauna assured. Finally, this publication will serve as a reminder of the sort of environmental stewards we are called upon to be and a milestone against which to measure our achievements for the benefit of future generations. — *Executive Director, Pennsylvania Fish Commission, Harrisburg.*

GLENN L. BOWERS — *Pennsylvania Game Commission*

The Pennsylvania Game Commission is responsible for all wild birds and mammals in the Commonwealth as mandated by law. The Commission's involvement in and endorsement of this publication stems from the recognition that some species are rarely seen or are not as common as they once were. Maybe they are secretive; more likely their scarcity or decline is the predictable result of habitat loss or deterioration. These species are the subject of this publication and of the Game Commission's special concern.

In effect, the Game Commission considers this benchmark publication to be a listing of research and management priorities. "*Endangered*" and "*Threatened*" species need first attention. As Durward Allen, in Part 1 of a "Report of the Committee on North American Wildlife Policy 1973" put it:

"In a sense, our program for wildlife is a holding action. Today and in the years immediately ahead, the first big job is to prevent irreversible losses — of species, populations, and life communities."

Also, mammal and bird species classified as "*Vulnerable*" or "*Status Undetermined*" must be studied. Perhaps certain ones will need constant monitoring. In the past, without periodic monitoring of population levels, some species declined unnoticed. All of a sudden, they were endangered and required concentrated effort to prevent their extinction or extirpation from Pennsylvania. We can no longer afford to take this shortsighted and expensive tack. Population monitoring and aquisition, and improvement of critical habitats can help prevent species from becoming endangered in the first place. This is not only a wise, but a fiscally conservative strategy. For example, eight of 13 birds (62%) listed as *"Endangered"* or *"Threatened"* in Pennsylvania are associated with wetland habitats. In a most basic sense, we can consider wetlands, too, as being endangered or threatened. Aquisition and sensitive management of such habitat is an obvious first step if we are to prevent, slow, or reverse population declines of wetland wildlife species.

It must be emphasized that with new knowledge and management, the status of some species will change. It is the Game Commission's goal to see that change is for the better, that a future such publication will list fewer and not more species as extirpated, endangered, or threatened in Pennsylvania. As public trustee in the task of wildlife conservation, we are committed to perpetuating this state's rich wildlife heritage intact for the use and enjoyment of future generations. — *Executive Director, Pennsylvania Game Commission, Harrisburg.*

PETER S. DUNCAN — *Department of Environmental Resources*

Article I, Section 27, of the Pennsylvania Constitution, known as the Environmental Rights Amendment states:

"The people have a right to clean air, pure water, and to the preservation of natural, scenic, historic, and aesthetic values of the environment. Pennsylvania's public natural resources are the common property of all the people, including generations yet to come. As a trustee of these resources, the Commonwealth shall conserve and maintain them for the benefit of all the people."

An important step in upholding the Environmental Rights Amendment is the identification of the elements of our natural heritage that are endangered or threatened, the species of special concern. This is the first logical step in the management and protection of any natural resource.

The Department of Environmental Resources is the agency responsible for environmental protection and the management of the water, air, soil, and floristic natural resources of the Commonwealth. The recently passed Wild Resources Conservation Act mandates that DER establish a list of endangered, threatened, and vulnerable plants and that it develop regulations and management programs to insure the protection and perpetuation of these species. The information provided in *Species of Special Concern* will be useful in the administration of a number of DER programs such as the Statewide Environmental Master Plan, water and sewage facilities planning, surface mine and water quality permits, public land management, and environmental review processes and wild plant management.

I see the publication of *Species of Special Concern in Pennsylvania* as a major accomplishment and an important step in protecting and managing the Commonwealth's natural resources. — *Secretary Department of Environmental Resources, Harrisburg.*

AQUATIC AND TERRESTRIAL HABITATS IN PENNSYLVANIA

FRED J. BRENNER

INTRODUCTION

The Commonwealth of Pennsylvania has a vast array of diverse and unique aquatic and terrestrial habitats occurring within its boundaries. These aquatic habitats include streams of all magnitudes as well as lakes and various types of wetlands, while terrestrial habitats include areas in various stages of succession from grasslands to climax forests. Rock outcroppings and talus slopes are other terrestrial habitats common to the mountainous regions of the Commonwealth. Caves are also common features in this region of Pennsylvania, especially in limestone formations. Many plants and animals have evolved over long periods of time in association with a particular habitat and, therefore, any alteration—either natural or man-related—will result in a change in size and composition of these communities. The overall objective of this chapter is to briefly describe the general characteristics of different habitats occurring in Pennsylvania as a guide to the individual species description. In general, these classifications are based on the previous descriptions by Erdman and Wiegman (1974) for natural areas of Pennsylvania. However, in some cases these descriptions have been modified in light of more recent and accepted classification systems.

AQUATIC HABITATS

Open water habitats include those areas of non-flowing, or slowly water greater than 2 m in depth with surface or near-surface vegetation along the edges. In a recent classification system, Cowardin et al. (1979) described open water habitats as characterized by permanently flooded lands lying below the deepwater boundary of wetlands. Deepwater habitats include environments where surface water is permanent and often deep, so that water, rather than air, is the principle medium in which the dominant organisms live regardless of whether or not they are attached to the substrate. The dominant plants are hydrophytes and the substrates are considered nonsoil because the water is too deep to support emergent vegetation (U.S. Soil Conservation Service, Soil Survey Staff, 1975).

Deep water habitats would include the limnetic zone and those portions of the littoral zone where the water depth is 2 m or greater. These areas include both natural and artificial lakes and ponds. Naturally deep water habitats would include kettle-hole, oxbow, and dune lakes, whereas artificial lakes include all those created by human activities such as flood control, recreation, or surface mining. Kettle-hole lakes occur only in the glaciated physiographic provinces of the northwestern and northeastern sections of Pennsylvania. Oxbow lakes are associated with large meandering streams or river systems. Those artificial systems created by damming a water course may either maintain a relatively stable water level for recreation or fluctuate depending on the degree of seasonal draw-down for flood control purposes.

RIVERINE SYSTEMS

A Riverine System includes all aquatic habitats contained within a channel (Fig. 1) with the exception of (1) habitats dominated by trees, shrubs, persistent emergents and emergent mosses or lichens or (2) water containing ocean-derived salts in excess of 0.5 percent (Cowardin et al., 1979). A channel is hereby defined as an open conduit naturally or artificially created, containing periodically or continuously moving water or connecting two bodies of standing water (Langbein and Iseri, 1960). Riverine systems are bounded on the landward side by upland, the channel bank or a wetland dominated by trees, shrubs, persistent emergents, emergent mosses or lichens (Cowardin et al., 1979). In braided streams, the system is bounded by the outer limits of the depression within which the braiding occurs.

Riverine systems terminate at the downstream end where the concentration of ocean-derived salts in the water exceeds 0.5 percent during the period of annual average flow or where the channel enters a lake. It terminates at the upstream end where tributary systems originate or where the channel leaves a lake. Springs discharging into a channel are gen-

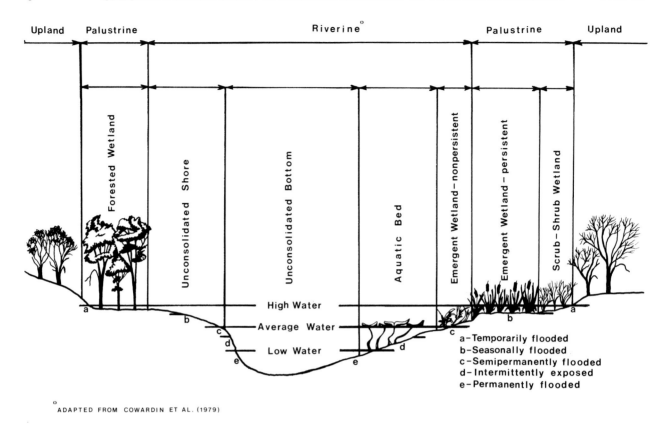

a–Temporarily flooded
b–Seasonally flooded
c–Semipermanently flooded
d–Intermittently exposed
e–Permanently flooded

ADAPTED FROM COWARDIN ET AL. (1979)

Fig. 1.—Illustration of a Riverine Wetland System as adapted from Cowardin et al. (1979).

erally considered part of the Riverine System. Flowing waters are classified according to the order of magnitude of stream size. Cowardin et al. (1979) divided the Riverine System into four sub-systems: the tidal, the lower perennial, the upper perennial, and the intermittant all of which may or may not be present in the same system. Each subsystem is defined in terms of water permanence, gradient, water velocity, substrate, and extent of flood plain development.

The *tidal system* is characterized by a low gradient (under 3 m/km), well-developed flood plain and water velocity fluctuating under tidal influence. The *lower perennial* subsystem has a typically low gradient, slow velocity, water flow throughout the year, and a substrate mainly of sand and mud. The *upper perennial* subsystem is characterized by a high gradient (over 3 m/km), swift velocity, water flow throughout the year and a substrate consisting of rock, cobbles, gravel, and occasional patches of sand. In this system the flood plain is not well developed. In the *intermittent* subsystem the channel contains flowing water for only part of the year which

may remain throughout the remainder of the year in isolated pools or be entirely absent.

AQUATIC-TERRESTRIAL TRANSITION

These habitats are adjacent to bodies of water, and are subjected to periodic flooding. The vegetational patterns are generally not well developed, but are, however, characterized by specific types of native vegetation. Some ecologists believe that, if these habitats occur along streams or rivers, they should be considered part of the Riverine System because their presence is a result of flooding. However, Reid and Wood (1976) proposed that a flood plain is a flat expanse of land bordering an old river that may never or only occassionally be flooded. Hence, it is this subsurface water that controls to a great extent the level of lake surfaces, the flow of streams, and the extent of swamps and marshes. These areas should, therefore, be considered as distinctive habitat types and not part of the Riverine System. Two of these areas are rare in Pennsylvania—the Tidal Mud Flat confined to the lower reaches of the Delaware River and the Sandy Lake

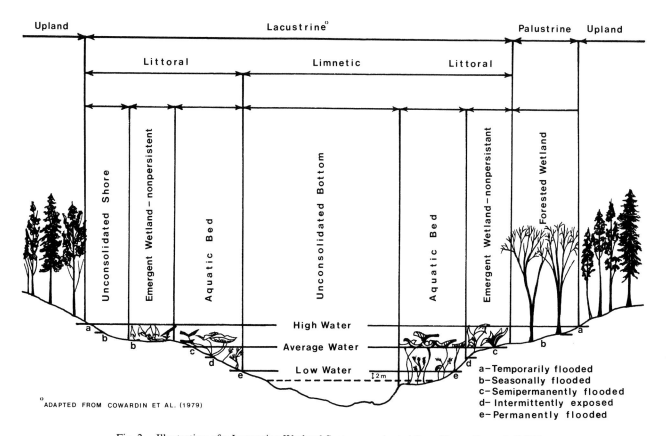

Fig. 2.—Illustration of a Lacustrine Wetland System as adapted from Cowardin et al. (1979).

Shore confined along Lake Erie, both of which contain distinctive and characteristic vegetative communities containing rare species.

WETLANDS

According to the classification system derived by Cowardin et al. (1979), wetlands are transitional lands between terrestrial and aquatic systems where the land is covered by shallow water or where the water table is generally at or near the surface. Wetlands must have one or more of the following three criteria: (1) at least periodically, the land must support hydrophytes predominantly, (2) the substrate is predominantly undrained hydric soil and (3) termed nonsoil, saturated with water or covered by shallow water at some time during the growing season each year.

In Pennsylvania, the term wetlands generally includes those areas with hydrophytes and hydric soils, commonly referred to as marshes, swamps, and bogs. The upland limit of wetlands is designated as (1) the boundary between land with predominantly hydrophytic cover and land with predominantly meso-

phytic or xerophytic cover, (2) the boundary between predominantly hydric and non-hydric soils, or (3) if vegetation is lacking, the boundary between land that is saturated sometime each year and land that is not.

The following discussion of wetland habitats is based on the classification system proposed by Cowardin et al. (1979). In Pennsylvania, two wetland systems would comprise the majority of these habitats.

The *Lacustrine System* includes wetlands and deep water habitats with the following three characteristics: (1) situated in a topographical depression or a dammed river channel (Fig. 2), (2) lacking trees, shrubs, persistent emergents, emergent mosses or lichens with greater than 30 percent coverage, and (3) total area exceeding 8 ha (20 acres). The Lacustrine System is bounded by upland or wetland dominated by trees, shrubs, persistant emergents, emergent mosses or lichens and permanently flooded lakes and reservoirs.

The second major type of wetland habitat is the *Palustrine System* which includes all nontidal wet-

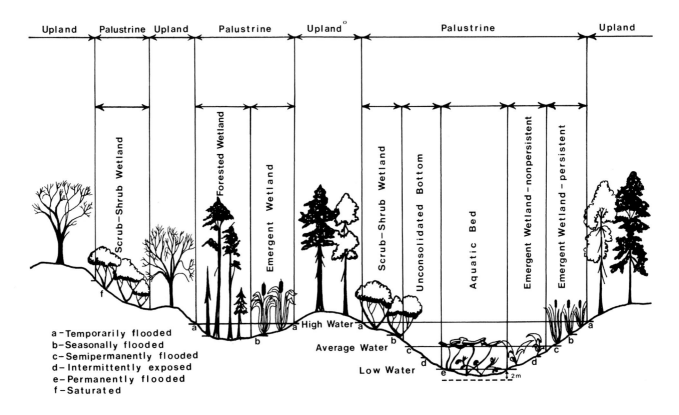

Fig. 3.—Illustration of a Palustrine Wetland System as adapted from Cowardin et al. (1979).

land dominated by trees, shrubs, persistent emergents, emergent mosses or lichens or tidal wetlands where salinity due to ocean-derived salts is below 0.5 percent (Fig. 3). Included within this system are the traditional wetlands such as bogs, marshes, and swamps. These systems are further subdivided into classes, subclasses and dominate types with "class" being the highest taxonomic unit below subsystem describing the general appearance of the habitat in terms of the dominant vegetation life form or the physiography and composition of the substrate, "subclass" defining the finer differences in life forms, and "dominant type" determining the dominant plant species.

Palustrine wetlands that occur in Pennsylvania are moss-wetlands or bogs and various subclasses of emergent-wetlands such as marshes and swamps. Moss-wetland, commonly referred to as bogs, include those areas where mosses cover substrate other than rocks and where emergent shrubs, or trees comprise less than 30 percent of the areal cover. In Pennsylvania, the principal moss species is Sphag-

num which forms a floating mat extending from the outer edges over the water surface. These areas are generally acidic and lack a regular flowing inlet or outlet.

Emergent wetlands are characterized by erect, rooted, herbaceous hydrophytes, including mosses and lichens. These wetlands are usually dominated by perennial plants that are present for most of the growing season. Emergent wetlands have a regular flowing inlet and outlet. In areas such as Pennsylvania with relatively stable climatic conditions, these wetlands have the same appearance. Emergent wetlands are generally referred to as marshes and are divided into two subclasses—"Persistent" and "Nonpersistent" with further subdivisions according to the dominant vegetation.

Persistent Emergent Wetlands are dominated by species that normally remain standing until the beginning of the next growing season. This subclass is found only in Estuarine and Palustrine systems. In an Estuarine System along the Atlantic coast, these areas are commonly dominated by various species of cordgrass (*Spartina* spp.), narrow leaved cattail (*Typha angustifolia*), and possibly southern wild rice (*Zizaniopsis millacea*) (Cowardin et al., 1979). *Palustrine Persistent Emergent Wetlands* are fresh water systems and contain a vast array of species including *Typha* spp., bullrushes (*Scirpus* spp.), saw grass (*Cladium jamaicensis*), sedges (*Carex* spp.), and reed grass (*Phragmites communis*). A variety of broad-leaved persistent emergents such as purple loosestrife (*Lythrum salicaria*), dock (*Rumex mexicanus*) and smartweeds (*Polygonum* spp.). In the subclass *Nonpersistent Wetlands,* the dominant vegetation are those species which fall to the surface of the substrate or below the water surface at the end of the growing season. Dominant species may include arrow arum (*Peltandra virginica*), pickleweed (*Pontederia cordata*) and arrowheads (*Sagittaria* spp.).

The other two classes of wetlands that occur in Pennsylvania are the *Scrub-Shrub* and *Forested Wetlands,* both of which have a defined inlet and outlet. The class—*Scrub-Shrub Wetlands*—includes those areas dominated by woody vegetation less than 6 m in height. These wetlands may be a successional stage leading to a Forested Wetland or relatively stable communities (Cowardin et al., 1979).

Subclasses and Dominant Types of Scrub-Shrub Wetland:

1. Broad-leaved deciduous. In an Estuarine System, these wetlands would be dominated by species such as sea-myrtle (*Baccharis halimifolia*) and marsh alder (*Iva frutescens*), whereas in a Palustrine System, alders (*Alnus* spp.), willows (*Salix* spp.), buttonbush (*Cephalanthus occidentalis*), red osier dogwood (*Cornus stolonifera*), and young red maples (*Acer rubrum*) are common species.

2. Needle-leaved Deciduous. The dominant vegetation of these wetlands are predominantly needle-leaf deciduous trees and shrubs such as young or stunted tamaracks (*Larix laricina*).

3. Broad-leaf Evergreen. These Palustrine Wetlands are typically found on organic soils and the dominant vegetation species such as laboratory tea (*Ledum groenlandicum*) and bog laurel (*Kalmia polifolia*).

4. Needle-leaved Evergreen. The dominant vegetation of these wetlands includes young or stunted black spruce (*Picea mariàna*) and other conifers.

5. Dead. These are wetlands created by a prolonged increase in the water table from an impoundment of water by beavers, man, or other activity.

The other class of wetlands common in Pennsylvania is the *Forested Wetland*. These wetlands are characterized by woody vegetation that is 6 m or taller (Cowardin et al., 1979). Forested wetlands are common in Pennsylvania as well as in other regions in the northeast and are commonly referred to as a swamp. Forest wetlands only occur in Palustrine and Estuarine systems.

Subclasses and Dominant Types of Forested Wetland:

1. Broad-leaved Deciduous. This is the most common forested wetland occurring in Pennsylvania. The common dominants includes such species as red maple (*Acer rubrum*), ashes (*Fraxinus pennsylvanica* and *F. nigra*), American elm (*Ulmus americana*), black gum (*Nyssa sylvatica*), swamp white oak (*Quercus bicolor*), and pin oak (*Q. palustris*). These wetlands commonly occur on mineral or decomposed organic soils.

2. Needle-leaved Deciduous. These wetlands commonly occur on organic soils with tamarack as a characteristic species.

3. Needle-leaved Evergreen. These wetlands also occur on organic soils with black spruce as the major dominant species. Black Spruce, however, is common on nutrient-poor soils while northern white cedar (*Thuja occidentalis*) dominates on more nutrient-rich soils.

4. Dead. As with Shrub Wetlands, dead forested wetlands occur as a result of impoundments either created by beavers, man or other activities.

The other aquatic habitat common to Pennsylvania are *springs* which are areas where ground water flows from the subterranean formations onto the surface or into a larger body of water. The chemical characteristics of these areas is dependent on the geological formation from which the water is derived.

GEOLOGIC COMMUNITIES

Three different habitats that support distinctive geologic communities have developed as a result of unique geologic formations occurring in different sections of Pennsylvania. The first of these are classified as rock outcrops and talus slopes that generally occur on steep or almost vertical slopes. These habitats occur primarily in the central and southwestern mountainous regions of the state. Vegetation on these sites is limited to small crevices. A talus slope is hereby defined as a sloping mass of rocky fragments which may or may not be associated with a rock outcropping. The plant communities on these areas are generally sparse with an irregular distribution. As with rock outcroppings, these habitats occur in mountainous sections of the state.

Another habitat that is maintained because of unique geologic and/or climatic conditions are areas commonly referred to as the "barrens." The sandy soils of these areas are usually low in nutrients and, thus, are infertile. The "barrens" area located in the Nittany Valley has a distinctive history in addition to its unique ecological characteristics. This area occupies some 20,000 ha extending from near Belle- fonte, Center County, to Birmingham, Huntington County. The soil is derived from the iron-bearing sandstone which accounts for its infertility. In some places the sandstone becomes pure sand reaching a depth of 21 m.

The first accounts of this region in 1784 refers to its as "The Great Pine Barrens." This area was lum- bered extensively for oaks, chestnut (*Castanea den- tata*), and pines which were the original forest cover. Exploitation of iron deposits began around 1800 and terminated shortly after the turn of the century. It was the "barrens" that provided Andrew Carnegie with the opportunity to found his iron and steel empire around the community of Scotia Benne or Scotia, as it was commonly called. This town was founded by Carnegie in honor of his home area in Scotland. The remaining trees were removed from the area to supply charcoal for the iron furnaces.

The dominant vegetation of the "barrens" is pri- marily oaks and blueberries (*Vaccinium* spp.) with occassional patches of pines, aspen (*Populus tremu- loides, P. grandidentata*), willows, and a few other hardwood species. Repeated fires in this region has destroyed the organic content of the soil which not only contributed to the lower fertility but also re- duced the moisture and heat retaining capacities of these sandy soils. In addition to the reduced soil fertility, the climatic conditions were also a factor in maintaining the plant communities characteristic of the area. The barrens average 45 frost-free days per year and temperatures as low as $-12°C$ have been recorded in the middle of May.

In addition to the sand barrens, shale barrens oc- cur in south-central Pennsylvania where outcrops of Brallier Shales of the Devonian Period are com- mon. The shale barrens are often less than 4 ha in size but they contain many endemic plant species because of the unusual soil conditions (Erdman and Wiegman, 1974). Serpentine outcrops are other bar- rens-type of habitats but these are restricted to southeastern Pennsylvania, primarily Chester and Delaware counties. These areas support a prairie- like plant community containing many endemic species.

The last geologic community to be discussed as a separate habitat is that of caves and rock shelters. A rock shelter is defined as an opening caused by an overhanging rock or created by an expansion of a joint or fracture in a sandstone formation. These caverns have a relatively shallow depth and are not a true cave. Caves, on the other hand, are generally formed in a limestone formation as a result of the erosive action of an underground stream although caves may also be formed in sandstone formations. These subterranean habitats may be extensive and are characterized by a fairly constant temperature (10°C) and high humidity. Many of these extensive cave systems have been opened to the public as a commercial enterprise (for example, Penn's Cav- erns, Indian Caverns, Laurel Caverns, and others), which may have been detrimental to the natural cave communities.

TERRESTRIAL HABITATS

Terrestrial habitats encompass diverse types of plant communities from cultivated fields to climax forests, however, because the primary objective of this chapter is to discuss the types of natural habitats in Pennsylvania, the majority of it will be devoted to that end.

GRASSLAND HABITATS

Old field communities are a common grassland habitat occurring throughout Pennsylvania. These generally represent areas that have been abandoned from agriculture and are in various stages of succes- sion, reverting back to a forest community. A few native grassland or prairie communities do, how- ever, occur in Pennsylvania such as the Blazing Star Meadow in Beaver County and Jennings Environ- mental Education Center, Butler County. Both of these areas support blazing star (*Liatris spicata*) communities (Jennings, 1953) while the endangered Massassauga rattlesnake (*Sistrurus catnatus*) also occurs in the Jennings Preserve. There are several other areas of similar quality occurring in Butler and adjacent counties (Erdman and Wiegman, 1974).

Prairie grassland communities also exist on the shale and serpentine barrens discussed previously. The plant communities occurring on the shale barrens include endemic species such as barrens ragwort (*Senecio antennariifolius*), Kate's Mountain clover (*Trifolium virginicum*), barren's bindweed (*Convolvulus spithamaeus*), and barrens evening primrose (*Oenothera argillicola*). The serpentine barrens plant communities include several prairie grasses unique to that region of Pennsylvania. All of these natural prairie communities are subjected to the continual invasion of woody vegetation and, therefore, in order to maintain these grasslands, they must be intensively managed. For example, the sections of Blazing Star communities at the Jennings Environmental Education Center are burned on a rotating basis in order to preserve the prairie community.

Grasslands are also being created by the reclamation of surface mines, often with exotic species. It would be possible, however, that by altering reclamation procedures, habitats could be created that would include both rare and endangered plant and animal species. For example, the development of grasslands as a result of strip-mining has been shown to attract bird species which did not occur in the area prior to mining (Whitmore, 1979). These habitats in Pennsylvania have been shown to support diverse plant and animal communities (Brenner, 1981, 1982). The concept of using mine land reclamation as a means to develop habitat for rare and endangered species should be given consideration by both the coal industry and enforcement agencies.

FOREST HABITATS

Pennsylvania is within the Eastern Deciduous Forest Biome of North America. Human disturbance along with variations in typography, climate, drainage patterns, geologic formations and soil types has resulted in a variety of primary and secondary communities. Braun (1950) divided Pennsylvania into four broad forest regions: beech-maple forest of glaciated regions, mixed mesophytic forest of southwestern Pennsylvania, hemlock-white pine-northern hardwood occupying the central plateaus and northeastern region, and oak-chestnut forest within the Piedmont and Ridge and Valley Provinces (fig. 1, Guilday, this volume).

These basic forest types have been redefined by Kuchler (1964) and the U.S. Forest Service (1968)

according to the dominant species which constitute each forest type. Kuchler (1964) redefined the boundaries proposed by Braun (1950) and, recognizing that the chestnut was no longer a dominant species, this region was redefined as Appalachian Oak Forest as was all the mixed mesophytic region with the exception of a narrow zone along the West Virginia border which was retained as mixed mesophytic.

In addition, Kuchler (1964) classified the pine-hickory-oak forest in the south-central region of the state as a principal forest type. The conifer bog and the red spruce-northern hardwood forest as defined by Kuchler only occurs in the state on a limited basis. The different forest types found in Pennsylvania will be described according to both the classification proposed by Kuchler as well as that used by the U.S. Forest Service (Ferguson, 1968; Powell and Considine, 1982). Kuchler described six different forest regions in Pennsylvania which were also used by Erdman and Wiegman (1974) in describing the natural areas of Pennsylvania. Hence, this classification will receive somewhat greater attention than the system used by the forest service.

The following forest types occurring in Pennsylvania are based on the descriptions of Kuchler (1964) and Erdman and Wiegman (1974):

1. Hemlock-Northern Hardwood. This forest type was probably common in the state prior to the extensive logging and fires that occurred in the late 1800's. This forest type is usually present in cooler climates so that the present warming trend and total removal of forest by logging may be the factors that resulted in a shift of this forest type to mixed oak communities. Several stands of the hemlock-northern hardwood forest, however, remain on plateau summits and the steep north slopes of the Ridge and Valley Provinces (fig. 1; Guilday, this volume). The Tionesta Scenic Area and Tionesta Research Natural Areas in McKean and Warren counties are examples of a hemlock-northern hardwood forest. In the Ridge and Valley Province, the original forests were comprised of nearly pure stands of hemlock along with a mixture of white pine (*Pinus strobus*), beech (*Fagus grandifolia*), and a mixture of various hardwoods. Successional communities are either mixed oak or composed of a mixture of aspens, birches (*Betula* spp.), red maple (*Acer rubrum*), black cherry (*Prunus serotina*) as well as the hemlock-northern hardwood species.

2. Beech-Maple Forest. This forest type occurred in northwestern Pennsylvania in an area delineated

by the boundaries of the Wisconsin Glaciation. The dominant species in the upland forest were beech and sugar maple (*Acer saccharum*) but repeated lumbering and farming have altered the species composition in this region. The older communities occurring in ravines are basically hemlock-northern hardwood forests while secondary forests may either be predominately beech or sugar maple or comprised of other species including aspen, red maple, black cherry, and white ash (*Fraxinus americana*). One of the best examples of virgin beech-sugar maple stands is Tryon's Woods located near Conneaut Lake, Crawford County and Jumbo Woods (State Game Lands 101) on the Crawford-Erie County Line.

3. Appalachian Oak Forest. These communities have the greatest distribution and abundance of all the forest types occurring in Pennsylvania. This forest is composed of a mixture of red (*Quércus rúbra*), white (*Q. álba*), black (*Q. velùtina*), scarlet (*Q. coccinea*) and chestnut (*Q. prinus*) oaks interspersed with pines (*Pinus* spp.), hemlock, maples, hickories, and other hardwoods. The areas originally occupied by this forest type (chestnut-oak, Braun, 1950) have either been logged extentensively and/or subjected to human habitation and farming. Hence, primeval stands are difficult to identify. It is possible, however, that virgin stands of oak forest may occur in the Pine Creek Gorge Natural Area located in the Tioga State Forest (Erdman and Wiegman, 1974). Virgin chestnut-oak stands may occur on some steep south slopes but few of these stands have been identified.

4. Mixed Mesophytic Forest. This forest type is the most diverse of the forest types occurring within the Eastern Deciduous Forest Biome. Pennsylvania is the northern limit of the mixed mesophytic forest and the chief indicator species of Braun (1950), neglected (white) basswood (*Tilia negléctea*), only occurs in southwestern Pennsylvania. In the northern regions, these communities retain the high canopy species diversity and abundant herbaceous layer but they also show a transition into other forest types. These forests currently possess a lack of old growth and have a prevelence of successional species. Hence, the original composition of these communities is not well understood. The Wissahickon Valley in Philadelphia is the best example of a mature second growth stand of mixed mesophytic forest occurring in Pennsylvania. This area is also of interest, because it represents one of the earliest attempts at land preservation in the country, dating from the 1870's (Erdman and Wiegman, 1974).

Table 1.—*Basis of stand classification by the U.S. Forest Service.*

Stand classification	Characteristics
Sawtimber	Commercial species of minimum diameter Breast height (DBH)—soft wood—22.5 cm; hardwood—27.5 cm and contains at least a 3.6 m merchantable saw log.
Pole-timber	Commercial species—DBH—soft wood—12.5–22.5 cm; hardwood—12.5–27.5 cm.
Sapling-seedling	Commercial species less than 12.5 cm DBH.

These four forest regions overlap in western Pennsylvania with Appalachian oak occurring on drier sites and with either mixed mesophytic or beech-maple forest being present on the moist slopes and river valleys while hemlock-hardwood communities persist in the steeper ravines.

5. Oak-Hickory-Pine Forest. The northern limit for this forest region is the Valley and Ridge Province in extreme south-central Pennsylvania. The key dominants of this forest as defined by Kuchler are not always present but these communities currently are composed of a mixture of oaks along with white pine (*P. strobus*), pitch pine (*P. rigida*), and Virginia pine (*P. virginiana*). The original species composition of these communities in Pennsylvania is unknown due in part to the absence of virgin stands of this community in the state.

6. Northern Hardwoods-Spruce Forest. These forest types originally occurred on the plateaus from New York to West Virginia. The best example of this forest type occurs in Hickory Run State Park in the Poconos which probably contains the only virgin spruce forest in Pennsylvania.

These forest types are based primarily on the original forest communities found in the state. However, these communities have been altered through extensive lumbering, fires, agriculture and other activities affecting both the size and species composition of these communities.

U.S. FOREST SERVICE CLASSIFICATION

A forest stand as defined by the U.S. Forest Service is a growth of trees on a minimum of 10 acres that is at least 10 percent stocked by trees of any size. Sawtimber stands (Table 1) are defined as an area in which at least 10 percent of the trees are growing stock trees and 50 percent or greater of the stand stocked with sawtimber that is at least equal

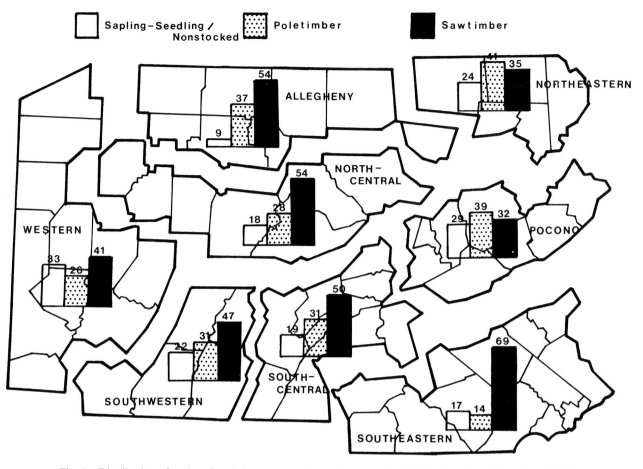

Fig. 4.—Distribution of various forest size classes in Pennsylvania as classified by Powell and Considine (1982).

to poletimber. Poletimber stands, on the other hand, are defined as an area at least 10 percent stocked with growing stock trees and 50 percent or more in sawtimber and poletimber, with poletimber exceeding the sawtimber.

While sapling and seedling stands are defined as an area where at least 10 percent of the area is stocked with growing-stock trees and sapling and/or seedlings make up the plurality of the stocking. A nonstocked area is hereby defined as forest lands that are less than 10 percent stocked with growing trees. The distinction of these various stands among the forest communities vary in the different geographic regions of the state. The proportion of the forest communities that is in sawtimber is greater in the southeast than it is in other regions of the state. Sawtimber represents 50 percent or more of the stands throughout the central region of Pennsylvania. However, sawtimber exceeds the other stand classes in all regions of the state except the Pocono region (Fig. 4) (Powell and Considine, 1982).

The species composition of these various regions has also been altered by a variety of natural and human activities. The U.S. Forest Service recognized nine basic forest types in Pennsylvania based on species composition. The following classification is based upon the majority of stocking by all live trees of various species. If no indicator species makes up the majority, the forest type is then determined on the basis of plurality of stocking (Ferguson, 1968).

1. White Pine: Forests in which 50 percent or more of the stand is eastern white pine. These forests also include a small acreage where hemlock is the dominant species.

2. Spruce: Forests in which 50 percent or more of the stand is any species of spruce.

3. Virginia: Forests in which 50 percent or more of the stand is either Virginia, pitch, or other pines, singularly or in combination.

4. Oak-Pine: Forests in which 50 percent or more of the stand is hardwood, usually upland oaks. Pines also make up 25–49 percent of the stand. This type

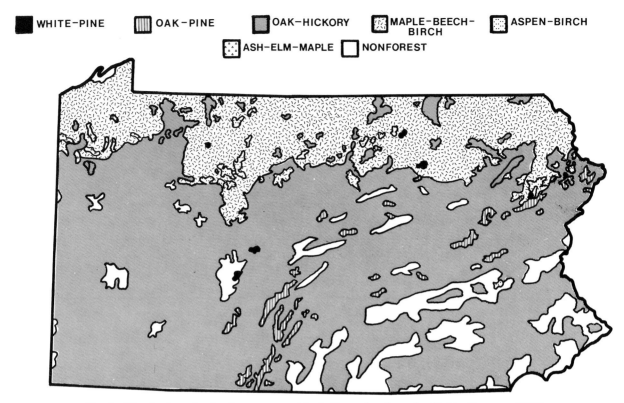

Fig. 5.—Distribution of major forest communities in Pennsylvania as classified by Ferguson (1968).

also includes a small acreage in eastern redcedar-hardwood type.

5. Oak-Hickory: Forests in which 50 percent or more of the stand is upland oaks or hickory, singularly or in combination, Where pines comprise 25–49 percent, it would be classified as oak-pine. This forest type also includes the yellow poplar-oak forest.

6. Oak-Gum: These for the most part are Riverine Forests in which 50 percent or more of the stand is black gum (*Nyssa sylvática*), sweet gum (*Liquidambar syraciflua*) or oaks, singularly or in combination. Where pines comprise 25–49 percent, the stand would be classified as oak-pine.

7. Elm-Ash-Red Maple: Forests in which 50 percent or more of the stand is American elm (*Ulmus americana*), black ash (*Fraxinus nigra*), or red maple, singularly or in combination. When all three species occur, it usually indicates wet soil conditions. Red maple stands on upland sites comprise the majority of the acreage on this broad forest type.

8. Maple-Beech-Birch: Forests in which 50 percent or more of the stand is sugar maple, beech, or

yellow birch (*Betula lutea*), singularly or in combination. This forest type includes extensive areas of black cherry.

9. Aspen-Birch: Forest in which 50 percent or more of the stand is aspen, paper birch (*B. papyrifera*), gray birch (*B. populifolia*), or pin cherry (*Prunus pennsylvanica*) singularly or in combination.

The oak-hickory forest is currently the dominant forest type occurring in Pennsylvania and, aside from the maple-beech-birch community, occurs primarily across the northern section of the state. Other minor forest types are scattered around the state (Fig. 5). Spruce forests are not considered a major forest type in Pennsylvania because their distribution is limited primarily to the Pocono region extending south to Bear Meadows in Center County. While Virginia pine-pitch pine forests also are not considered a major forest type in Pennsylvania, these species have been planted on surface coal mines during reclamation (Brenner et al., 1975). In general, the U.S. Forest Service assigns the northern one-third of Pennsylvania to the *Northern Hardwood Forest Section* of the Laurentian. Mixed Forest

Province and the southern two-thirds to the *Appalachian Oak Forest Section* of the Eastern Deciduous Forest Province (Bailey, 1980).

In summary, Pennsylvania possess a diversity of both aquatic and terrestrial habitat types including open water, wetlands, grasslands and forest communities. A large number of both plant and animals that are discussed throughout this volume have specialized and unique habitat requirements. Although many of these habitats have been or are currently being destroyed by natural and/or human activity, it may possible to create the specialized habitats required by some species during surface mine reclamation, land fills and other land restoration efforts. This will, however, require a re-evaluation of both governmental agencies and industry on the objectives of land restoration.

LITERATURE CITED

BAILEY, R. G. 1980. Description of the ecoregions of the United States. U.S. Dept. Agriculture Misc. Publ., 1391:1–77.

BRAUN, E. L. 1950. Deciduous forests of eastern North America. Hafner Publ. Co., New York, 596 pp.

BRENNER, F. J., R. H. CROWLEY, M. J. MUSAUS, and J. H. GOTH III. 1975. Evaluation and recommendations of strip-mine reclamation procedures for maximum sediment-erosion control and wildlife potential. Third Symp. Surface Mine Reclamation, II:3–23.

BRENNER, F. J., and J. KELLY. 1981. Characteristics of avian communities on surface mine lands in Pennsylvania. Environmental Management, 5:441–449.

BRENNER, F. J., R. B. KELLY, and J. KELLY. 1982. Mammalian community characteristics on surface mine lands in Pennsylvania. Environmental Management, 6:241–249.

COWARDIN, L. M., V. CARTER, F. C. GOLET, and E. T. LaROE. 1979. Classification of wetlands and deepwater habitats of the United States. U.S. Dept. of the Interior, FWS/OBS 79/81, 103 pp.

ERDMAN, K. S., and P. G. WIEGMAN. 1974. Preliminary list of natural areas in Pennsylvania. Western Pennsylvania Conservancy, Pittsburgh, 106 pp.

FERGUSON, R. M. 1968. The timber resources of Pennsylvania. U.S. Forest Service Resource Bull. NE-8, 147 pp.

JENNINGS, O. E. 1953. Wild flowers of western Pennsylvania and the upper Ohio basin. Univ. Pittsburgh Press, Pittsburgh, 574 pp.

KUCHLER, A. W. 1964. Manual to accompany the map of potential natural vegetation of the conterminous United States. Amer. Geogr. Soc. Spec. Publ., 36:1–116.

LANGBEIN, W. B., and R. T. ISERI. 1960. General introduction and hydrologic definitions manual of hydrology. Part 1. General surface-water techniques. U.S. Geol. Surv. Water Supply Publ. 1541-A, 20 pp.

POWELL, D. S., and F. J. CONSIDINE, JR. 1982. An analysis of Pennsylvania forest resources. U.S. Forest Service. Resource Bull. NE-69, 96 pp.

REID, G. K., and R. D. WOOD. 1976. Ecology of inland waters and estuaries. D. Van Nostrand and Co., New York, 485 pp.

U.S. SOIL CONSERVATION SERVICE, SOIL SURVEY STAFF. 1975. Soil taxonomy: a basic system of soil classification for making and interpreting soil surveys. U.S. Soil Conservation Service, Agric. Handbook, 436:1–754.

WHITMORE, R. C. 1978. Managing reclaimed surface mines in West Virginia to promote non-game birds. Pp. 381–388, *in* Proc. Surface Mining and Fish/Wildlife Needs in the Eastern United States (D. E. Samuel, J. R. Stauffer, C. H. Hocutt, and W. F. Mason, Jr., eds.), FWS/OBS 78/81. 388 pp.

Address: Biology Department, Grove City College, Grove City, PA 16127.

THE PHYSIOGRAPHIC PROVINCES OF PENNSYLVANIA

John E. Guilday

INTRODUCTION

Pennsylvania (117,412 square km) is a 480 km transit of the Appalachian Mountain system from tidewater at Marcus Hook, on upper Delaware Bay, to the shore of Lake Erie. Its irregular eastern boundary, formed by the Delaware River, is at approximately 74°43'W longitude. Its western boundary, surveyed in 1779, is at 80°31'W longitude. Except for a 65 km jog (surv: 1792) to the lake, the state is bounded on the north by latitude 42°N (surv: 1786–1787) and 260 km to the south by latitude 39°43'N (surv: 1763–1767, the Mason-Dixon Line).

The Commonwealth is divided into six physiographic provinces (Fig. 1)—Coastal Plain, Piedmont, Blue Ridge (and its geological continuum, a small portion of the New England province), Valley and Ridge, Appalachian Plateau, and Central Lowland. Their make-up reflects the variety of the rocks underlying them and the effects of past volcanic and sedimentary processes, crustal uplift, peneplanation, erosion, and glaciation (Fig. 2).

PROVINCES

COASTAL PLAIN PROVINCE

A narrow strip of eastern Delaware, Philadelphia, and Bucks county from five to eight km wide, along the west bank of the lower Delaware River in the southeastern corner of the state, is classified as Coastal Plain. The topography is low and gently rolling, sloping gradually toward the Delaware River. Elevation above sea level nowhere exceeds 18 m. This flat belt of unconsolidated sands and silts is primarily reworked Pleistocene and Holocene river sediments. Several low terraces along the Schuylkill River record successive relatively recent changes in sea level. The city of Philadelphia is built, in part, on a Pleistocene terrace of the Delaware River. The river in its lower reaches is influenced by the tide, and both fresh and brackish saltwater marshes occur regionally.

PIEDMONT PROVINCE

Piedmont Upland Section

Leaving the Coastal Plain and proceeding inland, a belt of low rounded hills, composed of Cambrian and Precambrian igneous and metamorphic crystalline rocks, schists, gneisses, and quartzites, rise gently about 60 m above the surrounding valleys. These Piedmont highlands are dissected by narrow valleys but the former plateau-like appearance of the uplands, although modified by prolonged erosion, is still apparent and topographic relief is slight, except near the rivers. West of the Susquehanna River the uplands continue to rise to a general elevation of 300 m above sea level, but the overall topography remains gently rolling. In western York County, the upland slopes end abruptly as a low ridge 200–300 m above sea level, overlooking the Hanover-York Valley. As the Susquehanna River enters these rocky uplands from the northwest, its valley constricts and the river has entrenched deeply so that local relief may be as much as 150 m. Many of its smaller direct tributaries such as Counselman Run, Oakland Run, and Otter Creek, in York County, and Ferncliff and Kelly Runs in Lancaster County, are cool rocky gorges with high stream gradients and occasional waterfalls, more reminiscent of northern Pennsylvania than of the Piedmont. The Piedmont Uplands, in Chester and Northumberland counties, have serpentine outcrops which form characteristic "barrens." Intrusive igneous rocks contain small amounts of lead, zinc, and chromite, formerly of some importance but no longer of commercial value.

Conestoga Valley Section

West of the Piedmont Uplands the Conestoga and Chester valleys are broad rolling plains with little relief, underlain by Cambrian and Ordovician limestones and shales. These sedimentary rocks are more easily eroded than the crystalline Piedmont Uplands, and the Lancaster and Chester valley plains lie at an altitude of 60–120 m above sea level. Precambrian volcanics are exposed in small areas of the Pigeon and Hellam hills, and the underlying

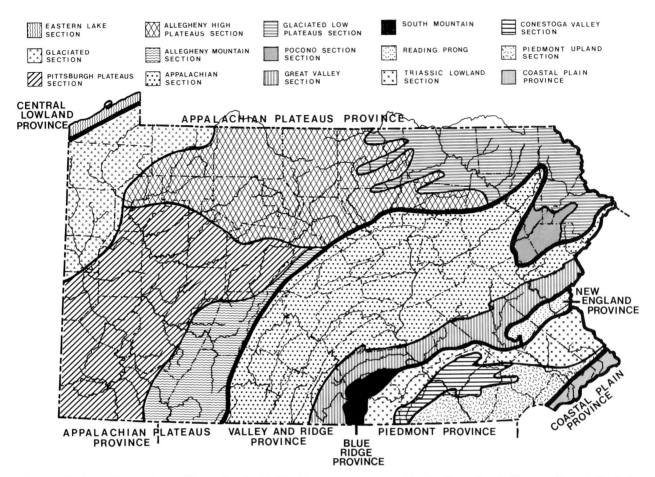

Fig. 1.—Physiographic provinces of Pennsylvania. Modified from a map prepared by the Pennsylvania Topographic and Geologic Survey, Arthur A. Socolow, State Geologist.

geological structure composed of distorted folds and thrust faults is complicated. Limestone areas of the valley contain sinkholes, disappearing streams, and some caves. The Lancaster, or Conestoga Valley, settled by the "Pennsylvania Dutch" in the late 1600's and the early 1700's, has been cleared and cultivated for over 250 years and remains one of the most productive of agricultural areas in Pennsylvania.

Triassic Lowlands Section

Proceeding north and west from the Piedmont Uplands and the Conestoga Valley, one encounters the broad 15 to 80 km wide Triassic Lowlands, trending southwest to northeast through Adams, York, Dauphin, Lebanon, and parts of Lancaster, Berks, Montgomery, and Bucks counties. Beyond the Delaware River, in New Jersey, the Triassic Lowlands continue north to the Hudson River. The

province is a lowland only in a structural sense. Topographically it is an uplifted plain composed of soft reddish freshwater sandstones and shales of Triassic age some 60 m higher than the older limestone lowlands to the north and south. The general level of this hilly plain rises 120–180 m above sea level. It is criss-crossed with dikes and sills of highly resistant volcanic rock, trap or diabase, that intruded in molten form through the Triassic strata, baking the adjacent rocks as it did so, and altering their makeup. These ridges rise above the general land level as outcrops of jumbled rocky woodlands, bypassed by agriculture. Two of the most famous volcanic structures of the Triassic Lowlands are Cemetery Ridge in Adams County, which the Confederate Army charged in vain during the battle of Gettysburg, and the picturesque Palisades of the Hudson, in New Jersey. The Cornwall Mine, south of Lebanon, provided the iron for Revolutionary

GEOLOGIC MAP OF PENNSYLVANIA

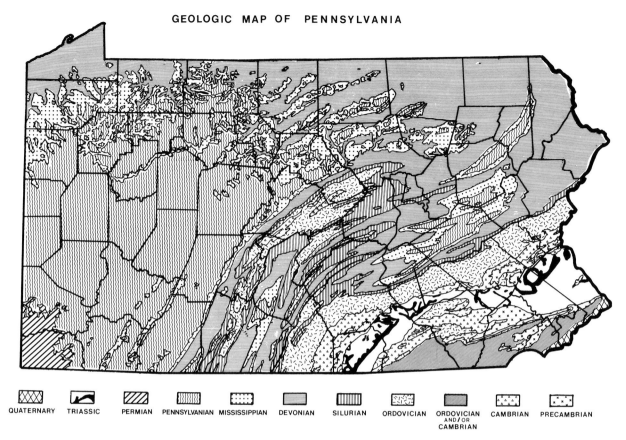

Fig. 2.—Geologic map of Pennsylvania. Modified from a map prepared by the Pennsylvania Topographic and Geologic Survey, Arthur A. Socolow, State Geologist.

War cannon and shot, and its magnetite ore body, associated with volcanic activity, was mined continuously from 1742 until 1973.

BLUE RIDGE AND NEW ENGLAND PROVINCES

South Mountain, in the Blue Ridge Province, and the Reading Prong, or Reading Hills, in the New England Province, are geologically related, although discontinuous in the state. They constitute a belt of dense Precambrian and Cambrian crystalline rocks lying between the Triassic Lowlands to the south, and the Paleozoic rocks of the Valley and Ridge Province to the northwest.

New England Province (Reading Prong)

The Reading Prong begins west of the Schuylkill River, as a series of isolated hills in Berks County, and extends east for 65 km to the Delaware River. It is a rugged range of hills composed of metamorphic and igneous granite, gneiss, schist, and quartzite. The average elevation of the Reading Hills varies from 250–300 m above sea level, some 90–120

m above the surrounding lowlands. Rounded summits rise more than 240 m above the Great Valley to the north, and reach a maximum height of 400 m above sea level. These hills are deeply dissected by stream valleys to a depth of 150 m. The residual loamy soils have been derived from the underlying igneous and metamorphic rocks. The rough terrain promotes erosion, but the soils are excellent for farming where slopes are not too extreme.

Blue Ridge Province (South Mountain Section)

South Mountain begins in Cumberland County, just south of Carlisle, runs south through western Adams and eastern Franklin counties for 65 km, where it crosses into Maryland to continue south to form the Catoctin Mountains and the Blue Ridge Mountains of Virginia. Rising abruptly between the Triassic Lowlands to the east and the Great Valley to the west, the hills of the South Mountain Section range from 450 m above sea level, in Cumberland County, to 630 m above sea level at Snowy Mountain, and 640 m above sea level at Big Pine Flat

Ridge, in Adams County. In Pennsylvania, these mountains are composed of almost flat-topped ridges, rocky tumbles, and deeply eroded valleys. Stream gradients are high, 90–120 m per km, and Conewego Creek has cut a deep 200-m gorge as it traverses the mountain. Geologically, South Mountain is a large, over-turned, faulted, asymmetrical anticline composed of erosion resistant Cambrian and Precambrian metamorphic and igneous rocks. Residual soils are primarily stony loam, normally well-drained and agriculturally important where the topography permits. South Mountain is a rugged, well-forested wildlife habitat in the midst of a highly populated agricultural region.

Valley and Ridge Province

(Ridge and Valley Section of some authors)

The remaining three-fourths of the state, the Valley and Ridge, Appalachian Plateau, and Central Lowlands Sections are underlain by sedimentary rocks that vary in age from Cambrian to lower Permian, and the topography is governed by the effects of erosion upon the rock layers of varying resistance and pitch. The Valley and Ridge Province is divided into the Great Valley Section to the southeast, and the rugged Appalachian Mountain Section to the north and west.

Great Valley Section

The Great Valley, known in Pennsylvania as the Lehigh, Lebanon, or Cumberland Valley, extends in an eastward-trending arc for 320 km from Franklin and eastern Fulton counties in the south, through parts of Cumberland, Dauphin, Lebanon, Berks, Lehigh, and Northampton counties in the east. It runs south into Maryland as the Hagerstown Valley, through Virginia as the Shenandoah Valley, and continues through Tennessee to northern Alabama. In Pennsylvania it forms a broad, undulating to moderately hilly, lowland plain, underlain by Ordovician shales and limestones, with elevations varying from 120–180 m above sea level. Its average width is 30 km, between the Piedmont Uplands and the Appalachian Mountains that flank it on the north and west. Except for the major rivers that cross the valley, the Susquehanna, the Schuylkill, the Lehigh, and the Delaware, there is little surface drainage. Stream gradients are gentle and there is some entrenching; meandering Conodoguinet Creek, a tributary of the Susquehanna River in Franklin and Cumberland counties, has entrenched to a depth of

40 m. A large portion of the drainage is subterranean in limestone areas, and the valley floor contains many sinkholes, disappearing streams, and other karst features. The residual soils are largely the result of solution and weathering of limestones, dolomites, and some shales, leaving a residue of deep, silt/clay loam, varying in color from brown to reddish. These soils, known as the Hagerstown-Frederick group, are some of the most productive and valuable farmlands in the state. They are also found on the Lancaster Plain and Chester Valley in the Piedmont Province to the southeast, and in some of the intermontane valleys of the Appalachian Mountain Section to the northwest of the valley, where similar limestone beds outcrop.

Appalachian Mountain Section

As one leaves the Great Valley and proceeds north or west, the character of the landscape changes abruptly. The Great Valley is bounded throughout its length by a mountain wall that extends for over 320 km, from the Maryland border in the south to the Delaware River in the northeast. Known at various parts along its length as Blue, Kittatinny, or First Mountain, it is one of the most striking geological features in the state. Rising 300 m above the Great Valley, it is the first of many parallel ridges of the Valley and Ridge Province to the west. Its even crest, broken only by water gaps, averages about 480 m above sea level, with occasional higher points of up to 670 m above sea level. The Appalachian Mountains proper constitute a 80 to 110 km-wide belt of northeast-southwest trending ridges and intermontane valleys. Geologically they are the eroded remnants of a former mountain system. The rock sequences, sedimentary marine and freshwater beds, ranging from Cambrian to Pennsylvanian in age, are the same as those found under the Appalachian Plateau to the west and north. But here, compressive forces have thrown the once level sedimentary beds into a series of long parallel trust-faults, anticlines, and synclines, the upper portions of which, constituting kilometers of missing sediments, have eroded away. The present deeply-etched topography is governed by the extent to which sedimentary beds of varying degrees of hardness have resisted erosion. The ridges are the upturned edges of dense sandstone beds, and the intermontane valleys were formed by stream erosion working on softer shales and limestones. Intermontane valleys are variously composed of Devonian, Cambrian, and Ordovician shales, limestones, and weak sandstones; the resistant ridges of Devonian and Silurian sandstones. The master stream of the area, the Susquehanna River, flows south and east across the Valley and Ridge Section at right angles cutting deep water gaps through the mountain ridges, but the secondary drainage is developed along the parallel intermontane valleys at right angles to the Susquehanna. The crestlines of the narrow mountain ridges are uninterrupted for great distances, except for an occasional wind or water gap, at a uniform elevation of from 430–550 m above sea level, although some may reach as high as 825 m above sea level. Many are simply straight along ridges trending north and east; others zigzag, are canoe-shaped, enclosing long mountain-walled valleys, or are elliptical. This seeming confusion is due to the plunging or emerging anticlinal and synclinal axes that govern the direction of the resistant sandstone and quartzite beds that form the ridge lines. Valley elevations vary from 460–490 m above sea level in the west, to about 120 m above sea level in the east. Local relief, from ridge top to adjacent valley, averages 240–300 m. Ridge tops are generally dry, sandy, and rocky with little residual soil. Exposures of the glaring white Tuscarora quartzite, a dense, Silurian, silicious sandstone, often occur as boulder fields, formed by frost action during the Pleistocene, that run for miles near the tops of the ridges. Broad Top Mountain, in northern Bedford, Fulton, and southern Huntingdon counties, is atypical, it is a 100 square km remnant of the Pennsylvanian rocks typical of the Appalachian Plateau, 65 km to the west, that has been preserved from erosion in a broad synclinal trough. The surface topography of Broad Top Mountain resembles the flat plateau surface, but it is technically a part of the Valley and Ridge Province.

Large areas of Mississippian and Pennsylvanian rocks, preserved in synclinal troughs, have been exposed in the northeastern portion of the Valley and Ridge Province. These rocks are coal-bearing, like Pennsylvanian strata in western Pennsylvania. This is the anthracite region—parts of Lackawanna, Luzerne, Carbon, Schuylkill, Columbia, Northumberland, and northern Dauphin counties.

Soil types throughout the Valley and Ridge Province are variable. Most of the section has stoney, shallow, well-drained, thin soils (lithosols). The crests and upper slopes of the ridges are often excessively dry and usually deficient in organic matter. Cultivation is limited largely to stream terraces and mountain benches. In some areas of Fulton, Mifflin,

Huntingdon, Blair, and Bedford counties, Ordovician and Cambrian limestones, similar to those of the Great Valley, outcrop in broad intermontane areas such as the Nittany Valley, producing fertile soils that are extensively farmed.

APPALACHIAN PLATEAU PROVINCE

The northern and western boundary of the Valley and Ridge Province is a sharp, well-defined escarpment, over 480 km in length, rising 300 m above the last of the intermontane valleys to the east. The escarpment, actually the western flank of the last major anticline of the Valley and Ridge Province, marks the beginning of the Appalachian Plateau which covers all of western Pennsylvania, half of Ohio, all of the northern counties of Pennsylvania, all of western New York south of the Mohawk River and east to and including the Catskill Mountains of southeastern New York. The plateau escarpment, known as Allegheny Mountain or Allegheny Front, extends from Bedford County in the south, north for 160 km through Blair and Center counties, then swings east through southern Clinton, Lycoming, Sullivan, and northern Luzerne counties where it is interrupted by the North Branch of the Susquehanna and Lackawanna river valleys. The escarpment rises again as the Moosic Mountains east of the Lackawanna River Valley, runs south through parts of Lackawanna, Luzerne, Carbon, Monroe, and Pike counties, outlining the Pocono Mountain Plateau. This escarpment marks portions of the eastern and southern rim of a vast elevated plateau composed of relatively horizontal beds of marine and freshwater Paleozoic sandstones, shales, limestones, and coal. The plateau surface slopes gently to the west and has been dissected throughout by the Ohio, Susquehanna, and Delaware river systems into a rugged hill and valley topography. Its original surface is still echoed, however, in the concordant heights of its hilltops. Because the Paleozoic rock sequence that forms the plateau was deposited in a geosyncline with its epicenter in northwestern West Virginia, the rocks become younger as one travels north or northeast from the Permian beds of Greene County, in the southwestern corner of the state, to older Pennsylvanian, Mississippian, and Devonian rocks underlying the northern and eastern portions of the plateau. The plateau surface, at present hilltop level, rises from about 400 m in the west, to a general height of about 750 m above sea level in the High Plateau Section of northcentral Pennsylvania, and to about 730 m above sea level along the Allegheny

Front. East of Potter County, the hilltops decline gradually from 730–580 m above sea level in western Bradford County to 425–365 m above sea level in eastern Bradford County. East of the North Branch of the Susquehanna River Valley the plateau surface rises again to over 600 m above sea level.

The Appalachian Plateau Province is so topographically variable that it is subdivided in Pennsylvania into six sections—Pittsburgh, Allegheny Mountain, Northcentral, Pocono Plateau, and Glaciated Northwest and Northeast. These differ among themselves in their degree of stream dissection, caused primarily by warping of the original plateau surface and by the effects of Pleistocene glaciation.

Pittsburgh Section

The terrain of the Pittsburgh Section is so maturely dissected that little of the original plateau remains. Major rivers, the Ohio and its tributaries, the Allegheny and the Monongahela, are entrenched to a depth of 120–150 m in broad flat valleys, over a km wide, with broad alluvial plains over a half km in width. Their immediate tributaries have cut severely into the plateau surface, often leaving deep V- and U-shaped valleys extensively lined with sandstone outcrops. Pleistocene terraces and elevated abandoned stream channels are apparent in some areas. The floors of the beds of the Allegheny, Beaver, and Ohio rivers are comprised of Pleistocene sands and gravels, up to 25 m in depth. Away from rivers, the entrenched valleys become shallower and lose themselves into the gently sloping hillsides. Hilltops are rounded and occasionally knoblike. Elevations range from 120–240 m above sea level in the major river valleys, to 360–490 m above sea level on the hilltops. From Pittsburgh south to Washington, Pennsylvania, in Allegheny and Washington counties, hilltop level is about 365–380 m above sea level, and local relief is between 75 and 105 m. South and west of Washington, in southern Washington and Greene counties, hills sharpen into ridges and increase in altitude to about 490 m above sea level. The residual soils of the uplands are derived from shale, thinly-bedded limestones, and sandstones. They are usually brown to gray-brown and overlie a heavy clay subsoil. Overgrazing and cultivation have resulted in severe slope-wash and many of the higher areas are covered thinly, if at all, with top soil. The Pittsburgh Section has been heavily mined for coal both by deep and strip mining of Pennsylvanian Age beds. In some areas, unreclaimed strip mine spoils are extensive, and many surface streams are polluted with acid mine drainage.

Allegheny Mountain Section

The Allegheny Mountain Section is the broad, tilted, eastern rim of the Appalachian Plateau. It includes the Allegheny Front itself, and the mountain ridges just to the west, Chestnut Ridge, Laurel Mountain, and Negro Mountain, parallel, northeast/southwest trending, truncated anticlines, rising above the horizontal Paleozoic strata of the plateau. Chestnut Ridge on the west rises 365 m above general plateau level and reaches a height of 847 m above sea level. Laurel Ridge, 16 km east, is slightly higher, 853 m above sea level, and Mt. Davis, in the Negro Mountains anticline, in southern Somerset county, reaches 979 m above sea level, the highest spot in the state. These ridges are supported by dense resistant sandstones. East of Laurel Ridge the general plateau surface rises rapidly, forming the flat, poorly-defined top of Allegheny Mountain, beyond whose eastward-facing escarpment lies the Valley and Ridge Province. The topography of the Allegheny Mountain Section varies from gently rolling hills to deeply incised mountain canyons. The general plateau level, exclusive of the Chestnut and Laurel anticlines, rises from a level of 425 m above sea level in the west, to well over 610 m above sea level in the east. Its eastern rim, Allegheny Front, reaches altitudes of 730–880 m above sea level in eastern Somerset, western Bedford, and Blair counties; its highest point, Blue Knob, 960 m above sea level, in western Bedford County, is the second highest point in the state. The major streams that drain the section, the Conemaugh River, Loyalhanna Creek, the Youghiogheny River, and the Castleman River, flow west across the path of the ridges and form spectacular water gaps over 300 m in depth, that expose the underlying Mississippian and older Devonian rocks forming the core of the ridges. Their tributaries are deep rocky gorges with high stream gradients and occasional waterfalls. Where the Youghiogheny River traverses the Pottsville sandstones at Ohiopyle in Somerset County, it flows over a broad 12 m waterfall with extensive stretches of white water. On the flat western surface of Allegheny Mountain, just west of the Front, drainage headwaters are sluggish and local swamps may occur, otherwise the section is well-drained. Upland soils are generally shallow, stoney, and in areas of weathered sandstones, dry and sandy.

Allegheny High Plateau

North and east of the Pittsburgh Section the surface of the plateau domes gradually from 400–425 m above sea level, in southwestern Pennsylvania, to over 760 m above sea level in Potter County. Streams become progressively more incised and local relief may be as much as 460 m in some parts of Potter County. Protected by horizontal beds of Mississippian or Devonian sandstones, the flat-topped hills lose their rolling aspect and become mesa-like in appearance as more of the original plateau surface remains between deeply entrenched valleys. The highest point on the general plateau surface, 783 m above sea level in Potter County, is a unique triple divide, north to the St. Lawrence River, south to the Gulf of Mexico, and east to the Atlantic Ocean. Eastward the plateau gradually declines toward the valley of the North Branch of the Susquehanna River and the hills become more rounded. Farther to the south, however, along the Allegheny Front, the plateau rim remains at a height of over 760 m, ending in the rugged North Mountain (790 m above sea level) and Dutch Mountain sections of Sullivan, western Wyoming, and Luzerne counties. The West Branch of the Susquehanna River and its tributaries have cut extensively into the plateau, forming V-shaped canyon-like valleys of up to 300 m in depth that drain much of the northern and eastern portions of the High Plateau. The headwaters of some of these streams—Pine Creek, Lycoming Creek, Loyalsock Creek, in Lycoming County, Fishing Creek in Luzerne County—have been affected by Pleistocene glaciation, and enormous amounts of meltwater released during the glacial meltback have produced deep rock-walled canyons up to 300 m in depth, forming some of Pennsylvania's most scenic areas. There are over 20 waterfalls in Ricketts Glen alone, a tributary of Fishing Creek, as it traverses the Allegheny Front in western Luzerne County. Soils are residual and formed from underlying Mississippian and Devonian sandstones and shales. The High Plateau is predominantly forested and agriculture is marginal compared to other areas of the state.

Glaciated Low Plateau Section

The Appalachian Plateau has been so extensively broached and dissected by the North Branch of the Susquehanna River that it is almost unrecognizable in the immediate vicinity of the river where hills are rounded and valley profiles are more gentle than

in the High Plateau Section to the west. The river is at an elevation of about 230 m above sea level in Bradford and Wyoming counties, but the plateau becomes more apparent toward the east, and hilltop levels rise gradually from 400–425 m to a maximum of 670–700 m in Susquehanna and Wayne counties. The plateau itself continues east of the Delaware River into southern New York State, where it forms the Catskill Mountains, rising to 900–1,220 m (maximum 1,275 m above sea level on Sliding Mountain). In eastern Wayne and Pike counties, where the plateau is cut by the Delaware River to a depth of about 200 m above sea level, there are spectacular cliffs, deep valleys, and waterfalls draining into the river. This section of the plateau is mantled with glacial till, and morainal features such as kettle-hole bogs and lakes, eskers, drumlins, and kames occur. In southern Wayne, Pike, and eastern Monroe counties the general surface of the Low Plateau Section declines from a maximum of 480 m above sea level in the west, to a minimum of 275 m above sea level in the east. Soils are primarily derived from glacial drift composed largely of sands and clays derived from the Devonian rocks of the plateau. They are thin, loamy, surface soils that vary in composition from fine to gravely. The blanket of glacial till is thin on the plateau and hilltops, but may be 8 m or more in thickness in the valleys. Much of the terrain is unsuitable for agriculture because it is poorly drained or too steep, and large areas are in forest.

Pocono Mountain Section

The Pocono Plateau Section is a flat tableland of little relief east of the North Branch–Lackawanna River Valley, rising 300 m above the Valley and Ridge Province to the south. Its rim is an escarpment formed by resistant Pocono sandstone, similar to the Allegheny Front to the west. Gentle uplands vary from 500–600 m above sea level. They are thinly mantled with glacial till and dotted with lakes, swamps, and other post-glacial features. The Pocono Plateau is ill-suited for agriculture. Its cool forests and lakelands have been developed for recreation and vacation sites.

Northwest Glaciated Plateau Section

The northwestern portion of the Allegheny Plateau has been mantled with glacial till and modified by ice-scour and glacial meltwater. Its southern boundary is defined largely by the terminal moraine deposits of the Wisconsinan glaciation. The terminal moraine is an 8 to 16 km wide band of low, rounded, often inconspicuous mounds of unsorted sands, clays, rounded pebbles and boulders. It marks the southern limit of the ice advance and extends for over 160 km in a northeasterly direction through parts of Beaver, Lawrence, Butler, Venango, Crawford, and Warren counties. The original plateau surface rises gently toward the east, but the general aspect of the Glaciated Section is of open shallow valleys with sluggish, often chaotic drainage, and little topographical relief. Glacial features such as eskars, kames, and drumlins, kettle hole bogs, lakes, and valley swamps are common throughout. Glacial till has filled many of the original plateau valleys with sand and gravel deposits, so that the preglacial topography has been altered. Ice advances have drastically affected drainage patterns in northwestern Pennsylvania. The upper Allegheny, which formerly drained north, was diverted south to join the present lower Allegheny River. The once northward-flowing Beaver River was reversed and forced to seek a new course to the southwest, the present Ohio River. McConnell's Mills Gorge, in Lawrence County, is a meltwater drainage channel from a former pro-glacial lake. Despite the large number of lakes in both the glaciated eastern plateau sections and the Northwestern Glaciated Section, there were none of very large size. The largest natural lake in the state is Conneaut Lake, in Crawford County, approximately 4 km long and 1 km wide, formed by a natural till dam. Pymatuning Lake, also in Crawford County, was formerly a 42 square km tamarack bog until it was converted into a lake in 1933. The province merges gradually into the Lake Erie shore lands. The general altitude varies from a low of 300–330 m above sea level in western Crawford, Mercer and Lawrence counties, to 510–550 m above sea level in Venango and western Warren counties. Transported soils tend to be stoney and poorly drained in the low areas and agriculture centers around dairy farming.

CENTRAL LOWLAND PROVINCE
Eastern Lake Section

Eighty km of the southcentral portion of the shore of Lake Erie, 174 m above sea level, lies within the borders of Pennsylvania. Former lake deposits, now dry land, extend 3 to 8 km inland rising about 60 m from the lake shore. Relief is so slight that the land appears flat except for low ridges paralleling the lake shore that mark former wave-cut beach lines made at a time when the lake level was higher, in late Pleistocene times. A few streams flow northwest across the lake plain, cutting through the lake deposits into the underlying Devonian shales and sandstones, forming deep precipitous valleys over 30 m in depth. The most interesting physiographic feature is Presque Isle, a 10-km peninsula extending into the lake enclosing Erie Bay. The peninsula, which sweeps to the east, expanding as it goes, is composed of sand deposits laid down by lake currents. Due to continuous deposition and erosion, plant successions extending over a period of some 600 years are unusually apparent, and the Peninsula has been the site of extensive botanical investigation.

CLIMATE

The climate of the state is part of a transcontinental pattern, but local weather is influenced by topography. Pennsylvania has a humid, continental, temperate climate with cold winters, hot summers, and constantly changing weather conditions. Prevailing winds are from the west. Precipitation usually occurs in episodes associated with frontal passages of northern or western air masses; during the warmer months the influence of moist, cyclonic air from the south is more apparent. Bailey (1980) includes the northern one-third of the state in his Warm Continental Division—coldest month below 0°C, warmest month less than 22°C, with adequate seasonal rainfall. The southern two-thirds of the state are included in the Hot Continental Division—coldest month below 0°C, warmest month greater than 22°C, with maximum rainfall in summer months.

Temperature and length of growing season (frost-free days, usually May through September) are influenced by elevation. Average temperatures are highest and growing season longest in low-lying sections such as the Upper Ohio Valley and the Susquehanna and Delaware lowlands. Conditions are harshest in higher and more northerly sectors. Mean annual temperature is 10°C, varying from 11°C on the southeastern Coastal Plain, to 8°C on the High Plateau, but temperatures as low as −40°C and as high as 43°C have been recorded. Growing season may be as long as 205 days in the Piedmont or Coastal Plain provinces, or as short as 100 days on the High Plateau in Potter County, where frosts have been recorded in every month of the year. Growing season may vary as much as 10 days in less than 15 km, depending upon altitude and exposure. Growing season averages 193 days on the Lake Erie Plain (180 m above sea level), 170 days in Allegheny County (400 m above sea level), but only 131 days in the Allegheny Mountains of Somerset County (700 m above sea level). Length of growing season may vary as much as 60 days in successive years (119 days in 1945, 179 days in 1946, Linesville, Crawford County; Richmond and Rosland, 1949).

Annual precipitation averages 105 cm, and is influenced by altitude. Precipitation averages 90 cm at the western border of the state, where the plateau surface is a low 400–500 m above sea level, but increases toward the east as the general plateau surface rises. It reaches a maximum of 125–140 cm at elevations of almost 1,000 m above sea level in southern Somerset County. There is a pronounced rainshadow effect east of the Allegheny Front, in Bedford and Fulton counties, where precipitation averages 25–28 cm less in the intermontane valleys of the Valley and Ridge Section than on the plateau

just to the west and 300 m higher. Precipitation also increases across the northern portions of the plateau to about 112 cm in northcentral Pennsylvania. East of this, it falls to 85–95 cm in the reduced elevations of the North Branch Susquehanna and Lackawanna river valleys, then rises to 122 cm on the elevated Pocono Plateau.

Winter snows occur throughout the state, their severity and duration dependent upon altitude. Snow cover is lightest and often discontinuous in the southeastern corner of the state. Highest snowfall occurs in the Allegheny Mountain Section (220 cm), and on the Pocono Plateau (125 cm). Throughout most of the northern portion of the state, snow cover may be expected from 15 November through 15 March.

Regional drought conditions may occur in summer and autumn months, but are usually of relatively short duration and seldom have lasting effect. Flash flooding may occur in areas of incised topography during summer thunderstorms, and regional flooding during periods of heavy spring rain combined with snow-melt. Tornadoes have been recorded, but are rare.

NATURAL REGIONS

The natural regions of the state are determined by physiography, climate, and the historical development of the flora and fauna. Primitively, before colonial deforestation, Pennsylvania was forest—a transition from the oak-rich deciduous woodlands of the southern Appalachians to the mixed, deciduous/coniferous, maple-beech-hemlock forests of the northern Appalachians. Major terrestrial habitats, other than forest-related, were not common. Grassland areas were confined to temporary riverine situations, beaver meadows, or isolated mountain glades. Swamp and bog habitats were locally common, particularly in glaciated areas, but these, too, were generally wooded. Open lakes were small and rare. Despite this seeming homogeneity of forest cover, local variations in elevation, weather, drainage, soils, exposure, affected the flora and fauna, producing a diversity in marked contrast to the apparent "sea of trees."

Pennsylvania straddles the Appalachian Mountain system at a point where elevations are at their lowest (100 m below the Catskills to the north, 200 m below the rugged peaks of West Virginia), and the Appalachian Plateau has been broached by the

major branches of the Susquehanna River system so that intermingling has occurred between the biota of the Coastal Plain to the east and that of the Central Lowlands to the west. As a result, Pennsylvania is a meeting ground not only of northern and southern, but of eastern and western faunal elements as well, producing a biological diversity not shared by some adjoining states.

There have been many generalized descriptions of the natural regions of the state (Rhoads, 1903; Luttringer, 1931; Todd, 1940; Dice, 1943; Jennings, 1953; Shelford, 1963; Bailey, 1980), based upon indicators such as climate, physiography, soils, vegetation types, faunal composition, etc. They differ in detail, but agree in the concept of a transitional biota. This transition can be visualized most readily by type of forest cover, usually the most conspicuous natural element. There are other characteristics, of course, but forest types provide a ready index. The forests of Pennsylvania are rich in species (278 native trees and shrubs, 16 of them oaks; Illick, 1923) and vary in composition, not only locally, but as one travels north or to higher elevations. In the lowland areas of the Pittsburgh Plateau Section in the southwest, and in the Great Valley, the Piedmont, and the Coastal Plain to the east, the forest is (in places was) dominated by white oak (*Quercus alba*), red oak (*Q. borealis*), black oak (*Q. velutina*), scarlet oak (*Q. coccinea*), with a rich mixture of other trees. This type of forest also occurs in the lower elevations of the Valley and Ridge Province, with varying mixtures of oaks, white pine (*Pinus strobus*), hemlock (*Tsuga canadensis*), and formerly chestnut (*Castanea dentata*), but at higher altitudes where accelerated drainage along ridge tops produces extremely dry soil conditions, drought or fire resistant trees such as chestnut oak (*Q. montana*), scrub oak (*Q. ilicifolia*), and pitch pine (*Pinus rigida*) predominate. Toward the north on the Appalachian Plateau, and in moist sheltered coves of the Valley and Ridge, the forests take on a more northern aspect as oak forest changes to one dominated by sugar maple (*Acer saccharum*), beech (*Fagus grandifolia*), and yellow birch (*Betula lutea*). Stands of white pine, hemlock, various birches (*Betula*), aspens (*Populus*), red maple (*Acer rubum*), and many other species occur in varying percentages. In areas of the High Plateau, such as on North Mountain, and in the Poconos, black and red spruce (*Picea mariana, P. rubens*) and tamarack (*Larix laricina*) are locally common, lending a true Canadian aspect to the High Plateau Section. This "Canadian flora" extends south in diluted form along the Allegheny Front to include the uplands of the Allegheny Mountain Section. Northern conifers, such as balsam fir (*Abies balsamea*) and red and black spruce, reach their southern limit in the state at Bear Meadows (545 m above sea level), in Centre County. Red spruce and balsam fir do not occur again for another 320 km to the south (Cranberry Glades, West Virginia, 1,100 m above sea level) (Core, 1966).

The U.S. Forest Service assigns the northern one-third of the state to the *Northern Hardwoods Forest Section* of the Laurentian Mixed Forest Province; the southern two-thirds to the *Appalachian Oak Forest Section* of the Eastern Deciduous Forest Province (Bailey, 1980). Shelford (1963) includes Pennsylvania in his *Northern Temperate Deciduous Forest Biome*—northwestern Pennsylvania in maple-beech, grading eastward to maple-beech-hemlock, with oak-chestnut in the southeast and south-central, and mixed deciduous in extreme southwest. One of the earliest general descriptions of the natural regions of the state utilizing Merriam's life zone concepts was that of Rhoads (1903). He assigned the Appalachian High Plateau, generally areas above 600 m, from Warren County in the west to Wayne County in the northeast, to the *Canadian Life Zone,* including a southern extension through the highlands of the Allegheny Mountain Section south to the Maryland border. Rhoads placed the present northwestern glaciated section of the Plateau, most of the Valley and Ridge Province, and the valley of the North Branch of the Susquehanna River, in his *Transition Zone* (Alleghenian of some authors), implying a change from southern oak forest to northern hardwoods. He mapped the southwestern Pittsburgh Plateau Section centered around the Upper Ohio Valley, and the eastern Piedmont and Coastal Plain area centered around the Susquehanna and Delaware River valleys, as *Austral Life Zone* (Carolinian of some authors), reflecting their southern affinities.

The distribution of forest types is also reflected in the ranges of many other plants as well as in those of invertebrates, amphibians, reptiles, birds, and mammals, all of which are influenced, directly or indirectly, by the same environmental parameters. This is a gross oversimplification, of course, and in many areas of the state does not apply due to local environmental restrictions, so that a forest subtype or small ecological community may retain its distinctive character as it fragments over broad areas to lose itself eventually in the changing regional picture.

The hand of man has changed the primitive picture, and is largely responsible for the Pennsylvania we see today. Stillwater habitats, once so rare in the state, have been augmented by damming. Marshlands have been expanded, particularly in the glaciated portions of the state. Lowland areas were cleared for farming at the earliest opportunity and, in unindustrialized portions of the larger valleys, in the Great Valley, the Piedmont, and in the lower hill country of the Appalachian Plateau, are in cleared farm fields and managed woodlots. Ninety percent of Lancaster County, for instance, was stripped of its original forest cover 250 years ago. Thousands of hectares of man-managed grasslands are devoted to dairy farming and livestock production in formerly forested areas.

The original forests were altered by clearing, repeated logging, burning, and reforestation. Less than 1 percent of the virgin forest remains, in small reserves primarily in areas unsuited for agriculture (Erdman and Wiegman, 1974). Except in these protected areas, and on slopes too steep for logging where fragments of the original forest still persist, all of the woodlands of the state are in some stage of regeneration, from brush and pole stages to approaching maturity. In the wake of logging and the abandoning of many small subsistence farms since the turn of the century, thousands of hectares of woodlands, particularly in the northern Appalachian Plateau Section, have regenerated to some degree. Forest recovery, often retarded by deer and livestock overgrazing, logging, and fires, has been greatest in the central High Plateau area, where such counties as Forest, Elk, or Cameron are 90 percent forested. Large areas of the coal mining regions of the state, the Pittsburgh Plateau Section, the Flat Top Mountain coal field, the anthracite region in the northeastern portion of the Valley and Ridge Section, have been biologically devastated by mining and stripping, leaving as a legacy eroding spoil banks, reduced water tables, acid and silt-polluted streams, and hundreds of square kilometers of "barrens."

In spite of 300 years of settlement and exploitation, however, there are many areas of the state which, if not primeval, still remain wild and unspoiled. Many significant habitat types occur that cannot be discussed in this short summary—the botanically unique shale barrens of the Valley and Ridge, the serpentine barrens of the Piedmont, boreal bogs, flood plain woodlands, unique gorge habitats, thousands of hectares of upland streams, extensive cliff outcrops, caves, and many other natural features that give such variety to Penn's Woods, and such fascination to its students.

LITERATURE CITED

BAILEY, R. G. 1980. Description of the ecoregions of the United States. U.S. Dept. Agriculture Misc. Publ., 1391:1–77.

CORE, E. L. 1966. Vegetation of West Virginia. McClain Printing Co., Parsons, West Virginia, 217 pp.

DICE, L. R. 1943. The biotic provinces of North America. Univ. Michigan Press, Ann Arbor, 78 pp.

ERDMAN, K. S., and P. G. WIEGMAN. 1974. Preliminary list of natural areas in Pennsylvania. Western Pennsylvania Conservancy, Pittsburgh, 106 pp.

ILLICK, J. S. 1923. Pennsylvania trees. Bull. Pennsylvania Dept. Forestry, 11:1–237.

JENNINGS, O. E. 1953. Wild flowers of western Pennsylvania and the upper Ohio basin. Univ. Pittsburgh Press, 1:lxxv + 574 pp; 2:xvi + 200 plates.

LUTTRINGER, L. A. JR. 1931. An introduction to the mammals of Pennsylvania. Bull. Pennsylvania Game Commission, Harrisburg, 15:1–66.

RHOADS, S. N. 1903. The mammals of Pennsylvania and New Jersey. Privately printed, Philadelphia, 266 pp.

RICHMOND, N. D., and H. R. ROSLAND. 1949. Mammal survey of northwestern Pennsylvania. Final report Pittman-Robertson Project 20-R, Pennsylvania Game Commission, Harrisburg, 67 pp.

SHELFORD, V. E. 1963. The ecology of North America. Univ. Illinois Press, Urbana, 610 pp.

TODD, W. E. C. 1940. Birds of western Pennsylvania. Univ. Pittsburgh Press, 710 pp.

Address: Section of Vertebrate Fossils, Carnegie Museum of Natural History, 4400 Forbes Ave., Pittsburgh, PA 15213. (Deceased 11/17/1982.)

DRAINAGE PATTERNS IN PENNSYLVANIA

Clark Shiffer

INTRODUCTION

Careful consideration of Fig. 1 reveals an orderly network of streams covering the length and breadth of Pennsylvania. The majority of these are part of a system of tributaries contributing to the three largest rivers of the Commonwealth—the Ohio, Susquehanna, and Delaware. Streams of the westernmost Ohio Basin drain some 41,450 square km, those of the centrally located Susquehanna Basin about 54,404 square km, and those of the easternmost Delaware Basin about 15,544 square km (Fig. 2). The Susquehanna River, in fact, has the largest drainage area of any United States river contributing its waters to the Atlantic Ocean. Pennsylvania is also unique with respect to containing three major river basins roughly resembling broad north-south bands. The smaller Lake Erie, Genesee River, and Potomac River drainages encompass the remainder of the streams within the Commonwealth (Fig. 2). Unlike the Ohio, Susquehanna, and Delaware drainages, these latter three are not subdivided into smaller drainage systems or subbasins.

PRESENT DRAINAGE PATTERNS

One of the major streams of the Ohio Drainage Basin is the Allegheny River, which arises near the New York border, flows northwestward into New York, then south into Pennsylvania, and pursues a meandering southerly course until joining with the Monongahela River at Pittsburgh to form the Ohio River. Major tributaries to the Allegheny include Brokenstraw Creek, French Creek, Oil Creek, Tionesta Creek, Clarion River, Redbank Creek, Mahoning Creek, Conemaugh River, Kiskiminetas River, and Loyalhanna Creek, the latter three of which flow generally northward and the remainder either southeasterly or southwesterly. The Youghiogheny River and Monongahela River flow northward from Maryland and West Virginia, respectively, and together with their tributaries drain the southcentral portion of the Ohio Basin. Much of the western portion of the basin is drained by the southward-flowing Shenango River and Beaver River and their tributaries, and the northward-flowing Chartiers Creek and Raccoon Creek, all of which flow into the Ohio River west of Pittsburgh.

The Susquehanna River, the major stream of the Susquehanna Drainage Basin, begins in New York, flows south into northeast Pennsylvania, then turns northwestward into New York before turning southward into Pennsylvania, where it continues a meandering southerly course to the Chesapeake Bay in Maryland. The Cowanesque River and Tioga River flow north, join at the New York border and their combined waters then flow northward into New York, where other tributaries join to form the Chemung River. The Chemung then flows south into Pennsylvania and soon joins the Susquehanna not far from final entry of that river into the Commonwealth. Other major tributaries of the Susquehanna include the Lackawanna River, West Branch Susquehanna River, and the Juniata River, the latter two, together with a number of important tributaries, combine to drain a large portion of the basin. While most of the streams in the northern and eastern portions of the basin flow in various southerly directions, those in the southcentral portion generally flow in a northerly direction.

Streams of the Potomac Drainage Basin, which is nestled in the southwesternmost portion of the Susquehanna Basin, all flow south into Maryland to empty their combined waters into the Potomac River.

The Delaware River forms the eastern boundary of Pennsylvania as it flows from the Catskill Mountains in New York south to Delaware Bay. Most of the streams in the Delaware Drainage Basin flow in a southeasterly direction. Major streams include the Lackawaxen River, Lehigh River, and Schuylkill River.

The Genesee River arises in northcentral Pennsylvania near the New York border and flows north into New York. Its drainage basin is the smallest in Pennsylvania.

Lake Erie Drainage Basin streams flow north to Lake Erie. Major streams include Elk Creek and Conneaut Creek, the latter emptying into Lake Erie in the northeast corner of Ohio.

31

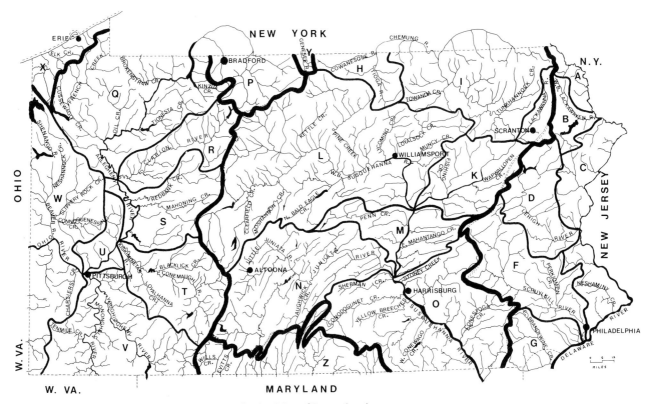

Fig. 1.—Map of Pennsylvania streams.

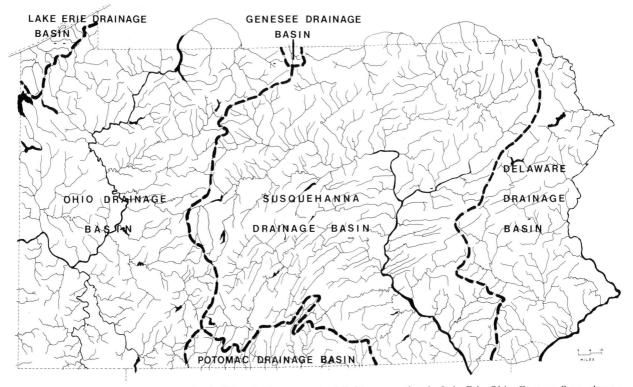

Fig. 2.—Pennsylvania drainage patterns. Dashed lines indicate watershed divides separating the Lake Erie, Ohio, Genesee, Susquehanna, Potomac, and Delaware basins.

PAST DRAINAGE PATTERNS

During the last 100,000 years, much of the northern portion of the North American Continent was covered by vast sheets of ice and snow. Four separate southward advances and subsequent northward retreats of these glacial sheets have been recorded by geologists, the last three of which reached southward into present-day Pennsylvania. The first two of these, termed the Kansan and Illinoian, reached farthest south, ultimately covering northwestern Pennsylvania north of a line drawn diagonally from extreme northwest McKean County south to northwest Beaver County, and much of northeastern Pennsylvania from northwest Potter County south to northeast Bucks County. The last, or Wisconsin glaciation, covered somewhat more than half the area covered during the previous advances, and retreated northward some 15,000 years ago.

Although drainage patterns in Pennsylvania probably remained relatively unchanged during millions of years preceding these "ice ages," and the Potomac and Delaware Basins have remained relatively unchanged, the upper Ohio and Susquehanna drainage basins were dramatically altered by glaciation. Prior to glaciation the upper Allegheny, Monongahela-Youghiogheny, and Beaver-Ohio drainages flowed northward into the Erian River, which flowed along the site of the present Lake Erie. The Erian River continued north to join with the Ontarian River flowing along the site of the present Lake Ontario. The northward-flowing Genesee and Susquenesca-Chenango river systems also flowed into the Ontarian River in what is now northern Pennsylvania and New York.

DRAINAGE PATTERN CHANGES—EFFECTS ON
FLORA AND FAUNA

Repeated glacial ebb and flow blocked the northward flow of these streams, shunting their waters southward and creating the present Great Lakes, Finger Lakes in New York, and numerous lakes, swamps, and marshes in the glaciated portions of Pennsylvania. The formerly separate upper Allegheny and Monongahela-Youghiogheny and Ohio drainages were now connected because of blockage of their former outlets and their combined waters shunted southward to the present Ohio River. This process of "stream capture" also occurred as glaciers blocked the northern outlets of the Genesee and Susquenesca-Chenango drainages, shunting their waters southward into the present Susquehanna drainage.

Concurrent with these changes in drainage patterns were changes in the distributions of both aquatic and terrestrial plants and animals. Contiguous populations of organisms were separated, and some exist today as "island," disjunct, or relict populations far removed from the more contiguous populations of their species. As stream systems were shunted into, or "captured by," other formerly separate stream systems, many organisms used these new routes to disperse into new and acceptable habitats. Some of these populations were subsequently separated as new drainage patterns were established and have evolved along different morphological or

genetic lines. Individuals comprising such populations may be recognized today as distinct species or subspecies, whose ranges may expand, contract or sometimes coincide. Geological events such as scouring and erosive action of flowing waters, along with climatic changes, have combined in a dynamic way in the past to shape present-day drainage patterns, and along with specific habitat requirements have determined the distributions of plants and animals in Pennsylvania.

Although human influence on the Pennsylvania landscape has steadily increased since the last ice age, these activities have not appreciably altered major drainage patterns. They have resulted, however, in the channelization and relocation of many stream portions across the Commonwealth, and the construction of canals, locks, and numerous impoundments along the courses of many free-flowing waters. Human activities have also influenced aquifers in various places by disrupting the flow of surface and subsurface waters thereby resulting in the drying up of wells, springs, or portions of streams. Ditching and diversion projects have also resulted in the drying up of swamps, bogs, and marshes and projects of this type may in the future connect discrete portions of drainage basins, thereby affecting flow regimes of major streams. Finally, human activities have resulted in the thermal and chemical degradation of free-flowing and impounded waters in various areas of Pennsylvania.

The distribution and relative abundance of Pennsylvania plants and animals has been increasingly affected in various ways as a result of these more recent activities. Many of the species discussed in this volume are especially sensitive to these changes, and thus have been negatively affected, but the sort of environmental degradation that has affected these species, if not checked, will ultimately affect the more common species, some of which are used by man for sport or profit.

Thus, while major geological and climatic events have largely created present-day drainage patterns in Pennsylvania, and will continue to be the major architects of these patterns, the future status and distribution of the Commonwealth's flora and fauna will, in the interim, depend largely on man's care and concern for the proper maintenance of this natural environment for their benefit—and his.

Address: Pennsylvania Fish Commission, Robinson Lane, Bellefonte, PA.

DEFINITIONS OF STATUS CATEGORIES

Frank Dunstan

Categories used to designate the status of organisms included in *Species of Special Concern in Pennsylvania* are defined below. In the case of species or subspecies whose ranges extend beyond the borders of the Commonwealth, the category to which the animal or plant is assigned is based on its status in Pennsylvania.

In the following definitions, "species" is used in a general sense to include: 1) full taxonomic species, 2) subspecies or varieties, and 3) particular populations of a species or subspecies that do not have formal taxonomic status. This use of the term agrees with that of the Federal Endangered Species Act of 1973.

Endangered. — Species in imminent danger of extinction or extirpation throughout their range in Pennsylvania if the deleterious factors affecting them continue to operate. These are species whose numbers have already been reduced to a critically low level or whose habitat has been so drastically reduced or degraded that immediate action is required to prevent their extirpation from the Commonwealth.

Threatened. — Species that may become endangered within the forseeable future throughout their range in Pennsylvania unless the causal factors affecting the organism are abated. These are species in which: 1) most or all populations within the Commonwealth are decreasing or whose populations have been heavily depleted by adverse factors — and while not actually endangered, are still in critical condition; or 2) populations which may be relatively abundant but are under severe threat from serious adverse factors that have been identified and documented.

Vulnerable. — Species not currently endangered or threatened but which may become endangered because: 1) they exist only in one or a few restricted geographic areas or habitats within Pennsylvania; or 2) they occur in low numbers over a relatively broad area of the Commonwealth; or 3) although relatively abundant, they are particularly susceptible to certain types of exploitation or environmental modification.

Status undetermined. — Species that may be included in one of the above categories but there is insufficient data available to provide an adequate basis for their assignment to a specific category. New information must be generated in order to determine the status of these species.

Extirpated. — Species that have disappeared from Pennsylvania since 1600 but still exist elsewhere.

Recently extinct. — Species, now extinct, that have occurred in Pennsylvania since 1600.

Address: Sanctuary Department, National Audubon Society, West Cornwall Road, Sharon, CT 06069.

35

CHAPTER 1
PLANTS

Spreading Globe-flower (*Trollius laxus*). Photograph by P. G. Wiegman.

CHAPTER 1—PLANTS

edited by

P. AUL G. W. IEGMAN

Western Pennsylvania Conservancy
316 Fourth Avenue
Pittsburgh, PA 15222

Table of Contents

INTRODUCTION

As of 1982 in Pennsylvania, plants are under the jurisdiction of the Pennsylvania Department of Environmental Resources. Prior to 1982, no state agency was responsible for the general protection of native plants, nor were there laws providing protection for specific species. However, land holding agencies such as the Bureau of State Forests, Bureau of State Parks, the Pennsylvania Fish Commission, and the Pennsylvania Game Commission recognized the need to regulate potentially damaging activities, and promulgated regulations controlling the picking, digging, or damaging of any plants on lands under their jurisdiction. Therefore, although specific plants were not protected, a general blanket regulation could be used to stop general destruction of plant species. Federal lands have similar regulations. Unfortunately, the plant regulations were applied in only the most flagrant cases, and the officers of the various agencies were unaware of rare or endangered species on the land they were responsible for managing.

Historically, there has been plant legislation in Pennsylvania, but from a different perspective. In the 1800's the state legislature passed the Noxious Weed Act. Rather than protecting native plants, the law prohibited the growing of certain alien species. The plants included were hemp (this is the proper name of the species otherwise called by the name of the drug associated with it—marijuana) (*Cannabis sativa* L.), chickory (*Cichorium intybus* L.), and Canada thistle (*Cirsium arvense* (L.) Scop.). Obviously these laws prohibiting the growth, and thus the spread of these noxious weeds had little effects. Recently the Noxious Weed law was resurrected and two species were added to the list, prohibiting their cultivation in Pennsylvania. These are Johnson grass (*Sorghum halrpense* (L.) Pers.) and multiflora rose (*Rosa multiflora* Thunb).

The Bureau of State Forests has a regulation prohibiting the picking of plants on land owned by the Bureau. However, collection of "ground-pine" is allowed, but only with a permit received from the required forestry office. Apparently the *Lycopodium* permit was instituted to control the collection of ground-pines for Christmas decorations. The efficiency of this regulation is unknown.

In 1982, the Pennsylvania Legislature passed the Wild Resources Conservation Act. This bill created the first legislation in Pennsylvania specifically designed to protect plants. The Department of Environmental Resources is empowered to "conduct investigations on wild plants in order to ascertain information relating to population, distribution, habitat needs, limiting factors, and other biological and ecological data to classify plants and to determine management measures necessary for their continued ability to sustain themselves successfully." The first responsibility of the Department is to establish a classification procedure and prepare an official list. Then regulations will be developed to set limitations related to collection, possession, and sale of wild plants.

Another feature of the bill is the establishment of a system of Wild Plant Sanctuaries. This land use designation can be placed on parcels of both private and public land. Once so designated, lands will be subject to the regulations developed by the Department of Environment Resources and the enforcement penalties of those regulations.

Prior to Pennsylvania's enactment of plant protection laws, Congress passed the Endangered Species Act of 1973 (P.L. 93-205). In 1975, the Smithsonian Institute published a list of extinct, endangered, and threatened plants in the United States. These species were accepted by the U.S. Fish and Wildlife Service and published in the *Federal Register* (vol. 40, no. 127, July 1975) as species proposed for listing. The U.S. Fish and Wildlife Service selected the Western Pennsylvania Conservancy to review those species native to the Commonwealth on the Smithsonian list.

The initial task was to review the 17 proposed species listed in the *Federal Register*. The review suggested species which should remain on the Federal list and ultimately be authorized as an endangered or threatened species as well as those considered for deletion from the proposed Federal list.

The Conservancy also evaluated species uncommon in Pennsylvania which might be additions to the federal list. This required an assessment of the Pennsylvania flora, especially those species of rare or infrequent occurrence. This project prepared in 1979 was the first Pennsylvania Plants of Special Concern (PPSC) list.

The list was compiled from original reports prepared by Keener and Wherry (1977), Buker (1975), and Henry and Buker (1963), as well as records from the Morris Arboretum, Carnegie Museum of Natural History Herbarium, Academy of Natural Science, and other references pertaining to the flora of Pennsylvania.

The original draft list contained plants occurring in four or less counties of Pennsylvania. Only full species were used, except where a variety appeared on the Federal list. In addition, the genus *Rubus* and the genus *Cratagus* were deleted due to the complexity and taxonomic problems of these taxa.

From the first draft list, a second draft was prepared including only those species generally occurring in two or less counties. Consideration was given in this process for the deletion of species with limited ranges, the area and size of the counties of occurrence, and the extent of development and alteration within those counties. For example, species occurring in the counties of Philadelphia, Bucks, and Delaware might be retained on the list because of the extensive development and small size of these combined counties. On the other hand, a species occurring in Tioga, Potter, and Clinton counties might be deleted.

The distributional information of the original Keener and Wherry list was drawn from the Flora of Pennsylvania records at Morris Arboretum, Philadelphia. These files in turn were based on the collections of Carnegie Museum of Natural History, Pennsylvania State University, the Academy of Natural Sciences in Philadelphia, the University of Pennsylvania, and the Plant Industry Herbarium in Harrisburg. Because the Carnegie Museum herbarium had been consulted nearly 20 years ago, it was necessary to review the second draft against the present records at Carnegie Museum of Natural History. The records of Carnegie Museum of Natural History were also reviewed for species occurring in two or less counties. This assured that any new species for the Commonwealth, which were not on the Morris Arboretum records, would be included.

All species on the second draft list were then reviewed in *Britton & Brown* (Gleason, 1952), *Gray's 8th* (Fernald, 1952), and *Jennings Wild Flowers of the Upper Ohio Valley* (Jennings, 1953). Special attention was paid to the range of the species, the habitat type, any particular reference to the rarity or commonness of the species, the distinctiveness of the species, and possible taxonomic problems.

The present proposed list of extirpated, endangered, threatened, and plant species of concern in Pennsylvania is a distillation of an earlier list of plants rare in the commonwealth (Wiegman, 1979).

This work is a further review of all species rare to Pennsylvania, and suggestions for placing 80+ species on an extirpated, endangered, threatened, or species of concern list depending on their individual status and concern for their future in Pennsylvania. In addition, it lists those plants presently being considered for Federal designation as endangered or under review (*Federal Register,* vol. 45, no. 202, December 1980).

Several drafts of these lists were prepared and circulated to interested amatuer and professional botanists in Pennsylvania. Dr. Alfred E. Schuyler of the Academy of Natural Sciences of Philadelphia and Dr. Frederick Utech of the Carnegie Museum of Natural History were of special help in providing their expert opinion as well as making herbarium materials available. Comments, criticism, and appropriate changes were received and incorporated when appropriate.

Nomenclature and author abbreviations follow Kartesz (1980), while those epithets in [ ] follow Gleason (1963). Some effort has been made to utilize a standard common name, and these follow Kartesz (1977). The following are the Extirpated, Threatened, and Vulnerable lists. The Endangered species are listed individually. Detailed accounts have been written only for the endangered species because accounts for the total of more than 370 species on the 1981 list would make this publication unnecessarily long.

Pennsylvania extirpated.—Species that have disappeared from Pennsylvania, but still exist elsewhere.

Sensitive Joint-Vetch—*Aeschynomene virginica* (L.) BSP

Black-Stemmed Spleenwort—*Asplenium resiliens* Kunze

American Barberry—*Berberis canadensis* Mill.

Atlantic White Cedar—*Chamaecyparis thyoides* (L.) BSP

Small White Lady's-Slipper—*Cypripedium candidum* Muhl. ex. Willd.

Long-Stemmed Water-Wort—*Elatin americana* (Pursh) Arn.

Schweinitz's Waterweed—*Elodea schweinitzii* (Planch.) Caspary

Parker's Pipewort—*Eriocaulon parkeri* Robins.

Wild Ipecac—*Euphorbia ipecacuanhae* L.

St. Peter's-Wort—*Hypericum stans* (Michx.) P. Adams & Robson

Ink-Berry—*Ilex glabra* (L.) Gray

Fir Clubmoss—*Lycopodium sabinifolium* Willd.

Nuttall's Mud-Flower—*Micranthemum micranthemoides* (Nutt.) Wettst.

Chammisso's Miner's-Lettuce—*Montia chamissoi* (Ledeb. ex. Spreng) Greene

Prairie White-Fringed Orchid—*Platanthera leucophaea* (Nutt.) Lindl.

Yellow Milkwort—*Polygala lutea* L.

Long-Stalked Crowfoot—*Ranunculus hederaceus* L.

Slender Marsh Pink—*Sabatia campanulata* (L.) Torr.

Sea Pink—*Sabatia stellaris* Pursh.

Pennsylvania threatened.—Plants and animals for which the available evidence indicates that they may become endangered or extirpated within the foreseeable future throughout their range in Pennsylvania, if the causal factors continue to operate. These are taxa:

Mountain Alder—*Alnus viridis* (Chaix) DC spp. *crispa* (Ait.) Turrell

Collin's Sedge—*Carex collinsii* Nutt.

Geyer's Sedge—*Carex geyeri* Boott.

Black Sedge—*Carex nigra* (L.) Reich.

Sartwell's Sedge—*Carex sartwellii* Dewey

Sedge—*Carex wiegandii* Mackenzie

Mouse-Ear Chickweed—*Cerastium arvense* (L.) var. *villossissimum* Penn.

Dichanthelium—*Dichanthelium leibergii* (Vasey) Freckmann

Beaked Spike-Rush—*Eleocharis rostellata* (Torr.) Torr.

Limestone Oak Fern—*Gymnocarpium robertianum* (Hoff.) Newm.

Coville's Rush—*Juncus gymnocarpus* Cov.

Southern Twayblade—*Listera australis* Lindl.

Large-Flowered Marshallia—*Marshallia grandiflora* Beadle & Boynton

Crested Yellow Orchid—*Platanthera cristata* (Michx.) Lindl.

Tuckerman's Pondweed—*Potamogeton confervoides* Reichenb.

Hill's Pondweed—*Potamogeton hillii* Morong.

Three-Toothed Cinquefoil—*Potentilla tridentata* (Soland.) Ait.

Capillary Beaked-Rush—*Rhynchospora capillacea* Torr.

Autumn Willow—*Salix serissima* (Bailey) Fern.

Northeastern Bullrush—*Scirpus ancistrochaetus* Schuyler

Ladies'-Tresses—*Spiranthes magnicamporum* Sheviak

October Ladies'-Tresses—*Spiranthes ovalis* Lindl.

Spring Ladies'-Tresses—*Spiranthes vernalis* Engelm. & Gray

Round-Leaved Fame-Flower—*Talinum teretifolium* Pursh.

Hairy Violet—*Viola villosa* Walt.

Pennsylvania vulnerable.—Species and subspecies of plants which, though not presently endangered or threatened, may become so.

Swamp-Pink—*Arethusa bulbosa* L.

Small Yellow Lady's-Slipper—*Cypripedium parviflorum* Salisb.

Showy Lady's-Slipper—*Cypripedium reginae* Walt.

Common Shooting-Star—*Dodecatheon meadia* L.

Showy Orchid—*Galearis spectabilis* (L.) Raf.

Checkered Rattlesnake-Plantain—*Goodyera tessellata* Lodd.

Golden-Seal—*Hydrastis canadensis* L.

Slender Blue Iris—*Iris prismatica* Pursh.

Michigan Lily—*Lilium michiganese* Farw.

Heart-Leaved Twayblade—*Listera cordata* (L.) R.Br.

American Lotus—*Nelumbo lutea* (Willd.) Pers.

Wild Ginseng—*Panax quinquefolius* L.

Christmas Mistletoe—*Phoradendron serotinum* (Raf.) M. C. Johnston

Leafy White Orchid—*Platanthera dilatata* (Pursh) Lindl. ex. Beck var. *dilatata*

Balsam Poplar—*Populus balsamifera* L.

Hooded Ladies'-Tresses—*Spiranthes romanzoffiana* Cham.

Nodding Pogonia—*Triphora trianthophora (Sw.) Rydb.*

SELECTED REFERENCES

BUKER, W. E. 1975. Rare western Pennsylvania plants. Unpublished List, Carnegie Museum of Natural History, Pittsburgh, Section of Plants, 1 p.

FERNALD, M. L. 1952. Gray's manual of botany. Hafner Press, New York, 8th ed., 1632 pp.

GLEASON, H. A. 1952. The New Britton and Brown illustrated flora of the northeastern United States and adjacent Canada, Volumes 1–3. Hafner Press, New York, Vol. 1, 482 pp.; Vol. 2, 655 pp.; Vol. 3, 589 pp.

GLEASON, H. A., and A. CRONQUIST. 1963. Manual of vascular plants of northeastern United States and adjacent Canada. Van Nostrand, Inc. New York, 810 pp.

HENRY, L. K., and W. E. BUKER. 1963–1964. Rare or otherwise noteworthy plants of western Pennsylvania. Trillia, 12:52–134.

JENNINGS, O. E. 1953. Wild flowers of Western Pennsylvania

and the Upper Ohio Basin, Vol. I. Univ. Pittsburgh Press, Pittsburgh, 600 pp.

KARTESZ, J. T., and R. KARTESZ. 1977. The biota of North America, Part I: Rare plants, Vol. I. Biota of North America Committee (BONAC), Pittsburgh, 360 pp.

———. 1980. A synonymized checklist of the vascular flora of the United States, Canada, and Greenland. The biota of North America, Vol. II. Univ. North Carolina Press, Chapel Hill, 498 pp.

WHERRY, E. T., and C. S. KENNER. 1977. A preliminary list of rare species of vascular plants native to Pennsylvania. Unpublished Report, Pennsylvania State University, University Park, 10 pp.

WIEGMAN, P. G. 1979. Rare and endangered vascular plant species in Pennsylvania. U.S. Fish and Wildlife Service, Endangered Species Office, Newton Corner, Massachusetts, 94 pp.

Paul G. Wiegman, *Western Pennsylvania Conservancy, 316 Fourth Avenue, Pittsburgh, PA 15222.*

ACKNOWLEDGMENTS

I would like to acknowledge the work of the U.S. Fish and Wildlife Service in the preparation of the original list of Endangered plant species. A very special thanks also goes to Sara Davison of The Nature Conservancy, Philadelphia, for her work in the preparation of numerous Species Accounts contained herein. We both acknowledge the considerable assistance of Carl Keener,

The Pennsylvania State University; Ernie Schuyler, Academy of Natural Sciences Philadelphia; and Dr. Fred Utech, Carnegie Museum of Natural History. The support of the Western Pennsylvania Conservancy and The Nature Conservancy was also very important in the preparation of these accounts.—*Paul G. Wiegman, Western Pennsylvania Conservancy.*

SPECIES ACCOUNTS

Endangered

MOUNTAIN CLUBMOSS
Lycopodium selago L.
Family Lycopodiaceae
Order Lycopodiales

DESCRIPTION: Mountain clubmoss is a robust, glossy clubmoss growing in fan-shaped clusters. The small leaves are lance-shaped and pointed and are arranged on the stem in eight longitudinal rows. The spore-bearing leaves resemble the true leaves, and contain the spores at the base of the leaf.

RANGE: Mountain clubmoss is a circumboreal species extending south to Oregon, Minnesota, and through New England, continuing along the mountains to North Carolina. In Pennsylvania, the distribution of this species is restricted to mountains of the northeastern part of the Commonwealth. The only herbarium specimen is from Monroe County near the Delaware Water Gap. It was collected by T. C. Porter in 1870. A recent report of *Lycopodium selago* at the Delaware Water Gap needs to be verified.

HABITAT: This species is located on rocks, mountain tops, and acid bog margins. It usually is found growing in fairly open areas. This is a boreal species with only limited habitat in Pennsylvania. It grows in association with other boreal and montane species.

BASIS OF STATUS CLASSIFICATION: The limited occurrence of this species in Pennsylvania is the basis for placing it on the Pennsylvania Plants of Special Concern list. Even though more suitable habitat can be found in the New England states, this species is still on the list of special concern in Massachusetts, Connecticut, Vermont, New Hampshire, and Maine. In the mountains of North and South Carolina, this clubmoss has a localized distribution. Thus this species is considered to be rare throughout its range in the eastern United States.

In Pennsylvania, *Lycopodium selago* is restricted to the mountains of the Delaware Water Gap. The main threat to this habitat type is recreation, particularly trampling. Because of the precarious and marginal habitat for this species in Pennsylvania, and its rarity in the remainder of its range, it is included in the "Endangered" category.

RECOMMENDATIONS: The locality where this species still occurs should be afforded special preservation status within the Delaware Water Gap National Recreational Area. The area should be delineated to prevent trampling and over collecting. Additional high ridges in the northeastern part of the Commonwealth and in the Ridge and Valley province should be searched for new localities.

PREPARED BY: Sara Davison, *1218 Chestnut Street, Suite 505, Philadelphia, PA 19107.*

MOUNTAIN CLUBMOSS (*Lycopodium selago*)

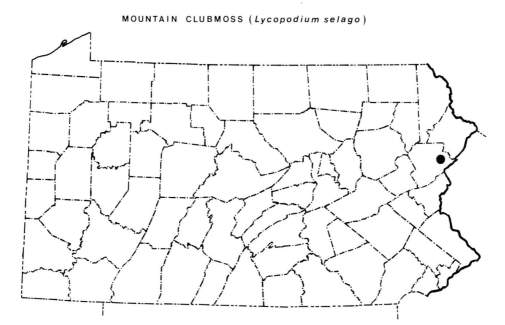

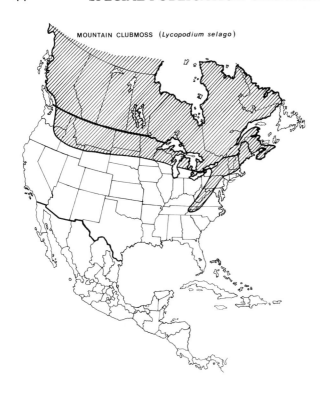

MOUNTAIN CLUBMOSS (*Lycopodium selago*)

Endangered

RIVER-BANK QUILLWORT
Isoetes riparia Engelm.
Family Isoetaceae
Order Isoetales

DESCRIPTION: At first glance, the river-bank quillwort can easily be mistaken for one of the ar-

row-heads that also occur in the intertidal zone. The dark green, wiry leaves come to a sharp point, and are thickened at the base by the cluster of whitish-brown spores. The roots are densely clustered and white. A final determination of this species, using the characters of the megaspores, can only be made with a microscope.

RANGE: The river-bank quillwort is found from New Jersey north to Maine. In Pennsylvania, this species occurs chiefly along the tidal portions of the Delaware River, but has also been collected at muddy shores of non-tidal rivers and lakes. Herbarium records have been reported from 14 Pennsylvania counties including, Bucks, Delaware, Franklin, Lacawanna, Lancaster, Lycoming, Monroe, Northampton, Northumberland, Philadelphia, Sullivan, Union, Wayne, and Wyoming. Because of the difficulty in identifying this species, some of the older records may be misidentified. *Isoetes riparia* was recently verified in Bucks County near Andalusia and Bristol. Historic stations in Philadelphia, Delaware, and Sullivan counties field checked in 1982 did not reveal this species. *Isoetes riparia* was first collected in Pennsylvania at Tinicum in 1864 by T. C. Porter.

HABITAT: This is a riverine species growing in gravelly mud or sand; not strictly limited to tidal rivers. This species also occurs in the middle to lower zone of the intertidal marsh. Vegetation in

RIVER-BANK QUILLWORT (*Isoetes riparia*)

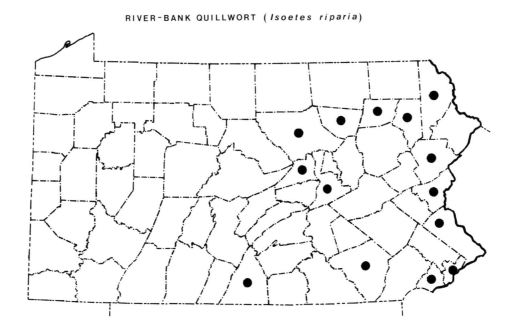

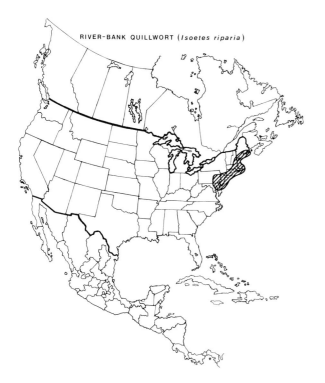

RIVER-BANK QUILLWORT (*Isoetes riparia*)

vania Plants of Special Concern list. This species is also on the list of special concern in New Hampshire.

Along the banks of the Delaware River, intertidal habitat has declined dramatically. Industrial activities such as dredging and filling, bulkheading, and pollution have all contributed to the destruction of intertidal habitat. In addition, the wake from heavy boat traffic is thought to contribute to the accelerated erosion of the river shoreline. Because of habitat destruction and few recently verified populations, the river-bank quillwort is included in the "Endangered" category.

RECOMMENDATIONS: The localities where this plant still remains should be afforded public or private preservation status. Further searching, particularly along inland rivers at historic collecting localities should continue.

PREPARED BY: Sara Davison, *1218 Chestnut Street, Suite 505, Philadelphia, PA 19107.*

this area is moderately sparce. It can often be found growing with *Sagittaria subulata, Sagittaria calycina,* and *Nuphar advena.*

BASIS OF STATUS CLASSIFICATION: The few and scattered localities for *Isoetes riparia* in Pennsylvania are the basis for placing it on the Pennsyl-

Endangered

SLENDER ROCK-BRAKE
Cryptogramma stelleri (S. G. Gmel.) Prantl.
Family Polypodiaceae
Order Filicales

DESCRIPTION: The slender rock-brake is a drooping, delicate fern with sterile and fertile (spore-bear-

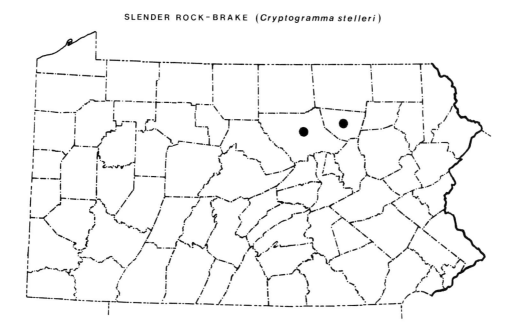

SLENDER ROCK-BRAKE (*Cryptogramma stelleri*)

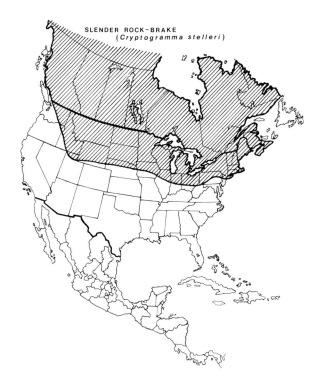

SLENDER ROCK-BRAKE
(*Cryptogramma stelleri*)

ing) fronds. The fertile fronds are narrower, more erect, and bear the spores along the leaf margins. The sterile fronds are broader and form the drooping base of the plant; they have a membraneous quality. Both fronds are "twice-cut." The fern takes root by putting forth short, densely rooting rhizomes, which are covered with pale brown scales.

RANGE: The slender rock-brake has a circumboreal distribution, in America from Newfoundland to Alaska south to northern New Jersey, Pennsylvania, West Virginia, Illinois, Iowa, Utah, and Washington. Herbarium records for the plant are from two Pennsylvania counties—Lycoming and Sullivan. One known locality near Lincoln Falls was relocated in 1982. There are three historical records which have not been recently relocated, although attempts were made in 1982. This species was first collected in Pennsylvania near Lincoln Falls in 1919.

HABITAT: Prime habitat for *Cryptogramma stelleri* is dripping, sandstone cliffs and limestone rock outcrops in partly to deeply shaded spots. This species is restricted to cool, wet rocky cliffs and outcrops associated with streams. Areas where this species is found also often contain *Asplenium trichomanes*, *Pilea pumila*, and *Circaea alpina*, and an abundance of mosses and liverworts.

BASIS OF STATUS CLASSIFICATION: The scattered and occasional distribution of *Cryptogramma stelleri* in Pennsylvania is the basis for placing it on the Pennsylvania Plants of Special Concern list. Although more common in Canada, a factor that would more likely put this species in the "rare" category, in Pennsylvania and New England very little suitable habitat is available. Wet cliff habitat, while quite inaccessible, can be dramatically disturbed by only a few rock climbers. In addition, the extremely moist conditions necessary for the slender rock-brake can be easily changed by altering the upstream water courses by damming and channelization.

Where it occurs, the slender rock-brake is usually abundant, but because it is difficult to find, it is often over collected. Outside of Pennsylvania, this fern is on the list of special concern in Maine, Massachusetts, New Hampshire, and Connecticut. Because of its rarity in Pennsylvania and New England, this species is included in the "Endangered" category.

RECOMMENDATIONS: The localities where this plant still occurs should be afforded public or private preservation status. Further searching in limestone and other wet cliff areas should be done.

PREPARED BY: Sara Davison, *1218 Chestnut Street, Suite 505, Philadelphia, PA 19107.*

Endangered

ARROWHEAD
Sagittaria calycina Engelm. var. *spongiosa* Engelm.
Family Alismataceae
Order Alismatales

DESCRIPTION: The leaves of this arrowhead, which originate from a common base, may or may not be flattened to form a blade. The bases of the leaves are very spongy. The small white flowers are borne on stalks shorter than the leaves, usually in groups of one to three. This species usually occurs singly in small tufts, and "disappears" at high tide.

RANGE: This arrowhead can be found from northeast New Brunswick to Virginia in brackish and fresh tidal marshes. In Pennsylvania, this species is found only along the Delaware River and its tidal tributaries. Herbarium specimens are only from Bucks County. Recently verified populations have been found at Neshaminy State Park and near Bristol. In Pennsylvania, this species was not collected

Arrowhead *Sagittaria calycina* var. *spongiosa*). Photograph by P. G. Wiegman.

ARROWHEAD (*Sagittaria calycina*)

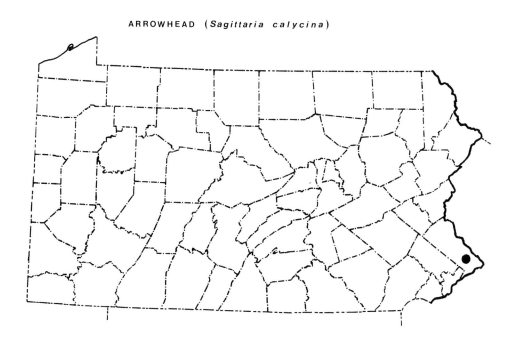

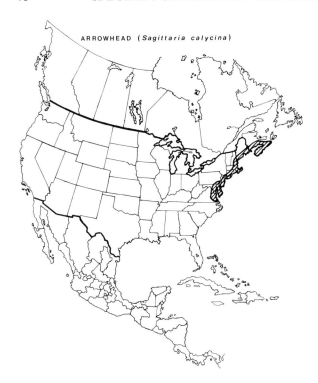

ARROWHEAD (*Sagittaria calycina*)

until the twentieth century. It probably was overlooked by early botanists because of its similarity to other arrowheads, and unpromising habitat.

HABITAT: This is a wetland species, which is restricted to freshwater intertidal shores. It may be found in muddy freshwater to brackish marshes, ponds, and sluggish streams where the vegetation is often quite open. In freshwater tidal areas, this species grows near the limits of the low tide mark. It can be found growing with *Sagittaria subulata* and *Zizania aquatica,* both of which are intertidal endemics.

BASIS OF STATUS CLASSIFICATION: The limited occurrence of *Sagittaria calycina* in Pennsylvania is the basis for placing it on the Pennsylvania Plants of Special Concern list. At some sites it is locally abundant and at others it is quite rare.

Sagittaria calycina is rare in the east as a result of habitat loss. Large tidal rivers such as the Delaware, Hudson, and the James are all heavily used for industrial purposes. Dredging and filling, pollution, and bulkheading have all contributed to the loss of intertidal marsh along these rivers. Because there are only two known localities for this species in Pennsylvania and because of its very threatened habitat, *Sagittaria calycina* is included in the "Endangered" category.

RECOMMENDATIONS: The localities where this plant still occurs should be afforded public or private preservation status. At Neshaminy State Park, areas containing *Sagittaria calycina* should be delineated and recreational activities focused elsewhere.

SELECTED REFERENCE:

FERREN, W. R., JR., and A. E. SCHUYLER. 1980. Intertidal vascular plants of river systems near Philadelphia. Proc. Acad. Nat. Sci. Philadelphia, 132:86–120.

PREPARED BY: Sara Davison, *1218 Chestnut Street, Suite 505, Philadelphia, PA 19107.*

Endangered

SUBULATA ARROWHEAD
Sagittaria subulata (L.) Buch.
Family Alismataceae
Order Alismatales

DESCRIPTION: This arrowhead has thin, strap-shaped leaves arising from a common base. The leaves are blunt tipped, dark green, and often covered with mud and algal growth. The flowers are small and white, in whorls of one to three. The plant is low-growing forming extensive turf-like carpets. It expands its colonies with long straight runners. It often grows under a canopy of *Nuphar advena, Scirpus pungens,* and *Zizania aquatica,* and "disappears" at high tide.

RANGE: This species ranges from Massachusetts to Florida in brackish to freshwater tidal mud. In Pennsylvania, the distribution is restricted to the freshwater tidal shores of the Delaware River and its tidal tributaries. Herbarium records in Pennsylvania are from the three counties of Bucks, Philadelphia, and Delaware.

Today, *Sagittaria subulata* has not been found below northeast Philadelphia. Populations have recently been verified around Bristol and Andalusia. Historically, *Sagittaria subulata* was common along the Delaware River, having been first collected in Pennsylvania in 1814 from Philadelphia.

HABITAT: This species is a strict intertidal endemic, growing in mud covered gravelly substrates along both fresh and brackish shorelines. The species grows from the middle intertidal zone all the way down to the low water mark, while another variety is a submerged deep water species over a similar range. *Sagittaria subulata* is frequently found growing with

SUBULATA ARROWHEAD (*Sagittaria subulata*)

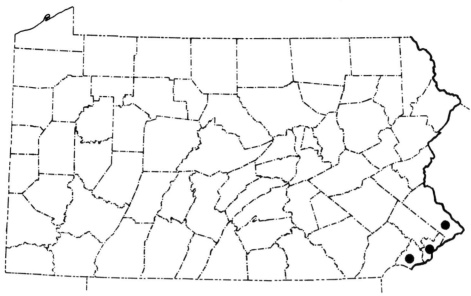

other intertidal or wetlands species such as *Isoetes riparia, Zizania aquatica,* and *Nuphar advena.*

BASIS OF STATUS CLASSIFICATION: The restricted habitat of *Sagittaria subulata* in Pennsylvania and within its total range is the basis for placing it on the Pennsylvania Plants of Special Concern

SUBULATA ARROWHEAD (*Sagittaria subulata*)

list. It is also on the special concern list in adjacent New Jersey, Delaware, and Maryland. Its intertidal habitat is threatened by dredging, filling, bulkheading, pollution, and other industrial and recreational uses. Because of the dramatic loss of habitat, *Sagittaria subulata* is included in the "Endangered" category.

RECOMMENDATIONS: The localities where this plant still remains should be afforded public or private preservation status. During the 404 permit review process, intact intertidal marshes should be identified to avoid conflicts with proposed development.

SELECTED REFERENCE:

FERREN, W. R., JR., and A. E. SCHUYLER. 1980. Intertidal vascular plants of river systems near Philadelphia. Proc. Acad. Nat. Sci. Philadelphia, 132:86–120.

PREPARED BY: Sara Davison, *1218 Chestnut Street, Suite 505, Philadelphia, PA 19107.*

Endangered

SMALL-WHORLED POGONIA
Isotria medeoloides (Pursh.) Raf.
Family Orchidaceae
Order Orchidales

DESCRIPTION: This delicate and inconspicuous little orchid, 15 to 25 cm tall, is a perennial herb

Small-whorled Pogonia (*Isotria medeoloides*). Photograph by P. G. Wiegman.

arising from a cluster of thickened roots. The erect stem bears a single whorl of usually five leaves near the top. The yellowish green flowers are borne just above the whorl of leaves. The short, arching sepals are 16 to 20 mm long and are the most conspicuous feature that separates *Isotria medeoloides* from the more common *Isotria verticillata*. The plant blooms in late May or early June.

RANGE: This species is found in Maine, New Hampshire, and Vermont, then south to North Carolina and Missouri. Apparently it occurs throughout

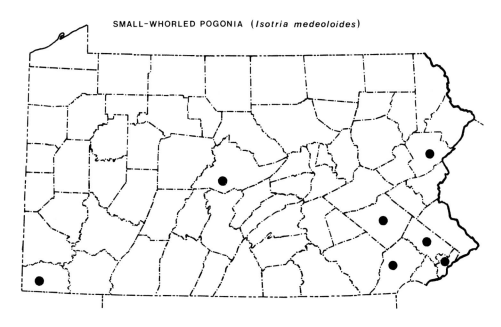

SMALL-WHORLED POGONIA (*Isotria medeoloides*)

Pennsylvania with possible exception of the extreme northwest.

There are Pennsylvania records for Berks, Montgomery, Philadelphia, Chester, Monroe, Centre, and Greene counties. The first records are from Chester County, 1884. The most recent collections are from Centre County, 1973, that population was still extant as of 1982. It is presently the only known population in Pennsylvania.

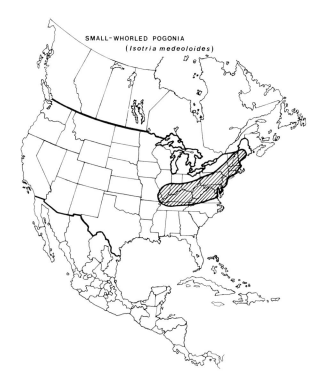

SMALL-WHORLED POGONIA
(*Isotria medeoloides*)

HABITAT: The small-whorled pogonia occurs in dry, generally acid woodlands. In Pennsylvania, the species is mostly found in oak or oak-hickory forests with rocky, acidic soils. This type of habitat is abundant in the Commonwealth as much of the central portion is vegetated with such woodland. Apparently, specific microhabitat factors are required by the species.

According to Correll (1950), *Isotria medeoloides* will produce leaves and flowers above the surface for a few years, then remain dormant, as a root stalk, for up to 20 years. This has not been substantiated, but is not unusual for other members of the orchid family to be found in great abundance one year, and not found in subsequent years at the same locality.

BASIS OF STATUS CLASSIFICATION: Isotria medeoloides is considered our rarest native orchid. It has been known to occur in 49 counties of 17 eastern states and Canada. Extant populations are currently known from 12 counties in 11 states. In Pennsylvania, the plant has been recorded from eight localities in seven counties. Today there are two remaining populations—one has two plants, the other three plants, both are in the same general locality.

Michigan and South Carolina have officially listed *Isotria medeoloides* as an endangered plant. In August 1982, the species was added to the Federal list of endangered plants, making it the first Federally listed plant in Pennsylvania. That listing applies to the plants total range, including, Connecticut, Georgia, Illinois, Massachusetts, Maryland, Nebraska,

Michigan, Missouri, Montana, New Hampshire, New Jersey, New York, North Carolina, Pennsylvania, Rhode Island, South Carolina, Virginia, and Vermont.

RECOMMENDATIONS: There are several reasons for the decline of *Isotria medeoloides.* Collection of extant populations have contributed to a gradual decline. Some collections of rare plants are for valid reasons, but collections by the wild flower gardeners and other unnecessary taking of specimens has also reduced their numbers. A more critical problem, however, is inadvertent habitat alteration.

Inadvertent alteration of the macrohabitat, especially from logging, and similar damage to the microhabitat from trampling or soil compaction are the most serious threats. The species occurs in a common habitat, oak-hickory woodlands. This forest type is extensively utilized for lumber and other wood products. *Isotria medeoloides* is at best inconspicuous even during the height of bloom. Furthermore, the species may remain dormant, or lead a saprophytic existance for long periods. Without extensive searching, and documentation of existing populations, inadvertent loss will continue.

Both localities in Centre County have been recently logged. Through the insistance of a local resident, who was aware of the plants, the land owners and logging contractors were notified and their operations were voluntarily restricted at the specific sites. In both cases, the populations were saved.

SELECTED REFERENCE:

CORRELL, D. S. 1950. Native orchids of North America, north of Mexico. Chronica Botanica Co., Waltham, Massachusetts, new series, 26:xv + 1–399 pp.

PREPARED BY: Paul G. Wiegman, *Western Pennsylvania Conservancy, 316 Fourth Avenue, Pittsburgh, PA 15222.*

Endangered

KIDNEY-LEAVED TWAYBLADE
Listera smallii Wieg.
Family Orchidaceae
Order Orchidales

DESCRIPTION: The kidney-leaved twayblade is a delicate erect herb with a single pair of opposite sessile leaves situated near the middle of the erect stem. The leaves are 1.5–3 cm long and broadly ovate. Flowers are borne at the top of a slender stalk.

The lateral petals and sepals are nearly alike giving the appearance of five similar petals, with one lower petal forming a declining lip. In *L. smallii* the lip is not cleft to the middle and is longer than the other petals. The kidney-leaved twayblade blooms from July to August.

RANGE: The kidney-leaved twayblade is known from central Pennsylvania south in the mountains to eastern Kentucky and North Carolina. In Pennsylvania, the plant has been collected in southern Centre, Huntingdon, and Somerset counties. They appear to be found only in the mountains of south-central Pennsylvania.

HABITAT: The general habitat description for this species is wooded slopes. In Pennsylvania, the recorded populations have been found in and around springs and seeps, or flood plains of small streams where there is a dense mat of sphagnum growing underneath rhododendron. Most of the plants are in small openings where there is direct sun for a short period.

SPECIAL OR UNUSUAL FEATURES: The three *Listera* species which occur in Pennsylvania are all on the Pennsylvania Plants of Special Concern list. They are *L. smallii* ("Endangered"), *L. australis* ("Threatened"), and *L. cordata* ("Species of concern"). The first, *L. smallii,* is the only species in Pennsylvania with the lip not divided to the middle, the other two have deeply cleft lips. All three are plants of sphagnum bogs or mossy edges of springs and small cold streams.

BASIS OF STATUS CLASSIFICATION: Due to the decline in occurrence, the relatively small total range, and the restricted habitat, *Listera smallii* has been placed in the "Endangered" category.

Kidney-leaved twayblade was collected in three counties from six localities in south-central Pennsylvania. The Centre County collections made in 1853, 1931, and 1937 are from Bear Meadows. A number of seeps and springs on the north side of the Bear Meadows Natural Area were examined in 1980, but *L. smallii* was not found.

In Huntingdon County, *L. smallii* was collected at Alan Seeger Natural Area in 1977 and 1978. A large vigorous population was still extant in 1980 and 1981.

The Somerset County records were collected in

Kidney-leaved Twayblade (*Listera smallii*). Photograph by P. G. Wiegman.

1898 from Big Springs near Petersburg. That locality was visited in 1981 and the species could not be found. In 1982, a small remnant of a sphagnum mat along a stream near Buckstown was located. No return visit was made, but this area is believed to be from the same tract where *L. smallii* was collected in 1898. Unfortunately, the sphagnum mat covers only a fraction of the natural bowl which was probably sphagnum bog in the past. The area is now a pasture.

The species is listed as endangered in New Jersey where it occurs at a single locality. In West Virginia, the plant is listed as rare, being found in five counties.

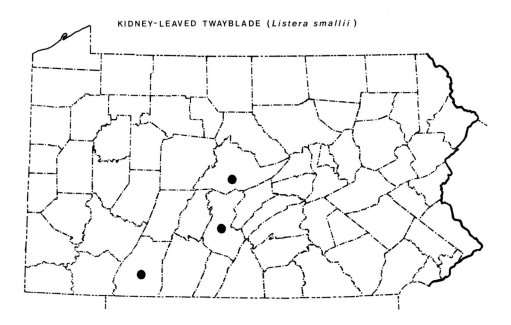

KIDNEY-LEAVED TWAYBLADE (*Listera smallii*)

RECOMMENDATIONS: Known occurrences of *Listera smallii* on public lands should be designated as Natural Areas and as Plant Sanctuaries under the Pennsylvania Act 163. This applies to, and has been carried out to some degree at, Alan Seeger Natural Area owned by the Pennsylvania Bureau of Forestry in Huntingdon County.

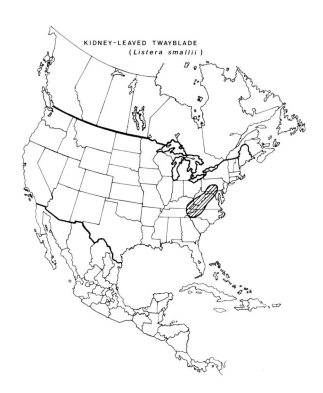

KIDNEY-LEAVED TWAYBLADE
(*Listera smallii*)

SELECTED REFERENCES:

CLARKSON, R. B., D. K. EVANS, R. FORTNEY, W. GRAFTON, and L. RADER. 1981. Rare and endangered vascular plant species in West Virginia. U.S. Fish and Wildlife Service, Washington, DC, iii + 76 pp.
JENNINGS, O. E. 1953. Wild flowers of western Pennsylvania and the Upper Ohio Basin. Univ. Pittsburgh Press, Pittsburgh, Pennsylvania 1:lxxv + 574 pp.
SNYDER, D. B., and V. E. VIVIAN. 1981. Rare and endangered vascular plant species in New Jersey. U.S. Fish and Wildlife Service, Washington, DC, viii + 98 pp.

PREPARED BY: Paul G. Wiegman, *Western Pennsylvania Conservancy, 316 Fourth Avenue, Pittsburgh, PA 15222.*

Endangered
BARRATT'S SEDGE
Carex barrattii Schw. & Torr.
Family Cyperaceae
Order Poales

DESCRIPTION: Pennsylvania has a large number of sedges, a complex group of plants that are distinct as species, but are difficult to separate due to their minute and often inconspicuous differences. Field identification is impossible in all except certain highly distinctive species. For a detailed description see Gleason (1952). Overall, the plant is a tuft of grass-like leaves arising from long thickened roots. The clusters are 30–80 cm tall and the principal blades 2–4 mm wide.

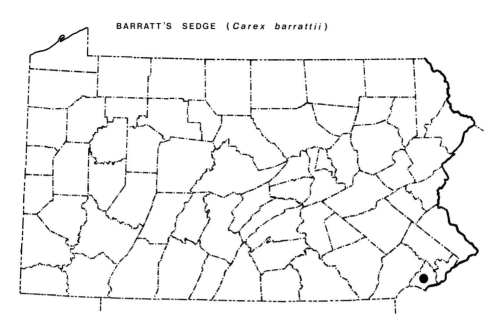

BARRATT'S SEDGE (*Carex barrattii*)

RANGE: Barratt's sedge occurs from Connecticut to North Carolina principally along the coast. In Pennsylvania, the species is found only in Delaware County, specifically in the Tinicum Marsh area.

HABITAT: As a coastal species, this sedge is found in wet ground of swamps and marshes near the coast. It is particularly noted for its occurrence in pine-barren wetlands.

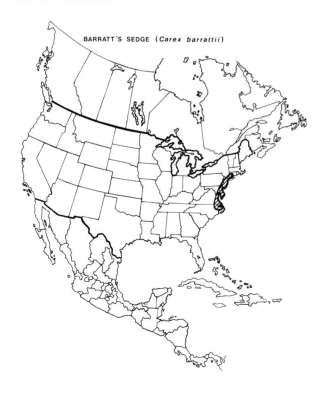

BARRATT'S SEDGE (*Carex barrattii*)

BASIS OF STATUS CLASSIFICATION: Barrett's sedge is listed as "Endangered" due to the scarcity of occurrence records within Pennsylvania, and the lack of recent observations. The plant has been collected only in the Tinicum Marsh area of Delaware County. Most of the collections were made in the late 1800's and early 1900's, the most recent collection made in 1914 at Essington. The other factor for its listing is the relatively small range and extreme pressure on the plants critical habitat.

New York lists the plant as "Northern Limit of Range," New Jersey as "Rare, Local and Declining," and Connecticut lists *Carex barrattii* as being at the "Northern Limit of Range and Local."

RECOMMENDATIONS: Because of the extensive industrial and residential development in the region that Barratt's sedge once occurred, probably the only remaining stands are within the protected Tinicum Wildlife Refuge. That area should be searched for the species, and if located, the area designated and protected to assure continued existence of the species.

SELECTED REFERENCES:

DOWHAN, J. J., and R. J. CRAIG. 1976. Rare and endangered species of Connecticut and their habitats. State Geological and Natural History Survey of Connecticut, Hartford, Connecticut, 6:v + 1–137.

GLEASON, H. A. 1952. The new Britton and Brown illustrated flora of the northeastern United States and adjacent Canada. Lancaster Press, Inc., Lancaster, Pennsylvania, 1:1xxxv + 1–482; 2:iv + 1–655; 3:iii + 1–589.

MEHRHOFF, L. J. 1978. Rare and endangered vascular plant species in Connecticut. U.S. Fish and Wildlife Service, Washington, DC, vii + 41 pp.

MITCHELL, R. S., C. J. SHEVIAK, and J. K. DEAN. 1980. Rare and endangered vascular plant species in New York State. U.S. Fish and Wildlife Service, Washington, DC, 38 pp.

MITCHELL, R. S., and C. J. SHEVIAK. 1981. Rare plants of New York state. State Univ. New York, Albany, New York State Mus., Bull., 445:vii + 1–96.

SNYDER, D. B., and V. E. VIVIAN. 1981. Rare and endangered vascular plant species in New Jersey. U.S. Fish and Wildlife Service, Washington, DC, viii–98 pp.

PREPARED BY: Paul G. Wiegman, *Western Pennsylvania Conservancy, 316 Fourth Avenue, Pittsburgh, PA 15222.*

Endangered

PRAIRIE DROPSEED
Sporobolus heterolepis (Gray) Gray
Family Gramineae
Order Poales

DESCRIPTION: Prairie dropseed is a tall grass with long, narrow, often rolled leaves. The inflorescence is usually cylindric to ovoid. Each spikelet is single-flowered with unequal glumes—the first being half as long as the second. It is an attractive perennial occurring in conspicuous tufts. The seeds drop quite soon after ripening and are dispersed, while the glumes are persistent; hence, the name dropseed.

RANGE: This grass is a prairie species ranging from Ontario to Saskatchewan south to Texas with oc-

casional disjunct occurrences in eastern Pennsylvania, Connecticut, and Quebec. Herbarium records in Pennsylvania for this species are from Lancaster and Chester counties. Recently verified populations have been found at Goat Hill barrens and New Texas barrens. These two sites are also the only historical collections for this species in Pennsylvania, the first made by Carter in 1866.

HABITAT: Prairie dropseed grows in dry open ground, such as prairies in the west and bluffs and serpentine outcrops in the east. It is found in sunny, exposed locations with sparce and low associated vegetation. In Pennsylvania, Connecticut, and Quebec, prairie dropseed has only been found on serpentine barrens; these populations are quite disjunct from the western populations. In Pennsylvania, it can be found growing with serpentine endemics such as *Aster depauperatus* and *Cerastium arvense* var. *villossissimum*.

BASIS OF STATUS CLASSIFICATION: The restricted distribution of *Sporobolus heterolepis* in Pennsylvania is the basis for placing it on the Pennsylvania Plants of Special Concern list. Although more common in the west, a factor that would more likely put this species in the "Rare" category, in Pennsylvania it is restricted to dry, open serpentine outcrops. Serpentine outcrops in the Commonwealth are restricted to Lancaster, Chester and Delaware counties in the Piedmont province. In the

PRAIRIE DROPSEED (*Sporobolus heterolepis*)

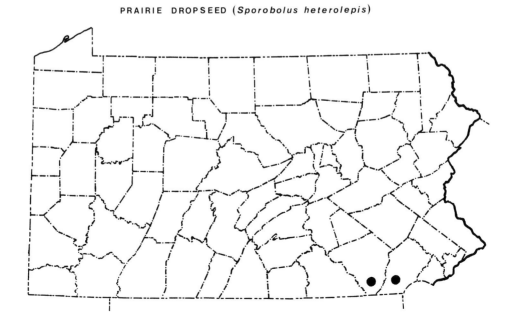

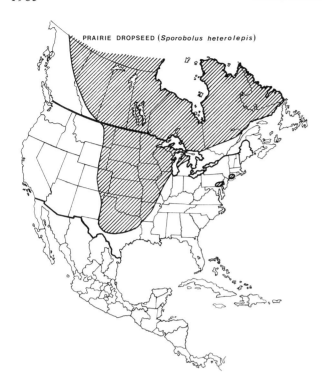

PRAIRIE DROPSEED (*Sporobolus heterolepis*)

past, serpentine barrens were exploited for their chrome deposits, and today are still quarried for road fill. Although unsuitable for cultivation, serpentine barrens were frequently pastured. Grazing, quarrying, and development continue to threaten the few serpentine barrens that remain in Pennsylvania. Because of the limited distribution of suitable habitat, and the threat to existing habitat, prairie dropseed is included in the "Endangered" category.

RECOMMENDATIONS: The two localities where this species still occurs should be afforded public or private preservation status.

SELECTED REFERENCE:

PENNELL, F. W. 1910. Flora of the Conowingo Barrens of southeastern Pennsylvania. Proc. Acad. Nat. Sci. Philadelphia, 62:541–584.

PREPARED BY: Sara Davison, *1218 Chestnut Street, Suite 505, Philadelphia, PA 19107.*

Endangered

WHITE MONKSHOOD
Aconitum reclinatum Gray
Family Ranunculaceae
Order Ranales

DESCRIPTION: The white monkshood is a low perennial herb arising from a short tuber. The pal-

mately, 5-cleft leaves are distinctive of both this species and the remainder of the genus. Stems of the plant are weak and reclining, usually climbing over surrounding larger herbs and shrubs. Occasionally the stems will reach lengths of 3 m.

The leaves are deeply cleft, mostly into five parts, but occasionally three parts, but not to the base. Of the two *Aconitum* in Pennsylvania, *A. uncinatum*, has smooth flower stalks and blue flowers. *Aconitum reclinatum* has a hairy flower stalk and white flowers with a prolonged spur-like projection. They bloom in late August or early September.

RANGE: This attractive native woodland species occurs in the mountains of southwestern Pennsylvania into West Virginia south to Virginia and Georgia. In Pennsylvania, the plant is known from the counties of Somerset and Fayette. The plant was first collected at Wymp's Gap, Fayette County in 1940 and again later in 1947. The Somerset County locality was discovered in 1977.

HABITAT: White monkshood prefers rich, generally moist mountain woods, usually along streams and adjacent flood plains. At both southwestern Pennsylvania localities, the plant is found on the floodplains of small streams.

SPECIALIZED OR UNIQUE CHARACTERISTICS: The genus *Aconitum* is represented by three native species in the eastern United States, none of which are abundant or widely distributed. Both *A. reclinatum* and *A. uncinatum* occur in Pennsylvania and are on the special concern list, the latter as "Threatened." *A. noveboracense* is listed in New York as "Endangered," but there are no records from Pennsylvania. This species also occurs in the unglaciated sections of Iowa and Wisconsin.

There are several *Aconitums* in cultivation. *A. napellus* L., a poisonous European cultivar, the source of the drug aconite and the alkaloid aconitine, has been noted in the wild.

BASIS OF STATUS CLASSIFICATION: During the initial development of the Pennsylvania Plants of Special Concern (PPSC) list, *Aconitum reclinatum* was listed as Extirpated, based on reports that the Fayette County locality had been strip mined. The Somerset County Record was unknown at that time. After the 1979 publication of the PPSC list,

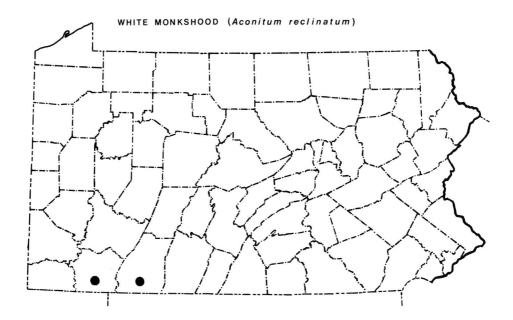

WHITE MONKSHOOD (*Aconitum reclinatum*)

the Somerset County Record came to light, and it was discovered that the Fayette County locality had not been destroyed. Therefore, the species was moved from "Extirpated" to "Endangered."

The present status is based on the relatively small range outside Pennsylvania, the few known localities within the Commonwealth, and the improbability of additional new localities since the plant is at its northern limit of range. Another contributory factor to the status is the generally sporadic distribution of the genus. Both species of *Aconitum* in Pennsylvania are local and thus on the PPSC list.

Aconitum reclinatum is on the West Virginia list as "Rare and Restricted."

RECOMMENDATIONS: Survival of *Aconitum reclinatum* in Pennsylvania can best be accomplished through securing the site of one of the extant populations and protecting the area against habitat changes that would eliminate the species.

Both known colonies have been recently surveyed, and the populations are intact. The Somerset County locality is close to a heavily used and potentially expandable road on the south side of Mount Davis. Apparently the plant has not been effected by disturbance at the location, or has recently colonized in the rather open habitat. This locality is not the original colony collected by Kunsman in 1977. However, this site would be difficult to protect from possible road salt damage, spraying of a nearby powerline right-of-way, or expansion of the road from Savage, Pennsylvania, to Mount Davis.

WHITE MONKSHOOD (*Aconitum reclinatum*)

The Fayette County locality is in a better position to be protected. There are several colonies of *Aconitum reclinatum* along Laurel Run east of Wymp's Gap. These were field surveyed in 1981 and 1982. At least one of the colonies is on Forbes State Forest. This area should be delineated and the tract considered for Natural Area Status under the Pennsylvania State Forest's Natural Area Program.

SELECTED REFERENCES:

FORTNEY, R. H., R. B. CLARKSON, C. N. HARVEY, and J. KARTESZ. 1978. Vascular plants. Rare and endangered species of West Virginia: a preliminary report. West Virginia Department of Natural Resources, Heritage Trust Program, Charleston, West Virginia, 1:vii + 1–96.

JENNINGS, O. E. 1953. Wild flowers of western Pennsylvania and the Upper Ohio Basin. Univ. Pittsburgh Press, Pittsburgh, Pennsylvania, 1:lxxv + 574 pp.

WHERRY, E. T., and C. S. KENNER. 1977. A preliminary list of rare species of vascular plants native to Pennsylvania. Pennsylvania State Univ., University Park, Pennsylvania, Unpublished Report, 8 pp.

PREPARED BY: Paul G. Wiegman, *Western Pennsylvania Conservancy, 316 Fourth Avenue, Pittsburgh, PA 15222.*

Endangered

SPREADING GLOBE-FLOWER
Trollius laxus Salisb.
Family Ranunculaceae
Order Ranales

DESCRIPTION: The spreading globe-flower is a low growing herb of alkaline wetlands. The leaves are broad palmately 5 or 7-parted, that strongly suggest the buttercup family. Generally, the plant is sprawling or at least partly reclining with the succulent stems supported by surrounding vegetation. In late April or early May a solitary large, terminal blossom is produced. Although the petals are inconspicuous, the flower has 5–7 greenish yellow showy sepals. Globe-flower resembles marsh marigold, *Caltha palustris,* and may be found in the same wetland, but the solitary flower and upper two sessile leaves, which surround the stem, are distinguishing characteristics.

RANGE: *Trollius laxus* occurs in the eastern U.S. from Connecticut westward into Michigan, and southward into Delaware. It potentially can be found throughout Pennsylvania; however, the distribution is very spotty. In eastern Pennsylvania, the plant is known from the upper Delaware River Valley, just south of the glaciated region. A few records have been found north of the Delaware Water Gap, but most collections have been made in the limestone region south of Kittantinny Ridge and around South Mountain.

In western Pennsylvania, all historic and extant populations are within the glaciated region. There is one record from the limestone valley region in central Pennsylvania.

HABITAT: Spreading globe-flower grows in calcareous, wet meadows and edges of swamps. The Northampton County, Pennsylvania, localities are open wet meadows with sparse to moderate shrub cover. Ground cover is tufted grasses or sedges surrounded by flowing surface water in finely braided rivulets. The water courses have mud bottoms. Individual *Trollius* plants grow on top of, or sprouting from, the sedge clumps, and are somewhat above the saturated soils of the rivulets.

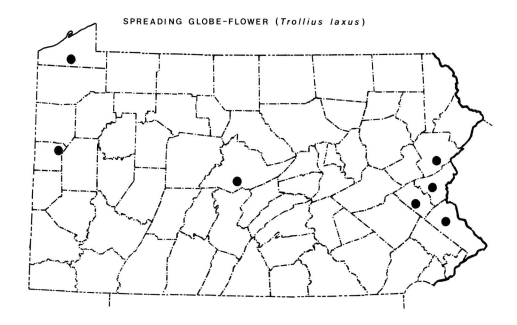

SPREADING GLOBE-FLOWER (*Trollius laxus*)

SPREADING GLOBE-FLOWER
(*Trollius laxus*)

Wetlands of this type are fed by diffuse sources of ground water surfacing at the base of small glacially formed knolls. At both the Northampton and Lawrence County localities, the ground water surfaces from unconsolidated glacial till.

The alkaline soil affinities of *Trollius laxus* are strong. Areas where *Trollius* occurs often contain other plants which require alkaline soils including *Parnassia glauca, Smilacina stellata, Geum rivale, Salix serrisima, Cypripedium reginae,* and *Rhynchospora capillacea.* Adjacent to the alkaline portions of the wet meadow, the soil chemistry apparently changes to a more acid reaction. *Trollius,* as well as other calcareous species, is lacking and replaced by more typical acid wetland species.

BASIS OF STATUS CLASSIFICATION: Trollius laxus occurs sporadically in rare edaphic conditions. The plant has been collected in seven counties of Pennsylvania, but recent field searches have located only three extant populations in two counties. All localities are in private ownership.

Habitat disturbance is the most serious threat to the survival of the populations. The wet, calcareous meadows are often used for agricultural activities and as pasture for grazing livestock. Drainage and conversion to cropland is easily accomplished. Although wetlands have received a generous amount of attention recently, and protective measures have

increased, these small wet meadows are overlooked when compared to larger swamps and marshes teeming with highly visible wildlife.

In addition to being a relatively inconspicuous habitat, calcareous wet meadows are rare in Pennsylvania. At present, there are only eight known areas where this unique habitat remains intact. Of these, three contain *Trollius laxus*; all of which are now being used for livestock pasture.

Proper habitat for *Trollius laxus* is greatly dependent on specific ground water amounts and chemistry. Apparently the recharge areas which supply the subsurface flow, composition of the rock strata or glacial materials through which the water flows, and the relief character of the discharge area all contribute to the uniqueness of these wetlands.

Disturbance of any of these factors can irrevocably alter the habitat and eliminate *Trollius.* Because the groundwater may originate some distance from the discharge area, the general development of the region is a potential threat.

Trollius laxus was originally proposed for the Federal list of Endangered Plants. It presently is classified as "Under Review." In Connecticut, the plant is classified as "Few—known from three or fewer vouchered stations, Rare—usually occurring as a single individual or very few individuals, and Ind—status indeterminate." New Jersey lists the plant as "Rare—not threatened with extinction, but requiring observation," Local, and southeast Limit of range. It is known to be extant at eight stations in New Jersey and was seen in 1980. New York lists the plant as "Rare," vulnerable to loss of habitat, and declining. The plant is gone from southern New York and extirpated from over half of the sites visited in 1979. Ohio lists the species as "Endangered." Delaware reports that "no authentic specimen is known."

RECOMMENDATION: Protection and preservation of *Trollius laxus* necessitates the protection of the immediate habitat, as well as the geologic and edaphic conditions that are necessary for the plants survival. The immediate habitat should be protected by outright purchase of the privately owned locations. Furthermore, it may be necessary to apply restrictive measures to surrounding lands to assure continual water supply to the wetlands.

SELECTED REFERENCES:

DOWHAN, J. J., and R. J. CRAIG. 1976. Rare and endangered species of Connecticut and their habitats. State Geological and Natural History Survey of Connecticut, Hartford, Connecticut, 6:v + 1–137.

FAIRBROTHERS, D. E., and M. Y. HOUGH. 1973. Rare or endangered vascular plants of New Jersey. New Jersey State Mus., Trenton, New Jersey, Sci. Notes, 14:1–53.

MEHRHOFF, L. J. 1978. Rare and endangered vascular plant species in Connecticut. U.S. Fish and Wildlife Service, Washington, DC, vii + 41 pp.

MITCHELL, R. S., C. J. SHEVIAK, and J. K. DEAN. 1980. Rare and endangered vascular plant species in New York state. U.S. Fish and Wildlife Service, Washington, DC, 38 pp.

MITCHELL, R. S., and C. H. SHEVIAK. 1981. Rare plants of New York state. State Univ. New York, Albany, New York State Mus., Bull., 445:viii + 1–96.

OHIO DEPARTMENT OF NATURAL RESOURCES. 1982. Rare species of native Ohio wild plants. Division of Natural Areas and Preserves, Columbus, Ohio, Unpublished Report, 20 pp.

SNYDER, D. B., and V. E. VIVIAN. 1981. Rare and endangered vascular plant species in New Jersey. U.S. Fish and Wildlife Service, Washington, DC, viii + 98 pp.

TUCKER, A. O., N. H. DILL, C. R. BROOME, C. E. PHILLIPS, and M. J. MACIARELLO. 1979. Rare and endangered vascular plant species in Delaware. U.S. Fish and Wildlife Service, Newton Corner, Massachusetts, x + 89 pp.

PREPARED BY: Paul G. Wiegman, *Western Pennsylvania Conservancy, 316 Fourth Avenue, Pittsburgh, PA 15222.*

Endangered

WATER PIGMY-WEED
Crassula aquatica (L.) Schoenl.
Family Crassulaceae
Order Rosales

DESCRIPTION: Water pigmy-weed is a small (20–100 mm) freely branching annual herb with narrow succulent leaves that are fused around the stem. The flowers form in late summer and are tiny, seldom exceeding 1 mm wide with four white or greenish-white petals. Each single flower grows at the point where the leaf and stem join.

RANGE: Crassula aquatica is the only species of this genus that occurs in northeastern North America. It can be found within the limits of tides from Quebec and Newfoundland to Maryland. In the southern United States it occurs in Louisiana and Texas. The plant is also a native of the Pacific Coast and Eurasia.

In Pennsylvania, the plant has been collected only from Bucks County at a single locality near Andalusia.

HABITAT: This plant occurs along open, muddy shores near the coast and usually within the limits of the tide. In Pennsylvania, the collections were made in fresh water intertidal areas near the mouth of a tributary stream. Collection notes state the plant was growing at the base of *Zizania* a few cm above the mud.

BASIS OF STATUS CLASSIFICATION: Crassula aquatica is classified as "Endangered" due to its limited occurrence in the Commonwealth, and the likelihood that it is no longer extant. Of the three specimens collected from Bucks County, two were taken on the same date in 1917, and the third at the

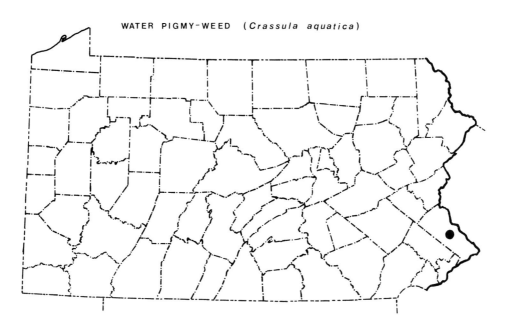

WATER PIGMY-WEED (*Crassula aquatica*)

WATER PIGMY-WEED (*Crassula aquatica*)

same locality in 1918 with a note "we could only find this one plant."

Crassula aquatica is listed in Delaware as southeastern limit of range, and possibly extirpated, with the last collection made in 1867. Maryland lists the species at a few sites with only one collection in 1950, the remainder in the 1800's. New York classifies it as "Restricted to Habitats Rare in the State." Connecticut lists *Crassula* as "Declining and Vulnerable with few sites."

RECOMMENDATIONS: This is one of several intertidal mud flat species, which need to be searched for in Pennsylvania and a clear statement of population status defined. Of the few sites with proper habitat, one or several should be identified and either public or private action taken to assure that the site is protected. The best solution would be acquisition by a conservation organization, with detailed management actions taken to protect the habitat from outside alteration.

SELECTED REFERENCES:

BROOME, C. R., A. O. TUCKER, J. L. REVEAL, and N. H. DILL. 1979. Rare and endangered vascular plant species in Maryland. U.S. Fish and Wildlife Service, Newton Corner, Massachusetts, vii + 64 pp.

DOWHAN, J. J., and R. J. CRAIG. 1976. Rare and endangered species of Connecticut and their habitats. State Geological and Natural History Survey of Connecticut, Hartford, Connecticut, 6:v + 1–137.

MEHRHOFF, L. J. 1970. Rare and endangered vascular plant species in Connecticut. U.S. Fish and Wildlife Service, Washington, DC, vii + 41 pp.

MITCHELL, R. S., C. J. SHEVIAK, and J. K. DEAN. 1980. Rare and endangered vascular plant species in New York state. U.S. Fish and Wildlife Service, Washington, DC, 38 pp.

MITCHELL, R. S., and C. J. SHEVIAK. 1981. Rare plants of New York state. State Univ. New York, Albany, New York State Mus., Bull., 445:xiii + 1–96.

TUCKER, A. O., N. H. DILL, C. R. BROOME, C. E. PHILLIPS, and M. J. MACIARELLO. 1979. U.S. Fish and Wildlife Service, Newton Corner, Massachusetts, x + 89 pp.

PREPARED BY: Paul G. Wiegman, *Western Pennsylvania Conservancy, 316 Fourth Avenue, Pittsburgh, PA 15222.*

Endangered

KATE'S MOUNTAIN CLOVER
Trifolium virginicum Small
Family Fabaceae
Order Rosales

DESCRIPTION: Kate's Mountain clover is a low-growing distinctive clover with a very thick, deep tap root. The pea-shaped flowers are white to yellow-pink. The leaves consist of linear to slightly rounded leaflets in groups of three. The stems, flower stalks, and underside of the leaflets are all thinly hairy. This perennial occurs singly in scattered clumps.

RANGE: Kate's Mountain clover is a shale barrens endemic whose total range is restricted to Virginia, West Virginia, Maryland, and Pennsylvania. Pennsylvania herbarium records for this species are from the counties of Bedford and Huntington. There are six historical localities in Pennsylvania centered around the Chaneysville area in Bedford County. Recent searches have revealed only one extant population in Pennsylvania.

HABITAT: The habitat of Kate's Mountain clover in Pennsylvania is south facing, open, dry slopes of Devonian shale in the Ridge and Valley province. This species is a strict endemic and has never been recorded from sites other than shale barrens. It occurs with other shale barrens endemics such as *Senecio antennariifolius* and *Pseudotaenidia montana*.

BASIS OF STATUS CLASSIFICATION: The nar-

Kate's Mountain Clover (*Trifolium virginicum*). Photograph by P. G. Wiegman.

row total range and restricted habitat within the range of *Trifolium virginicum* is the basis for placing it on the Pennsylvania Plants of Special Concern list. In addition, this species is never abundant where it occurs. A number of historical locations have been destroyed, including the type locality on Kate's Mountain in West Virginia. This species grows only in open, dry areas of the shale barrens community, and is quickly shaded out by higher vegetation or agressive exotics such as crown vetch. In addition, it is sensitive to deer and cattle grazing, and has been overcollected by eager botanists. Kate's Moun-

KATE'S MOUNTAIN CLOVER (*Trifolium virginicum*)

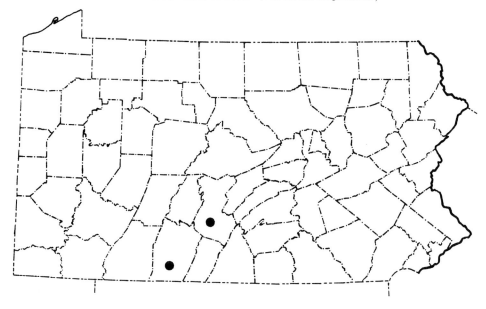

KATE'S MOUNTAIN CLOVER
(*Trifolium virginicum*)

tain clover is the most famous of the shale barrens endemic plants.

Trifolium virginicum is on the list of special concern in every state where it occurs. It is also under review for federal listing. Because of the overall rarity and degree of threat, "Endangered" is the appropriate category for this plant.

RECOMMENDATIONS: There should be additional searching for new locations for Kate's Mountain clover in the shale barrens area of Pennsylvania. The existing population should be afforded public or private preservation status with careful monitoring to detect any population changes.

SELECTED REFERENCES:

Duppstadt, W. H. 1972. Flora of Bedford County, Pennsylvania I. Plant communities. Castanea, 37:86–94.
Henry, L. K. 1954. Shale barrens flora in Pennsylvania. Proc. Pennsylvania Acad. Sci., 28:65–68.
Keener, C. S. 1970. The natural history of the mid-Appalachian shale barrens flora. Pp. 215–245, *in* The distributional history of the biota of the southern Appalachians. II. Flora. (P. C. Holt, ed.), Virginia Polytechnic Institute, Blacksburg, viii + 414 pp.

PREPARED BY: Sara Davison, 1218 Chestnut Street, Suite 505, Philadelphia, PA 19107.

Endangered

CANBY'S MOUNTAIN-LOVER
Pachistima canbyi Gray
Family Celastraceae
Order Celastrales

DESCRIPTION: Pachistima canbyi is a low growing, small woody evergreen shrub with opposite, narrowly crowded leaves. The tiny green four-parted flowers arise from the axils of the upper leaves. The plant seldom grows more than 40 cm in height, but colonies growing freely on rocky terrain can be extensive, covering 2000 to 4000 square m. The flowers bloom in April or May, but distinctive leaves and growth form allow the plant to be found and recognized throughout the year.

RANGE: Canby's mountain-lover can be found from the mountains of western Virginia west into southern Ohio, then south into eastern Kentucky. In Pennsylvania, there are only two known localities, both in central Bedford County. One is near St. Clairsville, and the other at Ashcom along the Raystown branch of the Little Juniata River.

HABITAT: The plant occurs in rocky well-drained upland woods throughout its range. In Pennsylvania, both colonies are at the upper lip of steep slopes above large streams. Also at both localities, the plant is climbing over exposed rock outcrops.

SPECIAL OR UNIQUE CHARACTERISTICS: The Family Celastraceae (Staff-Tree) is an unusual group of woody plants with simple opposite leaves. There are only three genera of the family in Pennsylvania, and they include *Celastrus* (Bittersweet) and *Euonymus* (*E. atropurpureus*—burning bush and *E. americanus* strawberry bush). Of the genus *Pachistima, P. canbyi* is the only one to occur in Pennsylvania. Another member of the genus occurs in the Pacific Coast states.

The plant is used commercially as an ornamental cover. It can be purchased from nurseries, and apparently much of the material sold is rooted from nursery stock, some may come from the wild.

BASIS OF STATUS CLASSIFICATION: Canby's mountain-lover has been proposed for "Endangered" status in Pennsylvania because of its relatively small range in the south-central Appalachian Mountains, scarcity in Pennsylvania with only two

Candy's Mountain-lover (*Pachistima canbyi*). Photograph by P. G. Wiegman.

occurrences, and possible depletion because of commercial value.

Herbarium records for *P. canbyi* are all from Bedford County. One locality is on a north-facing hillside near St. Clairsville. The plant has been seen and collected there as recently as 1977. The other occurrence is a rocky limestone cliff near Lutzville.

The most recent collection was in 1978, but the plant was seen in both 1980 and 1981.

West Virginia lists *P. canbyi* as "Restricted and Local." There are 12 localities in five counties. Ohio lists the species as "Endangered." The species has also been recommended for Federal listing, and is presently under review.

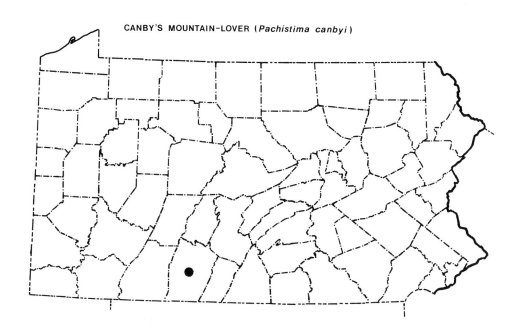

CANBY'S MOUNTAIN-LOVER (*Pachistima canbyi*)

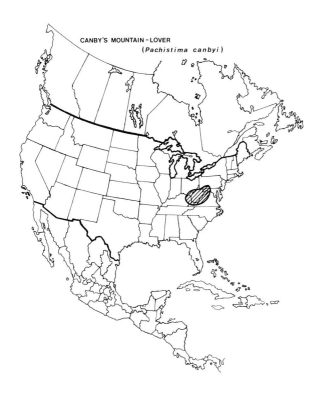

CANBY'S MOUNTAIN-LOVER
(*Pachistima canbyi*)

SELECTED REFERENCES:

CLARKSON, R. B., D. K. EVANS, R. FORTNEY, W. GRAFTON, and L. RADAR. 1981. Rare and endangered vascular plant species in West Virginia. U.S. Fish and Wildlife Service, Washington, DC, iii + 76 pp.

JENNINGS, O. E. 1953. Wild flowers of western Pennsylvania and the Upper Ohio Basin. Univ. Pittsburgh Press, Pittsburgh, Pennsylvania, 1:1xxv + 574 pp.

PREPARED BY: Paul G. Wiegman, *Western Pennsylvania Conservancy, 316 Fourth Avenue, Pittsburgh, PA 15222.*

Endangered

COAST VIOLET
Viola brittoniana Pollard
Family Violaceae
Order Violales

DESCRIPTION: Violets are a well known herb of eastern North America, being represented by about 50 species. The coast violet is one of the stemless species, with the leaves and flower stalks arising directly from the rhizome. Petaliferous flowers have stamens, which do not protrude, and non-petaled flowers are present and well developed. The leaves are without hair, sharply incised, and the leaf margins are sharply toothed. Flowers are rich violet with a prominent white throat, appearing in late April or early May.

RANGE: The coast violet occurs in coastal areas from southern Maine to North Carolina. The typical variety, var. *brittoniana,* is found over that complete range, and the var. *pectinata* is found only from Massachusetts to New Jersey, but always with the other.

In Pennsylvania, *Viola brittoniana* is known only from a few localities in Bucks and Philadelphia counties. The two primary sites are at Tullytown and Bristol along the Delaware River.

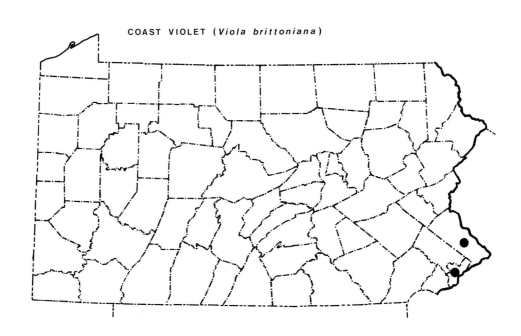

COAST VIOLET (*Viola brittoniana*)

COAST VIOLET (*Viola brittoniana*)

SELECTED REFERENCES:

Dowhan, J. J., and R. J. Craig. 1976. Rare and endangered species of Connecticut and their habitats. State Geological and Natural History Survey of Connecticut, Hartford, Connecticut, 6:v + 1–137.

Mehrhoff, L. J. 1978. Rare and endangered vascular plant species in Connecticut. U.S. Fish and Wildlife Service, Washington, DC, vii + 41 pp.

Mitchell, R. S., C. J. Sheviak, and J. K. Dean. 1980. Rare and endangered vascular plant species in New York State. U.S. Fish and Wildlife Service, Washington, DC, 38 pp.

Mitchell, R. S., and C. H. Sheviak. 1981. Rare plants of New York state. State Univ. New York, Albany, New York State Mus., Bull., 445:viii + 1–96.

PREPARED BY: Paul G. Wiegman, *Western Pennsylvania Conservancy, 316 Fourth Avenue, Pittsburgh, PA 15222.*

Endangered

MOUNTAIN PARSLEY
Pseudotaenidia montana Mackenzie
Family Umbelliferae
Order Umbellales

DESCRIPTION: Mountain parsley is a tall, smooth plant with ovate leaflets in a whorled arrangement. The stem of the leaflets becomes shorter towards the top of the plant. The yellow flowers are arranged in an umbel, characteristic for the family. There are both sterile and fertile flowers, which can be distinguished by the length of the flower stalk. In the fertile flowers, the flower stalk is twice as long as in the sterile flowers. The fruits are elliptic, ribbed, and brown. The plant has a thick, long root and a strong, somewhat unpleasant, odor.

RANGE: The range of mountain parsley includes southern Pennsylvania to western Virginia, Maryland, and West Virginia. In Pennsylvania, the distribution of this species is restricted to the south-central part of the Commonwealth where shale barrens communities develop. Pennsylvania herbarium records for the plant are from Bedford and Fulton counties. There are four historical localities, with recent records from around Chaneysville and Hewitt. One historic location has been destroyed.

HABITAT: Peaty or moist sandy soils along the coast are typical edaphic conditions for this plant. Open meadows and salt marsh is the preferred habitat.

BASIS OF STATUS CLASSIFICATION: The combination of few collections and lack of recent known occurrences are the reasons for placing the coast violet in the "Endangered" category. The scarcity of historic locations for the plant are indicative of the small amount of the typical habitat in Pennsylvania. The 15 specimens of this species now in Pennsylvania herbaria represent only five localities.

Of those specimens, 13 were collected in 1900 or before. Only two are modern, one in 1944 and one in the Bristol area collected in 1977.

New York and Connecticut list the plant as "Declining" because of the loss of habitat to general development.

RECOMMENDATIONS: Historic localities need to be checked to see if old populations are still extant. In addition, the coastal plain sections of Bucks, Philadelphia, and Chester counties should be examined for new localities. Once an adequate survey is completed, specific tracts of open coastal plain habitat should be protected.

HABITAT: This a strict shale barrens endemic. It occurs on wooded to open south-facing slopes of Devonian shale in the Ridge and Valley province, usually in a fairly open, savannah-like woodland. It is often growing under *Pinus virginiana* and several species of oaks.

Mountain Parsley (*Pseudotaenidia montana*). Photograph by P. G. Wiegman.

BASIS OF STATUS CLASSIFICATION: The restricted distribution and very few occurrences of *Pseudotaenidia montana* in Pennsylvania is the basis for placing it on the Pennsylvania Plants of Special Concern list. *Pseudotaenidia montana* is rare in Maryland but more abundant on shale barrens in West Virginia and Virginia. It is currently under

federal review, but because it is fairly secure in Virginia and West Virginia, it may be deleted from the federal review list.

Road work and highway construction have threatened and destroyed several locations. Because of the few locations and the loss of habitat, mountain parsley is included in the "Endangered" category.

MOUNTAIN PARSLEY (*Pseudotaenidia montana*)

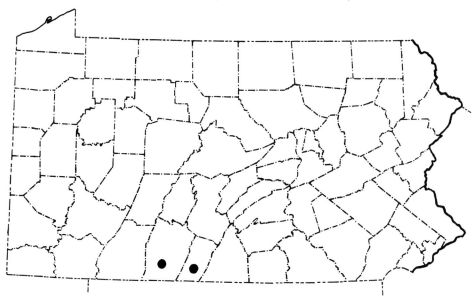

RECOMMENDATIONS: The localities where this plant still remains should be afforded public or private preservation status. More searching in the shale barrens region for new localities is needed.

SELECTED REFERENCES:

CRONQUIST, A. 1982. Reduction of *Pseudotaenidia* to *Taenidia* (Apiaceae). Brittonia, 34:365–367.

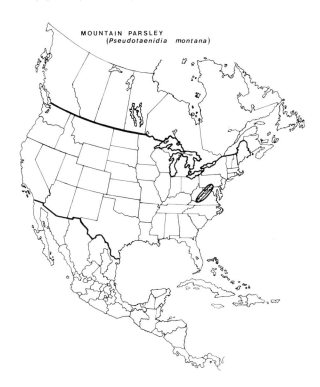

MOUNTAIN PARSLEY
(*Pseudotaenidia montana*)

HENRY, L. K. 1954. Shale barren flora in Pennsylvania. Proc. Pennsylvania Acad. Sci., 28:65–68.

KEENER, C. S. 1970. The natural history of the mid-Appalachian shale barrens flora. Pp. 215–245, *in* The distributional history of the biota of the southern Appalachians. II. Flora. (P. C. Holt, ed.), Virginia Polytechnic Institute, Blacksburg, viii + 414 pp.

WHERRY, E. T. 1937. Two plant-geographic notes. Castanea, 2(1):1–2.

PREPARED BY: Sara Davison, *1218 Chestnut Street, Suite 505, Philadelphia, PA 19107.*

Endangered

AWL-SHAPED MUDWORT
Limosella australis R.Br.
Family Schrophulariaceae
Order Scrophulariales

DESCRIPTION: The awl-shaped mudwort is a tiny, inconspicuous annual herb. The stems lay on the mud surface of intertidal flats and spread to form bunched colonies. Each stem node forms roots and a cluster of basal leaves, usually five to 10 per tuft. The linear leaves are 20–50 mm long and 1–2 mm wide. Flowers arise on peduncles shorter than the leaves and have five white petals 3–4 mm long and fused into a tube at the bottom. The awl-shaped mudwort blooms in August and September.

RANGE: The awl-shaped mudwort occurs along the Atlantic Coast from Newfoundland and Quebec south to Maryland. In Pennsylvania, the plant has been collected in Bucks and Delaware counties. In

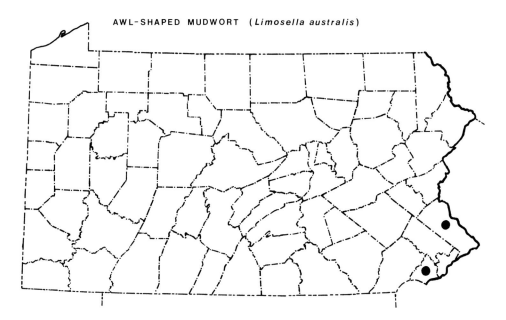

AWL-SHAPED MUDWORT (*Limosella australis*)

Bucks County, records are from the Delaware River near Andalusia, near the Philadelphia County line, and at Penrose Ferry. The Delaware County records are from Tinicum.

HABITAT: Limosella australis grows on intertidal mudflats in both fresh and brackish situations. It requires open areas with full sun and very little competition.

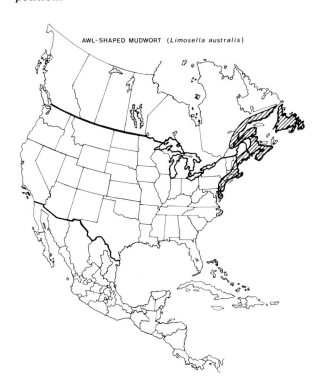

AWL-SHAPED MUDWORT (*Limosella australis*)

BASIS OF STATUS CLASSIFICATION: The range of *Limosella* is large, but the habitat in which it occurs is restricted and under heavy pressure from a wide variety of uses. These factors, along with the limited collection records of the species within Pennsylvania account for its ranking as "Endangered." Connecticut has listed the species as "Local and Threatened by urban development." New Jersey places it on their "Endangered" list, and notes that it is declining, local, and vulnerable with the loss of the plant due to filling and dredging operations. Maryland categorized the species as "Local" and Delaware lists *Limosella* as "Southeast Limit of Range and possibly Extirpated." The Pennsylvania records for this plant are all in the 1800's and it may well be extirpated.

RECOMMENDATIONS: The first step is a careful search of the mud flats in the lower Delaware River for suitable habitat and extant populations of the awl-shaped mudwort. If found, these areas should be protected from disturbances that would eliminate the plant. Public or private action will be needed, with the best method being acquisition of the site and suitable buffer for permanent protection. If already on public land, the area should be designated as a Plant Sanctuary under Pennsylvania Law.

SELECTED REFERENCES:

BROOME, C. R., A. O. TUCKER, J. L. REVEAL, and N. H. DILL. 1979. Rare and endangered vascular plant species in Maryland. U.S. Fish and Wildlife Service, Newton Corner, Massachusetts, vii + 64 pp.

Dowhan, J. J., and R. J. Craig. 1976. Rare and endangered species of Connecticut and their habitats. State Geological and Natural History Survey of Connecticut, Hartford, Connecticut, 6:v + 137 pp.

Mehrhoff, L. J. 1978. Rare and endangered vascular plant species in Connecticut. U.S. Fish and Wildlife Service, Washington, DC, vii + 41 pp.

Snyder, D. B., and V. E. Vivian. 1981. Rare and endangered vascular plant species in New Jersey. U.S. Fish and Wildlife Service, Washington, DC, viii + 98 pp.

PREPARED BY: Paul G. Wiegman, *Western Pennsylvania Conservancy, 316 Fourth Avenue, Pittsburgh, PA 15222.*

Endangered

KALM'S LOBELIA
Lobelia kalmii L.
Family Lobeliaceae
Order Campanulales

DESCRIPTION: Kalm's lobelia is an alternatively arranged herb with entire linear leaves and a raceme of small blue flowers. The lip of the corolla is united at the base forming a tube. Petals are an attractive sky blue with white centers; the upper lip is smooth at the base. The low plant occurs singly and in loose colonies amongst other low growing wildflowers. Kalm's lobelia blooms in late August or early September.

RANGE: This *Lobelia* can be found from Newfoundland to British Columbia, south into Pennsylvania, Ohio, and west to Illinois and Minnesota. In Pennsylvania, the distribution is probably throughout, but is restricted to specific habitats with moist alkaline soils. Herbarium records for the plant are from the counties of Northampton, Monroe, Lancaster, Butler, and Erie.

HABITAT: Kalm's lobelia occurs in calcareous areas of wetlands, wet meadows, lake edges, along streams, and spring heads. It usually is found in open, sunny, or lightly shaded areas. Associated vegetation is low and sparce.

The alkaline affinities of the species are strong. Areas where this species are found often contain other calceophiles such as *Trollius laxus* Salisb., *Salix serrisima* (Bailey) Fern., and *Cypripedium reginae* Walt.

BASIS OF STATUS CLASSIFICATION: The scattered and occasional distribution of *Lobelia*

kalmii in Pennsylvania is the basis for placing in on the Pennsylvania Plants of Special Concern list. Although common outside the Commonwealth, a factor that probably would place the plant in the "Rare" category, the species is restricted in Pennsylvania to moist alkaline soils. Alkaline or calcareous habitats in the Commonwealth are scarce and limited to a few geologic regions. Furthermore, these habitats have been directly and indirectly affected by agricultural activities and hence are declining in both number and extent. Mining of marl in the early 1900's was the first activity that destroyed large alkaline wetlands. Smaller, more localized habitats, often only a fraction of an acre, have been lost to generalized development of the landscape. Agricultural activities have expanded and techniques for draining these small wetlands have improved. Application of the improved techniques has lead to the loss of alkaline wetlands, and specialized species which inhabit them. Kalm's lobelia is one species that has suffered from habitat loss and is thus included in the "Endangered" category.

Other states listing *Lobelia kalmii* include: West Virginia (1978) and (1981) which categorizes it as "Rare, Vulnerable, Southern Limit of Range, and a Single W. Va. Station," Connecticut (1976) and (1978) lists the plant as "Local and Southern Limit of Range."

In Pennsylvania, Kalm's lobelia historically occurred at eight specific localities. At Presque Isle, Erie County, *Lobelia kalmii* was first collected in 1868 by T. C. Porter. Subsequent collections and sight records have been made up to, and including, September of 1982 when the plant was found at the eastern end of the Presque Isle peninsula on moist sand plains and around young ponds.

The only other western Pennsylvania locality for *Lobelia kalmii* was a small wetland 1.5 mi. west of West Liberty, Butler County. Here the plant was first collected in 1940 by Boardman. Subsequent collections were made in 1941 and 1951. A 1980 search failed to locate the species at this locality.

In eastern Pennsylvania, the plant was collected in the alkaline wetlands around Mt. Bethel, beginning in 1907, with subsequent specimens up to 1946. A site survey found *Lobelia kalmii* in a small wetland east of Mt. Bethel in 1980. The other alkaline wetlands in that vicinity were searched, but no plants were located. A Monroe County collection was made in 1910 by Pretz at Dodendorf Mountain near Saylorsburg, but the locality has not recently been surveyed.

Kalm's Lobelia (*Lobelia kalmii*). Photograph by P. G. Wiegman.

The only other stand of *Lobelia kalmii* was at Dillersville Swamp, Lancaster County. The first collection at this locality was made in 1856 by T. C. Porter. The most recent is a collection in 1909 by Carter. Schuyler (1980) made a survey of the wetland in 1977 and 1979 and did not locate the species.

RECOMMENDATIONS: The localities where this plant still remains should be afforded public or private preservation status. In the case of Presque Isle State Park, habitats containing *Lobelia kalmii* must be delineated and activities that are detrimental to the continued existence of the species ceased. Fur-

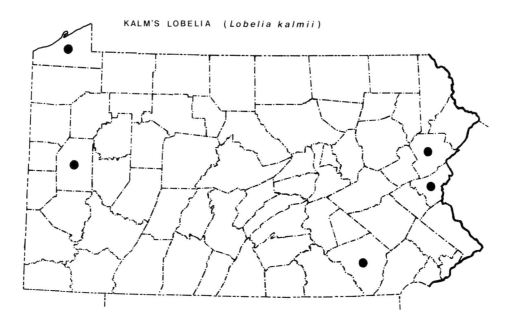

KALM'S LOBELIA (*Lobelia kalmii*)

thermore, areas on Presque Isle that are in early stages of becoming prime habitat for the plant should also be designated and the necessary use restrictions be established and enforced. The primary problem at the Presque Isle locality is trampling. The moist sand plain habitat where the largest *L. kalmii* pop-

ulations are located are close to Budney Beach at the eastern end of the peninsula. Crowding of the beaches and the growing number of people walking into the dunes and sand plains beyond the beach have increased the erosion and trampling of the habitats.

KALM'S LOBELIA (*Lobelia kalmii*)

SELECTED REFERENCES:

ARGUS, G. W., and D. J. WHITE. 1977. The rare vascular plants of Ontario. National Museum of Natural Sciences, Botany Division, Ottawa, Ontario, Syllogeus, 14:1–64.

CLARKSON, R. B., D. K. EVANS, R. FORTNEY, W. GRAFTON, and L. RADER. 1981. Rare and endangered vascular plant species in West Virginia. U.S. Fish and Wildlife Service, Washington, DC, iii + 76 pp.

DOWHAN, J. J., and R. J. CRAIG. 1976. Rare and endangered species of Connecticut and their habitats. State Geological and Natural History Survey of Connecticut, Hartford, Connecticut, 6:v + 1–137.

FORTNEY, R. H., R. B. CLARKSON, C. N. HARVEY, and J. KARTESZ. 1978. Vascular plants. Rare and endangered species of West Virginia: a preliminary report. West Virginia Department of Natural Resources, Heritage Trust Program, Charleston, West Virginia, 1:vii + 1–96.

MEHRHOFF, L. J. 1981. Rare and endangered vascular plant species in Connecticut. U.S. Fish and Wildlife Service, Washington, DC, vii + 41 pp.

SCHUYLER, A. E. 1980. Botanical degradation of Dillerville Swamp, Lancaster County, Pennsylvania. Bartonia, 47:1–2.

PREPARED BY: Paul G. Wiegman, *Western Pennsylvania Conservancy, 316 Fourth Avenue, Pittsburgh, PA 15222.*

Endangered

SWAMP BEGGAR-TICKS
Bidens bidentoides (Nutt.) Britt.
Family Asteraceae
Order Asterales

SWAMP BEGGAR-TICK (*Bidens bidentoides*)

DESCRIPTION: Swamp beggar-ticks are smooth dark green to red annual plants whose height varies depending on where it occurs in the intertidal zone. The leaves are lance-shaped and toothed. The small yellow disk flowers are packed into small heads with no ray flowers. The brown fruits are hairy and have small barbs. The absence of ray flowers helps distinguish this species from the co-occurring *Bidens laevis*.

RANGE: This beggar-tick is known only from tidal rivers of New York, New Jersey, Pennsylvania, Maryland, and Delaware. In Pennsylvania, it is restricted to the Delaware River and its tidal tributaries. Herbarium records are from three Pennsylvania counties—Bucks, Philadelphia, and Delaware. Recent populations have been seen at Neshaminy State Park and near Bristol.

Bidens bidentoides was first collected in Pennsylvania around Philadelphia by Thomas Nuttal in 1841. The historic localities on the lower Delaware River in Philadelphia and Delaware counties have all but been destroyed.

HABITAT: This is a strict intertidal endemic, restricted to the fresh water sections of tidal rivers occurring along tidal shores growing in mud covered sand and gravel. It often grows in the middle to upper zone of the intertidal marsh and is found with *Amaranthus cannabinus*, *Bidens laevis*, and *Zizania aquatica*. It has been seen growing in riprap and old cracked walls along the Delaware River.

SWAMP BEGGAR-TICK (*Bidens bidentoides*)

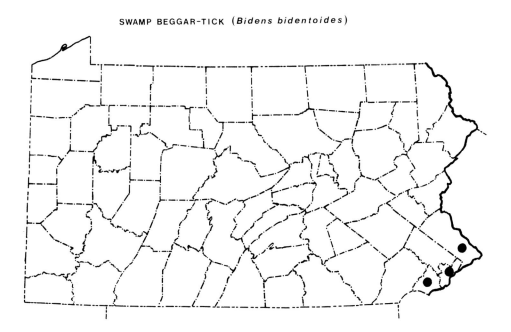

BASIS OF STATUS CLASSIFICATION: Of the eight historical records for this species, only four are believed to exist. *Bidens bidentoides* is never abundant where it occurs and its restricted distribution in Pennsylvania and throughout its range is the basis for placing it on the Pennsylvania Plants of Special Concern list. This species in under federal review as endangered throughout its range.

Freshwater intertidal habitats have probably undergone the greatest alteration of any habitat type in Pennsylvania. Dredging and filling, pollution, and heavy industrial and recreational use threatens these delicate marshes. Because of the dramatic loss of habitat, *Bidens bidentoides* is included in the "Endangered" category.

RECOMMENDATIONS: The localities where this plant still remains should be afforded public or private preservation status. At Neshaminy State Park, areas containing *Bidens bidentoides* should be delineated and recreational activities focused elsewhere.

SELECTED REFERENCE:

FERREN, W. R., JR., and A. E. SCHUYLER. 1980. Intertidal vascular plants of river systems near Philadelphia. Proc. Acad. Nat. Sci. Philadelphia, 132:86–120.

PREPARED BY: Sara Davison, *1218 Chestnut Street, Suite 505, Philadelphia, PA 19107.*

Endangered
RATTLESNAKE ROOT
Prenanthes racemosa Michx.
Family Compositae
Order Asterales

DESCRIPTION: Rattlesnake root is a tall 30–150 cm perennial herb with alternate leaves. The persistent lower basal leaves are broadly oblanceolate with long petioles. Leaves occurring on the stalks are reduced upwards toward the flowers. The narrow elongated flower-head has pink to purplish blossoms which are closely attached to the terminal of the stalk. The stems near the flowers, the flower stalks, and the flower receptacles are covered with long coarse hairs. Flowers are found in August and early September.

RANGE: The plant is known from Quebec to New Jersey west to Alberta, Canada and Colorado. Although the range appears to extend throughout most of northern Pennsylvania, the plant was only collected in 1977 at Plaingrove Bog, Lawrence County. Subsequent visits to this site have not rediscovered the plant.

HABITAT: Rattlesnake root is a plant of deep rich generally neutral soils. The locality at Plaingrove is known for several species with alkaline affinities, although *Prenanthes* is not specifically considered as a plant with alkaline affinities.

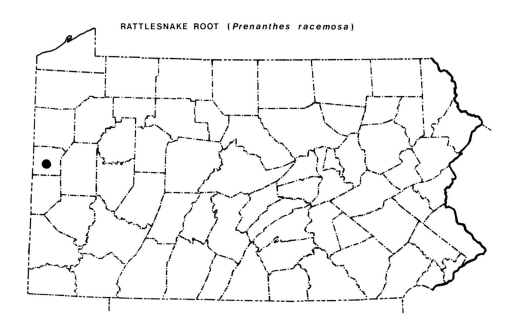

RATTLESNAKE ROOT (*Prenanthes racemosa*)

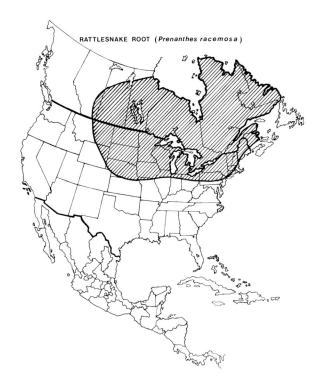

RATTLESNAKE ROOT (Prenanthes racemosa)

Other habitats noted for the plant include stream banks, moist meadows, and praries. Generally the species is one of the open sunny sites with deep, rich, moist soils.

BASIS OF STATUS CLASSIFICATION: Rattlesnake root is known from only a single locality, and has not been observed at that site for several years. In addition, the apparent affinity to habitats with non-acidic rocks, as compared to obligate calcophiles, and the scarcity of these habitats in Pennsylvania lead to the listing of the plant as "Threatened."

New York lists *Prenanthes racemosa* as "Threatened"; a western species at the eastern limit of range. Ohio lists the species as "Potentially Threatened." New Jersey lists the species as "Undetermined Status" and at its eastern limit of range.

RECOMMENDATION: Efforts need to be made to locate additional occurrences of this species, and steps taken to protect those areas. Habitat protection should consider those broader edaphic and water needs of this species and controls may need to be instituted to extend beyond the site that the plant grows. As a species of wet meadows, the ground water recharge areas that feed the wet meadows must

be protected to assure continuance of *Prenanthes* and other plants of the community.

SELECTED REFERENCES:

MEHRHOFF, L. J. 1978. Rare and endangered vascular plant species in Connecticut. U.S. Fish and Wildlife Service, Washington, DC, vii + 41 pp.
MITCHELL, R. S., C. J. SHEVIAK, and J. K. DEAN. 1980. Rare and endangered vascular plant species in New York state. U.S. Fish and Wildlife Service, Washington, DC, 38 pp.
MITCHELL, R. S., and C. J. SHEVIAK. 1981. Rare plants of New York state. State Univ. New York, Albany, New York State Mus., Bull., 445:viii + 1–96.
OHIO DEPARTMENT OF NATURAL RESOURCES. 1982. Rare species of native Ohio wild plants. Division of Natural Areas and Preserves, Columbus, Ohio, Unpublished Report, 20 pp.

PREPARED BY: Paul G. Wiegman, *Western Pennsylvania Conservancy, 316 Fourth Avenue, Pittsburgh, PA 15222.*

Endangered

CAT'S-PAW RAGWORT
Senecio antennariifolius Britt.
Family Compositae
Order Asterales

DESCRIPTION: Cat's-paw ragwort is a tall plant growing from a basal rosette with a thickened base from which yellow filamentous roots develop. The spoon-shaped rosette leaves are grey-green and very silky on the undersides. Few leaves develop on the stem. The yellow flowers are born in clustered heads. The plants are very conspicuous at the dispersal stage with their white bristles.

RANGE: This species is restricted to shale barrens communities of southern Pennsylvania, Maryland, Virginia, and West Virginia. Herbarium records in Pennsylvania for the plant are only from Fulton County. There are only two historic and recent locations for this plant, which are near the McConnelsburg and Harrisonville area.

HABITAT: This species is a strict shale barrens endemic, and is found with other shale barrens endemics such as *Trifolium virginicum* and other indicator species. The cat's-paw ragwort prefers upper slopes of south facing, steep, rocky shale barrens. The sites are in full sun, dry, and slightly acid. The plants are often nestled in crevices of the shale outcrops.

Cat's-paw Ragwort (*Senecio antennariifolius*). Photograph by P. G. Wiegman.

BASIS OF STATUS CLASSIFICATION: The restricted distribution and few localities of cat's-paw ragwort in Pennsylvania is the basis for placing it on the list of Pennsylvania Plants of Special Concern. In Virginia and West Virginia, it is abundant on shale barrens, and there are nine reported sites from Maryland. Like all the shale barrens endemics, Pennsylvania is the northern limit of their range. This species is under federal review as being endangered throughout its range.

Grazing and road construction are the greatest threats to this species. Because of its overall rarity

CAT'S-PAW RAGWORT (*Senecio antennariifolius*)

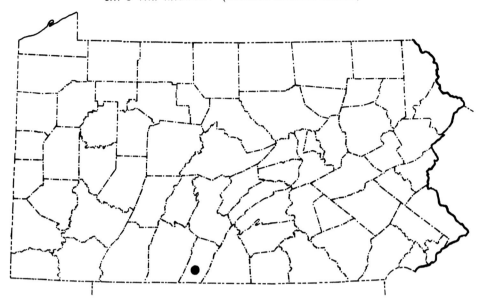

CAT'S PAW RAGWORT
(*Senecio antennariifolius*)

and extremely narrow range, the cat's-paw ragwort is included in the "Endangered" category.

RECOMMENDATIONS: The localities where this plant still occurs should be afforded public or private preservation status. Searching for new locations should continue.

SELECTED REFERENCES:

HENRY, L. K. 1954. Shale barrens flora in Pennsylvania. Proc. Pennsylvania Acad. Sci., 28:65–68.
KEENER, C. S. 1970. The natural history of the mid-Appalachian shale barrens flora. Pp. 215–245, *in* The distributional history of the biota of the southern Appalachians. II. Flora. (P. C. Holt, ed.), Virginia Polytechnic Institute, Blacksburg, viii + 414 pp.
WHERRY, E. T. 1937. Two plant-geographic notes. Castanea, 2:1–2.

PREPARED BY: Sara Davison, *1218 Chestnut Street, Suite 505, Philadelphia, PA 19107.*

CHAPTER 2
INVERTEBRATES

Regal Fritillary (*Speyeria idalia*). Photograph by P. A. Opler.

CHAPTER 2—INVERTEBRATES

edited by

PAUL A. OPLER

U.S. Fish and Wildlife Service
Editorial Office
Room 259 Aylesworth Hall
Colorado State University
Fort Collins, CO 80523

Table of Contents

INTRODUCTION

Assessing the entire invertebrate fauna of a state such as Pennsylvania is an impossible task. There are perhaps 20,000 or more such species in Pennsylvania, and the status of most would have to be "undetermined." At the beginning of this effort, it was decided that the concentration would be on several well-known insect groups, that is, butterflies and moths (Lepidoptera) and dragonflies (Odonata), as well as several groups of aquatic non-insectan invertebrates.

The butterflies, moths, and dragonflies form the core of this Chapter. A substantial number of members of the Lepidopterists' Society, mostly resident Pennsylvanians, gave freely of their data and opinions, while the review of moths and dragonflies was based largely on the personal efforts of Dale Schweitzer and Clark Shiffer, respectively. The three of us now present a brief introduction to butterflies, moths, and dragonflies.

Information concerning the continental distribution of each species in the text which follows is based primarily on previously published information, but may include more recent, unpublished information. Previously published information may no longer be valid, because of specimen misidentifications and/or re-evaluation of older records. While the continental distribution of these species remains imperfectly known, the maps depict what is believed, from various published and unpublished sources of information, to represent their approximate known distributions to date. One of the purposes of this publication is to motivate others with verifiable new information about the species, and their habits, habitats, and distribution, to add to the depth and breadth of our present body of knowledge.

Butterflies.—Initially, lists of potential Pennsylvania candidates were provided by Arthur Shapiro and George Ehle, both of whom were familiar with the butterflies of the Commonwealth. Then Opler abstracted records from the literature on individual data sheets for the recommended species. Next, copies of these sheets were mailed with self-return envelopes to all Pennsylvania members of the Lepidopterist's Society. The response was heart-warming, as 14 persons replied, not only with their records, but with their status assessments and comments as well. The significant amount of data received, together with the status recommendations, allowed the original 47 species suggested to be narrowed down to 12. Many of the species proved to be actually widespread in the Commonwealth and/or to have suffered no decline, while others were unpredictable, periodic colonists from the south. One species, the Diana fritillary (*Speyeria diana*) may have once occurred in the Commonwealth, but the records are uncertain and a status report was not prepared.

From a habitat standpoint, the butterflies of the southeastern serpentine barrens have suffered most, while other species of shale and sand barrens are of concern. Butterflies of wet meadows and freshwater marshes seem to have declined even more than agricultural conversion would imply. Because many of these species have caterpillars which overwinter, inordinate winter mortality from acid rain would seem to be the only plausible factor.

Moths.—There are probably about 1,100 species of "macro" moths breeding in Pennsylvania. Most of these are permanent residents. Probably less than 10 species have become extirpated in the Commonwealth since 1600. The most likely extirpations are *Catocala pretiosa* Lintner and *Pyreferra ceromatica* (Grote) both of which disappeared from vast areas of the northern United States between about 1890 and 1935. The disappearance of *P. ceromatica* probably was not due to human disturbance. Both of these species still exist southward.

All but one of the species covered here are known to occur in other states and all of them are probably more common elsewhere, although many are quite restricted in habitat throughout their range.

There appear to be various factors involved in human-induced declines of Pennsylvania Lepidoptera. Habitat destruction is by far the most important of these. Aerial spraying of insecticides over extensive forested areas has been implicated elsewhere for declines in certain Sphingidae and some Saturniidae but has probably not seriously affected many other species (certainly not the target species). Mercury vapor streetlights are sometimes mentioned in connection with the decline of these same two families. Other factors may be involved. Collecting has not been responsible for any significant declines of Lepidoptera in this Commonwealth or any nearby regions, and should be encouraged by all appropriate regulatory agencies. Private collectors have been the ultimate source of nearly all information available on the species discussed below.

From the compilation to follow it is apparent that pitch pine-bear oak barrens habitats contain a disproportionate number of species of some concern. It is likely that most of these species will prove to be more widespread in such habitats than is now known. Acid bogs are another habitat of concern but rather little collecting has been done in these habitats in Pennsylvania.

This list is extremely preliminary but compilation of a more useful one is not now possible—except perhaps for the butterflies. The biggest problem has been a lack of collecting. Pennsylvania has had rather few resident moth collectors and contains few habitats which would attract out-of-state collectors. Even the known barrens and bogs have been poorly worked because persons primarily desirous of specimens go to "classic" localities elsewhere (often in New Jersey) or obtain specimens by exchange. A coordinated collecting effort concentrating on unusual habitats would be quite instructive.

Most of the species listed are more common though local elsewhere (for example, the New Jersey Pine Barrens); however, we left out dozens which are nearly ubiquitous over sizeable areas outside of the state and probably occur in Pennsylvania mostly as strays or sporadic temporary populations. Numerous *Catacola* species (for example, *insolabilis, lacrymosa, robinsonii, angusii, nebulosa,* and *marmorata*) are probably in this category.

Some Pennsylvania Lepidoptera whose out-of-state ranges and habitats are rather restricted and might be vulnerable everywhere include *Hemileuca maia* (northern sand barrens strains only), *Merolonche dolli, Chaetoglaea cerata, Papaipema* new species, *Hydroecia stramentosa,* and *Datana ranaeceps* (northern population). Northern *H. maia* and *D. ranaeceps* populations are rather distinctive—more so than most so-called subspecies of butterflies named in this region.

The pine barrens at Nottingham (County) Park, Chester County, may be among the most important "unique" habitats in the Commonwealth. This is the only location in Pennsylvania known to us for *Caripeta aretaria, Zale curema, Zale obliqua,* and *Artace cribraria.* It also has (as of 1972) *H. maia* and (1971) *Citheronia sepulcralis,* two of the Commonwealth's more threatened Lepidoptera. We have heard of other supposedly largely obliterated barrens in southern York County which may contain these species also.

Dragonflies.—A total of 171 species of dragonflies and damselflies are now listed as valid members of the Pennsylvania Odonata fauna. Of these, 33, or about 19%, are treated in the following accounts. All are presently recorded from six or fewer counties, with the exception of *Anax longipes* (recorded from nine counties) and *Somatochlora elongata* (recorded from seven counties). An additional 24 species known from four or fewer counties have not been included; most of these are Coastal Plain inhabitants found primarily along the eastern edge or southeastern corner of the Commonwealth. The only *Neurocordulia* species recorded for the Commonwealth (*obsoleta* and *yamaskanensis*) have not been treated in the accounts since, like most species of *Neurocordulia,* they are probably more widespread than the occasional captures of nymphs or crepuscular adults would indicate.

Most of the species treated herein are inhabitants of bogs, boggy ponds, and spring-fed streams and rivers. All of the species listed as possibly extirpated are river inhabitants, thus indicating that this aquatic habitat has suffered the greatest physical/chemical changes detrimental to Pennsylvania Odonata. Bogs, boggy ponds, and spring-fed streams are special habitats which support a specialized flora and fauna requiring their limited combination of physical/

chemical conditions, and are sensitive to change. Although man has created for his own uses a variety of aquatic habitats around the Commonwealth, which largely benefit the more common and adaptable Odonata, he is not able to create the sorts of habitats required by these species of concern. Such habitats must be the focus of man's concern and protected if they and their unique living things are to remain a part of our environment.

In addition to the many persons named in the published references following each account, who contributed information on Pennsylvania Odonata, the following have provided more recent informa-tion, thus making the accounts more complete: Dr. Frank L. Carle, Warren, New Jersey; Dr. Thomas W. Donnelly, Binghamton, New York; Dr. Kenneth J. Tennessen, Florence, Alabama; and Dr. Harold B. White, III, Newark, Delaware.

Paul A. Opler, *U.S. Fish and Wildlife Service, Editorial Office, Room 259 Aylesworth Hall, Colorado State University, Fort Collins, CO 80523;* Dale F. Schweitzer, *Museum of Comparative Zoology, Harvard University, Cambridge, MA 02138;* Clark Shiffer, *Pennsylvania Fish Commission, Robinson Lane, Bellefonte, PA 16823.*

ACKNOWLEDGMENTS

Clark Shiffer (Pennsylvania Fish Commission, Bellefonte) and Dale F. Schweitzer (Cambridge, MA) provided major sections of this chapter on dragonflies and moths, respectively. Their efforts are greatly appreciated.

Arthur M. Shapiro (University of California, Davis) and George Ehle (Lancaster, PA) provided the initial lists and advice on butterfly candidates to the Chapter's editor, as he had no forehand knowledge of the Commonwealth's fauna or conditions.

The following members of the Lepidopterist's Society have made extensive efforts to survey and collect Pennsylvania butterflies and they willingly provided data and recommendations which permitted accurate status accounts to be prepared: Richard W. Boscoe (Lafayette Hill), William F. Boscoe (Willow Grove), George Ehle (Lancaster), Frank D. Fee (State College), Thomas Greager (Greensburg), David F. Hess (Macomb, Illinois), Gerald McWilliams (Union City), Mark Minno (Fort Lauderdale, Florida), Breten G. Murray (Villanova), Charles G. Oliver (Scottsdale), John M. Prescott (Erie), C. E. Schildknecht (Gettysburg), and Thomas S. Williams (Glenside).

In addition, David M. Wright (Waynewood) provided literature records, Michael Bentzien (Jacksonville, Florida) wrote species accounts for beetles, and Arnold Norden (Towson, Maryland) provided data on the Refton Cave Planarian—their assistance is also gratefully acknowledged.—Paul A. Opler, *U.S. Fish and Wildlife Service.*

SPECIES ACCOUNTS

Threatened

REFTON CAVE PLANARIAN
Sphalloplana pricei (Hyman)
Family Planariidae
Order Tricladida
Class Turbellaria

DESCRIPTION: The Refton cave planarian is a pure white troglobitic flatworm, which is up to 2.8 cm long and 0.35 cm wide when mature. The anterior end has a straight or very slightly bulging frontal margin. There are no auricular projections. Refer to Kenk's (1977) monograph for further details.

RANGE: The Refton cave planarian is known only from three caves in Dauphin, Lancaster, and Mifflin counties, Pennsylvania. It has been found only in Refton Cave, Lancaster County, since the 1930s.

HABITAT: The species is found only within the dark zone of caves where it lives under water on rotting wood and the surface of rocks.

SPECIALIZED OR UNIQUE CHARACTERISTICS: The flatworm is completely white and lacks light sensitive pigments. Both characteristics are typical of cave-dwelling invertebrates.

BASIS OF STATUS CLASSIFICATION: Because this species has apparently lost two of its three known populations any threat to the third would be a serious event in this species' future.

RECOMMENDATIONS: Survey historical populations and seek cooperative agreement with landowner for protection of Refton Cave.

ACKNOWLEDGMENTS: Arnold Norden recommended that this species be included and provided pertinent literature references.

REFTON CAVE PLANARIAN (*Sphalloplana pricei*)

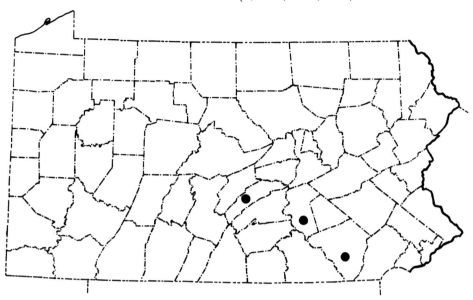

SELECTED REFERENCES:

HOLSINGER, J. R. 1976. The cave fauna of Pennsylvania. Pp. 72–87, *in* Geology and biology of Pennsylvania caves (W. B. White, ed.), Pennsylvania Geol. Surv. (4th Series), Gen. Geol. Rept., 66:iii + 1–103.

KENK, R. 1977. Freshwater triclads (Turbellaria) of North America. IX. The genus *Sphalloplana*. Smithsonian Contr. Zool., 246:iii + 1–38.

PREPARED BY: Paul A. Opler, U.S. Fish and Wildlife Service, Editorial Office, Room 259 Aylesworth Hall, Colorado State University, Fort Collins, CO 80523.

Threatened

REGAL FRITILLARY
Speyeria idalia (Drury)
Family Nymphalidae
Order Lepidoptera

DESCRIPTION: The regal fritillary is a large nymphalid with 10–11 cm wingspan. The forewings are predominantly red orange with black markings. The hindwings are black with marginal white spots above and grayish black with scattered ovoid silvery markings scattered below.

RANGE: The original range of this species covered approximately the northeast quadrant of the United States and a few localities in extreme southern Canada. The metropolis of the species is in the tall grass prairie biome. Generally, in Pennsylvania the species has been found in the southern half of the Commonwealth, but some notable exceptions occur. Significant declines have occurred in the southeastern portion, as well as the general area around Pittsburgh. In the last 10 years the regal fritillary has been found in only nine of 34 known localities: near Greensburg, Westmoreland Co.; Dent's Run, Elk Co.; Gettysburg National Battlefield, Adams Co.; Gilbert, Monroe Co. (since destroyed); Monroe Furnace, Huntingdon Co. (only one male); Patience, Bedford Co. (since destroyed); Phoenixville, Chester Co. and Presque Isle State Park and Erie, Erie Co. (John M. Prescott, personal communication).

HABITAT: In Pennsylvania the species is found in low wet meadows, upland pastures, and infrequently mowed fields. Important factors usually are some dampness, extensiveness of habitat, presence of caterpillar host (*Viola* spp.), and adult nectar sources, especially *Cirsium* and *Asclepias*.

LIFE HISTORY AND ECOLOGY: This butterfly has a single annual generation with adult flight from late June to mid August. The eggs are laid in late summer and the caterpillars do most of their feeding during spring and early summer. Males usually emerge a week or so prior to females, and some individuals disperse widely from the colonies, for example, the Monroe Furnace record. The species is probably a good colonizer if suitable habitats are available. Colonies do not require pristine habitat;

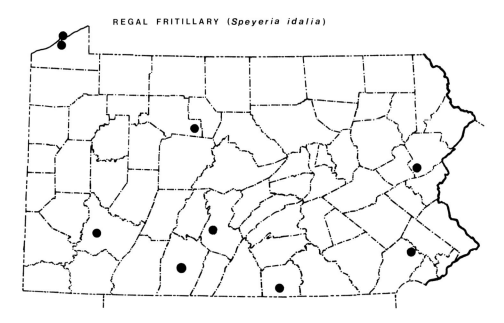

REGAL FRITILLARY (*Speyeria idalia*)

in fact, annual mowing may be beneficial in some instances.

SPECIALIZED OR UNIQUE CHARACTERISTICS: The regal fritillary has no close relatives and is one of the more spectacular eastern butterflies.

BASIS OF STATUS CLASSIFICATION: The

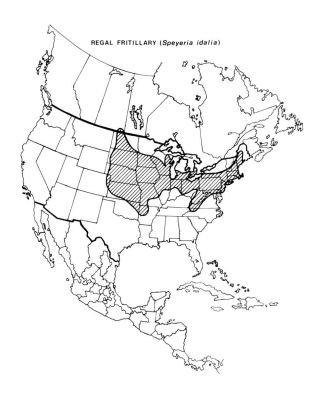

REGAL FRITILLARY (*Speyeria idalia*)

species has declined drastically in the Commonwealth and only four good colonies are known at present. Most of these are on private land and could be inadvertently destroyed. A major cause of decline has been conversion of hay fields and grazing lands to mechanically manipulated croplands. The species may be susceptible to acid rain or pesticide drift.

RECOMMENDATIONS: Ensure proper management of extant colonies. Surveys should be carried out for additional colonies. Experiments should be conducted to see if larvae are sensitive to acid rain.

ACKNOWLEDGMENTS: The following Lepidopterist's Society members contributed data and/or recommendations: G. Ehle, B. Murray, A. M. Shapiro, T. A. Greager, C. E. Schildknecht, F. D. Fee, and T. Williams.

SELECTED REFERENCES:

HOVANITZ, W. H. 1963. Geographical distribution and variation of the genus *Argynnis*. II. *Argynnis idalia*. J. Res. Lepid., 1:117–123.

HOWE, W. H. 1975. The butterflies of North America. Doubleday Co., New York, xiii + 633 pp.

PERKINS, P. D. 1980. North American insect status review. Unpublished Contract Report to Fish and Wildlife Service, Dept. of Entomology, Smithsonian Institution, Washington, D.C.

SHAPIRO, A. M. 1966. The butterflies of the Delaware Valley. Amer. Ent. Soc., Special Publ., vi + 79 pp.

——. 1971. Postglacial biogeography and the distribution of *Poanes viator* and other marsh butterflies. J. Res. Lepid., 9: 125–155.

PREPARED BY: Paul A. Opler, *U.S. Fish and Wildlife Service, Editorial Office, Room 259 Aylesworth Hall, Colorado State University, Fort Collins, CO 80523.*

Threatened

TAWNY CRESCENT
Phyciodes batesii (Reakirt)
Family Nymphalidae
Order Lepidoptera

DESCRIPTION: The tawny crescent is a small nymphalid closely related to the abundant pearl crescent (*Phyciodes tharos*). The tawny crescent may be distinguished by its more extensive black markings above and the relatively plain marked hindwings beneath.

RANGE: The tawny crescent occurs in the northern United States and extreme southern Canada west to the Rocky Mountains. Several small populations have been reported in the Appalachians extending south to Georgia. In Pennsylvania, scattered populations are known from the eastern and central portions of the Commonwealth, but none have been found in the last decade. Several older records may represent misidentifications.

HABITAT: Dry, open hillside fields with the caterpillar host, blue wood aster (*Aster undulatus*), are the primary habitat of the tawny crescent.

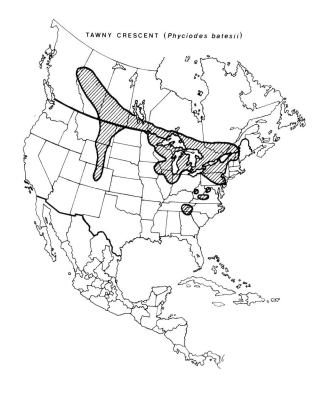

LIFE HISTORY AND ECOLOGY: The tawny crescent has a single annual generation with adults in flight during late May and June. The larvae are gregarious and overwinter at the base of their aster host plant.

BASIS OF STATUS CLASSIFICATION: The tawny crescent apparently has declined dramatical-

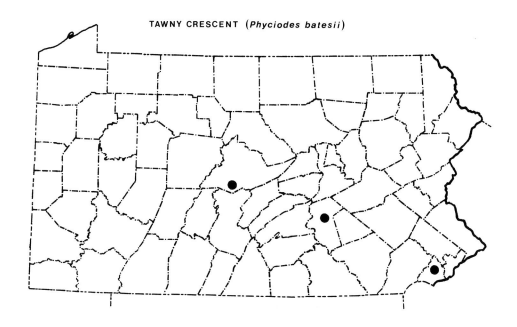

ly, but there is no reason to believe that it has completely disappeared from Pennsylvania.

RECOMMENDATIONS: Every effort should be made to locate colonies of this species. If found, their habitat should be protected. Studies should be undertaken to see if the larvae are susceptible to acid rain.

ACKNOWLEDGMENTS: The following Lepidopterist's Society members provided data and/or recommendations: R. W. Boscoe, W. F. Boscoe, D. Schweitzer, F. D. Fee, A. M. Shapiro, and T. Williams.

SELECTED REFERENCES:

FORBES, W. T. M. 1944. The genus *Phyciodes* (Lepidoptera, Nymphalidae). Entomol. Amer. (n.s.), 24:139–207.
HOWE, W. H. 1975. The butterflies of North America. Doubleday Co., New York, xiii + 633 pp.
SHAPIRO, A. M. 1966. The butterflies of the Delaware Valley. Amer. Ent. Soc., Special Publ., vi + 79 pp.

PREPARED BY: Paul A. Opler, *U.S. Fish and Wildlife Service, Editorial Office, Room 259 Aylesworth Hall, Colorado State University, Fort Collins, CO 80523.*

Threatened

BUCKMOTH
Hemileuca maia (Drury)
Family Saturniidae
Order Lepidoptera

DESCRIPTION: The buckmoth may be mistaken for a member of the *H. lucina*-complex that occurs in moist habitats, but this species has not been observed in Pennsylvania. The buckmoth is black with yellowish white bands across all wings at least partially enclosing on eyespot on each wing. The male has a red tuft at tip of its abdomen. The buckmoth is a day flier. Males are large (50 mm); females are larger. Larvae are blackish with spines capable of inflicting a painful sting, and the young are gregarious. Older larvae usually have some yellowish speckling on their body and some brownish or reddish speckling on spines. Larvae feed from May to July; adult moths fly in the fall. All stages are illustrated by Holland (1903).

RANGE: The buckmoth was reported by Tietz from State College, Centre County; Fayetteville, Franklin County; Eighty Four, Washington Co.; and Mt. Airy (Philadelphia), Philadelphia County; larvae were found at Nottingham Barrens, Chester County in June 1972 (Schweitzer). Isolated populations occur in Ohio, New England (some extirpated), and near Albany, New York (declining). It is widespread in

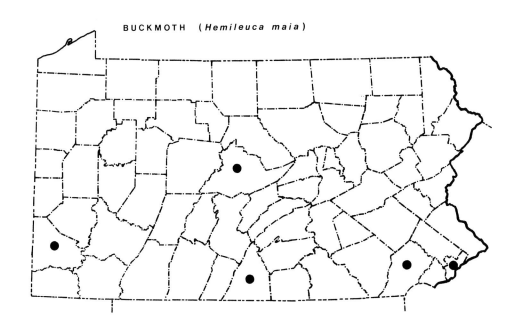

BUCKMOTH (*Hemileuca maia*)

BUCKMOTH (*Hemileuca maia*)

the pine barrens of Long Island and New Jersey. It seems rather widespread in diverse habitats from western Virginia and Missouri southward to northern Florida and westward to central Texas.

HABITAT: Northward it apparently occurs exclusively in open scrub oak barrens, almost always on sandy soil. It occurs also in open sandy oak woods in southern New Jersey. Habitat southward is variable, but often includes turkey oak barrens in Florida.

LIFE HISTORY: Eggs are laid in clusters on small oaks. Larvae hatch in May and feed gregariously during the day on oaks (usually *Quercus ilicifolia*) until the fourth (of six) instar. Then they disperse and may feed on a variety of woody shrubs but primarily still on oaks. Older larvae are solitary or stay in groups of about two to four and often leave the bush when not feeding. Pupation is in the soil, in some populations with a slight cocoon. Pupation takes place in late July and August and moths emerge in October or early November (in southern New Jersey), but fairly often not until the following year.

SPECIALIZED OR UNIQUE CHARACTERISTICS: This is one of two or three eastern outliers of an essentially desert genus. These attractive moths are easily noticed where they are common.

BASIS OF STATUS CLASSIFICATION: In most situations, the habitat of this species can be maintained only by recurrent fires. Suppression of such fires for more than 30 years can eliminate this species due to habitat loss. Because this moth also requires very poor dry soils, the species is exceedingly vulnerable to human development projects because suitable sites seldom develop in these new areas to replace those which are lost. Apparently this moth is highly vulnerable to repeated gypsy moth spraying.

RECOMMENDATIONS: It is likely that only public acquisition and fire management of appropriate scrub oak barrens can perpetuate this species in the Commonwealth into the next century. Many other unusual Lepidoptera occur in such places.

SELECTED REFERENCES:

DIRIG, R., and J. F. CRYAN. 1975. Endangered pine bush lepidoptera. Privately published, Albany, New York, 12 pp.

FERGUSON, D. C. 1971. The moths of America north of Mexico. Fasc. 20.2A. Bombycoidea: Saturniidae comprising subfamilies Citheroniiae Hemileucinae (part). E. W. Classey Limited and RBD Publications Inc., London, 153 pp.

HOLLAND, W. J. 1903. The moth book. Doubleday, Page & Company, New York, vii + 479 pp.

PREPARED BY: Dale F. Schweitzer, *Museum of Comparative Zoology, Harvard University, Cambridge, MA 02138.*

Threatened

SUGAR MAPLE LONGHORN BEETLE
Dryobius sexnotatus Linsley
Family Cerambycidae
Order Coleoptera

DESCRIPTION: The sugar maple longhorn beetle is a large (25 mm), elongate, yellow beetle with six black bands crossing the head, thorax, and abdomen. The legs and antennae are brown. The antennae are one and a half (males) to one and a quarter (females) times as long as the body. A detailed description of the larva is provided by Perry et al. (1974).

RANGE: The beetle has been recorded from Alabama, Arkansas, Indiana, Kansas, Kentucky, Louisiana, Maryland, Michigan, Missouri, Ohio, Oklahoma, Pennsylvania, Tennessee, and Virginia (Perry et al., 1974). A recent survey of North American entomological collections (Perkins, 1980) revealed 117 specimens from seven states. Pennsylvania rec-

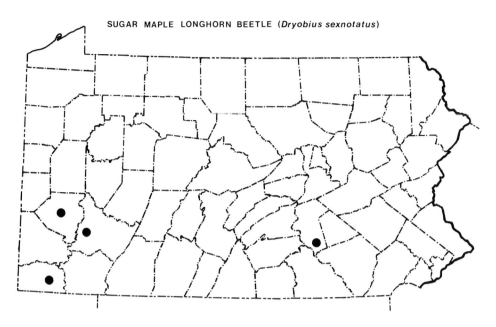

SUGAR MAPLE LONGHORN BEETLE (*Dryobius sexnotatus*)

ords for the sugar maple longhorn beetle include Jeanette, Westmoreland County; Middletown, Dauphin County; Pittsburgh, Allegheny County; and Greene County. Most records after 1942 in Pennsylvania are specimens collected by Surdick and Gifford in three areas in Greene County (Perry et al., 1974).

LIFE HISTORY AND ECOLOGY: The biology of

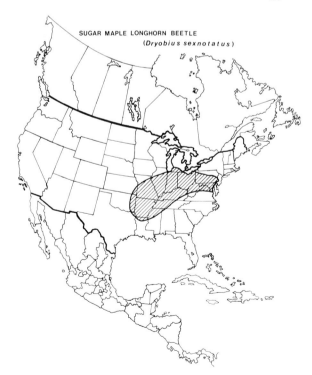

SUGAR MAPLE LONGHORN BEETLE
(*Dryobius sexnotatus*)

this species has been summarized by Perry et al. (1974). The principal host tree is sugar maple (*Acer saccharum*), but larvae have apparently been collected from beech (*Fagus grandifolia*). Specimens have also been reported from basswood (*Tilia americana*) and elm (*Ulmus*). In sugar maple, the larvae excavate meandering galleries deep into the heartwood. Feeding continues after the maple has died and the bark has fallen off. The larval stage may last from two to three years. The larvae apparently pupate near the surface of the tree. Adults have been collected from March to September, walking on maple trunks and flying in the vicinity of the trees. The sugar maple host trees observed in Pennsylvania were old trees, at least 1 m in diameter. Colonies of the beetle may be dependent on overmature host trees. The sugar maple longhorn beetle appears to be dependent on climax eastern hardwood forest habitat.

BASIS OF STATUS CLASSIFICATION: The scarcity of recent collection records for this beetle indicates a decline over its range. One known colony in Greene County, Pennsylvania, apparently became extinct after 1960 (Perry et al., 1974). No concerted collecting efforts have been made for the beetle over its range, but it appears that its status may be precarious in Pennsylvania.

RECOMMENDATIONS: Search known collecting sites for the beetle. Survey remaining mature sugar maple stands for the species. Alternate hosts (beech or basswood) must be utilized where the beetle occurs outside the range of sugar maple (that is, Alabama, Arkansas, Louisiana, and Oklahoma), and probably are used in Pennsylvania as well. Mature stands of these tree species should be surveyed for the beetles. Within Pennsylvania, protection should be given to stands of sugar maple or other host tree species which support colonies of the beetle.

SELECTED REFERENCES:

LINSLEY, E. G. 1964. The Cerambycidae of North America. Part V. Univ. California Publ. Entomol., 22:7–9.

PERKINS, P. D. 1980. North American insect status review. Final report of research study conducted by Department of Entomology of Smithsonian Institution under contract 14-16-0009-79-052 to Office of Endangered Species of U.S. Fish and Wildlife Service, Department of Interior, pp. 261–265.

PERRY, R. H., R. W. SURDICK, and D. M. ANDERSON. 1974. Observations on the biology, ecology, behavior, and larvae of *Dryobius sexnotatus* Linsley (Coleoptera : Cerambycidae). Coleopterists' Bull., 28:169–176.

PREPARED BY: Michael M. Bentzien, *U.S. Fish and Wildlife Service, 2747 Art Museum Drive, Jacksonville, FL 32207.*

Vulnerable

SPOTTED BLUE DARNER
Aeshna clepsydra Say
Family Aeshnidae
Order Odonata

DESCRIPTION: The spotted blue darner is a blue darner dragonfly of slender aspect (total length, 56–70 mm). It is remarkable within the genus for the variegated pattern of thoracic markings. Males have a brown body, and the eyes, face, variegated thoracic pattern, and abdominal spots are pale blue to blue-green. Females have a brown body with light yellow-green markings or blue markings similar to those found in the males. An ovipositor and associated structures are present on the underside of abdominal segments 8 and 9.

RANGE: The spotted blue darner has been recorded from Ontario, Quebec, and Nova Scotia, Canada, and from Connecticut, Indiana, Iowa, Maine, Massachusetts, Michigan, New Hampshire, New Jersey, New York, Ohio, Pennsylvania, and Wisconsin. In Pennsylvania, it is known from Bradford, Pike, Sullivan, and Susquehanna counties.

HABITAT: This species inhabits lentic habitats, primarily small lakes or the embayments and backwaters of large lakes, in forested or glaciated terrain. In Pennsylvania, *A. clepsydra* has been taken at five lakes only in the four counties previously listed, all within one of the glaciated portions of the Commonwealth.

LIFE HISTORY AND ECOLOGY: Adult flights occur from June to early October somewhere within the range, but the main portion of the flight period is probably in August and September. Capture dates for Pennsylvania specimens fall within this latter period. Males patrol the lake edges, close to the water, from mid-morning to late afternoon during sunny weather. They also may be encountered in

Male, Spotted Blue Darner (*Aeshna clepsydra*). Photograph by C. N. Shiffer.

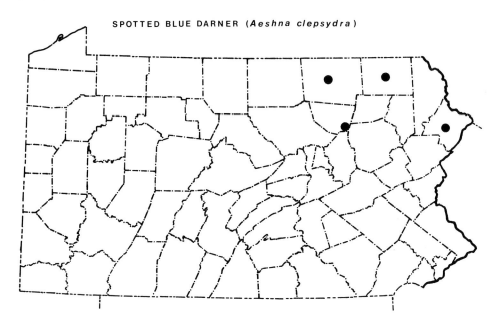

SPOTTED BLUE DARNER (*Aeshna clepsydra*)

open places, resting flat against tree trunks in the sunshine, at varying distances from water. Females do not patrol the lakeshore like the males, but fly there furtively from place to place, stopping to oviposit in plant material or wet wood. Patrolling males seize females along the lakeshore and the coupled pair then fly to some tree trunk away from the water to complete mating.

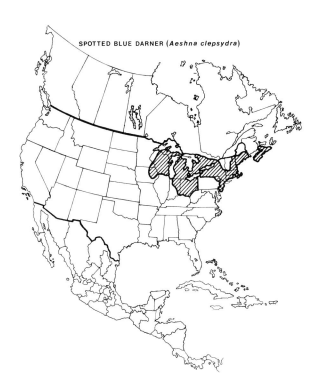

SPOTTED BLUE DARNER (*Aeshna clepsydra*)

Developmental time for eggs and nymphs has not been recorded, but some eggs may not hatch until the following spring or summer. Nymphs may require several winters to reach mature size. During transformation to the adult stage, the nymphs climb to wooded or aquatic vegetation at or near the shore. Adults do not wander far from the breeding sites, resembling *A. mutata* in this respect.

BASIS OF STATUS CLASSIFICATION: Aeshna clepsydra is presently known from only three specimens from Promised Land Lake and Pecks Ponds in Pike County, one specimen from Ganoga Lake in Sullivan County, and several specimens from Silver Lake in Susquehanna County. The Pike County lakes are owned by the Department of Environmental Resources; the Sullivan County and Susquehanna County lakes are privately owned. A more substantial number of individuals and specimens are known from Sunfish Pond in Bradford County, which is part of a county park. The Pike and Sullivan county records date back 20 to 40 years.

RECOMMENDATIONS: Additional surveys are necessary to determine the possible occurrence of this species at historic and other suitable habitats in the Commonwealth, particularly in the northeastern sector. Barring unforeseen habitat changes, the location of one known colony of the species within a county park should continue to offer it protection.

SELECTED REFERENCES:

BEATTY, A. F., and G. H. BEATTY. 1971. The distribution of Pennsylvania Odonata. Proc. Pennsylvania Acad. Sci., 45: 147–167.

BEATTY, G. H., and A. F. BEATTY. 1968. Check list and bibliography of Pennsylvania Odonata. Proc. Pennsylvania Acad. Sci., 42:120–129.

BEATTY, G. H., A. F. BEATTY, and C. N. SHIFFER. 1969. A survey of the Odonata of central Pennsylvania. Proc. Pennsylvania Acad. Sci., 43:127–136.

WALKER, E. M. 1958. The Odonata of Canada and Alaska. Univ. Toronto Press, Toronto, 2:1–318.

PREPARED BY: Clark Shiffer, *Pennsylvania Fish Commission, Robinson Lane, Bellefonte, PA 16823.*

Vulnerable

SPRING BLUE DARNER
Aeshna mutata Hagen
Family Aeshnidae
Order Odonata

DESCRIPTION: The spring blue darner is the only northeastern U.S. representative of the *Aeshna multicolor*-group of blue darner dragonflies. Body length is 74–80 mm. Males have a brown body, and the face, eyes, thoracic stripes, and abdominal spots are of a bright, intense cerulean blue. Superior append- ages on the end of male abdomen are bifurcated at tip in a peculiar beaklike formation. Females have a brown body with blue-green or yellow-green mark- ings, and plain elliptical abdominal appendages. The undersides of abdominal segments 8 and 9 on the female contain a sharp egg-laying organ (ovi- positor) and associated structures.

RANGE: Historically, the spring blue darner has been recorded from one site in Ontario, Canada, and from Indiana, Kentucky, Massachusetts, Mich- igan, Ohio, Pennsylvania, Virginia, and West Vir- ginia. Sight records in Pennsylvania are from Cam- bria and Centre counties; specimen records are from Centre, Cumberland, Erie, and Huntingdon coun- ties.

HABITAT: Throughout its range, this species has been recorded as occurring at relatively shallow len- tic habitats, ranging in type from woodland swamps and bog-margined permanent and temporary ponds to glaciated, moderate-sized or larger lakes. Spat- terdock (*Nuphar* spp.) and white waterlilies (*Nym- phaea* spp.) are often conspicuous elements of the aquatic vegetation.

In Pennsylvania, the species has been recorded from most of the lentic habitat types previously list-

Male, Spring Blue Darner (*Aeshna mutata*). Photograph by C. N. Shiffer.

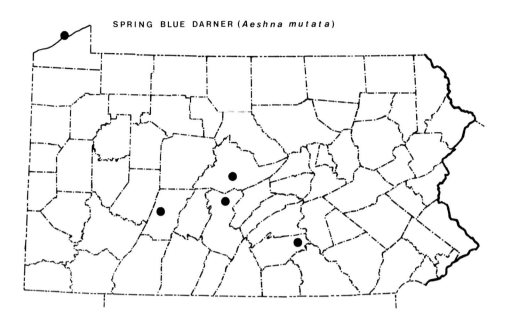

SPRING BLUE DARNER (*Aeshna mutata*)

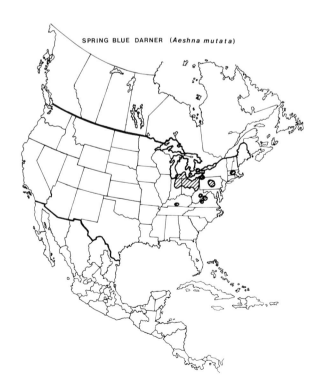

SPRING BLUE DARNER (*Aeshna mutata*)

ed, but is presently known to occur consistently only at "Ten Acre Pond," Scotia, Centre County. This pond is located just outside the boundary of State Game Lands 176 in a wooded area commonly known as "The Barrens." Surface acreage of the pond may slightly exceed 10 acres in the spring, while in the autumn and winter it is almost dry in most years.

Extensive beds of spatterdock are prominent in this pond and buttonbush (*Cephalanthus occidentalis*) grows on slightly higher ground.

LIFE HISTORY AND ECOLOGY: Throughout the historic range of this species adult flights have been noted from May to the end of August. In Pennsylvania, flying adults begin to appear near the end of May or the beginning of June and continue flying until the end of July most years, although numbers decline after the middle of July. Males fly repeatedly over and around the spatterdock beds during sunny weather from 9 AM to late afternoon, searching for females. Females fly singly to the spatterdock beds with low, more direct flight, and may be seized by watchful males. The copulatory position is achieved soon after seizure and the pair flies into some nearby tree to complete the mating process.

Mated females return unaccompanied to the spatterdock beds, coming to rest primarily on spatterdock flowers which are located several cm above the water's surface. Each female then probes the flower stem beneath the surface and deposits eggs singly in slits cut by the ovipositor. They may thus oviposit in more than one flower stem before leaving the site, but will return to oviposit on successive days. The recent observation of a female ovipositing at the base of a clump of rice cut-grass (*Leersia oryzoides*) with the abdomen partly submerged suggests that plants other than spatterdock may be used occasionally.

The length of time required for egg and nymphal

development has not been reported for this species, although eggs probably hatch within 30 days, and the first nymphs to hatch probably complete development within a year, but others may require several winters to complete the life cycle. Nymphs complete development within spatterdock beds and transform to the adult stage on emergent spatterdock or sedge leaves.

Except for individual vagrants, as with other members of the genus, adults do not wander widely from breeding sites. They tend to breed only at certain types of geographically separated, lentic habitats.

SPECIALIZED OR UNIQUE CHARACTERISTICS: Among large Pennsylvania Odonata, this species is unique with respect to the intensity and extent of blue color and is a striking and beautiful insect. The species may have developed an interesting relationship with spatterdock inasmuch as all stages of the life cycle usually center around spatterdock beds, but the use of rice cut-grass as an oviposition site indicates some flexibility in this regard.

BASIS OF STATUS CLASSIFICATION: Although recorded from one Canadian Province and eight states, the species has been collected at only one locality in Canada, Kentucky, Massachusetts, and West Virginia, three localities in Michigan and Virginia, seven in Ohio, and four in Indiana. At present, it appears that viable colonies may exist only in Virginia, several Ohio localities and one locality in Pennsylvania, because all previous reports of occurrence date back 20–80 years. With the exception of these localities and one Indiana swamp, which was converted to farmland, most previous records are one-time occurrences representing relatively few specimens.

RECOMMENDATIONS: Annexation of "Ten Acre Pond," and the surrounding tract of land to Game Lands 176 would undoubtedly help assure the continued survival of this uncommon species as part of the Pennsylvania fauna. Although individuals have been encountered at several smaller ponds within the Game Lands, numbers and extent of habitat are so small that "Ten Acre Pond" undoubtedly constitutes critical habitat for the species in Pennsylvania, and serves as one of the few known habitats for viable colonies of the species within its present range.

SELECTED REFERENCES:

BEATTY, G. H., and A. F. BEATTY. 1969. Evolution and speciation in the subgenus *Schizuraeschna,* with observations on *Aeshna* (Schizuraeschna) *mutata* Hagen (Odonata). Proc. Pennsylvania Acad. Sci., 43:147–152.

CARLE, F. L. 1979. Environmental monitoring potential of the Odonata, with a list of rare and endangered Anisoptera of Virginia, United States. Odonatologica, 8:319–323.

NEEDHAM, J. G., and M. J. WESTFALL, JR. 1955. A manual of the dragonflies of North America (Anisoptera). Univ. of California Press, Berkeley and Los Angeles, 615 pp.

WALKER, E. M. 1958. The Odonata of Canada and Alaska. Univ. Toronto Press, Toronto, 2:1–318.

PREPARED BY: Clark Shiffer, *Pennsylvania Fish Commission, Robinson Lane, Bellefonte, PA 16823.*

Vulnerable

LONG-LEGGED GREEN DARNER
Anax longipes Hagen
Family Aeshnidae
Order Odonata

DESCRIPTION: This dragonfly is a large (total length, 75–87 mm) green darner with long hind legs. The face, eyes, thorax, and first two abdominal segments are green. The remainder of the abdomen is orange-red in males and duller red-brown in females. The legs are black with reddish femora. Hind femora are 15–18 mm in length. The undersides of abdominal segments 8 and 9 in females possess an ovipositor and associated structures.

RANGE: The long-legged green darner occurs from Florida and Mississippi north to Massachusetts, and west to Indiana, Oklahoma, and Texas. It is also found in Haiti, Jamaica, and the Bahamas, and Mexico south to Brazil. In Pennsylvania, sight records are known from Allegheny, Huntingdon, Lackawanna, Luzerne, Westmoreland, and York counties; specimens are available from Centre, Delaware, and Wayne counties.

HABITAT: The long-legged green darner is found near relatively shallow lentic habitats, usually ponds with a variety of emergent and submerged aquatic vegetation, in wooded or partly wooded areas. It is also recorded as occurring around slow streams, particularly bayous in southern U.S.

Occurrences in Pennsylvania are all from ponds or small lakes, but the species is presently known to occur consistently only at "Ten Acre Pond," Scotia, Centre County. This is the same habitat de-

Male, Long-legged Green Darner (*Anax longipes*). Photograph by C. N. Shiffer.

scribed under the account for *Aeshna mutata*; this pond is remarkable for the mutual occurrence of northern (boreal) and southern (austral) Odonata species, which are uncommon in Pennsylvania.

LIFE HISTORY AND ECOLOGY: Although adult flights occur throughout the year in the southern portion of the range, the Pennsylvania flight period extends from the third week in May to the end of July. The large and striking males fly in an aimless manner over the breeding sites on sunny days from about 0900 hr until late afternoon. They fly from 1–1.5 m above the surface of the water and may pause to hover briefly. Females fly more directly and closer to the water, seeking sites for oviposition in submerged and floating vegetation. Males seize unmated females as they fly close to the water and the coupled pair then settle on woody or non-herbaceous vegetation at heights of 1.2 m or more above ground to complete mating.

Mated females return to the water with low, direct flight, ovipositing alone in floating or barely sub-

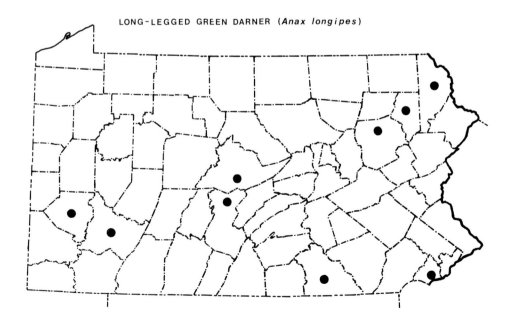

LONG-LEGGED GREEN DARNER (*Anax longipes*)

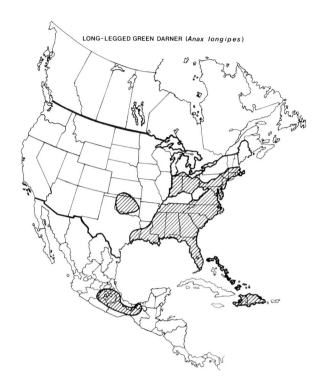

LONG-LEGGED GREEN DARNER (*Anax longipes*)

merged vegetation. Although males may attempt seizure, these mated females strike out with their legs and their whirring wings cause the males to withdraw.

Eggs probably hatch within a month and nymphs probably develop rapidly, reaching the next to the last stage of their development before autumn. Nymphs complete development the following spring or early summer, although some may require a second winter for development. Nymphs ascend the stems and leaves of aquatic vegetation to transform to the adult stage.

SPECIALIZED OR UNIQUE CHARACTERISTICS: The orange-red abdomen and long hind legs are unique among species of the genus *Anax*.

BASIS OF STATUS CLASSIFICATION: Although *A. longipes* has been sighted at various places in Pennsylvania (one to three males each time), this fact only attests to the tendency of the strong-flying members of the genus, males particularly, to wander far from breeding sites. Reports of established colonies are less common. Pennsylvania specimen records for the species from Delaware and Wayne counties date back about 45 to 75 years and the Delaware County site is no longer extant. "Ten Acre Pond," Centre County, is presently the only known

site in Pennsylvania of a viable colony of *A. longipes*.

RECOMMENDATIONS: Comments concerning annexation of "Ten Acre Pond" in the account of *Aeshna mutata* would apply to this species as well. Individuals of *A. longipes* have not been encountered at other ponds on Game Lands 176.

SELECTED REFERENCES:

BEATTY, A. F., and G. H. BEATTY. 1971. The distribution of Pennsylvania Odonata. Proc. Pennsylvania Acad. Sci., 45: 147–167.
BEATTY, G. H., and A. F. BEATTY. 1968. Check list and bibliography of Pennsylvania Odonata. Proc. Pennsylvania Acad. Sci., 42:120–129.
BEATTY, G. H., A. F. BEATTY, and C. N. SHIFFER. 1969. A survey of the Odonata of central Pennsylvania. Proc. Pennsylvania Acad. Sci., 43:127–136.
BICK, G. H. 1953. The occurrence of *Anax longipes* Hagen in Mississippi. Ent. News, 640:230–232.

PREPARED BY: Clark Shiffer, *Pennsylvania Fish Commission, Robinson Lane, Bellefonte, PA 16823.*

Vulnerable

HOWE'S SNAKE DARNER
Ophiogomphus howei (Bromley)
Family Gomphidae
Order Odonata

DESCRIPTION: Howe's snake darner is the smallest species of its genus and family in North America (total length, 31–34 mm). Howe's snake darner possesses a greenish yellow face; green (mature insect) or yellow (immature insect) thorax with mid-dorsal, shoulder, and lateral brown stripes; black legs with greenish yellow on hind portion of bases; black abdomen with dorsal and lateral spots and streaks of yellow. There is a ridge at the rear of the head (occiput) of the female with a pair of short, sharp, widely separated spines. Wings of both sexes are tinged with yellow, which is deeper basally, covering two-thirds of hind wing in female.

RANGE: This species is known historically only from Amherst, Massachusetts (1 female—holotype); Fort Washington at Lemoyne, Cumberland County, Pennsylvania (1 male allotype—associated with the holotype by supposition); Pennsylvania Fish Commission Great Bend Access Area, N. Branch Susquehanna River, Susquehanna County, Pennsyl-

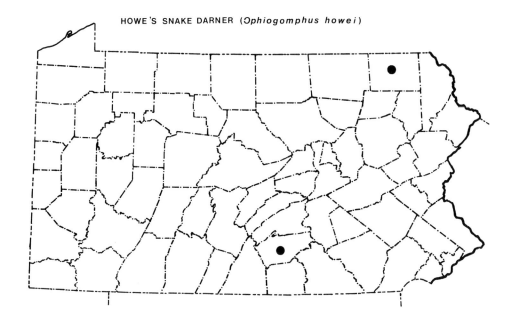

HOWE'S SNAKE DARNER (*Ophiogomphus howei*)

vania; eastern Kentucky; New River in Virginia (Grayson and Carroll counties) and North Carolina (Alleghany County).

HABITAT: The habitat of Howe's snake darner is unpolluted, moderate-sized portions of large rivers with gravelly to sandy substrate.

HOWE'S SNAKE DARNER (*Ophiogomphus howei*)

LIFE HISTORY AND ECOLOGY: Adults are recorded as appearing as early as 30 April in Virginia in 1977, but flights occur primarily in May and June in all parts of the range. Although numbers of larvae and exuviae have been taken, adults have not been seen or taken in large numbers after the period of larval emergence and transformation. Adults may spend considerable time perched on sunlit leaves high above the water. They have been observed on such sites late in the day in Virginia and were noted leaving such sites late in the afternoon in Pennsylvania and flying over the surface of the river. One male was observed patrolling a water-filled ditch near the New River (Frank Carle, personal communication).

Although the time required for egg and nymphal development is not known, the collection of several distinct sizes of nymphs in Virginia may indicate a two-year life cycle. When ready to transform to the adult stage, nymphs climb to bare mud banks, tree rootlets, or other vegetation along the river's edge. Exuviae (nymphal skins) may thus be found 1.2 m or more above the river as spring high water levels return to normal.

SPECIALIZED OR UNIQUE CHARACTERISTICS: The small size and present limited and disjunct occurrence of this species within rivers of ancient orgin makes it one of scientific interest.

BASIS OF STATUS CLASSIFICATION: This

species is certainly one of the rarest of North American Odonata. Until the discovery of the New River colony, *O. howei* was known only from three specimens, the two type specimens and an immature female collected at Great Bend Access Area, Susquehanna County.

Although this species is under no known immediate threat to its existence at present, plans to build dams within recent years on the New River and North Branch Susquehanna River would have eliminated half of the sites where *O. howei* is presently known to occur. Future deterioration of water quality or physical makeup of these critical habitats would quickly downgrade the status of *O. howei*.

RECOMMENDATIONS: Continued monitoring of water quality and physical makeup of the North Branch Susquehanna River in northern Pennsylvania and southern New York will be necessary to prevent changes deleterious to aquatic organisms. Political support and strict enforcement of federal and state laws and regulations pertinent to maintenance of a quality environment, which take into account the continued existence of organisms like *Ophiogomphus howei,* will also be necessary.

SELECTED REFERENCES:

BROMLEY, S. W. 1924. A new *Ophiogomphus* (Aeshnidae: Odonata) from Massachusetts. Entomol. News, 35:343–344.
CALVERT, P. P. 1924. The supposed male of *Ophiogomphus howei* Bromley (Odon.: Aeshnidae). Entomol. News, 35:345–347.
KENNEDY, J. H., and H. B. WHITE, III. 1979. Description of the nymph of *Ophiogomphus howei* (Odonata:Gomphidae). Proc. Entomol. Soc. Washington, 81:64–69.

PREPARED BY: Clark Shiffer, *Pennsylvania Fish Commission, Robinson Lane, Bellefonte, PA 16823.*

Vulnerable

ABBREVIATED CLUBTAIL
Gomphus abbreviatus Hagen
Family Gomphidae
Order Odonata

DESCRIPTION: The abbreviated clubtail is a small, stocky dragonfly, with the terminal abdominal segments somewhat widened and bearing short, widely-spread appendages in the male. Total length is about 35 mm. This species has a greenish yellow face and thorax; thorax with broad mid-dorsal and paired shoulder stripes of dark-brown; black abdomen, with

Male, Abbreviated Clubtail (*Gomphus abbreviatus*). Photograph by C. N. Shiffer.

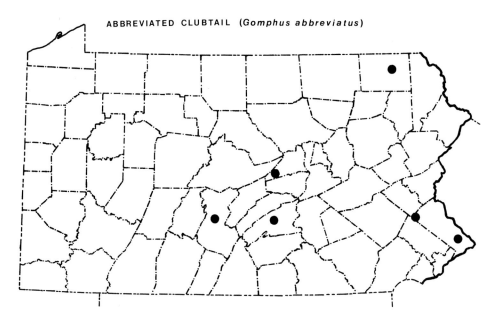

ABBREVIATED CLUBTAIL (*Gomphus abbreviatus*)

yellow spear-shaped dorsal markings and broad, brighter yellow markings on sides of segments 7, 8, and 9. Females possess an occiput with two short, widely-spread spines and are more brightly marked with yellow on the abdomen.

RANGE: Historically, this species has been recorded locally from Maine to South Carolina and Georgia and west to Ohio. In Pennsylvania, the abbreviated clubtail has been recorded from one or two sites in Bucks, Huntingdon, Perry, Susquehanna, and Union counties.

HABITAT: The abbreviated clubtail prefers low to moderate gradient streams and rivers with gravelly to rocky substrate, in partly open country.

LIFE HISTORY AND ECOLOGY: The adult flight period is recorded as extending from late April in the south to early July in the north. The main flight period is probably from mid-May to the end of June in most areas. Males may be seen in sunny weather, from mid-morning to mid-afternoon, flying over riffle areas within 0.6–0.9 m of the surface of the water. Not infrequently, they hover for varying periods, facing upstream. At other times, they will perch on rocks projecting from the riffles, on vegetation along the bank, or near the ground in clearings away from the water. Females frequently perch on vegetation away from the water, returning to riffle areas only to oviposit. Oviposition is accomplished as the female flies close to the water, dipping the end of the abdomen at various spots between projecting stones and washing a group of eggs off with each dip.

Egg and nymphal developmental time are unknown, but several winters may be required for the completion of nymphal growth. Emergence and transformation occur during high springtime water levels. Larvae climb stream banks, trees, tree roots, or herbaceous vegetation at or near the edge of the

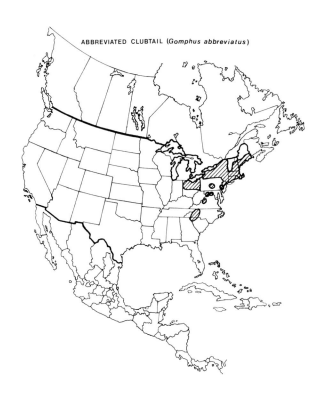

ABBREVIATED CLUBTAIL (*Gomphus abbreviatus*)

water. Transformation usually occurs before midday. Large numbers of transforming adults have been noted at one site in Maine and one in Pennsylvania.

When the body and wings are sufficiently hardened, the fresh adults (tenerals) fly away from the water and may be encountered feeding in fields or open areas for nearly a week. When fully mature, they begin to frequent the riffle areas and do not wander far from the breeding sites.

SPECIALIZED OR UNIQUE CHARACTERISTICS: This species is one of the smallest of the family Gomphidae and the subgenus *Hylogomphus*, and, like other species of the subgenus, is locally distributed.

BASIS OF STATUS CLASSIFICATION: Confirmation of the continued occurrence of this species at most historic sites within its range is needed. In Pennsylvania, *G. abbreviatus* has been encountered in largest numbers at Finland, Bucks County. Although the last records from this locality date back to the mid-1950s, the species probably still exists there, because water quality in Unami Creek is still suitable. A visit to one site in Perry County in 1976 indicated the continued occurrence of the species there. The unique Huntingdon County record dates back 50 years. Although nymphs of this species have been reared from the Union County site, adults have not been encountered. Water quality at this location is good, and the species should still occur there. Both nymphs and adults are recorded for the Susquehanna County site.

RECOMMENDATIONS: The maintenance of the sort of physical habitat and water quality conditions required by *G. abbreviatus* is of utmost importance to our aquatic invertebrate fauna. In addition, more systematic surveys are needed to establish the possible occurrence of this species within historic and other suitable habitats.

SELECTED REFERENCES:

BEATTY, A. F., and G. H. BEATTY. 1971. The distribution of Pennsylvania Odonata. Proc. Pennsylvania Acad. Sci., 45:147–167.
BEATTY, G. H., A. F. BEATTY, and C. N. SHIFFER. 1969. A survey of the Odonata of central Pennsylvania. Proc. Pennsylvania Acad. Sci., 43:127–136.
———. 1970. A survey of the Odonata of eastern Pennsylvania. Proc. Pennsylvania Acad. Sci., 44:141–152.
CARLE, F. L. 1979. Two new *Gomphus* (Odonata: Gomphidae) from eastern North America with adult keys to the subgenus *Hylogomphus*. Ann. Entomol. Soc. Amer., 72:418–426.

PREPARED BY: Clark Shiffer, *Pennsylvania Fish Commission, Robinson Lane, Bellefonte, PA 16823.*

Vulnerable

ROGER'S CLUBTAIL
Gomphus rogersi Gloyd
Family Gomphidae
Order Odonata

DESCRIPTION: Roger's clubtail is an average-sized gomphine dragonfly (total length, about 48 mm), heavily marked with black. In the male, the ground color of the face and thorax is light gray-green; top of head between eyes black; face, front, and shoulder area of thorax heavily striped with black; legs black, with pale greenish streak at base of front pair; wings clear with fumose brownish color at tips; abdomen largely black, except for small dorsal spear-shaped pale green markings and dull yellow edgings on sides of segments 7, 8, and 9. End segments of abdomen are only slightly widened; male terminal appendages with superior ante-apical tooth, moderately slender, subequal in length and widely divergent. Females lack these appendages and have a ground body color of greenish-yellow.

RANGE: This species is known locally from Delaware (Harold B. White, III, personal communication), Kentucky (Frank Carle, personal communication), Georgia (Sidney W. Dunkle, personal communication), North Carolina, South Carolina (Ken Tennessen, personal communication), Pennsylvania, Tennessee, Virginia (Frank Carle, personal communication), and West Virginia (nymphs only). It has been recorded in Pennsylvania from five sites in Huntingdon County, one site in Butler, Clearfield, Forest, and Fulton counties, respectively and from one sight record in Centre County. Published records from Elk and Somerset counties lack substantiation and a Franklin County record has proven erroneous.

HABITAT: Roger's clubtail prefers relatively small spring-fed streams with sandy, gravelly, or silty substrate. It prefers streams flowing through forested to partly forested areas or open meadow terrain, with open, sunny, and partially shaded areas.

Male, Roger's Clubtail (*Gomphus rogersi*). Photographs by C. N. Shiffer.

LIFE HISTORY AND ECOLOGY: Adult flights occur from mid-April to mid–late July somewhere in the range, but are most often encountered in June. Both sexes are rather localized with respect to their occurrence along the length of preferred streams; that is, they are generally encountered along a very limited portion of the stream. Males may be seen on sunny days, from mid-morning to late afternoon, resting on herbaceous vegetation close to the water, or on logs, or rocks, usually in the sun, but sometimes in shaded areas. They occasionally patrol slowly, 0.3–0.6 m above the stream, pausing to hover before coming to rest on streamside perches or flying to vegetation in full sun away from the edge of the water. Both sexes spend much time perched on sunlit tree leaves some distance above the water. Females oviposit in flight, near a mid-stream clump of grasses or sedges, by dipping the tip of the abdomen into the water.

The time required for egg and nymphal development is unknown, but nymphs may require several winters to complete development. Nymphal

Female, Roger's Clubtail (*Gomphus rogersi*). Photograph by C. N. Shiffer.

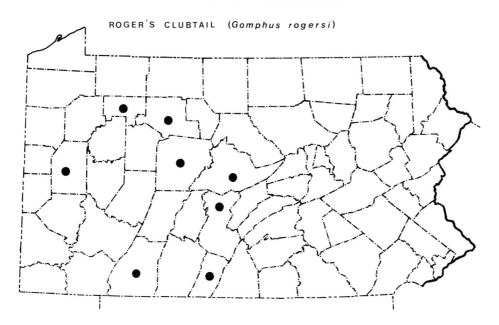

ROGER'S CLUBTAIL (*Gomphus rogersi*)

emergence and transformation to the adult stage occur during early to mid-morning hours on stream banks or vegetation not far from the edge of the water.

Adults are most commonly found in the immediate vicinity of the breeding sites, showing no disposition to wander from their preferred habitats.

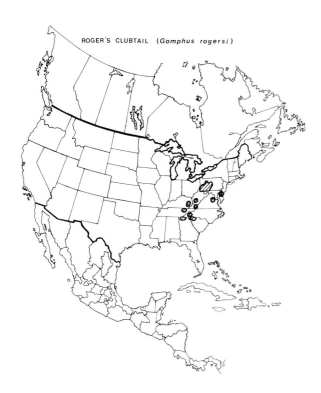

ROGER'S CLUBTAIL (*Gomphus rogersi*)

SPECIALIZED OR UNIQUE CHARACTERISTICS: This species is one of several closely related species assigned to the subgenus *Gomphurus* which differ enough in various characteristics from most species in the subgenus to possibly warrant separate taxonomic status.

BASIS OF STATUS CLASSIFICATION: This species is quite local throughout its known range. In Pennsylvania, with the exception of two sites in Huntingdon County, all records consist of single collections of one or several specimens of adults or nymphs per locality. The specimens collected at the Butler County site are now represented only by fragments. These specimens (one male, one female) were collected nearly 40 years ago. The figures of the male appendages labelled *Gomphus consanguis* (a closely related species with a slightly different range) in the Needham and Westfall Manual were those of this now-destroyed male. Other records consist mostly of nymphs which were reared, and date from 15–25 years ago. Water quality and physical makeup of the habitat at some of these sites would appear to be suitable for occurrence of the species. The one Huntingdon County site near Whipple Dam has produced adults and nymphs since the mid-fifties, although in low total numbers. Nymphal material from this site was the basis for the original description of the nymph of *G. rogersi*. (In this same paper the true identity of *G. rogersi* was established. For nearly 20 years following its original description, *G.*

rogersi was confused with, and listed as, *G. consanguis*.)

RECOMMENDATIONS: Historic sites for *G. rogersi* should be revisited to ascertain the present status of the species. Several of these sites, including the one near Whipple Dam, are on state forest land in close proximity to state parks, offering some protection to the species and its habitat. One Huntingdon County site is a Pennsylvania State University recreation area. Additional surveys may reveal other sites for *G. rogersi* in Pennsylvania, a state with the largest known number of sites for the species within its present range. As is true for all aquatic organisms in Pennsylvania, the safeguarding of water quality and environmental integrity throughout the Commonwealth is essential to the continued existence of *G. rogersi*.

SELECTED REFERENCES:

BEATTY, G. H., A. F. BEATTY, and C. N. SHIFFER. 1969. A survey of the Odonata of central Pennsylvania. Proc. Pennsylvania Acad. Sci., 43:127–136.

CARLE, F. L. 1979. Environmental monitoring potential of the Odonata, with a list of rare and endangered Anisoptera of Virginia, United States. Odonatologica, 8:319–323.

GLOYD, L. K. 1936. Three new North American species of Gomphinae (Odonata). Occas. Papers Mus. Zool., Univ. Michigan, 326:1–18.

NEEDHAM, J. G., and M. J. WESTFALL, JR. 1955. A manual of the dragonflies of North America (Anisoptera). Univ. California Press, Berkeley and Los Angeles, 615 pp.

WESTFALL, M. J., JR., and R. P. TROGDON. 1962. The true *Gomphus consanguis* Selys (Odonata: Gomphidae). Florida Entomol., 45:29–41.

PREPARED BY: Clark Shiffer, *Pennsylvania Fish Commission, Robinson Lane, Bellefonte, PA 16823.*

Vulnerable

SCUDDER'S CLUBTAIL
Gomphus scudderi Selys
Family Gomphidae
Order Odonata

DESCRIPTION: Scudder's clubtail is a darkly-marked gomphine dragonfly with a thin abdomen, the terminal segments of which are noticeably broadened. Total length is about 58 mm. This species possesses a pale greenish face and a thorax heavily marked with dark brown stripes; the thorax has broad brown stripings on front, shoulder, and side areas. The abdomen is dark brown with pale greenish dorsal triangles and oblique lateral markings presenting a ringed appearance; widened segments 7–9 are marked with dorsal triangles and broad lateral markings of yellow. Males display terminal appendages, which are moderately stout, apically tapered, and widely divergent. Females are similar to the males with one pair of short, inconspicuous terminal appendages.

RANGE: Historically, Scudder's clubtail has been recorded from Nova Scotia, Ontario, and Quebec, Canada, and from Maine to Georgia, west to Michigan and Wisconsin. It is known in Pennsylvania from sites in Clarion, Clearfield, Clinton, and Jefferson counties.

HABITAT: Forest streams or slow rivers with alternating riffles and pools and a gravelly to rocky or sandy substrate are the preferred habitat of Scudder's clubtail.

LIFE HISTORY AND ECOLOGY: The adult flight period extends from late June to early October over the range of the species, with the main portion of the period being July to September. Although large numbers of exuviae may be found, adults are not as evident. Males may be seen flying over riffles or perched on bank vegetation. Females are seen less often, visiting the streams only to oviposit by flying close to the water along a sheltering bank and dipping the end of the abdomen to the surface in various places.

Egg and nymphal developmental times are not known, but several winters are probably spent in the nymphal stage. Emergence and transformation occur during the morning hours and may be more pronounced during mid-day. Exuviae may be found on stream banks, tree rootlets, or other vegetation not far from the water. Adults do not wander widely, but stay in the immediate vicinity of the breeding sites.

SPECIALIZED OR UNIQUE CHARACTERISTICS: This is a species of local occurrence. Adults are seldom encountered in large numbers.

BASIS OF STATUS CLASSIFICATION: The Clarion and Clearfield county records date back 40 to 45 years, and these are the only known collections of adults. The deterioration of water quality in the Clarion River and West Branch Susquehanna River, due primarily to acid mine drainage, make it un-

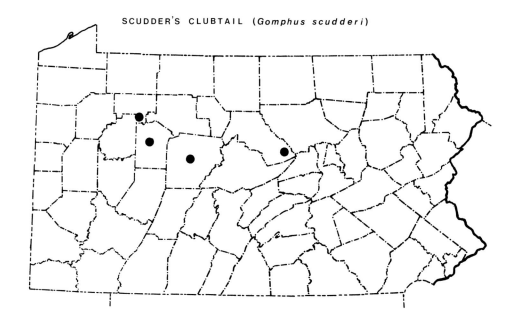

SCUDDER'S CLUBTAIL (*Gomphus scudderi*)

likely that *G. scudderi* still occurs at those sites. The most recent collections, in Clinton and Jefferson counties, are of nymphs only. Water quality and habitat conditions at these sites are still suitable for the species.

RECOMMENDATIONS: Statements under previous species accounts concerning the need to safe-guard the integrity of our environment would apply here as well. Further surveys of suitable habitats will be necessary to establish the further occurrence of *G. scudderi* in this Commonwealth.

SELECTED REFERENCES:

BEATTY, A. F., and G. H. BEATTY. 1971. The distribution of Pennsylvania Odonata. Proc. Pennsylvania Acad. Sci., 45: 147–167.
BEATTY, G. H. and A. F. BEATTY. 1968. Check list and bibliography of Pennsylvania Odonata. Proc. Pennsylvania Acad. Sci., 42:120–129.
BEATTY, G. H., A. F. BEATTY, and C. N. SHIFFER. 1969. A survey of the Odonata of central Pennsylvania. Proc. Pennsylvania Acad. Sci., 43:127–136.
WALKER, E. M. 1958. The Odonata of Canada and Alaska. Univ. Toronto Press, Toronto, 2:1–318.

PREPARED BY: Clark Shiffer, *Pennsylvania Fish Commission, Robinson Lane, Bellefonte, PA 16823.*

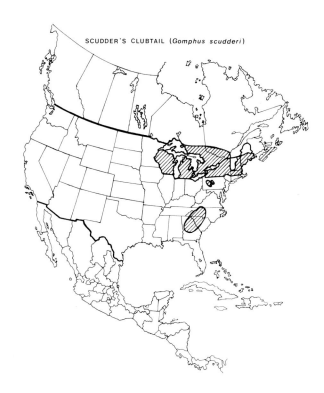

SCUDDER'S CLUBTAIL (*Gomphus scudderi*)

Vulnerable

SLENDER BOG SKIMMER
Somatochlora elongata (Scudder)
Family Libellulidae
Order Odonata

DESCRIPTION: The slender bog skimmer is a medium-sized (total length, 52–62 mm) dark brown dragonfly with a metallic sheen to the thorax and abdomen. The face of this species is yellowish, marked with dark metallic blue to blue-green; the

Male (upper) and female (lower), Slender Bog Skimmer (*Somatochlora elongata*). Photographs by C. N. Shiffer.

thorax is dark brown, with two prominent light yellow stripes or elongate spots on each side, and with metallic bronzy blue-green reflections; the abdomen is black with dull bronzy bluish sheen, and with large pale markings on basal segments. The superior appendages at end of the abdomen of the male are moderately long and slender with recurved tips. The female is similar to the male, but with prominent scoop-shaped vulvar lamina (plate covering the genital opening) on underside of abdominal segments 8 and 9.

RANGE: Historically, this species is known from the Canadian maritime provinces, west to Ontario, south to Wisconsin and Minnesota, east to New England, and south along the mountains into Georgia. It is known in Pennsylvania from one site each in Centre, Clearfield, Clinton, Huntingdon, Somerset, and Union counties and two sites in McKean County.

HABITAT: The slender bog skimmer inhabits areas with spring-fed, low gradient creeks and streams in bogs or boggy surroundings.

LIFE HISTORY AND ECOLOGY: Adult flights occur from mid-June in the south to early September in the north, but may be most commonly encountered, at most localities, from mid-July through August. Males fly slowly up and down the center or over the shady, ponded expanses or embayments of small streams, or the edges of larger streams. On sunny days, they can be seen flying in a series of forward movements interrupted by periods of momentary hovering within 0.3 m of the water. Females visit the water on sunny or warm, overcast days, only to oviposit, choosing a spot among moss-covered rocks or a mossy area along the bank. There they hover close to the stream, alternately dipping the tip of the abdomen one or two times to the wet moss above the water and then to the water itself.

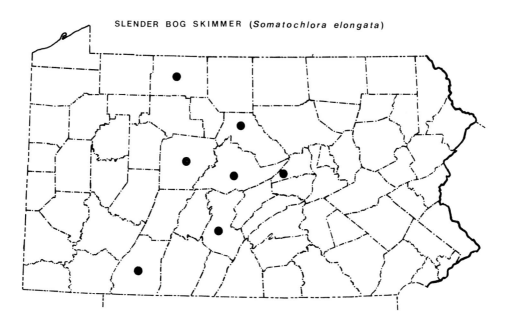

SLENDER BOG SKIMMER (*Somatochlora elongata*)

Eggs are thus deposited among the moss filaments in successive small batches, and the ovipositor is cleared of debris when dipped to the water.

Eggs hatch the following spring, and larvae spend at least several winters in the feeding and growing stage. Larvae may crawl a moderate distance from the water to transform to the adult stage on woody or herbaceous vegetation. Transformation normally takes place during the early morning hours.

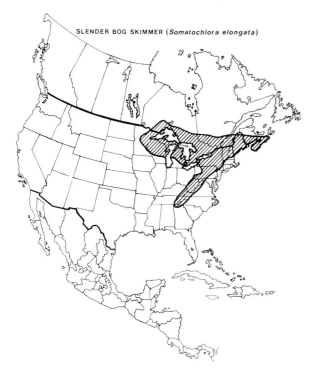

SLENDER BOG SKIMMER (*Somatochlora elongata*)

Freshly-transformed adults may move up to a mile from the breeding site before becoming reproductively mature. After 1 to 2 weeks adults return to the breeding sites, where males are especially evident as they patrol over the water. Mature adults remain in the vicinity of the breeding sites for the remainder of their lives, which on an individual basis is about 1 month.

SPECIALIZED OR UNIQUE CHARACTERISTICS: Somatochlora elongata is not generally distributed, but may occur locally in moderate numbers in areas where boggy terrain is more generally distributed.

BASIS OF STATUS CLASSIFICATION: Some protection may be accorded the species in Centre, Clearfield, and Clinton counties. The Centre County site is a National Natural Landmark; the Clearfield County site is a state park, and a portion of the Clinton County site has been designated a state natural area. The Huntingdon County site is on state forest land. Other sites, however, are under private control. The Union County record is based on a single reared nymph; the species is otherwise unknown from the county. The Somerset County record of a single adult dates back about 44 years; the species is otherwise unknown from that county. The species may still occur at the McKean County sites, although increased oil and gas well activity could pose a threat to its existence.

RECOMMENDATIONS: Additional surveys should be conducted to determine the possible occurrence of *S. elongata* at other sites in Pennsylvania and the integrity of present habitats for the species safeguarded.

SELECTED REFERENCES:

BEATTY, A. F., and G. H. BEATTY. 1971. The distribution of Pennsylvania Odonata. Proc. Pennsylvania Acad. Sci., 45: 147–167.
BEATTY, G. H., and A. F. BEATTY. 1968. Check list and bibliography of Pennsylvania Odonata. Proc. Pennsylvania Acad. Sci., 42:120–129.
WALKER, E. M. 1925. The North American dragonflies of the genus *Somatochlora*. Univ. Toronto Studies, Biol. Ser., 26: 1–202.
WALKER, E. M., and P. S. CORBET. 1975. The Odonata of Canada and Alaska. Univ. Toronto Press, Toronto, 3:1–307.

PREPARED BY: Clark Shiffer, *Pennsylvania Fish Commission, Robinson Lane, Bellefonte, PA 16823.*

Vulnerable

FORCIPATE BOG SKIMMER
Somatochlora forcipata (Scudder)
Family Libellulidae
Order Odonata

DESCRIPTION: Somatochlora forcipata is one of the smaller species of the genus (total length, 43–51 mm). The face of this species is yellowish with dark metallic greenish markings; the thorax is dark brown with two well-defined elongate yellow spots on each side, and with metallic blue-green reflections; the abdomen is black with a dull metallic greenish sheen, marked on sides of second and third segments with several pale yellow spots and smaller spots of dull yellow-brown on rear lateral portions of segments 4–9. In males, the abdominal appendages have slender apices, slightly bowed, and forcipate when viewed from the top. On the underside of females, abdominal segments 8 and 9 have narrow scoop-shaped vulvar lamina.

RANGE: Historically, the forcipate bog skimmer has been recorded sparingly in western Canada from Alberta and the Northwest Territories, becoming more common eastward to New Brunswick and Newfoundland; in the United States from Michigan east to the New England states, south to Pennsylvania and West Virginia (Pocahontas County). It is known in Pennsylvania from Clearfield, Clinton, Monroe, and Tioga counties.

HABITAT: The forcipate bog skimmer prefers spring runs or seeps in, or associated with, sphagnum bogs.

LIFE HISTORY AND ECOLOGY: Adult flights occur within the range of the species from the latter part of May to the end of August. In Pennsylvania, the flight period extends from 5 June to 1 August, with most records from mid-June to mid-July. Until reproductive maturity is reached, both sexes are en-

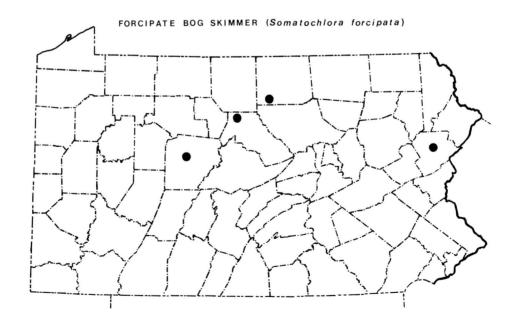

FORCIPATE BOG SKIMMER *(Somatochlora forcipata)*

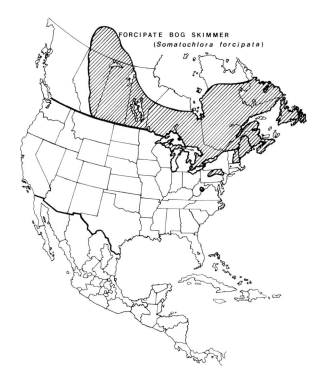

BASIS OF STATUS CLASSIFICATION: Although all known sites of occurrence in Pennsylvania remain suitable for the species, only one site is known for each of the four counties. A single adult has been taken at each of the sites in Clearfield, Monroe, and Tioga counties. The Monroe County bog is owned by Lafayette College; the Clearfield County site is part of a state park; the Tioga County bog is a state natural area. A portion of the Clinton County bog is also a state natural area, and is the only site which has produced adults of *S. forcipata* nearly every year since 1958. All other site records date back from 10 to 40 years.

RECOMMENDATIONS: Considering the suitability of habitat conditions at the Clearfield, Monroe, and Tioga county sites, further surveys should be conducted there to ascertain the present status of the species. Further surveys of other bogs, particularly in the northeastern portion of the Commonwealth, may reveal additional sites of occurrence. The environmental integrity of presently known sites must be safeguarded if *S. forcipata* is to remain a part of the Pennsylvania fauna.

SELECTED REFERENCES:

BEATTY, A. F., and G. H. BEATTY. 1971. The distribution of Pennsylvania Odonata. Proc. Pennsylvania Acad. Sci., 45: 147–167.

BEATTY, G. H., and A. F. BEATTY. 1968. Check list and bibliography of Pennsylvania Odonata. Proc. Pennsylvania Acad. Sci., 42:120–129.

SHIFFER, C. N. 1969. Occurrence and habits of *Somatochlora incurvata,* new for Pennsylvania. Michigan Entomol. 2:75–76.

WALKER, E. M. 1925. The North American dragonflies of the genus *Somatochlora.* Univ. Toronto Studies, Biol. Ser., 26: 1–202.

WALKER, E. M., and P. S. CORBET. 1975. The Odonata of Canada and Alaska. Univ. Toronto Press, Toronto, 3:1–307.

PREPARED BY: Clark Shiffer, *Pennsylvania Fish Commission, Robinson Lane, Bellefonte, PA 16823.*

countered on sunny days flying at average heights of 0.9–3 m above the ground in clearings, alighting occasionally on shrubs or the foliage of trees. Mature males frequent the vicinity of small spring runs or seeps in sunny weather, pausing frequently to hover at heights of about 1.2 m or less. Females fly to these sites with lower, more direct flight, and oviposit among cattails or other concealing vegetation by hovering close to the water and dipping the abdomen to its surface at intervals, washing off clusters of eggs. Males may seize females during this time and the coupled pair then fly to the foliage or branchlets of nearby trees or shrubs to complete mating.

Eggs hatch the following spring, and nymphs grow slowly, requiring at least several winters to complete development. Transformation occurs on woody or herbaceous vegetation not far above the water or sphagnum moss. Although adults are sometimes seen flying at some height above the ground, they do not wander far from the breeding sites.

SPECIALIZED OR UNIQUE CHARACTERISTICS: This species of predominately Canadian distribution reaches its southernmost known range limits in Pennsylvania and West Virginia. It appears to be rather restricted to the habitat previously mentioned.

Vulnerable

MICHIGAN BOG SKIMMER
Somatochlora incurvata Walker
Family Libellulidae
Order Odonata

DESCRIPTION: This is a little-known species of above-average size for the genus (total length, about

Male (upper) and female (lower), Michigan Bog Skimmer (*Somatochlora incurvata*). Photograph by C. N. Shiffer.

63 mm). The face of the Michigan bog skimmer is yellowish brown with dark, metallic greenish markings; the thorax is brown with metallic blue-green reflections and a pair of dull yellowish-brown elongate spots on each side; the abdomen is black with dull greenish sheen, pale areas on sides of segments 2 and 3, and smaller dull yellow-brown spots on rear lateral portions of segments 4 to 9. In males, the abdominal appendages possess acute and sinuous apices in side view, close together at the base and forcipate when viewed from the top. Females are similar to males, with narrow, elongate scoop-shaped vulvar lamina.

RANGE: Somatochlora incurvata is known only from the Canadian provinces of Ontario (one male—

Nippissing District) and Nova Scotia, and in the U.S. from northern Michigan, Maine (Mt. Desert Island), and Pennsylvania (Bradford and Clinton counties).

HABITAT: This species is associated with small pools of apparently still, but not stagnant, spring water in sphagnum bogs.

LIFE HISTORY AND ECOLOGY: Adult flights have been recorded from the latter half of July to the middle of October. In Pennsylvania, a single teneral female was taken on 29 June, which is probably very close to the usual time of emergence and transformation in the Commonwealth. Aside from this early date, adults have been recorded here from

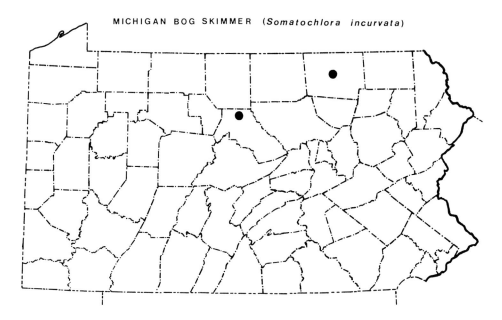

MICHIGAN BOG SKIMMER (*Somatochlora incurvata*)

15 July to 25 August. Males may be seen in sunny weather usually in the mid-morning to mid-afternoon. They fly in a random manner within several cm of bog vegetation, pausing occasionally to hover over the larger pools or to perch in an oblique position on bare twigs. Females have been observed to be most active on warm, but overcast, days when very few males are evident. They fly among bog

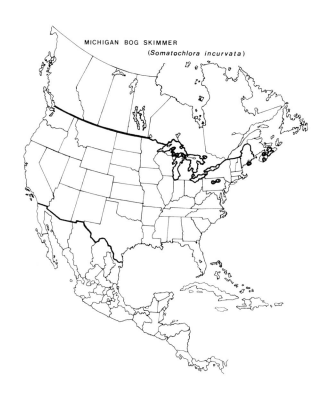

MICHIGAN BOG SKIMMER
(*Somatochlora incurvata*)

shrubs with direct and furtive flight, seeking appropriate places in sphagnum depressions in which to oviposit. Oviposition is accomplished as the female hovers alone, close to the water or wet mud, often turning slowly about and dipping the abdomen to its surface at closely spaced intervals.

The nymph of *S. incurvata* is currently unknown as is the time for egg development, although eggs probably hatch in the spring or summer of the year following their deposition. Nymphs most likely require a minimum of two winters to reach maturity. As is the case with other *Somatochlora* species, transformation probably occurs on vegetation close to the water or sphagnum moss. Adults apparently do not wander far from the vicinity of the breeding sites, but young adults may be seen flying at great heights during the time required to reach reproductive maturity.

SPECIALIZED OR UNIQUE CHARACTERISTICS: This species is certainly among the most uncommon of North American Odonata. Its disjunct pattern of distribution is of scientific interest.

BASIS OF STATUS CLASSIFICATION: The Bradford County record is based on a single female collected in 1979 by Frank Fee. The Clinton County bog at Tamarack is presently the only known site for a colony of *S. incurvata* in the Commonwealth and is the southernmost known locality for the species within its range. Adults have been encountered at this bog nearly every year since its original discovery in 1969.

Although the upper portion of the Tamarack bog is a state natural area, the surrounding forest and remainder of the bog are under private control. Within the last several years most of the mixed co-nifer-hardwood tract on the western boundary was clearcut. The loss of this forest environment has apparently not adversely affected the population of *S. incurvata,* but the similar removal of forest on the eastern boundary could prove detrimental to the bog and its inhabitants. Loss of the proper humidity gradient, feeding sites and shelter during the period of maturation prior to breeding, could adversely affect a number of invertebrate species.

RECOMMENDATIONS: Most critical to the con-tinued survival of *S. incurvata* at the Tamarack bog is the maintenance of the environmental integrity of the bog itself. The quality and quantity of spring water at the upper end of the bog, which flows through the bog mat and forms Drury Run, must be safeguarded.

Although the collection site for the Bradford County female is not a colony site for this species, there are nearby habitats indicated on topographic maps that may prove to be breeding sites. These probable habitats are outside, but close to, the boundary of Game Lands No. 12. The annexation of these habitats to the present Game Lands would help assure their future integrity. Should a colony of *S. incurvata* be found at these sites, such action could be of critical importance to the future exis-tence of this species.

SELECTED REFERENCES:

BEATTY, A. F., and G. H. BEATTY. 1971. The distribution of Pennsylvania Odonata. Proc. Pennsylvania Acad. Sci., 45: 147–167.
BEATTY, G. H., and A. F. BEATTY. 1968. Check list and bib-liography of Pennsylvania Odonata. Proc. Pennsylvania Acad. Sci., 42: 120–129.
SHIFFER, C. N. 1969. Occurrence and habits of *Somatochlora incurvata,* new for Pennsylvania. Michigan Entomol., 2:75–76.
WALKER, E. M. 1925. The North American dragonflies of the genus *Somatochlora.* Univ. Toronto Studies, Biol. Ser., 26: 1–202.
WALKER, E. M., and P. S. CORBET. 1975. The Odonata of Can-ada and Alaska. Univ. Toronto Press, Toronto, 3:1–307.

PREPARED BY: Clark Shiffer, *Pennsylvania Fish Commission, Robinson Lane, Bellefonte, PA 16823.*

Vulnerable
LINED BOG SKIMMER
Somatochlora linearis (Hagen)
Family Libellulidae
Order Odonata

DESCRIPTION: The lined bog skimmer is a species of slender aspect and above-average size for the ge-nus (total length, 58–68 mm). The face of this species is dull yellow-brown with dark metallic blue mark-ings; the thorax is brown with metallic greenish re-flections, and is unique within the genus in lacking light markings; the abdomen is long and slender, dark brown with dull greenish sheen, several large pale areas at sides of segment 2, and dull, incon-spicuous yellow-brown spots on rear lateral portions of segments 4 to 8. The male possesses abdominal appendages widened toward the apex, bifid in lateral view, and scalloped in the middle when viewed from the top. Females are similar in appearance to males, with downwardly-directed, compressed, and point-ed vulvar lamina (ovipositor) on the underside of abdominal segments 8 and 9.

RANGE: Historically, *Somatochlora linearis* has been recorded from Florida and Louisiana, north to New England, and west to Illinois, Oklahoma, and eastern Texas. It is recorded in Pennsylvania from Bucks, Centre, and Greene counties.

HABITAT: The lined bog skimmer prefers forest streams of low gradient with shallow riffles and pools, which become intermittent in late summer, that flow over a substrate of fine shaly gravel and coarse sand underlain by firm shale or bedrock.

LIFE HISTORY AND ECOLOGY: Adult flights occur within their range from early June to early October. Limited Pennsylvania records indicate a flight period from mid-June through August. July and August are probably the months when most adults are encountered in many parts of the range. Young adults of both sexes fly high about trees in clearings in the vicinity of the breeding sites. When mature, the males may be seen patrolling sections of the streams, about 0.6–0.9 m above the water, pausing occasionally to hover. Females frequent the streams primarily to oviposit, during periods of de-clining water levels when flow becomes intermittent. Areas of low-flowing riffles or moist substrate, or portions of pools, are selected for ovipositing. Flying

LINED BOG SKIMMER (*Somatochlora linearis*)

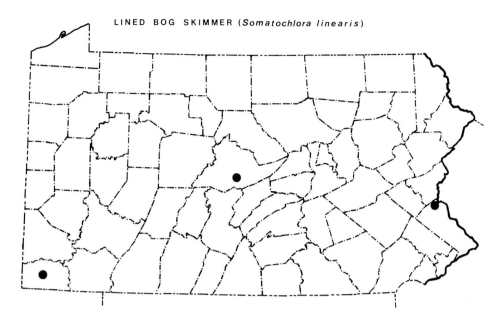

close to the water or substrate, the female touches the tip of the abdomen to the surface at various spots, sometimes more than once in the same place.

Developmental time for eggs and nymphs is unknown, but nymphs probably overwinter at least 2 years. Emergence and transformation occur on various supports not far from the water. Adults are not found far from the breeding sites.

LINED BOG SKIMMER (*Somatochlora linearis*)

SPECIALIZED OR UNIQUE CHARACTERISTICS: This is the only species of the genus which lacks light thoracic markings. The male abdominal appendages are similar to only one other species in the genus. The intermittent stream habitat is shared by few other Pennsylvania Odonata species.

BASIS OF STATUS CLASSIFICATION: The Centre County record consists of a single male and the Greene County records consist of a male and female taken on different dates in 1961. Only the Bucks County locality has produced adults on more than one occasion. This latter site is not far from a state park, and the disconnected tracts of State Game Lands No. 56 are also nearby.

RECOMMENDATIONS: Maintenance of the physical conditions and flow regimes of the streams favored by *S. linearis* is necessary for its continued survival. Although the Bucks County stream flows through privately owned property, at least one tributary arises on Game Lands.

SELECTED REFERENCES:

BEATTY, A. F., and G. H. BEATTY. 1971. The distribution of Pennsylvania Odonata. Proc. Pennsylvania Acad. Sci., 45: 147–167.
BEATTY, G. H., and A. F. BEATTY. 1968. Check list and bibliography of Pennsylvania Odonata. Proc. Pennsylvania Acad. Sci., 42:120–129.
WALKER, E. M. 1925. The North American dragonflies of the genus *Somatochlora*. Univ. Toronto Studies, Biol. Ser., 26: 1–202.

WHITE, H. B. III, G. H. BEATTY, and A. F. BEATTY. 1968. The Odonata fauna of Bear Meadows, a boreal bog in central Pennsylvania. Proc. Pennsylvania Acad. Sci., 42:130–137.

PREPARED BY: Clark Shiffer, *Pennsylvania Fish Commission, Robinson Lane, Bellefonte, PA 16823.*

Vulnerable

DWARF SKIMMER
Nannothemis bella (Uhler)
Family Libellulidae
Order Odonata

DESCRIPTION: The dwarf skimmer is the smallest species of North American dragonflies of the suborder Anisoptera (total length, about 20 mm). This species has a white face with prominent black marks; yellow thorax with black stripings in young males and females, becoming light powdery blue in mature males; black abdomen with yellow spots, also turning light powdery blue in mature males; male abdominal appendages light yellow. Males have clear wings; females have wings tinged with amber on the basal half.

RANGE: Nannothemis bella is known from the Canadian provinces of Ontario and Quebec, and in the United States from Maine to Florida and Mississippi, north to Illinois and Wisconsin. Pennsylvania records are from Lehigh, Monroe, Philadelphia, Pike, and Schuylkill counties.

HABITAT: Primary habitat of the dwarf skimmer includes small pools of water in sphagnum bogs or in boggy situations associated with the backwaters of ponds or lakes, in forested or open terrain.

LIFE HISTORY AND ECOLOGY: The adult flight period spans mid-April to early September over the entire range. The few Pennsylvania records range from mid-June to the latter part of July. Mature males may be seen on sunny days, flying quickly from perch to perch on low-growing vegetation near the water, pausing to rest for varying periods with the wings slanted downwards over each side of the thorax. Females spend much of their time in areas of higher vegetation away from water, visiting the small pools only to oviposit. Males may seize females arriving at the pools and the pair then come to rest on nearby vegetation to complete mating. Oviposition may then be performed by the female alone, or in concert with the male, as he retains a hold on the head of the female with his abdominal appendages. The single female or the pair then hover over the small pools, close to the water, making several dips to its surface to wash off a cluster of eggs. The process may be interrupted by brief rests on nearby vegetation.

The tiny nymphs may require two winters to reach maturity. Transformation to the adult stage takes place on vegetation not far above the water. Adults are found only in and about the breeding habitat.

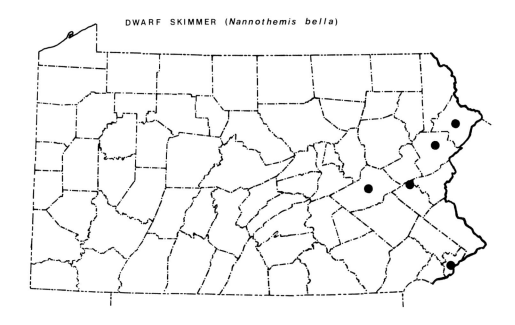

DWARF SKIMMER (*Nannothemis bella*)

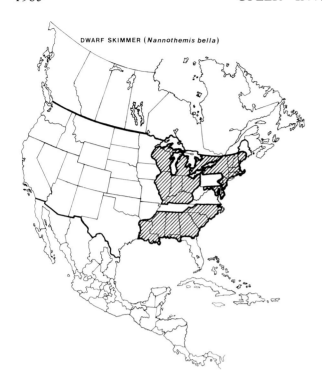

DWARF SKIMMER (*Nannothemis bella*)

SPECIALIZED OR UNIQUE CHARACTERIS-TICS: This dragonfly is one of the smallest species of Odonata in the world. It is a characteristic, but locally distributed, species of bog habitats.

BASIS OF STATUS CLASSIFICATION: Occurrence records for Lehigh and Philadelphia counties date back to the beginning of the century, while those for Pike and Monroe counties date back 30 to 35 years, and the Schuylkill County record dates back 10 years. It is doubtful that *N. bella* still occurs at the Philadelphia and Lehigh county sites. The species probably still occurs at the Pike, Monroe, and Schuylkill county sites. The Monroe County bog is the same habitat referred to under the account of *Somatochlora forcipata*. The sites in Pike and Schuylkill counties are associated with small privately owned recreational lakes.

RECOMMENDATIONS: Further surveys in the northeastern portion of the Commonwealth may reveal additional sites for *N. bella*. Considering the local pattern of distribution for the species, only some of the many bogs in this portion of the Commonwealth may prove to be suitable sites. Historic sites should be revisited to ascertain the present status of the species, and the environmental integrity of fragile bog habitats for this and associated species safeguarded.

SELECTED REFERENCES:

BEATTY, A. F., and G. H. BEATTY. 1971. The distribution of Pennsylvania Odonata. Proc. Pennsylvania Acad. Sci., 45: 147–167.

BEATTY, G. H., and A. F. BEATTY. 1968. Check list and bibliography of Pennsylvania Odonata. Proc. Pennsylvania Acad. Sci., 42:120–129.

NEEDHAM, J. G., and M. J. WESTFALL, JR. 1955. A manual of the dragonflies of North America (Anisoptera). Univ. California Press, Berkeley and Los Angeles, 615 pp.

WALKER, E. M., and P. S. CORBET. 1975. The Odonata of Canada and Alaska. Univ. Toronto Press, Toronto, 3:1–307.

PREPARED BY: Clark Shiffer, *Pennsylvania Fish Commission, Robinson Lane, Bellefonte, PA 16823.*

Vulnerable

BLACK-BANDED BANDWING
Calopteryx aequabilis (Say)
Family Calopterygidae
Order Odonata

DESCRIPTION: Calopteryx aequabilis is a damselfly of average size for the genus (total length, 45–50 mm), with the usual metallic green body color, and clear to yellow-tinted wings, which in the male are dark brown to black on the apical third. The black-banded bandwing possesses a dull black face with paler markings at sides and metallic greenish highlights; metallic green to blue-green thorax and abdomen with bronzy highlights. Females are similar to males, but with duller body color and apical wing coloring ranging in intensity from dark brown to light yellow-brown; underside of segments 8 and 9 with an ovipositor and associated structures.

RANGE: The black-banded bandwing is nearly transcontinental in northern U.S. and occurs in Canada from southern Saskatchewan, Manitoba, Ontario, and Quebec to Nova Scotia. In Pennsylvania, it is known only from Black Moshannon State Park, Centre County (one male), Penns Creek in Centre, Mifflin, and Union counties, Unami Creek at Finland, Bucks County, and Starrucca Creek and Susquehanna River, Susquehanna County.

HABITAT: Spring-fed streams (small rivers) with rocks of moderate to large size in wooded to partly open terrain are the preferred habitat of this species.

LIFE HISTORY AND ECOLOGY: Adult flights have been recorded from mid-May to mid-Septem-

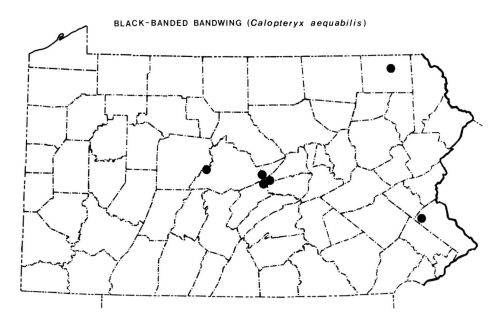

BLACK-BANDED BANDWING (*Calopteryx aequabilis*)

ber. Pennsylvania records encompass a period from late May to mid-July. Both sexes may be seen along the streamside, perched on leaves in dappled sunshine, or, in the case of males particularly, making short flights from perch to perch. Males often skirmish, within 30 cm of the surface of the stream, by flying about one another in tight circles, until one individual breaks away, closely pursued for a short distance by the other. Both then perch in different areas.

Females oviposit in various plants, while completely underwater and unattended by males. They may remain submerged for 30 minutes, inserting eggs singly in slits made in plant leaves or stems with the ovipositor. After ovipositing, they float to the surface and fly to a streamside perch.

Nymphal development may encompass 2 or 3 years. Transformation occurs on wooded or herbaceous vegetation near the stream bank.

BASIS OF STATUS CLASSIFICATION: Despite the wider distribution of this species outside Pennsylvania, its known occurrence in the Commonwealth is limited. The only records for Bucks County date back 27 years, although the species probably still occurs there. The earliest Penns Creek record dates back to 1938, and the species has been taken subsequently, at various locations along this stream, nearly every year since 1950. The record of a single male at Black Moshannon State Park, Centre County, is unique, and dates back to the mid-1950s. The Susquehanna County records are recent.

RECOMMENDATIONS: Water quality is presently being monitored and safeguarded at both Penns Creek and Unami Creek. Continued concern for the environmental integrity of all streams where the species occurs will be necessary if *C. aequabilis* is to remain one of the unique elements of Pennsylvania's fauna.

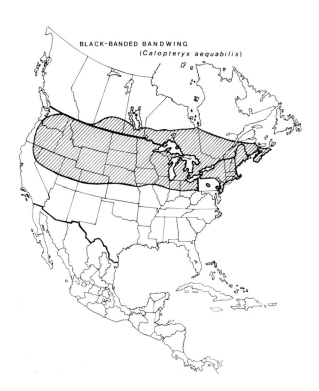

BLACK-BANDED BANDWING
(*Calopteryx aequabilis*)

SELECTED REFERENCES:

BEATTY, G. H., and A. F. BEATTY. 1968. Check list and bibliography of Pennsylvania Odonata. Proc. Pennsylvania Acad. Sci., 42:120–129.

BEATTY, G. H., A. F. BEATTY, and C. N. SHIFFER. 1969. A survey of the Odonata of central Pennsylvania. Proc. Pennsylvania Acad. Sci., 43:127–136.

MARTIN, R. D. C. 1939. Life histories of *Agrion aequabile* and *Agrion maculatum*. Ann. Ent. Soc. Amer., 32:601–619.

WAAGE, J. K. 1975. Reproductive isolation and the potential for character displacement in the damselflies, *Calopteryx maculata* and *C. aequabilis* (Odonata: Calopterygidae). Syst. Zool., 24:24–36.

WALKER, E. M. 1953. The Odonata of Canada and Alaska. Univ. Toronto Press, Toronto, 1:1–292.

PREPARED BY: Clark Shiffer, *Pennsylvania Fish Commission, Robinson Lane, Bellefonte, PA 16823.*

Vulnerable

LATERAL BLUET
Enallagma laterale Morse
Family Coenagrionidae
Order Odonata

DESCRIPTION: The lateral bluet is a small damselfly of local occurrence (total length, about 27 mm). Males possess a face, thorax, and abdomen with a pale blue ground color; thorax with wide mid-dorsal black stripe and narrow black shoulder stripe; abdomen marked with black on terminal portion of segments 2–5, the black occupying half of the length of segment 5, three fourths of the length of segment 6, and nearly all of segment 7. Segments 8 and 9 are largely blue, segment 8 has a black lateral spot or dash, and segment 10 is black. Male superior appendages are short and shallowly bifid in lateral view. Females possess an ovipositor and associated structures on underside of segments 8 and 9.

RANGE: Historically, this damselfly is recorded locally in Maine, Massachusetts, New Hampshire, New York (Long Island), New Jersey, Pennsylvania, and Indiana. It is known in Pennsylvania only from Elk Lake near Eldredsville, Sullivan County.

HABITAT: Enallagma laterale prefers ponds or small lakes associated with bogs or surrounded in part by boggy vegetation; most often found in glaciated terrain.

LIFE HISTORY AND ECOLOGY: Adult flights have been recorded from the beginning of June to mid-July. The few Pennsylvania records are centered around the end of June and the first week in July. Tandem pairs were reportedly taken on Cape Cod, Massachusetts, on 13 June, when individuals were observed in abundance. The acknowledged rarity of this small damselfly is in keeping with the paucity of published observations concerning its habits and behavior. There are no published reports concerning the female, beyond the first record of capture on Cape Cod in 1953. There are no reports concerning nymphs. In Pennsylvania, only one female has been taken in the total of 28 specimens.

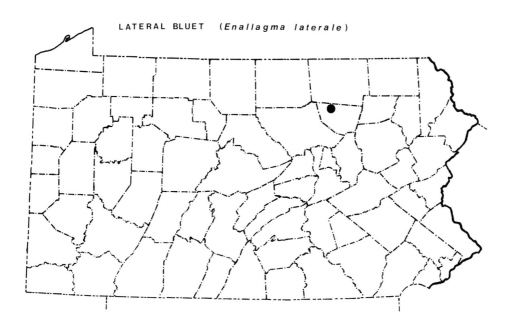

LATERAL BLUET   (*Enallagma laterale*)

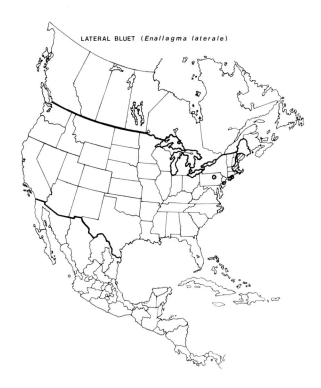

LATERAL BLUET (*Enallagma laterale*)

BEATTY, G. H., and A. F. BEATTY. 1968. Check list and bibliography of Pennsylvania Odonata. Proc. Pennsylvania Acad. Sci., 42:120–129.

BEATTY, G. H., A. F. BEATTY, and C. N. SHIFFER. 1969. A survey of the Odonata of central Pennsylvania. Proc. Pennsylvania Acad. Sci., 43:127–136.

BICK, G. H., and J. C. BICK. 1980. A bibliography of reproductive behavior of Zygoptera of Canada and coterminous United States. Odonatologica, 9:5–18.

GIBBS, R. H., JR., and S. P. GIBBS. 1954. The Odonata of Cape Cod, Massachusetts. New York Entom. Soc., 62:167–184.

MORSE, A. P. 1895. New North American Odonata. Psyche, 7: 274–276.

PREPARED BY: Clark Shiffer, *Pennsylvania Fish Commission, Robinson Lane, Bellefonte, PA 16823.*

Vulnerable

GIANT SWALLOWTAIL
Papilio cresphontes Cramer
Family Papilionidae
Order Lepidoptera

OTHER NAMES: Orange dog; *Papilio cresphontes pennsylvanicus.*

DESCRIPTION: The giant swallowtail is a large black and yellow swallowtail, which is about 130 mm in wingspan. It differs from the widespread tiger swallowtail (*Papilio glaucus*) by having the yellow and black areas diagonal (rather than a vertical tiger striped pattern), having an almost solid yellow abdomen, and having fluted yellow-centered tails on the hindwings.

RANGE: This species is widespread from the central United States south to Central and South America. In southern areas, it may be a pest of citrus crops. The species is found primarily in the southern half of Pennsylvania. Recent records are lacking from the southwest corner of the Commonwealth. At present the best colonies occur at Spring Creek, Centre Co.; Gettysburg National Battlefield, Adams Co.; Gifford Pinchot Park, York Co. This butterfly may be found in small numbers in Chester, Philadelphia, and Montgomery counties.

HABITAT: This species prefers somewhat open hilly areas, often near streams. These areas provide proper situations for its caterpillar host, prickly ash (*Zanthoxylum americanum*), adult patrolling areas, as well as nectar sources.

BASIS OF STATUS CLASSIFICATION: The disjunct occurrence of *E. laterale* in Sullivan County, Pennsylvania, is in keeping with previous remarks concerning the species. The author visited Elk Lake in 1974 and among many specimens of *Enallagma* captured, four were *laterale*. Most were specimens of the superficially similar *ebrium*. Nothing distinctive was noted about the behavior of the few individuals of *laterale*. Camp Brule is a Boy Scout Camp located at Elk Lake. Scouts were using the camp during the 1974 visit and it continues to be used by such groups. The environmental integrity of the lake and its surroundings was secure in 1974, and the author is confident that it will remain such under the scrutiny of the Boy Scout conservation ethic.

RECOMMENDATIONS: It is to be hoped that the Boy Scouts of America will retain control over the environmental integrity of Elk Lake in order that *Enallagma laterale* may continue to occur there. Further survey of other possible habitats in the glaciated portion of northeastern Pennsylvania may reveal further colonies of the species.

SELECTED REFERENCES:

BEATTY, A. F., and G. H. BEATTY. 1971. The distribution of Pennsylvania Odonata. Proc. Pennsylvania Acad. Sci., 45: 147–167.

Giant Swallowtail (*Papilio cresphontes*). Photograph by G. O. Krizek.

LIFE HISTORY AND ECOLOGY: This butterfly has two adult flights each year—mid May–early June, then again in August. The winter is passed in the chrysalid. Most populations have low density and adult males require bluffs, open hillsides, or open streambeds over which to patrol.

SPECIAL OR UNIQUE CHARACTERISTICS: This is the largest butterfly in the United States.

BASIS OF STATUS CLASSIFICATION: In Pennsylvania, the giant swallowtail is at the northern edge of its range. Some decline has occurred, but not

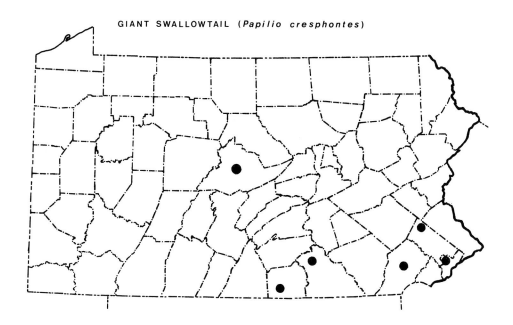

GIANT SWALLOWTAIL (*Papilio cresphontes*)

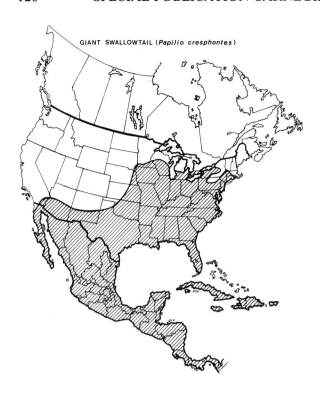

GIANT SWALLOWTAIL (*Papilio cresphontes*)

terist's Society members provided data and/or recommendations on this species: R. W. Boscoe, G. Ehle, A. M. Shapiro, T. A. Greager, and C. Schildknecht.

SELECTED REFERENCES:

HOWE, W. H. 1975. The butterflies of North America. Doubleday Co., New York, xiii + 633 pp.
SHAPIRO, A. M. 1966. Butterflies of the Delaware Valley. Amer. Ent. Soc., Spec. Publ., vi + 79 pp.

PREPARED BY: Paul A. Opler, *U.S. Fish and Wildlife Service, Editorial Office, Room 259 Aylesworth Hall, Colorado State University, Fort Collins, CO 80523.*

Vulnerable

FROSTED ELFIN
Incisalia irus (Godart)
Family Lycaenidae
Order Lepidoptera

OTHER NAME: Callophrys irus.

DESCRIPTION: The frosted elfin is a small plain brown or grayish hairstreak with small tail-like projections from the hindwings. The butterfly, which is about 30 mm in wingspan, is further distinguished from its close relative, *Incisalia henrici,* by the long stigma on the male's forewings and the gray "frosting" on the hindwing beneath.

enough to place it in the threatened category. There may be other extant populations.

RECOMMENDATIONS: Ensure that appropriate habitat is maintained at known colonies. Surveys should be conducted for other populations.

ACKNOWLEDGMENTS: The following Lepidop-

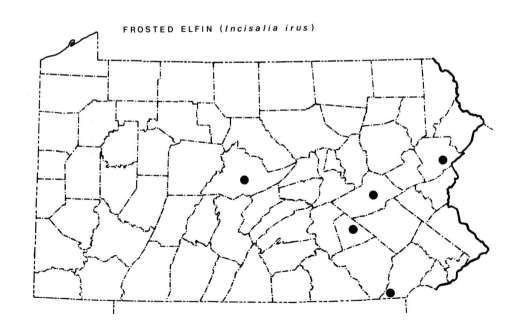

FROSTED ELFIN (*Incisalia irus*)

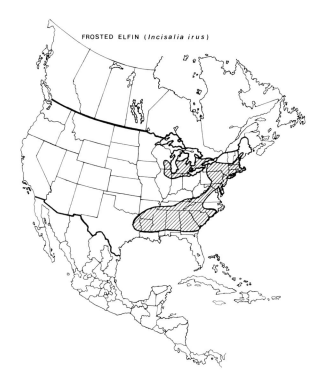

FROSTED ELFIN (*Incisalia irus*)

RANGE: The frosted elfin is generally found in southern Canada and the eastern half of the United States. In Pennsylvania it is restricted to barrens habitats in the southeastern and central portions of the Commonwealth. At present it is known to occur at only five of 23 historical localities in the Commonwealth.

HABITAT: Throughout its range the frosted elfin is best found on barrens, whether or not they be of the sand, shale, or serpentine variety. Other important habitat attributes are the presence of suitable caterpillar host plants; in Pennsylvania it is wild indigo, *Baptisia tinctoria.*

LIFE HISTORY AND ECOLOGY: The frosted elfin has a single adult flight each year (21 April–29 June) with most records during May. Winter is passed in the chrysalid stage in litter at the base of the host plant, wild indigo. The host is an early seral plant and burning or some other form of disturbance is necessary to provide suitable growth conditions.

BASIS OF STATUS CLASSIFICATION: The fact that the butterfly has not been found at most of its localities during the last 10 years and its special habitat requirements justify the designated status.

RECOMMENDATIONS: Field surveys should be conducted for additional localities. Habitat requirements, including controlled burning or other manipulation, should be studied.

ACKNOWLEDGMENTS: The following individuals contributed data or recommendations to this report: D. Schweitzer, F. D. Fee, A. M. Shapiro, R. W. Boscoe, and W. F. Boscoe.

SELECTED REFERENCES:

HOWE, W. H. 1975. The butterflies of North America. Doubleday Co., New York, xiii + 633 pp.
SHAPIRO, A. M. 1966. The butterflies of the Delaware Valley. Amer. Ent. Soc., Spec. Publ., vi + 79 pp.

PREPARED BY: Paul A. Opler, *U.S. Fish and Wildlife Service, Editorial Office, Room 259 Aylesworth Hall, Colorado State University, Fort Collins, CO 80523.*

Vulnerable

BOG COPPER
Lycaena epixanthe (Boisduval and LeConte)
Family Lycaenidae
Order Lepidoptera

OTHER NAME: Epidemia epixanthe.

DESCRIPTION: The bog copper is a small butterfly, which is 20–25 mm in wingspan. The male has a faint purplish gloss above, whereas the female is grayer and duller. Both sexes are a yellow tan color beneath with a wavy reddish band on the margin of the hindwing. Its flight is extremely weak and fluttery. No other Pennsylvania butterfly is similar to it.

RANGE: This species occurs from southern Canada and northern states from the maritimes west to Minnesota. In Pennsylvania, the bog copper is known from only five localities north of the maximum glacial extent. Only three of the colonies have been verified in the last 10 years (Crystal Lake Camp, Sullivan Co.; near Elgin, Erie Co.; near LeRoy, Bradford Co.).

HABITAT: The bog copper is found only in acid bogs with a growth of the caterpillar host, cranberry (*Vaccinium macrocarpon*).

Bog Copper (*Lycaena epixanthe*). Photograph by C. N. Shiffer.

LIFE HISTORY AND ECOLOGY: The bog copper has a single annual flight (24 June to 11 July). The winter is passed as a first instar caterpillar within the egg, and development is completed during the following spring.

BASIS OF STATUS CLASSIFICATION: Because the bog copper is found in so few localities, and because these habitats might be susceptible to peat mining or other perturbations, the present status was felt to be appropriate.

ACKNOWLEDGMENTS: The following individuals contributed data or status recommendations:

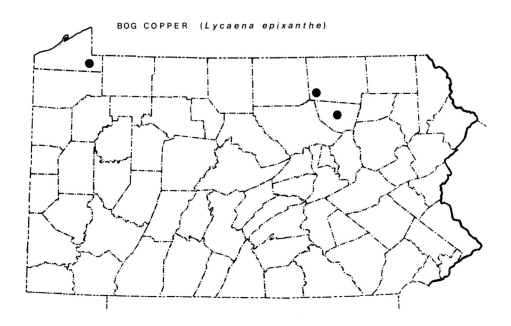

BOG COPPER (*Lycaena epixanthe*)

G. Ehle, G. M. McWilliams, F. D. Fee, A. M. Shapiro, R. W. Boscoe, W. F. Boscoe, and B. Murray.

SELECTED REFERENCES:

HOWE, W. H. 1975. The butterflies of North America. Doubleday Co., New York, xiii + 633 pp.

PREPARED BY: Paul A. Opler, *U.S. Fish and Wildlife Service, Editorial Office, Room 259 Aylesworth Hall, Colorado State University, Fort Collins, CO 80523.*

Vulnerable

NORTHERN METALMARK
Calephelis borealis (Grote and Robinson)
Family Riodinidae
Order Lepidoptera

DESCRIPTION: The northern metalmark is a small butterfly of about 20 mm wingspan. The butterfly is orange brown above with some black markings and orange below with linear metallic markings.

RANGE: This species occurs from extreme southern New York thence southwest through mountains in New Jersey, Pennsylvania, Maryland, Virginia, and West Virginia. Another group of populations is known in the midwest from the general area of the lower Ohio Valley. In Pennsylvania, the northern metalmark is known at present only at Spring Creek, Centre Co., although four other populations occurred at one time in extreme southeastern Pennsylvania. The latter four populations are now extirpated due to construction projects.

HABITAT: The habitat of the northern metalmark is closely associated with serpentine and shale barrens. The caterpillar host is reported to be *Senecio*

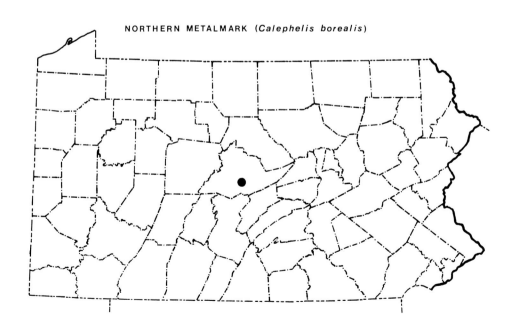

NORTHERN METALMARK (*Calephelis borealis*)

obovatus, but other composites may also serve as hosts. Favored adult nectar sources are sunflower-like plants and butterflyweed (*Asclepias tuberosa*).

LIFE HISTORY AND ECOLOGY: This butterfly has a single annual flight each year (late June–early July). The caterpillars overwinter near the base of the host plant. Most colonies seem to occur in the general vicinity of woodlands near streams or ravines.

SPECIAL OR UNIQUE CHARACTERISTICS: The northern metalmark is the only member of its family in Pennsylvania.

BASIS OF STATUS CLASSIFICATION: The fact that only one known colony is still extant in the Commonwealth, its occurrence on Fish Commission property, and the likely occurrence of additional populations in the shale barrens seem to justify the assigned status.

RECOMMENDATIONS: Obtain the cooperation of the Pennsylvania Fish Commission for protection of the Spring Creek habitat. Also surveys of likely shale barrens habitat in Bedford County should be conducted for this butterfly.

ACKNOWLEDGMENTS: Data or recommendations were provided by F. D. Fee, D. Schweitzer, B. Murray, R. W. Boscoe, and A. M. Shapiro.

SELECTED REFERENCES:

Howe, W. H. 1975. The butterflies of North America. Doubleday Co., New York, xiii + 633 pp.
Shapiro, A. M. 1966. The butterflies of the Delaware Valley. Amer. Ent. Soc., Spec. Publ., vi + 79 pp.

PREPARED BY: Paul A. Opler, *U.S. Fish and Wildlife Service, Editorial Office, Room 259 Aylesworth Hall, Colorado State University, Fort Collins, CO 80523.*

Vulnerable

HARRIS' CHECKERSPOT
Chlosyne harrisii (Scudder)
Family Nymphalidae
Order Lepidoptera

DESCRIPTION: This species is 40–50 mm in wingspan. The wings above are light orange brown with basal and marginal black markings. The hindwing below has a pattern of checkered orange red and white marks. The Harris' checkerspot is somewhat similar to the silvery crescent, particularly above.

RANGE: Harris' checkerspot has been recorded from the maritime provinces of Canada west to Manitoba and south to Pennsylvania, Ohio, Indiana, Illinois, Michigan, and Wisconsin. In Pennsylvania, it is known only from the northern half, particularly in the central mountainous area.

HABITAT: The Harris' checkerspot is found in damp meadow areas, particularly if they are brushy and have stands of blue flag (*Iris* sp.) and the host plant, *Aster umbellatus.*

LIFE HISTORY AND ECOLOGY: The adults occur in a single mid-summer flight (4 June–3 July). The larvae are gregarious and overwinter on the host plant.

BASIS FOR STATUS CLASSIFICATION: Although the species is fairly widespread in Pennsylvania and relatively few colonies have been extirpated, the fact that most colonies are small and localized, combined with the vulnerability of wet meadow habitats, justifies the status.

HARRIS' CHECKERSPOT (*Chlosyne harrisii*)

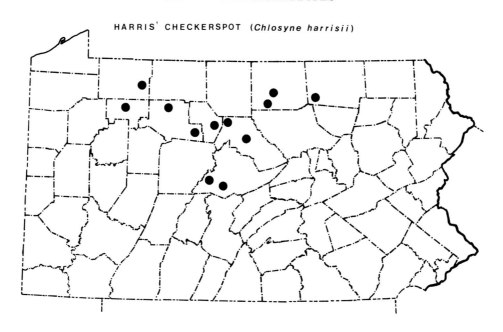

RECOMMENDATIONS: Continue to monitor known colonies and search for additional populations.

ACKNOWLEDGMENTS: The following Lepidopterist's Society members contributed data or recommendations: F. D. Fee, G. Ehle, T. A. Greager, G. M. McWilliams, A. M. Shapiro, C. G. Oliver, R. W. Boscoe, and W. F. Boscoe.

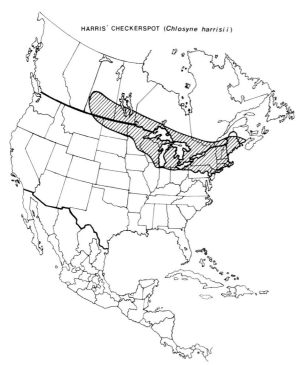

HARRIS' CHECKERSPOT (*Chlosyne harrisii*)

SELECTED REFERENCES:

Howe, W. H. 1975. The butterflies of North America. Doubleday Co., New York, xiii + 633 pp.

PREPARED BY: Paul A. Opler, *U.S. Fish and Wildlife Service, Editorial Office, Room 259 Aylesworth Hall, Colorado State University, Fort Collins, CO 80523.*

Vulnerable

NORTHERN PEARL CRESCENT
Phyciodes pascoensis Wright
Family Nymphalidae
Order Lepidoptera

OTHER NAMES: Phyciodes arctica; P. pascoensis.

DESCRIPTION: The northern pearl crescent is extremely similar to the ubiquitous and protean pearl crescent. This species is larger (40 mm wingspan), and the male has orange antennal knobs and a relatively large unmarked orange area in the dorsal marginal area of the hindwings.

RANGE: The range of *Phyciodes pascoensis* includes the maritime provinces south to Maine, New Hampshire, and northern New York, thence west across the northern states and southern Canada to eastern Oregon, Washington, and British Columbia, and south in the Rocky Mountains to northern New Mexico, and the White Mountains of Arizona. The northern pearl crescent also occurs south in the Ap-

NORTHERN PEARL CRESCENT (*Phyciodes pascoensis*)

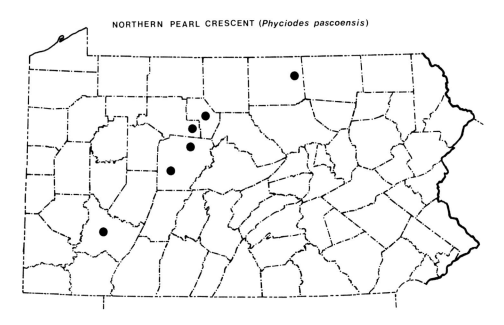

palachians to Pennsylvania, West Virginia, Virginia, and possibly North Carolina. In Pennsylvania, the northern pearl crescent is known from two localities in Clearfield County, and one locality in Bradford, Cameron, Elk, and Westmoreland counties.

HABITAT: This species is found in open fields or

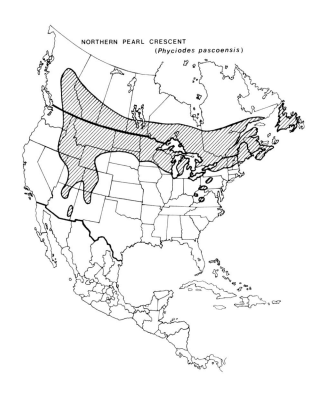

NORTHERN PEARL CRESCENT
(*Phyciodes pascoensis*)

clearings surrounded by wooded areas. Colonies are usually adjacent to small streams.

LIFE HISTORY AND ECOLOGY: The northern pearl crescent has only one or two adult flights each year. The first is in late June and early July, while the second is only partial and occurs in late August. Winter is passed by partially grown larvae at the base of host asters.

BASIS FOR STATUS CLASSIFICATION: The fact that only two colonies are known and that both occur on private land is the basis for the vulnerable assignment.

RECOMMENDATIONS: Ensure habitat protection of known colonies, and conduct searches for additional colonies.

ACKNOWLEDGMENTS: Charles G. Oliver provided data and recommendations.

SELECTED REFERENCES:

OLIVER, C. G. 1979. Genetic differentiation and hybrid viability within and between some Lepidoptera species. Amer. Nat., 114:681–694.

PREPARED BY: Paul A. Opler, *U.S. Fish and Wildlife Service, Editorial Office, Room 259 Aylesworth Hall, Colorado State University, Fort Collins, CO 80523.*

Vulnerable

BLACK DASH
Euphyes conspicua (Edwards)
Family Hesperiidae
Order Lepidoptera

OTHER NAME: Pontiac skipper.

DESCRIPTION: The black dash is a medium-sized (30 mm wingspan) yellow-orange and black skipper, with a heavy black stigma and conspicuous yellow patch in the center of an orange hindwing beneath. Many other skippers are quite similar and the reader should refer to a standard reference such as Klots (1951) or Howe (1975) for the finer distinctions.

RANGE: Two major populations of the species occur—one from central New England south to Maryland and another in the upper Midwest from Ohio west to Iowa and Minnesota. Small outliers occur in southeastern Virginia, the southern Appalachians, and eastern Nebraska. In Pennsylvania, the black dash is known primarily from southeastern and south-central portions of the Commonwealth. Only eight of 15 colonies are known to be extant with most losses in the lower Delaware Valley. There are probably more colonies awaiting discovery.

HABITAT: Freshwater marshes, bogs, and broad boggy creeks are the favored habitats of the black dash. In Pennsylvania, all the localities are south of the maximum glacial advance. Nectar sources favored by adults are swamp milkweed (*Asclepias incarnata*), buttonbush (*Cephalanthus occidentalis*), and Canada thistle (*Cirsium arvense*). Another important element is the presence of suitable caterpillar host plants, in this case sedges, particularly *Carex stricta*.

LIFE HISTORY AND ECOLOGY: The black dash has but a single adult flight each year (29 June to 12 August). The larvae probably overwinter in shelters with development completed during the following spring.

BASIS OF STATUS CLASSIFICATION: The black dash is placed in the vulnerable category as almost half of the known colonies have not been reported in the last 10 years, and at least several are known to have been lost. The fragility of the habitat of this butterfly, as well as the probability that additional colonies exist are other factors relevant to this category.

RECOMMENDATIONS: Status of all colonies

Black Dash (*Euphyes conspicua*). Photograph by P. A. Opler.

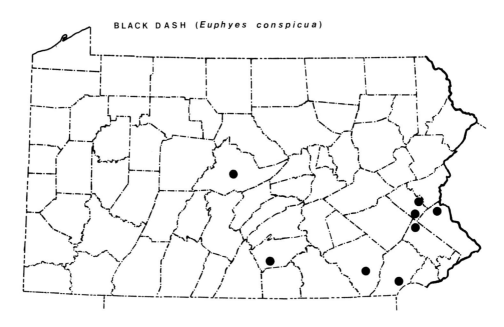

BLACK DASH (*Euphyes conspicua*)

should be monitored on a periodic basis. Steps must be taken to ensure proper management/protection of colonies on public land. Field studies need to be carried out to locate additional populations.

ACKNOWLEDGMENTS: The following lepidopterists contributed data and/or recommendations: T. Williams, A. M. Shapiro, W. F. Boscoe, G. Ehle, F. D. Fee, R. W. Boscoe.

BLACK DASH (*Euphyes conspicua*)

SELECTED REFERENCES:

HOWE, W. H. 1975. The butterflies of North America. Doubleday Co., New York, xiii + 633 pp.

KLOTS, A. B. 1951. A field guide to the butterflies. Houghton Mifflin Co., New York, 349 pp.

SHAPIRO, A. M. 1966. The butterflies of the Delaware Valley. Amer. Ent. Soc., Spec. Publ., vi + 79 pp.

———. 1971. Postglacial biogeography and the distribution of *Poanes viator* and other marsh butterflies. J. Res. Lepid., 9: 125–155.

PREPARED BY: Paul A. Opler, *U.S. Fish and Wildlife Service, Editorial Office, Room 259 Aylesworth Hall, Colorado State University, Fort Collins, CO 80523.*

Vulnerable

DION SKIPPER
Euphyes dion (Edwards)
Family Hesperiidae
Order Lepidoptera

DESCRIPTION: The dion skipper is a medium-sized skipper (40–50 mm wingspan), which is predominantly black above with small yellow orange areas in the central portion of each wing in the male. The wings below are predominantly orange with a central yellow "slash" on the hindwings.

RANGE: The range of the dion skipper consists of several population aggregates extending from southern New England and coastal Virginia west to southern Minnesota and extreme eastern Nebraska. In

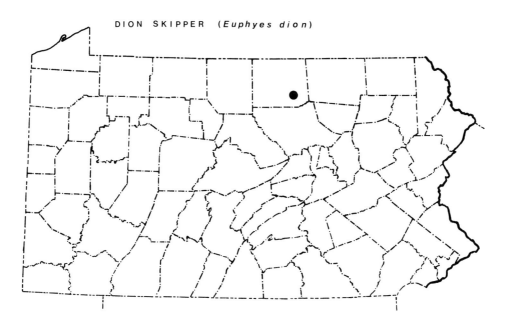

DION SKIPPER (*Euphyes dion*)

Pennsylvania, one colony is known to occur in a Tioga County bog (1979–1980), while Shapiro (1971) shows a single record in extreme western Pennsylvania.

HABITAT: Freshwater marshes or bogs with a growth of sedge are the preferred habitat of the dion skipper. Important habitat elements include the caterpillar host plant, *Carex lacustris,* and adult nectar sources such as swamp milkweed (*Asclepias incarnata*).

LIFE HISTORY AND ECOLOGY: The dion skipper has a single adult flight each year (late June to late July). The larvae feed in leaf shelters and overwinter partially grown. Adult males perch and actively interact with neighboring males while awaiting receptive females.

BASIS OF STATUS CLASSIFICATION: The facts that the dion skipper is presently known only from one locality in Pennsylvania and that its bog habitat is potentially vulnerable constitute sufficient grounds for the present assignment.

RECOMMENDATIONS: Continue to monitor the Tioga County colony. Conduct survey for other populations.

ACKNOWLEDGMENTS: The following lepidopterists provided data and/or recommendations: F. D. Fee, R. W. Boscoe, A. M. Shapiro.

SELECTED REFERENCES:

HOWE, W. H. 1975. The butterflies of North America. Doubleday Co., New York, xiii + 633 pp.
SHAPIRO, A. M. 1971. Postglacial biogeography and the distribution of *Poanes viator* and other marsh butterflies. J. Res. Lepid., 9:125–155.

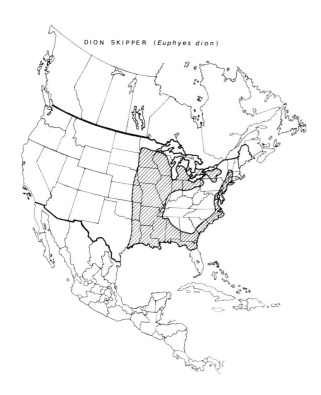

DION SKIPPER (*Euphyes dion*)

PREPARED BY: Paul Opler, *U.S. Fish and Wildlife Service, Editorial Office, Room 259 Aylesworth Hall, Colorado State University, Fort Collins, CO 80523.*

Vulnerable

PINE-DEVIL MOTH
Citheronia sepulcralis Grote and Robinson
Family Saturniidae
Order Lepidoptera

DESCRIPTION: The pine-devil moth is a large dusky gray moth usually with pink on hind wings and with an inordinately large body. The purplish brown larvae are approximately 100 mm in length with six thoracic and one caudal yellowish horns and many similar but smaller tubercles. They are generally found on pitch, red, and probably Virginia pines but generally avoid white pine.

RANGE: It is rare in hard pine stands (planted or native) in Delaware, Chester, Schuylkill, and Snyder counties and reported from Williamsport, Lycoming County, and Clark Valley, Dauphin County. It was formerly known from Cape Cod and southern Maine southward to eastern Pennsylvania and on to Florida.

LIFE HISTORY AND ECOLOGY: Eggs are laid mostly in June and hatch in about 2 weeks. Larvae feed on pine needles until August, then pupate in the ground and overwinter there.

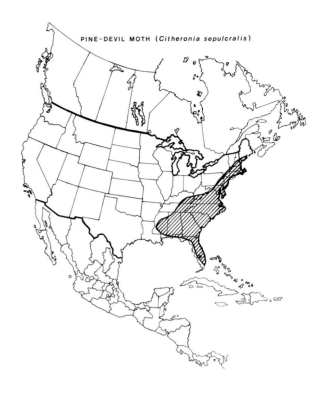

BASIS FOR STATUS CLASSIFICATION: Members of the family Saturniidae (esp. Citheroniinae) generally decline sharply immediately after aerial spraying programs, but in New England some populations have recovered rapidly following termination of spraying. However, all large Citheroniinae (*C. sepulcralis, C. regalis,* and *Eacles imperialis*) were

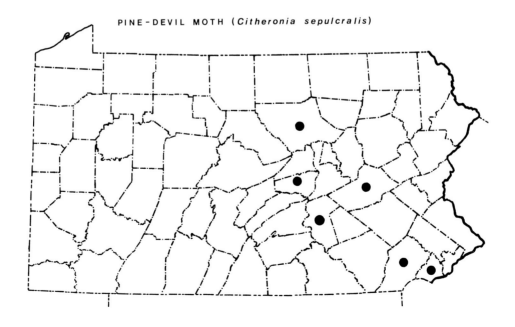

apparently entirely eliminated from southern New England. Thus gypsy moth spraying may be an imminent threat to *C. sepulcralis,* although whether current insecticides would be as destructive as DDT is unknown.

SELECTED REFERENCES:

FERGUSON, D. C. 1971. The moths of America north of Mexico. Fasc. 20.2A. Bombycoidea: Saturniidae comprising subfamilies Citheroniinae Hemileucinae (part). E. W. Classey Limited and RBD Publications Inc., London, 153 pp.

HOLLAND, W. J. 1903. The moth book. Doubleday, Page and Company, New York, vii + 479 pp.

PREPARED BY: Dale F. Schweitzer, *Museum of Comparative Zoology, Harvard University, Cambridge, MA 02138.*

Vulnerable

DOLL'S MEROLONCHE
Merolonche dolli Barnes and McDunnough
Family Noctuidae
Order Lepidoptera

DESCRIPTION: This moth is almost 40 mm in wing expanse. The forewings are white with black shades and markings, and the hind wings are white. Although this is the only eastern species of the genus, the adults are similar to the 'Daggers' (*Acronicta*). A similar species is illustrated by Holland (1903: Plate 18, Fig. 7).

RANGE: This moth is known to range from New Brunswick south to southeastern Pennsylvania and southern New Jersey. In Pennsylvania, during the 1970s it was found at Spinnerstown, Bucks County, and near Auburn, Schuylkill County.

HABITAT: This species is found in areas with acidic soil, most often in pitch pine-oak scrub or bogs (New Jersey).

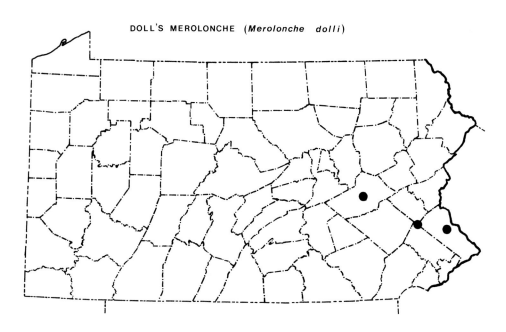

DOLL'S MEROLONCHE (*Merolonche dolli*)

LIFE HISTORY AND ECOLOGY: The adult moths occur in a single flight during April and early May. The larvae presumably do their feeding during May and June. This moth was raised once on cranberry, but this plant is not found everywhere the species occurs. It is likely that other heath family (Ericaceae) members are also utilized by the caterpillars.

BASIS FOR STATUS CLASSIFICATION: This species may have one of the most restricted ranges of any noctuid in the northeastern states (excluding, of course, those endemic to southern New Jersey), and is probably among the rarest macro-moths occurring in Pennsylvania.

RECOMMENDATIONS: Locate and seek protection for the two known Pennsylvania sites.

SELECTED REFERENCES:

FORBES, W. T. M. 1954. Lepidoptera of New York and neighboring states. Part III. Noctuidae. Mem. Cornell Univ. Agr. Expt. Sta., 329:1–433.
HOLLAND, W. J. 1903. The moth book. Doubleday, Page and Company, New York, vii + 479 pp.

PREPARED BY: Dale F. Schweitzer, *Museum of Comparative Zoology, Harvard University, Cambridge, MA 02138.*

Vulnerable

BARRENS CHAETOGLAEA
Chaetoglaea tremula Harvey
Family Noctuidae
Order Lepidoptera

DESCRIPTION: This moth has a wing span of 42–46 mm. The wings are variably colored—brown, dull pink, or gray—and are glossy in fresh individuals. It may be distingushed from similar noctuid moths in that its antemedial line on the forewing is toothed where it crosses vein A (Forbes, 1954). A color illustration is given by Holland (1903: Plate 26, Fig. 41).

RANGE: This moth occurs on the Coastal Plain from Maine south to central Florida, thence west to Arkansas and Texas. In Pennsylvania, it is known only from the vicinity of Scranton, Lackawanna County.

HABITAT: In Pennsylvania, this species is found on pitch pine-bear oak barrens.

LIFE HISTORY AND ECOLOGY: The moths have a single flight in September and October. The eggs overwinter and hatch during May. The larvae feed for about 6 weeks, then aestivate until late August when they pupate. The host plants are small oaks and low heaths. One caterpillar was found feeding

BARREN CHAETOGLEA (*Chaetoglaea tremula*)

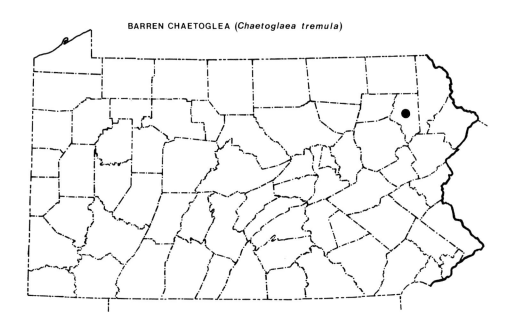

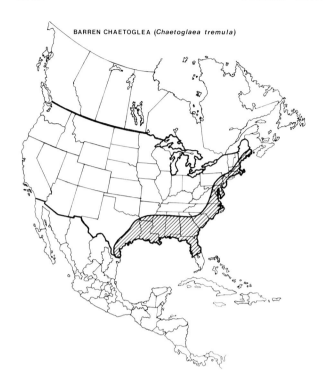

BARREN CHAETOGLEA (*Chaetoglaea tremula*)

BASIS OF STATUS CLASSIFICATION: The species has an extremely limited range in Pennsylvania.

RECOMMENDATIONS: Ascertain location and status of populations near Scranton. Determine if conservation actions are required.

SELECTED REFERENCES:

FORBES, W. T. M. 1954. Lepidoptera of New York and neighboring states. Part III. Noctuidae. Mem. Cornell Univ. Agr. Expt. Sta., 329:1–433.
HOLLAND, W. J. 1903. The moth book. Doubleday, Page and Company, New York, vii + 479 pp.

PREPARED BY: Dale F. Schweitzer, *Museum of Comparative Zoology, Harvard University, Cambridge, MA 02138.*

Vulnerable

BARRENS XYLOTYPE
Xylotype capax (Grote)
Family Noctuidae
Order Lepidoptera

on blueberry (*Vaccinium pennsylvanica*) in Massachusetts.

Although the habitats are generally maintained by fire, the species has no mechanism to survive its occurrence; therefore it needs a sufficiently large area that has a mosaic of recently burned and unburned scrub oak thickets. Such a habitat would prevent all of the population from being burned at once.

DESCRIPTION: This moth ranges from 40 to 47 mm in wing expanse. Its forewings are blue gray shaded with darker fuscous. The normal noctuid lines are present and are double with paler filling (Forbes, 1954). The species was illustrated by Holland (1903: Plate 25, Fig. 21).

RANGE: The species ranges along the Atlantic Coast from York County, Maine, south to Washington,

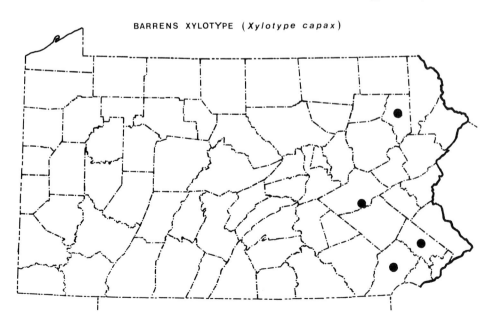

BARRENS XYLOTYPE (*Xylotype capax*)

BARRENS XYLOTYPE (*Xylotype capax*)

D.C., and the Delmarva Peninsula. In Pennsylvania, it is known from Lambs Creek, Blue Mountain near Auburn, Schuylkill County, Flourtown, Montgomery County, Scranton, Lackawanna County, and the Nottingham barrens, Chester County.

HABITAT: The moth is found in acidic habitats where pitch pine is present. These include barrens, bogs, and acidic swamplands.

LIFE HISTORY AND ECOLOGY: The single adult generation flies in October. Eggs hatch the following April or early May and the caterpillars feed until June when they pupate in the soil and aestivate until autumn. In the laboratory, a wide array of deciduous trees and shrubs are acceptable to the larvae. The natural foodplants are unknown, but may be blueberries (*Vaccinium*) and bear oak (*Quercus ilicifolia*) in Pennsylvania.

BASIS OF STATUS CLASSIFICATION: The moth is found in relatively few colonies. In addition, periodic fires or other management procedures may be necessary to provide suitable habitat.

RECOMMENDATIONS: Surveys to locate populations and to investigate native host plants and habitat are needed.

ACKNOWLEDGMENTS: Mr. Eric Quinter, American Museum of Natural History, New York, provided data on this moth as well as several other species.

SELECTED REFERENCES:

FORBES, W. T. M. 1954. The Lepidoptera of New York and neighboring states. Part III. Noctuidae. Mem. Cornell Univ. Agr. Expt. Sta. 329:1–433.
HOLLAND, W. J. 1903. The moth book. Doubleday, Page and Company, New York, vii + 479 pp.

PREPARED BY: Dale F. Schweitzer, *Museum of Comparative Zoology, Harvard University, Cambridge, MA 02138.*

Status Undetermined

SOUTHERN BOG DARNER
Gomphaeschna antilope (Hagen)
Family Aeshnidae
Order Odonata

DESCRIPTION: The southern bog darner is a slim and little-known darner dragonfly (total length, 52–60 mm). This species possesses a dull greenish brown face; brown thorax with pale green and yellow-brown markings in a variegated pattern, especially so on the sides; brown abdomen with a pattern of pale greenish to yellow-brown dorsal and lateral irregular marks on each segment. The superior abdominal appendages of the male are relatively straight and of thin aspect; the inferior appendage is shallowly forked. Females are similar to males; the undersides of abdominal segments 8 and 9 carry the ovipositor and related structures; abdominal appendages are very short.

RANGE: Gomphaeschna antilope has been recorded from Florida and Louisiana north to Ohio, Pennsylvania, and New Jersey. It is known in Pennsylvania from Allegheny, Delaware, Philadelphia, and Venango counties.

HABITAT: The southern bog darner inhabits areas of naturally acidic sphagnaceous pools or gently flowing streams in shaded, swampy woods, or partly wooded terrain.

LIFE HISTORY AND ECOLOGY: Flying adults have been recorded from early March to mid-July. Pennsylvania dates range from May to mid-July. Although little has been published concerning the

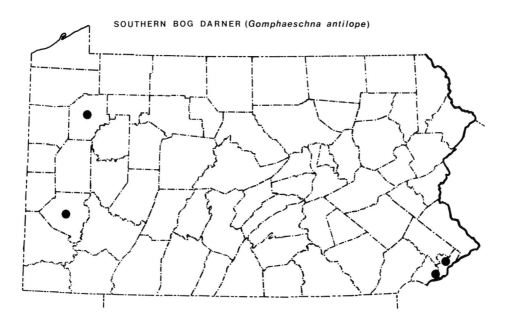

SOUTHERN BOG DARNER (*Gomphaeschna antilope*)

habits of adults, the author has observed both sexes outside Pennsylvania in both dense and sparse woods along swamp streams. Females were noted flying in an irregular flight pattern some distance above ground among trees, coming to rest for varying periods on tree trunks. Males have been observed flying among trees in swamp woods, coming to rest on sunlit patches on tree trunks or on the foliage of white cedar trees. Oviposition in this species has not been recorded, but the closely-related *G. furcillata* has been observed inserting eggs in dead wood above water. The process is probably similar for *G. antilope* and wet, partly decayed wood is probably used. Dunkle (1977) reared this species from a single nymph found clinging to the underside of a barkless log in a shallow, sphagnaceous cypress swamp pool. A nymph of *G. furcillata* was also collected and reared from this same habitat.

Transformation, as reported for *G. furcillata,* occurs on herbaceous or other vegetation not far from the water. The process is probably similar for *G. antilope.* Although adults are not often encountered, even in the vicinity of breeding sites, they have been found in city buildings, often at some distance above ground. Most of the Allegheny and Philadelphia county records consist of one or more individuals which flew into office buildings or museums. In Philadelphia, specimens were found on the 9th and 14th floors of office buildings.

SOUTHERN BOG DARNER (*Gomphaeschna antilope*)

BASIS OF STATUS CLASSIFICATION: All Pennsylvania records for this species date back 40 to 100 years, and most of these are for specimens encountered in Philadelphia and Pittsburgh. The Delaware County site is now essentially part of Philadelphia, and the Venango County site is surrounded by a number of oil and gas wells and active strip mines. Considering the infrequent and unusual occurrences of *G. antilope* within its range, and in the Commonwealth, its present status is not at all predictable.

RECOMMENDATIONS: Gomphaeschna antilope has apparently been an infrequently encountered species historically, and its habits and particular habitat requirements therefore have remained virtually unknown. Recent collections of the species and observations of adults and nymphs have provided some information about its occurrence and habitat needs. Swampy habitat of the type that may be required by *G. antilope* is often drained, filled, or the recipient of various pollutants. If this species and the valuable aspects of its habitat are to exist in the future, the environmental integrity of the habitat must be maintained.

SELECTED REFERENCES:

BEATTY, A. F., and G. H. BEATTY. 1971. The distribution of Pennsylvania Odonata. Proc. Pennsylvania Acad. Sci., 45: 147–167.

BEATTY, G. H., and A. F. BEATTY. 1968. Check list and bibliography of Pennsylvania Odonata. Proc. Pennsylvania Acad. Sci., 42:120–129.

BEATTY, G. H., A. F. BEATTY, and C. N. SHIFFER. 1970. A survey of the Odonata of eastern Pennsylvania. Proc. Pennsylvania Acad. Sci., 43:141–152.

DUNKLE, S. W. 1977. Larvae of the genus *Gomphaeschna* (Odonata:Aeshnidae). Florida Entomol., 60:223–225.

GLOYD, L. K. 1940. On the status of *Gomphaeschna antilope* (Hagen). Occas. Paper Mus. Zool., Univ. Michigan, 415:1–14.

PREPARED BY: Clark Shiffer, *Pennsylvania Fish Commission, Robinson Lane, Bellefonte, PA 16823.*

Status Undetermined
BLUE-NOSED DARNER
Nasiaeschna pentacantha (Rambur)
Family Aeshnidae
Order Odonata

DESCRIPTION: The blue-nosed darner is an average-sized darner dragonfly (total length, about 73 mm) with a prominent, forwardly-produced face and a long, tapering abdomen. The face of this species is pale greenish-brown, with a pair of blue-green spots on top; the thorax is brown with paired green stripings on front and sides; the abdomen is brown, marked with a pattern of irregular blue-green spots on top and sides of each segment. Abdominal appendages of males are small and bowed in profile. Females are similar to males but with a stout ovipositor and associated structures on underside of abdominal segments 8 and 9.

RANGE: The species has been recorded from the Canadian provinces of Ontario and Quebec; in the U.S. from New Hampshire west to Illinois, Iowa and Wisconsin, and south to Florida and Texas. It is known in Pennsylvania only from a single nymph taken in Mercer County.

HABITAT: The primary habitat of *Nasiaeschna pentacantha* is low gradient streams flowing through wooded swamps or swampy terrain, and the backwaters of lakes in swampy terrain.

LIFE HISTORY AND ECOLOGY: The flight period extends from early March to late August. Males may be seen during sunny weather flying slowly back

Female, Blue-nosed Darner (*Nasiaeschna pentacantha*). Photograph by C. N. Shiffer.

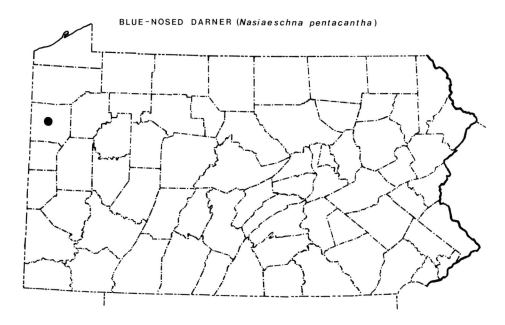

BLUE-NOSED DARNER (*Nasiaeschna pentacantha*)

and forth over a limited area of water about 0.6–1.3 m above its surface. During these flights the wings are vibrated rapidly and there are occasional hovering pauses. Females are less evident, flying among aquatic vegetation in shaded or partly shaded areas. Eggs are inserted singly in wet, decaying leaves or wood.

Although developmental time for eggs and nymphs

is not known, nymphs probably require several winters to reach maturity. Transformation occurs on vegetation near the water. Adults are seen most often in the vicinity of breeding sites.

BASIS OF STATUS CLASSIFICATION: Although known only from a single nymph taken from French Creek, Mercer County, it is likely that this species occurs at other sites, particularly in the northwestern portion of the Commonwealth. The species is somewhat locally distributed throughout its range and this is probably the case in Pennsylvania.

RECOMMENDATIONS: Additional surveys in the northwestern counties will be necessary to determine the present status of the species.

SELECTED REFERENCES:

BEATTY, A. F., and G. H. BEATTY. 1971. The distribution of Pennsylvania Odonata. Proc. Pennsylvania Acad. Sci., 45: 147–167.

BEATTY, G. H., and A. F. BEATTY. 1968. Check list and bibliography of Pennsylvania Odonata. Proc. Pennsylvania Acad. Sci., 42:120–129.

NEEDHAM, J. G., and M. J. WESTFALL, JR. 1955. A manual of the dragonflies of North America (Anisoptera). Univ. California Press, Berkeley and Los Angeles, 615 pp.

WALKER, E. M. 1958. The Odonata of Canada and Alaska. Univ. Toronto Press, Toronto, 2:1–318.

PREPARED BY: Clark Shiffer, *Pennsylvania Fish Commission, Robinson Lane, Bellefonte, PA 16823.*

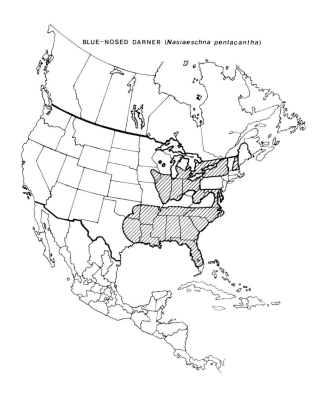

BLUE-NOSED DARNER (*Nasiaeschna pentacantha*)

Status Undetermined

OBSCURE CLUBTAIL
Progomphus obscurus (Rambur)
Family Gomphidae
Order Odonata

DESCRIPTION: The obscure clubtail is an average-sized gomphine dragonfly (total length, about 53 mm) of dull brown color and with pale yellow superior abdominal appendages. This species possesses a dull pale greenish face; largely dull, dark brown thorax, marked on front with a pair of downwardly divergent pale yellow stripes and on sides with larger pale yellowish areas between brown stripings on sutures; dark brown abdomen, with pale yellow-orange on sides and top of segments 1 to 7. Males have moderately stout superior abdominal appendages, with divergent and upturned apices. Females are similar to males, with a short vulvar lamina on the underside of abdominal segment 8.

RANGE: This species is recorded from Florida to Texas, north to New Hampshire and west to Missouri, Michigan, and Oregon, although not known that far west at present. It is recorded in Pennsylvania from Allegheny, Dauphin, Fayette, Juniata, and Perry counties.

HABITAT: This species may be sought around lake shores and moderate-sized, brown water to clear, streams and rivers of low to moderate gradient, where sand and gravel substrate predominate.

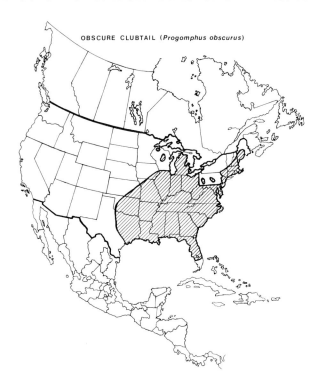

OBSCURE CLUBTAIL (*Progomphus obscurus*)

LIFE HISTORY AND ECOLOGY: Adult flights have been recorded from February to September. Nearly all Pennsylvania records are for the month of June. Males frequent the vicinity of lake margins or riffle areas in streams during sunny weather, flying low over the water or coming to rest on projecting sand bars, twigs, or branches. Numbers of individuals may be encountered along particular portions

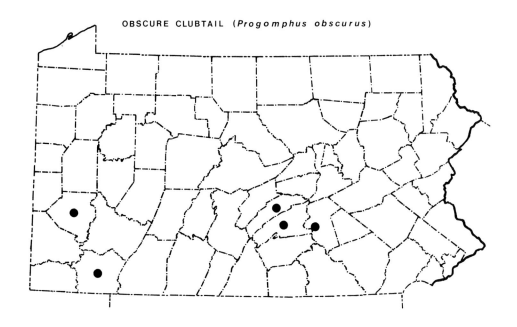

OBSCURE CLUBTAIL (*Progomphus obscurus*)

of streams or lake shores. Females visit the water only to oviposit by flying about and tapping the surface here and there and washing a small cluster of eggs from the end of the abdomen.

Nymphal development may require several years. When ready to transform, nymphs crawl only a short distance from the water; emergence often occurs on a nearly horizontal surface. While adults are to be found resting on bare, open patches of ground a short distance from the water, they do not seem to wander widely from breeding sites.

BASIS OF STATUS CLASSIFICATION: Although recorded from five Pennsylvania counties, collection records date back about 20 to 80 years, and consist of about a dozen adult specimens and several nymphs. At least one locality has been rendered unsuitable as a habitat due to acid mine drainage. The species should still occur at several historic localities.

RECOMMENDATIONS: More intensive surveys of unpolluted riverine habitats where sand and gravel substrate prevail may yield additional specimens of *Progomphus obscurus.* The species may have been more widespread in such habitats in Pennsylvania before the influence of various factors detrimental to its survival. The restoration and maintenance of good water quality in many of our rivers is essential for the continued survival of a number of species like *Progomphus obscurus.*

SELECTED REFERENCES:

BEATTY, A. F., and G. H. BEATTY. 1971. The distribution of Pennsylvania Odonata. Proc. Pennsylvania Acad. Sci., 45: 147–167.
BEATTY, G. H., and A. F. BEATTY. 1968. Check list and bibliography of Pennsylvania Odonata. Proc. Pennsylvania Acad. Sci., 42:120–129.
NEEDHAM, J. G., and M. J. WESTFALL, JR. 1955. A manual of the dragonflies of North America (Anisoptera). Univ. California Press, Berkeley and Los Angeles, 615 pp.

PREPARED BY: Clark Shiffer, *Pennsylvania Fish Commission, Robinson Lane, Bellefonte, PA 16823.*

Status Undetermined

BROTHERLY CLUBTAIL
Gomphus fraternus (Say)
Family Gomphidae
Order Odonata

DESCRIPTION: The brotherly clubtail is an average-sized gomphine dragonfly (total length, about 50–55 mm) of dull greenish-yellow color and widened abdominal end segments. The face is greenish-yellow; the thorax has somewhat divided brown shoulder stripes, an incomplete mid-lateral brown stripe, and a usually complete brown stripe behind this one; the abdomen is black with interrupted dorsal stripe of yellow on segments 2–8, and wider yellow markings on lateral margins of segments 7–9, segment 10 yellow beneath. Females are similar in

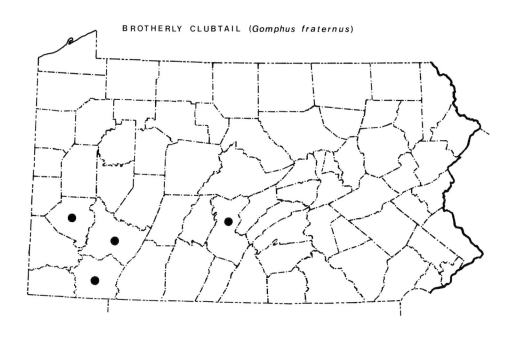

BROTHERLY CLUBTAIL (*Gomphus fraternus*)

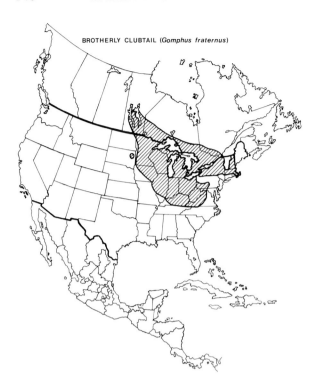

BROTHERLY CLUBTAIL (*Gomphus fraternus*)

appearance to males but with a bifurcated vulvar lamina on the underside of abdominal segments 8 and 9.

RANGE: Gomphus fraternus has been recorded from the Canadian provinces of Manitoba, Quebec, and Ontario; in the U.S. from northern Florida west to Texas, north to Iowa, South Dakota, and Wisconsin, and east to New Hampshire, although it is not present in many of these areas today. In Pennsylvania, it has been recorded from Allegheny, Fayette, Huntingdon, and Westmoreland counties.

HABITAT: Wave-washed lake shores and turbulent portions of small to large rivers are the preferred habitat of the brotherly clubtail.

LIFE HISTORY AND ECOLOGY: The adult flight period ranges from early April in the south to early August in the north. The few Pennsylvania records indicate a flight period from May to late June. Males may be encountered flying over the turbulent portions of streams or resting on mid-stream boulders, streamside vegetation, or on the ground in open areas away from the shore. Females visit the water only to oviposit by flying here and there close to the surface, and dipping the tip of the abdomen to wash off a cluster of eggs.

When ready to transform, nymphs travel only a short distance from water.

BASIS OF STATUS CLASSIFICATION: Only four adult specimens are known from Pennsylvania. The few dates of collection date back 30 to 80 years and at least one of the historic localities has been rendered unsuitable as a habitat due to acid mine drainage.

RECOMMENDATIONS: Further surveys are needed to confirm the possible occurrence of *G. fraternus* at other localities in Pennsylvania. The reclamation of historic habitats for this species, and a host of other species, must be vigorously pursued.

SELECTED REFERENCES:

BEATTY, A. F., and G. H. BEATTY. 1971. The distribution of Pennsylvania Odonata. Proc. Pennsylvania Acad. Sci., 45: 147–167.
BEATTY, A. F., G. H. BEATTY, and H. B. WHITE, III. 1969. Seasonal distribution of Pennsylvania Odonata. Proc. Pennsylvania Acad. Sci., 43:119–126.
BEATTY, G. H., and A. F. BEATTY. 1969. Check list and bibliography of Pennsylvania Odonata. Proc. Pennsylvania Acad. Sci., 42:120–129.
WALKER, E. M. 1958. The Odonata of Canada and Alaska. Univ. Toronto Press, Toronto, 2:1–318.

PREPARED BY: Clark Shiffer, *Pennsylvania Fish Commission, Robinson Lane, Bellefonte, PA 16823.*

Status Undetermined

FORKED CLUBTAIL
Gomphus furcifer Hagen
Family Gomphidae
Order Odonata

DESCRIPTION: The forked clubtail is a darkly-marked gomphine of average size (total length, 46–54 mm); the male appendages have very slender incurved apices. Face and ground color of the thorax are pale gray-green; thorax is marked with dark brown on front and at shoulder; abdomen is black with slender dorsal markings of pale green on segments 3–8, segment 10 brighter yellow on top, and segments 7–10 edged with yellow on lateral margins; appendages are yellow.

RANGE: The range of this species is from the Canadian Provinces of Ontario and Quebec; in the U.S. from New England west to Minnesota, south to Iowa and Virginia, and north to Pennsylvania and New

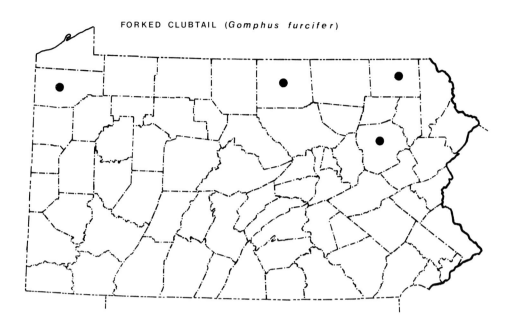

FORKED CLUBTAIL (*Gomphus furcifer*)

Jersey. It is known in Pennsylvania from Crawford, Luzerne, Susquehanna, and Tioga counties.

HABITAT: Boggy ponds and quiet backwaters of streams or larger lakes with extensive growth of aquatic macrophytes are the preferred habitat of the forked clubtail.

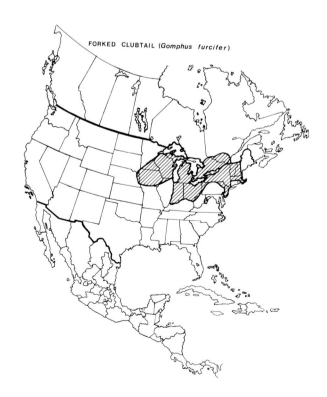

FORKED CLUBTAIL (*Gomphus furcifer*)

LIFE HISTORY AND ECOLOGY: Adult flights are recorded within the range from May to early August. The few Pennsylvania records nearly span the month of June and early July. Males fly close to the water in sunny weather, landing often upon water lily leaves or floating mats of vegetation, where they remain perched for varying periods of time. They may also be encountered on the ground in open areas a short distance from the water.

Although oviposition has not been described in this species, it is probably similar to oviposition as practiced by the related *Gomphus villosipes* Selys. Females of *G. villosipes* hover at various places along the weedy margins of slow-water areas, close to the water, and dip the tip of the abdomen to the surface, sometimes making a number of dips at nearly the same place.

Nymphs usually transform on water lily leaves or other floating vegetation in a nearly horizontal position.

BASIS OF STATUS CLASSIFICATION: This species is currently represented in Pennsylvania by three nymphs from Crawford County, one adult male from Luzerne County, three adult males from Susquehanna County, and three adult males from Tioga County. Collection records date back 8 to 15 years. It is probable that *G. furcifer* occurs at other suitable habitats in the northern tier counties and the northeastern and northwestern portions of the Commonwealth.

RECOMMENDATIONS: Historic sites for the species should still be suitable. The Luzerne County site is a county park and the Tioga County site is a state park. Further surveys will be necessary to ascertain the possible occurrence of *G. furcifer* at other suitable localities, although the species may prove to be somewhat locally distributed.

SELECTED REFERENCES:

BEATTY, A. F., and G. H. BEATTY. 1971. The distribution of Pennsylvania Odonata. Proc. Pennsylvania Acad. Sci., 45: 147–167.

BEATTY, A. F., G. H. BEATTY, and H. B. WHITE, III. 1969. Seasonal distribution of Pennsylvania Odonata. Proc. Pennsylvania Acad. Sci., 43:119–126.

BEATTY, G. H., and A. F. BEATTY. 1968. Check list and bibliography of Pennsylvania Odonata. Proc. Pennsylvania Acad. Sci., 42:120–129.

WALKER, E. M. 1958. The Odonata of Canada and Alaska. Univ. Toronto Press, Toronto, 2:1–318.

PREPARED BY: Clark Shiffer, *Pennsylvania Fish Commission, Robinson Lane, Bellefonte, PA 16823.*

Status Undetermined

WILLIAMSON'S BOG SKIMMER
Somatochlora williamsoni Walker
Family Libellulidae
Order Odonata

DESCRIPTION: Williamson's bog skimmer is an average-sized *Somatochlora* (total length, 53–60 mm) with obscure lateral thoracic stripes. The face is yellow-brown with dark metallic blue markings; the thorax is brown with metallic blue-green reflections and obscure lateral stripes; the abdomen is black with dull metallic blue-green sheen and dull pale spots on sides of segment 2. In males, superior appendages are moderately long, with a small lateral, basal tooth, tapering to recurved apices. In females, there is a long, laterally-compressed and pointed ovipositor on the underside of abdominal segments 8 and 9.

RANGE: Historically, this species is recorded from the Canadian provinces of Manitoba, Ontario, and Quebec and in the U.S. from New England, south to New York, Pennsylvania, and Tennessee, and west to Michigan and Minnesota. It has been recorded in Pennsylvania from Hartstown, Crawford County.

HABITAT: The habitat of *Somatochlora williamsoni* is quiet, boggy streams in partially forested terrain.

LIFE HISTORY AND ECOLOGY: The adult flight period occurs from about mid-June to mid-September throughout the range. Pennsylvania dates are 13–17 July. Mature males fly slowly, within 30 cm or less of the stream, often in shady or partially shaded areas, frequently hovering for varying periods along the bank. When flying in open, sunny areas, their flight is at a greater height. Females may occasionally be seen during feeding flights near dusk,

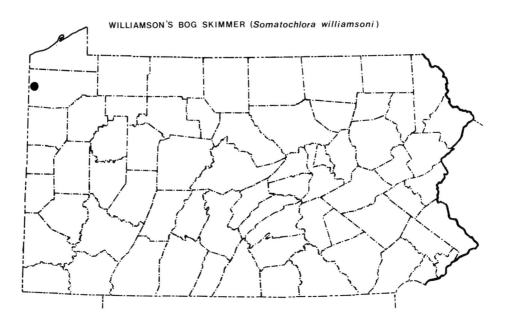

WILLIAMSON'S BOG SKIMMER (*Somatochlora williamsoni*)

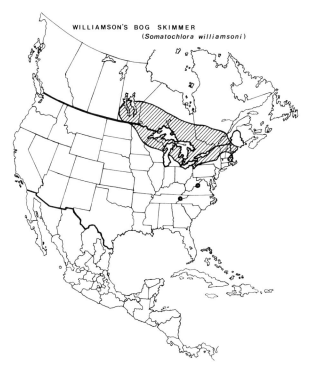

WILLIAMSON'S BOG SKIMMER
(*Somatochlora williamsoni*)

but are generally secretive. They oviposit near the stream bank by hovering within 15 cm of the surface, the abdomen held obliquely upward, dipping the tip of the abdomen to the shore substrate several or more times and then alternately tapping the water. Oviposition in this species is thus reminiscent of the manner of oviposition in *S. elongata*. Nymphal development time is unknown, but may encompass several winters. Transformation occurs on vegetation not far above the water's surface.

Young adults fly near the tops of trees at heights of 9–15 m, staying within a limited area. They generally frequent clearings and may wander up to 1.6 km from the breeding sites.

BASIS OF STATUS CLASSIFICATION: Although the only record of occurrence for this species in Pennsylvania (three males, one female in 1922) dates back many years, suitable habitat for the species is still to be found at Hartstown. The glaciated portions of the Commonwealth, particularly the northeast, would appear to contain suitable habitat for *S. williamsoni.*

RECOMMENDATIONS: The Hartstown locality should be revisited. Other habitats in the glaciated portions of the Commonwealth may well prove to contain colonies of *S. williamsoni* upon investigation.

SELECTED REFERENCES:

BEATTY, A. F., and G. H. BEATTY. 1971. The distribution of Pennsylvania Odonata. Proc. Pennsylvania Acad. Sci., 45: 147–167.

BEATTY, A. F., G. H. BEATTY, and H. B. WHITE, III. 1969. Seasonal distribution of Pennsylvania Odonata. Proc. Pennsylvania Acad. Sci., 43:119–126.

BEATTY, G. H., and A. F. BEATTY. 1968. Check list and bibliography of Pennsylvania Odonata. Proc. Pennsylvania Acad. Sci., 42:120–129.

WALKER, E. M. 1925. The North American dragonflies of the genus *Somatochlora.* Univ. Toronto Studies, Biol. Ser., 26: 1–202.

WALKER, E. M., and P. S. CORBET. 1975. The Odonata of Canada and Alaska. Univ. Toronto Press, Toronto, 3:1–307.

PREPARED BY: Clark Shiffer, *Pennsylvania Fish Commission, Robinson Lane, Bellefonte, PA 16823.*

Status Undetermined

ELEGANT SKIMMER
Dorocordulia lepida (Hagen)
Family Libellulidae
Order Odonata

DESCRIPTION: The elegant skimmer is one of the smaller members of the subfamily Corduliinae, resembling a diminutive *Somatochlora* (total length, 37–43 mm). The face of this species is dark bronzy green on top, pale yellowish-brown on sides; the thorax is brown with metallic bronzy green reflections, and is moderately hairy; the abdomen is black with dull metallic blue-green sheen. Tips of male superior abdominal appendages are divergent when viewed from above. Females are similar to males, but with dull yellow-brown markings on lateral portions of abdominal segments and a bifurcated vulvar lamina on underside of segments 8 and 9.

RANGE: This species has been recorded from the Canadian provinces of New Brunswick and Nova Scotia and in the U.S. from the New England states west to Indiana and south to Maryland—primarily coastal. In Pennsylvania, it is known from Bradford, Centre, Lackawanna, Monroe, Susquehanna, and Wayne counties.

HABITAT: Boggy ponds and small lakes are the preferred habitats of *Dorocordulia lepida.*

LIFE HISTORY AND ECOLOGY: Adult flights occur from June through August within the range, and this approximates the seasonal distribution in

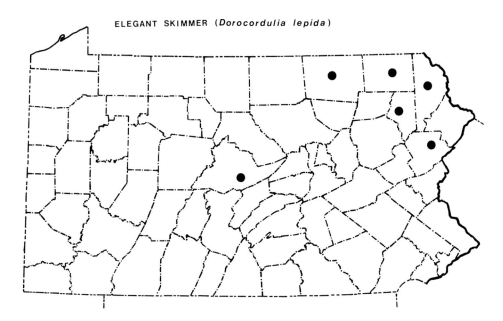

ELEGANT SKIMMER (*Dorocordulia lepida*)

Pennsylvania. Males fly over quiet water or boggy terrain in sunny weather, within 2 m of the water or ground, patrolling over limited areas. Females visit the water to oviposit by flying close to the water, dipping down to its surface to touch the tip of the abdomen, and washing off a cluster of eggs.

Nymphs transform on stumps, branchlets, or emergent vegetation in relatively shallow water. Adults are encountered in open areas away from the

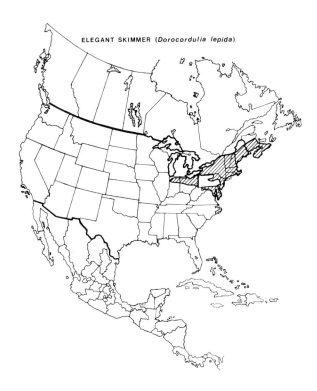

ELEGANT SKIMMER (*Dorocordulia lepida*)

water in early life. After about a week spent feeding in these areas, adults are reproductively mature and return to the breeding sites.

BASIS OF STATUS CLASSIFICATION: Although *D. lepida* has been recorded from six Pennsylvania counties, its status in several of these counties is uncertain. The Wayne County record of a single female dates back about 80 years, although the species may still occur in Wayne County. The Centre County record, also of a single female, dates back about 30 years, and no other individuals have been recorded at that locality. One Susquehanna County collection is recent but other records for this and the other counties date back 7 to 10 years; however, *D. lepida* probably still occurs at each of these localities. One site is part of state game lands, three are county parks, and one site is protected as a unique natural area. Although the species probably occurs at other suitable boggy habitats in northeastern Pennsylvania, the vulnerability of these habitats makes its future uncertain.

RECOMMENDATIONS: Additional surveys will be necessary to ascertain the occurrence of *D. lepida* at other than historic localities. Historic localities should be revisited.

SELECTED REFERENCES:

BEATTY, A. F., and G. H. BEATTY. 1971. The distribution of Pennsylvania Odonata. Proc. Pennsylvania Acad. Sci., 45: 147–167.

BEATTY, A. F., G. H. BEATTY, and H. B. WHITE, III. 1969.
  Seasonal distribution of Pennsylvania Odonata. Proc. Penn-
  sylvania Acad. Sci., 43:119–126.
BEATTY, G. H., and A. F. BEATTY. 1968. Check list and bib-
  liography of Pennsylvania Odontata. Proc. Pennsylvania
  Acad. Sci., 42:120–129.
WALKER, E. M., and P. S. CORBET. 1975. The Odonata of Can-
  ada and Alaska. Univ. Toronto Press, Toronto, 3:1–307.

PREPARED BY: Clark Shiffer, *Pennsylvania Fish Commission, Robinson Lane, Bellefonte, PA 16823.*

Status Undetermined

CANADIAN WHITE-FACED SKIMMER
Leucorrhinia proxima Calvert
Family Libellulidae
Order Odonata

DESCRIPTION: The Canadian white-faced skimmer is a dragonfly of above average size for the genus (total length, 33–36 mm). The face of this species is white; the thorax is brown with black markings on front and sides, those on sides forming a rough letter N; the abdomen is black beyond pale brownish-red basal segments, becoming whitish basally in mature individuals, particularly males. Females similar in appearance to males, but with very short, widely-divergent lobes comprising the vulvar lamina (ovipositor) on the underside of abdominal segments 8 and 9.

RANGE: It is known from nearly all of Canada, and in the U.S. from Washington to New England and south to New York, Pennsylvania, and Virginia. It is known in Pennsylvania from Bradford, Luzerne, Susquehanna, and Wayne counties.

HABITAT: Open portions of bogs or boggy swamps are the primary areas preferred by the Canadian white-faced skimmer.

LIFE HISTORY AND ECOLOGY: Adult flights occur from mid-May to late August within the range. In Pennsylvania, adults have been collected in June, July, and August. Males may be seen in sunny weather flying within 30 cm of the surface of the water in a random manner, coming to rest on twigs or rocks with the wings slanted downward. Females visit the water with low, more direct flight and are seized by watchful males. The copulatory position is assumed shortly after seizure and a pair then flies to the foliage of a nearby tree to complete mating. The females return alone to the water to oviposit among emergent vegetation by flying here and there close to the surface and tapping the abdomen to wash off a cluster of eggs.

Nymphs crawl a short distance above the water on emergent vegetation to transform. Young adults frequent clearings a short distance from the breeding sites.

BASIS OF STATUS CLASSIFICATION: Although Pennsylvania populations of *L. proxima* are undoubtedly at the southernmost edge of the range of the species, the status of these populations is not

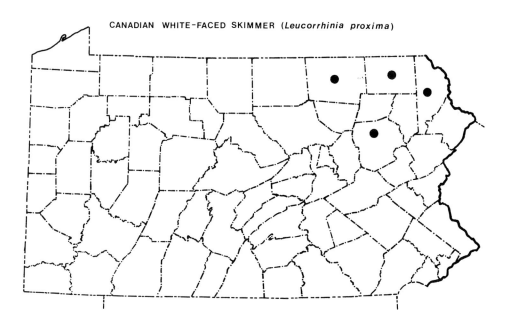

CANADIAN WHITE-FACED SKIMMER (*Leucorrhinia proxima*)

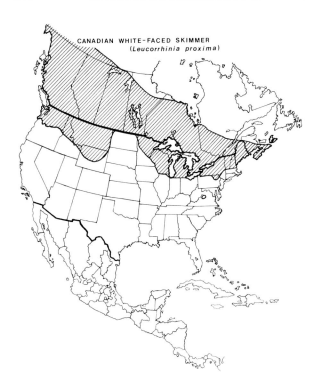

itats required by *L. proxima* must be protected from destruction.

SELECTED REFERENCES:

BEATTY, A. F., and G. H. BEATTY. 1971. The distribution of Pennsylvania Odonata. Proc. Pennsylvania Acad. Sci., 45: 147–167.

BEATTY, A. F., G. H. BEATTY, and H. B. WHITE, III. 1969. Seasonal distribution of Pennsylvania Odonata. Proc. Pennsylvania Acad. Sci., 43:119–126.

BEATTY, G. H., and A. F. BEATTY. 1968. Check list and bibliography of Pennsylvania Odonata. Proc. Pennsylvania Acad. Sci. 42:120–129.

WALKER, E. M., and P. S. CORBET. 1975. The Odonata of Canada and Alaska. Univ. Toronto Press, Toronto, 3:1–307.

PREPARED BY: Clark Shiffer, Pennsylvania Fish Commission, Robinson Lane, Bellefonte, PA 16823.

Status Undetermined

TITIAN RUBY-SPOT
Hetaerina titia (Drury)
Family Calopterygidae
Order Odonata

known. The species may occur locally in suitable habitats, particularly in the north-central and northeastern portions of the Commonwealth.

RECOMMENDATIONS: Suitable habitat in the north-central and northeastern portions of the Commonwealth should be investigated to ascertain the occurrence and status of this species. The bog hab-

DESCRIPTION: The titian ruby-spot is a stream damselfly of relatively southern distribution, with variously-darkened wings. Total length is 39–48 mm. Males have a face and body that are largely dull blackish-brown with dull reddish sheen on front of thorax and darker markings on side of thorax of dull greenish sheen; forewings are bright red at base and

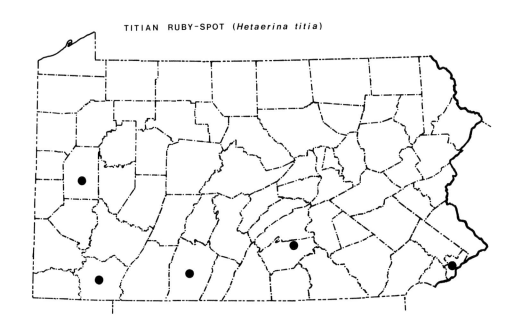

TITIAN RUBY-SPOT (*Hetaerina titia*)

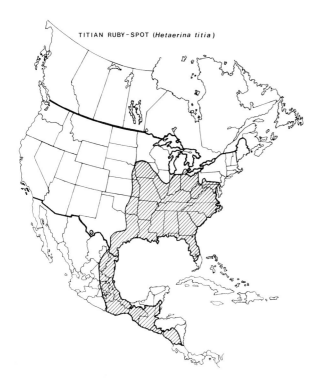

TITIAN RUBY-SPOT (*Hetaerina titia*)

clear beyond; hindwings are dark red-brown at base and essentially clear with darkened apices, or variously pigmented with an outwash of dark blackish-brown that may cover the entire wing. Females possess a body that is lighter brown with metallic green thoracic markings; both fore- and hindwings are suffused throughout with amber to blackish. An ovipositor and associated structures are on the underside of segments 8 and 9.

RANGE: The titian ruby-spot has been recorded from northwest Idaho, east to southern Michigan and southern Pennsylvania, south to Florida, southern and eastern Texas and Central America, north to eastern Oklahoma, eastern Kansas, and southeastern Nebraska, although it is not currently present in some of these areas. In Pennsylvania, it has been taken from Bedford, Butler, Cumberland, Fayette, and Philadelphia counties.

HABITAT: This species frequents shaded to semi-shaded portions of small to moderate-sized streams with sandy to gravelly or rock substrate.

LIFE HISTORY AND ECOLOGY: Adults are recorded in flight throughout the range between late March and mid-November. Most northern records indicate a mid- to late summer flight period, where occurrences are much less common than farther south. The few Pennsylvania records encompass the period between late August and early September. Both sexes may be seen perched from 5 to 25 cm above the stream on leaves or twigs of vegetation overhanging the water. Males change perch sites at intervals, coming to rest for a brief period on the leaves of herbage growing nearer the water. They may also skirmish briefly by flying around one another in horizontal, circular patterns about 8 cm above the water. One then briefly chases the other until they come to rest on widely separated perches.

Unmated females fly into the territories of waiting males and hover, whereupon they are seized by the male. Each tandem pair then comes to rest on vegetation within the male territory to complete copulation.

Mating may take several minutes, after which the couple fly in tandem to the more swiftly-flowing parts of the stream, where the female oviposits alone on vegetation while submerged. Males may remain perched nearby during oviposition, which may last up to 30 min. Single mated females refuse advances of males by spreading the wings and bending the abdomen forward.

BASIS FOR STATUS CLASSIFICATION: Although "Philadelphia" is listed as a type locality for *Hetaerina tricolor,* generally considered a color form of *H. titia,* the locality data is questionable. At any rate, it is not likely that *H. titia* presently occurs there. Three specimens were taken above Ohiopyle, Fayette County, in 1901 and that locality is not presently suitable Odonata habitat. The Cumberland County record is a single female taken in 1909. Two males were taken at different sites in Butler County, one in 1945 and one in 1965. It is possible that *H. titia* occurs at other localities in southern Pennsylvania, but consideration of the sporadic occurrences of the species in the north makes its status in the Commonwealth uncertain.

RECOMMENDATIONS: Conoquenessing Creek and Little Conoquenessing Creek in Butler County are the streams along which *H. titia* was collected. These streams may yet be suitable habitat, and should be revisited. Plans in relatively recent years to build dams on these streams would render portions of them unsuitable habitat for *H. titia* and other organisms requiring stream conditions.

SELECTED REFERENCES:

BEATTY, G. H., and A. F. BEATTY. 1968. Check list and bibliography of Pennsylvania Odonata. Proc. Pennsylvania Acad. Sci., 42:120–129.

BEATTY, G. H., A. F. BEATTY, and C. N. SHIFFER. 1970. A survey of the Odonata of eastern Pennsylvania. Proc. Pennsylvania Acad. Sci., 44:141–152.

JOHNSON, C. 1961. Breeding behavior and oviposition in *Hetaerina americana* (Fabricius) and *H. titia* (Drury) (Odonata: Agridae). Canadian Entomol., 93:260–266.

———. 1973. Distributional patterns and their interpretation in *Hetaerina* (Odonata:Calopterygidae). Florida Entomol., 56:24–42.

PREPARED BY: Clark Shiffer, *Pennsylvania Fish Commission, Robinson Lane, Bellefonte, PA 16823.*

Status Undetermined

TWO-SPOTTED DANCER
Argia bipunctulata (Hagen)
Family Coenagrionidae
Order Odonata

DESCRIPTION: The two-spotted dancer is the smallest species of the genus (total length, 27–30 mm) in our fauna, resembling an *Enallagma* in color pattern. The eyes, face, and ground color of body are pale blue. The thorax has wide black mid-dorsal and shoulder stripes; abdominal segments 2–5 have a terminal black band, segment 6 black on terminal half, segment 7 all black, and segments 8–10 blue. Females have an ovipositor and associated structures on underside of segments 8 and 9.

RANGE: This species occurs from New York, south to northern Florida, eastern Texas, and eastern Oklahoma, west and southwest to southern Missouri, Tennessee, Virginia, West Virginia, Ohio, and southern Michigan. In Pennsylvania, it is recorded from "Pa."—no locality or date, and Tannersville, Monroe County.

HABITAT: The habitat of *Argia bipunctulata* is shallow spring seeps in bogs or sphagnaceous situations in the open.

LIFE HISTORY AND ECOLOGY: Little published ecological information is available for this species. However, what information is available indicates that adults are in flight within the range between late April and the end of August. The few Pennsylvania records encompass a period from late June to the third week in July. Both sexes are seen in sunny weather flying low over the open sphagnaceous areas of their habitat. Like most species of *Argia,* flights are brief, from one resting place to another. Because of their small size and color pattern, adults resemble some species of *Enallagma* more than most *Argia* species.

There seems to be no account of oviposition, and the nymph remains undescribed.

BASIS OF STATUS CLASSIFICATION: Only 10 specimens of this species have apparently been collected in Pennsylvania, most of which are from Tannersville. The records date back 30 to 35 years. Hab-

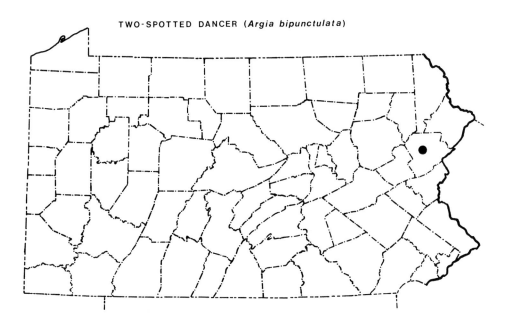

TWO-SPOTTED DANCER (*Argia bipunctulata*)

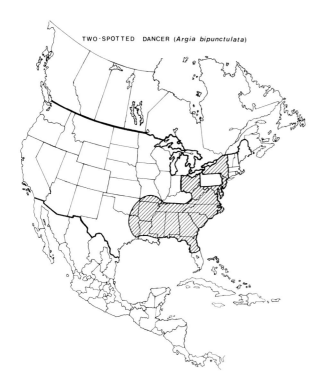

TWO-SPOTTED DANCER (*Argia bipunctulata*)

itat similar to areas of the New Jersey Pine Barrens, where *A. bipunctulata* is more commonly encountered, exists in various places in northeastern Pennsylvania. It is likely that additional localities for this species will be found after adequate search. The species is one of the few members of its genus that inhabits sphagnaceous spring seeps, and, like its preferred habitat, is local in occurrence.

RECOMMENDATIONS: Adequate searches for this species should be undertaken, and the environmental integrity of its habitat safeguarded.

SELECTED REFERENCES:

BEATTY, A. F., and G. H. BEATTY. 1971. The distribution of Pennsylvania Odonata. Proc. Pennsylvania Acad. Sci., 45: 147–167.
BEATTY, G. H., and A. F. BEATTY. 1968. Check list and bibliography of Pennsylvania Odonata. Proc. Pennsylvania Acad. Sci., 42:120–129.
BICK, G. H. 1957. The Odonata of Louisiana. Tulane Stud. Zool. 5:71–135.

PREPARED BY: Clark Shiffer, *Pennsylvania Fish Commission, Robinson Lane, Bellefonte, PA 16823.*

Status Undetermined

EASTERN DANCER
Argia tibialis (Rambur)
Family Coenagrionidae
Order Odonata

DESCRIPTION: The eastern dancer is a species of average size for the genus (total length, 30–38 mm) in which the males have the front of the thorax pale brownish-purple and the sides becoming white with age. Males have a pale blue face; thorax is pale brownish-purple on front, pale yellow on sides, and becomimg white with age, a narrow dark band on middle of thorax in front and wide black shoulder

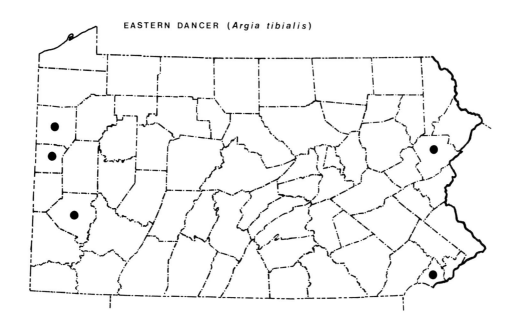

EASTERN DANCER (*Argia tibialis*)

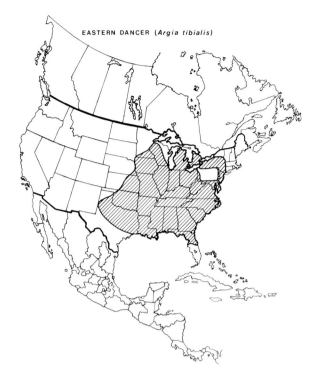

EASTERN DANCER (*Argia tibialis*)

stripes; abdomen is mostly black with last two segments mostly blue, but black along lower margins. Females similar in appearance to males, but with pale rings on front of abdominal segments 3–7 and pale lower margins on segments 2–7; an ovipositor and associated structures on underside of segments 8 and 9.

RANGE: This species occurs from Florida to Texas, north to New Jersey and southern Ontario, Canada, west to southern Minnesota, Kansas, and Oklahoma. In Pennsylvania, it is known from Allegheny, Delaware, Lawrence, Mercer, and Monroe counties.

LIFE HISTORY AND ECOLOGY: Adult flights occur within the range from mid-March to mid-September. Pennsylvania records encompass a period from about mid-June to the end of August. Both sexes may be encountered in shady to partly shady areas along streams, perched most often on vegetation or rocks projecting from the water. Unlike many other *Argia* species, they seem to prefer perching on vegetation, rather than bare sunny spots on the ground. Their flight is similar to other species of the genus, which make short flights from one resting place to another.

Despite its wide occurrence in eastern United States, there is no published information concerning aspects of its life history and reproduction.

BASIS OF STATUS CLASSIFICATION: Only about 10 specimens of *A. tibialis* have been collected in the Pennsylvania counties previously listed. Dates of collection range back 20 to 93 years. It is most likely that this species occurs at other locations in the southern portion of the Commonwealth, but have simply been overlooked.

RECOMMENDATIONS: Historic localities for the species should be revisited to ascertain its present status, and additional surveys should be conducted in the southern portion of the Commonwealth.

SELECTED REFERENCES:

BEATTY, A. F., and G. H. BEATTY. 1971. The distribution of Pennsylvania Odonata. Proc. Pennsylvania Acad. Sci., 45: 147–167.

BEATTY, G. H., and A. F. BEATTY. 1968. Check list and bibliography of Pennsylvania Odonata. Proc. Pennsylvania Acad. Sci., 42:120–129.

BICK, G. H., and J. C. BICK. 1980. A bibliography of reproductive behavior of Zygoptera of Canada and coterminous United States. Odonatologica, 9:5–18.

WALKER, E. M. 1953. The Odonata of Canada and Alaska. Univ. Toronto Press, Toronto, 1:1–292.

PREPARED BY: Clark Shiffer, *Pennsylvania Fish Commission, Robinson Lane, Bellefonte, PA 16823.*

Status Undetermined

RESOLUTE DAMSEL
Coenagrion resolutum (Hagen)
Family Coenagrionidae
Order Odonata

DESCRIPTION: The resolute damsel is a damselfly of moderate size (total length, 23–31 mm), resembling some of the species of *Enallagma*. Males display a pale green face marked with black; rear of the head is pale greenish-yellow; the thorax is pale greenish-yellow with broad black shoulder stripes; the abdomen is pale blue, yellow-green below, with segments 3–5 black on top for half their length, segments 5 and 6 nearly all black on top, segments 8 and 9 all blue, segment 10 black on top. Females are either colored like the male or display pale yellow-green to brownish colors, and possess an ovipositor and associated structures on underside of segments 8 and 9.

RANGE: The resolute damsel occurs through nearly all of Canada, from Newfoundland to Hudson Bay

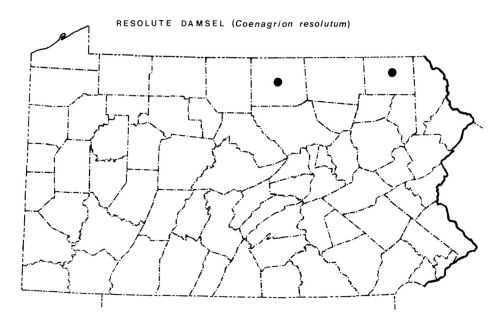

RESOLUTE DAMSEL (*Coenagrion resolutum*)

and Alaska, south to Vermont, New Hampshire, northern Pennsylvania, west to Oregon and south to California, Nevada, and Colorado. This species is known in Pennsylvania from three males collected at Weirs Pond, Susquehanna County and a single male obtained at Hills Creek State Park, Tioga County.

HABITAT: The resolute damsel prefers still marshy

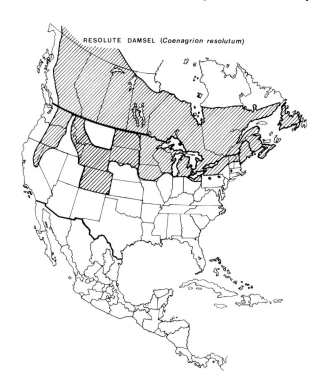

RESOLUTE DAMSEL (*Coenagrion resolutum*)

or boggy waters that are somewhat shaded in the southern part of the range.

LIFE HISTORY AND ECOLOGY: The adult flight period is recorded as occurring from about mid-May to mid-August, within some part of the range. The Pennsylvania captures were on 13 and 24 June. Both sexes may be seen during fair weather flying low over the breeding sites, or resting on shrubbery nearby. Pairing and oviposition begin about the first of June. Oviposition is performed in tandem, the male retaining his hold upon the female's prothorax with the terminal abdominal appendages and maintaining an oblique or vertical position above her by stiffening his abdominal segments. He thus appears to be "standing upright on his tail." Pairs move from one aquatic plant to another, the female depositing eggs in underwater portions of each.

Eggs hatch within 3 weeks and nymphs are full-grown, or nearly so, by mid-September. Further development is arrested in early October and nymphs remain in their final stages through the winter. They may survive being frozen during this time, and begin development to their final stage the following May. Emergence and transformation to the adult stage begin in late May and may continue until the third week in June. Most individuals emerge within the first 10 days of the season, however. Adults do not seem to wander more than 90–120 m from the breeding sites.

BASIS FOR STATUS CLASSIFICATION: Further search in the northern portion of the Commonwealth, at suitable boggy habitats, should reveal additional occurrences of this species. It is undoubtedly at or near the southern limits of its range in eastern North America, and may thus be of local occurrence in our Commonwealth. Prior to the capture of the single male in Tioga County, the genus *Coenagrion* was unknown in Pennsylvania.

RECOMMENDATIONS: Hills Creek State Park should be revisited to determine the current status of the species. Additional suitable habitats in northern Pennsylvania should be searched for possible occurrence of this species.

SELECTED REFERENCES:

SAWCHYN, W. W., and C. GILLOTT. 1975. The biology of two related species of coenagrionid dragonflies (Odonata:Zygoptera) in western Canada. Canadian Entomol., 107:119–128.
SHIFFER, C. N. 1974. Two species of Odonata new to Pennsylvania. Ent. News, 85:170.
WALKER, E. M. 1953. The Odonata of Canada and Alaska. Univ. Toronto Press, Toronto, 1:1–292.

PREPARED BY: Clark Shiffer, *Pennsylvania Fish Commission, Robinson Lane, Bellefonte, PA 16823.*

Status Undetermined

BOREAL BLUET
Enallagma boreale Selys
Family Coenagrionidae
Order Odonata

DESCRIPTION: The boreal bluet is a large northern *Enallagma* (total length, 28–35 mm) with the blue and black color pattern characteristic of many species in the genus. In males, the face is pale blue to greenish-blue; the thorax is blue to pale bluish-green with a broad mid-dorsal black stripe and a pair of heavy black shoulder stripes that widen below; the abdomen is pale blue with small black spots on the top of segments 1 and 2, the terminal third of segments 3–5 black, the terminal three quarters of segment 6 black, nearly all of segment 7 black, segments 8 and 9 all blue, segment 10 black on top; superior appendages are blunt, rounded, and notched on the lower rear margin in side view. Females are either colored like the male or yellowish-green and have an ovipositor and associated structures on the underside of segments 8 and 9.

RANGE: The boreal bluet occurs in nearly all of Canada from Newfoundland to the Yukon and Alaska, south to Massachusetts, New York, Pennsylvania, and southwest to the higher altitudes of Arizona, New Mexico, and California. It is known in Pennsylvania only from Centre (one male), Pike (one male), Monroe (three females, three males), and Susquehanna (one male) counties.

HABITAT: Ponds and boggy or marshy lakes, mostly in glaciated terrain, are the preferred habitats of the boreal bluet.

LIFE HISTORY AND ECOLOGY: Adult flights occur between late April and mid-October some-

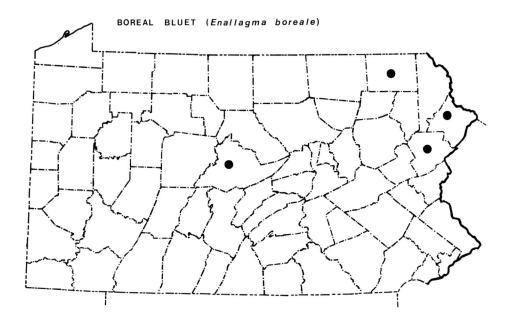

BOREAL BLUET (*Enallagma boreale*)

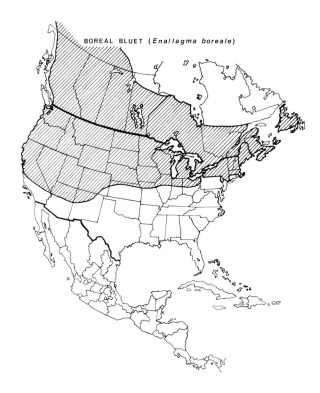

BOREAL BLUET (*Enallagma boreale*)

where within the range. Pennsylvania dates are between mid-June and 1 August. Pairing begins soon after the period of emergence. Oviposition may be performed by the female alone or in tandem with a male, and usually above water. The period of pairing and oviposition may last about a month in most parts of the range and the total period of adult activity is about a month and a half in most places.

Nymphs probably overwinter in the final stages of development and emerge the following spring. Transformation occurs on various kinds of emergent vegetation, not far above the water.

BASIS OF STATUS CLASSIFICATION: Pennsylvania records for this boreal species are few, but it is likely that additional localities will be found in the glaciated northeastern portion of the Commonwealth. The boggy lakes and ponds of the Poconos region would be especially good habitat for this and other boreal species.

RECOMMENDATIONS: Further surveys in the northeastern portions of the Commonwealth should reveal other occurrences of *E. boreale*. The environmental integrity of that region of the Commonwealth must continue to be valued and safeguarded.

SELECTED REFERENCES:

BEATTY, G. H., and A. F. BEATTY. 1968. Check list and bibliography of Pennsylvania Odonata. Proc. Pennsylvania Acad. Sci., 2:120–129.
BEATTY, G. H., A. F. BEATTY, and C. N. SHIFFER. 1969. A survey of the Odonata of central Pennsylvania. Proc. Pennsylvania Acad. Sci., 43:127–136.
WALKER, E. M. 1953. The Odonata of Canada and Alaska. Univ. Toronto Press, Toronto, 1:1–292.

PREPARED BY: Clark Shiffer, *Pennsylvania Fish Commission, Robinson Lane, Bellefonte, PA 16823.*

Status Undetermined

OLYMPIA MARBLE
Euchloe olympia Edwards
Family Pieridae
Order Lepidoptera

DESCRIPTION: The Olympia marble is a medium white butterfly (3–4 cm in wingspan) with some black on the forewing tips above and green marbling on the hind wings below. Actually, when examined under a microscope, the 'green' marbling is seen to be a mixture of yellow and black scales.

RANGE: This species occurs in local colonies scattered from the central Appalachians across the Great Lakes states and plains to the Rocky Mountain front and southern Alberta. In Pennsylvania, the Olympia marble is known only from an area near Inglesmith in Bedford County. This is the northernmost occurrence of the species in the Appalachian region.

HABITAT: In the central Appalachians including the Pennsylvania locality and those to the south in adjacent Allegany County, Maryland, this butterfly is strictly limited to Devonian shale barrens habitats (Clench and Opler, 1983). The species is found in somewhat open areas in the barrens and is usually found flying along ridge-tops or through clearings.

LIFE HISTORY AND ECOLOGY: The Olympia marble has only a single adult flight each spring, usually in late April and early May at our latitude. Eggs are laid singly on rock cress (*Arabis*) and the young caterpillars hatch in less than a week. They feed on the flowers and unopened buds of their plant host and then wander off the plant when fully fed. They then pupate on some dead plant material. The

Olympia Marble (*Euchloe olympia*). Photograph by G. O. Krizek.

chrysalids remain in a dormant state until the following spring (Opler, 1974).

BASIS OF STATUS CLASSIFICATION: This species has been found only once or twice in Pennsylvania in the extremely limited northern extension of the Braillier Shale Formation. The status of its populations and their conservation status is un-known. In adjacent Maryland, the species is locally common and occurs on land in a protected category.

RECOMMENDATIONS: Survey likely shale barren localities and determine the conservation status of areas where the species is found. After this initial groundwork, the appropriate state agencies must decide if further steps are necessary.

OLYMPIA MARBLE (*Euchloe olympia*)

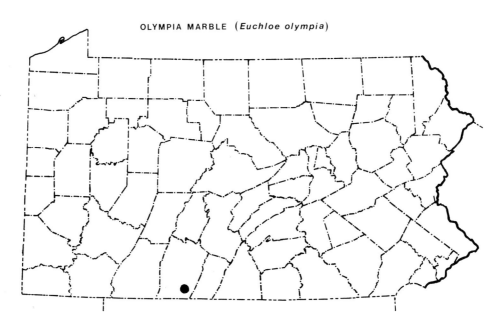

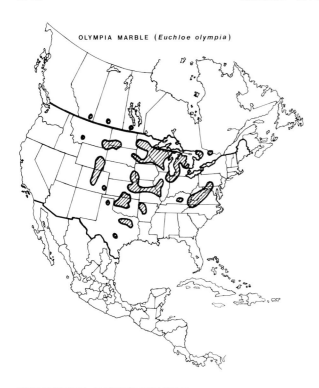

OLYMPIA MARBLE (*Euchloe olympia*)

SELECTED REFERENCES:

CLENCH, H. K., and P. A. OPLER. 1983. Studies on Nearctic *Euchloe.* Part 8. Distribution, ecology, and variation of *Euchloe olympia* (Pieridae) populations. Ann. Carnegie Mus., 52:41–54.

OPLER, P. A. 1974. Studies on Nearctic *Euchloe.* Part 7. Life histories and immature stages. J. Res. Lepid., 13:1–20.

PREPARED BY: Paul A. Opler, *U.S. Fish and Wildlife Service, Editorial Office, Room 259 Aylesworth Hall, Colorado State University, Fort Collins, CO 80523.*

Status Undetermined

PINK-EDGED SULFUR
Colias interior (Scudder)
Family Pieridae
Order Lepidoptera

DESCRIPTION: This is a medium-sized (30–40 mm wingspan) lemon yellow butterfly with black wing margins. The species is very similar to the common sulfur (*Colias philodice*), but differs by having the wing fringes more widely pink and only a single round discocellular spot on the underside of the hind wings.

RANGE: The species occurs from Labrador south to New England thence westward to Minnesota and southern Saskatchewan, with isolated colonies occurring in the mountains of Pennsylvania, Virginia, and West Virginia. In Pennsylvania, the pink-edged sulfur is known only from one beaver meadow in Elk Township, Tioga State Forest, Tioga County.

Pink-edged Sulfur (*Colias interior*). Photograph by G. O. Krizek.

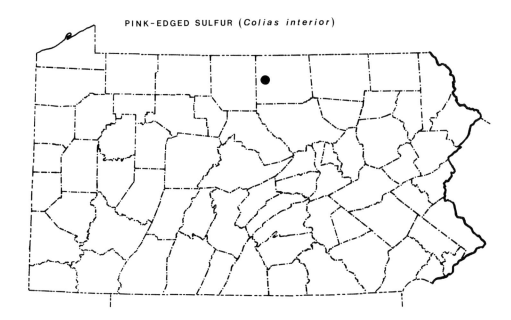

PINK-EDGED SULFUR (*Colias interior*)

HABITAT: The pink-edged sulfur is generally found in moist bogs, muskegs, or other areas with an abundance of blueberries (*Vaccinium*), the caterpillar food plants.

LIFE HISTORY AND ECOLOGY: There is a single annual generation with adults in flight from late June to early August (Klots, 1951). Winter is passed by the first instar caterpillar, and feeding is completed the following spring on young blueberry foliage.

SPECIALIZED OR UNIQUE CHARACTERISTICS: This is the only single-brooded eastern sulfur butterfly, and it is a good indicator of acidic habitats.

BASIS OF STATUS CLASSIFICATION: Although known from only a single Pennsylvania locality, the record is more than 10 years old. In addition, intensive survey may reveal other colonies.

RECOMMENDATIONS: Conduct additional surveys to determine present status and threats, as well as possible new locations.

ACKNOWLEDGMENTS: R. W. Boscoe, F. D. Fee, and A. M. Shapiro made recommendations.

SELECTED REFERENCES:

HOVANITZ, W. H. 1950. The biology of *Colias* butterflies. I. The distribution of the North American species. Wasmann J. Biol., 8:49–75.

KLOTS, A. B. 1951. A field guide to butterflies of North America, east of the Great Plains. Houghton Mifflin Co., Boston, 349 pp.

SHAPIRO, A. M. 1969. New distributional data on three northeastern United States butterflies. J. Lepid. Soc., 23:265–269.

PREPARED BY: Paul A. Opler, U.S. Fish and Wildlife Service, Editorial Office, Room 259 Aylesworth Hall, Colorado State University, Fort Collins, CO 80523.

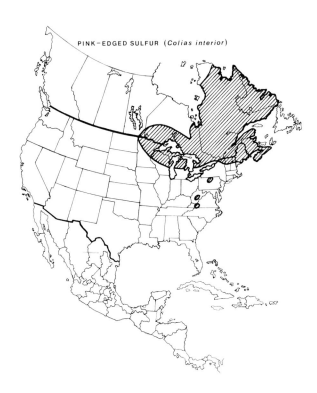

PINK-EDGED SULFUR (*Colias interior*)

Status Undetermined

HOARY ELFIN
Incisalia polios (Cook and Watson)
Family Lycaenidae
Order Lepidoptera

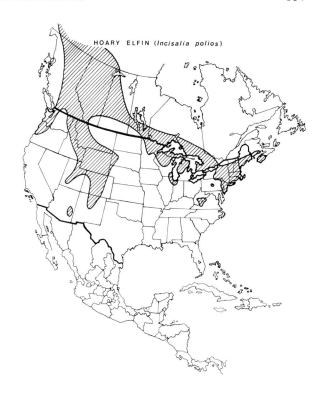

DESCRIPTION: This is a small (25 mm wingspan) reddish brown butterfly with much gray scaling on the outer margin of the underside of the hindwing. It differs from similar elfins by its almost complete lack of short tail-like projections from the outer hind wing margins.

RANGE: The hoary elfin occurs in New England west through Great Lake Region to Rocky Mountains and southwestern Canada (British Columbia and Alberta). Along the Atlantic seaboard, the isolated southernmost populations occur in the New Jersey pine barrens, near Philadelphia, and in the Virginia mountains. The species has not been found in Pennsylvania for over a decade.

HABITAT: This species occurs in barrens, sand plains, or rocky outcrops where suitable hosts are present.

LIFE HISTORY AND ECOLOGY: The hoary elfin has a single annual adult flight each spring (late March to early May). Eggs are laid on host leaves, and the larvae develop directly to the pupal stage. Winter is passed by the pupa. The caterpillars feed on bearberry (*Arctostaphylos uva-ursi*) and trailing arbutus (*Arbutus*).

BASIS OF STATUS CLASSIFICATION: The hoary elfin has not been reported from Pennsylvania since Shapiro's (1966) treatment. The species is either possibly extant in small local colonies or extirpated.

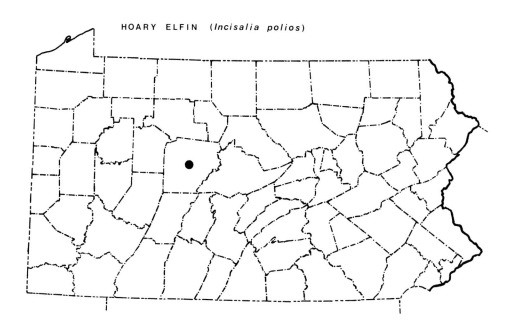

HOARY ELFIN (*Incisalia polios*)

RECOMMENDATIONS: Conduct status survey of historical colonies, and search other possible sites during mid- to late April.

ACKNOWLEDGMENTS: R. W. Boscoe, W. F. Boscoe, F. D. Fee, and A. M. Shapiro made status recommendations.

SELECTED REFERENCES:

FERRIS, C. D., and M. S. FISHER. 1973. *Callophrys* (*Incisalia*) *polios* (Lycaenidae): distribution in North America and description of a new subspecies. J. Lepid. Soc., 27:112–118.
SHAPIRO, A. M. 1966. Butterflies of the Delaware Valley. Amer. Entomol. Soc., Spec. Publ., vi + 79 pp.

PREPARED BY: Paul A. Opler, *U.S. Fish and Wildlife Service, Editorial Office, Room 259 Aylesworth Hall, Colorado State University, Fort Collins, CO 80523.*

Extirpated

GREEN-FACED CLUBTAIL
Gomphus viridifrons Hine
Family Gomphidae
Order Odonata

This species is distinguished from others of the subgenus *Hylogomphus* (*abbreviatus* and *brevis*) in Pennsylvania by its essentially unmarked greenish face. It is historically recorded locally from Ontario, Canada, and from Alabama, Indiana, Kentucky, Michigan, New York, North Carolina, Ohio, Pennsylvania, Tennessee, Virginia, and West Virginia. In Pennsylvania, it is recorded only from "the Ohio River" and the Youghiogheny River at Ohiopyle, Fayette County. A single teneral adult female was taken on 3 May 1899, at "the Ohio River," two adult males at Ohiopyle on 25 June 1900 and a single adult female at Ohiopyle on 28 June 1900. Since that time, water quality in both rivers has been degraded by various pollutants, or there have been changes in their physical characteristics, that have been detrimental to *Gomphus viridifrons* and other organisms. The Youghiogheny River at Ohiopyle continues to receive acid mine drainage from the Casselman River upstream. Although water quality has fluctuated somewhat during the last 10 years, the long-term conditions necessary for the survival of organisms like *G. viridifrons* will require elimination of the sources of pollution. If and when this is done, there is a very real possibility that *G. viridifrons* could once again be a member of the Pennsylvania fauna.

SELECTED REFERENCES:

BEATTY, A. F., and G. H. BEATTY. 1971. The distribution of Pennsylvania Odonata. Proc. Pennsylvania Acad. Sci., 45: 147–167.
BEATTY, A. F., G. H. BEATTY, and H. B. WHITE, III. 1969. Seasonal distribution of Pennsylvania Odonata. Proc. Pennsylvania Acad. Sci., 43:119–126.
BEATTY, G. H., and A. F. BEATTY. 1968. Check list and bibliography of Pennsylvania Odonata. Proc. Pennsylvania Acad. Sci., 42:120–129.
WALKER, E. M. 1958. The Odonata of Canada and Alaska. Univ. Toronto Press, Toronto, 2:1–318.

PREPARED BY: Clark Shiffer, *Pennsylvania Fish Commission, Robinson Lane, Bellefonte, PA 16823.*

Extirpated

LINED CLUBTAIL
Gomphus lineatifrons Calvert
Family Gomphidae
Order Odonata

This species, the second largest of the subgenus *Gomphurus*, was described by Calvert (1921). Two females, collected at Weaver, Perry County, on 17 June 1917, were named as allotype and paratype specimens, respectively, thus making Weaver a type locality for the species. No other adult or larval specimens of *G. lineatifrons* are known from Pennsylvania, although the species is recorded from the adjacent states of New York, Ohio, Virginia, and West Virginia.

The small village of Weaver was situated along Little Juniata Creek, approximately five miles from its junction with the Susquehanna River at Duncannon. Water quality in the creek remains good, although it is more forested and narrower than streams in other states where *G. lineatifrons* has been collected.

SELECTED REFERENCES:

BEATTY, A. F., and G. H. BEATTY. 1971. The distribution of Pennsylvania Odonata. Proc. Pennsylvania Acad. Sci., 45: 147–167.
BEATTY, A. F., G. H. BEATTY, and H. B. WHITE, III. 1969. Seasonal distribution of Pennsylvania Odonata. Proc. Pennsylvania Acad. Sci., 43:119–126.
BEATTY, G. H., and A. F. BEATTY. 1968. Check list and bibliography of Pennsylvania Odonata. Proc. Pennsylvania Acad. Sci., 42:120–129.
CALVERT, P. P. 1921. *Gomphus dilatatus, vastus,* and a new species, *lineatifrons.* Trans. Amer. Entomol. Soc., 47:221–232.

Male, Lined Clubtail (*Gomphus lineatifrons*). Photograph by C. N. Shiffer.

Female, Lined Clubtail (*Gomphus lineatifrons*). Photograph by C. N. Shiffer.

WESTFALL, M. J., JR. 1974. A critical study of *Gomphus modestus* Needham, 1942, with notes on related species (Anisoptera: *Gomphidae*). Odonatologica, 3:63–73.

PREPARED BY: Clark Shiffer, *Pennsylvania Fish Commission, Robinson Lane, Bellefonte, PA 16823.*

Extirpated

WIDE-TAILED CLUBTAIL
Gomphus ventricosus Walsh
Family Gomphidae
Order Odonata

This species, one of the smallest of the subgenus *Gomphurus,* is not common anywhere in its range from eastern Canada, south to Tennessee and west to Wisconsin and Minnesota. Pennsylvania records encompass a period from late May to mid-July and date back about 65 to 70 years. Less than a dozen adult specimens were collected, most from along the Susquehanna River at Dauphin or Inglenook, both of which are in Dauphin County. One adult female was taken at York in York County, collection date unknown.

Although the Susquehanna River at these locations has been the recipient of various pollutants over the years, at present the water quality is considered to be good.

SELECTED REFERENCES:

BEATTY, A. F., and G. H. BEATTY. 1971. The distribution of Pennsylvania Odonata. Proc. Pennsylvania Acad. Sci., 45: 147–167.
BEATTY, G. H., and A. F. BEATTY. 1968. Check list and bibliography of Pennsylvania Odonata. Proc. Pennsylvania Acad. Sci., 42:120–129.
NEEDHAM, J. G., and M. J. WESTFALL, JR. 1955. A manual of the dragonflies of North America (Anisoptera). Univ. California Press, Berkeley and Los Angeles, 615 pp.
WALKER, E. M. 1958. The Odonata of Canada and Alaska. Univ. Toronto Press, Toronto, 2:1–318.

PREPARED BY: Clark Shiffer, *Pennsylvania Fish Commission, Robinson Lane, Bellefonte, PA 16823.*

Extirpated

RIVER CLUBTAIL
Gomphus amnicola (Walsh)
Family Gomphidae
Order Odonata

This species, smallest of the subgenus *Stylurus,* is characterized by the triradiate yellow markings on the otherwise nearly black front of the thorax. Although recorded from Quebec, Canada, south to Louisiana, and west to Kansas, Nebraska, Iowa, Minnesota, and Wisconsin, the species is not common. *G. amnicola* is known in Pennsylvania only from seven specimens collected in Dauphin and Perry counties in June and July. All records date back about 65 to 70 years. Like *Gomphus ventricosus, G. amnicola* was an inhabitant of the Susquehanna River not far from Harrisburg.

SELECTED REFERENCES:

BEATTY, A. F., and G. H. BEATTY. 1971. The distribution of Pennsylvania Odonata. Proc. Pennsylvania Acad. Sci., 45: 147–167.
BEATTY, G. H., and A. F. BEATTY. 1968. Check list and bibliography of Pennsylvania Odonata. Proc. Pennsylvania Acad. Sci., 42:120–129.
WALKER, E. M. 1958. The Odonata of Canada and Alaska. Univ. Toronto Press, Toronto, 2:1–318.

PREPARED BY: Clark Shiffer, *Pennsylvania Fish Commission, Robinson Lane, Bellefonte, PA 16823.*

Extirpated

MARKED CLUBTAIL
Gomphus notatus Rambur
Family Gomphidae
Order Odonata

Another member of the subgenus *Stylurus,* the marked clubtail is historically recorded from Manitoba, Ontario, and Quebec, Canada and in the U.S., from New York, south to Alabama and Georgia, and west to Michigan and Wisconsin. This species is known in Pennsylvania only from a single male adult collected 6 August 1921, at Wall, Allegheny County. Wall is situated close to Turtle Creek, a tributary of the Monongahela River, both of which received acid mine drainage and other pollutants for many years.

SELECTED REFERENCES:

BEATTY, A. F., and G. H. BEATTY. 1971. The distribution of Pennsylvania Odonata. Proc. Pennsylvania Acad. Sci., 45: 147–167.
BEATTY, G. H., and A. F. BEATTY. 1968. Check list and bibliography of Pennsylvania Odonata. Proc. Pennsylvania Acad. Sci., 42:120–129.
WALKER, E. M. 1958. The Odonata of Canada and Alaska. Univ. Toronto Press, Toronto, 2:1–318.

PREPARED BY: Clark Shiffer, *Pennsylvania Fish Commission, Robinson Lane, Bellefonte, PA 16823.*

Extirpated

OBLIQUE CLUBTAIL
Gomphus plagiatus Selys
Family Gomphidae
Order Odonata

This member of the subgenus *Stylurus* is widely distributed from Ontario, Canada, south to Florida and Texas, and north to Iowa and Michigan, but is uncommon in the north. Pennsylvania records consist of seven specimens collected in July and August in Philadelphia and Delaware counties as early as 1805. Urbanization in the southeastern corner of Pennsylvania and the progressive deterioration of various habitats has been responsible for the demise of *G. plagiatus* and other species which once occurred there.

SELECTED REFERENCES:

BEATTY, A. F., and G. H. BEATTY. 1971. The distribution of Pennsylvania Odonata. Proc. Pennsylvania Acad. Sci., 45: 147–167.
BEATTY, A. F., G. H. BEATTY, and H. B. WHITE, III. 1969. Seasonal distribution of Pennsylvania Odonata. Proc. Pennsylvania Acad. Sci., 43:119–126.
BEATTY, G. H., and A. F. BEATTY. 1968. Check list and bibliography of Pennsylvania Odonata. Proc. Pennsylvania Acad. Sci., 42:120–129.
WALKER, E. M. 1958. The Odonata of Canada and Alaska. Univ. Toronto Press, Toronto, 2:1–318.

PREPARED BY: Clark Shiffer, Pennsylvania Fish Commission, Robinson Lane, Bellefonte, PA 16823.

Extirpated

ALLEGHENY RIVER SKIMMER
Macromia alleghaniensis Williamson
Family Macromiidae
Order Odonata

This member of a genus of swift-flying, green-eyed dragonflies was originally described from specimens collected at Ohiopyle, Fayette County, thus making Ohiopyle the type locality for the species. Seven specimens from the type locality were collected in June 1900 and September 1901. The species is otherwise known in Pennsylvania from a reared larva taken in Bucks County about 30 years ago. Although known from Alabama, Florida, Georgia, Kentucky, Maryland, New Jersey, North Carolina, Ohio, Pennsylvania, Tennessee, and Virginia, *M. alleghaniensis* is relatively abundant in the north only in the New Jersey Pine Barrens. The southeastern Penn-

sylvania specimen may have been the product of oviposition by a stray female.

The present unsuitability of the Youghiogheny River at Ohiopyle as habitat for various aquatic organisms has already been noted in the account of *Gomphus viridifrons.* The optimistic comment concerning the possible future occurrence of *G. viridifrons* at Ohiopyle would also apply in the case of *M. alleghaniensis.*

SELECTED REFERENCES:

BEATTY, A. E., and G. H. BEATTY. 1971. The distribution of Pennsylvania Odonata. Proc. Pennsylvania Acad. Sci., 45: 147–167.
BEATTY, G. H., and A. F. BEATTY. 1968. Check list and bibliography of Pennsylvania Odonata. Proc. Pennsylvania Acad. Sci., 42:120–129.
BEATTY, G. H., A. F. BEATTY, and H. B. WHITE, III. 1969. Seasonal distribution of Pennsylvania Odonata. Proc. Pennsylvania Acad. Sci., 43:119–126.
WILLIAMSON, E. B. 1909. The North American dragonflies of the genus *Macromia.* Proc. U.S. Nat. Mus., 37:369–398.

PREPARED BY: Clark Shiffer, Pennsylvania Fish Commission, Robinson Lane, Bellefonte, PA 16823.

Extirpated

DOTTED SKIPPER
Hesperia attalus (Edwards)
Family Hesperiidae
Order Lepidoptera

The dotted skipper is a medium skipper in which the male has a long narrow black "sex brand" on the dorsal surface of the forewing. The hind wing below is orange with a series of white dots. This species is similar to the more widespread Leonard's skipper (*Hesperia leonardus*). Reliable identification can only be made by a qualified lepidopterist.

This species occurs from Massachusetts west to Wisconsin and Nebraska, thence south to Florida, the Gulf Coast, and Texas. In Pennsylvania, it has been found only in Delaware County. No specimens have been taken since 1966 and the species is probably extirpated. Its habitat is wet meadows, primarily on coastal plain.

The dotted skipper, unlike its relative the Leonard's skipper, has two adult flights annually (June, August). Development of the autumnal brood is direct, but first instar larvae leading to the following late spring brood probably hibernate. The host plants are grasses, most likely *Andropogon* species. The adults are low fliers, and utilize thistles as a primary nectar source.

ACKNOWLEDGMENTS: Recommendations were made by W. F. Boscoe, A. M. Shapiro, and T. Williams.

SELECTED REFERENCES:

KLOTS, A. B. 1951. A field guide to the butterflies of North America, east of the Great Plains. Houghton Mifflin Co., Boston, 349 pp.
SHAPIRO, A. M. 1966. Butterflies of the Delaware Valley. Amer. Ent. Soc., Spec. Publ., vi + 79 pp.

PREPARED BY: Paul A. Opler, *U.S. Fish and Wildlife Service, Editorial Office, Room 259 Aylesworth Hall, Colorado State University, Fort Collins, CO 80523.*

Extirpated

AROGOS SKIPPER
Atrytone agrogos Boisduval and LeConte
Family Hesperiidae
Order Lepidoptera

OTHER NAME: Iowa skipper.

This is a small (2.6–2.8 cm wing span) orange and black skipper. In the male, the dorsal surfaces of the wings are orange rimmed with black. Below the wings are orange with the hind wings having the veins lined with paler orange.

The Arogos skipper has two groups of populations, one extending along the Atlantic coastal plain form New Jersey to Florida and another in the central plains. It occurs primarily in grassy fields in sandy regions or on serpentine barrens. In Pennsylvania, it is known from only two sites in Bucks County. This skipper has not been observed for more than 15 years and is probably extirpated.

The Arogos skipper has two adult flights each year. The adults visit thistle flowers for nectar, and the caterpillars feed on various grasses, especially *Andropogon*. The species may depend on fire to renew its habitat. Habitat protection and management may be necessary, if new populations are located.

ACKNOWLEDGMENTS: The following provided status recommendations or comments: R. W. Boscoe, W. F. Boscoe, F. D. Fee, A. M. Shapiro, and T. S. Williams.

SELECTED REFERENCES:

HEITZMAN, J. R. 1966. The life history of *Atrytone agrogos* (Hesperiidae). J. Lepid. Soc., 20:177–181.
SHAPIRO, A. M. 1966. Butterflies of the Delaware Valley. Amer. Ent. Soc., Spec. Publ., vi + 79 pp.

PREPARED BY: Paul A. Opler, *U.S. Fish and Wildlife Service, Editorial Office, Room 259 Aylesworth Hall, Colorado State University, Fort Collins, CO 80523.*

Extirpated

KARNER BLUE BUTTERFLY
Lycaeides melissa samuelis
Family Lycaenidae
Order Lepidoptera

This is a small butterfly, 23 mm in wingspan. The adults are gray white below with scattered black spots. There is a marginal band of metallic spots on the ventral hindwing. Above, the males are deep blue with a black marginal line on all wings, while the female is a warm brown with orange margins. Similar species are the spring azure (*Celastrina ladon*) and the eastern tailed blue (*Everes comyntas*).

This butterfly ranges from southern New Hampshire and New York west to eastern Iowa and southern Wisconsin. The species has disappeared from many localities where it once occurred. In Pennsylvania, it is definitely known to have occurred only at White Mills, Wayne County, but it has not been found there since around the turn of the century. The butterfly is believed to be extirpated in the Commonwealth.

This butterfly is a denizen of pine-oak sand barrens and plains. Within these areas its colonies are found in open areas where its host plant lupine (*Lupinus perennis*) thrives. Because suitable habitats depend on periodic disturbance, usually fire, the species is of necessity an excellent colonizer, at least on a local scale.

SELECTED REFERENCES:

DIRIG, R., and J. F. CRYAN. 1975. Endangered pine bush Lepidoptera. Privately published, Albany, New York, 12 pp.
HOWE, W. H. 1975. The butterflies of North America. Doubleday Co., New York, xiii +633 pp.
PERKINS, P. D. 1980. North American insect status review. Unpublished Contract Report to U.S. Fish and Wildlife Service, Department of Entomology, Smithsonian Institution, Washington, D.C.

PREPARED BY: Paul A. Opler, *U.S. Fish and*

Wildlife Service, Editorial Office, Room 259 Aylesworth Hall, Colorado State University, Fort Collins, CO 80523.

Extirpated

CHESTNUT CASE-BEARER MOTH
Coleophora leucochrysella Clemens
Family Coleophoridae
Order Lepidoptera

The adult chestnut case-bearer moth is 14 to 15 mm in wing span. The wings are unmarked white. The species is best identified by its case. The species was originally described from Pennsylvania, probably Easton, Northampton County. According to Forbes (1923), the moth was common wherever the host, American chestnut (*Castanea dentata*), was found.

The chestnut case-bearer moth feeds only on the leaves of American chestnut. The young larva mines chestnut leaves, while the older stages make a pistol-shaped case within which they live. The case is attached to host leaves and the larva inserts its head within the leaf tissue to feed. There is one generation each year, the adults emerging in June, with larval stages feeding during summer and fall.

The moth has not been reported for several decades. It may have become extinct, coincident with the decimation of its plant host, American chestnut, by blight.

SELECTED REFERENCES:

BUSCK, A. 1903. Notes on Brackenridge Clemens' types of Tineina. Proc. Washington Ent. Soc., 5:181–235.
CLEMENS, V. 1863. American micro-lepidoptera. Proc. Ent. Soc. Philadelphia, 2:4–22.
FORBES, W. T. M. 1923. The Lepidoptera of New York and neighboring states. Mem. Cornell Univ. Agr. Expt. Sta., 68:1–729.

PREPARED BY: Paul A. Opler, U.S. Fish and Wildlife Service, Editorial Office, Room 259 Aylesworth Hall, Colorado State University, Fort Collins, CO 80523.

Extirpated

AMERICAN CHESTNUT CLEARWING MOTH
Synanthedon castaneae (Busck)
Family Sesiidae
Order Lepidoptera

This is a wasp-like moth with black body with small amounts of yellow. It has transparent wings, except for black margins and veining, and is virtually identical to the ubiquitous lesser peach clearwing moth (*Synanthedon pictipes*).

This species formerly occurred from Orange and Suffolk counties, New York, south to South Carolina. It probably occurred throughout the Appalachian range of American Chestnut (*Castanea dentata*). The American chestnut clearwing moth bored into bruised trunk tissue of the American chestnut. In Pennsylvania, it was known from Centre, Cumberland, Dauphin and Luzerne counties, but probably occurred throughout the Commonwealth wherever the American chestnut grew. This moth had a single adult flight each year from late May to early July. The only known host was the American chestnut (Englehardt, 1946). The larvae overwintered in their burrows until spring.

This moth has not been found anywhere in its range since 1936. The last Pennsylvania records were in 1917. If individuals of this species can be located, they might be useful in transferring the attenuated strain of "Chestnut Blight" (Opler, 1978).

SELECTED REFERENCES:

ENGLEHARDT, G. P. 1946. The North American clear-wing moths of the family Aegeriidae. Bull. U.S. Nat. Mus., 190:1–222.
OPLER, P. A. 1978. Insects of American chestnut: possible importance and conservation concern. Pp. 83–85, *in* Proc. American Chestnut Symp. (W. MacDonald, ed.), West Virginia Univ., Morgantown, vi + 122 pp.

PREPARED BY: Paul A. Opler, U.S. Fish and Wildlife Service, Editorial Office, Room 259 Aylesworth Hall, Colorado State University, Fort Collins, CO 80523.

Extirpated

YPONOMEUTID MOTH
Swammerdamia castaneae Busck
Family Yponomeutidae
Order Lepidoptera

This is a small moth (12 mm wing span) with cream white head and thorax and violet gray forewings. This small moth was known from Connecticut, Kentucky, New Hampshire, and Pennsylvania. It may have occurred more widely through the range of American chestnut, because its primary habitat was deciduous forests that included the American chestnut as one element. The caterpillar fed in an open web on top of American chestnut (*Castanea dentata*) leaves during early July. The caterpillar formed a white spindle-shaped web, and the adult emerged in August.

This moth has not been seen for several decades and may be extinct. Living individuals should be sought in remnant stands of American chestnut during July. The moth may occur on Allegheny chinkapin (*Castanea pumila*) and this potential host should be surveyed as well.

SELECTED REFERENCES:

BUSCK, A. 1914. Descriptions of new microlepidoptera of forest trees. Proc. Ent. Soc. Washington 16:143–163.

DUCKWORTH, W. D. 1965. North American moths of the genus *Swammerdamia* (Lepidoptera: Yponomeutidae). Proc. U.S. Nat. Mus. 116:549–555.

FORBES, W. T. M. 1923. The Lepidoptera of New York and neighboring states. Mem. Cornell Univ., Agric. Expt. Sta., 68:1–729.

PREPARED BY: Paul A. Opler, *U.S. Fish and Wildlife Service, Editorial Office, Room 259 Aylesworth Hall, Colorado State University, Fort Collins, CO 80523.*

Extirpated

WHITE AND ORANGE DAGGER
Acronicta albarufa (Grote)
Family Noctuidae
Order Lepidoptera

OTHER NAME: Apatela albarufa.

This moth varies from 30 to 35 mm in wing expanse. The thorax and forewing are a glossy bluegray. The markings are very similar to *Acronicta ovata,* and the moths should be identified by specialists.

Originally, the range of this moth extended from Ontario and Massachusetts south to Georgia and west to Manitoba, Colorado and New Mexico. In Pennsylvania, there are records from Beaver and Wayne counties (Tietz, 1952). In the Northeast, the preferred habitat is sand barrens with stands of bear oak (*Quercus ilicifolia*). The adults have a single annual flight from late May to July. In 1982, Schweitzer raised adults from caterpillars found on bear oak at Plymouth, Massachusetts.

During this century, this moth has declined or disappeared in Pennsylvania, New York, New England, and the New Jersey Pine Barrens. Within the Northeast since 1965, it has been located only at Plymouth, Massachusetts, and southern New Jersey. The cause of this long-term decline is not obvious.

SELECTED REFERENCES:

FORBES, W. T. M. 1954. Lepidoptera of New York and neighboring states. Part III. Noctuidae. Mem. Cornell Univ. Agr. Expt. Sta., 329:1–433.

TIETZ, H. M. 1952. The Lepidoptera of Pennsylvania, a manual. Pennsylvania State College Agric. Exper. Sta., State College, xii + 194 pp.

PREPARED BY: Dale F. Schweitzer, *Museum of Comparative Zoology, Harvard University, Cambridge, MA 02138.*

Extirpated

AMERICAN BURYING BEETLE
Nicrophorus americanus (Olivier)
Family Silphidae
Order Coleoptera

OTHER NAMES: Sexton beetle or carrion beetle.

The largest carrion beetle in North America, with adults measuring from 25–40 mm in total length. The terminal segments of the antennae are club-like and red. The pronotum has a red disc, distinguishing this from other species of *Nicrophorus*. The elytra are short, exposing the terminal three abdominal segments. The thorax has golden hairs; the abdomen brown hairs.

The species appears to have formerly been widespread throughout forested portions of the eastern United States (east of the 100th meridian). The beetle has become increasingly rare in collections since 1920. Only two specimens are known to have been collected in the U.S. since 1960. This decrease appears to have taken place throughout the range of the species. Major North American museum collections contain only 11 specimens of the beetle from Pennsylvania. It has been recorded from Philadelphia, Philadelphia County, Pittsburgh, Allegheny County, "Angora" (county unknown), and from Erie, Lancaster County.

This beetle probably has only a single annual generation. In related species of *Nicrophorus*, overwintered adult beetles search for the carcasses of small vertebrates in the spring. Male-male and female-female fighting may occur at a carcass. One male-female pair excavates a burrow under the partially buried carcass, and forms a ball of carrion on which the female lays the eggs. After the eggs hatch, the female feeds the larvae by regurgitation. Larvae are unable to reach the adult stage without maternal care. The male may aid in feeding larvae to a lesser extent. It has been suggested that *Nicrophorus americanus* utilizes principally fish or reptile carrion for its food supply, but this is not definitely known. The species has been collected from April to September.

The decline of *Nicrophorus americanus* in the United States is indicated by its decreasing representation in collections, despite increasing collecting effort for Coleoptera in later years. The most recent collection dates include a 1974 record for Kentucky; 1972 near Harrow, Ontario, Canada; 1971 for a Tennessee location; 1966 for Columbia, Missouri; and a 1965 record for Hovey Lake, Indiana. Efforts by coleopterists to locate populations of the beetle in the last few years have failed. Dr. Louis J. Milne of the University of New Hampshire has made particular efforts to locate a population of this beetle without success.

ACKNOWLEDGMENTS: The following persons have contributed information on *Nicrophorus americanus*: Dr. Louis J. Milne of the University of New Hampshire; Mr. Robert Anderson and Dr. Stewart Peck of Carleton University, Ottawa, Canada; and Mr. Roy Latham, of Orient, New York.

SELECTED REFERENCES:

MADGE, R. B. 1958. A taxonomic study of the genus *Nicrophorus* in America north of Mexico (Coleoptera, Silphidae). Master's thesis, Department of Entomology, Univ. Illinois, Urbana.

PERKINS, P. D. 1980. North American insect status review. Final report of research study conducted by Department of Entomology of Smithsonian Institution under contract 14-16-0009-79-052 to Office of Endangered Species of U.S. Fish and Wildlife Service, Department of Interior.

PREPARED BY: Michael M. Bentzien, *U.S. Fish and Wildlife Service, 2747 Art Museum Drive, Jacksonville, FL 32207.*

CHAPTER 3
FISHES

Blue Sucker (*Cycleptus elongatus*). Photograph supplied by National Fisheries Center, U.S. Fish and Wildlife Service, Kearneyville, WV 25430.

CHAPTER 3—FISHES

edited by

EDWIN L. COOPER
Department of Biology
The Pennsylvania State University
University Park, PA 16802

Table of Contents

INTRODUCTION

Some of the earliest ichthyologists to work in North America, such as Cope, Baird, Lesueur, and Fowler, have contributed to our understanding of the original distribution of fishes in Pennsylvania. Yet it was not until the recent period from 1960 to 1980, that a detailed account of fish distribution in the Commonwealth was available. The present compilation is based on extensive recent collections by personnel of the U.S. Fish and Wildlife Service, the Pennsylvania Fish Commission, and The Pennsylvania State University. It is thought to be complete in comparison with the scattered reports and specimens of the earlier collectors.

Status of Vulnerability

Of the 182 species reliably reported from Commonwealth waters over the years, 120 remain as thriving populations under no recognized threat to their existence; 28 species have been extirpated, and 27 are either vulnerable or their population status is undetermined. Based on the judgment of Clark N. Shiffer, Endangered Species Coordinator for the Pennsylvania Fish Commission, and his Advisory Committee on Fishes, only three species are considered as threatened, and an additional four species are listed as endangered in Pennsylvania waters. Of these latter two groups, only the shortnose sturgeon is on the federal endangered list, and the status of the eastern sand darter is considered as threatened in North America.

There are several possible additions or deletions to these categories for Pennsylvania. The silver lamprey has never been reported as a spawning population, but it is likely that feeding adults are present in Lake Erie. The mosquitofish has been occasionally introduced in the Philadelphia area but there is no evidence of continued survival of these populations. The pink salmon has been reported at various sites in Lake Erie, but no voucher specimens are available, and two specimens reputed to be pink salmon were misidentified. There are old reports of the river carpsucker and the highfin carpsucker from the Beaver River and elsewhere in the Ohio drainage; most of these were re-identified as the quillback, but one specimen has been identified by Carter R. Gilbert as a juvenile of either the river carpsucker or the highfin carpsucker.

Finally, in a very early collection of fishes from the Monongahela River, the slenderhead darter was reported as common. Two specimens of this darter from this collection have been identified by Reeve M. Bailey as the newly recognized sharpnose darter. It is thus likely that the slenderhead darter has never been taken in Pennsylvania.

Exotics

There are very few exotic species remaining as reproducing populations in Pennsylvania, compared with the large number of native forms. The common carp and the goldfish are so widespread and successful that, despite their undesirability, they are likely to be permanent species in our fauna. The brown trout and, to a lesser extent, the rainbow trout spawn successfully and are a valuable part of sport fishery management.

Several other species have been introduced for management purposes with variable success. The kokanee (landlocked sockeye) is present in at least one lake; coho and chinook salmon are stocked as an important sport fishery in Lake Erie. Atlantic salmon are stocked occasionally as fish become available. Many other species such as the redear sunfish, striped bass, threadfin shad, alewife, and the Amur pike have been introduced for management purposes, but there is little evidence so far that these populations will spread and become permanent additions to our fauna.

Losses to Native Fauna

Of the 28 species believed to be extirpated from our fauna, 10 were large river forms in the Ohio River drainage. Many of these, such as the shovelnose sturgeon, the paddlefish, the skipjack herring, the blue sucker, and the blue catfish remain as viable species in the Mississippi drainage. It is unlikely that these will reinvade Pennsylvania waters due to the large number of lock-and-dam installations that curtail movement. However, the reappearance of sauger, smallmouth buffalo, and spotted bass in Pennsylvania portions of the Ohio River in recent years helps to confirm the idea that water quality there is improving.

Lake Erie has also suffered loss of several species that probably will not return—the longjaw cisco, the lake herring, the lake whitefish, the mooneye, and the blue pike. The presumed extirpation of the spoonhead sculpin and the deepwater sculpin from Lake Erie may be an artifact of inadequate collecting in the deep, cold waters of the central basin.

Another group of species has probably been permanently lost to the fauna in the small coastal plain of southeastern Pennsylvania due to pollution, industrial development, and loss of marsh habitat. Species such as the ironcolor shiner, pirate perch, mud sunfish, blackbanded sunfish, and swamp darter are highly dependent on a clear, weedy, low-gradient habitat that has been almost completely obliterated in this area.

The apparent extirpation of the black bullhead, previously reported in Pennsylvania is an enigma that is difficult to understand when compared with the reported abundance of the black bullhead in Ohio. It is admittedly difficult to separate this species from the brown bullhead, but no validated specimens of the black bullhead have been found in Pennsylvania since 1938.

Recent Additions to Native Fauna

There are only a few species that have been added to previous lists of fishes recorded from Pennsylvania. It is likely that these were present previously, but were discovered only as a result of more intensive collecting. Two specimens of the ghost shiner were identified from thousands of mimic shiners taken from the Monongahela River in 1978. A small population of the northern brook lamprey was discovered in Conneaut Creek, identified by both ammocoetes and spawning adults; this fills in a gap in the known distribution of this species in streams tributary to Lake Erie from Ohio east to New York.

The Potomac sculpin has been added to the list recently as a result of the recognition of this species as distinct from the mottled sculpin. Other species that were reported as very rare or possibly present have been found as a result of specific searches in likely localities. These include the Iowa darter, the channel darter, the blacknose shiner, and the redfin shiner. And, two specimens of the popeye shiner were recently discovered by Carter R. Gilbert in an 1853 collection from the Clarion River.

Freshwater Forms Versus Marine Forms

It has been difficult to draw lines between marine, estuarine, and freshwater forms that occur in the Delaware River or the Schuylkill River at some time in their life cycle. Sturgeons, anadromous shads, white perch, and striped bass are included here as freshwater forms along with the inland silversides. Other species which possibly could be listed include the hogchoker and the sheepshead minnow. Many other marine forms are usually not considered in the fauna of Pennsylvania although stragglers may be found occasionally in freshwater.

Edwin L. Cooper, *Department of Biology, The Pennsylvania State University, University Park, PA 16802.*

ACKNOWLEDGMENTS

Many persons have contributed to the species accounts which follow, and these are identified at the end of each account. In addition, there are a few individuals who have helped in the many field collections which have made this compilation possible. I would like to especially thank the following persons and their organizations for their encouragement and advice: Joseph A. Boccardy and John K. Andersen, of the U.S. Fish and Wildlife Service; Clark N. Shiffer of The Pennsylvania Fish Commission; and Charles C. Wagner, my research associate at The Pennsylvania State University.—Edwin L. Cooper, *Pennsylvania State University.*

SPECIES ACCOUNTS

Endangered

SHORTNOSE STURGEON
Acipenser brevirostrum Lesueur
Family Acipenseridae
Order Acipenseriformes

DESCRIPTION: A species of sturgeon that is distinguished from *A. oxyrhynchus,* with which it occurs sympatrically along the Atlantic Coast of the United States and extreme eastern Canada, in having a wider mouth (62 percent versus 55 percent of interorbital width); blackish (versus pale) viscera; a shorter and blunter snout; almost complete absence of postdorsal shields; preanal shields arranged in a single (versus a double) row; a pigmented (versus whitish) anal fin; and a slightly higher total gill raker count (22–29, mean 25.5 as compared to 17–27, mean 21.6). The most conspicuous difference between the two species, however, is in the pigmentation of the lateral scutes, which are much paler

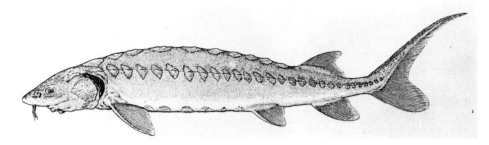

Shortnose Sturgeon (*Acipenser brevirostrum*). Figure from Vladykov and Greeley. Mem. Sears Found. Marine Res., 1:37, 1963.

than the background of the body in *A. brevirostrum,* but are the same shade as the background in *A. oxyrhynchus. A. brevirostrum* probably is the smallest species of *Acipenser,* the largest recorded specimen (a female from the Connecticut River) measuring 1,003 mm total length. The weight of this individual was not recorded, but probably was in excess of 4.5 kg, this calculation based on the weight of 3.9 kg for an 884 mm female.

RANGE: Confined to the western north Atlantic Ocean, where it ranges from southern New Brunswick (St. Johns River) to extreme northeastern Florida. Apparently not uncommon, historically, throughout range (largest populations believed to have occurred from Potomac to Connecticut rivers; Scott and Crossman (1973), but now widely extirpated from middle sections of Atlantic Coast. Only records between Maine and South Carolina within the past 30 years are from Hudson River (New York)

and Connecticut River (Massachusetts) (Gruchy and Parker, 1980), and the Delaware River, at Newbold Island, near Bordentown, New Jersey (four specimens collected in 1971; W. F. Smith-Vaniz, personal communication). Although the latter four specimens were actually taken on the New Jersey side of the river, this record is considered positive evidence of the continued presence of this species in Pennsylvania. Largest and most stable populations today are in the northern and southern parts of its range, from Massachusetts to New Brunswick (Scott and Crossman, 1973; Dadswell, 1975; McCleave et al., 1977; Taubert, 1980) and from South Carolina to Florida, respectively (Loyacano and Gilbert, 1979; Gilbert and Heidt, 1979). A detailed distribution map appears in Gruchy and Parker (1980). In Pennsylvania, the shortnose sturgeon apparently was once common in the Delaware River (the type locality; type specimen ANSP 16953) (Lesueur, 1818; Ryder, 1890; Fowler, 1906), and, as

SHORTNOSE STURGEON (*Acipenser brevirostrum*)

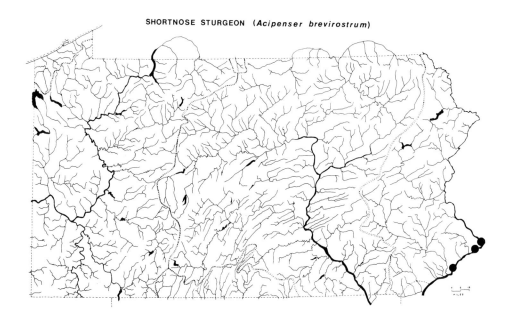

SHORTNOSE STURGEON
(*Acipenser brevirostrum*)

more rapid growth of the latter specimens once they enter the sea.

This species, as is true of all sturgeons, is a bottom feeder, and consumes bottom invertebrates of varying size, as well as plant material intermingled with mud.

SPECIALIZED OR UNIQUE CHARACTERISTICS: The most interesting aspect of *Acipenser brevirostrum,* as well as sturgeons in general, is its evolutionary position. Sturgeons are among the most primitive living fishes, with a fossil history that extends back at least 100 million years.

BASIS OF STATUS CLASSIFICATION: The shortnose sturgeon is classified as endangered in Pennsylvania, as is also the case nationally.

RECOMMENDATIONS: It seems obvious that extensive domestic and industrial pollution in the lower Delaware River during the past century has had a detrimental effect on this species. Whether or not the discovery of *A. brevirostrum* (in 1971) in the river represents re-establishment after a long absence or continued presence of a small residual population cannot be determined, because no monitoring program was carried out over the years. Success of this species can only be assured by continued efforts to maintain and improve water quality of the river.

indicated above, apparently still exists there in limited numbers. There appear to be no records of this species from the Susquehanna River drainage (Fowler, 1948; Vladykov and Greeley, 1963).

HABITAT: Acipenser brevirostrum occurs in the lower sections of large rivers and in coastal marine habitats (mostly estuaries) along the Atlantic coast (habitat type II-C-2). It may spend most of the year in brackish or completely saline estuarine situations, and move into fresh water only to spawn.

LIFE HISTORY AND ECOLOGY: The shortnose sturgeon spawns in rivers during early spring, and females with roe have been taken as late as 21 April. Males mature when only 508 mm total length; females mature at about 610 mm.

The early life history is unknown. Few small individuals have been recorded, the smallest individual known being about 185 mm total length. Age determination, based on otolith readings, show that *A. brevirostrum* is a slow-growing species; specimens from the Hudson River measuring nearly 430 mm total length were 4 years old, and a 890 mm individual from the same river was calculated to be 15 years of age. The early growth rates of *A. brevirostrum* and *A. oxyrhynchus* are very similar, and the difference in maximum size evidently results from

SELECTED REFERENCES:

DADSWELL, M. J. 1975. Biology of the shortnose sturgeon (*Acipenser brevirostrum*) in the St. John River estuary, in New Brunswick, Canada. Huntsman Marine Lab., St. Andrews, N.B., Canada, 67 pp.
FOWLER, H. W. 1906. The fishes of New Jersey. Ann. Rept. New Jersey State Mus. Pt. II:35–477.
———. 1948. A list of the fishes recorded from Pennsylvania. Bull. Pennsylvania Bd. Fish Commissioners, 7:3–26.
GILBERT, R. J., and A. R. HEIDT. 1979. Movements of shortnose sturgeons, *Acipenser brevirostrum* (Acipenseridae), in the Altamaha River, Georgia. ASB Bull., 26(2):35.
GRUCHY, C. G., and B. PARKER. 1980. *Acipenser brevirostrum* Lesueur, shortnose sturgeon. P. 38, *in* Atlas of North American freshwater fishes (D. S. Lee et al.), North Carolina State Mus. Nat. Hist., Raleigh, x + 854 pp.
LESUEUR, C. A. 1818. Description of several species of chondropterygious fishes of North America, with their varieties. Trans. Amer. Phil. Soc., n.s., 1:383–394.
LOYACANO, H. A., and C. R. GILBERT. 1979. Status report: Fishes. Pp. 68–72, *in* Proceedings of the first South Carolina endangered species symposium (D. M. Forsythe and W. B. Ezell, Jr., eds.), 201 pp.
MCCLEAVE, J. D., S. M. FRIED, and A. K. TOWT. 1977. Daily

movements of shortnose sturgeon, *Acipenser brevirostrum,* in a Maine estuary. Copeia, 1977:149–157.

RYDER, J. A. 1890. The sturgeon and sturgeon industries of the eastern coast of the United States, with an account of experiments bearing upon sturgeon culture. Bull. U.S. Fish Comm. (1888), 8:231–328.

SCOTT, W. B., and E. J. CROSSMAN. 1973. Freshwater fishes of Canada. Bull. Fish. Res. Bd. Canada, 184:xi + 1–966.

TAUBERT, B. D. 1980. Reproduction of shortnose sturgeon (*Acipenser brevirostrum*) in Holyoke Pool, Connecticut River, Massachusetts. Copeia, 1980:114–117.

VLADYKOV, V. D., and J. R. GREELEY. 1963. Order Acipenseroidei. Pp. 24–60, *in* Fishes of the western North Atlantic, Mem. Sears Found. Mar. Res., 1(3):vi–xxi + 1–630.

PREPARED BY: Carter R. Gilbert, *Florida State Museum, University of Florida, Gainesville, FL 32611.*

Endangered

LAKE STURGEON
Acipenser fulvescens Rafinesque
Family Acipenseridae
Order Acipenseriformes

OTHER NAMES: Freshwater sturgeon, rock sturgeon, red sturgeon.

DESCRIPTION: Adult lake sturgeon are pentagonal in cross section, generally 0.9 to 1.5 m in length with weights up to 36 kg. Males are usually smaller than females. There are five rows of pointed bony plates (one dorsal, two lateral, two ventral), which gradually become worn with age, along the length of the body. It has a protrusible mouth posterior to the eyes preceded by four barbels. Teeth, branchiostegal rays, and opercula are absent. This sturgeon has a large simple gas bladder, rectum with spiral valve, and numerous pyloric caeca. It differs from the shortnose sturgeon by having 33 short, blunt gill rakers (range 25 to 40) and the mouth width more than 62 percent of the interorbital width. The lake sturgeon differs from the shovelnose sturgeon in having a spiracle and an incompletely mailed caudal peduncle. Adult lake sturgeon are olive brown to gray on the sides and back, with a white belly. The peritoneum is clear to lightly speckled. Young lake sturgeon less than 300 mm in length have two large black spots on the upper surface of the snout which disappear with age. There are many smaller black spots on the body.

RANGE: Saskatchewan River in Alberta and Saskatchewan east to southern Quebec, south along the Appalachian mountains through western Pennsylvania, and the Mississippi River Valley to northern Alabama and Mississippi. North through the midwest, all of the Great Lakes, eastern Nebraska, and the eastern part of the Dakotas. Vladykov and Greeley (1963) indicate that it may be found in Labrador. Historical records for Pennsylvania include the Ohio River Basin in Allegheny, Clarion, Indiana, and Warren counties and Lake Erie in Erie County.

HABITAT: It generally inhabits quiet water of large rivers and lakes with rock, pebble, or sand bottom. Less often found where bottom is mud. A sea-res-

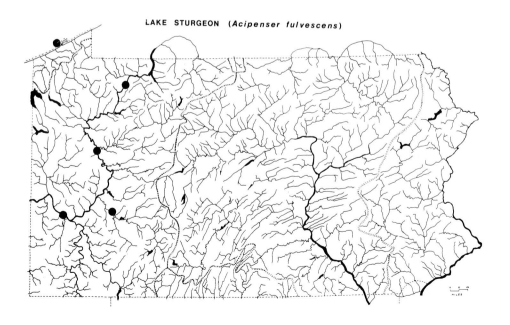

LAKE STURGEON (*Acipenser fulvescens*)

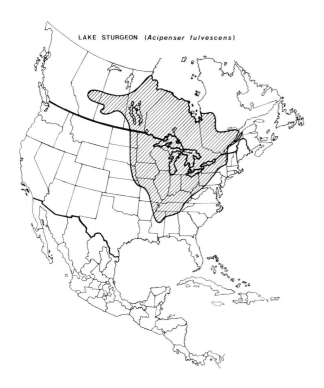

LAKE STURGEON (Acipenser fulvescens)

idence stage has not been found although lake sturgeon do inhabit brackish water.

LIFE HISTORY AND ECOLOGY: Spawning extends from early May to late June, at an optimum water temperature between 13 and 18°C. Males migrate to the spawning grounds before the females, as early as ice-out. Spawning sites are sandy or rocky areas of rivers in swift water or rapids at 0.6 to 5 m depth. Spawning has been reported in wave action over rocky ledges and off rocky islands. Females in spawning condition may produce up to 885,000 eggs (extrapolation based on body weight indicates a maximum of 3 million) although not all eggs are shed at one time. Spawning probably occurs over a few days. Eggs are adhesive and are laid indiscriminately, adhering to bottom debris. There is no nest construction or parental care. Ripe eggs are black, 2.7–3.5 mm in diameter, and hatch in 5–8 days at 15.6–17.8°C. The larvae are 8 mm total length and have a large yolk sac that is utilized for 9 to 18 days. Feeding begins at about 16 days at which time the young resemble the adults. Early growth is rapid; the young may reach 123 mm total length during September of their first year. Sexual maturity is attained at an average of 18 years. Females spawn at intervals of 4 to 6 years and males at intervals of 2 to 3 years.

Using cross sections of pectoral rays for age determination, lake sturgeon in the Lake Winnebago region of Wisconsin reached 13 kg in 20 years and 35 kg in 40 years. Females can live 25 years longer than males, and the greatest age is reached in slower-growing, northern populations. The oldest lake sturgeon from the Lake Winnebago region was 82 years old. A 94 kg specimen from Lake of the Woods was 154 years old. Larger sturgeon have been reported— 106 kg from Lake of the Woods, Ontario in 1965; 141 kg, apparently the largest on record, from Batchewana Bay, Lake Superior in 1922. The lake sturgeon is a bottom feeder, consuming crayfish, clams, snails, invertebrates, insect larvae, and some plants. Only a small proportion of its diet is fish eggs. Mussels, clams, and snails are important foods in Ohio Rivers. Tendepedid larvae are important in Lake Winnebago and mayflies and aquatic sow bugs in small lakes. Feeding ceases during the spawning period.

SPECIALIZED OR UNIQUE CHARACTERISTICS: The slow growth rate and lengthy maturation period of lake sturgeon are important in view of management practices. Spawning intervals of more than 2 years create conditions that require special regulations.

BASIS OF STATUS CLASSIFICATION: The lake sturgeon catch in Lake Erie was 5 million pounds in 1885, but had declined to one million pounds in 1895. A similar decline occurred in Lake of the Woods, which at one time provided 20 percent of the total landings. In recent years, total landings have declined from 194,638 pounds (1961) to 85,723 pounds (1966). There is no recent record of lake sturgeon in Pennsylvania. It was listed as threatened by Deacon et al. (1979) over its range in North America.

RECOMMENDATIONS: Overfishing in the late 1880's combined with modification of spawning habitat by dams, pollution, and siltation have undoubtedly reduced the lake sturgeon population. Strict adherence to fishing regulations and continued improvement of aquatic habitats is needed to insure future successful spawning.

SELECTED REFERENCES:

DEACON, J. E., G. KOBETICH, J. D. WILLIAMS, and S. CONTRERAS. 1979. Fishes of North America, endangered, threatened, or of special concern. Fisheries, 4:29–44.

FOWLER, H. W. 1940. A list of fishes recorded from Pennsylvania. Pp. 59–78, *in* Biennial Rept. Pennsylvania Bd. Fish Comm., 129 pp.

HARKNESS, W. J. K., and J. R. DYMOND. 1961. The lake sturgeon. The history of its fishery and problems of conservation. Ontario Dept. Lands and Forests, Fish and Wildl. Branch, 121 pp.

PROBST, R. T., and E. L. COOPER. 1955. Age, growth, and production of the lake sturgeon (*Acipenser fulvescens*) in the Lake Winnebago region, Wisconsin. Trans. Amer. Fish. Soc., 84:207–227.

ROUSSOW, G. 1957. Some considerations concerning spawning periodicity. J. Fish. Res. Bd. Canada, 14:553–572.

TRAUTMAN, M. B. 1957. The fishes of Ohio with illustrated keys. Ohio State Univ. Press, Columbus, v–xvii + 683 pp.

VLADYKOV, V. D., and J. R. GREELEY. 1963. Order Acipenseroidei. Pp. 24–60, *in* Fishes of the western North Atlantic, Mem. Sears Found. Marine Res., 1(3):vi–xxi + 1–630.

PREPARED BY: John E. Cooper, *Rt. 2, Box 241A, Greenville, NC 27834.*

Endangered

GHOST SHINER
Notropis buchanani Meek
Family Cyprinidae
Order Cypriniformes

OTHER NAMES: Once considered a subspecies of the mimic shiner, *Notropis volucellus.*

DESCRIPTION: This shiner is a small, yellowish-colored minnow with silvery sides and very little pigmentation, seldom exceeding 50 mm. The body is rather deep and slab-sided. The ghost shiner is

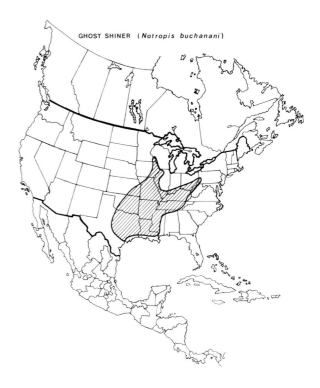

GHOST SHINER (*Notropis buchanani*)

very similar morphologically to the mimic shiner, but lacks the sensory canal and pores beneath the eye. It has no special breeding coloration, but males develop small pearl organs on head and body.

RANGE: The ghost shiner is restricted to the Mississippi River drainage and Gulf Coast tributaries in Texas. It was not reported in Pennsylvania prior

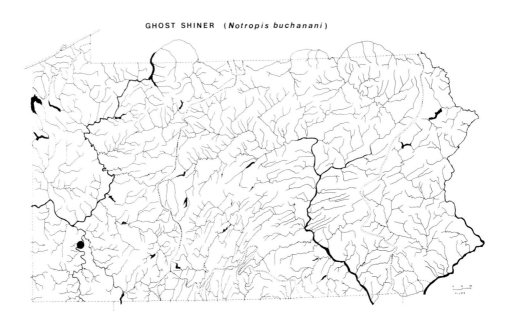

GHOST SHINER (*Notropis buchanani*)

to the capture of two specimens from the Monongahela River near Elizabeth in the spring of 1978.

HABITAT: It usually occurs in schools in midwater, associated with other shiners. It is found in large sluggish streams, occupying the quiet backwaters with clear water and little current.

LIFE HISTORY AND ECOLOGY: This species has not been studied extensively because it is seldom abundant at any locality. Its life history is therefore imperfectly known. Spawning occurs in the spring over sluggish riffles of sand or fine gravel, but there is no nest building or parental care. The food habits have not been studied, but presumably the ghost shiner eats small invertebrates as do similar small shiners. It is often sympatric with the mimic shiner and is frequently mistaken as young for that species. It is rather curious that the ghost shiner has been collected over a wide geographic area but seldom abundant enough to offer a chance for detailed study.

BASIS OF STATUS CLASSIFICATION: The apparent rarity of this species in Pennsylvania may be an artifact in that no intensive sampling has been conducted in its prime habitat, the quiet backwaters of the Ohio River drainage. Until this can be done, it seems advisable to list the species as endangered.

RECOMMENDATIONS: No effort has been made to protect this species since its presence has only recently been established. More information is necessary before definitive recommendations are advisable.

SELECTED REFERENCES:

BAILEY, R. M. 1951. A check list of the fishes of Iowa with keys for identification. Pp. 187–238, *in* Iowa Fish and Fishing, Iowa State Cons. Comm., Ames, 238 pp.

CLAY, W. M. 1975. The fishes of Kentucky. Kentucky Dept. Fish and Wildl. Resources, Frankfort, 416 pp.

MEEK, S. E. 1895. A list of fishes and mollusks collected in Arkansas and Indian Territory in 1894. Bull. U.S. Fish Comm., 15:341–349.

PFLIEGER, W. L. 1975. The fishes of Missouri. Missouri Dept. Conserv., Western Publ. Co., Jefferson City, 343 pp.

RENO, H. W. 1966. The infraorbital canal, its lateral-line ossicles and neuromasts, in the minnows *Notropis volucellus* and *N. buchanani.* Copeia, 1966:403–413.

PREPARED BY: Edwin L. Cooper, *The Pennsylvania State University, University Park, PA 16802.*

Endangered

SMALLMOUTH BUFFALO
Ictiobus bubalus (Rafinesque)
Family Catostomidae
Order Cypriniformes

OTHER NAMES: Razor-backed buffalo, quillback buffalo; *Amblodon bubalus.*

DESCRIPTION: This is a dark-colored sucker with a deep, slab-sided body and large scales. The dorsal fin has a long base, and the anterior rays are somewhat elongated but not as extreme as the quillback. The mouth is smaller than in other buffalofishes and nearly horizontal. Adults commonly reach 750 mm in length and occasionally weigh as much as 18 kg.

RANGE: The smallmouth buffalo is widely distributed throughout the Mississippi River drainage and Gulf Coast tributaries west of Alabama. In Pennsylvania, it was reported in 1820 as common in the Ohio River as far as Pittsburgh, but was not reported in recent years from these waters until the collection of one specimen in the Monongahela River in 1978.

Smallmouth Buffalo (*Ictiobus bubalus*). Photograph by E. L. Cooper.

SMALLMOUTH BUFFALO (*Ictiobus bubalus*)

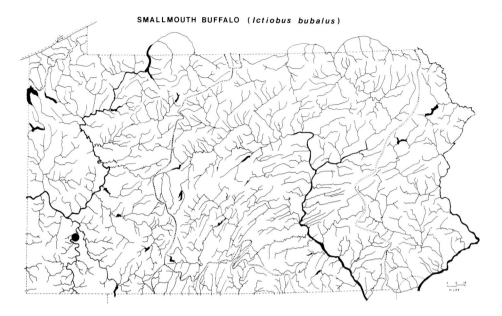

HABITAT: The smallmouth buffalo has a preference for large, deep, flowing rivers with less turbidity than for other buffalofishes. It is also found in lakes and sloughs connected to large river systems. With continued improvement in water quality of the upper Ohio River drainage, it is expected that this species will expand its range and increase in abundance in the large rivers of western Pennsylvania.

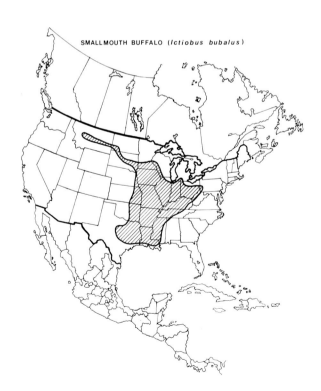

SMALLMOUTH BUFFALO (*Ictiobus bubalus*)

LIFE HISTORY AND ECOLOGY: The smallmouth buffalo has been an important commercial fish in the Mississippi River drainage and offers some recreation for spear-fishermen. In reservoirs it spawns on shoals in the spring, but no spawning observations have been reported in streams. It has been observed apparently feeding on gravelly riffles of streams. Detailed food studies indicate that it is versatile in items of food consumed ranging from a large variety of insects, algae, and aquatic plants in rivers to a concentration on zooplankton in large reservoirs. It is a long-lived fish, reaching at least an age of 13 years.

BASIS OF STATUS CLASSIFICATION: Because of its recent upstream occurrence in the headwaters of the Ohio River after a long period of absence from Pennsylvania waters, it appears advisable to consider this species as endangered. With continued improvement in water quality of large river systems, the smallmouth buffalo should increase its range and abundance.

RECOMMENDATION: No additional special regulations are considered necessary at the present time until more information is obtained on its occurrence in Pennsylvania waters.

SELECTED REFERENCES:

FORBES, S. A., and R. E. RICHARDSON. 1920. The fishes of Illinois. Illinois Nat. Hist. Surv., Urbana, 357 pp.
MCCOMISH, T. S. 1967. Food habits of bigmouth and small-

mouth buffalo in Lewis and Clark Lake and the Missouri River. Trans. Amer. Fish. Soc., 96:70–74.

PFLIEGER, W. L. 1975. The fishes of Missouri. Missouri Dept. Conserv., Western Publ. Co., Jefferson City, 343 pp.

RAFINESQUE, C. S. 1819. Prodrome de 70 nouveaux genres d'animaux decoverts dans l'interieur des Etats-Unis d'Amerique durant l'annee 1818. J. Physique, Paris, 88:417–429.

———. 1820. Ichthyologia Ohiensis, or natural history of the fishes inhabiting the River Ohio and its tributary streams, preceded by a physical description of the Ohio and its branches. Publ. for author by W. G. Hunt, Lexington, Kentucky, 90 pp.

PREPARED BY: Edwin L. Cooper, *The Pennsylvania State University, University Park, PA 16802.*

Threatened

NORTHERN BROOK LAMPREY

Ichthyomyzon fossor Reighard and Cummins
Family Petromyzontidae
Order Petromyzontiformes

OTHER NAMES: Michigan brook lamprey, brook lamprey; *Ichthyomyzon (Reighardina) unicolor.*

DESCRIPTION: This is a small, non-parasitic lamprey which seldom exceeds a length of 150 mm. The buccal funnel is small; when expanded it is not wider than the rest of the head. Teeth in the buccal disc are small and blunt, and are occasionally missing. The anal fin is well developed, particularly in the female.

RANGE: This species is found throughout the Great Lakes and Upper Mississippi River drainages from Quebec west to Minnesota and south to Missouri and Kentucky. Recent collections in one small stream in Pennsylvania indicate a scattered distribution along the southern tributaries of Lake Erie from New York to Ohio. It was not reported from Pennsylvania prior to 1968 and is apparently restricted to a small headwater portion of Conneaut Creek in Crawford County.

HABITAT: The larval stages (ammocoetes) are most common in slow current of headwater streams. Most of their time is spent in U-shaped burrows in bottom material of silt and sand. After metamorphosis, sexually mature adults spawn on riffles, chiefly among or beneath stones from 75 to 150 mm in diameter. Spawning nests are ill-defined, little more than small areas where sand or pebbles have been cleared away from under stones. Experiments indicate that a preference for weak light determines the burrowing habitat for spawning.

LIFE HISTORY AND ECOLOGY: The northern brook lamprey is thought to be the non-parasitic form derived from the parasitic silver lamprey, *Ichthyomyzon unicuspis.* Eggs are deposited in a gravel redd in moderate current with no parental care after spawning. Larval forms spend 3 or 4 years in a U-shaped burrow in the bottom growing to a size somewhat exceeding the adult size. After a rest-

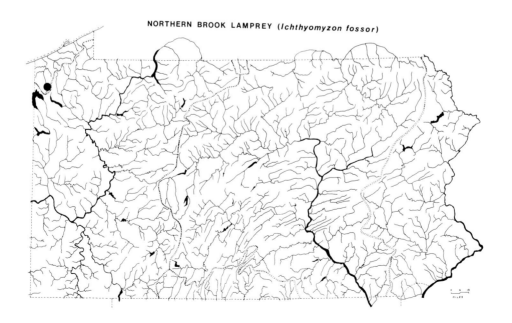

NORTHERN BROOK LAMPREY (*Ichthyomyzon fossor*)

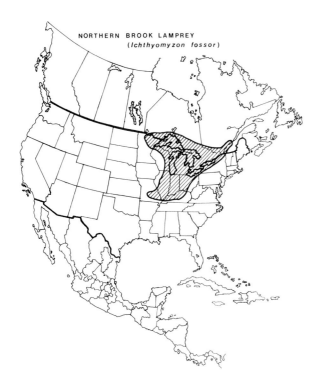

NORTHERN BROOK LAMPREY
(Ichthyomyzon fossor)

RECOMMENDATIONS: No protection measures are considered necessary at the present time. In the event of loss of this restricted habitat, it might be possible to introduce this species into similar habitats from existing populations outside Pennsylvania.

SELECTED REFERENCES:

CHURCHILL, W. S. 1947. The brook lamprey in the Brule River. Trans. Wisconsin Acad. Sci. Arts Ltrs., 37:337–346.

HUBBS, C. L., and M. B. TRAUTMAN. 1937. A revision of the lamprey genus *Ichthyomyzon*. Misc. Publ. Mus. Zool., Univ. Michigan, 35:1–110.

OKKELBERG, P. 1922. Notes on the life-history of the brook lamprey, *Ichthyomyzon unicolor*. Occas. Papers Mus. Zool., Univ. Michigan, 125:1–14.

REIGHARD, J., and H. CUMMINS. 1916. Description of a new species of lamprey of the genus *Ichthyomyzon*. Occas. Papers Mus. Zool., Univ. Michigan, 31:1–12.

VLADYKOV, V. D. 1949. Quebec lampreys. I. List of species and their economical importance. Contr. Quebec Dept. Fisheries, 26:1–67.

PREPARED BY: Edwin L. Cooper, *The Pennsylvania State University, University Park, PA 16802.*

ing period, during which the ammocoete transforms into the sexually mature form, the adults move to the nearest suitable riffle, spawn, and die. There is no active feeding during the adult stage. Compared with other sympatric lamprey species, the northern brook lamprey seldom is found to be abundant.

BASIS OF STATUS CLASSIFICATION: This lamprey has a very restricted distribution in the headwaters of a single stream in Pennsylvania and is not abundant there. Populations are found at scattered localities throughout a wide range but apparently demand clean, gravelly, headwater tributaries most often found in glaciated areas. Populations have small home ranges and are vulnerable to localized disturbances of their restricted habitat.

Threatened

SILVER CHUB
Hybopsis storeriana (Kirtland)
Family Cyprinidae
Order Cypriniformes

OTHER NAMES: Storer's chub, lake minnow.

DESCRIPTION: The silver chub is a silvery minnow with no dark lateral stripe along mid-side of body; lowermost ray of caudal fin depigmented, in contrast to other parts of fin; a well-developed barbel nearly always present at posterior end of maxillary (that is, at corner of mouth); origin of dorsal fin in advance of insertion of pelvics, and notably closer

Silver Chub (*Hybopsis storeriana*). Photograph by E. L. Cooper.

SILVER CHUB (*Hybopsis storeriana*)

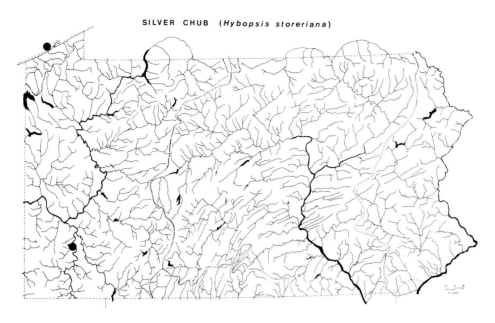

to tip of snout than base of caudal fin; mouth included (that is, "underslung") and nearly horizontal; body moderately stout; eye moderately large, about 1.5 to 1.75 times in snout length; snout fairly long, but rather blunt; lateral line complete and nearly straight; pharyngeal teeth 1,4–4,1; anal rays usually 8; lateral-line scales 38–41. Maximum total length 231 mm.

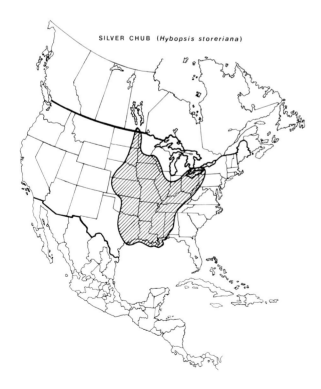

SILVER CHUB (*Hybopsis storeriana*)

RANGE: The silver chub is distributed in the Mobile Bay basin west to Mississippi River, with semidisjunct population in Brazos River, Texas. It is also present north throughout most of Mississippi basin, except for upper half of Missouri River drainage, and in upper (that is, southern) sections of Red River of North drainage in Minnesota, North Dakota, and southern Manitoba. In Great Lakes basin, this minnow is found only in Lake Erie and its largest tributaries. A detailed distribution map appears in Gilbert (1980).

In Pennsylvania, *Hybopsis storeriana* was once present in the Ohio River drainage, but has not been recorded since before 1900. It may have been common in Lake Erie, although ecological deterioration there during the past 25 years may have resulted in a recent decline in abundance. The only confirmed records of this species from the Commonwealth are by Evermann and Bollman (1886), who stated that it was "abundant" in the Monongahela River, at Monongahela City; and a recent (1971) collection from Lake Erie, near the mouth of Walnut Creek (specimen in Pennsylvania State University collection). Inasmuch as surveys of sections of the upper Ohio River drainage during the past 40 years (Raney, 1938; Hendricks et al., 1979) have failed to reveal this species, it is now presumed to be extirpated from this part of the Commonwealth. Its decline in adjacent sections of the Ohio River, in Ohio, has been shown by Trautman (1957), who indicated that only one post-1900 record occurred above the mouth of the Muskingum River. The paucity of confirmed records from the Pennsylvania section of Lake Erie, however, may be due in large degree to lack of collecting effort (or rather to lack of effort to save museum specimens), at least prior to the 1950's. There are numerous records from adjacent areas in Ohio (Trautman, 1957), although it should be noted that the species has always attained its greatest abundance in the western half of the lake. It is possible that the silver chub now is indeed rare from the Pennsylvania section of the lake, considering the overall environmental deterioration that has occurred during the past 25 years.

HABITAT: The silver chub is typically a large-river species (usually occurring in streams over 30 m in width), and is usually found over a bottom of clean gravel and sand (habitat type II-C-2). Considering the extensive siltation that has occurred throughout the Ohio River since the turn of the century, it is not surprising that this species has disappeared from this area. Although rarely found in lakes, it is (or has been) common in Lake Erie, where it typically occurs in water from 1 to 20 m in depth. Scott and Crossman (1973), however, noted that the species was always absent from seine hauls (either day or night) of even 1.2 m depth, and all specimens caught in Canadian waters were taken in small-mesh gill nets.

LIFE HISTORY AND ECOLOGY: The study by Kinney (1954), on the Lake Erie population, is the most comprehensive work done on this species. His findings have been summarized by Scott and Crossman (1973). Spawning occurs mostly in June (possibly late May), although spawning behavior and place of spawning were not noted. Most reproduction occurs at temperatures above 21°C. Individuals rarely live longer than 3 years, and those that survive into the fourth year die soon after spawning. Young individuals consumed cladocerans, copepods, and chironomids, but the major food supplies of adults were mayflies of the genus *Hexagenia,* until these disappeared from the Lake Erie fauna; then a greater use was made of chironomids and *Gammarus.*

BASIS OF STATUS CLASSIFICATION: Although *Hybopsis storeriana* is probably extirpated from the Ohio River, in Pennsylvania, it presumably persists in Lake Erie, where it has survived the extreme environmental degradation that began during the mid-1950's. Although conditions in Lake Erie have begun to improve, the silver chub should presently be considered a threatened species.

RECOMMENDATIONS: Carefully monitor the presence of this species in Lake Erie, in order to determine trends in abundance. Also monitor for possible presence of residual populations in Ohio River and its largest tributaries. Because of the restriction of *Hybopsis storeriana* to large bodies of water, it appears that the protection and/or restoration of this type of habitat is the only feasible way of managing and perpetuating this species.

SELECTED REFERENCES:

EVERMANN, B. W., and C. H. BOLLMAN. 1886. Notes on a collection of fishes from the Monongahela River. Ann. New York Acad. Sci., 3:335–340.
GILBERT, C. R. 1980. *Hybopsis storeriana* (Kirtland), silver chub. P. 194, *in* Atlas of North American freshwater fishes (D. S. Lee et al.), North Carolina State Mus. Nat. Hist., Raleigh, x + 854 pp.
HENDRICKS, M. L., J. R. STAUFFER, JR., C. H. HOCUTT, and C. R. GILBERT. 1979. A preliminary checklist of the fishes of the Youghiogheny River. Nat. Hist. Misc., 203:1–15.
KINNEY, E. C., JR. 1954. A life history study of the silver chub, *Hybopsis storeriana* (Kirtland), in western Lake Erie with notes on associated species. Unpublished Ph.D. disser., Ohio State Univ., Columbus, 99 pp.
RANEY, E. C. 1938. The distribution of the fishes of the Ohio drainage basin of western Pennsylvania. Unpublished Ph.D. disser., Cornell Univ., Ithaca, New York, 102 pp.
SCOTT, W. B., and E. J. CROSSMAN. 1973. Freshwater fishes of Canada. Bull. Fish. Res. Bd. Canada, 184:1–966.
TRAUTMAN, M. B. 1957. The fishes of Ohio. Ohio St. Univ. Press, Columbus, v–xvii + 683 pp.

PREPARED BY: Carter R. Gilbert, *Florida State Museum, University of Florida, Gainesville, FL 32611.*

Threatened

EASTERN SAND DARTER
Ammocrypta pellucida (Putnam)
Family Percidae
Order Perciformes

OTHER NAMES: Etheostoma pellucidum Baird, *Pleurolepis pellucidus* Baird, *Vigil pellucidus* Baird.

DESCRIPTION: The specific name *pellucida* is derived from the Latin "pellucidus" which means clear or transparent and refers to the body color of the species. Young are somewhat white or silvery in color while adults, especially breeding males, are more yellow. Nine to 14 oblong, olive colored spots

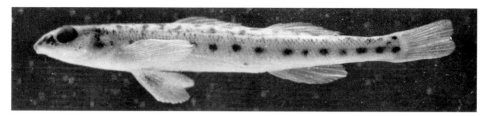

Eastern Sand Darter (*Ammocrypta pellucida*). Photograph by E. L. Cooper.

are present on the lateral line and 12 to 16 small olive spots are present on the midline of the dorsum. The body is very elongate, standard length is seven to ten times the body depth.

It is the only member of its genus found in Pennsylvania. It is distinguished from other Pennsylvania darters by the transparent color of its flesh.

RANGE: The eastern sand darter is distributed throughout most of the Ohio River basin from Pennsylvania to the Wabash River in the northern tributaries and to the Cumberland River in the southern tributaries. It is also present in Lake Erie, Lake St. Clair, and southern Lake Huron and their tributaries. A disjunct population is present in the St. Lawrence-Lake Champlain drainage near Montreal (Williams, 1975). The eastern sand darter has been reported from seven locations in Pennsylvania. It was first reported from Pennsylvania by Cope (1869) based on specimens from the Youghiogheny River. These specimens no longer exist and the Youghiogheny population has probably been extir-

pated due to severe acid mine pollution in the early twentieth century.

Evermann and Bollman (1886) reported on collections made in the Monongahela River in 1885 by C. H. Bollman. They listed *A. pellucida* as "common everywhere in suitable places." One specimen (Field Museum of Natural History 1095) collected by C. H. Bollman in the Monongahela River in Washington Co. is apparently the only *A. pellucida* specimen remaining from those collections.

There are five known collections of the eastern sand darter from Lake Erie in the vicinity of Erie. The most recent collection indicates that this species was still present in 1983 but it is threatened here.

Several collections of *A. pellucida* are known from two sites in French Creek near Venango and 2 mi west of Mill Village.

HABITAT: The eastern sand darter inhabits lakes and low gradient streams or rivers and is usually found in sandy substrates (Lachner et al., 1950; Langlois, 1954). This marked preference for sandy

EASTERN SAND DARTER (*Ammocrypta pellucida*)

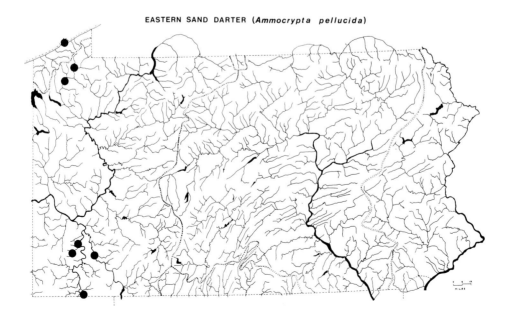

EASTERN SAND DARTER (*Ammocrypta pellucida*)

substrates is related to its habit of burying itself headfirst in the sand with only its eyes visible above the substrate. The adaptive value of this behavior may be concealment from predators or conservation of energy (Williams, 1975).

LIFE HISTORY AND ECOLOGY: Very little is known of the life history and ecology of the eastern sand darter. The primary food item of specimens from Illinois was midge larvae of the genus *Chironomus*. Midge larvae also comprised 90 percent of the stomach contents of specimens from Bass Island, Lake Erie (Turner, 1921).

Spawning takes place in the Ohio Basin from the first part of June through July while spawning in the Great Lakes and St. Lawrence River occurs 2 to 3 weeks later (Williams, 1975).

BASIS OF STATUS CLASSIFICATION: Currently, only two populations are known to exist in the state. A population still exists in the Pennsylvania waters of Lake Erie but only two specimens have been collected since 1907. A second population exists in French Creek but it has suffered declines as well.

RECOMMENDATIONS: An extensive distributional survey is necessary to determine the present distribution of the eastern sand darter in Pennsylvania. Because siltation is thought to be a major factor in the decline of this species, special attention should be focused on identifying and eliminating silt loads in areas where it is found.

SELECTED REFERENCES:

COPE, E. D. 1869. Synopsis of the cyprinidae of Pennsylvania. Trans. Amer. Phil. Soc., 13:351–399.
EVERMANN, B. W., and C. H. BOLLMAN. 1886. Notes on a collection of fishes from the Monongahela River. Ann. New York Acad. Sci., 3:335–340.
LACHNER, E. A., E. F. WESTLAKE, and P. S. HANDWERK. 1950. Studies on the biology of some percid fishes from western Pennsylvania. Amer. Midland Nat., 43:92–111.
LANGLOIS, T. H. 1954. The west end of Lake Erie and its ecology. J. W. Edwards, Inc., Ann Arbor, Michigan, 479 pp.
TURNER, C. L. 1921. Food of the common Ohio darters. Ohio J. Sci., 22:41–62.
WILLIAMS, J. D. 1975. Systematics of the percid fishes of the subgenus *Ammocrypta*, genus *Ammocrypta*, with descriptions of two new species. Bull. Alabama Mus. Nat. Hist., 1:1–56.

PREPARED BY: Michael L. Hendricks, *Lake Erie Research Unit, Fairview Fish Culture Station, P.O. Box 531, Fairview, PA 16415.*

Vulnerable

ATLANTIC STURGEON
Acipenser oxyrhynchus Mitchill
Family Acipenseridae
Order Acipenseriformes

OTHER NAMES: Sea sturgeon, common sturgeon, sharpnose sturgeon; *Acipenser sturio.*

DESCRIPTION: The Atlantic sturgeon is a large heavy-bodied fish with small caudal peduncle and heterocercal tail. Scales are absent from the body being replaced by five rows of hooked bony scutes. The head is long and tapering to an upturned snout; mouth inferior and protrusible. A large fish reaching a size of 3 m and a weight of 273 kg. The color is blue black on the back, grading to a white belly.

RANGE: The Atlantic sturgeon is distributed on the Atlantic Coast from Labrador to Florida, and runs into large rivers to spawn. It is replaced in the Gulf of Mexico as far west as Mississippi by a similar subspecies. In Pennsylvania, it is occasionally taken in the Delaware River, but seldom in abundance.

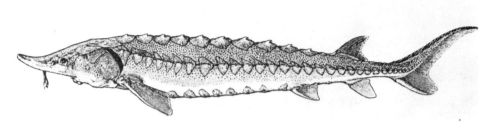

Atlantic Sturgeon (*Acipenser oxyrhynchus*). Figure from Vladykov and Greeley. Mem. Sears Found. Marine Res., 1:47, 1963.

HABITAT: The Atlantic sturgeon is anadromous, running from the sea into large rivers such as the Hudson River to spawn. The young may spend 3 to 4 years in freshwater before returning to the sea. Most adult fish spend most of their time in the estuary or nearby areas of the sea, but a few tagged fish wandered as far as 563 km from freshwater and were recaptured on Georges Bank in the North Atlantic Ocean. Judging from its diet, the sturgeon is a benthic form at all stages of its life history.

LIFE HISTORY AND ECOLOGY: Spawning occurs in freshwater, and in the Delaware River, where this occurs over a hard clay bottom when water temperatures reach 13°C in the spring. Because spawning occurs in deep channels, no actual spawning behavior has been observed. The adhesive, dark brown eggs can be recovered attached to vegetation or stones in fast current. The young gradually descend to the estuary or coastal marine waters, re-

turning as spawning females after at least 10 years growth and a minimum size of 68 kg. The Atlantic sturgeon reaches a size of 2.7 m and 159 kg in about 60 years.

The food of the sturgeon is a wide variety of bottom dwelling plant and animal materials. In freshwater, aquatic insects and invertebrates are common; in the ocean this often changes to molluscs, annelids, crustaceans, and small fishes.

The Atlantic Sturgeon is a good food fish and supports a small commercial fishery in many large estuaries such as those of the St. Lawrence and Hudson Rivers. The flesh is prized as a smoked fish and the eggs are sometimes processed into caviar. The fishery is small compared to the managed sturgeon populations of eastern Europe.

SPECIALIZED OR UNIQUE CHARACTERISTICS: Sturgeons grow slowly and mature at large sizes and advanced ages. For this reason, exploita-

ATLANTIC STURGEON (*Acipenser oxyrhynchus*)

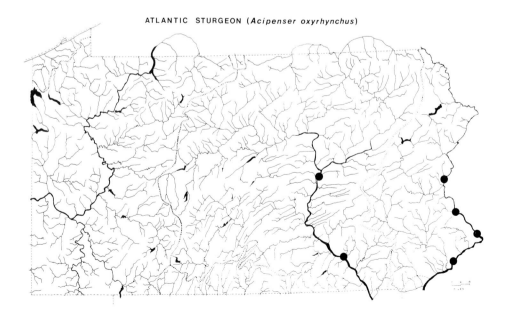

ATLANTIC STURGEON (*Acipenser oxyrhynchus*)

tion of immature fish is exceedingly detrimental to the population, and has resulted in commercial extirpation in local areas.

BASIS OF STATUS CLASSIFICATION: Atlantic sturgeon populations in the Delaware estuary have greatly declined in recent years, and may be nearly extirpated. A combination of overfishing and habitat deterioration may make it difficult to restore these populations to former levels of abundance.

SELECTED REFERENCES:

HALL, A. J. 1978. The Hudson: that river's alive. National Geographic, 153(1):62–88.
LEIM, A. H., and W. B. SCOTT. 1966. Fishes of the Atlantic Coast of Canada. Bull. Fish. Res. Bd. Canada, 155:1–485.
MITCHILL, S. L. 1815. Fishes of New York. Trans. Lit. Phil. Soc., New York, 1:355–492.
SCOTT, W. B., and E. J. CROSSMAN. 1973. Freshwater fishes of Canada. Bull. Fish. Res. Bd. Canada, 184:1–966.
VLADYKOV, V. D., and G. BEAULIEU. 1946. Etudes sur l'esturgeon (*Acipenser*) de la province de Quebec. Quebec Dept. Pecheries 18:1–62.
———, and J. R. GREELEY. 1963. Order Acipenseroidei. Pp. 24–60, *in* Fishes of the western North Atlantic, Mem. Sears Found. Marine Res., 1(3):vi–xxi + 1–630.

PREPARED BY: Edwin L. Cooper, *The Pennsylvania State University, University Park, PA 16802.*

Vulnerable

SPOTTED GAR
Lepisosteus oculatus (Winchell)
Family Lepisosteidae
Order Semionotiformes

OTHER NAMES: Shortnose gar, garpike, billfish; *Lepidosteus oculatus, Cylindrosteus oculatus, Lepisosteus productus.*

DESCRIPTION: The spotted gar is a very elongate fish, completely armored with tile-like scales. The head is long and the elongate jaws carry needle-like teeth. Dorsal and anal fins are located near the tail. The tail fin is rounded with upturned spinal axis. It is distinguished from longnose gar by shorter snout and prominent brown spots on snout and head. The spotted gar is the smallest of the gars, growing to a length of about 600 mm.

RANGE: The spotted gar ranges throughout most of the Mississippi River drainage and sparingly into the lower Great Lakes. In Pennsylvania, it is restricted to bays and sloughs of the Presque Isle peninsula of Lake Erie. It is not common and rarely seen or distinguished from the longnose gar.

HABITAT: Throughout its range, the spotted gar is most abundant in warm, shallow, weedy bays or sloughs away from the main current. Along the Gulf Coast it is frequently found in brackish water.

LIFE HISTORY AND ECOLOGY: Spawning occurs in the spring in quiet bays filled with aquatic vegetation, or over cleaned beds of gravel in shallow streams. Their food, even as young, is mainly fish, but in brackish water large numbers of shrimp and crabs occur in the diet along with many kinds of fish. All of the gars, including this species, are considered as undesirable by fish managers, presumably because of their predation on young sport fishes and consequently are seldom protected by fishing regulations. Virtually nothing is known about the dynamics of gar populations despite much effort to eradicate these species.

UNIQUE CHARACTERISTICS: The few species of extant gars in North America with their ganoid scales and heavily vascularized swim bladder are relicts of an ancient order of fishes which evolved millions of years ago. They are known as fossils dating from the Jurassic period.

SPOTTED GAR (*Lepisosteus oculatus*)

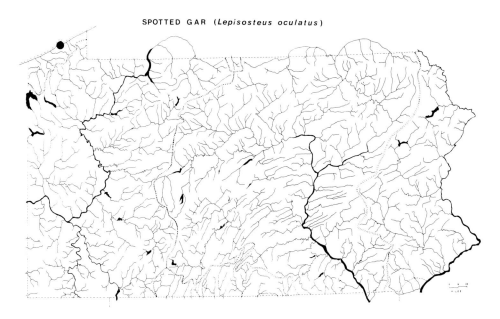

BASIS OF STATUS CLASSIFICATION: This species is considered as vulnerable because of the limited habitat found along the Presque Isle area of Lake Erie. No attempts have been made to transplant this species to similar habitats outside its normal range. Because of its presumed reputation as an undesirable predator, it is not likely that measures to protect this species would be favored by fish managers.

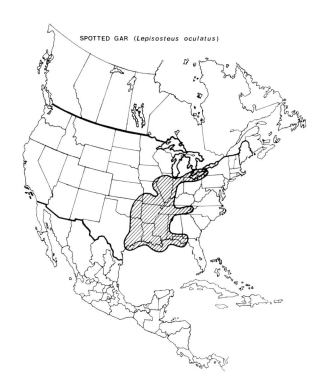

SPOTTED GAR (*Lepisosteus oculatus*)

SELECTED REFERENCES:

BONHAM, K. 1941. Food of gars in Texas. Trans. Amer. Fish. Soc., 70:356–362.

GOODYEAR, C. P. 1967. Feeding habits of three species of gars, *Lepisosteus,* along the Mississippi Gulf Coast. Trans. Amer. Fish. Soc., 96:297–300.

SCOTT, W. B., and E. J. CROSSMAN. 1973. Freshwater fishes of Canada. Bull. Fish. Res. Bd. Canada, 184:1–966.

SUTTKUS, R. D. 1963. Order Lepisostei. Pp. 61–88, *in* Fishes of the western North Atlantic, Mem. Sears Found. Mar. Res., 1(3):vi–xxi + 1–630.

WINCHELL, A. 1864. Description of a garpike, supposed to be new—*Lepidosteus* (*Cylindrosteus*) *oculatus.* Proc. Acad. Nat. Sci. Philadelphia, 16:183–185.

PREPARED BY: Edwin L. Cooper, *The Pennsylvania State University, University Park, PA 16802.*

Vulnerable

LAKE TROUT
Salvelinus namaycush (Walbaum)
Family Salmonidae
Order Salmoniformes

OTHER NAMES: Togue, Grey trout, Mackinaw trout; *Salmo namaycush, Cristivomer namaycush.*

DESCRIPTION: The largest of the chars, reported in excess of 45 kg, the lake trout has a typical trout or salmon body shape with small scales. It lacks the red spots on the body, and the tail is more forked, than the similar brook trout. It differs from all of

LAKE TROUT (*Salvelinus namaycush*)

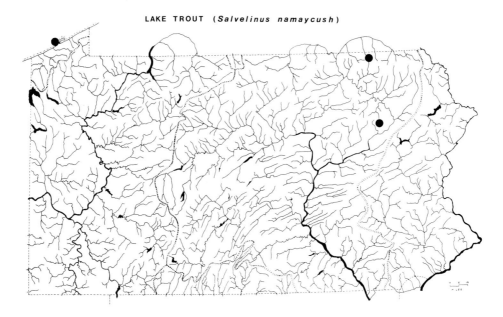

the Pacific salmon, and the black-spotted trouts in having teeth restricted to the head of the vomer.

RANGE: The lake trout is widely distributed throughout northern North America, coinciding with the limits of glaciation. It reaches its southern limit in New York and Michigan in the east and in Idaho and Montana in the west. It has been introduced

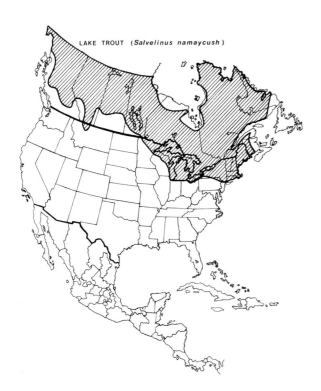

LAKE TROUT (*Salvelinus namaycush*)

elsewhere. In Pennsylvania it was native only to Lake Erie and in Silver Lake, Susquehanna County.

HABITAT: The lake trout is recognized as a cold-water benthic species in oligotrophic lakes. In the far north, it occasionally occurs in large rivers, but is less tolerant than the Arctic char in these waters.

LIFE HISTORY AND ECOLOGY: The lake trout is an autumn spawner in lakes on rocky shoals in deep water, but some populations run into large tributary streams to spawn at night. It grows more slowly than other chars, but, because of its extreme longevity, reaches a large size. Adult lake trout eat mostly fish, but will feed on many other organisms including plankton and benthos as available. The lake trout is seldom considered as good a sport fish as other salmonids, but it has been a favorite species in the Great Lakes commercial fishery for many years because of its excellent eating qualities. A hybrid with the brook trout, known as the splake, has been used in some management programs with good results.

BASIS OF STATUS CLASSIFICATION: In Pennsylvania, the restricted occurrence of oligotrophic lakes means that lake trout populations will never be widespread, and these habitats are continually threatened by cultural eutrophication.

RECOMMENDATIONS: To safeguard native or introduced populations of lake trout, deep, cold-water lakes must be protected from excessive fertilization and indiscriminate use of pesticides that threaten early life history stages.

SELECTED REFERENCES:

CLEMENS, W. A., J. R. DYMOND, N. K. BIGELOW, F. B. ADAMSTONE, and W. J. K. HARKNESS. 1923. The food of Lake Nipigon fishes. Publ. Ontario Fish. Res. Lab., 16:171–188.

ESCHMEYER, P. H. 1955. The reproduction of lake trout in southern Lake Superior. Trans. Amer. Fish. Soc., 84:47–74.

GREELEY, J. R. 1936. Fishes of the area with annotated list. Pp. 45–88, in A biological survey of the Delaware and Susquehanna watersheds, Suppl. to 25th Ann. Rept. (1935), New York Conserv. Dept. Biol. Surv., 10:1–356.

KENNEDY, W. A. 1954. Growth, maturity and mortality in the relatively unexploited lake trout, Cristivomer namaycush, of Great Slave Lake. J. Fish. Res. Bd. Canada, 11:827–852.

LOFTUS, K. H. 1958. Studies on river-spawning populations of lake trout in eastern Lake Superior. Trans. Amer. Fish. Soc., 87:259–277.

MARTIN, N. V. 1966. The significance of food habits in the biology, exploitation, and management of Algonquin Park, Ontario lake trout. Trans. Amer. Fish. Soc., 95:415–422.

———, and N. S. BALDWIN. 1960. Observations on the life history of the hybrid between eastern brook trout and lake trout in Algonquin Park, Ontario. J. Fish. Res. Bd. Canada, 17:541–551.

McCRIMMON, H. R. 1958. Observations on the spawning of lake trout, Salvelinus namaycush, and the post-spawning movement of adult trout in Lake Simcoe. Canadian Fish Culturist, 23:3–11.

SCOTT, W. B., and E. J. CROSSMAN. 1973. Freshwater fishes of Canada. Bull. Fish. Res. Bd. Canada, 184:1–966.

PREPARED BY: Edwin L. Cooper, *The Pennsylvania State University, University Park, PA 16802.*

Vulnerable
GRAVEL CHUB
Hybopsis x-punctata Hubbs and Crowe
Family Cyprinidae
Order Cypriniformes

OTHER NAMES: Spotted chub.

DESCRIPTION: The gravel chub is a slender, terete minnow with a long snout and an underslung, horizontal mouth with a well-defined barbel at each corner (that is, at tip of maxillary); color silvery on sides and belly (olive green dorsally), with sides of body having small, irregularly-spaced x-shaped markings; no intensification of pigment on fins; origin of dorsal fin slightly in advance of insertion of pelvic fins; pharyngeal teeth 4–4; anal rays 7; lateral-line scales 38–45. The maximum size is usually about 80 mm standard length (largest known specimen 89 mm).

RANGE: The gravel chub has a wide but spotty distribution from south-central Arkansas north to southeastern Minnesota and east to southern Ontario (Thames River system), southwestern New York, and northwestern Pennsylvania. It is apparently absent from areas south of Ohio River, and extirpated from Ontario and from many other localities where formerly found. In Pennsylvania, all known locality records (the most recent in 1971) are from the Allegheny River proper or from the lowermost part of French Creek, in Venango and War-

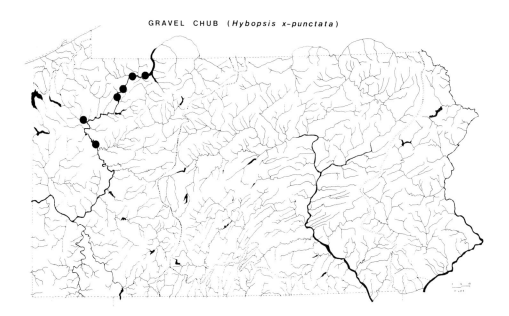

GRAVEL CHUB (*Hybopsis x-punctata*)

GRAVEL CHUB (*Hybopsis x-punctata*)

ren counties. A detailed distribution map appears in Gilbert (1980).

HABITAT: As its vernacular name implies, *Hybopsis x-punctata* is closely restricted to a fine sand-gravel (occasionally rocky) substrate with no vegetation, in areas of moderate flow (usually riffles) in clear to moderately turbid waters of large creeks and rivers (habitat types II-B-2 and II-C-2). Water depth usually is from 0.3 to 1.2 m in these areas. Trautman (1957), discussing Ohio populations, indicated that rocky areas are occupied when the preferred substrate becomes covered by silt.

LIFE HISTORY AND ECOLOGY: Nothing is known regarding the life history of this species. Trautman (1957) observed feeding competition between the gravel chub and the closely related spotted chub (*Hybopsis dissimilis*). He also noted that *H. x-punctata* seems to prefer slightly deeper, more slowly flowing waters in comparison with the other species.

SPECIALIZED OR UNIQUE CHARACTERISTICS: Hybopsis x-punctata is one of only a few species that is highly specific to a gravel substrate. Other Pennsylvania species so restricted ecologically are the popeye shiner (*Notropis ariommus*) and

Tippecanoe darter (*Etheostoma tippecanoe*). Since this type of habitat is more susceptible to siltation than most, it is not surprising that all three species are sporadically distributed throughout their ranges. Apparently *H. x-punctata* is somewhat more adaptable to change than the other two (particularly *H. ariommus*), at least in Pennsylvania, judging from its somewhat wider distribution in the state.

BASIS OF STATUS CLASSIFICATION: All Pennsylvania records for the gravel chub are from the main channel of the Allegheny River or from the lowermost part of a main tributary (French Creek). Dam construction or unrestricted pollution in this area would probably eliminate the species from the state, hence the basis of its "vulnerable" classification.

RECOMMENDATIONS: Strict pollution controls, intelligent farming practices, and restrictions on further dam building on the Allegheny River would probably assure the continued existence of this species in Pennsylvania.

SELECTED REFERENCES:

GILBERT, C. R. 1980. *Hybopsis x-punctata* Hubbs and Crowe, Gravel chub. P. 196, *in* Atlas of North American freshwater fishes (D. S. Lee et al.), North Carolina State Mus. Nat. Hist., Raleigh, x + 854 pp.

TRAUTMAN, M. B. 1957. The fishes of Ohio. Ohio State Univ. Press, Columbus, v–xvii + 683 pp.

PREPARED BY: Carter R. Gilbert, *Florida State Museum, University of Florida, Gainesville, FL 32611.*

Vulnerable

BRIDLE SHINER
Notropis bifrenatus (Cope)
Family: Cyprinidae
Order: Cypriniformes

OTHER NAMES: Bridled shiner, bridled minnow; *Hybopsis bifrenatus, Notropis cayuga, Notropis kendalli.*

DESCRIPTION: The bridle shiner is a small, slender minnow, less than 50 mm in standard length. Outside the breeding season, both sexes are straw-colored on the upper sides and silvery white below, with an intense black lateral band extending from the base of the tail forward to the tip of the snout,

Bridle Shiner (*Notropis bifrenatus*). Photograph by E. L. Cooper.

but not onto the chin. The fins are transparent. In breeding season, the sides of the male become yellow below the black lateral band. The unpaired fins become yellow in both sexes. The male develops minute tubercles on the pectoral fins and head. The lateral line is typically incomplete, though it may become complete or nearly so in large individuals. There are usually 7 anal rays and 0, 4–4, 0 pharyngeal teeth.

Among northeastern shiners in its range, the presence of the dark lateral band, dark snout, pale chin, 7 anal rays, and the incomplete lateral line are diagnostic. The large, pointed anal and dorsal fins, the large eyes, and the regularly arranged, almost hexagonal predorsal scales are also useful characters.

RANGE: From the upper St. Lawrence and southern Maine south and west to Lake Ontario and south to the Neuse drainage in North Carolina, including eastern Long Island, upper Delmarva Peninsula, and the upper Susquehanna drainage in New York (Harrington, 1947*a*; Jenkins and Zorach, 1970). It is rare or local south of the Potomac and in some northern parts of its range.

In Pennsylvania, its historic range is the Delaware River and tributaries from Brodhead Creek south, and the lower Susquehanna drainage in York and Lancaster counties. There is one upper Susquehanna record, from Buffalo Creek at Lewisburg (ANSP 80518). The bridle shiner was described from Pennsylvania, from "near the mouth of a stream which flows into the Schuylkill River at Conshohocken" (Cope, 1869).

HABITAT: The bridle shiner occurs in shallow, clear, slow-moving, or still water with moderate or abun-

BRIDLE SHINER (*Notropris bifrenatus*)

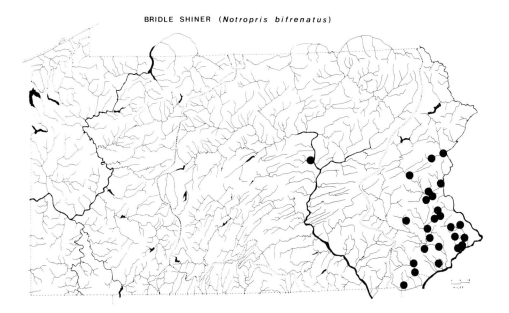

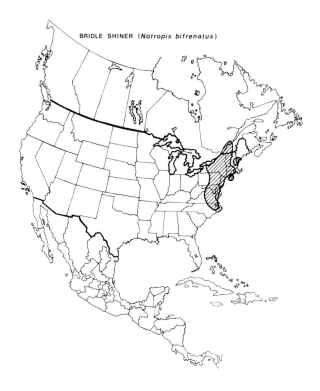

BRIDLE SHINER (Notropis bifrenatus)

dant vegetation, over sand, mud or detritus. Given these conditions, it is found in a variety of situations, including lakes (northern part of range), large rivers, small rivers and creeks, and in low salinity portions of estuaries in the southern part of its range. It is often abundant where found.

LIFE HISTORY AND ECOLOGY: Spawning is protracted, being said to occur in May and June in Pennsylvania (Fowler, 1909), mid-May through mid-June in Oneida Lake, New York, and June and July in Connecticut and in New Hampshire (Harrington, 1947a). In Harrington's study, spawning occurred at water temperatures of 14–27°C and was sporadic within the spawning period. Spawning occurred near the surface of shallow water over beds of vegetation. The eggs sink and are adhesive at laying. See Harrington (1947a, 1947b, 1950, 1951, 1957) for further information on the sexual cycle and development.

Males mature at about 25 mm standard length, whereas females mature at about 30 mm (Harrington, 1948a). Young males grow faster than females, and almost all males are probably sexually mature by their second summer, whereas many females may not spawn until their third summer. Mortality is high, and Harrington observed no individual older than 3 summers (2+ years old).

The bridle shiner is often considered an important forage fish, especially for pickerel, with which it often occurs.

Bridle shiners feed in the lower water column, in vegetation, or on the bottom (Harrington, 1948b). The main foods are aquatic insects, primarily chironomids, and microcrustacea, primarily cladocerans. Adults primarily take insects, whereas young (9–18 mm) primarily take microcrustacea. Other foods which are taken in high volumes at times are plant matter, molluscs, terrestrial insects, amphipods, hydrachnids (water mites), and fish eggs (for example, from sunfish nests).

BASIS OF STATUS CLASSIFICATION: Historically, the bridle shiner was abundant in the Delaware River and its tributaries in New Jersey (Abbott, 1874) and Pennsylvania (Bean, 1891). These accounts and the number of records suggest that it was the most common small shiner in southeast Pennsylvania at least until 1920. Currently, it appears to be common only in parts of upper Bucks and adjacent Montgomery counties.

The shrinking distribution parallels increasing urban, industrial, suburban, and agricultural development of its range in Pennsylvania, especially around Philadelphia, Bristol, Tullytown, Allentown, and Bethlehem. The resultant siltation, dredging, increased turbidity, pollution, and other changes have decreased aquatic vegetation and/or lowered water quality. The habitat specificity of the bridle shiner probably makes it extremely vulnerable to these changes. The bridle shiner is subject to the same pressures over much of its total range, and it may be declining over large parts of its range. Although a number of recent records exist, it is probably declining in New York. Once abundant in northwestern and southwestern New Jersey, it has been recorded recently in only one New Jersey locality.

Upper Bucks County, its prime remaining range in Pennsylvania, is subject to increasing development. Based on historical precedent, this is likely to reduce the range of the bridle shiner even further. The Northeast Branch of Perkiomen Creek, in which it is common, is the proposed receiving tributary for diversions of Delaware River water for Limerick Generating Station. The effects of this on stream morphology and aquatic vegetation are unclear.

RECOMMENDATIONS: Because the bridle shiner is common within its preferred habitat, clear, vegetated streams, and subject to little direct human depredation, habitat protection is the critical factor in protecting the bridle shiner. Because it has been reported from a number of sites and may still occur at some of these, greater documentation of its current distribution would be useful.

SELECTED REFERENCES:

ABBOTT, C. C. 1874. Notes on the cyprinoids of central New Jersey. Amer. Nat., 8:326–338.

———. 1875. Notes on some fishes of the Delaware River. U.S. Comm. of Fish and Fisheries, Rept. 1875(1878), pp. 825–845.

BEAN, T. H. 1891. The fishes of Pennsylvania. Report of the Pennsylvania State Comm. Fisheries for 1889–1891, pp. 1–149.

COPE, E. D. 1869. Synopsis of the Cyprinidae of Pennsylvania. Trans. Amer. Phil. Soc., 13:351–399.

FOWLER, H. W. 1909. A synopsis of the Cyprinidae of Pennsylvania. Proc. Acad. Nat. Sci. Philadelphia, 60:517–553.

HARRINGTON, R. W. 1947a. The breeding behavior of the bridled shiner, Notropis bifrenatus. Copeia, 1947:186–192.

———. 1947b. The early life of the bridled shiner, Notropis bifrenatus (Cope). Copeia, 1947:97–102.

———. 1948a. The life cycle and fertility of the bridled shiner, Notropis bifrenatus (Cope). Amer. Midland Nat., 39:83–92.

———. 1948b. The food of the bridled shiner, Notropis bifrenatus (Cope). Amer. Midland Nat., 40:353–361.

———. 1950. Preseasonal breeding by the bridled shiner, Notropis bifrenatus induced under light-temperature control. Copeia, 1950:304–311.

———. 1951. Notes on spawning in an aquarium by the bridled shiner, Notropis bifrenatus, with counts of the eggs deposited. Ichthyological Notes, 1:85–86.

———. 1957. Sexual photoperiodicity of the cyprinid fish, Notropis bifrenatus (Cope) in relation to the phases of its annual reproductive cycle. J. Exp. Zool., 135:529–553.

JENKINS, R. E., and T. ZORACH. 1970. Zoogeography and characters of the American cyprinid fish, Notropis bifrenatus. Chesapeake Science, 11:174–182.

PREPARED BY: Richard J. Horwitz, *Division of Limnology and Ecology, Academy of Natural Sciences of Philadelphia, 19th and the Parkway, Philadelphia, PA 19103.*

Vulnerable

BLACKNOSE SHINER
Notropis heterolepis Eigenmann and Eigenmann
Family Cyprinidae
Order Cypriniformes

OTHER NAMES: Blacknose dace, Muskoka minnow.

DESCRIPTION: Attaining an average length of about 64 mm, this minnow is most characterized by vertical black crescents within the lateral band. Convex surfaces of the crescents are directed anteriorly. The lateral band is dark and extends around the body and across the snout, but not onto the chin. Overall color is silvery.

RANGE: The range of this shiner is from the Hudson Bay drainage in Canada east to Nova Scotia. It is common in Great Lakes drainage of Michigan and Minnesota east through New York to Maine. The blacknose shiner was recently extirpated from most of midwest although glacial relict populations occurred farther south. One population still remains in northern Tennessee.

HABITAT: The blacknose shiner prefers cool, quiet, vegetated streams and lakes over bottoms of sand and gravel although Tennessee populations are in warm, weedless streams.

LIFE HISTORY AND ECOLOGY: Little is known of its habits, but this shiner probably spawns in spring and summer over sandy bottoms. Foods likely consist of small insects and crustaceans associated with aquatic vegetation.

BASIS OF STATUS CLASSIFICATION: Although reported from the northwestern portion of the Ohio drainage in Pennsylvania this species is

Blacknose Shiner (*Notropis heterolepis*). Photograph by E. L. Cooper.

BLACKNOSE SHINER (*Notropis heterolepis*)

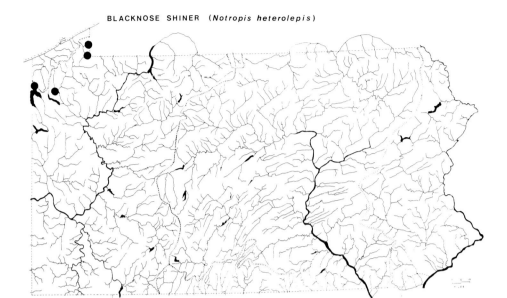

vulnerable to increased stream turbidity and siltation which have caused its demise in the midwest.

RECOMMENDATIONS: Agricultural runoff must be held to a minimum. A current distributional study is needed to delimit the present range.

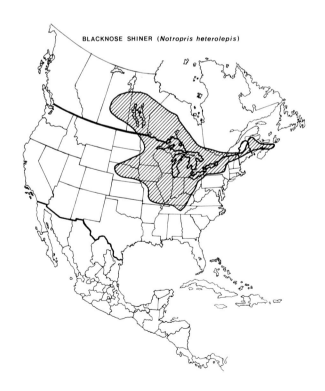

BLACKNOSE SHINER (*Notropris heterolepis*)

SELECTED REFERENCES:

SCOTT, W. B., and E. J. CROSSMAN. 1973. Freshwater fishes of Canada. Bull. Fish. Res. Bd. Canada, 184:1–966.
TRAUTMAN, M. B. 1957. The fishes of Ohio with illustrated keys. Ohio State Univ. Press, Columbus, v–xvii + 683 pp.

PREPARED BY: Robert W. Malick, Jr., *Ichthyological Associates, Inc., Three Mile Island Aquatic Study, P.O. Box 223, Etters, PA 17319.*

Vulnerable

LONGNOSE SUCKER
Catostomus catostomus (Forster)
Family Catostomidae
Order Cypriniformes

OTHER NAMES: Sturgeon sucker, finescale sucker, red-sided sucker; *Catostomus griseus, Catostomus longirostris, Cyprinus catostomus.*

DESCRIPTION: The longnose sucker is a terete, streamlined fish with slender snout and inferior mouth. Breeding males develop a wide rosy stripe along sides of body and numerous small pearl organs on anal fin and ventral lobe of the caudal fin. Adults are usually dark on the back with light coloration on belly. Dwarf forms of this species are recognized in the Appalachians and other localities. In the east, it is distinguished from the sometime sympatric white sucker by its more terete head and longer snout.

Longnose Sucker (*Catostomus catostomus*). Photograph by E. L. Cooper.

RANGE: The longnose sucker is widely distributed across northern North America from Quebec to Alaska. In Pennsylvania, it occurs as a disjunct distribution in the headwaters of the Youghiogheny River, possibly as a relict population isolated in this stream system by glacial rearrangement of the upper Ohio and Great Lakes watersheds. It is common throughout most of its northern range.

HABITAT: The longnose is a versatile sucker found in both lakes and streams, adapting its spawning requirements to utilize gravel riffles of streams or lake shoals. The Great Lakes populations often migrate short distances into streams in huge numbers to spawn, the young quickly returning to the lakes.

LIFE HISTORY AND ECOLOGY: Longnose suckers spawn in the spring; several males congregate on a gravel riffle and spawn with ripe females as they enter the area. There is no nest preparation or egg care, but gravel areas soon become free of silt due to the activity of the spawning group. The young disperse rapidly to lakes, or remain dispersed throughout the stream system.

Growth rate is extremely variable from one locality to another, mature longnose suckers in Pennsylvania streams seldom exceed 250 mm in length, whereas those in lake populations often are twice that size. The food is also highly variable with a large number of benthic invertebrates being the principal diet. Throughout the Great Lakes area, this fish seldom is used by man either as a commercial fish or as a sport fish, the numerous small bones in the flesh being a chief deterrent. However in the far northern part of its range, it is extensively used as food for dogs.

BASIS OF STATUS CLASSIFICATION: Although no protection has been given to this species in Pennsylvania or Maryland, the small relict pop-

LONGNOSE SUCKER (*Catostomus catostomus*)

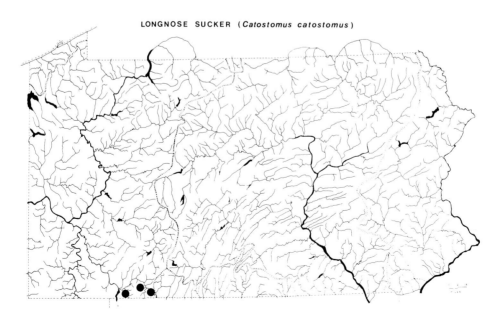

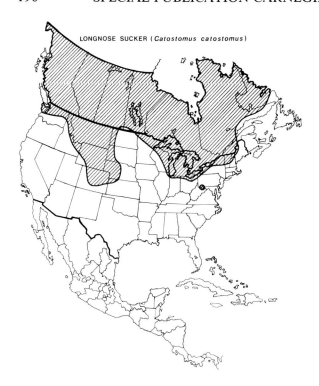

LONGNOSE SUCKER (*Catostomus catostomus*)

SELECTED REFERENCES:

FORSTER, J. R. 1773. An account of some curious fishes, sent from Hudson Bay. Phil. Trans. Roy. Soc. London, 63:149–160.

GEEN, G. H., T. G. NORTHCOTE, G. F. HARTMAN, and C. C. LINDSEY. 1966. Life histories of two species of catostomid fishes in Sixteenmile Lake, British Columbia, with particular reference to inlet stream spawning. J. Fish. Res. Bd. Canada, 23:1761–1788.

HARRIS, R. H. D. 1962. Growth and reproduction of the longnose sucker, *Catostomus catostomus* (Forster), in Great Slave Lake. J. Fish. Res. Bd. Canada, 19:113–126.

KENDALL, W. C., and W. A. DENCE. 1929. The fishes of the Cranberry Lake Region. Bull. New York State Coll. Forestry at Syracuse, 2:219–309.

RAWSON, D. S., and C. A. ELSEY. 1950. Reduction in the longnose sucker population of Pyramid Lake, Alberta, in an attempt to improve angling. Trans. Amer. Fish. Soc., 78:13–31.

SCOTT, W. B., and E. J. CROSSMAN. 1973. The freshwater fishes of Canada. Bull. Fish. Res. Bd. Canada, 184:1–966.

PREPARED BY: Edwin L. Cooper, *The Pennsylvania State University, University Park, PA 16802.*

Vulnerable

SPOTTED SUCKER
Minytrema melanops (Rafinesque)
Family Catostomidae
Order Cypriniformes

OTHER NAMES: Striped sucker, black sucker, black-nosed sucker, sand sucker.

DESCRIPTION: This is a sucker with an elongate body and with mouth small, horizontal, inferior, and protrusible, but little overhung by snout; body with brown to black spots on base of exposed parts of each scale, the spots on sides more conspicuous

ulation occurring in a very limited geographic area is vulnerable to extirpation. It is of inestimable value as an historical oddity, left behind by the glacier and now completely isolated from the major centers of its species distribution.

RECOMMENDATIONS: The populations existing in a few localities should be watched with the view to affording some protection if the ecology of these streams begins to change. The fish is not highly vulnerable to exploitation under present conditions and publicity should be avoided that might result in increased exploitation.

Spotted Sucker (*Minytrema melanops*). Photograph by C. A. Purkett.

SPOTTED SUCKER (*Minytrema melanops*)

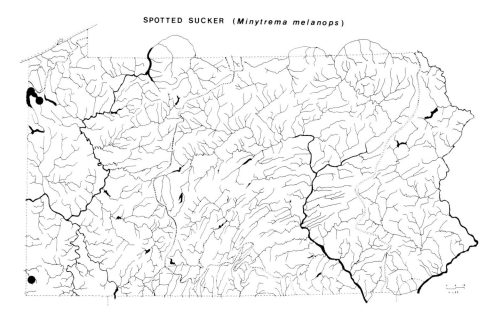

than those on the darker back, and forming 8–10 obvious horizontal rows on sides of body (spots less well developed in young); dorsal surface of head, back, caudal peduncle and upper sides of body dark green, olive to brown; dorsal, caudal and sometimes anal fin gray to olive, the paired fins dusky to white; dorsal fin rounded at tip, somewhat emarginate, with

11 or 12 principal rays; anal rays 7; lateral scales usually 43 to 45; lateral line rarely complete or conspicuous.

Total length of adults is usually from 230–280 mm and weight is 170 to 792 g. Dwarf forms may mature at 150 mm total length. Maximum total length is about 450 mm; maximum weight about 1,360 g.

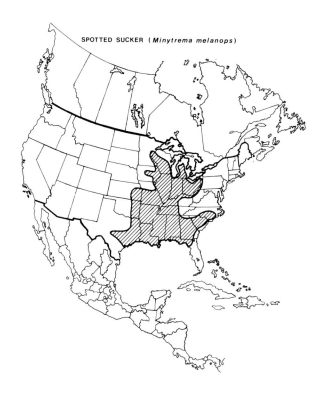

SPOTTED SUCKER (*Minytrema melanops*)

RANGE: The range of the spotted sucker is the lower Great Lakes basin (Lakes Erie, Huron and Michigan) of Ohio, Michigan, Wisconsin, and Ontario; upper Mississippi Valley in Wisconsin, Minnesota, and Iowa; south to Gulf slope drainages from Texas (Colorado River drainage) to Florida (Suwannee River drainage), and north on Atlantic slope to Cape Fear drainage of North Carolina. A detailed distribution map appears in Gilbert and Burgess (1980).

In Pennsylvania, the spotted sucker is recorded only from Pymatuning Lake (upper Shenango River system), in Crawford County, and from the Wheeling Creek system, Washington County, with collections having been made as recently as 1976–1977.

HABITAT: It occurs typically in lakes, overflow ponds, sloughs, oxbows, and those sections of streams with low or base gradients; and with clean, sandy, gravel or hard clay bottoms and relatively little siltation (habitat types I-A-various categories and II-B-2 and II-C-2).

LIFE HISTORY AND ECOLOGY: Several papers have been published on the life history and ecology of this species, mostly dealing with work done in Oklahoma. Spawning occurs from early March to early May (Georgia and Florida), late April to May (Oklahoma), or late spring or early summer farther north. Spawning activity typically occurs in riffle areas above pools, at temperatures ranging from 12–19.5°C (Georgia) or from 15–18°C (Oklahoma). Young-of-the-year in Ohio were 51–102 mm total length by October, and adults are usually 230–380 mm total length and weigh 170–792 g. Dwarf forms may be mature as small as 150 mm. Maximum age calculated for Minnesota individuals was 6 years. Food consists of molluscs and other invertebrates, mainly immature insects.

BASIS OF STATUS CLASSIFICATION: The spotted sucker is classified as vulnerable, on the basis of its limited range in extreme western Pennsylvania.

RECOMMENDATIONS: Monitor likely looking habitats in western Pennsylvania, in order to determine other areas where this species occurs. Prevent alteration of habitat in these areas.

SELECTED REFERENCE:

GILBERT, C. R., and G. H. BURGESS. 1980. *Minytrema melanops* (Rafinesque), spotted sucker. P. 408 *in* Atlas of North American freshwater fishes (D. S. Lee et al.), North Carolina State Mus. Nat. Hist., Raleigh, x + 854 pp.

PREPARED BY: Carter R. Gilbert, *Florida State Museum, University of Florida, Gainesville, FL 32611.*

Vulnerable

MOUNTAIN MADTOM
Noturus eleutherus Jordan
Family Ictaluridae
Order Siluriformes

DESCRIPTION: The mountain madtom is a catfish of the genus *Noturus* that lacks posterior extensions of the premaxillary tooth patch; adipose fin adnate to caudal fin, but low and almost separated from caudal by a distinct notch (the notch more pronounced than in any other member of the genus); upper jaw only slightly longer than lower jaw and barely projecting beyond it; blackish saddle band on caudal peduncle not extending to distal edge of adipose fin, thus leaving edge of that fin colorless; caudal fin without a mid-caudal bar; color relatively uniform, with saddle bars and other body markings usually faint; caudal peduncle rather slender, its depth usually contained more than one time in snout length; posterior teeth of pectoral spine well developed, about seven in number; anterior serrae on pectoral spine weakly developed.

Adult size ranges from 26–63 mm standard length; maximum size 73 mm.

MOUNTAIN MADTOM (*Noturus eleutherus*)

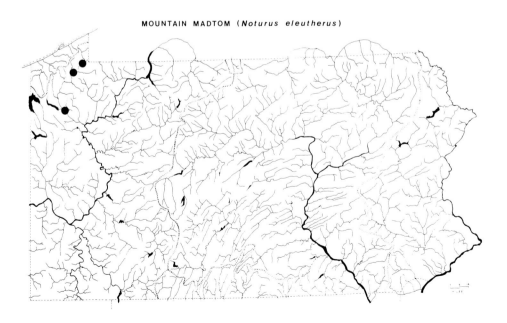

MOUNTAIN MADTOM (*Noturus eleutherus*)

RANGE: This catfish occurs in the Red and Ouachita river systems, Oklahoma and Arkansas, and Tennessee River drainage of Georgia, Tennessee, and Virginia; northeast throughout Ohio River basin to northern Indiana and northwestern Pennsylvania. It is most common in the upper Tennessee drainage of eastern Tennessee and western Virginia. A detailed distribution map appears in Rohde (1980).

In Pennsylvania, both known localities of occurrence (three separate collections) are in French Creek, tributary to Allegheny River, in Crawford and Erie counties. Specimens have been collected as recently as 1977.

HABITAT: Noturus eleutherus inhabits large or moderately large, moderate to swiftly flowing creeks and rivers (habitats II-B-2 and II-C-2). It has been taken principally in streams containing medium or large stones, rubble, gravel, and sand, in water of little or moderate turbidity. It is usually found in riffles or rapids, and dense submergent vegetation attached to the rocks and rubble is sometimes present. This species appears to be one of the more sensitive to siltation or other forms of pollution.

LIFE HISTORY AND ECOLOGY: No specific life history or ecological studies have been conducted on this species. As is true of ictalurid catfishes in general, and species of *Noturus* in particular, the mountain madtom is active only at night, retiring during the day to cover in deeper water and/or burrowing into the substrate. Although the food of *N. eleutherus* has not been analyzed, studies involving the food of other madtoms indicate that small aquatic invertebrates and small fish comprise the most common items. Trautman (1957), studying Ohio populations, found that young-of-the-year ranged from 25–58 mm total length and yearlings from 36–64 mm.

SPECIALIZED OR UNIQUE CHARACTERISTICS: Because of the sensitivity of this madtom to siltation and pollution, it is a valuable "marker" species in environmental studies.

BASIS OF STATUS CLASSIFICATION: Because of the apparently limited distribution of the mountain madtom in Pennsylvania, as well as its sensitivity to ecological perturbations, this species is classified as "vulnerable."

RECOMMENDATIONS: Monitor known localities where this species is found, attempt to find additional localities, and protect those areas of occurrence from ecological modification.

SELECTED REFERENCES:

ROHDE, F. C. 1980. *Noturus eleutherus* Jordan, mountain madtom. P. 451, *in* Atlas of North American freshwater fishes (D. S. Lee et al.), North Carolina State Mus. Nat. Hist., Raleigh, x + 854 pp.
TRAUTMAN, M. B. 1957. The fishes of Ohio. Ohio State Univ. Press, Columbus, v–xvii + 683 pp.

PREPARED BY: Carter R. Gilbert, *Florida State Museum, University of Florida, Gainesville, FL 32611.*

Vulnerable

TADPOLE MADTOM
Noturus gyrinus (Mitchill)
Family Ictaluridae
Order Siluriformes

OTHER NAMES: Tadpole stonecat, tadpole cat.

DESCRIPTION: This is a small madtom which seldom exceeds 90 mm in length. It possesses typical madtom characters of adipose fin connected to caudal fin and four pairs of barbels—1 pair on snout,

Tadpole Madtom (*Noturus gyrinus*). Photograph by E. L. Cooper.

1 pair at edges of mouth, and 2 pairs on chin. Unique characters include tadpole-like shape; pot-bellied forward and long, rounded caudal fin. The dorsal spine is sharp but without barbs; pectoral spines sharp and unserrated but deeply grooved with associated poison glands. The body color is generally dark but ranges from dull golden yellow to olive gray; lower body lighter than upper. A dark gray streak outlines the vertebral column and branches into dark lines over muscle segments.

RANGE: The tadpole madtom occurs in fresh and slightly brackish water of Atlantic Coastal Plain from New York to Florida and along Gulf slope to Texas; north throughout most of Mississippi, Missouri, and Ohio river systems to North Dakota, Wisconsin, Minnesota, and southern Canada. It is absent from the Appalachian highlands and introduced to Idaho and Oregon.

HABITAT: Active primarily at night like all madtoms, this secretive species inhabits clear to moderately turbid waters with little current. It is often common where cover is abundant, particularly submergent vegetation.

LIFE HISTORY AND ECOLOGY: Food consists of crustaceans, immature aquatic insects, and occasionally small fish. This species spawns in summer; egg clusters enclosed within a gelatinous envelope are deposited in dark cavities. Average number of eggs per female ranges from about 50 to 100. Most specimens mature during their second summer and rarely live beyond 3 years.

TADPOLE MADTOM (*Noturus gyrinus*)

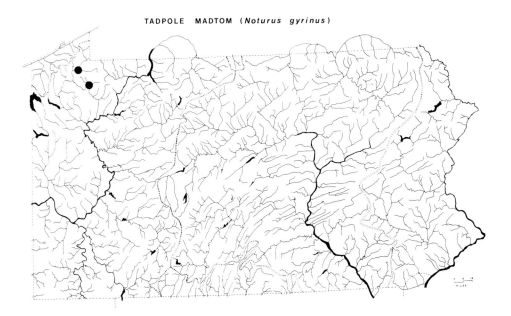

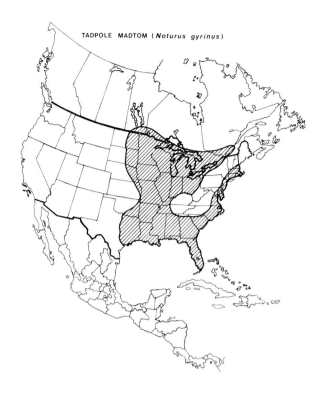

TADPOLE MADTOM (*Noturus gyrinus*)

habitat. These factors have led to the increased decimation of the species in recent decades in Illinois.

RECOMMENDATIONS: The status of the tadpole madtom within Pennsylvania is vulnerable, and the species is indeed rare. A distributional study is needed to delimit the exact range. Habitat protection is essential.

SELECTED REFERENCE:

TAYLOR, W. R. 1969. A revision of the catfish genus *Noturus* Rafinesque with an analysis of higher groups in the Ictaluridae. Bull. U.S. Nat. Mus. 282: v–vi + 1–315.

PREPARED BY: Robert W. Malick, Jr., *Ichthyological Associates, Inc., Three Mile Island Aquatic Study, P.O. Box 223, Etters, PA 17319.*

Vulnerable

NORTHERN MADTOM
Noturus stigmosus Taylor
Family Ictaluridae
Order Siluriformes

SPECIALIZED OR UNIQUE CHARACTERISTICS: An excellent bait fish.

BASIS OF STATUS CLASSIFICATION: Recent collecting has revealed this species at two Crawford County locations. Other populations may exist but increased water turbidity and silting could destroy

DESCRIPTION: The northern madtom is a catfish of the genus *Noturus* that lacks posterior extensions of the premaxillary tooth patch; adipose fin adnate to caudal fin, but high and almost separated from caudal by a distinct notch (nearly as pronounced as

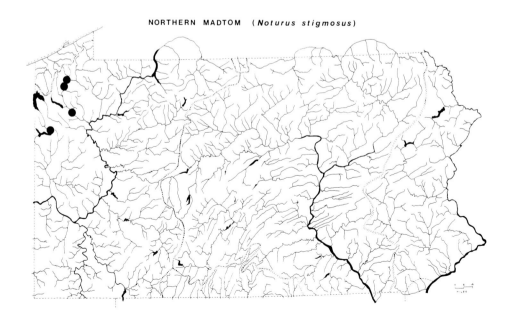

NORTHERN MADTOM (*Noturus stigmosus*)

NORTHERN MADTOM (*Noturus stigmosus*)

in *Noturus eleutherus,* with which this species has, in the past, been mistakenly confused). It also shares, with *N. eleutherus,* the characters of an upper jaw only slightly longer than lower jaw and barely projecting beyond it; blackish saddle band on caudal peduncle usually not extending to distal edge of adipose fin, thus leaving the outer part of that fin colorless (some individuals from southern part of range may have saddle reaching edge of fin); and posterior teeth of pectoral spine well developed, about seven or eight in number. It differs from *N. eleutherus* in a number of features, the most obvious of which are: (a) caudal fin with a mid-caudal bar; (b) body usually mottled; (c) light, short "saddles" along midline of back immediately anterior and immediately posterior to dorsal fin; (d) adipose fin slightly higher; (e) caudal peduncle deeper, usually contained 1.1 times or less in snout length; and (f) anterior serrae on pectoral spine somewhat better developed.

Noturus stigmosus matures at about 37 mm standard length, with the largest specimen recorded about 100 mm. It thus reaches a substantially larger size than *N. eleutherus,* the largest recorded individual of that species only 73 mm.

RANGE: The northern madtom occurs in tributaries of Mississippi River in western Mississippi and Tennessee, north throughout much of Ohio River basin to northern Indiana and extreme western Pennsylvania; also in western Lake Erie drainage in Ohio, Indiana, and Michigan. A detailed distribution map appears in Rohde (1980).

In Pennsylvania, all known localities are either from the Shenango River (near Delaware Grove), in Mercer County, or from three localities on French Creek, in Crawford County. The last known collection from any of these localities was made in 1959.

HABITAT: This catfish typically occurs in large creeks and small rivers, with bottom usually of shifting sand and mud (but not heavy silt) and water varying from clear to turbid, with moderate current (habitat types II-B-1 and II-C-1). Although present in riffles, the faster, more turbulent situations are usually avoided. Little cover is usually present, except for limbs and debris.

LIFE HISTORY AND ECOLOGY: Taylor (1969) reported that egg masses, containing from 89–141 eggs, were found in the Huron River, Michigan, in late July. An incomplete brood, taken at the same time, included 61 young. Spawning occurs under stones, or in cans, boxes, or other submerged objects affording protection. The male guards the nest and brood, as is true of other ictalurid catfishes.

Trautman (1957) showed young-of-the-year individuals (collected in October) to range from 25–59 mm total length, yearlings from 36–64 mm, and adults usually from 56–97 mm.

SPECIALIZED OR UNIQUE CHARACTERISTICS: As is true also of *Noturus eleutherus,* as well as most other members of the genus, this is one of the better "marker" species, and one of the first to disappear with the advent of ecological disturbance.

BASIS OF STATUS CLASSIFICATION: Because of the limited distribution of the northern madtom in Pennsylvania, as well as its sensitivity to ecological changes, this species is classified as "vulnerable."

RECOMMENDATIONS: Inasmuch as this species has not been reported from the state since 1959, efforts should be made to determine if it is still present at those localities where originally reported. Further surveys should be conducted to determine if the species exists at other localities. Areas of occurrence should be protected from further ecological disturbance.

SELECTED REFERENCES:

Rohde, F. C. 1980. *Noturus stigmosus* Taylor, northern madtom. P. 469, *in* Atlas of North American freshwater fishes (D. S. Lee et al.), North Carolina State Mus. Nat. Hist., Raleigh, x + 854 pp.

Taylor, W. R. 1969. A revision of the catfish genus *Noturus* Rafinesque, with an analysis of higher groups in the Ictaluridae. Bull. U.S. Nat. Mus., 282:v–vi + 1–315.

Trautman, M. B. 1957. The fishes of Ohio. Ohio State Univ. Press, Columbus, v–xvii + 683 pp.

PREPARED BY: Carter R. Gilbert, *Florida State Museum, University of Florida, Gainesville, FL 32611.*

Vulnerable

BANDED SUNFISH
Enneacanthus obesus (Girard)
Family Centrarchidae
Order Perciformes

OTHER NAMES: Sphagnum sunfish; *Pomotis guttatus, Pomotis obesus.*

DESCRIPTION: The body is short, elliptical, deep, and strongly compressed. The lateral line is usually incomplete, distinguishing it from its close relative, the bluespotted sunfish. The olive green body has numerous green, gold, and purple spots. Gold spots and lines are found on the cheeks. A black opercular spot is present, edged in purple or gold. Coloration is enhanced in breeding males. Young and adults exhibit five to eight dark, vertical bars, which are three to four scales in width.

RANGE: The banded sunfish occurs farther north than other Enneacanthini sunfishes. It is mostly restricted to the Atlantic Coastal Plain. Occurring sparsely as far north as southern New Hampshire, the banded sunfish occupies most major river systems from New Jersey to northern Florida. Collections in Pennsylvania are mostly limited to the Delaware River in the Philadelphia area.

HABITAT: The three sunfishes of the tribe Enneacanthini prefer sluggish, acidic, heavily vegetated streams and ponds. This habitat does not occur to any great extent in Pennsylvania.

LIFE HISTORY AND ECOLOGY: This species is morphologically and behaviorally adapted to nutrient poor, dystrophic habitats. These adaptations include small size and vertical banding to aid concealment, a rounded caudal fin for quick bursts of speed, and reduced mouth size for capturing small prey. Spawning is similar to other sunfishes. Breeding may begin earlier, and become more protracted than many of its larger sunfish relatives.

BASIS OF STATUS CLASSIFICATION: Relatively few collections of the blackbanded sunfish in Pennsylvania indicate that it has never been abundant there. One specimen collected as recently as 1978 suggests that a small population exists in the lower Delaware. The lack of suitable habitat, and the industrialization of the lower Delaware River area probably is related to the decline of this species.

BANDED SUNFISH (*Enneacanthus obesus*)

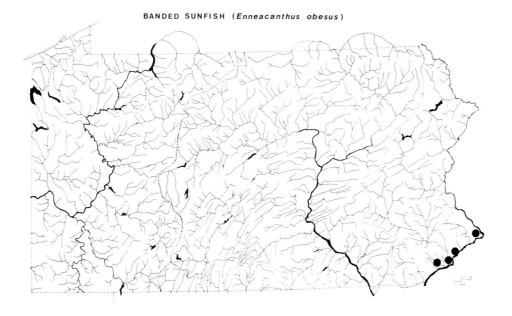

BANDED SUNFISH (*Enneacanthus obesus*)

RECOMMENDATIONS: Because this species is abundant throughout the rest of its distribution outside of Pennsylvania, no management programs are recommended. The recent collection of a specimen near Tinicum Marsh Sanctuary may indicate that a protected population exists in the area.

SELECTED REFERENCES:

BREDER, C. M., JR., and D. E. ROSEN. 1966. Modes of reproduction in fishes. Crown Publishers, New York, New York, 941 pp.

HARDY, J. D., JR. 1978. Development of the fishes of the mid-Atlantic Bight; an atlas of egg, larval and juvenile stages. U.S. Fish Wildl. Serv., 3:1–394.

LEE, D. S., and C. R. GILBERT. 1978. *Enneacanthus obesus.* P. 589, *in* Atlas of North American freshwater fishes (D. S. Lee et al.), North Carolina State Mus. Nat. Hist., Raleigh, x + 854 pp.

TRUITT, R. V., B. A. BEAN, and H. W. FOWLER. 1929. The fishes of Maryland. Bull. Maryland State Conserv. Dept., 3:1–120.

PREPARED BY: James R. Lebo, *90221 Territorial Road, Junction City, OR 97448.*

Vulnerable

SPOTTED BASS
Micropterus punctulatus (Rafinesque)
Family Centrarchidae
Order Perciformes

OTHER NAMES: Kentucky bass, yellow bass, speckled bass; *Calliurus punctulatus, Micropterus salmoides, Micropterus pseudaplites.*

DESCRIPTION: The prominent row of horizontal spots present below the lateral line has given rise to the common name. Further distinguishing characteristics are an irregular longitudinal stripe of merging dark blotches—dark olive, variegated markings often roughly diamond shaped above the lateral band; a prominent dark spot on the tip of the opercle and at the base of the caudal fin and a shallow emargination between the spined and soft-rayed portions of the dorsal fin. The upper jaw extends beneath the posterior portion of the eye; the head is more elongated and pointed than that of either the largemouth or smallmouth bass. Adults are commonly 250 to 430 mm in length and weigh 270 to 1,580 g. Individuals weighing more than 1,800 g are rare.

RANGE: Spotted bass occur naturally in the Ohio River drainage from West Virginia, North Carolina, and Ohio, through Indiana, Illinois, Kentucky, and Tennessee; in the central and lower Mississippi Riv-

Spotted Bass (*Micropterus punctulatus*). Photograph by C. A. Purkett.

SPOTTED BASS (*Micropterus punctulatus*)

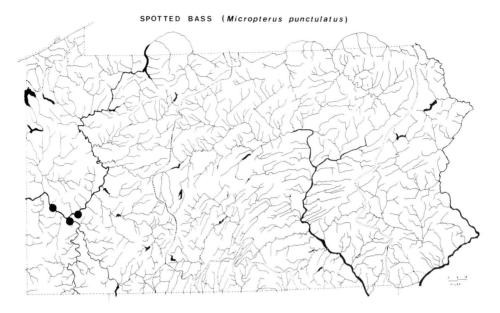

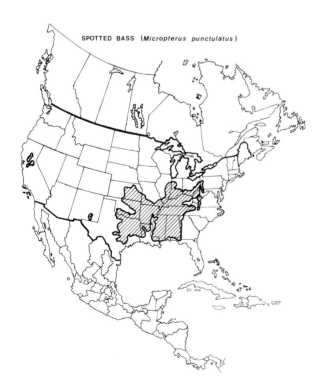

SPOTTED BASS (*Micropterus punctulatus*)

er drainage in Missouri, Kansas, Oklahoma, Arkansas, Louisiana, and Mississippi, and in parts of the Gulf Coast drainage of Georgia, Florida, Alabama, and Texas.

The spotted bass is by far the most abundant black bass in the Ohio River downstream from southern Ohio despite heavy plantings of smallmouth and largemouth bass. The spotted bass appears to be

more tolerant of turbidity in the northern part of its range than the other resident black basses.

As of 1974, the most northern collection of the species in the Ohio River was located near Wheeling, West Virginia. However, since this date, the spotted bass has been collected at several locations in the Ohio River basin within Pennsylvania. It seems that this species is gradually extending its range northward after apparent localized extirpation.

HABITAT: In the northern section of its range the spotted bass is most abundant in moderate to large streams having a low gradient and long deep pools where medium to high turbidity does not appear to restrict its abundance.

The spotted bass generally inhabits permanent flowing waters that are warmer and slightly more turbid than those where the smallmouth bass occur. It is largely replaced by the smallmouth bass in cool spring-fed streams, and by the largemouth bass in standing waters.

LIFE HISTORY AND ECOLOGY: Maturity occurs typically at an age of 2 or 3 years in most waters by which time the spotted bass will usually have reached a length of slightly more than 200 cm; females are generally larger than males. Spotted bass usually begin nesting a few days later than smallmouth bass at temperatures varying from 13 to 23°C. Rocky and gravelly substrates near cover are preferred. The diet consists of crayfish, forage fish, and aquatic invertebrates. Zooplankton form the main diet of all young bass until they are old enough to engulf small fish or other animals.

BASIS OF STATUS CLASSIFICATION: If water quality continues to improve it seems likely that the spotted bass will increase in occurrence in Pennsylvania as it reinvades suitable habitat. However, since the spotted bass has yet to be collected in any abundance, it would be prudent to maintain a vulnerable species classification at this time.

SELECTED REFERENCES:

GILBERT, R. J. 1979. *Micropterus punctulatus* (Rafinesque), spotted bass. P. 607, *in* Atlas of North American freshwater fishes (D. S. Lee et al.), North Carolina State. Mus. Nat. Hist., Raleigh, x + 854 pp.

HOWLAND, J. W. 1931. Studies on the Kentucky Black Bass (*Micropterus pseudoplites* Hubbs). Trans. Amer. Fish. Soc., 61:89–94.

———. 1932. Experiments in the propagation of spotted black basses. Trans. Amer. Fish. Soc., 62:185–188.

HUBBS, C. L. 1927. *Micropterus pseudoplites,* a new species of black bass. Occas. Papers Mus. Zool., Univ. Michigan, 184: 1–12.

———, and R. M. BAILEY. 1940. A revision of the black basses (*Micropterus* and *Huro*) with descriptions of four new forms. Misc. Publ. Mus. Zool., Univ. Michigan, 48:1–51.

TRAUTMAN, M. B. 1957. Fishes of Ohio. Ohio State Univ. Press, Columbus, v–xvii + 683 pp.

VOGELE, L. E. 1975. The spotted bass. Pp. 34–44, *in* Black bass biology and management (H. Clapper, ed.), National Symposium on the Biology and Management of Centrarchid Basses, Tulsa, Oklahoma, 534 pp.

PREPARED BY: Paul E. McKeown, *Canberra-RMC, Environmental Services Division, P.O. Box 10, Drumore, PA 17518.*

Vulnerable

BLUEBREAST DARTER
Etheostoma camurum (Cope)
Family Percidae
Order Perciformes

DESCRIPTION: This is a deep-bodied, colorful darter with a blunt snout and squarish tail; seldom exceeds 55 mm in length. It is distinguished from close relatives in the subgenus *Nothonotus* (in Pennsylvania, spotted darter, *E. maculatum,* and tippecanoe darter, *E. tippecanoe*) by broad orange red to rusty margins on dorsal and caudal fins edged with white. The background color is blue green to blue black. The back is traversed by eight to 10 obscure brownish saddles; sides crossed by eight to 11 vertical, dark bars; and 10 to 15 horizontal lines between scale rows on posterior two-thirds of body. Often several rows of red spots are present on the sides of males. Two light yellow spots are located at base of caudal fin. Fins of females are finely barred. Females are colored less brilliantly than males; colors of both sexes fade quickly in preservative.

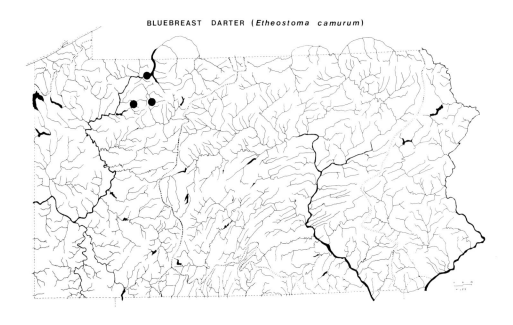

BLUEBREAST DARTER (*Etheostoma camurum*)

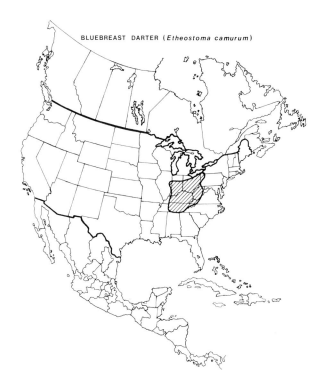

BLUEBREAST DARTER (*Etheostoma camurum*)

RANGE: This darter occurs from the Allegheny River in northwestern Pennsylvania, west through the Ohio River Basin to the Tippecanoe River in Indiana and the Vermilion River in Illinois, and south through the Kanawha and Monongahela rivers in West Virginia to the Tennessee and Cumberland drainages in Tennessee, Virginia, and Kentucky.

HABITAT: The bluebreast darter is found in fast runs and riffles of medium to large streams over firm substrates of rock and rubble. It exhibits a marked preference for sections up to 30 cm in depth.

LIFE HISTORY AND ECOLOGY: This darter spawns during late spring through summer. The female is buried in substrate and clasped by male from above. Eggs are buried among sand and fine gravel, beside large rocks and in riffles. Food consists of benthic insects, mostly fly larvae.

SPECIALIZED OR UNIQUE CHARACTERISTICS: This fish is sexually dimorphic; male coloration is more brilliant than that of female.

BASIS OF STATUS CLASSIFICATION: The bluebreast darter is currently restricted to scattered localities of the upper Allegheny River in northwestern Pennsylvania where it is never abundant.

RECOMMENDATIONS: Habitat protection of the larger streams this darter inhabits is essential.

SELECTED REFERENCES:

MOUNT, D. I. 1959. Spawning behavior of the bluebreast darter, *Etheostoma camurum* (Cope). Copeia, 1959:240–243.
TRAUTMAN, M. B. 1957. The fishes of Ohio with illustrated keys. Ohio State Univ. Press, Columbus, v–xvii + 683 pp.
ZORACH, T. 1972. Systematics of the percid fishes, *Etheostoma camurum* and *E. chlorobranchium* new species, with a discussion of the subgenus *Nothonotus*. Copeia, 1972:427–447.

PREPARED BY: Robert W. Malick, Jr., *Ichthyological Associates, Inc., Three Mile Island Aquatic Study, P.O. Box 223, Etters, PA 17319.*

Vulnerable

IOWA DARTER
Etheostoma exile (Girard)
Family Percidae
Order Perciformes

OTHER NAMES: Boleichthys exilis, Poecilichthys exilis.

DESCRIPTION: The Iowa darter is a short slender fish with seven or eight dorsal saddles and 10 lateral blotches that are vertically elongated. Usually brownish or olive in color, they have a distinct teardrop and preorbital bar, barred fins, a well developed caudal fin, and large pectoral fins. The cheeks, opercles, nape, and belly are scaled with the breast usually naked. The lateral line is incomplete and highly flexed with 18 to 28 pored scales in the lateral series.

RANGE: The Iowa darter occurs throughout much of the interior of southern Canada and northern United States and is common throughout the Great Lakes drainage. In Pennsylvania it is presently limited to Lake Pleasant and Lake LaBoeuf, both tributaries of French Creek in Erie County, and is locally common in Presque Isle Bay.

HABITAT: The Iowa darter occurs in well vegetated lakes and low gradient rivers and streams. It usually can be found in protected cover with sand, mud, or clay substrates. In lakes, it prefers sandy to muddy bottoms with submerged vegetation.

LIFE HISTORY AND ECOLOGY: Spawning takes place in April and May along lake shores and slow flowing streams, over sandy to muddy bottoms with

Iowa Darter (*Etheostoma exile*). Photograph supplied by National Fisheries Center, U.S. Fish and Wildlife Service, Kearneyville, WV 25430.

organic debris. First the males come from deeper water setting up large, strongly intraspecific territories. Later, the females move from territory to territory mating with several different males.

Young darters begin feeding on copepods and cladocerans, with midge larvae, mayfly larvae, and amphipods the primary diet of adults and juveniles. Little information is known on the rate of growth, but adults may live at least 3 years.

This species is a glacial relict species that can apparently withstand cooler waters than other darters, because it is found farther north than other darters. One of the limiting factors of the Iowa darter is its intolerance of turbid, muddy waters with low visibility, which destroys its food supply.

BASIS OF STATUS CLASSIFICATION: The Iowa darter probably never was abundant in Pennsylva-

nia. It is now limited to a few localities in the glaciated northwest corner of the Commonwealth where clear, weedy, quiet areas exist. It is locally common in Presque Isle Bay.

RECOMMENDATIONS: None. Other populations of the Iowa darter may be found in suitable habitat in northwestern Pennsylvania.

SELECTED REFERENCES:

FORBES, S. A., and R. E. RICHARDSON. 1908. The fishes of Illinois. Illinois State Lab. Nat. Hist., Urbana, 357 pp.

HUBBS, C. L., and K. F. LAGLER. 1958. Fishes of the Great Lakes Region. Univ. Michigan Press, Ann Arbor, 314 pp.

LEE, D. S., and C. R. GILBERT. 1978. *Etheostoma exile* (Girard), Iowa darter. P. 646, *in* Atlas of North American freshwater fishes (D. S. Lee et al.), North Carolina State Mus. Nat. Hist., Raleigh, x + 854 pp.

IOWA DARTER (*Etheostoma exile*)

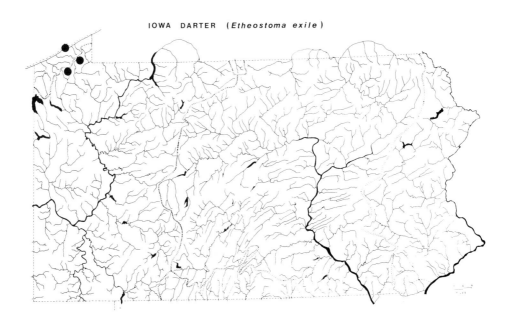

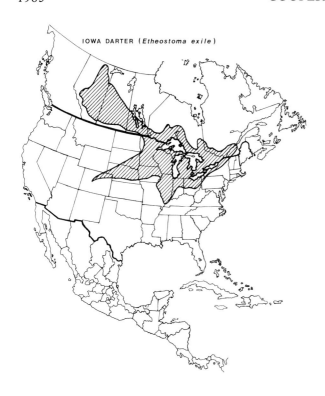

IOWA DARTER (*Etheostoma exile*)

RICHARDSON, L. R. 1938. A note on variation in squamation of the cheek operculum in two etheostomid fishes from Quebec. Copeia, 1938:126–128.

SMITH, P. W. 1979. The fishes of Illinois. Univ. Illinois Press, Urbana, 314 pp.

TURNER, C. L. 1921. Food of the common Ohio darters. Ohio J. Sci., 22:41–62.

WINN, H. E. 1958. Comparative reproductive behavior and ecology of fourteen species of darters (Pisces-Percidae). Ecol. Monogr., 28:155–191.

PREPARED BY: William L. Goodfellow, Jr., *Johns Hopkins University, Applied Physics Laboratory, Shady Side, MD 20887.*

Vulnerable

SPOTTED DARTER
Etheostoma maculatum Kirtland
Family Percidae
Order Perciformes

DESCRIPTION: This is a colorful darter with a sharply pointed snout and slightly rounded tail; the standard length rarely exceeds 70 mm. It is distinguished from close relatives in the subgenus *Nothonotus* (in Pennsylvania, bluebreast darter, *E. camurum,* and tippecanoe darter, *E. tippecanoe*) by light margins on dorsal and caudal fins and scattered red, side spots surrounded by dark halos. Horizontal lines between scale rows on side are limited to posterior one-third of body. The fins of females are heavily spotted. Adult males are olivaceous with a light belly; adult females are greenish with irregular dark markings.

RANGE: This darter is known from French Creek of the Allegheny River drainage in southwestern New York and northwestern Pennsylvania, west through the Ohio River basin to north-central Indiana, and south through the Cumberland and Tennessee rivers in Kentucky and Tennessee.

HABITAT: It is found either adjacent to or in swift deep riffles of large streams over a substrate of large rubble.

LIFE HISTORY AND ECOLOGY: The spotted darter spawns in midsummer. About 65 eggs per spawning act are laid in several layers on the undersides of large rocks at depths up to 60 cm. Prob-

Spotted Darter (*Etheostoma maculatum*). Photograph by E. L. Cooper.

SPOTTED DARTER (*Etheostoma maculatum*)

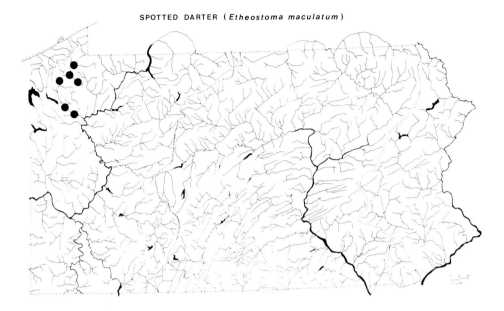

ably from two to four spawning acts occur each season. A territorial male guards each nest. The diet is dominated by midge larvae.

SPECIALIZED OR UNIQUE CHARACTERISTICS: This fish is sexually dimorphic; male coloration more brilliant than that of female.

BASIS OF STATUS CLASSIFICATION: The

SPOTTED DARTER (*Etheostoma maculatum*)

spotted darter is presently uncommon at scattered localities in French Creek, northwestern Pennsylvania.

RECOMMENDATIONS: Protect the habitat and monitor population trends.

SELECTED REFERENCES:

RANEY, E. C., and E. A. LACHNER. 1939. Observations on the life history of the spotted darter, *Poecilichthys maculatus* (Kirtland). Copeia, 1939:157–165.

TRAUTMAN, M. B. 1957. The fishes of Ohio with illustrated keys. Ohio State Univ. Press, Columbus, v–xvii + 683 pp.

WINN, H. E. 1958. Comparative reproductive behavior and ecology of fourteen species of darters (Pisces-Percidae). Ecol. Monogr., 28:155–191.

ZORACH, T., and E. C. RANEY. 1967. Systematics of the percid fish, *Etheostoma maculatum* Kirtland, and related species of the subgenus *Nothonotus*. Amer. Midland Nat., 77:296–322.

PREPARED BY: Robert W. Malick, Jr., *Ichthyological Associates, Inc., Three Mile Island Aquatic Study, P.O. Box 223, Etters, PA 17319.*

Vulnerable

CHANNEL DARTER
Percina copelandi (Jordan)
Family Percidae
Order Perciformes

OTHER NAMES: Copeland's darter; *Hadropterus copelandi, Cottogaster copelandi, Rheocrypta copelandi.*

Channel Darter (*Percina copelandi*). Photograph by E. L. Cooper.

DESCRIPTION: The channel darter is an elongate, slender fish which seldom exceeds 50 mm. The color is sandy with brown speckles; dark lateral stripe broken into numerous oblong to round blotches. Breeding males become dark about the head and pelvic fins, with blue and green colors along the sides. The species is unique in this genus in that it lacks a frenum which fastens the upper jaw firmly to the snout.

RANGE: This darter has a wide disjunct distribution from Oklahoma and Louisiana northeast to the Great Lakes drainage. In Pennsylvania, it is found in Lake Erie tributaries and in the upper Allegheny River drainage.

HABITAT: The channel darter is usually restricted to large rivers and their main tributaries, occurring on fine gravel shoals or riffles. It over-winters in quiet backwaters over organic debris. It apparently needs moderate current and clean fine gravel substrate for spawning and feeding.

LIFE HISTORY AND ECOLOGY: Spawning occurs in early summer in Michigan. Adults migrate to form large breeding aggregations in fast current over a mixed substrate of rocks, gravel, and sand. They apparently avoid areas of soft bottom. Males guard territories within the spawning area and mate promiscuously with females invading their territory. No care of eggs and young occurs after spawning.

The food of channel darters is varied, with some individuals eating mostly algae and organic debris, others consuming small mayfly and midge larvae. The lack of zooplankton in lake forms indicates that the channel darter is primarily a benthic feeder.

CHANNEL DARTER (*Percina copelandi*)

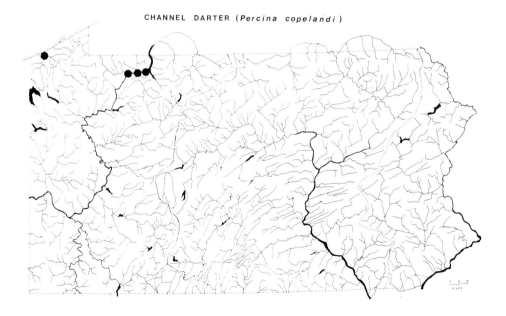

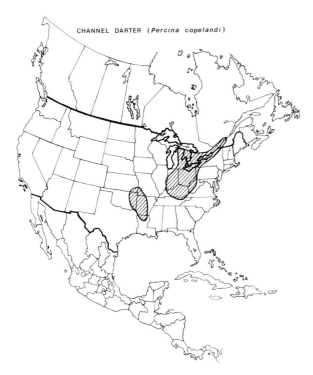

CHANNEL DARTER (*Percina copelandi*)

There are no detailed growth studies, but males grow larger than females, sometimes reaching a size of 60 mm. The ecology of this species, which is seldom abundant at any locality, is not well understood. It probably is used as food for predators but is of some interest in that it is one of a few darters that feeds on algae and detritus to a large extent.

BASIS OF STATUS CLASSIFICATION: The channel darter must be considered as vulnerable in Pennsylvania due to its scarcity and because it occurs in only a few localities. Its habitat requirement of clean substrate in lakes, and rapid current over clean riffles for spawning makes it vulnerable to pollution.

SELECTED REFERENCES:

CROSS, F. B., and J. T. COLLINS. 1975. Fishes in Kansas. Univ. Kansas, Mus. Nat. Hist., Publ. Ed. Ser., 3:1–189.

JORDAN, D. S. 1877. Notes on Cottidae, Etheostomatidae, Percidae, Centrarchidae, Aphredoderidae, Dorysomatidae and Cyprinidae, with revisions of the genera and descriptions of new or little known species. Bull. U.S. Nat. Mus. 10:1–116.

SCOTT, W. B., and E. J. CROSSMAN. 1973. Freshwater fishes of Canada. Bull. Fish. Res. Bd. Canada, 184:1–966.

TRAUTMAN, M. B. 1957. The fishes of Ohio. Ohio State Univ. Press, Columbus, v–xvii + 683 pp.

TURNER, C. L. 1921. Food of the common Ohio darters. Ohio J. Sci., 22:41–62.

WINN, H. E. 1953. Breeding habits of the percid fish, *Hadropterus copelandi* in Michigan. Copeia, 1953:26–30.

PREPARED BY: Edwin L. Cooper, *The Pennsylvania State University, University Park, PA 16802.*

Vulnerable

GILT DARTER
Percina evides (Jordan and Copeland)
Family Percidae
Order Perciformes

OTHER NAMES: Hadropterus evides, Alvordius evides, Ericosma evides.

DESCRIPTION: The gilt darter is a rather robust fish with a series of dark blotches along the sides, and dark cross bars on the back. It grows to a size of about 88 mm. The color is dark olive on the back, shading to lighter green and yellow colors on the sides and belly. A well-developed dusky bar is present beneath the eye. Breeding males develop bright orange and yellow colors on the head, throat and some fins.

RANGE: The gilt darter has a disjunct distribution, presumably reduced from a former wide range throughout the upper Mississippi and Ohio River drainages. In Pennsylvania it is present only in the upper Allegheny River.

HABITAT: This darter is found in clear medium-sized streams over gravel or rubble bottom in riffles with moderate to fast current. It has apparently disappeared from suitable habitats in some rivers due to impoundment, siltation and industrial pollution. In others, such as the Allegheny River, it remains a rare inhabitant which was considered rare at least 40 years ago.

LIFE HISTORY AND ECOLOGY: Except for Denoncourt's unpublished thesis (1969) virtually nothing is known of its life-history. Breeding males are larger, more brilliantly colored with reds and greens, and are more tuberculate. They spawn in the spring on deep riffles. In contrast with very abundant populations of sympatric darters such as the greenside, the rainbow, and the variegate darter, the gilt darter is only occasionally collected in a few selected riffles.

BASIS OF STATUS CLASSIFICATION: The gilt darter must be considered as vulnerable because of the very small populations present only in the main

GILT DARTER (*Percina evides*)

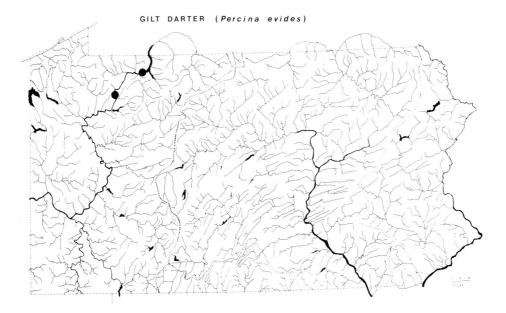

stem of the upper Allegheny River. It is somewhat surprising that a species that was rare in 1936 continues to maintain small populations in this river in 1975.

SELECTED REFERENCES:

DENONCOURT, R. F. 1969. A systematic study of the gilt darter *Percina evides* (Jordan and Copeland) (Pisces: Percidae). Un-

publ. Ph.D. thesis, Cornell Univ., Ithaca, New York, 216 pp.

GREELEY, J. R. 1938. Fishes of the area with annotated list. Pp. 48–73, *in* A biological survey of the Allegheny and Chemung watersheds, Suppl. Ann. Rept., New York State Conserv. Dept., 27:1–287.

JORDAN, D. S. 1877. On the fishes of northern Indiana. Proc. Acad. Nat. Sci. Philadelphia, 29:42–82.

PFLIEGER, W. L. 1975. The fishes of Missouri. Missouri Dept. Conserv., Western Publ. Co., Jefferson City, 343 pp.

RANEY, E. C. 1938. The distribution of the fishes of the Ohio drainage basin of western Pennsylvania. Unpubl. Ph.D. thesis, Cornell Univ., Ithaca, New York, 102 pp.

TRAUTMAN, M. B. 1957. The fishes of Ohio. Ohio State Univ. Press, Columbus, v–xvii + 683 pp.

GILT DARTER (*Percina evides*)

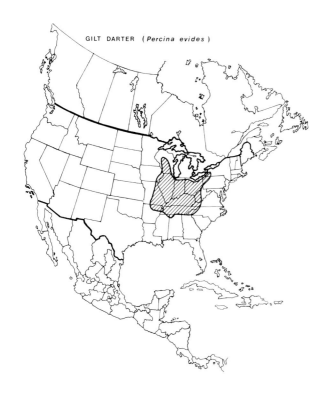

PREPARED BY: Edwin L. Cooper, *The Pennsylvania State University, University Park, PA 16802.*

Vulnerable

FRESHWATER DRUM
Aplodinotus grunniens Rafinesque
Family Sciaenidae
Order Perciformes

OTHER NAMES: Sheepshead, freshwater sheepshead, croaker, white perch; *Corvina oscula, Sciaena oscula.*

DESCRIPTION: The freshwater drum is a deep-bodied, robust fish with a long dorsal fin extending from near the operculum to the caudal fin. The head profile is steep, the mouth is nearly horizontal. Two skeletal characteristics are unique; the stout pha-

Freshwater Drum (*Aplodinotus grunniens*). Photograph by C. A. Purkett.

ryngeal arches adapted for crushing molluscs and very enlarged saccular otoliths. The background color is greenish-brown on the back, grading to a white belly. The body is covered with large silvery scales, small scales extending onto the base of the soft dorsal fin. The second ray of the anal fin is enlarged into a stout spine.

RANGE: The freshwater drum has an extensive north–south range from Hudson Bay, Canada, to Guatemala in Central America. The drum is absent from the East Coast, but common throughout the Great Lakes and Mississippi River drainages. In Pennsylvania it was once common in the Allegheny and Monongahela Rivers, but during the past 25 years it has been found only in Lake Erie.

HABITAT: The freshwater drum is considered to be a benthic form of large rivers and turbid lakes tolerating eutrophic conditions. With continued improvement in water quality of the upper Ohio River it would not be surprising to find the freshwater drum re-establishing its former abundance in the Allegheny River. The sauger is a good example of a fish which has re-established itself in recent years.

LIFE HISTORY AND ECOLOGY: Despite the long time this fish has been important commercially, details of its spawning have not been described. It is apparently a communal, pelagic spawner in the evening. During spawning, all drums and croakers emit characteristic drumming sounds by means of mus-

FRESHWATER DRUM (*Aplodinotus grunniens*)

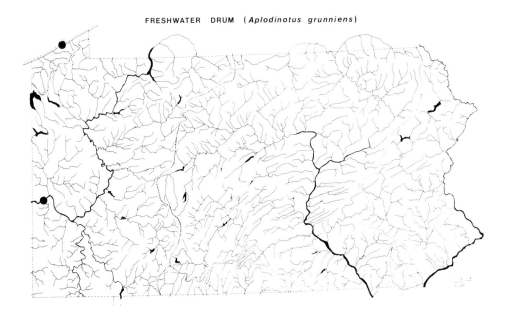

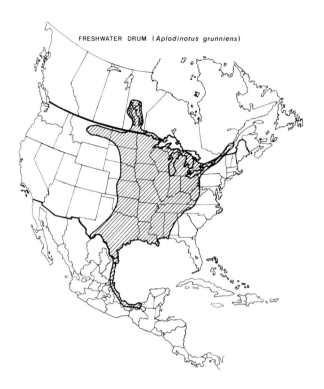

FRESHWATER DRUM (*Aplodinotus grunniens*)

cles vibrating the swim bladder. The eggs are semi-buoyant.

The food of the drum is highly variable but large numbers of molluscs are utilized when available. In other areas, a common food progression occurs from zooplankton and aquatic insects to crayfish and forage fishes as the fish grows. The drum lives for at least 15 years and reaches a weight of more than 6.8 kg. It is taken occasionally by anglers, but is becoming more important as a food fish as stocks of the more desirable species such as blue pike or walleye have declined.

SPECIALIZED OR UNIQUE CHARACTERISTICS: The freshwater drum is unique in being the only freshwater representative of a marine family of many species.

BASIS OF STATUS CLASSIFICATION: It is classed as vulnerable because it has disappeared from areas of former abundance in Pennsylvania and now is found only in Lake Erie. It is still widely distributed and abundant in other areas of North America.

SELECTED REFERENCES:

DAIBER, F. C. 1952. The food and feeding relationship of the freshwater drum, *Aplodinotus grunniens* Rafinesque in western Lake Erie. Ohio J. Sci., 52:35–46.
———. 1953. Notes on the spawning population of the freshwater drum (*Aplodinotus grunniens* Rafinesque) in western Lake Erie. Amer. Midland Nat., 50:159–171.
DENDY, J. S. 1946. Food of several species of fish, Norris Reservoir, Tennessee. J. Tennessee Acad. Sci., 21:105–127.
EDSALL, T. A. 1967. Biology of the freshwater drum in western Lake Erie. Ohio J. Sci., 67:321–340.
FORBES, S. A., and R. E. RICHARDSON. 1920. The fishes of Illinois. Illinois Nat. Hist. Surv., Urbana, 357 pp.
RAFINESQUE, C. S. 1819. Prodrome de 70 nouveaux genres d'animaux decouverts dans l'interieur des Etats-Unis d'Amerique durant l'annee 1818. J. Physique, Paris, 88:417–429.

PREPARED BY: Edwin L. Cooper, *The Pennsylvania State University, University Park, PA 16802.*

Status Undetermined

LONGNOSE GAR
Lepisosteus osseus (Linnaeus)
Family Lepisosteidae
Order Semionotiformes

OTHER NAMES: Gar, garpike, billfish, needlenose gar; *Lepidosteus osseus, Esox osseus.*

DESCRIPTION: The longnose gar is an elongate fish with a narrow, elongate upper and lower jaws fitted with numerous needle-like teeth. The body is completely plated with rhombic, ganoid scales forming a complete bony covering. The dorsal and anal fins are short and placed far back toward the tail. The caudal fin is rounded with upturned vertebral axis. A few spots are present on the posterior body and fins but are lacking on head and jaws. This

Longnose Gar (*Lepisosteus osseus*). Photograph by E. L. Cooper.

LONGNOSE GAR (*Lepisosteus osseus*)

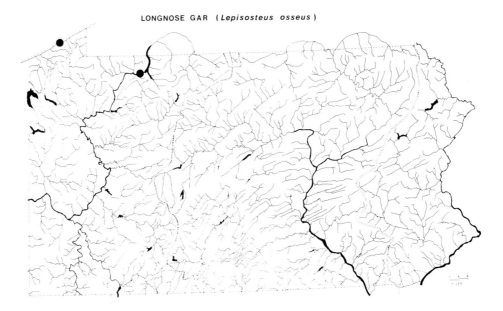

species is a medium-sized gar sometimes reaching a length of 1,500 mm.

RANGE: This gar is widely distributed throughout the Mississippi River drainage and into the lower Great Lakes; also common along the Gulf of Mexico and up the Atlantic Coast as far as New Jersey, in both fresh and brackish water. In Pennsylvania it is reported at widely scattered localities, but only taken consistently in the Presque Isle peninsula area of Lake Erie.

HABITAT: The longnose gar is found in a wide variety of habitats, but typically prefers sluggish pools, and backwaters of streams or shallow weedy bays of warm water lakes. Along the coast, it frequently invades brackish water estuaries.

LIFE HISTORY AND ECOLOGY: The longnose gar spawns in the spring in the warm weedy shallows of lakes, or occasionally migrates into shallow tributary streams to spawn. No nest is built, and the eggs are scattered at random, adhering to submerged vegetation. The young gar have an adhesive pad on the tip of the snout by which they adhere to vegetation to avoid being smothered in the bottom silt.

   The food of the longnose gar is almost entirely fish, even in brackish water where shrimp and crabs are commonly taken by the spotted gar. Because of this predatory habit, gar are often condemned as undesirable and have led some fish managers to control gar populations by netting, poisoning, and electrofishing. However, there is still little knowledge of either the dynamics of gar populations or of their effect on other fish populations.

SPECIALIZED OR UNIQUE CHARACTERISTICS: Gars are unique in retaining primitive characters such as ganoid scales, and a vascularized swimbladder which enables them to breathe at-

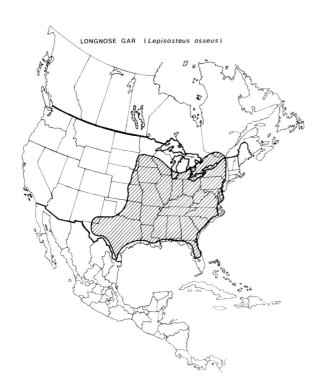

LONGNOSE GAR (*Lepisosteus osseus*)

mospheric oxygen. They are the remaining few species of a group of primitive fish known as fossil forms dating back at least to the Jurassic period.

BASIS OF STATUS CLASSIFICATION: Because of its unpopularity with anglers and fish managers, the longnose gar is always vulnerable to elimination in the Commonwealth. It is found in a very limited habitat in Pennsylvania, although it is common in other parts of its range in North America.

SELECTED REFERENCES:

LAGLER, K. F., D. B. OBRECHT, and G. V. HARRY. 1943. The food and habits of gars (*Lepisosteus* spp.) considered in relation to fish management. Invest. Indiana Lakes Streams, Indiana Dept. Conservation, 2:118–135.

LINNAEUS, C. 1758. Systema naturae per regna tria naturae, secundum classes, ordines, genera, species, cum characteribus, differentiis, synonymis, locis. Laurentii Salvii, Holmiae, 10th ed., 1:1–824.

MANSUETI, A. J., and J. D. HARDY, JR. 1967. Development of fishes of the Chesapeake Bay Region. Part 1. Nat. Res. Inst., Univ. Maryland, Baltimore, 202 pp.

NETSCH, N. F. 1967. Food and feeding habits of longnose gar in central Missouri. Proc. Southeastern Assoc. Game Fish. Comm., 18:506–511.

NETSCH, N. F., and A. WITT, JR. 1962. Contributions to the life history of the longnose gar (*Lepisosteus osseus*) in Missouri. Trans. Amer. Fish. Soc., 91:251–262.

SCOTT, W. B., and E. J. CROSSMAN. 1973. Freshwater fishes of Canada. Bull. Fish. Res. Bd. Canada, 184:1–966.

PREPARED BY: Edwin L. Cooper, *The Pennsylvania State University, University Park, PA 16802.*

Status Undetermined

BOWFIN
Amia calva Linnaeus
Family Amiidae
Order Amiiformes

OTHER NAMES: Dogfish, grindle, mudfish; *Amia ocellicaudata, Amiatus calva.*

DESCRIPTION: The bowfin is a stout-bodied, cylindrical fish with a long, low dorsal fin and a rounded tail. The oval gular plate on the ventral surface of the head is a unique skeletal character among North American fishes. A prominent black spot is present near the upper base of the tail. Young are marbled with yellow and black markings on sides of head, body, and fins. The bowfin grows to a large size sometimes exceeding 7 kg.

Bowfin (*Amia calva*). Photograph by E. L. Cooper.

RANGE: The bowfin has a wide range throughout the Mississippi River and Great Lakes drainages and along the Gulf of Mexico and Atlantic Coast as far north as the Susquehanna River. In Pennsylvania it is now restricted to the Presque Isle peninsula area of Lake Erie, and has been introduced into a few other localities.

HABITAT: The bowfin occupies many different habitats, but avoids swift current or excessive turbidity. They adapt readily to roadside ditches, swamps, and sloughs utilizing their vascularized swimbladder as an air breathing organ for respiration. Introduced populations often thrive under conditions that would be unfavorable to other fishes.

LIFE HISTORY AND ECOLOGY: The bowfin spawns in the spring in flooded marshes over submerged vegetation. The male prepares a shallow nest and guards the eggs and young until the young reach a size of 75 to 100 mm. Growth is rapid and adults reach a size of 500 mm in about 5 years.

Bowfins are largely piscivorous, with crayfish also an important food source. For this reason, they have historically been considered as undesirable predators on game fishes. In recent years, however, they have been introduced into lakes to help control stunted panfishes. There are few data to support either of these ideas.

SPECIALIZED OR UNIQUE CHARACTERISTICS: The bowfin is a sole species remaining in North America of a primitive order of fishes dating back in the fossil record for at least 180 million years. The gular plate and highly vascularized swimbladder are also rare characteristics found in few other species.

BASIS OF STATUS CLASSIFICATION: The bowfin is regarded as status undetermined in Pennsylvania because few data are available for it in the Commonwealth and because of its restricted habi-

BOWFIN (*Amia calva*)

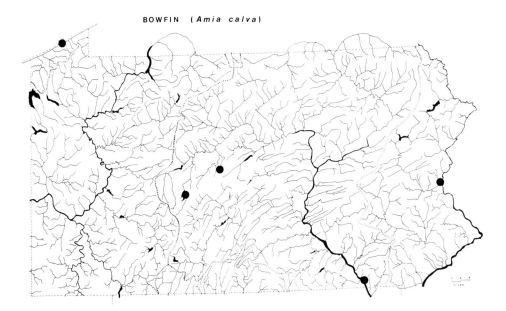

tat. Attempts to establish populations in other localities have not been clear successes, but some persist. Due to its wide distribution and large populations existing outside Pennsylvania there is no cause for intensive protection.

SELECTED REFERENCES:

BERRY, F. H. 1955. Food of the mudfish (*Amia calva*) in Lake Newman, Florida in relation to its management. Quart. J. Florida Acad. Sci., 18:69–75.

BEVELANDER, G. 1934. The gills of *Amia calva* specialized for respiration in an oxygen deficient habitat. Copeia, 1934:123–127.

BREDER, C. M., JR. 1928. On the appetite of *Amiatus calva* (Linnaeus). Copeia, 1928:54–56.

DOAN, K. H. 1938. Observations on dogfish (*Amia calva*) and their young. Copeia, 1938:204.

LINNAEUS, C. 1766. Systema naturae per regna tria naturae, secundum classes, ordines, genera, species, cum characteribus, differentiis, synonymis, locis. Laurentii Salvii, Holmiae, 12th ed., 1(1):1–532.

SCOTT, W. B., and E. J. CROSSMAN. 1973. Freshwater fishes of Canada. Bull. Fish. Res. Bd. Canada, 184:1–966.

PREPARED BY: Edwin L. Cooper, *The Pennsylvania State University, University Park, PA 16802.*

Status Undetermined

HICKORY SHAD
Alosa mediocris (Mitchill)
Family Clupeidae
Order Clupeiformes

OTHER NAMES: Hickory jack, tailor shad, freshwater tailor; *Pomolobus mediocris, Clupea mediocris.*

DESCRIPTION: The hickory shad is a fusiform, shad-like fish with large silvery scales and a protruding lower jaw. Readily separated from other silvery fishes by the saw-like scutes along the midbelly. It is easily distinguished from other sympatric clupeids such as the alewife, the blueback herring, and the American shad by the very small number (19–

BOWFIN (*Amia calva*)

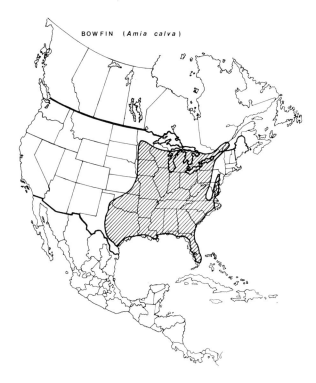

HICKORY SHAD (*Alosa mediocris*)

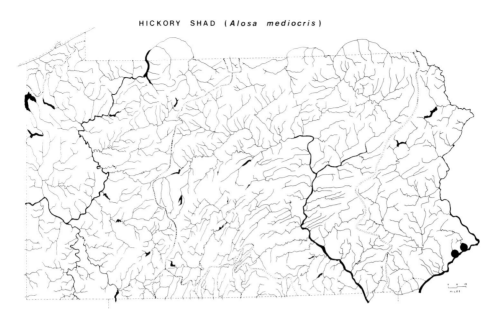

21) of gill rakers on the lower limb of the first arch. There is a dark shoulder spot followed by several obscure spots along the sides. This shad seldom exceeds a weight of 900 g.

RANGE: The hickory shad is anadromous along the Atlantic Coast from Maine to Florida. It is only geographically separated from the skipjack herring of the Mississippi and Gulf Coast drainages, considered to be the other species of a very similar pair. In Pennsylvania, it is sometimes reported in the lower Delaware River, but there has not been any recently collected specimens.

HABITAT: The hickory shad is an anadromous coastal form which comes from unknown marine areas to spawn in freshwater streams in the spring. The scarcity of young and juveniles in collections has led investigators to speculate that they quickly migrate downstream to deep waters of large bays or into the ocean for feeding and growth. The only possible habitat in Pennsylvania would therefore be the lower part of the Delaware River as spawning adults.

LIFE HISTORY AND ECOLOGY: Aside from its spawning migrations and early life history stages in freshwater, the life history of the hickory shad is largely unknown. They spawn in the lower reaches of fresh water including the tidal zone, depositing their semibuoyant eggs at random on shoals. The young spend only a short time in fresh water, then move to deeper bays or the ocean. The food of adult fish includes a wide variety of pelagic and benthic forms; fishes, squids, crabs, and other crustaceans are commonly found in stomachs. Historically, the hickory shad was marketed together with the alewife and blueback herring as river herrings, but was not as highly prized as the American shad as a food fish. It is now a respectable sport fish on its migratory runs in many coastal streams.

HICKORY SHAD (*Alosa mediocris*)

BASIS OF STATUS CLASSIFICATION: The hickory shad is classed as status undetermined on the basis of its restricted spawning habitat, and the somewhat degraded chemical conditions of the Delaware River in that area. Few data are available concerning the species in Pennsylvania. There is little danger of extinction of the species because of its wide geographic distribution along the Atlantic coast.

SELECTED REFERENCES:

BIGELOW, H. B., and W. C. SCHROEDER. 1953. Fishes of the Gulf of Maine. U.S. Fish Wildl. Serv., Fish. Bull., 53:1–577.

HILDEBRAND, S. F. 1963. Family Clupeidae. Fishes of the western North Atlantic. Mem. Sears Found. Mar. Res., 1:257–442.

———, and W. C. SCHROEDER. 1928. Fishes of Chesapeake Bay. Bull. U.S. Bur. Fish., 43(part 1):1–366.

MANSUETI, R. J. 1958. The hickory shad unmasked. Nature Mag., 51:351–354, 386.

———. 1962. Eggs, larvae, and young of the hickory shad, *Alosa mediocris* with comments on its ecology in the estuary. Chesapeake Sci., 3:173–205.

MASSMANN, W. H., and R. S. BAILEY. 1956. The shad in Virginia waters. Virginia Wildl., April, 4 pp.

MITCHILL, S. L. 1814. Report in part of Samuel L. Mitchill, M. D. on the fishes of New York. D. Carlisle, New York, 28 pp.

PREPARED BY: Edwin L. Cooper, *The Pennsylvania State University, University Park, PA 16802.*

Status Undetermined

HORNYHEAD CHUB
Nocomis biguttatus Kirtland
Family Cyprinidae
Order Cypriniformes

OTHER NAMES: Hybopsis biguttata, Nocomis kentuckiensis, Semotilus biguttatus.

DESCRIPTION: The hornyhead chub is a stout minnow with terminal maxillary barbels and large scales. Breeding males develop large pearl organs on top of the head from the snout to the occiput. The color is usually greenish-brown, shading to lighter colors on the ventral sides. Breeding males develop rosy, blue, and green colors along the sides. Maximum size is about 130 mm for males, females are somewhat smaller.

RANGE: The fish is widely distributed in the glaciated areas of the upper Mississippi River and Great Lakes drainages, with a western extension of its range into Kansas, Arizona, and Colorado. In Pennsylvania it is confined to the glaciated northwestern corner of the Commonwealth. In the 1930's it was found at more localities than during the past 25 years.

HABITAT: The hornyhead chub is restricted to warm, clear, gravelly creeks of moderate size with some current. It is not found in lakes or ponds, apparently requiring a moderate current over a gravel riffle for successful spawning. Temperatures suitable for trout are apparently too cold for the hornyhead chub.

LIFE HISTORY AND ECOLOGY: In the spring the male prepares a nest consisting of a pile of small stones by carrying them individually to a selected spot on a riffle. The chubs deposit their eggs in this stone pile and then desert the nest. Many other minnows also utilize chub nests for spawning, and minnow hybrids are not uncommon in these localities. The chubs grow to about 130 mm in 4 years with males slightly exceeding females in growth rate. Their food is varied, ranging from a predominance of algae in the young to a preference for aquatic insects, snails, and crustaceans in the larger chubs. They are a favorite bait fish because of their hardiness in tanks or in bait buckets.

Hornyhead Chub (*Nocomis biguttatus*). Photograph by E. L. Cooper.

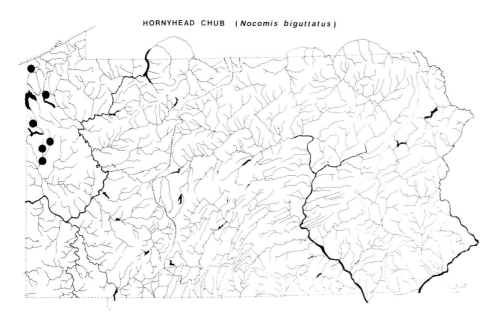

HORNYHEAD CHUB   (*Nocomis biguttatus*)

BASIS OF STATUS CLASSIFICATION: The current status of this species is undetermined due to its restricted distribution and appears to have declined in abundance over the past 50 years as once clear, gravelly streams became degraded. It is not presently in danger of extinction because of its widespread distribution outside Pennsylvania.

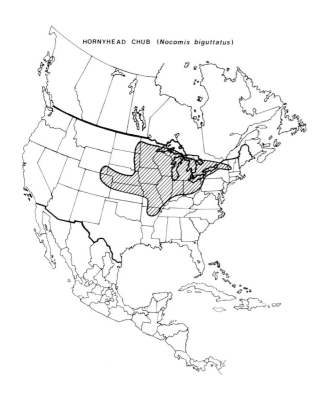

HORNYHEAD CHUB (*Nocomis biguttatus*)

SELECTED REFERENCES:

DEACON, J. E., and A. L. METCALF. 1961. Fishes of the Wakarusa River in Kansas. Univ. Kansas Publ., Mus. Nat. Hist., 13:309–322.

GERKING, S. D. 1945. Distribution of the fishes of Indiana. Invest. Indiana Lakes Streams, 3:1–137.

HANKINSON, T. L. 1932. Observations on the breeding behavior and habitats of fishes in southern Michigan. Papers Michigan Acad. Sci. Arts Ltrs., 15:411–425.

KIRTLAND, J. P. 1841. Descriptions of the fishes of the Ohio River and its tributaries. Boston J. Nat. Hist., 3:338–352, 469–482; 4:16–26, 303–308; 5:21–32.

LACHNER, E. A. 1952. Studies of the biology of the cyprinid fishes of the chub genus *Nocomis* in northeastern United States. Amer. Midland Nat., 48:433–466.

SCOTT, W. B., and E. J. CROSSMAN. 1973. The freshwater fishes of Canada. Bull. Fish. Res. Bd. Canada, 184:1–966.

PREPARED BY: Edwin L. Cooper, *The Pennsylvania State University, University Park, PA 16802.*

Status Undetermined

RIVER REDHORSE
Moxostoma carinatum (Cope)
Family Catostomidae
Order Cypriniformes

OTHER NAMES: Placopharynx carinatus, Placopharynx duquesnii.

DESCRIPTION: The river redhorse has a moderately stout body, often quite compressed in adult males. The snout profile is slightly rounded and ex-

RIVER REDHORSE (*Moxostoma carinatum*)

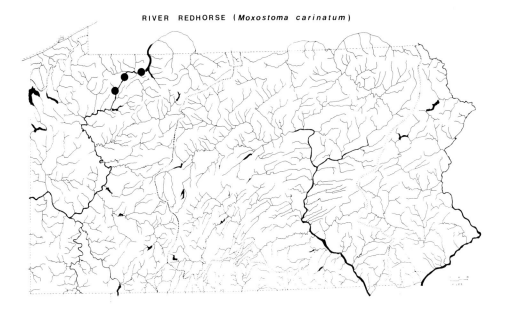

ceeding the upper lip in adults. The posterior margin of the lips forms a slightly obtuse angle, and the lip surfaces are deeply plicate. The margin of the dorsal fin is straight or concave. The anal fin of the males is elongate; the caudal fin with upper lobe is usually longer than the lower. The pharyngeal arch is very stout with molariform teeth, unique among redhorses. The color in adults is yellowish, brassy or bronzy. The caudal fin is bright red; the lower fins are orange to reddish orange. The largest redhorses reach a size of 750 mm and 2.7 to 3.6 kg.

RANGE: The range of the river redhorse is centered in mid-Mississippi and Ohio River drainages with disjunct populations in Michigan, Quebec, Mississippi, and Alabama. In Pennsylvania it is now known only from the Allegheny River.

HABITAT: It is usually found in large rivers and the lower portion of their main tributaries. It has been taken less often in smaller streams than all other species of redhorses. It largely avoids base-gradient streams in regions of little relief.

LIFE HISTORY AND ECOLOGY: Stomach analysis indicates that bivalve molluscs and aquatic insects are common food items. The large molar teeth are apparently an adaptation for crushing hard shelled molluscs. The large sizes attained, especially by males, appears to be due both to faster growth than other redhorses, and to a greater longevity. A 600 mm fish from the Allegheny River showed at least 14 winter marks on its scales.

The river redhorse is a late spawner compared with other redhorses, varying from mid-April in Alabama to early June in Quebec. An upriver migration for spawning was reported in Ohio by Trautman (1957). The male prepares a redd on a gravel riffle or run and one or more males spawns with a female. No parental care or defense of territory follows the spawning.

RIVER REDHORSE (*Moxostoma carinatum*)

SPECIALIZED OR UNIQUE CHARACTERIS-TICS: The apparent rarity of this species may be due in part to its preferred habitat in large rivers or reservoirs which seldom are sampled adequately. However, these river systems in western Pennsylvania have been polluted severely in the past and only a small amount of suitable habitat remains for this species.

BASIS OF STATUS CLASSIFICATION: Only a few large and old specimens have been taken in Pennsylvania in recent years. Until better data are obtained on possible spawning and recruitment of this species in the upper Ohio River watershed, the species should be considered as status undetermined.

SELECTED REFERENCES:

CLAY, W. M. 1975. The fishes of Kentucky. Kentucky Dept. Fish and Wildl. Res., Frankfort, 416 pp.

COPE, E. D. 1870. Partial synopsis of the freshwater fishes of North Carolina. Proc. Amer. Philos. Soc., 11:448–495.

FORBES, S. A. 1890. Studies of the food of freshwater fishes. Bull. Illinois State Lab. of Nat. Hist., 2:433–473.

FOWLER, H. W. 1919. A list of the fishes of Pennsylvania. Proc. Biol. Soc. Washington, 32:49–74.

HACKNEY, P. A., W. M. TATUM, and S. L. SPENCER. 1967. Life history of the river redhorse, *Moxostoma carinatum* (Cope) in the Cahaba River, Alabama, with notes on the management of the species as a sport fish. Proc. Ann. Conf. Southeastern Game Fish Comm., 21:324–332.

JENKINS, R. E. 1970. Systematic studies of the catostomid tribe Moxostomatini. Unpublished Ph.D. thesis, Cornell Univ., Ithaca, New York, 799 pp.

SCOTT, W. B., and E. J. CROSSMAN. 1973. Freshwater fishes of Canada. Bull. Fish. Res. Bd. Canada, 184:1–966.

TRAUTMAN, M. B. 1957. The fishes of Ohio. Ohio State Univ. Press, Columbus, v–xvii + 683 pp.

PREPARED BY: Edwin L. Cooper, *The Pennsylvania State University, University Park, PA 16802.*

Status Undetermined

BLACK BULLHEAD
Ictalurus melas (Rafinesque)
Family Ictaluridae
Order Siluriformes

OTHER NAMES: Black catfish, yellow belly bullhead, horned pout; *Silurus melas, Ameiurus melas.*

DESCRIPTION: A robust bullhead of dark color. Maximum length is usually 300 mm. The general body color is black, dark brown, or olive dorsally; sides with lustrous gold green sheen, ventrally dusky, white, or yellow; pale ventral color extending upward across the base of the caudal fin; fins dusky with darker margins, fin rays lighter than the membranes between; barbels gray, black, or mottled; pectoral fin spines weakly barbed; caudal fin moderately broad and truncate.

RANGE: They extend from northwestern New York, southwestward in the Mississippi drainage west of the Appalachians to the Mobile Bay drainage of Alabama, west and south to Texas and extreme

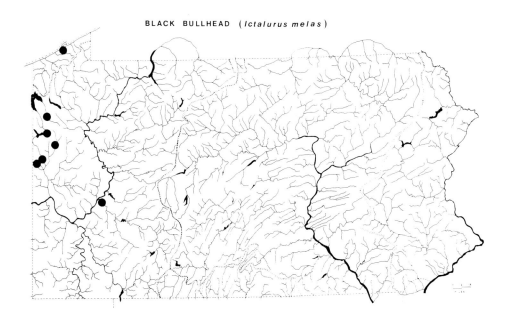

BLACK BULLHEAD (*Ictalurus melas*)

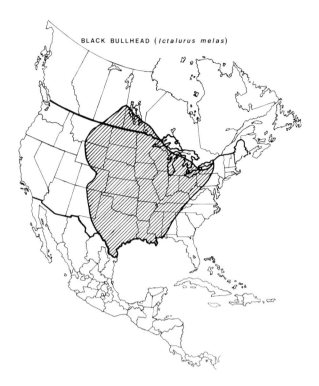

BLACK BULLHEAD (*Ictalurus melas*)

northern Mexico, north through the eastern portions of states from New Mexico to Montana and Saskatchewan, east through southern Manitoba to southwestern Ontario. It has been introduced in Arizona, California, Connecticut, Nevada, and Washington.

HABITAT: The black bullhead is found in lower portions of low-gradient, small to medium-size streams, ponds, and soft-bottom areas of lakes or impoundments.

LIFE HISTORY AND ECOLOGY: Spawning may occur from May to July or August. The female excavates a nest in shallow water in areas of heavy to moderate submerged vegetation. Silt and debris are fanned from the excavation, and gravel pushed toward the periphery with the snout.

The pair butt one another, and each slides its barbels over the other, prior to spawning. The male "embraces" the female during egg deposition, his caudal fin draped over her head. Spawning may take place five times in 1 hour, between which the deposited eggs are fanned by the female. Both sexes share in guarding and fanning the eggs after a day.

Eggs may hatch in 5 days if temperatures are high, and the young are herded about in a spherical mass until they reach about 25 mm. The parents then desert them.

Adults are mostly nocturnal, whereas the young are active and feed at dawn and dusk.

In one study both adults and young were considered to be selective planktivores. Other food items reported include insect larvae and pupae, clams, snails, crustaceans, plant material, leeches, and fishes.

BASIS OF STATUS CLASSIFICATION: Fowler (1919) listed this species as the black cat and reported it "Abundant and frequently marketed at Erie." Prior to 1982, the only verified specimens of *I. melas* from Pennsylvania were those reported by Raney (1938) in Lawrence, Mercer, and Westmoreland counties collected in 1934 and 1935. These specimens have been deposited in the University of Michigan Museum of Zoology and the Cornell University collections. In 1982, several specimens were collected in a tributary to the Beaver River in Lawrence County.

RECOMMENDATIONS: Further survey in western and northwestern Pennsylvania, particularly in the Shenango River drainage, may produce additional specimens of this species.

SELECTED REFERENCES:

DARNELL, R. M., and R. R. MEIEROTTO. 1965. Diurnal periodicity in the black bullhead, *Ictalurus melas* (Rafinesque). Trans. Amer. Fish. Soc., 94:1–8.

FOWLER, H. W. 1919. A list of the fishes of Pennsylvania. Proc. Biol. Soc. Washington, 32:49–74.

RANEY, E. C. 1938. The distribution of fishes of the Ohio drainage basin of western Pennsylvania. Unpublished Ph.D. thesis, Cornell Univ., Ithaca, New York, 102 pp.

REPSYS, A. J., R. L. APPLEGATE, and D. C. HALES. 1976. Food and food selectivity of the black bullhead, *Ictalurus melas*, in Lake Poinsett, South Dakota. J. Fish. Res. Bd. Canada, 33:768–775.

WALLACE, C. R. 1967. Observations on the reproductive behavior of the black bullhead (*Ictalurus melas*). Copeia, 1967: 852–853.

PREPARED BY: Clark N. Shiffer, *Pennsylvania Fish Commission, Robinson Lane, Bellefonte, PA 16823.*

Status Undetermined

FOURSPINE STICKLEBACK
Apeltes quadracus (Mitchill)
Family Gasterosteidae
Order Gasterosteiformes

OTHER NAMES: Stickleback, pinfish, mud-perch; *Gasterosteus apeltes, Gasterosteus quadracus.*

FOURSPINE STICKLEBACK (*Apeltes quadracus*)

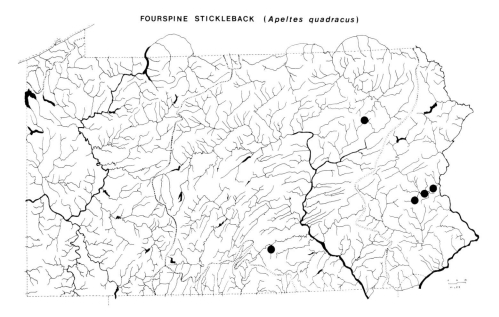

DESCRIPTION: The fourspine sticklebacks are diminutive fishes with stout dorsal, anal, and pelvic spines. The body tapers abruptly to a slender caudal peduncle. The skin is naked, without scales, bony plates, or prickles. Their color is dark-green to brown above grading to a light-colored belly. The maximum size reported is less than 50 mm.

RANGE: They are an Atlantic Coast form common

FOURSPINE STICKLEBACK (*Apeltes quadracus*)

from North Carolina to Quebec and Newfoundland. They have been introduced to nearby fresh waters in several places. In Pennsylvania, it was probably native to the lower Delaware River watershed, but has been successfully introduced into two Susquehanna River basin localities (Harvey's Lake, Luzerne County, and Big Spring, Cumberland County).

HABITAT: The fourspine stickleback is typically a marine and brackish water estuarine species found along mud flats or in dense vegetation. It seldom ventures far into fresh water. However, it is well acclimated to freshwaters in many disjunct localities from Nova Scotia to New York and Pennsylvania. In freshwater it shows a preference for quiet bays or weed beds along stream edges.

LIFE HISTORY AND ECOLOGY: The fourspine stickleback, like all other sticklebacks, has an elaborate breeding ritual with males constructing an enclosed nest of twigs and aquatic plants. Eggs are deposited in the nest where they are aerated and guarded by the male until after hatching. The life span for males is 1 or at most 2 years; females may live 1 year longer. The food is largely pelagic zooplankton, limited because of the small size of the fish. It is occasionally used as bait for sport fishing, but its chief interest is as a test animal for ecological study. An interesting behavior of the fourspine stickleback is that it is permitted to pick off the external parasites of the sympatric rainwater killifish. This symbiotic cleaning behavior is common among many marine fishes and shrimps.

The fourspine stickleback is extremely euryhaline, tolerating salinities from freshwater to complete seawater concentrations. Local populations are highly sedentary and could be easily extirpated as a result of environmental disturbances.

BASIS OF STATUS CLASSIFICATION: The introduced, freshwater populations in Pennsylvania must be considered as status undetermined. There is little evidence that these populations have spread even short distances from the stocking site over the past 25 years. Elsewhere along the Atlantic Coast, this species is in no danger of population decline or extirpation.

SELECTED REFERENCES:

BIGELOW, H. B., and W. C. SCHROEDER. 1953. Fishes of the Gulf of Maine. U.S. Fish Wildl. Serv., Fish. Bull., 53:1–577.

MITCHILL, S. L. 1815. On the fishes of New York. Notice in Trans. Linn. Soc. London, 11:424.

NELSON, J. S. 1968. Salinity tolerance of brook stickleback, *Culaea inconstans,* freshwater ninespine sticklebacks, *Pungitius pungitius,* and freshwater fourspine sticklebacks, *Apeltes quadracus.* Canadian J. Zool., 46:663–667.

REISMAN, H. M. 1963. Reproductive behavior of *Apeltes quadracus,* including some comparisons with other gasterosteid fishes. Copeia, 1963:191–192.

SCOTT, W. B., and E. J. CROSSMAN. 1973. Freshwater fishes of Canada. Bull. Fish. Res. Bd. Canada, 184:1–966.

TYLER, A. V. 1963. A cleaning symbiosis between the rainwater killifish, *Lucania parva* and the stickleback, *Apeltes quadracus.* Chesapeake Sci., 4:105–106.

PREPARED BY: Edwin L. Cooper, *The Pennsylvania State University, University Park, PA 16802.*

Status Undetermined
WARMOUTH
Lepomis gulosus (Cuvier)
Family Centrarchidae
Order Perciformes

OTHER NAMES: Warmouth bass, goggle-eye, stump-knocker; *Cyprinus coronarius, Chaenobryttus coronarius, Chaenobryttus gulosus, Pomotis gulosus.*

DESCRIPTION: The warmouth is a darkly mottled thick-bodied sunfish somewhat resembling the rock bass. Its affinity for other sunfishes in the genus *Lepomis* is shown by the presence of three anal spines. A large head with a very large mouth easily distinguishes this species from most other sunfishes. It seldom exceeds a length of 200 mm.

RANGE: The warmouth is widely distributed throughout east and central United States from Wisconsin and Michigan south to Texas and Florida. In Pennsylvania, it is rare in scattered localities over the Commonwealth.

HABITAT: This sunfish is found usually in lakes and ponds over a muddy bottom, but is occasionally taken in sluggish areas of warmwater streams, es-

WARMOUTH (*Lepomis gulosus*)

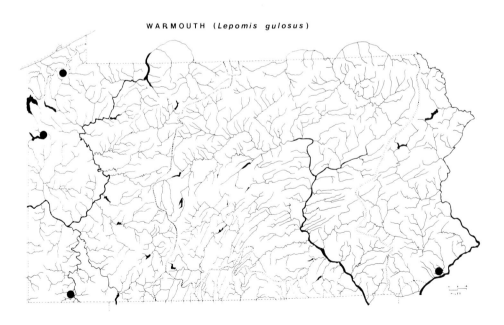

WARMOUTH (*Lepomis gulosus*)

pecially associated with dense weed beds. Stumps, logs, or other debris offer good hiding places in habitats lacking weeds.

LIFE HISTORY AND ECOLOGY: As is the case with all sunfishes, the male constructs a shallow nest near cover and guards the eggs and the young for a short period after hatching. Nests are usually found singly, rather than in large colonies such as in the bluegill. Their food is varied, ranging from zooplankton and small insects in newly hatched fry to larger insects and crayfish as the fish became larger. Growth is similar among the sexes, with an average size of about 150 mm reached in 4 years. Some fish live as long as 9 years.

Warmouths are important sport fish only in the lower Mississippi River drainage and states bordering the Gulf of Mexico. In the north, other sunfishes such as the bluegill and the rockbass are more abundant and popular among anglers. Managers have expressed some preference for the warmouth for the reason that it seldom overpopulates its habitat, thus not often producing a worthless stunted population of panfish.

BASIS OF STATUS CLASSIFICATION: The warmouth in Pennsylvania is widely scattered but occurs in very small numbers at any locality. Com-

petition with other sunfishes such as the bluegill, the green sunfish and the pumpkinseed probably is a factor contributing to its lack of success, as is the limited amount of preferred warmwater weedy habitat.

SELECTED REFERENCES:

Cuvier, G. A., and M. A. Valenciennes. 1828–1849. Histoire naturelle des poissons. Levrault, Strasborg, Paris, vol. 3.

Flemer, D. A., and W. S. Woolcott. 1966. Food habits and distribution of the fishes of Tuckahoe Creek, Virginia, with special emphasis on the bluegill, *Lepomis m. macrochirus* Rafinesque. Chesapeake Sci., 7:75–89.

Forbes, S. A., and R. E. Richardson. 1920. The fishes of Illinois. Illinois Nat. Hist. Surv., Urbana, 357 pp.

Larimore, R. W. 1957. Ecological life history of the warmouth (Centrarchidae). Bull. Illinois Nat. Hist. Surv., 27:1–83.

Lewis, W. M., and T. S. English. 1949. The warmouth, *Chaenobryttus coronarius* (Bartram) in Red Haw Hill Reservoir, Iowa. Iowa State Coll. J. Sci., 23:317–322.

Raney, E. C. 1965. Some pan fishes of New York — rock bass, crappies and other sunfishes. The Conservationist, New York Cons. Dept., 19(6):19–35.

PREPARED BY: Edwin L. Cooper, *The Pennsylvania State University, University Park, PA 16802.*

Status Undetermined

LONGHEAD DARTER
Percina macrocephala (Cope)
Family Percidae
Order Perciformes

OTHER NAMES: Bighead darter; *Hadropterus macrocephalus, Etheostoma macrocephalum.*

DESCRIPTION: The longhead darter is elongated with a long conical snout, and reaching a size of 100 mm. Noticeably bicolored, the upper parts are brown with black markings, the lower sides nearly white. There is a prominent tear-drop below the eye. The lateral blotches are broadly connected forming a wide, lateral band ending with a small discrete black spot at the base of the tail.

RANGE: The longhead darter has a restricted range on the west slope of the Appalachians from New York to Tennessee and North Carolina. In Pennsylvania it is now found only in French Creek and in the headwaters of the Allegheny River.

HABITAT: This species is found only in upland streams or large rivers, most frequently inhabiting

Longhead Darter (*Percina macrocephala*). Photograph by E. L. Cooper.

fast, rocky riffles. It is sometimes found in large pools below riffles, but only where the current is sufficient to keep the bottom free of silt.

LIFE HISTORY AND ECOLOGY: Little life history information is available, but they probably spawn in late spring or early summer; however, no actual observations have been reported. They grow to about 100 mm in 3 to 4 years and feed on small crayfish and larger insects.

SPECIALIZED OR UNIQUE CHARACTERISTICS: The habitat requirement for moderate current flowing over a clean stony substrate in large streams makes this species a good indicator of clean streams.

BASIS OF STATUS CLASSIFICATION: Originally found by Cope (1869) in the Youghiogheny River in Pennsylvania, this species is now absent or rare throughout much of its former range. It is taken regularly, but only in small numbers, in restricted localities of the Allegheny River and French Creek. The very restricted area and demanding habitat renders this species highly vulnerable to stream dredging or siltation.

SELECTED REFERENCES:

BEAN, T. H. 1892. The fishes of Pennsylvania. *In* Rept. State Comm. Fisheries for 1889–90–91, Harrisburg, Pennsylvania, 149 pp.

CLAY, W. M. 1975. The fishes of Kentucky. Kentucky Dept. Fish Wildl. Resources, Frankfort, 416 pp.

COPE, E. D. 1869. Synopsis of the Cyprinidae from Pennsylvania. Trans. Amer. Philo. Soc., 13(n.s.):351–410.

DEACON, J. E. et al. 1979. Fishes of North America, endangered, threatened, or of special concern: 1979. Pp. 30–44, *in* Fisheries, 4(2):1–69.

PAGE, L. M. 1978. Redescription, distribution, variation and life history notes on *Percina macrocephala* (Percidae). Copeia, 1978:655–664.

LONGHEAD DARTER (*Percina macrocephala*)

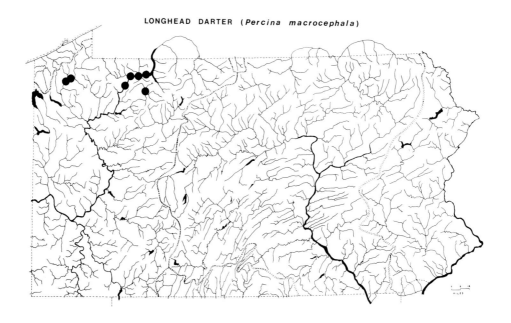

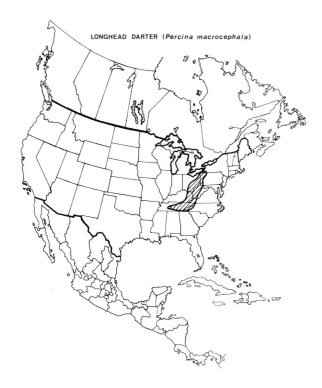

LONGHEAD DARTER (*Percina macrocephala*)

TRAUTMAN, M. B. 1957. The fishes of Ohio. Ohio State Univ. Press, Columbus, v–xvii + 683 pp.

PREPARED BY: Edwin L. Cooper, *The Pennsylvania State University, University Park, PA 16802.*

Extirpated

SHOVELNOSE STURGEON
Scaphirhynchus platorynchus (Rafinesque)
Family Acipenseridae
Order Acipenseriformes

OTHER NAMES: Hackleback, switchtail; *Accipenser platorynchus, Acipenser cataphractus.*

DESCRIPTION: One of the smallest sturgeons, it is easily distinguished from *Acipenser* by a wide and depressed snout, greatly elongate caudal peduncle and tail filament, fringed barbels and no spiracles. The color is pale yellow to brown on the back and sides, with a white belly. Females are usually larger than males, but average only about 630 mm and weigh about 1,360 g.

RANGE: The shovelnose sturgeon occurs in the Mississippi River and its major tributaries from

Montana, Minnesota, and Ohio south to Louisiana. The species was reported in the Ohio River as far upstream as Pittsburgh in the early 1800's, but has not been collected for many years.

HABITAT: This sturgeon is a large river form, apparently needing long stretches of flowing water to complete its life cycle. It is a benthic form, tolerant of high turbidity, usually found in deep channels over a sand or gravel bottom.

LIFE HISTORY AND ECOLOGY: Spawning probably occurs in the spring in fast water of channels over a stony bottom, although spawning has never been observed. Young, almost 25 mm in length, have been collected in Missouri in June. Spawning adults are 5 to 7 years old.

The food of this species is benthic in origin, including aquatic insects and molluscs, taken from clean sand and gravel bottoms in fast current. In the 1800's, this fish was marketed commercially as fresh or smoked sturgeon, and its eggs were mixed with those of paddlefish for caviar.

BASIS OF STATUS CLASSIFICATION: Although it was reported by Rafinesque (1820) in the Ohio River as far east as Pittsburgh, no specimens are available which were collected in Pennsylvania.

SELECTED REFERENCES:

BAILEY, R. M., and F. B. CROSS. 1954. River sturgeons of the American genus *Scaphirhynchus*: characters, distribution, and synonymy. Papers Michigan Acad. Sci. Arts Ltrs., 39:169–208.
FORBES, S. A., and R. E. RICHARDSON. 1920. The fishes of Illinois. Illinois Nat. Hist. Surv. Div., Urbana, 357 pp.
HELD, J. W. 1969. Some early foods of the shovelnose sturgeon in the Missouri River. Trans. Amer. Fish. Soc., 98:514–517.
PFLIEGER, W. L. 1975. The fishes of Missouri. Missouri Dept. Conserv., Western Publ. Co., Jefferson City, 343 pp.
RAFINESQUE, C. S. 1820. Ichthyologia Ohiensis, or natural history of the fishes inhabiting the River Ohio and its tributary streams, preceded by a physical description of the Ohio and its branches. Printed for the author by W. G. Hunt, Lexington, Kentucky, 90 pp.
SMITH, P. W. 1979. The fishes of Illinois. Illinois State Nat. Hist. Surv., Urbana, 314 pp.
TRAUTMAN, M. B. 1981. The fishes of Ohio. Ohio State Univ. Press, Columbus, rev. ed., 782 pp.

PREPARED BY: Edwin L. Cooper, *The Pennsylvania State University, University Park, PA 16802.*

Extirpated

PADDLEFISH
Polyodon spathula (Walbaum)
Family Polyodontidae
Order Acipenseriformes

OTHER NAMES: Spoonbill, spoonbill cat, shovelnose cat, boneless cat; *Squalus spathula, Polyodon feuille, Polyodon folium.*

DESCRIPTION: The paddlefish is a unique fish that cannot be confused with any other fish found in the United States and Canada. Possessing an elongated paddle-shaped snout, smooth skin, and a heterocercal tail, the paddlefish is easily recognizable. The mouth is large, without teeth, and located far back on the underside of the head. On the snout a pair of inconspicuous barbels are positioned ventroposteriorly. The eyes are small, placed at the front edge of the mouth, and directed down and forward. The pointed opercular flap is long, reaching beyond the pectoral fins. The dorsal fin is posterior to the pelvic fin and contains 50–60 fin rays; the pelvic fin is sub-abdominal; and the anal fin is slightly larger than the dorsal (50–60 fin rays) and slightly posterior. The body is naked, except for a small patch of scales on the upper lobe of the tail fin. The skeleton is composed of cartilage rather than bone. The color ranges from bluish-gray to olive gray on the upper parts to white or silvery on the belly.

DISTRIBUTION: The paddlefish was once common to most large water bodies in the Mississippi Valley and Gulf slope drainages. The range of the paddlefish has undergone a drastic decline since the early 1900's, possibly due to impoundments and less favorable water quality.

Historically the paddlefish has been collected from Pennsylvania, but it is unknown from recent collections. Specimens have been reported from Lake Erie, the Allegheny River, and the Kiskiminetas River.

HABITAT: Paddlefish occur primarily in quiet or slow-flowing waters rich in zooplankton. During spawning, however, they prefer free-flowing river with gravel bars.

LIFE HISTORY AND ECOLOGY: During spring flooding both males and females move upstream. Spawning takes place from April to June over sand and gravel bars in strong currents. The complete spawning act has not been reported, but it is generally believed that several males spawn with one female. The eggs are adhesive.

Young paddlefish feed on zooplankton, and aquatic and terrestrial insects. Feeding is accomplished by swimming slowly, with mouth open filtering water through gill rakers. Adult paddlefish will also eat larger insects and small fish.

Growth during the first two years can be rapid with an average daily increment of 4.3 mm. The average length of females tends to be larger than males, but no sexual difference in growth rate was noted. Individuals 20 years old are common and some live 30 years or more.

BASIS OF STATUS CLASSIFICATION: No records more recent than 1919 are known from Pennsylvania waters. Recent surveys by the Ohio River

Paddlefish (*Polyodon spathula*). Photograph supplied by National Fisheries Center, U.S. Fish and Wildlife Service, Kearneyville, WV 25430.

Valley Water Sanitation Commission and Preston and White (1978) document its presence no closer to Pennsylvania than mile point 436 of the Ohio River. Impoundments preventing upstream migration, destruction of habitat, and unfavorable water conditions have contributed to the extirpation of the paddlefish in Pennsylvania.

SELECTED REFERENCES:

CARLSON, D. M., and P. S. BONISLAWSKY. 1981. The paddlefish (*Polyodon spathula*) fisheries of the midwestern United States. Fisheries, 6:17–22; 26–27.

FRITZ, R. B. 1966. Unusual food of a paddlefish (*Polyodon spathula*) in Tennessee. Copeia, 1966:356.

HOUSER, A., and M. G. BROSS. 1959. Observations on the growth and reproduction of the paddlefish. Trans. Amer. Fish. Soc., 88:50–52.

MEYER, F. P., and J. H. STEVENSON. 1962. Studies on the artificial propagation of the paddlefish. Progr. Fish-Cult., 24:65–67.

PRESTON, H. R., and G. E. WHITE. 1978. Summary of Ohio River fishery surveys, 1968–76. Environ. Protection Agency, 903/ 9-78-009.

PURKETT, C. A., JR. 1961. Reproduction and early development of the paddlefish. Trans. Amer. Fish. Soc., 90:125–129.

———. 1963. The paddlefish fishery of the Osage River and Lake of the Ozarks, Missouri. Trans. Amer. Fish. Soc., 92:239–244.

RUELLE, R., and P. L. HUDSON. 1977. Paddlefish (*Polyodon spathula*): growth and food of young of the year and a suggested technique for measuring length. Trans. Amer. Fish. Soc., 106:609–613.

PREPARED BY: William L. Goodfellow, Jr., *Johns Hopkins University, Applied Physics Laboratory, Shady Side, MD 20887*; Reinald E. Smith, Jr., *NUS Corporation, 1910 Cochran Road, Manor Oak II, Pittsburgh, PA 15220.*

Extirpated

SHORTNOSE GAR
Lepisosteus platostomus Rafinesque
Family Lepisosteidae
Order Semionotiformes

OTHER NAMES: Stub-nose gar, duck-bill gar; *Lepidosteus platystomus, Cylindrosteus platostomus.*

DESCRIPTION: The shortnose gar has a shorter and broader snout than the longnose gar, and is distinguished from the spotted gar by the lack of discrete spots on the front half of the body, including the head and snout. Adults are usually less than 600 mm in length. The body is dark green or brown, shading along the sides to a white belly. Tile-like scales completely encase the body in a flexible, bony armor.

RANGE: The shortnose gar is confined to the more sluggish parts of the Mississippi River drainage. Although reported in early collections from the Ohio River and Lake Erie waters of Pennsylvania, there is some doubt as to the accuracy of these reports. Valid records exist, however, for the similar spotted gar from these localities.

HABITAT: Commonly found in quiet pools, backwaters and oxbows of large rivers, this gar is very tolerant of turbidity.

LIFE HISTORY AND ECOLOGY: Spawning occurs in early summer, with two or more males accompanying a female as they swim over shallow weed beds. The eggs are laid in small batches, and attach to each other and to vegetation by sticky threads. The predatory nature of this gar and its poor quality as a sport fish, or for eating, has resulted in a widespread reputation as a worthless nuisance.

BASIS OF STATUS CLASSIFICATION: It is doubtful that the species was ever present in Pennsylvania; it has been missing from the Commonwealth fauna for many years.

RECOMMENDATIONS: No measures should be taken to encourage the extralimital spread of this predator into Pennsylvania waters.

SELECTED REFERENCES:

COKER, R. E. 1930. Studies of common fishes of the Mississippi River at Keokuk. U.S. Bur. Fish. Bull., 45:141–225.

FORBES, S. A., and R. E. RICHARDSON. 1920. The fishes of Illinois. Illinois Nat. Hist. Surv. Div., Urbana, 357 pp.

FOWLER, H. W. 1919. A list of the fishes of Pennsylvania. Proc. Biol. Soc. Washington, 32:49–74.

LAGLER, K. F., C. B. OBRECHT, and G. V. HARRY. 1943. The food and habits of gars (*Lepisosteus spp.*) considered in relation to fish management. Invest. Indiana Lakes and Streams, 2:117–135.

PFLIEGER, W. L. 1975. The fishes of Missouri. Missouri Dept. Conserv., Western Publ. Co., Jefferson City, 343 pp.

POTTER, G. E. 1924. Food of the short-nosed gar-pike (*Lepidosteus platystomus*) in Lake Okoboji, Iowa. Proc. Iowa Acad. Sci. 30:167–170.

———. 1927. Ecological studies of the short-nosed gar-pike (*Lepidosteus platystomus*). Univ. Iowa Stud. Nat. Hist., 11:17–27.

SMITH, P. W. 1979. The fishes of Illinois. Illinois State Nat. Hist. Surv., Urbana, 314 pp.

PREPARED BY: Edwin L. Cooper, *The Pennsylvania State University, University Park, PA 16802.*

Extirpated

SKIPJACK HERRING
Alosa chrysochloris (Rafinesque)
Family Clupeidae
Order Clupeiformes

OTHER NAMES: River herring, blue herring, golden shad; *Pomolobus chrysochloris, Clupea chrysochloris.*

DESCRIPTION: The skipjack herring is a fusiform, shad-like fish with large silvery scales and protruding lower jaw, displaying iridescent green and golden colors in life. It is readily separated from other silvery fishes like the mooneye or quillback by the saw-like scales along the midline of the belly. It is more slender than the gizzard shad or the Alabama shad.

RANGE: The skipjack herring is a highly migratory form restricted to large streams of the Mississippi River drainage and a few other streams tributary to the Gulf of Mexico. It is only geographically separated from the hickory shad of the Atlantic Coast, and considered to be the other species of a similar pair.

HABITAT: This herring usually travels in schools in large rivers, often leaping from the water when feeding in fast current.

LIFE HISTORY AND ECOLOGY: The skipjack spawns over a prolonged period in spring and early summer, depositing its eggs at random over coarse sand and gravel bars of the main river channel. The diet consists mostly of small fishes and larger invertebrates. The skipjack never was an important commercial fish largely because it was considered inferior in flavor to the shad and other river species, and full of small bones. However, it was historically very important as a host for the glochidia of the niggerhead freshwater mussel, prized in the pearl button industry.

BASIS OF STATUS CLASSIFICATION: It is possible that the species never has been collected from Pennsylvania, but Rafinesque reported it as migratory in the Ohio River but that "it seldom goes as far as Pittsburgh." There are no recent collections of this species in the Commonwealth.

The species was apparently extirpated from much of the Upper Mississippi River and Ohio River drainages when impoundments and navigational locks impeded its spawning migrations.

SELECTED REFERENCES:

COKER, R. E. 1930. Studies of common fishes of the Mississippi River at Keokuk. Bull. U.S. Bur. Fisheries, 45:141–225.
FORBES, S. A., and R. E. RICHARDSON. 1920. The fishes of Illinois. Illinois Nat. Hist. Surv., Urbana, 357 pp.
PFLIEGER, W. L. 1975. The fishes of Missouri. Missouri Dept. Conserv., Western Publ. Co., Jefferson City, 343 pp.
RAFINESQUE, C. S. 1920. Ichthyologia ohiensis, or natural history of the fishes inhabiting the River Ohio and its tributary streams, preceded by a physical description of the Ohio and its branches. Printed for the author by W. G. Hunt, Lexington, Kentucky, 90 pp.
TRAUTMAN, M. B. 1957. The fishes of Ohio. Ohio State Univ. Press, Columbus, v–xvii + 683 pp.

PREPARED BY: Edwin L. Cooper, *The Pennsylvania State University, University Park, PA 16802.*

Extirpated

GOLDEYE
Hiodon alosoides (Rafinesque)
Family Hiodontidae
Order Osteoglossiformes

OTHER NAMES: Winnipeg goldeye, western goldeye, yellow herring, toothed herring, shad mooneye.

DESCRIPTION: The goldeye is a silvery, slab-sided fish that superficially resembles members of the herring family (Clupeidae), and was long thought to be closely related. In addition to a number of internal anatomical differences, the goldeye differs from local species of Clupeidae in having no scutes on the belly; teeth on tongue and jaws; few, short, and knob-like gill rakers; and a well-developed lateral line.

Hiodon alosoides differs from *H. tergisus* (the only other living member of the family Hiodontidae) in having the origin of the dorsal fin slightly behind (rather than in front of) the origin of the anal fin, dorsal rays 9–10 (versus 11–12), anal rays usually 29–34 (versus 26–29), and the iris of the eye golden (versus silvery).

Maximum total length about 500 mm; maximum weight 1,400 g.

Goldeye (*Hiodon alosoides*). Photograph by E. L. Cooper.

RANGE: Lower Mississippi River basin from Louisiana and Mississippi north to the Ohio River basin and throughout the Great Plains into extreme northwestern Canada, almost to the mouth of the MacKenzie River, Northwest Territories. There are widely disjunct populations in tributaries of James Bay, Ontario and Quebec. It is absent from the entire Great Lakes basin. A detailed distribution map appears in Gilbert (1980).

In Pennsylvania, the species is known from a total of 11 museum specimens (three series, all in the Academy of Natural Sciences of Philadelphia collection) from the Youghiogheny and Beaver rivers, the most recent ones taken in 1880 (Fowler, 1911, 1919). Precise locality data do not accompany any of the three series.

HABITAT: The goldeye is typically found in turbid, often quiet waters of large rivers and lakes, as well as adjacent backwaters. It is generally found in water that is more turbid than that inhabited by *Hiodon tergisus* (habitat type II-C-2).

LIFE HISTORY AND ECOLOGY: The goldeye is a fairly important commercial species, especially in Canada. For this reason, several biological studies have been published, the most detailed by Kennedy and Sprules (1967). Scott and Crossman (1973) have summarized the information appearing in this and other studies, and the following is taken from that source.

In Canada, spawning occurs from May to early July (starting just after the ice breaks up), and takes place at temperatures of 10–12°C in pools of rivers or backwaters of lakes. Actual spawning has not been observed, but is assumed to occur at night. The egg complement of adult females (300–375 mm fork length) ranges from 5,000 to over 25,000, with the eggs being semi-buoyant. Hatching occurs in about 2 weeks.

Age at sexual maturity varies with sex, and increases from south to north. In northern Alberta it is 6 to 9 years for males and 7 to 10 years for females. Farther south, in Manitoba, it is 2 to 3 years less, and in South Dakota some males mature at age 1.

Age-growth studies conducted in various parts of Canada (Ontario, Manitoba and Alberta) indicate that individuals may live a maximum of 8 to 15 years, depending on locality.

Goldeyes are generally omnivorous in their diet, and there is no indication of any specific food preferences. During summer, much of their food is taken at the surface, whereas at other times of the year it may be from deeper water.

SPECIALIZED OR UNIQUE CHARACTERISTICS: The most interesting aspect of the goldeye is its systematic position. As a member of the order Osteoglossiformes, it is one of only two living species (the other being the mooneye) of this rather primitive order of fishes found in the Northern Hemisphere. All other living members of the order occur in tropical areas of both the old and new worlds.

BASIS OF STATUS CLASSIFICATION: Inasmuch as the last confirmed record of *Hiodon alosoides* from Pennsylvania dates from 1880, the species is assumed to be extirpated from the Commonwealth. The tolerance of this species to turbidity suggests that industrial pollution, not deforestation and increased agriculture, has been responsible for its disappearance.

RECOMMENDATIONS: Pollution abatement in the upper Ohio River, together with intensive surveys of this area, will be needed if there is any hope of rediscovering this species in the Commonwealth. If a population is eventually discovered here, every effort should be made to maintain suitable environmental conditions.

SELECTED REFERENCES:

FOWLER, H. W. 1911. Notes on clupeoid fishes. Proc. Acad. Nat. Sci. Philadelphia, 63:204–221.

———. 1919. A list of the fishes of Pennsylvania. Proc. Biol. Soc. Washington, 32:49–74.

GILBERT, C. R. 1980. *Hiodon alosoides* (Rafinesque), goldeye. P. 74, *in* Atlas of North American freshwater fishes (D. S. Lee et al.), North Carolina State Mus. Nat. Hist., Raleigh, x + 854 pp.

KENNEDY, W. A., and W. M. SPRULES. 1967. Goldeye in Canada. Bull. Fish. Res. Bd. Canada 161:1–45.

SCOTT, W. B., and E. J. CROSSMAN. 1973. Freshwater fishes of Canada. Bull. Fish. Res. Bd. Canada, 184:viii–xi + 1–966.

PREPARED BY: Carter R. Gilbert, *Florida State Museum, University of Florida, Gainesville, FL 32611.*

Extirpated

MOONEYE
Hiodon tergisus Lesueur
Family Hiodontidae
Order Osteoglossiformes

OTHER NAMES: Toothed herring, river whitefish, fresh-water herring, shiner.

DESCRIPTION: A silvery, slab-sided fish that superficially resembles members of the herring family (Clupeidae), and was once thought to be closely related. In addition to a number of internal anatomical differences, the mooneye differs from local species of Clupeidae in having no scutes on the belly; teeth on tongue and jaws; gill rakers few, short and knob-like; and a well-developed lateral line.

Hiodon tergisus differs from *H. alosoides* (the only other living member of the family Hiodontidae) in having the origin of the dorsal fin slightly in front of (rather than behind) the origin of the anal fin, dorsal rays 11–12 (versus 9–10), anal rays usually 26–29 (versus usually 29–34), and the iris of the eye silvery (versus golden). Maximum total length is 445 mm; maximum weight is almost 1,140 g.

RANGE: The mooneye is found in the Mobile Bay basin west to Mississippi River basin, north throughout most of Mississippi Valley (but excluding most of Great Plains region). It is also found in parts of Great Lakes basin (lakes Erie and Ontario, and certain tributaries of Lake Michigan), ranging down into middle St. Lawrence River. The range of the mooneye extends north into Hudson Bay basin of south-central Canada, with semi-disjunct population in James Bay region, Ontario and Quebec. A detailed distribution map appears in Gilbert (1980).

The mooneye formerly ranged up the Ohio River into Pennsylvania. Kirtland (1847) indicated this species was abundant in the Ohio River, in Ohio, during the early to middle-1800's, but Trautman (1957) showed that it has decreased greatly in abundance and range, in this area, since that time. Evidently Lesueur's (1818) original description, which was based in part on specimens from the Ohio River, at Pittsburgh, is the only evidence confirming the former presence of this species in the Ohio River drainage of Pennsylvania. A specimen reported by Fowler (1911, 1919) from Lake Erie, at Erie, was collected in July 1907, and is in the collection of the Academy of Natural Sciences of Philadelphia (ANSP 23342).

HABITAT: The mooneye occurs in large rivers and (to a lesser extent) lakes, generally in water that is clearer and less turbid than that inhabited by *Hiodon alosoides* (habitat type II-C-2). Reduction in water clarity and generally deteriorating environmental conditions have caused this species to disappear from many areas where formerly found.

LIFE HISTORY AND ECOLOGY: Inasmuch as this species is less important commercially than the goldeye (*Hiodon alosoides*), less attention has been paid to its biology and life history. Johnson (1951) and Van Oosten (1961) have provided the most authoritative information on this species, and Trautman (1957) and Scott and Crossman (1973) have presented comprehensive summaries.

Spawning occurs in April and May, and may extend into early June. As a rule, mooneyes migrate in large numbers up large, clear streams to spawn. The number of eggs per female varies from 10,000–20,000. Sexual maturity, in males, is achieved at 3 years of age, but females do not mature before 5 years. Males also die earlier, thus resulting in skewed sex ratios (predominantly females) among larger individuals. Food mostly comprises small fish and a wide variety of aquatic and terrestrial invertebrates, particularly insects and crayfish.

SPECIALIZED OR UNIQUE CHARACTERISTICS: The most interesting aspect of the mooneye is its systematic position. As a member of the order Osteoglossiformes, it is one of only two living species (the other being the goldeye) of this rather primitive order of fishes found in the Northern Hemisphere.

All other living members of the order occur in tropical areas of both the old and new worlds.

BASIS OF STATUS CLASSIFICATION: Inasmuch as there are no definite records of the mooneye from the Ohio River drainage of Pennsylvania since its original description in 1818, it is presumed to be extirpated from that part of the state. The absence of records from Lake Erie since 1907 also suggests its extirpation there. Although it cannot be confirmed, it is possible that the mooneye was present in limited numbers in Lake Erie waters of Pennsylvania at least into the mid-1950's, at which time a drastic decline in ecological conditions in the lake began to occur.

RECOMMENDATIONS: Although chances are remote that *Hiodon tergisus* still occurs in the Ohio River, in Pennsylvania, any "herring-like" fish taken should be carefully examined with this possibility in mind. The possibilities of finding this species in Lake Erie are better, inasmuch as a partial ecological restoration of this lake has occurred in recent years. Should the species be found, every effort should be made to maintain suitable environmental conditions.

SELECTED REFERENCES:

Fowler, H. W. 1911. Notes on clupeoid fishes. Proc. Acad. Nat. Sci. Philadelphia, 63:204–221.
———. 1919. A list of the fishes of Pennsylvania. Proc. Biol. Soc. Washington, 32:49–74.
Gilbert, C. R. 1980. *Hiodon tergisus* Lesueur, mooneye. P. 75, *in* Atlas of North American freshwater fishes (D. S. Lee et al.), North Carolina State Mus. Nat. Hist., Raleigh, x + 854 pp.
Johnson, G. H. 1951. An investigation of the mooneye (*Hiodon tergisus*). Abstr. 5th Tech. Sess. Res. Council Ontario, p. 16.
Kirtland, J. P. 1847. Descriptions of the fishes of Lake Erie, the Ohio River and their tributaries. Boston J. Nat. Hist., 5:330–344.
Lesueur, C. A. 1818. Descriptions of several new species of North American fishes. J. Acad. Nat. Sci. Philadelphia, 1:222–235, 359–368.
Scott, W. B., and E. J. Crossman. 1973. Freshwater fishes of Canada. Bull. Fish. Res. Bd. Canada, 184:viii–xi + 1–966.
Trautman, M. B. 1957. The fishes of Ohio. Ohio State Univ. Press, Columbus, v–xvii + 683 pp.
Van Oosten, J. 1961. Records, ages, and growth of the mooneye, *Hiodon tergisus,* of the Great Lakes. Trans. Amer. Fish. Soc., 90:170–174.

PREPARED BY: Carter R. Gilbert, Florida State Museum, University of Florida, Gainesville, FL 32611.

Extirpated

LONGJAW CISCO
Coregonus alpenae (Koelz)
Family Salmonidae
Order Salmoniformes

OTHER NAMES: Longjaw chub; *Leucichthys alpenae, Leucichthys johannae.*

DESCRIPTION: A slender cisco of the Great Lakes, highly variable in body shape, seldom exceeding 300 mm in length, except in Lake Michigan. The overall coloration is silvery with iridescent colors of pink, green, or blue on live specimens. The extreme variability of body form and meristic characters makes exact identification difficult. The long and heavy lower jaw is the best single distinguishing feature serving to separate this species from the lake herring or the lake whitefish.

RANGE: The longjaw cisco is commonly found only in lakes Huron and Michigan, with a small population present in the "deep hole" of Lake Erie as late as 1957. It is now believed to be extirpated from Lake Erie and remains in small numbers only in the other two Great Lakes.

HABITAT: One of several deep-water chubs of the Great Lakes, the longjaw cisco seldom is found in water shallower than 6 m. It lives commonly at depths of 90 m, moving to about the 30 m level to spawn.

LIFE HISTORY AND ECOLOGY: Spawning apparently takes place in November judging from the change in condition of the gonads and the development of pearl organs on the males. Growth is rapid for this deep-water form and sexual maturity is usually reached at a size of 250 to 300 mm, age of 4 or 5 years. Some fish live at least 9 years. The food consists almost entirely of the pelagic crustaceans *Mysis relicta* and *Pontoporeia* sp.

The longjaw cisco was once harvested intensively by a commercial fishery as one of the fat ciscoes preferred for smoking. It was also part of the food supply for the lake trout and burbot before these species were severely reduced by predation by the sea lamprey. The cause of the marked decline of the longjaw is not well understood, but over-fishing, changes in water quality of their deep-water habitat brought about by increased eutrophication, and the great increase in the smelt population could be involved.

Longjaw Cisco (*Coregonus alpenae*). Figure from Koelz. U.S. Bur. Fish. Doc., 1048:364, 1929.

SELECTED REFERENCES:

BERSAMIN, S. V. 1958. A preliminary study of the nutritional ecology and food habits of the chubs (*Leucichthys* spp.) and their relation to the ecology of Lake Michigan. Papers Michigan Acad. Sci. Arts Ltrs., 43:107–118.
KOELZ, W. 1924. Two new species of cisco from the Great Lakes. Occas. Papers Mus. Zool., Univ. Michigan, 146:1–8.
———. 1929. Coregonid fishes of the Great Lakes. Bull. U.S. Bur. Fisheries, 43:297–643.
SCOTT, W. B., and S. H. SMITH. 1962. The occurrence of the longjaw cisco, *Leucichthys alpenae,* in Lake Erie. J. Fish. Res. Bd. Canada, 19:1013–1023.

PREPARED BY: Edwin L. Cooper, *The Pennsylvania State University, University Park, PA 16802.*

Extirpated

CISCO OR LAKE HERRING
Coregonus artedii Lesueur
Family Salmonidae
Order Salmoniformes

OTHER NAMES: Tullibee, shallowwater cisco; *Leucichthys nipigon, Leucichthys eriensis, Leucichthys artedi, Argyrysomus eriensis.*

DESCRIPTION: The cisco is an elongate, pelagic fish of lakes. The body is fusiform, somewhat compressed, but its shape varies from lake to lake. Small pearl organs are well developed on scales of spawning males. The color is silvery with iridescent colors on fresh specimens. Its variable shape from lake to lake has resulted in taxonomic confusion of the cisco and other close relatives, leading some ichthyologists to consider the cisco as a highly variable *Coregonus artedii* complex.

RANGE: The cisco is a wide-ranging species throughout all of the Great Lakes drainage and of many smaller lakes of Canada from Quebec to Saskatchewan and the Northwest Territories. The

species was named in 1818 from material collected from Lake Erie at Buffalo, New York, by Lesueur. The most recent specimens from the Pennsylvania waters of Lake Erie were collected in 1957, but the cisco persists as a commercial fish in other parts of its range. It was introduced into Harvey's Lake, Luzerne County between 1969 to 1972 by the Pennsylvania Fish Commission but there is no evidence that a successful reproducing population has become established.

HABITAT: The cisco is mainly a lake species although it may occur in large rivers. It is a pelagic, schooling species preferring cool, well-oxygenated water. Its potential habitat in Pennsylvania is therefore limited to Lake Erie and a very few oligotrophic lakes similar to Harvey's Lake.

LIFE HISTORY AND ECOLOGY: Spawning occurs over a gravel or stony bottom of lake shallows in the late fall. The eggs are broadcast and then deserted by the parents. The eggs hatch in the spring. Sexual maturity and growth rate are variable from lake to lake, but maturity is commonly attained at a size of 300 mm and 4 years of age. The maximum age has been recorded at about 13 years and 1,360–1,815 g ciscoes are occasionally taken in the Prairie Provinces of Canada.

The cisco is primarily a sight feeder on zooplankton, but a wide variety of organisms, from microcrustaceans to small minnows are eaten. It is an important forage species for large predators such as lake trout, and historically has supported a commercial fishery in Lake Erie that amounted to 22 million kg in 1918.

SELECTED REFERENCES:

KOELZ, W. 1929. Coregonid fishes of the Great Lakes. Bull. U.S. Bur. Fisheries, 43:297–643.
LESUEUR, C. A. 1818. Descriptions of several new species of

North American fishes. J. Acad. Nat. Sci. Philadelphia, 1:222–235; 359–368.

McPhail, J. D., and C. C. Lindsey. 1970. Freshwater fishes of northwestern Canada and Alaska. Bull. Fish. Res. Bd. Canada, 173:1–381.

Scott, W. B., and E. J. Crossman. 1973. Freshwater fishes of Canada. Bull. Fish. Res. Bd. Canada, 184:1–966.

Van Oosten, J. 1929. Life history of the lake herring (*Leucichthys artedi* LeSueur) of Lake Huron as revealed by its scales, with a critique of the scale method. Bull. U.S. Bur. Fisheries, 44:265–428.

PREPARED BY: Edwin L. Cooper, *The Pennsylvania State University, University Park, PA 16802.*

Extirpated

LAKE WHITEFISH
Coregonus clupeaformis (Mitchill)
Family Salmonidae
Order Salmoniformes

OTHER NAMES: Common whitefish, Great Lakes whitefish; *Coregonus albus, Salmo clupeaformis.*

DESCRIPTION: The lake whitefish is an elongate fish of large lakes, generally more robust than ciscoes. The snout of the lake whitefish projects beyond the lower jaw, whereas the lower jaw usually protrudes beyond the upper jaw in the ciscoes. Breeding males and some females develop pearl organs on scales on flanks above and below the lateral line. The color is silvery but usually with darkened scale margins; fins are usually clear but sometimes tipped with black. The morphometric variation of the lake whitefish and its similarity to some Eurasian forms has created taxonomic confusion of this group. The recognition of dwarf and normal races occurring in the same lake also has added to difficulty of correctly outlining its phylogenetic relationship. Hybrids between lake whitefish and the cisco have also been reported.

RANGE: The lake whitefish has a wide distribution in northern North America from the Canadian Maritimes south to the Great Lakes and west to Alaska. It formerly was abundant in Lake Erie, reaching a peak of production in the commercial fishery of 3.2 million kg in 1949, but few specimens have been taken from Lake Erie since 1965. It is reported present in Otsego Lake, New York, a headwaters of the Susquehanna River, but has never been collected from deep oligotrophic lakes in Pennsylvania within this watershed.

HABITAT: Like the cisco, the lake whitefish is principally a lake species although it occurs in some large rivers of Canada. It is a cool water species, retreating to the well-oxygenated hypolimnion of lakes during summer stratification. Such a combination of habitat requirements greatly restricts its potential distribution and abundance in Pennsylvania.

LIFE HISTORY AND ECOLOGY: Spawning occurs in late autumn or winter usually in shallow-water, gravelly shoals. The eggs are broadcast without nest building or parental care. Eggs hatch in the spring and the young form loose schools along steep shorelines, descending to deep water as temperatures rise.

Historically, lake whitefish attained sizes over 9 kg, and lived for more than 25 years, but now large and old fish are seldom reported except in Great Slave Lake, Canada, or other lightly exploited populations.

Adult whitefish are mainly bottom feeders, eating a wide variety of invertebrates and small fish. The major predators of lake whitefish, besides man, are the lake trout, northern pike, burbot, and walleye, with yellow perch and the cisco sometimes feeding on small whitefish.

Lake Whitefish (*Coregonus clupeaformis*). Figure from Brice. Manual of Fish Culture, U.S. Comm. Fish and Fisheries, p. 119, 1898.

SELECTED REFERENCES:

FENDERSON, O. C. 1964. Evidence of subpopulations of lake whitefish, *Coregonus clupeaformis,* involving a dwarfed form. Trans. Amer. Fish. Soc., 93:77–94.

KOELZ, W. 1929. Coregonid fishes of the Great Lakes. Bull. U.S. Bur. Fisheries, 43:297–643.

LINDSEY, C. C., J. W. CLAYTON, and W. G. FRANZIN. 1970. Zoogeographic problems and protein variation in the *Coregonus clupeaformis* whitefish species complex. *In* Biology of coregonid fishes, Univ. Manitoba Press, Winnipeg, Canada, 560 pp.

MACCRIMMON, H. R., and E. SKOBE. 1970. The fisheries of Lake Simcoe. Ontario Dept. Lands and Forests, Fish and Wildlife Branch, Toronto, 140 pp.

MITCHILL, S. L. 1818. Memoir on ichthyology. The fishes of New York described and arranged. Amer. Month. Mag. Crit. Rev., 1817–1818, 2:241–248, 321–328.

SCOTT, W. B., and E. J. CROSSMAN. 1973. Freshwater fishes of Canada. Bull. Fish. Res. Bd. Canada, 184:1–966.

PREPARED BY: Edwin L. Cooper, *The Pennsylvania State University, University Park, PA 16802.*

Extirpated

POPEYE SHINER
Notropis ariommus (Cope)
Family Cyprinidae
Order Cypriniformes

DESCRIPTION: The popeye shiner is a species of *Notropis* characterized by an unusually large eye (largest of any member of the genus). The eye is half again as long as the snout and length of head is only two and a half times the length of the eye. The color of the body is generally silvery, without dark stripe along the mid-side. A predorsal stripe is prominent and fairly dark. The origin of the dorsal fin is situated slightly posterior to the insertion of the pelvic fins. The mouth is moderately oblique, and situated at about a 10–15° angle to the horizontal. Pharyngeal teeth are usually 2,4–4,2. Anal rays usually number 9. The number of body-circumferential scales usually is 24 or 25. The number of predorsal scales usually is 15–18. The maximum size is about 80 mm standard length.

Many references to *Notropis ariommus* between 1939 and 1969 actually refer to *Notropis telescopus,* a much more common species that occurs sympatrically with the true *N. ariommus* in the Cumberland and Tennessee River drainages of Kentucky and Tennessee.

RANGE: Notropis ariommus ranges (or formerly ranged) from the Tennessee River drainage of northern Alabama and northwestern Georgia northward to northern Indiana, northwestern Ohio, and western Pennsylvania. The absence of recent records from Alabama (since 1889), Indiana (since 1890), Ohio (since 1893), and Pennsylvania (since 1853) attest to the drastic overall decline in the range and abundance of this species. A detailed distribution map appears in Gilbert (1980).

The only record of this species from Pennsylvania is based on two specimens collected, by S. F. Baird, from the mouth of the Clarion River (where it enters the Allegheny River), at Foxburg, Clarion County, in 1853. These specimens are deposited in the fish collection of the Museum of Comparative Zoology, Harvard University. According to E. L. Cooper (in litt.), the lower Clarion River has been polluted for many years, and an environmentally sensitive species such as *N. ariommus* would stand little chance of survival under these conditions.

Although the popeye shiner has apparently disappeared completely from most of the northern parts of its range, there are two fairly recent collections (in 1953 and 1956) from the Cheat River (upper Monongahela system) in northern West Virginia (Gilbert, 1969). Its presence here (in an area not far from the Pennsylvania state line) provides some degree of optimism that the species may still survive in Pennsylvania.

HABITAT: Notropis ariommus characteristically occurs in relatively clear, flowing, weedless, medium-large to medium-sized creeks and rivers (habitat types II-B-1 and III-B-1). In addition, it appears to be closely confined to areas having a gravel substrate. Its restriction to this type of bottom probably accounts in large degree for the widespread disappearance of this species over much of its former range (Gilbert, 1969), inasmuch as a gravel bottom, which has little relief and a minimum of interstices, is easily covered by silt and sediments. In those areas where the popeye shiner still occurs (almost all of which are in the southern half of its range), the water is usually clear, or when turbidity does exist the condition is usually temporary.

LIFE HISTORY AND ECOLOGY: Nothing has been published on the life history or ecology of this species. Its unusually large eye and its customary occurrence in clear water strongly indicate that *N.*

ariommus is a sight feeder. Its diet presumably consists largely of small aquatic invertebrates.

SPECIALIZED OR UNIQUE CHARACTERISTICS: Only a few North American freshwater fish species appear to be closely confined to a gravel substrate. Of those, the Tippecanoe darter (*Etheostoma tippecanoe*) and gravel chub (*Hybopsis x-punctata*), in addition to the popeye shiner, are known from Pennsylvania. Presence of either of the first two species at a locality could possibly be an indication that *N. ariommus* may be there also.

BASIS OF STATUS CLASSIFICATION: Absence of *Notropis ariommus* from any fish collections from Pennsylvania during the past 130 years strongly indicates that the species is no longer present, and thus accounts for its present classification.

RECOMMENDATIONS: The search should be continued for this species in the Ohio River drainage of western Pennsylvania, with particular attention being paid to relatively undisturbed areas in which a gravel substrate is present. Localities at which either *Etheostoma tippecanoe* or *Hybopsis x-punctata* are present should be given special attention. Should populations of the popeye shiner eventually be discovered in the Commonwealth, every effort should be made to see that the habitat remains undisturbed.

SELECTED REFERENCES:

GILBERT, C. R. 1969. Systematics and distribution of the American cyprinid fishes *Notropis ariommus* and *Notropis telescopus.* Copeia, 1969:474–492.

———. 1980. *Notropis ariommus* (Cope), popeye shiner. P. 229, *in* Atlas of North American freshwater fishes (D. S. Lee et al.), North Carolina State Mus. Nat. Hist., Raleigh, x + 854 pp.

PREPARED BY: Carter R. Gilbert, *Florida State Museum, University of Florida, Gainesville, FL 32611.*

Extirpated

IRONCOLOR SHINER
Notropis chalybaeus (Cope)
Family Cyprinidae
Order Cypriniformes

DESCRIPTION: The ironcolor shiner is a small, moderately deep-bodied and laterally compressed species of *Notropis* that is principally characterized by a usually intensely black lateral stripe extending from the tip of the snout to the base of the tail, and a combination of 2,4–4,2 pharyngeal teeth and 8 anal rays. The only soft-rayed fishes occurring in eastern Pennsylvania (specifically in the Delaware River drainage) that also have a black lateral stripe and with which *N. chalybaeus* might be confused are *Notropis bifrenatus, Notemigonus crysoleucas* (young only) and *Erimyzon oblongus* (young only). *N. chalybaeus* is distinguished from *N. bifrenatus* in having 2,4–4,2 (versus 4–4) pharyngeal teeth; 8 (versus 7) anal rays; a greater number of predorsal scales (17–19 versus 12–14), which are also more irregularly placed both in the predorsal and anterior dorso-lateral areas; predorsal and anterior dorso-lateral scales more narrowly outlined with pigment; a considerable amount of black pigment on chin, lower lip and inside of mouth (versus little or no pigment in these areas); lateral stripe uniformly pigmented behind head (versus lateral stripe in this area underlain by a zig-zag pigment pattern); origin of dorsal fin slightly posterior to (versus directly above) insertion of pelvic fins. *N. chalybaeus* differs from young *Notemigonus crysoleucas* in pharyngeal-tooth count (2,4–4,2 versus 5–5), anal-ray count (8 versus 11 to 13), in lacking a hard, fleshy, scaleless keel on mid-line of belly from anus to pelvic fins; in having a narrower, more intensely black, lateral line; a less compressed body; a less oblique mouth; and a much less decurved lateral line on the anterior part of the body. *N. chalybaeus* differs from *Erimyzon oblongus* (a species of Catostomidae) in a wide range of family-level characters, the most obvious of which are the position and nature of the mouth (terminal and non-suctorial in *N. chalybaeus*; subterminal and suctorial in *E. oblongus*); morphology of the pharyngeal arch (thicker, with no more than 4 teeth per row in *N. chalybaeus* versus thinner, with numerous teeth in a single row in *E. oblongus*); and relative position of the anal fin (distance from anal origin to caudal base contained less than 2.5 times, versus more than 2.5 times, in distance from anal origin to tip of snout). In addition, *N. chalybaeus* has 8 dorsal fin rays, as compared with 9 or 10 dorsal rays in *E. oblongus*. The maximum standard length is about 45 mm, usually closer to 40 mm.

RANGE: This species is found in lowlands from the Hudson River, New York, south to tributaries of Lake Okeechobee, Florida, and west to the Sabine

River, Louisiana and Texas, with a disjunct population to the west in the San Marcos River, Texas. It is also found north to the Wolf River system, in central Wisconsin, and east to extreme south-central Michigan. A detailed distribution map appears in Swift (1980).

It was formerly found in extreme eastern Pennsylvania, in tributaries of the Delaware River, where it was recorded from several localities in Bucks, Northampton, and Montgomery counties (Fowler, 1909, 1919). Fowler (1948) also indicated that it occurred in Philadelphia County, although no museum specimens from there appear to be extant. There apparently are no confirmed records of *N. chalybaeus* from Pennsylvania since 1917, and in this regard the distributional history of the species in the Commonwealth closely parallels that of *Aphredoderus sayanus*. These species, together with *Acantharchus pomotis*, *Enneacanthus chaetodon*, *Enneacanthus obesus*, and *Etheostoma fusiforme*, occur in predominantly lowland habitats, which are essentially limited, in Pennsylvania, to the Delaware River valley. This type of habitat has been greatly modified in this area over the past 60 years. *Notropis chalybaeus*, as well as the other species mentioned above, are not rare in the southern half of New Jersey, where suitable habitat is common.

HABITAT: *N. chalybaeus* is typically found in small, low-gradient acidic streams, usually with a sandy substrate and some submergent and/or partly emergent vegetation (habitat types II-A-2 and II-B-2).

LIFE HISTORY AND ECOLOGY: The only detailed life-history study of *Notropis chalybaeus* was carried out in northern Florida (Marshall, 1947). Breeding in that area occurs from early April to late September, at water temperatures ranging from about 15–25°C. However, breeding seasons normally are more protracted to the south, and in Maryland this species was found to spawn in late spring (Schwartz, 1963) (that is, late May to late June, possibly into July). Breeding occurs during daylight hours. The eggs apparently are broadcast into the water in areas of minimal current, without nest construction or subsequent parental care.

The ironcolor shiner normally swims in open water, in small to medium-sized schools of mixed age composition. It feeds on small aquatic and terrestrial insects, as well as other invertebrates, which are usually taken in the upper part of the water column.

The average or maximum age of this species has not been determined, but is probably about 2 years, or possibly 3 years as is the case of other *Notropis* species of similar size.

BASIS OF STATUS CLASSIFICATION: The ironcolor shiner is classified as extirpated in Pennsylvania, inasmuch as it apparently has not been collected in the state in over 60 years. Because the area of southeastern Pennsylvania where the species was once found has been the site of heavy commercial and industrial development for many years, it is highly questionable whether the fish still occurs there, although it is still common in adjacent parts of New Jersey. On the other hand, it should be noted that little scientific collecting has been done in this part of Pennsylvania for many years.

RECOMMENDATIONS: Re-collection must be done in those areas where *Notropis chalybaeus* was once known to occur, as well as in other suitable-looking areas if they exist. If discovered, efforts should be made to maintain the habitat in its natural state.

SELECTED REFERENCES:

FOWLER, H. W. 1909. A synopsis of the Cyprinidae of Pennsylvania. Proc. Acad. Nat. Sci. Philadelphia, 60:517–553.
———. 1919. A list of the fishes of Pennsylvania. Proc. Biol. Soc. Washington, 32:49–74.
———. 1948. A list of the fishes recorded from Pennsylvania. Bull. Pennsylvania Bd. Fish Commissioners, 7:3–26.
MARSHALL, N. 1947. Studies on the life history and ecology of *Notropis chalybaeus* (Cope). Quart. J. Florida Acad. Sci., 9:163–188.
SCHWARTZ, F. J. 1963. The fresh-water minnows of Maryland. Maryland Conserv., 40(2):19–29.
SWIFT, C. C. 1980. *Notropis chalybaeus* (Cope), ironcolor shiner. P. 250, *in* Atlas of North American freshwater fishes (D. S. Lee et al.), North Carolina State Mus. Nat. Hist., Raleigh, x + 854 pp.

PREPARED BY: Carter R. Gilbert, *Florida State Museum, University of Florida, Gainesville, FL 32611.*

Extirpated

BLACKCHIN SHINER
Notropis heterodon (Cope)
Family Cyprinidae
Order Cypriniformes

DESCRIPTION: The blackchin shiner is one of the

Blackchin Shiner (*Notropis heterodon*). Photograph by E. L. Cooper.

smaller species of *Notropis,* rarely exceeding 70 mm total length. It is characterized by a black stripe along the side of the body that extends from tip of snout to base of tail. The margins of the scales are more intensely pigmented than the centers in striped area along the mid-side of body, resulting in a characteristic zig-zag pattern from the back of the head to the base of the tail. The chin is darkly pigmented; the fins are without distinct markings. The origin of dorsal fin is directly above the insertion of the pelvics. The mouth is distinctly oblique, forming an angle of approximately 35–45° to the horizontal. The lateral line is incomplete. The pharyngeal teeth are usually 1,4–4,1; the anal rays are usually 8. There are 34–37 lateral-line scales.

This shiner most closely resembles the bridled shiner (*Notropis bifrenatus*) (of Atlantic slope drainages), which typically has 4–4 pharyngeal teeth and 7 anal rays, and which also differs in various pigmentary details. To a lesser extent, the blackchin shiner resembles the blacknose shiner (*Notropis heterolepis*) (with which *N. heterodon* often occurs sympatrically), a slightly larger species having a less oblique mouth, longer snout, no pigment on chin, crescentic (rather than zig-zag) markings along midside of body, and usually 4–4 pharyngeal teeth and 8 anal rays.

RANGE: The range of *Notropis heterodon* is centered in the Great Lakes and extreme upper Mississippi River basins, in northern United States and southern Canada, from western Minnesota and Iowa (extirpated in the latter state) east to eastern New York (Lake Champlain system). It was formerly present in northern Ohio and northwestern Pennsylvania, but is now believed to be extirpated from both states. A detailed distribution map appears in Gilbert (1980).

Apparently the only valid records of this species from Pennsylvania are from Conneaut Lake, west of Conneaut, Crawford County. Two series, comprising a total of 63 specimens, were collected by E. C. Raney on 7 June 1938, and are housed in the Cornell University fish collection (CU 39945 and CU 41007).

HABITAT: The blackchin shiner is highly partial to clear, cool lakes (occasionally quiet streams), with dense submergent vegetation and a silt-free (though often muddy) bottom (habitat type I-A-3). The species may be common where these conditions exist, particularly in the glacial lakes that are prevalent in Minnesota, Wisconsin, Michigan, and parts of New York and southeastern Ontario. Consistently clear water, in particular, appears necessary for its survival, and in areas where turbidity has increased, either on a permanent or seasonal basis, the species has rapidly disappeared (Trautman, 1957). The type of habitat described above is scarce in a largely unglaciated state such as Pennsylvania. Under these circumstances, the extreme scarcity (possible extirpation) of the species from the state is understandable.

LIFE HISTORY AND ECOLOGY: Despite the abundance of the blackchin shiner throughout parts of its range, little has been published on its life history and ecology (for best summaries of available information see Adams and Hankinson (1928), Trautman (1957), and Scott and Crossman (1973)). Keast (1965), in a study conducted in Lake Opinicon, Ontario, considered it to be a specialized feeder, the great bulk of food consumed during summer months consisting of cladocerans and flying insects (mainly small dipterans) taken at the surface. Adams and Hankinson (1928), summarizing previous works, reported unicellular and filamentous algae, fish eggs, entomostracans, chironomids (larvae, pupae and adults), oligochaete worms, and small crustaceans as comprising part of its diet. Although age-growth studies of this species have not been done, individuals presumably do not live more than 2 years (most probably only live 1 year), based on data obtained for other *Notropis* species of comparable size.

SPECIALIZED OR UNIQUE CHARACTERISTICS: Probably the one feature that sets *Notropis heterodon* apart from virtually all other Pennsylvania freshwater fishes is its close association with quiet, consistently clear, heavily vegetated bodies of water, and its rapid disappearance once such conditions are no longer present. A number of other species (for example, *Lepomis macrochirus, Lepomis gibbosus,* and *Micropterus salmoides,* to name a few) are also characteristic of such a habitat, but, in contrast to the blackchin shiner, may remain when these conditions are temporarily, or even permanently, modified.

BASIS OF STATUS CLASSIFICATION: This species likely has been neither common nor widespread in Pennsylvania, and probably existed only in a limited part of the Commonwealth in pre-colonial times. Its rapid disappearance from Ohio, where it once was common in the area centering around Sandusky Bay and the Bass Islands, was discussed by Trautman (1957), who indicated the absence of any verified records from the state during the past 40 years. In Iowa, the species has not been collected in any of that state's rivers since before 1900, nor from the few glacial lakes in the north-central part of the state since the early 1930's (Harlan and Speaker, 1956). Its disappearance from these states probably parallels closely the fate of the species in Pennsylvania.

RECOMMENDATIONS: Although it appears likely that *Notropis heterodon* no longer occurs in Pennsylvania, efforts should be made to find the species in potentially favorable habitats, particularly in Conneaut Lake. Should such efforts be successful, steps should be taken to ensure habitat stability of the area(s) where the species is found.

SELECTED REFERENCES:

ADAMS, C. C., and T. L. HANKINSON. 1928. The ecology and economics of Oneida Lake fish. Roosevelt Wild Life Annals, 1:235–548.
GILBERT, C. R. 1980. *Notropis heterodon* (Cope), blackchin shiner. P. 271, *in* Atlas of North American freshwater fishes (D. S. Lee et al.), North Carolina State Mus. Nat. Hist., Raleigh, x + 854 pp.
HARLAN, J. R., and E. B. SPEAKER. 1956. Iowa fish and fishing. Third Edition. Iowa St. Conserv. Comm., x + 377 pp.
KEAST, A. 1965. Resource subdivision amongst cohabiting fish species in a bay, Lake Opinicon, Ontario. Publ. Great Lakes Res. Div., Univ. Michigan, 13:106–132.
SCOTT, W. B., and E. J. CROSSMAN. 1973. Freshwater fishes of Canada. Bull. Fish. Res. Bd. Canada, 184:viii–xi + 1–966.
TRAUTMAN, M. B. 1957. The fishes of Ohio. Ohio St. Univ. Press, Columbus, v–xvii + 683 pp.

PREPARED BY: Carter R. Gilbert, *Florida State Museum, University of Florida, Gainesville, FL 32611.*

Extirpated

NORTHERN REDBELLY DACE
Phoxinus eos (Cope)
Family Cyprinidae
Order Cypriniformes

OTHER NAMES: Redbelly dace, red bellied dace.

DESCRIPTION: The northern redbelly dace is a small minnow seldom exceeding 60 mm in length. The body is somewhat rounded in cross section. The mouth is small and not reaching beyond the anterior edge of the eye. Scales are small with a lateral line usually terminating near the pelvic fins. The intestine is longer than the body with two cross-wise coils in addition to the main loop. Breeding tubercles are in 4 or 5 rows across the breast. Brilliant colors of breeding males are characterized by yellowish fins and a red belly flanked above by the first of two midlateral bands which both proceed posteriorly. The central and dominant lateral band originates on the snout, extends through the eye, and terminates at the base of the caudal fin, sometimes as a black spot. The background color of immature or non-breeding specimens is olive green to dark brown.

RANGE: Their range extends from Nova Scotia south to New York and northern Pennsylvania, west through the Great Lakes drainage to Colorado and northern British Columbia, and south to the upper Missouri River drainage.

HABITAT: The northern redbelly dace is found in quiet, often stained and acidic waters of beaver ponds, small lakes, and boggy creeks often over bottoms of detritus or silt.

LIFE HISTORY AND ECOLOGY: Spawning oc-

Northern Redbelly Dace (*Phoxinus eos*). Photograph by E. L. Cooper.

curs in late spring through summer. The eggs are deposited and fertilized within masses of filamentous algae. Growth is slow with most specimens maturing in the second or third summer. The maximum age is 6 to 8 years with few fish living beyond the fifth summer. Their food includes diatoms, filamentous algae, zooplankton, and aquatic insects.

BASIS OF STATUS CLASSIFICATION: It was originally described from Meshoppen Creek, Susquehanna County, Pennsylvania, in 1862. Currently, it is not found within the Commonwealth.

RECOMMENDATIONS: Intensive surveying across the northern tier of the state is needed to determine if this species is present.

SELECTED REFERENCES:

COOPER, G. P. 1935. Some results of forage fish investigations in Michigan. Trans. Amer. Fish. Soc., 65:132–142.
LEGENDRE, P. 1969. Two natural hybrids of the cyprinid fish *Chrosomus eos.* Unpublished M.S. thesis, McGill Univ., 119 pp.

PREPARED BY: Robert W. Malick, Jr., *Ichthyological Associates, Inc., Three Mile Island Aquatic Study, P.O. Box 223, Etters, PA 17319.*

Extirpated

BULLHEAD MINNOW
Pimephales vigilax (Baird and Girard)
Family Cyprinidae
Order Cypriniformes

OTHER NAMES: Fathead; *Ceratichthys vigilax, Cliola vigilax.*

DESCRIPTION: The bullhead minnow is a species of average size for the genus, length of 75 mm. Its color is dusky yellowish dorsally, silvery below; a dark lateral band; dorsal fin with a dark an-

terior spot and a small dark spot at base of caudal fin; peritoneum is silvery; teeth 4–4.

RANGE: The species ranges from the Mississippi River basin in Minnesota and South Dakota south to Mexico, Texas, Louisiana, and Mississippi, eastward to Georgia, Alabama, and Ohio.

HABITAT: The bullhead minnow lives in rivers of various sizes especially where the current is rapid and the bottom clean.

LIFE HISTORY AND ECOLOGY: This species is reported to spawn in late spring and early summer. Spawning males develop blackish heads, dark backs, a row of 5 tubercles just above the upper lip, and a row of 4 tubercles between and above the nostrils. Nest cavities are excavated and guarded by the male.

The chief food of fry in one study was found to be bottom ooze. Adults are recorded as feeding on seeds, fruits, algae, and other vegetation, and on small snails and other bottom-dwelling animals.

BASIS OF STATUS CLASSIFICATION: Although there are no known specimens of *P. vigilax* from Pennsylvania, the species was reported (as "*Cliola vigilax*") to be abundant at several places in the vicinity of Monongahela City, just south of Pittsburgh (Evermann and Bollman, 1866). Both the Monongahela River and a tributary stream, Pigeon Creek, were reported to contain the species. These waters have been, and continue to be, the recipient of acid mine drainage and other pollutants. Recent collections in Pigeon Creek revealed good numbers of the similar bluntnose minnow, *Pimephales notatus,* but no *P. vigilax* (Edwin Cooper, personal communication).

RECOMMENDATIONS: Further survey of suitable streams in the Monongahela drainage may reveal the existence of *P. vigilax.* The restoration of

Bullhead Minnow (*Pimephales vigilax*). Photograph by C. A. Purkett.

water quality in the Monongahela River and various tributaries is necessary if *P. vigilax* and other species are ever to be a viable component of the Pennsylvania fauna.

SELECTED REFERENCES:

EDDY, S., and J. C. UNDERHILL. 1974. Northern fishes. Univ. Minnesota Press, Minneapolis, 3rd ed., 414 pp.

EVERMANN, B. W., and C. H. BOLLMAN. 1886. Notes on a collection of fishes from the Monongahela River. Ann. New York Acad. Sci., 3:335–340.

FORBES, S. A., and R. E. RICHARDSON. 1920. The fishes of Illinois. Illinois State Journal Co., State Printers, Springfield, Illinois, 2nd ed., 357 pp.

PARKER, H. L. 1964. Natural history of *Pimephales vigilax* (Cyprinidae). Southwestern Nat., 8:228–235.

STARRETT, W. C. 1950. Food relationships of the minnows of the Des Moines River, Iowa. Ecology, 31:216–233.

PREPARED BY: Clark N. Shiffer, *Pennsylvania Fish Commission, Robinson Lane, Bellefonte, PA 16823.*

Extirpated

BLUE SUCKER
Cycleptus elongatus (Lesueur)
Family Catostomidae
Order Cypriniformes

OTHER NAMES: Missouri black horse, gourd-seed sucker, suckerel.

DESCRIPTION: The blue sucker has a slender, elongate body, in combination with a small, elongated head; dorsal fin long, containing from 30–37 rays; anteriormost dorsal rays notably longer than those following, thus resulting in a distinctly concave shape to the fin; mouth included (that is, "underslung"), the lips strongly papillose; eye small, measuring about 3.5 times in length of snout; lateral line complete, the lateral-line scales 53–59; color dark bluish. Adult size ranges from 400–930 mm total length.

RANGE: The blue sucker occurs in the Rio Grande drainage of Texas, New Mexico, and Mexico east to Mobile Bay basin of Alabama and Mississippi. It is found north throughout most of Mississippi River basin to Montana eastward to Ohio and (formerly) western Pennsylvania. This sucker is apparently absent from the Great Lakes basin. A detailed distribution map appears in Gilbert (1980).

In Pennsylvania, *Cycleptus elongatus* once occurred in the Ohio River upstream at least to Pittsburgh (Rafinesque, 1820). This is substantiated by a specimen from the Kiskiminetas River, in the Academy of Natural Sciences of Philadelphia collection (ANSP 23789), collected by E. D. Cope, presumably during the 1860's (Fowler, 1919, 1948). The species probably occurred in Pennsylvania well into the 20th century, based on a report of fishermen having taken occasional specimens (none of which apparently reached museum collections) from 1925–1950 between Marietta, Ohio, and the Pennsylvania state line (Trautman, 1957).

HABITAT: The blue sucker is found in the largest rivers and lower parts of their major tributaries (habitat type II-C-2). It usually inhabits channels and flowing pools with a moderate current, but seems to do well in at least some artificial impoundments (habitat types I-A-1 and I-A-2). The bottom type usually consists of exposed bed-rock, often in combination with hard clay, sand, and gravel. Although Trautman (1957) indicated that this species is intolerant of highly turbid conditions, its natural presence throughout much of the Missouri River suggests that this is not entirely true.

LIFE HISTORY AND ECOLOGY: Brown (1971), discussing Montana populations, stated that the blue sucker feeds mainly on aquatic insects and other small invertebrates, but also utilizes plant material. Spawning occurs in April or May in Kansas and Montana, when the water temperature reaches 10–15°C. Adults probably winter in deep pools and move upstream in spring to spawn on riffles. May reach 10 years of age.

SPECIALIZED OR UNIQUE CHARACTERISTICS: The blue sucker is strictly confined to large bodies of water, and thus is particularly susceptible to pollution of major waterways. Inasmuch as it seems to be tolerant of high turbidity levels, one may assume that industrial pollution in the upper Ohio River has caused its disappearance from Pennsylvania.

BASIS OF STATUS CLASSIFICATION: In view of the fact that *Cycleptus elongatus* has not been seen in Pennsylvania for many years, it is assumed to be extirpated from the Commonwealth.

RECOMMENDATIONS: Continued searches for this fish must be made in the Commonwealth. Although it has not been recorded from Pennsylvania for many years, water-quality improvement in the upper Ohio River would likely result in re-establishment of this species in the Commonwealth.

SELECTED REFERENCES:

Brown, C. J. D. 1971. Fishes of Montana. Big Sky Books, Montana State Univ., Bozeman, 207 pp.

Fowler, H. W. 1919. A list of the fishes of Pennsylvania. Proc. Biol. Soc. Washington, 32:49–74.

———. 1948. A list of the fishes recorded from Pennsylvania. Bull. Pennsylvania Bd. of Fish Commissioners, 7:3–26.

Gilbert, C. R. 1980. *Cycleptus elongatus* (Lesueur), blue sucker. P. 396, *in* Atlas of North American freshwater fishes (D. S. Lee et al.), North Carolina State Mus. Nat. Hist., Raleigh, x + 854 pp.

Rafinesque, C. S. 1820. Ichthyologia Ohiensis, or natural history of the fishes inhabiting the River Ohio and its tributary streams, preceded by a physical description of the Ohio and its branches. Printed for the author by W. G. Hunt, Lexington, Kentucky, 90 pp.

Trautman, M. B. 1957. The fishes of Ohio. Ohio State Univ. Press, Columbus, v–xvii + 683 pp.

PREPARED BY: Carter R. Gilbert, *Florida State Museum, University of Florida, Gainesville, FL 32611.*

Extirpated

LAKE CHUBSUCKER
Erimyzon sucetta (Lacépède)
Family Catostomidae
Order Cypriniformes

OTHER NAMES: Western lake chubsucker, pin sucker; *Cyprinus sucetta, Moxostoma oblongum, Labeo elegans.*

DESCRIPTION: The lake chubsucker is one of the smallest suckers, seldom exceeding 250 mm in length. The body is robust and laterally compressed, greatest depth about one-quarter to one-third of length; mouth subterminal and protrusible; head about one-fifth the body length; lateral line absent; longitudinal scale rows 36–38; scales deeper than long, somewhat smaller on dorsum between head and origin of single dorsal fin; color is dull silver bronze with a dark mid-lateral band, very distinct in young, becoming broken into diffuse blotches or bands in adults.

RANGE: The range extends from eastern Minnesota to extreme southern Ontario and northern New York, south through the Mississippi drainage; west to the Guadalupe River system, Texas; east to Florida and north along the Atlantic slope to southeastern Virginia.

HABITAT: This sucker inhabits lakes, ponds, and stream pools, where the water is clear, with submerged aquatic vegetation and sand or mud bottoms.

LIFE HISTORY AND ECOLOGY: Spawning occurs usually during a 2 week period between early spring and mid-summer in streams. Males may clean a gravelly nesting area, or eggs may be deposited over submerged vegetation. The eggs are nonadhesive and may number from 3,000–20,000.

Hatching occurs within a week at temperatures of 22°–29°C.

The food of both fry and adults is cladocera, chironomid larvae, and copepods, and doubtless other bottom organisms.

BASIS OF STATUS CLASSIFICATION: Although the closely related creek chubsucker, *Erimyzon oblongus,* has been taken in the Delaware and Susquehanna drainages in Pennsylvania, no specimens of that species are known from the Ohio

Lake Chubsucker (*Erimyzon sucetta*). Photograph by E. L. Cooper.

drainage. Fowler (1919, 1940) records the "Chub Sucker" (referred to *Erimyzon sucetta oblongus* (Mitchill) in 1919, and *Erimyzon oblongus* in 1940) from the Erie Basin in Erie County, in addition to the Delaware and Susquehanna drainages. Erie County specimens would most likely refer to *E. sucetta* and not *E. oblongus,* but there are currently no Erie County specimens of either to confirm this. Adding to the uncertainty concerning the provenance of the Erie County records is the fact that many literature records of occurrence list the creek chubsucker as a subspecies of *E. sucetta.* Additionally, Van Meter and Trautman (1970) list both *E. sucetta kennerlyi* and *E. oblongus claviformis* from Lake Erie and tributary waters; the latter ". . . occurring sporadically eastward to Pennsylvania."

RECOMMENDATIONS: Clearly, further attention should be paid to any specimens of chubsuckers obtained in the Lake Erie area in order to clarify the status of *Erimyzon sucetta* in Pennsylvania.

SELECTED REFERENCES:

BENNETT, G. W., and W. F. CHILDERS. 1966. The lake chubsucker as a forage fish. Prog. Fish Cult., 28:89–92.
COOPER, G. P. 1935. Some results of forage fish investigations in Michigan. Trans. Amer. Fish. Soc., 65:132–142.
FOWLER, H. W. 1919. A list of the fishes of Pennsylvania. Proc. Biol. Soc. Washington, 32:49–74.
———. 1940. A list of the fishes recorded from Pennsylvania. Bull. Pennsylvania Bd. Fish Comm., 7:1–25.
LACÉPÈDE, B. G. 1803. Histoire naturelle des poissons. Vol. 5, Plassen, Paris, 803 pp.
PFLIEGER, W. L. 1975. The fishes of Missouri. Missouri Dept. Conserv., Western Publ. Co., Jefferson City, 343 pp.
VAN METER, H. D., and M. B. TRAUTMAN. 1970. An annotated list of the fishes of Lake Erie and its tributary waters exclusive of the Detroit River. Ohio J. Sci., 70:65–78.

PREPARED BY: Clark N. Shiffer, *Pennsylvania Fish Commission, Robinson Lane, Bellefonte, PA 16823.*

Extirpated
BIGMOUTH BUFFALO
Ictiobus cyprinellus (Valenciennes)
Family Catostomidae
Order Cypriniformes

OTHER NAMES: Redmouth buffalo, buffalofish, bullfish; *Sclerognathus cyprinella, Megastomatobus cyprinella.*

DESCRIPTION: The bigmouth buffalo is a deep bodied, compressed sucker with large scales and a long dorsal fin. It can easily be confused with a carp, but lacks barbels around the terminal mouth. The peritoneum is black, and the intestine is very long with at least 4 loops. The color is olive green to brown with fins of somewhat lighter shades. It differs from the smallmouth buffalo in having a large terminal mouth.

RANGE: This fish is restricted to the Mississippi River and its larger tributaries, and in Lake Erie where it may have been introduced. It also occurs in Canada in the Red River system of Manitoba and Saskatchewan. In Pennsylvania, it has been collected only in Lake Erie.

HABITAT: The bigmouth buffalo is common only in large, sluggish rivers, oxbows, and flood plain lakes. Apparently this species is more tolerant of turbidity than other buffalofishes. It often occurs in schools at midwater depths.

LIFE HISTORY AND ECOLOGY: In the spring, adults migrate from lakes to small tributaries or flooded marshes to scatter their adhesive eggs over vegetation or rocky shoals. The young feed on benthic midges and other invertebrates; large buffalofish feed in midwater schools on microcrustaceans. One of the larger buffalofishes, it commonly reaches a size of 13 kg. It is seldom caught by hook and line, but is a commercial species of some importance taken in trammel nets or hoop nets. It is considered a fine food fish.

BASIS OF STATUS CLASSIFICATION: The only known specimen from the Pennsylvania waters of Lake Erie was collected in 1925. It is now presumed to be extirpated in that area.

RECOMMENDATIONS: None. The recent improvement in water quality and fish diversity in Lake Erie may be favorable to an increase in this species.

SELECTED REFERENCES:

BRADY, L., and A. HULSEY. 1959. Propagation of buffalofishes. Proc. Ann. Conf. Southeastern Assn. Game Fish Comm., 13:80–90.

CANFIELD, H. L. 1922. Care and feeding of buffalofish in ponds. U.S. Bur. Fish., Econ. Circ., 56:1–3.

JOHNSON, R. P. 1963. Studies on the life history and ecology of the bigmouth buffalo, *Ictiobus cyprinellus* (Valenciennes). J. Fish. Res. Bd. Canada, 20:1397–1429.

McCOMISH, T. S. 1967. Food habits of bigmouth and smallmouth buffalo in Lewis and Clark Lake and the Missouri River. Trans. Amer. Fish. Soc., 96:70–74.

MINCKLEY, W. L., J. E. JOHNSON, J. N. RINNE, and S. E. WILLOUGHBY. 1970. Foods of buffalofishes, genus *Ictiobus* in central Arizona reservoirs. Trans. Amer. Fish. Soc., 99: 333–342.

MOEN, T. 1954. Food of the bigmouth buffalo, *Ictiobus cyprinellus* (Valenciennes) in northwest Iowa lakes. Proc. Iowa Acad. Sci., 61:561–569.

PFLIEGER, W. L. 1975. The fishes of Missouri. Missouri Dept. Conserv., Western Publ. Co., Jefferson City, 343 pp.

SCOTT, W. B., and E. J. CROSSMAN. 1973. Freshwater fishes of Canada. Bull. Fish. Res. Bd. Canada, 184:1–966.

PREPARED BY: Edwin L. Cooper, *The Pennsylvania State University, University Park, PA 16802.*

Extirpated

BLUE CATFISH
Ictalurus furcatus (Lesueur)
Family Ictaluridae
Order Siluriformes

OTHER NAMES: Blue cat, chuckle-headed cat; *Pimelodus furcatus, Amiurus nigricans.*

DESCRIPTION: The blue catfish is a long and slender fish with a long, straight-edged anal fin and deeply forked tail. The juveniles are not spotted as in the channel catfish, and the fins are long and pointed.

RANGE: The blue catfish is restricted to large river tributaries of the Mississippi River and the Gulf of Mexico. It was reported in the Monongahela River of Pennsylvania in 1886 but has not been taken there in recent years.

HABITAT: It is found only in deep channels of large rivers or tidal canals. It is apparently highly mobile, because populations decline rapidly in impoundments. It is quite tolerant of brackish water along the Gulf Coast.

LIFE HISTORY AND ECOLOGY: Like other catfishes, the male guards eggs and young in a hollow excavated in the bank of a river. The young grow very fast, and this species reaches a weight of 21 kg in about 11 years. It is the largest of the catfishes, reported at more than 45 kg.

Adults feed mostly on crayfishes and fishes, but young fish take aquatic insects and other invertebrates. Under culture conditions they can be trained to accept pelleted foods readily. This is an excellent game fish and food fish, and is cultured widely for food and for introduction into natural habitats.

BASIS OF STATUS CLASSIFICATION: In 1886, Evermann et al. reported the presence of this fish in the Monongahela River. This is the only record for Pennsylvania, and the blue catfish is now presumed to be extirpated. No attempt has been made to reintroduce this species into Pennsylvania waters.

RECOMMENDATIONS: None. With the continued improvement of water quality in the Upper Ohio River drainage, this species may again return to Pennsylvania waters.

SELECTED REFERENCES:

BROWN, B. E., and J. S. DENDY. 1961. Observations on the food habits of the flathead and blue catfish in Alabama. Proc. Southeastern Assn. Game, Fish Comm., 15:219–222.

DARNELL, R. M. 1958. Food habits of fishes and larger invertebrates of Lake Pontchartrain, Louisiana, an estuarine community. Univ. Texas Publ., Inst. Mar. Sci., 5:353–416.

EVERMANN, B. W., and C. H. BOLLMAN. 1886. Notes on a collection of fishes from the Monongahela River. Ann. New York Acad. Sci., 3:335–340.

JENKINS, R. M. 1956. Growth of blue catfish (*Ictalurus furcatus*) in Lake Texoma. Southwestern Nat., 1:166–173.

LAMBOU, V. W. 1961. Utilization of macrocrustaceans for food by freshwater fishes in Louisiana and its effects on the determination of predator-prey relations. Progr. Fish-Cult., 23:18–25.

PERRY, W. G. 1973. Notes on the spawning of blue and channel catfish in brackish water ponds. Progr. Fish-Cult., 35:164–166.

SMITH, P. W. 1979. The fishes of Illinois. Illinois State Nat. Hist. Surv., Urbana, 314 pp.

WALBURG, C. H. 1964. Fish population studies, Lewis and Clark Lake, Missouri River, 1956 to 1962. U.S. Fish. Wildlife Serv., Spec. Sci. Rept.-Fish., 482:1–27.

PREPARED BY: Edwin L. Cooper, *The Pennsylvania State University, University Park, PA 16802.*

Extirpated

PIRATE PERCH
Aphredoderus sayanus (Gilliams)
Family Aphredoderidae
Order Percopsiformes

DESCRIPTION: A small to medium-sized, darkish fish with an undivided dorsal fin located slightly closer to tip of the snout than to base of the tail. The species' most distinctive feature is the position of the anal opening, which is located more posteriorly and "migrates" forward as the fish increases in size. The dorsal, pelvic, and anal fins have three, one, and two spines, respectively. These spines are small and not readily noticeable. The caudal fin is weakly emarginate, almost rounded. The scales are distinctly ctenoid. Size of adults is 64–144 mm total length.

Two distinct subspecies are recognized (*A. s. sayanus* and *A. s. gibbosus*), the nominal form occurring on the Atlantic coast, and the subspecies *gibbosus* living in the Mississippi Valley and parts of the lower Great Lakes basin.

RANGE: The pirate perch is widespread throughout lowlands of the Atlantic and Gulf slopes and the Mississippi Valley, where it is particularly common in more southern parts of the range. Disjunct populations occur in the Lake Erie and Lake Ontario drainages, in western New York. A detailed distribution map appears in Lee (1980). In Pennsylvania, all records are from the lower Delaware River drainage, in Bucks, Delaware and Philadelphia counties (Fowler, 1919). These are represented by five series (totalling 20 specimens), from three separate localities, in the collection of the Academy of Natural Sciences of Philadelphia, all of which were collected between 1899–1917.

The extremely limited range of *Aphredoderus sayanus* in Pennsylvania is a reflection of the small amount of suitable habitat available in the Commonwealth, rather than basic rarity of the species or drastic and widespread ecological alterations (although such changes may be involved in its apparent extirpation from the Commonwealth). Its naturally restricted range here is reflected in similar distribution patterns of several other species of lowland affinities, such as *Notropis chalybaeus, Acantharchus pomotis, Enneacanthus chaetodon, Enneacanthus obesus* and *Etheostoma fusiforme*. All of these species are present, and in most cases common, in adjacent areas of New Jersey.

HABITAT: They are found in lakes, ponds, quiet pools, and backwaters of low-gradient streams containing an abundance of aquatic plants, organic debris, or other cover (habitat types I-A-various categories and I-B-various categories).

Pirate Perch (*Aphredoderus sayanus*). Photograph by C. A. Purkett.

LIFE HISTORY AND ECOLOGY: The pirate perch is a solitary, secretive, nocturnal fish that hides during the day in thick growths of vegetation or organic debris. Its food consists entirely of animal matter, and is comprised of immature aquatic insects, small crustaceans, and occasionally small fish. Spawning occurs during May in the middle parts of its range, but probably occurs somewhat earlier to the south. The breeding habits are not known, but it has been suggested that the pirate perch builds a nest that is guarded by both parents. However, the anterior position of the anus indicates that the eggs are incubated in the gill cavities (this has yet to be proved), as is true of some cavefish species (of the closely related family Amblyopsidae), in which the anus is similarly situated (Pflieger, 1975). Studies conducted in Oklahoma indicate that *Aphredoderus sayanus* lives a maximum of 4 years (Hall and Jenkins, 1954).

SPECIALIZED OR UNIQUE CHARACTERISTICS: Aphredoderus sayanus is of scientific interest because it is the only living species of the family Aphredoderidae, fossil representatives of which are known from western North America, but not from other continents. The order to which this family belongs (Percopsiformes) is also entirely confined to North America, and includes the families Percopsidae (trout-perches) and Amblyopsidae (cavefishes).

BASIS OF STATUS CLASSIFICATION: The pirate perch is classified as extirpated in Pennsylvania, inasmuch as it apparently has not been collected in the Commonwealth in over 60 years. Because the area of southeastern Pennsylvania where the species was once found has been the site of heavy commercial and industrial development for many years, it is highly questionable whether the fish still occurs there. It should be noted that little scientific collecting has been done in this area for many years.

RECOMMENDATIONS: Recollection in those areas where *Aphredoderus sayanus* was once known to occur, as well as in other suitable-looking areas if they exist. If discovered, efforts should be made to maintain the habitat in its natural state.

SELECTED REFERENCES:

FOWLER, H. W. 1919. A list of the fishes of Pennsylvania. Proc. Biol. Soc. Washington, 32:49–74.

HALL, G. E., and R. M. JENKINS. 1954. Notes on the age and growth of the pirate perch, *Aphredoderus sayanus,* in Oklahoma. Copeia, 1954:69.

LEE, D. S. 1980. *Aphredoderus sayanus* (Gilliams), pirate perch. P. 484, *in* Atlas of North American freshwater fishes (D. S. Lee et al.), North Carolina State Mus. Nat. Hist., Raleigh, x + 854 pp.

PFLIEGER, W. L. 1975. The fishes of Missouri. Missouri Dept. Conserv., Western Publ. Co., Jefferson City, viii + 343 pp.

PREPARED BY: Carter R. Gilbert, *Florida State Museum, University of Florida, Gainesville, FL 32611.*

Extirpated

MUD SUNFISH
Acantharchus pomotis (Baird)
Family Centrarchidae
Order Perciformes

OTHER NAMES: Bass sunfish.

DESCRIPTION: The mud sunfish is a stout fish, a maximum of 203 mm in length, with an oblong body that is more similar to the basses than other sunfish. The caudal fin is rounded. There are five gill rakers in the upper limb and two in the lower limb. It is the only centrarchid with cycloid scales. The color is olive green with three to six lateral bands of gold, green, and bronze. These bands are particularly noticeable during spawning. Lateral line scales number 43. Fins: D. XI–XII, 10–12. A. IV–VI, 9–12.

RANGE: The mud sunfish occurs from southeastern New York to northern Florida along the Atlantic Coastal Plain. Pennsylvania records are Delaware River in Bucks County (Fowler, 1938).

HABITAT: This fish is found in tidal and non-tidal lowland streams (most often freshwater) in sluggish, turbid water.

LIFE HISTORY AND ECOLOGY: Little is known of the habits of the mud sunfish. It appears to be nocturnal and remains hidden for most of the time in aquatic grasses and under banks that have submerged roots. Spawning occurs in May and June in Delaware and perhaps in late April. The male guards the nest, which is saucer-shaped and about 300 mm in diameter. The mud sunfish is reported to produce an audible grunting sound, either by grating the pharyngeal teeth or by vibrating muscles in the gas bladder. In light of its nocturnal habits, the grunting may have a reproductive significance. Age and growth have had little study. In Maryland (from 13 specimens) it reached 25 mm total length at age I, 90 mm at age III, and 160 mm at age VII, the oldest fish found. The Maryland fish required 4 years to reach 70 g in weight and 7 years to reach 140 g. The Maryland population apparently grew faster than a comparable New York population after the third year.

SPECIAL OR UNIQUE CHARACTERISTICS: The life history and habits are largely unknown because of the secretive and nocturnal behavior of the mud sunfish.

BASIS OF STATUS CLASSIFICATION: It is listed as endangered by Miller (1972) over its range although Wang and Kernehan (1979) do not agree with the designation for Delaware. The last known collection of mud sunfish in Pennsylvania was in 1938.

RECOMMENDATIONS: An intensive survey of the remaining areas of Bucks County, Pennsylvania, that afford suitable habitat should be undertaken to more closely define the status.

SELECTED REFERENCES:

BAIRD, S. F. 1855. Fishes observed on the coasts of New Jersey and Long Island during the summer of 1854. Ann. Rept. Smithsonian Inst., 9:317–325.

BREDER, C. M., JR., and D. E. ROSEN. 1966. Modes of reproduction in fishes. Natural History Press, Garden City, New York, 941 pp.

FOWLER, H. W. 1938. Notes on Pennsylvania fishes. Repts. Pennsylvania Bd. Fish. Comm., pp. 101–108.

———. 1940. A list of the fishes recorded from Pennsylvania. Pp. 59–78, *in* Biennial Rept. Pennsylvania Bd. Fish. Comm., 129 pp.

HARDY, J. D., JR. 1978. Development of fishes of the Mid-Atlantic Bight, An atlas of egg, larval, and juvenile stages. Vol. III. Aphredoderidae through Rachycentridae. U.S. Dept. Interior, FWS/OBS-78/12, 394 pp.

MANSUETI, R., and H. J. ELSER. 1953. Ecology, age and growth of the mud sunfish, *Acantharchus pomotis*, in Maryland. Copeia, 1953:117–119.

MILLER, R. R. 1972. Threatened freshwater fishes of the United States. Trans. Amer. Fish. Soc., 101:239–252.

RANEY, E. C. 1965. Some panfishes of New York. New York Conserv. Dept., Div. Conserv. Educ., 16 pp.

SHIFFER, C. 1979. Pennsylvania endangered fishes, reptiles, and amphibians. Pennsylvania Fish Comm., 3 pp. (mimeo).

WANG, J. C. S., and R. KERNEHAN. 1979. Fishes of the Delaware estuaries. Ecological Analysts, Inc., Towson, Maryland, 410 pp.

PREPARED BY: John E. Cooper, *Rt. 2, Box 241A, Greenville, NC 27834.*

Extirpated

BLACKBANDED SUNFISH
Enneacanthus chaetodon (Baird)
Family Centrarchidae
Order Perciformes

OTHER NAMES: Pomotis chaetodon, Mesogonistius chaetodon.

DESCRIPTION: This small sunfish has a short, deep, strongly compressed body. It has a round caudal fin and small mouth. The body is dark olive green above and dingy white below. Dorsal, anal, and caudal fins exhibit mottling. Pelvic fins are red anteriorly, black medially, and yellow posteriorly. Pectoral fins are colorless or olive green. The black opercular spot is approximately one-half the diameter of the eye. This species is characterized by the presence of six to eight dark brown or black irregular, vertical bars along the sides of the body. Spawning females become more brilliant in coloration, whereas spawning males become pale and transparent.

RANGE: The distribution pattern of *E. chaetodon* shows localizations of populations. A northern section is centered in New Jersey on the coastal side of the Fall Line, and includes portions of Pennsylvania, Delaware, and Maryland. The area between the Cape Fear River system and the Edisto River system in South Carolina is occupied by a central population. Scattered populations in northern Florida and southern Georgia represent a southern section. Few records exist for Pennsylvania, but other collections have been made from the New Jersey side of the Delaware River.

HABITAT: The blackbanded sunfish prefers shallow, quiet, non-turbid, densely vegetated, darkly stained, acidic waters of streams, margins of rivers, ponds, and lakes. This habitat is abundant along the coastal plain. The lack of collections in Pennsylvania reflects the scarcity of this habitat in the state.

LIFE HISTORY AND ECOLOGY: This sunfish is well adapted to its habitat. Its small size and vertical banding aid in concealment. A rounded caudal fin allows for sudden thrusts. Primary food items are chironomids, caddis larvae, gammarids, dragon fly larvae, and vegetative matter. Toleration of low oxygen concentration is also an important adaptation of this species to its preferred habitat.

Spawning begins in March in North Carolina, within a temperature range of 15–25°C. Nests are constructed in sand or gravel among vegetation or within the vegetation itself. Once the eggs are laid, the male fans them to prevent siltation.

BASIS OF STATUS CLASSIFICATION: No individuals have been taken in Pennsylvania in recent years. There is a lack of preferred habitat in Pennsylvania along the coastal plain.

RECOMMENDATIONS: No action is recommended. This sunfish is abundant in its preferred habitat, which is restricted in the Commonwealth. Pennsylvania is outside of its major center of abundance and now presents only marginal habitat.

SELECTED REFERENCES:

BREDER, C. M., JR., and D. E. ROSEN. 1966. Modes of reproduction in fishes. Crown Publishers, New York, New York, 941 pp.

HARDY, J. D., JR. 1978. Development of the fishes of the mid-Atlantic Bight; an atlas of egg, larval and juvenile stages. Vol. III. Aphredoderidae through Rachycentridae. U.S. Dept. Interior, FWS/OBS-78/12, 394 pp.

JENKINS, R. E., L. A. REVELLE, and T. ZORACH. 1975. Records of the blackbanded sunfish, *Enneacanthus chaetodon,* and comments on the southeastern Virginia freshwater ichthyofauna. Virginia J. Sci., 26:128–134.

LEE, D. S. 1980. *Enneacanthus chaetodon,* blackbanded sunfish. Pp. 587, *in* Atlas of North American freshwater fishes (D. S. Lee et al.), North Carolina State Mus. Nat. Hist., Raleigh, x + 854 pp.

SCHWARTZ, F. J. 1961. Food, age, growth, and morphology of the blackbanded sunfish, *Enneacanthus c. chaetodon* in Smithville Pond, Maryland. Chesapeake Sci., 2:82–88.

SWEENEY, E. F. 1972. The systematics and distribution of the centrarchid fish Tribe Enneacanthini. Unpublished Ph.D. thesis, Boston Univ., Boston, Massachusetts.

TRUITT, R. V., B. A. BEAN, and H. W. FOWLER. 1929. The fishes of Maryland. Maryland State Conserv. Dept., 120 pp.

PREPARED BY: James R. Lebo, *90221 Territorial Road, Junction City, OR 97448.*

Extirpated

LONGEAR SUNFISH
Lepomis megalotis (Rafinesque)
Family Centrarchidae
Order Perciformes

OTHER NAMES: Northern longear, Great Lakes longear; *Icthelis megalotis, Xenotis megalotis.*

DESCRIPTION: A deep-bodied, laterally compressed sunfish with a length of 75–200 mm. The head is deep and narrow, about one-third of the total body length; opercular flap is angled upward, long and wide, black with pale red to yellowish-blue margin; body color is orange brown with orange and blue lateral spots, the side of the head and opercle are orange with blue streaks; lateral line scales number 33–45, usually 35; 10–11 spines of the first dorsal fin are low and even; flexible gill rakers are short, thick and blunt.

RANGE: Its range extends from southern Ontario southwestward through the Mississippi drainage to western Florida, west and south to northeastern Mexico and New Mexico, north to Oklahoma, and the eastern parts of the states to Minnesota, east to Quebec and southern New York.

HABITAT: It is found in quiet, shallow, clear, moderately warm waters of small streams and upland parts of rivers, ponds, and small lakes.

LIFE HISTORY AND ECOLOGY: Spawning occurs from mid-June to August when water temperatures are 23 to 25°C. Males construct saucer-shaped nests in shallow water in gravel, sand, or hard mud. Nests may be situated close together near the shoreline and males vigorously defend these against encroaching conspecifics and other bottom-feeding fishes.

Males spawn with more than one female, chasing these from the nest once the spawning act is completed. Eggs are then fanned and guarded until hatching 3–5 days later. Fry are also guarded by the male for several days. The young grow relatively slowly and reach sexual maturity in 2 to 4 years.

Food consists mostly of mature insects, often taken at the surface, along with leeches and other aquatic invertebrates.

BASIS OF STATUS CLASSIFICATION: Fowler (1919), referring to this species, reported "I have seen it from the Kiskiminetas River, where it was obtained by Cope." Acid mine drainage has since rendered this stream unsuitable for this and other species. The only other known occurrence of *L. megalotis* in Pennsylvania was reported by Raney (1938). His specimens were obtained in Erie and Mercer counties, and have been deposited in the University of Michigan Museum of Zoology and Cornell University collections.

Longear Sunfish (*Lepomis megalotis*). Photograph by E. L. Cooper.

RECOMMENDATIONS: It is reasonable to assume that additional specimens of *L. megalotis* should be found in western and northwestern Pennsylvania upon adequate survey. The species is particularly likely to be found in the Shenango River drainage.

SELECTED REFERENCES:

ADAMS, C. C., and T. L. HANKINSON. 1928. The ecology and economics of Oneida Lake fish. Bull. New York State Coll. Forestry, 1:235–548.

FOWLER, H. W. 1919. A list of the fishes of Pennsylvania. Proc. Biol. Soc. Washington, 32:49–74.

HUCK, L. E., and G. E. GUNNING. 1967. Behavior of the longear sunfish, *Lepomis megalotis* (Rafinesque). Tulane Stud. Zool., 14:121–131.

RAFINESQUE, C. S. 1820. *Ichthyologica Ohiensis,* or natural history of the fishes inhabiting the River Ohio and its tributary streams, preceded by a physical description of the Ohio and its branches. Printed for the author by W. G. Hunt, Lexington, Kentucky, 90 pp.

RANEY, E. C. 1938. The distribution of fishes of the Ohio drainage basin of western Pennsylvania. Unpublished Ph.D. thesis, Cornell Univ., Ithaca, New York, 102 pp.

———. 1965. Some pan fishes of New York. New York Conserv. Dept., Div. Conserv. Educ., 16 pp.

WITT, A., JR., and R. C. MARZOLF. 1954. Spawning and behavior of the longear sunfish, *Lepomis megalotis megalotis.* Copeia, 1954:188–190.

PREPARED BY: Clark N. Shiffer, *Pennsylvania Fish Commission, Robinson Lane, Bellefonte, PA 16823.*

Extirpated

SWAMP DARTER
Etheostoma fusiforme (Girard)
Family Percidae
Order Perciformes

DESCRIPTION: A small, elongate darter which rarely exceeds 45 mm in length. It is distinguished from other darters by an arched, incomplete lateral line which terminates near the end of the spinous dorsal fin. Body color varies with the color of water from which the fish was taken, but is usually tan to olivaceous. Eight to 12 dark saddles traverse the dorsal surface. Eight to 13 dark brown or black blotches often fuse into a dark lateral band with a spot usually present at the base of the tail. Scattered melanophores are present on the cheek; dorsal, caudal, and anal fins; and on the underside from vent to tail. Dorsal fin melanophores on breeding males often coalesce into a solid black band.

RANGE: It is found along the Atlantic Coastal Plain below the Fall Line from southeastern Maine throughout most of peninsular Florida west along the Gulf Coastal Plain to the Texas-Louisiana border and north in the Mississippi drainage to Oklahoma and Tennessee. It has also been introduced into a few ponds within the French Broad River system near Asheville, North Carolina.

HABITAT: The swamp darter occurs primarily in ponds, bogs, lakes, sloughs, swamps, and backwaters of streams and is found only rarely in flowing waters, then not in abundance. It is usually found over bottoms of mud or detritus or in or near aquatic vegetation such as water hyacinth, arrowhead, and pickerel weed. It is able to withstand warm (29–32°C) and stagnant water.

LIFE HISTORY AND ECOLOGY: Although reproductive behavior has not been observed in the wild, specimens held in aquaria spawned on floating plants or algae without exhibiting aggressiveness or territoriality. Evidence suggests that most specimens live for only 1 year. Food items include midge larvae and copepods. They are often parasitized by glochidia (clam larvae).

BASIS OF STATUS CLASSIFICATION: The last swamp darters to be taken from Pennsylvania waters were collected from Mill Creek, tributary to the Delaware River at Bristol, Bucks County. It was abundant in collections from this location in 1905 and 1911, but has not been found within the Commonwealth since.

RECOMMENDATIONS: The swamp darter likely fell prey to decreasing water quality and habitat destruction within the Delaware River drainage. It is not expected to be found now within Pennsylvania as water quality in the Delaware River drainage has continued to decrease since its last collection.

SELECTED REFERENCE:

COLLETTE, B. B. 1962. The swamp darters of the subgenus Hololepis (Pisces, Percidae). Tulane Stud. Zool., 9:115–211.

PREPARED BY: Robert W. Malick, Jr., Ichthyological Associates, Inc., Three Mile Island Aquatic Study, P.O. Box 223, Etters, PA 17319.

Extirpated

SHARPNOSE DARTER
Percina oxyrhyncha (Hubbs and Raney)
Family Percidae
Order Perciformes

OTHER NAMES: No other common names are employed for this species, but it has been occasionally misclassified as Percina macrocephala or Percina phoxocephala.

DESCRIPTION: The sharpnose darter is a relatively large darter that reaches a size of 97 mm standard length. It is characterized by a long tapered snout (hence the species name of oxyrhyncha), abundant small scales, and a rather drab coloration. It has 10 to 12 lateral squarish blotches, one dark spot located medianly on the caudal fin; a small squarish nuchal blotch; and a nearly horizontal mouth that is terminal in position. The body is drab brown, becoming more yellow ventrally. Paired fins, anal fin, and second dorsal are slate colored. The first dorsal fin has a wide dusky margin, with a red band above and a narrow dark margin. The caudal fin is brown at the base, yellowish on the middle part of all membranes, with a dusky margin. There is a dark line from the snout through the eye to the upper end of the gill cleft.

RANGE: The sharpnose darter is known exclusively from northward-flowing tributaries of the Ohio River drainage from the Monongahela River drainage in southwest Pennsylvania to the Green River in Kentucky. It is known from only one collection of two specimens in Pennsylvania, collected in 1885 by Evermann and Bollman from the Monongahela River, at Lock No. 9, Monongahela City. The next closest locality is the Cheat River at the mouth of Big Sandy Creek, Preston County, West Virginia, where nine specimens were collected in 1959.

HABITAT: Large adult sharpnose darters have a distinct preference for high gradient stream areas with a large rubble and boulder substrate; they may be collected in deep runs or turbulent riffles. Smaller adults are often collected over gravel and small rubble riffles in moderate current. Juveniles have been collected over clean sand or gravel in areas of slight to moderate current.

LIFE HISTORY AND ECOLOGY: Etheostoma blennioides, E. flabellare, and E. osburni are species commonly associated with it in the Greenbrier River, West Virginia. It hybridizes with Percina roanoka in New River, Virginia. Otherwise, the biology of this species is unknown.

SPECIALIZED OR UNIQUE CHARACTERISTICS: This species is difficult to collect by conventional seining techniques; thus its absence in earlier surveys of the Monongahela drainage in Pennsylvania may be an artifact of inadequate sampling.

BASIS OF STATUS CLASSIFICATION: This species is known historically from Pennsylvania only by two specimens collected in 1885. Recent surveys of the Monongahela River, including rotenone samples of navigation locks, have failed to yield additional specimens. Thus, the sharpnose darter is considered as extirpated in Pennsylvania, with the area of greatest potential for its occurrence to be the Cheat and Monongahela drainages near the West Virginia state line.

RECOMMENDATIONS: Collections should be made in the Cheat River of Pennsylvania to determine if the sharpnose darter still exists in this drainage.

SELECTED REFERENCES:

DENONCOURT, R. F., C. H. HOCUTT, and J. R. STAUFFER, JR. 1977. Notes on the habitat, description and distribution of the sharpnose darter, *Percina oxyrhyncha.* Copeia, 1977: 168–171.

EVERMANN, B. W., and C. H. BOLLMAN. 1886. Notes on a collection of fishes from the Monongahela River. Ann. New York Acad. Sci., 3:335–340.

HOCUTT, C. H., R. F. DENONCOURT, and J. R. STAUFFER, JR. 1978. Fishes of the Greenbrier River, West Virginia, with drainage history of the central Appalachians. J. Biogeogr., 5:59–80.

———, and P. S. HAMBRICK. 1973. Hybridization between the darters *Percina crassa roanoka* and *Percina oxyrhyncha* (Percidae: Etheostomatini), with comments on the distribution of *Percina crassa roanoka* in New River. Amer. Midland Nat., 90:397–405.

———, J. R. STAUFFER, JR., T. Y. BARILA, and R. F. DENONCOURT. In press. Fishes of the Monongahela National Forest, with a provisional key to the fishes of West Virginia. U.S. Forest Service, Spec. Sci. Rept., 111 pp.

HUBBS, C. L., and E. C. RANEY. 1939. *Hadropterus oxyrhynchus,* a new percid fish from Virginia and West Virginia. Occas. Papers Mus. Zool., Univ. Michigan, 396:1–9.

THOMPSON, B. A. 1979. *Percina oxyrhyncha* (Hubbs and Raney), sharpnose darter. P. 733, *in* Atlas of North American freshwater fishes (D. S. Lee et al.), North Carolina State Mus. Nat. Hist., Raleigh, x + 854 pp.

PREPARED BY: Charles H. Hocutt, *Horn Point Environmental Laboratory, University of Maryland, Box 775, Cambridge, MD 21613.*

Extirpated
BLUE PIKE
Stizostedion vitreum glaucum Hubbs
Family Percidae
Order Perciformes

OTHER NAMES: Blue walleye.

DESCRIPTION: The walleye and blue pike are similar in all respects except for the following characteristics of blue pike given by Hubbs (1926): smaller in size (908 g); a slower rate of growth; and larger, more closely set eyes. The size of the eyes differentiates blue pike from walleye: in blue pike, the interorbital width is 1.4 or more times in eye length; in walleye, the interorbital width is 1.4 or less times in eye length. This characteristic is illustrated by Hubbs (1926) and Trautman (1957). The color of the blue pike is gray blue on the body without mottling (no trace of yellow) and whitish-blue on the pelvic fins.

RANGE: The blue pike was originally believed to be found only in Lake Erie (not in tributaries), but apparently is also present in Lake Ontario. Confusion occurs concerning the range because of the supposed intergradation between the walleye and blue pike. Each of these has also been reported to hybridize with sauger. The gray blue walleye of Lake Nipissing, Ontario, has been considered by some to be blue pike.

HABITAT: The blue pike originally occurred in the deep clear waters of lakes Erie and Ontario. There appears to be an annual movement into shallower water in fall and winter. The largest population in Lake Erie is in the eastern two-thirds of the lake.

LIFE HISTORY AND ECOLOGY: The blue pike is said to spawn in deeper water than the walleye but nothing else is known of the early life history. Blue pike reach 50.8–127 mm total length in October of their first year and adults are 229–406 mm in length. Maximum size and age is uncertain because of intergradation with walleye. The intergrades (gray-pike) have a maximum weight of 3,178 g. Young blue pike feed on cladocerans and invertebrates. Adults eat fish, particularly yellow perch and freshwater drum. Some adult populations are reported to feed solely on emerging insects during part of the year.

SPECIALIZED OR UNIQUE CHARACTERISTICS: Much discussion has occurred concerning the specific or subspecific status of the blue pike. In some geographical areas, its characteristics appear to be consistent, whereas in other areas there is a profusion of intergrades with the walleye. In addition, many color variations of the walleye, some resembling the blue pike, are abundant in the Ohio drainage where the blue pike historically is not found. Bluish-colored walleyes with no trace of yellow are found in Lake Erie. These specimens have been 3,632 g or more which is too large for blue pike.

BASIS OF STATUS CLASSIFICATION: Once abundant in Lake Erie and economically important since 1850, it has been rarely seen in the past thirty years.

RECOMMENDATIONS: A study of the meristic and morphometric characters combined with protein isolation would help determine the specific status.

SELECTED REFERENCES:

DEACON, J. E., G. KOBETICH, J. D. WILLIAMS, and S. CONTRERAS. 1979. Fishes of North America, endangered, threatened, or of special concern: 1979. Fisheries, 4:29–44.

FOWLER, H. W. 1940. A list of the fishes recorded from Pennsylvania. Pp. 59–78, *in* Biennial Rept. Pennsylvania Board Fish Comms., 129 pp.

HUBBS, C. 1926. A checklist of the fishes of the Great Lakes and tributary waters, with nomenclatorial notes and analytical keys. Misc. Publ. Mus. Zool., Univ. Michigan, 15:1–77.

KENDALL, W. C. 1920. The relationship of the so-called blue pike and yellow pike of Lake Erie and Lake Ontario. Trans. Amer. Fish. Soc., 50:257–267.

SCOTT, W. B., and E. J. CROSSMAN. 1973. Freshwater fishes of Canada. Bull. Fish. Res. Bd. Canada, 184:1–966.

SHIFFER, C. 1979. Pennsylvania endangered fishes, reptiles, and amphibians. Pennsylvania Fish Comm., 3 pp. (mimeo).

STONE, F. L. 1948. A study of the taxonomy of the blue and the yellow pike-perches (*Stizostedion*) of Lake Erie and Lake Ontario. Unpublished Ph.D. thesis, Univ. Rochester, New York, 164 pp.

TRAUTMAN, M. B. 1957. The fishes of Ohio with illustrated keys. Ohio State Univ. Press, Columbus, v–xvii + 683 pp.

PREPARED BY: John E. Cooper, *Rt. 2, Box 241A, Greenville, NC 27834.*

Extirpated
SPOONHEAD SCULPIN
Cottus ricei (Nelson)
Family Cottidae
Order Perciformes

OTHER NAMES: Rice's sculpin, spoon head muddler; *Cottopsis ricei, Cottus pollicaris, Uranidia pollicaris.*

DESCRIPTION: The spoonhead sculpins are small benthic fishes with flattened head, fusiform body, and laterally compressed caudal peduncle. Adult size is usually less than 75 mm. They have a large hooked spine on the preopercle. The scales are replaced by small prickles on the body. Their color is dark brown or tan with darker blotches on the back. It is the most distinctive sculpin in North America, easily distinguished from all others.

RANGE: It is restricted in North America to the Great Lakes and most of Canada from the St. Lawrence River west to Saskatchewan and the Northwest Territories. In Pennsylvania it has been reported only from the deep waters of Lake Erie, but there are no recent records. Many of the records are from stomachs of lake trout and burbot.

HABITAT: In the southern part of its range, it is restricted to the deep waters of the Great Lakes occurring over a sand, gravel, or bedrock bottom. In northern Canada it is also frequently taken in large muddy rivers extending into brackish water. Its potential habitat in Pennsylvania appears to be restricted to the deep waters of Lake Erie.

LIFE HISTORY AND ECOLOGY: Virtually nothing is known about this secretive, deep water form. Mature males and females have been taken in summer but no spawning observations have been reported. Their food presumably consists of large zooplankton and aquatic insects. They have some value as forage for lake trout or burbot, a single lake trout stomach contained 33 sculpins. Their chief interest is as a glacial relict species with a unique northern distribution.

SELECTED REFERENCES:

DEASON, H. J. 1939. The distribution of cottid fishes in Lake Michigan. Papers Michigan Acad. Sci. Arts Ltrs., 24:105–115.

MCPHAIL, J. D., and C. C. LINDSEY. 1970. Freshwater fishes of northwestern Canada and Alaska. Bull. Fish. Res. Bd. Canada, 173:1–381.

NELSON, E. W. 1876. A partial catalogue of the fishes of Illinois. Bull. Illinois Mus. Nat. Hist., 1:33–52.

SCOTT, W. B., and E. J. CROSSMAN. 1973. Freshwater fishes of Canada. Bull. Fish. Res. Bd. Canada, 184:1–966.

TRAUTMAN, M. B. 1957. The fishes of Ohio. Ohio State Univ. Press, Columbus, v–xvii + 683 pp.

PREPARED BY: Edwin L. Cooper, *The Pennsylvania State University, University Park, PA 16802.*

Extirpated

DEEPWATER SCULPIN
Myoxocephalus thompsoni (Girard)
Family Cottidae
Order Perciformes

OTHER NAMES: Fourhorn sculpin, deep-water blob; *Triglopsis thompsoni, Cottus quadricornis.*

DESCRIPTION: The deepwater sculpin is a small benthic fish with flattened head, and body tapering abruptly to a slender caudal peduncle. Two dorsal fins are distinctly separated, differing from all other sculpins in this respect. Maximum size is about 100 mm. Scales are lacking, and the body is sparsely covered with prickles.

RANGE: The geographic distribution is in question due to the taxonomic confusion between freshwater and marine forms. As now considered, the deepwater sculpin is confined to large northern freshwater lakes of North America from the Great Lakes northwest into the Northwest Territories of Canada, and in a few lakes in Europe and Asia. In Pennsylvania it has been reported from the deep water of Lake Erie but there are no recent records.

HABITAT: This fish inhabits water so deep that its presence is usually known only from stomachs of lake trout and burbot taken in gill nets set at depths of more than 300 m.

LIFE HISTORY AND ECOLOGY: Almost nothing is known about the life history of this species. Mature females have been taken in midsummer, but no spawning has been observed. Their food consists of large zooplankton and a few midge larvae, but detailed studies have not been done. Its chief interest lies in its scientific curiosity as a glacial relict species associated with a few cold water zooplankton and other fishes.

SELECTED REFERENCES:

DEASON, H. J. 1939. The distribution of cottid fishes in Lake Michigan. Papers Michigan Acad. Sci. Arts Ltrs., 24:105–115.
GIRARD, C. F. 1852. Contributions to the natural history of the freshwater fishes of North America. I. A monograph of the cottoids. Smithsonian Contrib. Knowl., 3(3):1–80.
MCPHAIL, J. D., and C. C. LINDSEY. 1970. Freshwater fishes of northwestern Canada and Alaska. Bull. Fish. Res. Bd. Canada, 173:1–381.
SCOTT, W. B., and E. J. CROSSMAN. 1973. Freshwater fishes of Canada. Bull. Fish. Res. Bd. Canada, 184:1–966.

PREPARED BY: Edwin L. Cooper, *The Pennsylvania State University, University Park, PA 16802.*

CHAPTER 4
AMPHIBIANS AND REPTILES

Timber Rattlesnake (*Crotalus horridus*). Photograph by R. L. Pitler.

Chapter 4 — Amphibians and Reptiles

edited by

C. J. McCoy

Section of Amphibians and Reptiles
Carnegie Museum of Natural History
4400 Forbes Ave.
Pittsburgh, PA 15213

Table of Contents

INTRODUCTION

Amphibians and reptiles in Pennsylvania are under jurisdiction of the Pennsylvania Fish Commission, an independent state agency financed by revenues from fishing license sales. Prior to 1973, the only regulations affecting Pennsylvania amphibians and reptiles were the old "frog, tadpole, and terrapin" laws, that had been carried in the "Pennsylvania Fish Law," essentially unchanged, since the early 1900's. These regulations provided bag limits and seasons, and prohibited some methods of taking frogs, tadpoles, and turtles. These regulations were designed to control the harvest of frogs and turtles by anglers, rather than to protect Pennsylvanian populations of these species. Moreover the regulations were vague, and subject to great latitude in both interpretation and enforcement.

In 1973 the Pennsylvania Legislature, under pressure from bordering states, declared the bog turtle (*Clemmys muhlenbergii*) an endangered species in Pennsylvania. Although this initial endangered species legislation was not the result of a balanced approach to protection of threatened species, the wording of prohibited acts and penalties to be imposed were carefully thought-out and have served as the model for subsequent endangered species laws.

In 1974 the Pennsylvania Fish Commission officially assumed responsibility for all the native amphibians and reptiles of the Commonwealth, and a herpetology advisory committee was established. This committee, which meets annually or semiannually to consider problems concerning conservation of amphibians and reptiles in Pennsylvania, consists of representatives from museums, zoos, universities, and amateur herpetological groups.

On 1 January 1978 the Pennsylvania Fish Commission adopted, upon recommendation of the herpetology advisory committee, an official list of endangered and threatened amphibians and reptiles. This list was adapted from one published by the Society for the Study of Amphibians and Reptiles (Ashton 1976, Endangered and threatened amphibians and reptiles in the United States. SSAR Herpetological Circular 5, 65 pp.). The Pennsylvania Fish Commission list recognizes three status categories: endangered, threatened, and status undetermined (suspected of being endangered or threatened, but requiring further study). Eighteen forms were listed, as follows: *Endangered*—eastern tiger salamander (*Ambystoma t. tigrinum*), eastern mud salamander (*Pseudotriton m. montanus*), New Jersey chorus frog (*Pseudacris triseriata kalmi*), southern leopard frog (*Rana sphenocephala = Rana utricularia*), eastern mud turtle (*Kinosternon s. subrubrum*), red-bellied turtle (*Pseudemys rubriventris*), bog turtle (*Clemmys muhlenbergii*), Blanding's turtle (*Emydoidea blandingii*), midland smooth softshell (*Trionyx m. muticus*), and eastern massasauga (*Sistrurus c. catenatus*); *Threatened*—green salamander (*Aneides aeneus*); *Status Undetermined*—northern goal skink (*Eumeces a. anthracinus*), broad-headed skink (*Eumeces laticeps*), Kirt-

land's snake (*Clonophis kirtlandii*), eastern hognose snake (*Heterodon platyrhinos*), eastern kingsnake (*Lampropeltis g. getulus*), rough green snake (*Opheodrys aestivus*), and timber rattlesnake (*Crotalus horridus*).

The list proposed here by the Amphibian and Reptile Committee of the Pennsylvania Biological Survey includes the same 18 species, and differs only in the names of the status categories and placement of species in the categories. Four species (eastern tiger salamander, eastern mud salamander, Blanding's turtle, and midland smooth softshell) have been removed from the Endangered category and placed in the Recently Extirpated category. Four species that are peripheral in Pennsylvania, and occur at only one or a few localities, are placed in the Vulnerable category (green salamander, broad-headed skink, eastern kingsnake, rough green snake). Also placed in the Vulnerable category is the timber rattlesnake, a species that is under heavy pressure from commercial and sport exploitation and habitat destruction. The northern coal skink, Kirtland's snake, and eastern hognose snake remain in the Status Undetermined category.

C. J. McCoy, *Section of Amphibians and Reptiles, Carnegie Museum of Natural History, 4400 Forbes Ave., Pittsburgh, PA 15213.*

ACKNOWLEDGMENTS

Individuals too numerous to list have provided locality data, information, and experience for this review of Pennsylvania's amphibians and reptiles of special concern. We acknowledge their invaluable contributions. Compilation of distributional data was supported by grants from the Appalachian Audubon Society, Audubon Society of Western Pennsylvania, Conococheague Audubon Society, Greater Wyoming Valley Audubon Society, Stephen H. Harwig, Juniata Valley Audubon Society, Lehigh Valley Audubon Society, Lycoming Audubon Society, National Audubon Society, Pennsylvania Fish Commission. Philadelphia Herpetological Society, Seven Mountains Audubon Society, Tiadaughton Audubon Society, Valley Forge Audubon Society,

Western Pennsylvania Conservancy, and Wyncote Audubon Society. For assistance in arranging this funding I thank Ralph W. Abele and Clark N. Shiffer, Pennsylvania Fish Commission; Frank Dunstan, National Audubon Society; John D. Groves and Malvin L. Skaroff, Philadelphia Herpetological Society; John K. Hanes, Audubon Society of Western Pennsylvania; and Paul G. Wiegman, Western Pennsylvania Conservancy.

The major share of credit for this chapter, however, belongs to the members of the Amphibian and Reptile Committee of the Pennsylvania Biological Survey—Carl H. Ernst, John D. Groves, Howard K. Reinert, and Stephen R. Williams.—C. J. McCoy, *Carnegie Museum of Natural History.*

SPECIES ACCOUNTS

Endangered

NEW JERSEY CHORUS FROG
Pseudacris triseriata kalmi Harper
Family Hylidae
Order Anura

OTHER NAMES: Kalm's chorus frog, striped chorus frog, swamp cricket frog.

DESCRIPTION: A small (2–4 cm), slender greenish-gray to brown frog with three distinct brown or black stripes down the back. The stripes may be interrupted, forked, or reduced to spots in some specimens. A lateral dark stripe extends from the snout to the groin on each side. There is a light cream or white line under the eye, and along the margin of the upper lip. The legs are blotched or spotted. The ventral side is white. Adult males are smaller than the females and have a dark gray or brown throat during the breeding season. This subspecies can be distinguished from the upland chorus frog (*Pseudacris triseriata feriarum*) by having a more robust body and broader, usually well-defined and continuous dorsal stripes.

Tadpoles reach a length of 2.5–3.0 cm and are brownish above with small gold spots scattered over the dorsum of the body. The ventral surface is bronze and strongly iridescent. The tail crest is moderately high, extending onto the body dorsally, and has small black flecks that are most numerous on the dorsal crest but not conspicuously concentrated along the rim.

RANGE: The New Jersey chorus frog occurs along the Atlantic Coastal Plain from Staten Island, New York, south to the southern tip of the Delmarva Peninsula, westward onto the edge of the Piedmont in New Jersey and southeastern Pennsylvania. In Pennsylvania, this frog is known from Bucks, and Montgomery counties, and published reports are available from Philadelphia and Chester counties. Intergradation with the upland chorus frog presumably occurs at Piedmont margin localities.

HABITAT: This frog occurs in a variety of moist to wet habitats, including wet meadows, flood plains, forest swamps, along streams, ditches, and canals and around temporary and permanent water bodies. During the warmer months it is active on the ground in leaf litter along the edges of moist forests or woods. It will also seek subterranean shelter during hot, dry periods.

LIFE HISTORY AND ECOLOGY: Breeding in the New Jersey chorus frog occurs primarily in late February to early May, but may also take place during the summer months. Heavy warm rains stimulate breeding activities. Calling males produce a series of short trills that steadily rise in pitch, best imitated by running a thumb along the teeth of a plastic

New Jersey Chorus Frog (*Pseudacris triseriata kalmi*). Photograph supplied by Philadelphia Zoological Society.

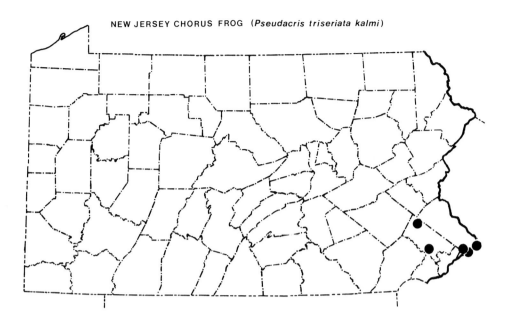

NEW JERSEY CHORUS FROG (*Pseudacris triseriata kalmi*)

comb. Eggs are produced in clutches ranging from 20 to 150 eggs. The loose cluster of eggs is always attached to sticks or other aquatic vegetation in shallow water. The incubation period varies from 5 to 20 days depending on water temperature. Tadpoles metamorphose in about 40 to 60 days from hatching, usually in May and June. Newly transformed frogs are 9–12 mm in length.

Hibernation occurs in terrestrial situations, usually under logs or rocks, or in ant mounds or rodent burrows. This frog has been reported to hibernate with snakes and other amphibians. Predators of adult chorus frogs include large spiders, snakes and small mammals. Salamander larvae, aquatic invertebrates and fish have been reported to prey on the tadpoles of this species.

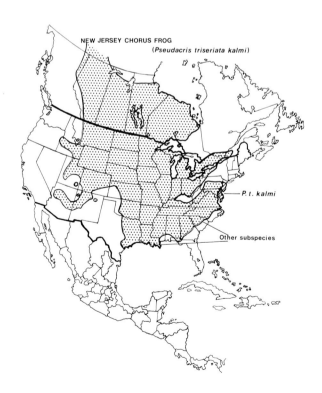

NEW JERSEY CHORUS FROG
(*Pseudacris triseriata kalmi*)

P. t. kalmi

Other subspecies

SPECIALIZED OR UNIQUE CHARACTERISTICS: As the most northeastern member of the genus, this frog is of great biogeographical and evolutionary interest. Its relationship to the upland subspecies of *Pseudacris triseriata,* and to the southern chorus frog (*Pseudacris nigrita*), need further study.

BASIS FOR STATUS CLASSIFICATION: Alteration of habitat by industrialization and urbanization in southeastern Pennsylvania has greatly depleted suitable habitat as well as the species in the Commonwealth.

RECOMMENDATIONS: The New Jersey chorus frog is currently protected as an endangered species by the Pennsylvania Fish Law (section 251.1). A complete study to determine its distribution, population dynamics, and ecological requirements in Pennsylvania is needed to plan possible further management to ensure survival of this frog in the Commonwealth.

SELECTED REFERENCES:

Bragg, A. N. 1948. Observations on the life history of *Pseudacris triseriata* (Weid) in Oklahoma. Wasmann Collector, 7:149–168.

Harper, F. 1955. A new chorus frog (*Pseudacris*) from the eastern United States. Nat. Hist. Misc., 150:1–6.

Whitaker, J. O., Jr. 1971. A study of the western chorus frog, *Pseudacris triseriata,* in Vigo County, Indiana. J. Herpetology, 5:127–150.

Wright, A. H., and A. A. Wright. 1949. Handbook of frogs and toads of the United States and Canada. Comstock Publ. Co., Ithaca, New York, xii + 640 pp.

PREPARED BY: John D. Groves, *Reptile Department, Philadelphia Zoological Garden, Philadelphia, PA 19104.*

Endangered

COASTAL PLAIN LEOPARD FROG
Rana utricularia Harlan
Family Ranidae
Order Anura

OTHER NAMES: Leopard frog, southern leopard frog, meadow frog, grass frog. For at least 50 years, this species has been known in the scientific literature under the names of *Rana pipiens sphenocephala* and/or *Rana sphenocephala.*

DESCRIPTION: A medium-sized frog (5–13 cm) with a slender, narrow head and pointed snout. The ground color is green or brownish-green with numerous elongated or round dark spots, which are sometimes bordered in white or yellow. The sides are variously spotted or darkly mottled. The limbs are spotted, and when the hindlimbs are folded the spots form dark bands. A light spot is usually present in the center of the tympanum. A light-colored dorsolateral glandular ridge extends from behind the eye to the groin. This species can easily be confused with the northern leopard frog (*Rana pipiens pipiens*) and the pickerel frog (*Rana palustris*), both of which occur in Pennsylvania. It can be distinguished from the former by its longer more pointed head, the presence of the light tympanic spot and the reduction or absence of distinct dark lateral spots. It can be distinguished from the pickerel frog by the elongate round spots on the back (pickerel frogs have square blotches) and by the absence of yellow or orange on concealed portions of the hind legs.

The tadpoles of this frog, as well as other members of the genus *Rana,* cannot be readily distinguished in the field. For identification and description of tadpoles, the reader is referred to Wright (1929) and Altig (1970).

RANGE: The coastal plain leopard frog occurs throughout the Atlantic Coastal Plain from southern

Coastal Plain Leopard Frog (*Rana utricularia*). Photograph supplied by Philadelphia Zoological Society.

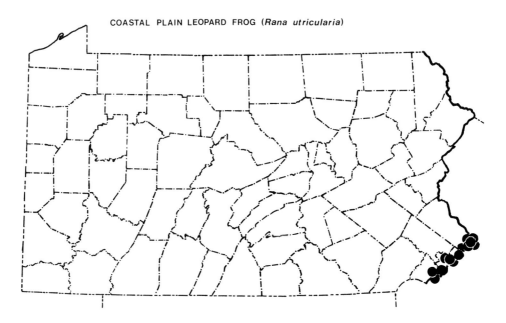

COASTAL PLAIN LEOPARD FROG (*Rana utricularia*)

New York to northern Florida and west in the Mississippi Valley to eastern Oklahoma, Texas, and Kansas. In Pennsylvania, this frog is recorded from Bucks, Delaware and Philadelphia counties, in the southeastern portion of the state. Specimens referred to this species from Chester County appear to be misidentified *Rana pipiens* and *Rana palustris* (Groves, in prep.).

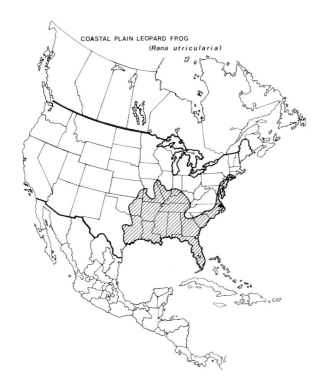

COASTAL PLAIN LEOPARD FROG
(*Rana utricularia*)

HABITAT: This frog inhabits a variety of aquatic habitats, including ponds, lakes, swamps, wet meadows, rivers, and streams. During periods of rainy or humid weather it may wander into any habitat that provides sufficient moisture. It is found most often in permanent and semi-permanent woodland ponds and coastal marshes. Although primarily a Coastal Plain frog, this species has invaded Piedmont areas by following streams and river valleys.

LIFE HISTORY AND ECOLOGY: Little is known concerning the life history of this frog in Pennsylvania. The following information is derived from published statements from populations throughout the Atlantic coastal region and from personal observations of this species in Maryland.

Breeding begins after the first warm rains in early March and continues through April, however, breeding may start as early as February in some years depending on temperature conditions. Calling males produce a series of guttural croaks and clucks similar to the sound made by rubbing a finger across an inflated balloon. Males usually call from shallow water along the edges of ponds, lakes and other water bodies, but underwater vocal behavior has also been reported. Eggs are laid in gelatinous masses, each containing several hundred to several thousand eggs, usually in shallow water. Several clutches of eggs may be produced during the breeding season by each female. Egg masses are generally attached to aquatic vegetation at or near the water surface. Eggs require 15 to 20 days to hatch depending on water temperatures. The tadpoles transform later in the same season, between June and August. Newly transformed frogs are 16 to 30 mm in length.

A wide variety of terrestrial and aquatic insects are eaten by the adult frogs, whereas tadpoles feed on algae, decaying plant debris, and some aquatic invertebrates. Many vertebrates and aquatic invertebrates prey on the adults and larvae of this species.

Some males may be heard calling throughout the active season (March to October), but eggs from summer and autumn choruses are not known in our area. Hibernation takes place under leaves or mud underwater, where the frogs remain inactive during the winter months.

SPECIALIZED OR UNIQUE CHARACTERISTICS: This species and other closely related frogs of the genus *Rana* have been used for biological research and commercial purposes. Comparative morphological and life history studies of this species from various parts of its range have shown wide variation of ecological and evolutionary interest.

BASIS OF STATUS CLASSIFICATION: The rapid depletion of habitat by industrialization along the Delaware River, and the continued urbanization of this region has made the species extremely rare in Pennsylvania. Although now virtually discontinued, the commercial interest in this frog has in the past contributed to the decline of the few known populations in the Commonwealth.

RECOMMENDATIONS: The coastal plain leopard frog is presently protected as an endangered species under the Pennsylvania Fish Law (section 251.1). It is illegal to catch, take, kill, or possess this frog in the Commonwealth. A thorough study of the few existing populations is needed to determine basic life history and ecological information that can be used to develop effective management practices. Although the habitats of some populations in the state are currently under protection by governmental and private organizations, additional habitat preservation is urgently needed.

SELECTED REFERENCES:

ALTIG, R. 1970. A key to the tadpoles of the Continental United States and Canada. Herpetologica, 26:180–207.

HUDSON, R. G. 1956. The leopard frog *Rana pipiens sphenocephala* in southeastern Pennsylvania. Herpetologica, 21:148–150.

PACE, A. E. 1974. Systematic and biological studies of the leop-ard frogs (*Rana pipiens* complex) of the United States. Misc. Publ. Mus. Zool., Univ. Michigan, 148:1–140.

WRIGHT, A. H. 1929. Synopsis and description of North American tadpoles. Proc. U.S. Nat. Mus., 74:1–70.

WRIGHT, A. H., and A. A. WRIGHT. 1949. Handbook of frogs and toads of the United States and Canada. Comstock Publ. Co., Ithaca, New York, xii + 640 pp.

PREPARED BY: John D. Groves, *Reptile Department, Philadelphia Zoological Garden, Philadelphia, PA 19104.*

Endangered
EASTERN MUD TURTLE
Kinosternon subrubrum subrubrum (Lacépède)
Family Kinosternidae
Order Testudines

OTHER NAMES: Mud digger, mud tortoise, Pennsylvania tortoise.

DESCRIPTION: A small turtle (7–10 cm) with an olive, brown or almost black oval-shaped carapace. The plastron is yellowish, with variable amounts of brown, particularly along the sutures. The head is brown to grayish and usually streaked or spotted with yellowish markings. The young of this species are darker in color than the adults, and have a mid-dorsal and lateral keels on the carapace. Adult males have a well-developed blunt spine on the end of the tail and rough scale patches on the insides of the hind legs. This species can be distinguished from the stinkpot (*Sternotherus odoratus*), the only similar species of turtle in our area, by its larger double-hinged plastron (stinkpots have a single anterior hinge).

RANGE: The eastern mud turtle occurs from Long Island south in the Coastal Plain to the Gulf Coast, and west to the Mississippi Valley. In Pennsylvania, it is known only from Bucks, Delaware, and Philadelphia counties, in the southeastern portion of the Commonwealth. Two specimens in the Carnegie Museum of Natural History from Warrendale, Allegheny County, Pennsylvania, are now considered doubtful records.

HABITAT: The eastern mud turtle is an inhabitant of shallow ponds, lakes, and slow-moving water courses with soft bottoms and abundant aquatic vegetation. Frequently, it occupies muskrat lodges. This species has a high tolerance for brackish water and is often found in tidal marshes or on offshore islands.

Eastern Mud Turtle (*Kinosternon s. subrubrum*). Photograph by R. W. Barbour.

LIFE HISTORY AND ECOLOGY: The eastern mud turtle is primarily aquatic, but will venture into terrestrial situations in search of food, particularly in the morning or early evening. During periods of severe drought this turtle will burrow into the mud bottom of a dried-up pool and aestivate until rains replenish the water. During cold months of the year this species hibernates, usually in an aquatic situation, but it may move to areas away from the water and dig a burrow or retreat under logs or in vegetable

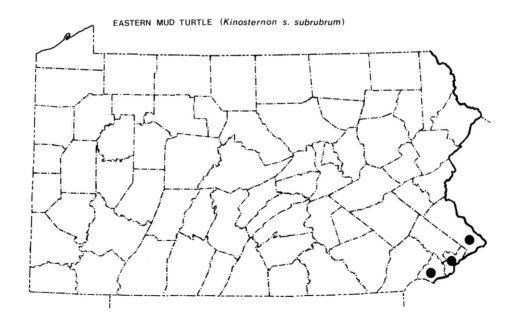

EASTERN MUD TURTLE (*Kinosternon s. subrubrum*)

EASTERN MUD TURTLE
(Kinosternon s. subrubrum)

K. s. subrubrum

Other subspecies

debris. Food of the mud turtle consists of insects, aquatic invertebrates, amphibians, carrion, and aquatic vegetation. Adults will generally eat most available food types, but juveniles prefer aquatic insects, carrion, and algae. Courtship and copulation occur from mid-March through June. One to five hard-shelled eggs are laid in June through August. The eggs are usually placed in a nest barely scratched in the ground under objects such as logs or boards, or in piles of vegetation. The nest is nearly always in sandy, loamy soils near water and usually in open ground. Hatching occurs in late August and September, but some hatchlings may remain in the nest throughout the winter and emerge the following spring. Predators of the mud turtle include snakes, birds, and small mammals. Due to their terrestrial activities, this turtle is often killed in large numbers by automobiles.

SPECIALIZED OR UNIQUE CHARACTERISTICS: Largely a scavenger, this species as well as other members of their family are important components of the environment. They are particularly adapted to forage on land, or in fresh and brackish water, feeding on a large variety of food types.

BASIS OF STATUS CLASSIFICATION: Although common elsewhere in its range, this turtle

appears extremely rare in Pennsylvania, with only a few known specimens being available for study. The continued destruction of habitat by industrialization along the Delaware River, and urban spread throughout southeastern Pennsylvania, have greatly contributed to the alarming decline of this species in the Commonwealth.

RECOMMENDATIONS: The eastern mud turtle is presently afforded protection as an endangered species under the Pennsylvania Fish Law (section 251.1). It is illegal to catch, take, kill, or possess this turtle unless authorized by the Pennsylvania Fish Commission. It is recommended that a thorough survey of existing populations be instituted to determine current population status and basic ecological information. It is further recommended that all available public and privately owned habitat be protected by state statutes to ensure the continued survival of the turtle in the state.

SELECTED REFERENCES:

ERNST, C. H., and R. W. BARBOUR. 1972. Turtles of the United States. Univ. Press Kentucky, Lexington, 347 pp.
BENNETT, D. H. 1972. Notes on the terrestrial wintering of mud turtles (*Kinosternon subrubrum*). Herpetologica, 28:245–247.
IVERSON, J. B. 1972. *Kinosternon subrubrum*. Cat. Amer. Amphib. Rept., 193.1–193.4.

PREPARED BY: John D. Groves, *Reptile Department, Philadelphia Zoological Garden, Philadelphia, PA 19104.*

Endangered

RED-BELLIED TURTLE
Pseudemys rubriventris (LeConte)
Family Emydidae
Order Testudines

OTHER NAMES: Red-bellied terrapin, slider, skillpot.

DESCRIPTION: A large (to 40 cm) freshwater turtle with an elongated dark brown to black carapace that is sawtoothed posteriorly, and bears red or yellow markings. The second pleural scute has a wide red or yellow central mark which is forked at the upper or lower end, or at both ends. Each marginal scute has a red bar on the upper surface and a dark blotch with a light central spot on the lower surface. The bright carapace markings fade with age as the adults become progressively more melanistic. The juvenile plastron is coral-red with a dark central mark that spreads along the seams. This mark fades

Red-bellied Turtle (*Pseudemys rubriventris*). Photograph by R. W. Barbour.

with age and adults usually have plain reddish-yellow plastrons. The bridge has a wide dark bar. The olive-colored head bears several yellow stripes. One passes forward between the eyes and joins, above the nostrils, two others from the temples, forming a prefrontal arrow. There are also five to eight yellow stripes behind the eyes. The tip of the upper jaw has a prominent notch with a toothlike cusp on each side.

Males have long, thick tails with the vent beyond the carapacial margin, elongate foreclaws, and flatter shells. Females grow slightly larger and have more domed carapaces.

The only native Pennsylvanian turtle resembling the red-bellied turtle is the painted turtle, *Chrysemys picta,* but it is smaller, has a smooth posterior margin on its carapace, and two large yellow marks on each side of the head.

RANGE: This species is found along the Atlantic Coastal Plain from central New Jersey south to northeastern North Carolina and westward up the Potomac River to eastern West Virginia. Isolated colonies exist in Massachusetts.

In Pennsylvania, the red-bellied turtle is currently restricted to a few isolated colonies in the Delaware drainages of Bucks, Philadelphia, and Delaware counties, and the Potomac drainage. It occurs in

Manor and Silver lakes in Bucks County, and in the Tinicum marshes and Darby Creek in Philadelphia and adjacent Delaware County. They may also occur in the Springton Reservoir in Delaware County (Conant, 1951; John D. Groves, personal communication). John D. Groves, Curator of Reptiles, Philadelphia Zoological Garden, has been observing these colonies for several years and feels that none probably contain more than 30 individuals. Records from the Potomac drainage are based on a specimen captured (and subsequently released) at Fannettsburg Dam on the West Branch of Conococheague Creek, Franklin County (C. Shiffer, personal communication), and specimens from near Fairfield, Adams County.

HABITAT: Throughout its range, this turtle is usually associated with relatively deep water bodies, low gradient rivers, and associated floodplain marshes, ponds, and oxbows. It often frequents brackish waters near the mouths of rivers, as evidenced by occasionally having barnacles attached to its shell (Arndt, 1975). A soft bottom and available basking sites are necessary. Common aquatic plants form the staples of its diet, and must be present.

LIFE HISTORY AND ECOLOGY: Little is known

RED-BELLIED TURTLE (*Pseudemys rubriventris*)

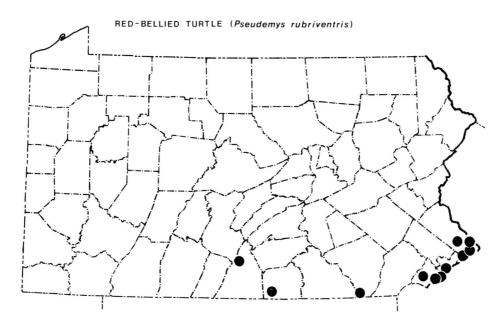

of the natural history of *P. rubriventris*. It is primarily vegetarian, feeding on such aquatic plants as *Sagittaria,* but it also takes crayfish, snails, and tadpoles. It spends much of the day basking in the sun on rocks and logs, but is extremely wary and slips into the water at the slightest sign of danger.

Courtship and mating have not been described.

Nesting occurs primarily in June. The nest is dug in sandy clay or loam soil, usually in full sunlight. A typical nest is flask-shaped, and measures about 10 cm deep and 10 cm wide at the bottom, with a 7 to 8 cm opening at the top. About 12 to 16 elliptical eggs, measuring about 34 by 24 mm, are laid. After an incubation period of from 70 to 80 days the young (average carapace length, 30 mm) hatch in September.

SPECIALIZED OR UNIQUE CHARACTERISTICS: The median ridges on the crushing surfaces of the jaws are tuberculate, an adaptation for feeding on aquatic vegetation. The hind toes are strongly webbed for swimming.

BASIS OF STATUS CLASSIFICATION: In the past, *Pseudemys rubriventris* was locally common, and ranged as far up the Delaware River as Trenton (the type-locality) and also in some of its tributaries such as the Schuylkill River and Darby Creek. It also once occurred in the lower Susquehanna River (Roddy, 1928; John W. Price, personal communication). However, habitat destruction, industrial pollution, and possibly collection of these edible turtles for food, have caused almost total disappearance from Pennsylvania. The habitat in the Tinicum marshes and Silver Lake is poor and the populations there are probably declining. The habitat conditions at Manor Lake are very good and its population appears stable. Conditions at Springton Reservoir are good, but the population size is un-

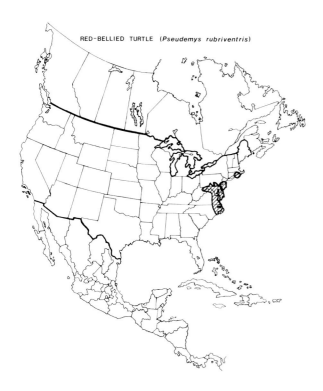

RED-BELLIED TURTLE (*Pseudemys rubriventris*)

known. The status of populations in the Potomac drainage is unknown.

RECOMMENDATIONS: The Tinicum marshes, Manor and Silver lakes, and Springton Reservoir are currently under some kind of protection, and this should stop the destruction of the critical habitat. Also, since the red-bellied turtle has been placed on the state list as an endangered species, collection of specimens is prohibited. However, pollution of the Delaware River and its major tributaries continues, and this could cause the extirpation of the species in Pennsylvania. If these waterways are sufficiently cleaned, and appropriate habitats restored, *Pseudemys rubriventris* could possibly be re-established at additional localities.

It is recommended that the red-bellied turtle population size at Springton Reservoir be determined, and if the population size warrants, that waterbody and Manor Lake be declared protected sanctuaries for this turtle.

SELECTED REFERENCES:

ARNDT, R. G. 1975. The occurrence of barnacles and algae on the red-bellied turtle, *Chrysemys r. rubriventris* (LeConte). J. Herpetol., 9:357–359.

CONANT, R. 1951. The red-bellied terrapin, *Pseudemys rubriventris* (LeConte) in Pennsylvania. Ann. Carnegie Mus., 32:281–290.

RODDY, H. J. 1928. Reptiles of Lancaster County and the state of Pennsylvania. Publ. Dept. Nat. Sci., Franklin and Marshall Coll., Science Press, Lancaster, Pennsylvania, 53 pp.

PREPARED BY: Carl H. Ernst, Department of Biology, George Mason University, Fairfax, VA 22030.

Endangered

BOG TURTLE
Clemmys muhlenbergii (Schoepff)
Family Emydidae
Order Testudines

OTHER NAMES: Muhlenberg's turtle.

DESCRIPTION: A small (to 11.5 cm) semiaquatic turtle with a black, mahogany, or light brown carapace and a large bright blotch on each side of the head. The elongated carapace has a central keel, is somewhat domed, and has a smooth posterior margin. Each scute may have a light central area. The undersides of the marginal scutes and the bridge are the same color as the carapace. The hingeless plastron is usually brown or black, but may contain a few dispersed yellow marks. The skin is brown and often contains some reddish or orange pigment. The head is brown and there is a large, usually orange but sometimes red or yellow, blotch above and behind the tympanum.

Males have concave plastrons and long, thick tails with the vent beyond the carapacial margin. Females have flat plastrons and shorter, narrower tails with the vent beneath the carapace.

Bog turtles may be confused with wood turtles, *Clemmys insculpta,* but the latter is larger, has a very rough shell with a saw-toothed posterior margin and lacks the bright orange or yellow neck patch. Old spotted turtles, *Clemmys guttata,* which have lost their spots have flatter shells and lack the bright neck patch. Old box turtles, *Terrapene carolina,* may resemble bog turtles in color, but they always have a hinged plastron.

RANGE: The bog turtle has a discontinuous range in the eastern United States. Its main area of distribution lies from eastern New York and western Massachusetts and Connecticut southward through New Jersey and eastern Pennsylvania to northern Delaware and Maryland. It is also found in northwestern New York, northwestern Pennsylvania, and from southwestern Virginia through western North Carolina to northern Georgia.

Today, *Clemmys muhlenbergii* is most prevalent in the Delaware and Susquehanna drainages of southeastern and south-central Pennsylvania, where it ranges from Monroe and Northampton counties southwestward to Cumberland, Adams, and Franklin counties. There are also colonies in the Pymatuning area of Crawford County and in Mercer and Butler counties, northwestern Pennsylvania.

HABITAT: The bog turtle prefers marshy meadows and sphagnum bogs (rush-sedge and mixed forb marshes) with clear running shallow water and mud bottoms. Here it lives among and within the bunches of *Carex,* cattails, and the tussocks of other grasses and sedges; at night and during inclement weather it crawls inside clumps of grass stalks for protection. It also uses them as sites for basking and laying eggs.

LIFE HISTORY AND ECOLOGY: Clemmys muhlenbergii is a secretive animal, spending much of its time hidden, but some individuals are usually active during the hours of 0800 to about 1800 from April through June, and again in September. Many

Bog Turtle (*Clemmys muhlenbergii*). Photograph by R. W. Barbour.

estivate under the mud, in grass tussocks, or in muskrat burrows to escape the hot, dry weather of July and August. Hibernation occurs from October into March in the mud of a waterway or in a muskrat burrow. All activities are carried out within a very small home range, averaging only 1.28 hectares.

Bog turtles are omnivores, eating plant and ani-mal foods both in the water and on land. Plant foods include various filamentous algae, berries, and seeds of pondweed (*Potamogeton*) and sedge (*Carex*). In-sects of various groups make up the bulk of the food. Other animals eaten include snails, slugs, earth-worms, and carrion.

Courtship and mating occur during May and early

BOG TURTLE (*Clemmys muhlenbergii*)

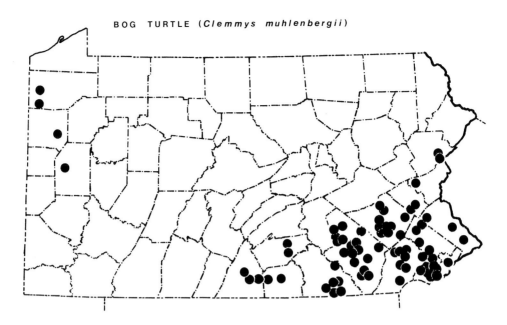

June. Males become quite active and search out females during this period. Courtship behavior has not been adequately described. In a Lancaster County colony, males pursued females in shallow water, captured them, and simply tried to mount them from the rear by hooking the claws of all four feet under the marginal scutes of the female. Occasionally the males would bite at the head or legs of the

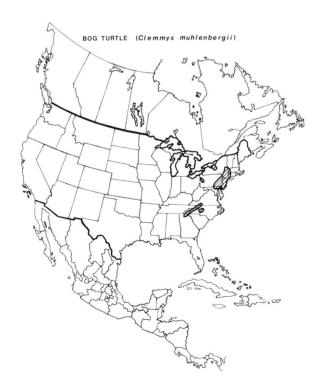

BOG TURTLE (*Clemmys muhlenbergii*)

female. Eggs are laid in June or July. Apparently a nest cavity is seldom constructed in the wild, although a nest sometimes occurs in captivity (Arndt 1977). Instead, the 3 to 5 eggs are laid, and often left partially exposed, in sedge tussocks or under sphagnum moss. The white elliptical eggs average 30 by 16 mm and weigh 4 to 5 g. Apparently only one clutch is laid a year. In nature, hatching probably occurs in August or September. Incubation periods for eggs laid in captivity ranged from 50 to 59 days (Arndt 1977). Hatchlings average about 25 mm in carapace length.

Colonies of *C. muhlenbergii* are small, usually ranging between 30 and 300 individuals. However, due to their secretive habits, accurate estimation of population size and density is difficult.

BASIS OF STATUS CLASSIFICATION: Although widespread throughout southeastern Pennsylvania, none of the colonies, as stated above, contain many individuals. This makes entire colonies vulnerable to extinction through natural predation, habitat destruction, or human exploitation for pets. Also, their preferred habitat represents one of the last stages in the natural succession that occurs as a water body fills with sediment, and becomes land (hydrarch succession). So, such habitats are at best transitory, and inevitably colonies must emigrate to other suitable areas or perish. Unfortunately, the available wetland habitats are rapidly disappearing under shopping centers, housing developments and superhighways, giving the bog turtle little chance to survive.

In the past bog turtles, due to their apparent rarity, commanded a high price in the animal trade, and many colonies were totally eliminated for sale as pets. Fortunately, every state in which these turtles occur now protects them from commercial exploitation.

RECOMMENDATIONS: Monitoring of existing colonies must continue to prevent commercial exploitation or inadvertent habitat destruction. Priority must be given the turtle as an endangered species when construction projects (public or private) threaten habitats. These efforts, and establishment of additional bog turtle preserves, may assure the survival of the bog turtle for the foreseeable future.

SELECTED REFERENCES:

ARNDT, R. G. 1977. Notes on the natural history of the bog turtle, *Clemmys muhlenbergi* (Schoepff), in Delaware. Chesapeake Sci., 18:67–76.

BARTON, A. J., and J. W. PRICE, SR. 1955. Our knowledge of the bog turtle, *Clemmys muhlenbergi,* surveyed and augmented. Copeia, 1955:159–165.

BLOOMER, T. J., and R. J. HOLUB. 1977. The bog turtle, *Clemmys muhlenbergi*—a natural history. Herp: Bull. New York Herpetol. Soc., 13(2):9–23.

BURY, R. B. 1979. Review of the ecology and conservation of the bog turtle, *Clemmys muhlenbergii.* U.S. Dept. Int., Fish Wildl. Serv., Spl. Sci. Report—Wildl., 219:1–9.

ERNST, C. H. 1977. Biological notes on the bog turtle, *Clemmys muhlenbergii.* Herpetologica, 33:241–246.

ERNST, C. H., and R. B. BURY. *Clemmys muhlenbergii.* 1977 Catalogue of American Amphibians and Reptiles, 204.1–204.2.

LANDRY, J. L. 1979. A bibliography of the bog turtle, *Clemmys muhlenbergii* (biology, ecology and distribution). Smithsonian Herpetol. Inform. Serv., 44:1–21.

NEMURAS, K. T. 1967. Notes on the natural history of *Clemmys muhlenbergi.* Bull. Maryland Herpetol. Soc., 3:80–96.

PREPARED BY: Carl H. Ernst, *Department of Biology, George Mason University, Fairfax, VA 22030.*

Endangered

EASTERN MASSASAUGA

Sistrurus catenatus catenatus (Rafinesque)
Family Viperidae
Order Squamata

OTHER NAMES: Swamp rattlesnake, snapper.

DESCRIPTION: The massasauga is a small, stout-bodied rattlesnake averaging 49.9 cm in total length with the largest Pennsylvania specimens rarely exceeding 75.0 cm. The color pattern is a series of large, dark brown to black, mid-dorsal blotches and two to three rows of lateral blotches set upon a light gray ground color. The tail has three to six dark cross-bands. The venter is black, occasionally mottled with white. The small rattle sounds like the buzz of an insect and is barely audible beyond 5 m. Massasaugas have a generally mild disposition and rarely rattle, even when approached.

RANGE: The range of the eastern massasauga extends from central New York and western Pennsylvania westward through Ohio, southwestern Ontario, Michigan, Indiana, Illinois, southern Wisconsin, extreme southeastern Minnesota, and eastern Iowa to central Missouri where it intergrades with the subspecies *Sistrurus catenatus tergeminus.*

Historically the massasauga occurred in Allegheny, Butler, Crawford, Lawrence, Mercer, and Venango counties in western Pennsylvania. A 1978 survey revealed extant populations only in Butler, Mercer, Venango, and possibly Crawford counties.

HABITAT: Low-lying, poorly drained, open habitats and "old field" situations are generally favored. Recent research has revealed the occurrence of a seasonal shift in habitat utilization by the massasauga in Pennsylvania. Suitable hibernacula are usually situated in the vicinity of mixed forb and rush–sedge marshes. Consequently, these vegetational zones are frequented in the spring and autumn. During the summer months slightly higher and drier vegetational zones dominated by goldenrods, asters, dogwoods, and poverty grass are used extensively by this species.

LIFE HISTORY AND ECOLOGY: In Pennsylvania, female massasaugas produce biennial broods containing an average of seven offspring. The young, which measure approximately 23.6 cm, are born in August or early September. Mating has been observed in late July and August.

Rodents and shrews compose the bulk of the diet; however, newborn snakes feed readily upon other small snakes. Additional observed food items of Pennsylvania specimens include crayfish (W. B. Allen, personal communication) and frogs.

Hibernation usually occurs in crayfish burrows, but any excavation that extends below the water table will be used. The snakes apparently pass the winter submerged in water, lifting their heads to the

Eastern Massasauga (*Sistrurus c. catenatus*). Photograph by H. K. Reinert.

surface periodically for air. The hibernation period begins in middle to late October and ends in late March or early April.

The activity range of individual massasaugas averages slightly less than 1 hectare. Daily movements average a distance of only 9 m. Massasaugas are largely diurnal in their movements, and activity is positively correlated with increased atmospheric relative humidity.

SPECIALIZED OR UNIQUE CHARACTERISTICS: The uniqueness of the massasauga extends beyond the fact that it is one of the three species of venomous snakes found in Pennsylvania. This small rattlesnake is also part of the unique fauna and flora that remains as the last vestige of the post-glacial prairie that once extended throughout the northwestern portion of the state.

EASTERN MASSASAUGA (*Sistrurus c. catenatus*)

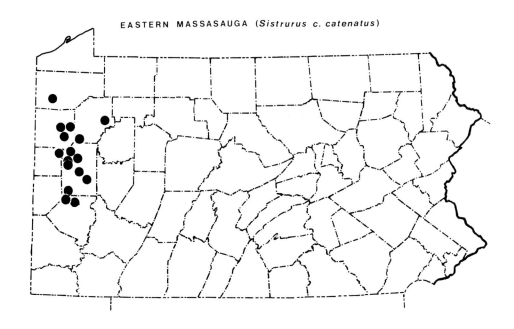

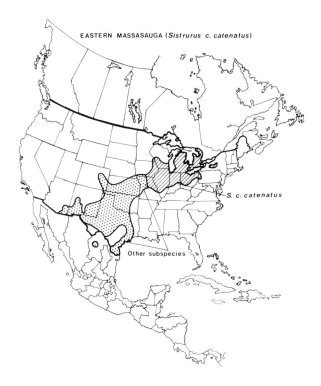

EASTERN MASSASAUGA (*Sistrurus c. catenatus*)

S. c. catenatus

Other subspecies

BASIS OF STATUS CLASSIFICATION: During 1977, nineteen locations of historical occurrence were surveyed for the presence of massasaugas and/or suitable habitat. Extant populations were verified at six localities, and suitable habitat remained at four additional sites. The remaining nine localities either lacked suitable habitat, or had such severely decreased habitat that the presence of the massasauga was considered doubtful. Seven of the localities with extant populations or potentially suitable habitat also exhibited signs of habitat deterioration. Damming, highway construction, urban expansion, forest succession, surface mining, and agriculture are the six major factors responsible for altering massasauga habitats. This loss of habitat has substantially decreased the geographic distribution of this species in Pennsylvania and may result in the fragmentation and isolation of populations.

RECOMMENDATIONS: The massasauga was officially listed as an endangered species by the Pennsylvania Fish Commission in 1978. This action prohibits the catching, taking, killing, or possession of specimens under penalty of a $500.00 fine. While this constitutes an important step in the protection of remaining populations, it does not confront the major problem of habitat loss. It is recommended that construction, mining, damming, and drainage

operations to be performed in Butler, Mercer, and Venango counties be carefully evaluated for their possible effect upon massasauga habitat. In addition, three localities with extant populations are currently in Commonwealth ownership. These sites should be carefully managed to maintain suitable habitat conditions. Acquisition of additional sites should be considered.

SELECTED REFERENCES:

ATKINSON, D. A., and M. G. NETTING. 1927. The distribution and habits of the massasauga. Bull. Antivenin Inst. America, 1:40–44.

REINERT, H. K. 1981. Reproduction by the massasagua (*Sistrurus catenatus catenatus*). Amer. Midland Nat., 105:393–395.

REINERT, H. K., and W. R. KODRICH. 1978. The occurrence of the massasauga in Pennsylvania. Clarion State College, Dept. Biol., Special Report to the PA Fish Commission, 45 pp.

———. 1982. Movements and habitat utilization by the massasauga, *Sistrurus catenatus catenatus*. J. Herpetol., 16:162–171.

SWANSON, P. L. 1930. Notes on the massasauga. Bull. Antivenin Inst. America 4:70–71.

———. 1952. The reptiles of Venango County, Pennsylvania. Amer. Midland Nat., 47:161–182.

PREPARED BY: Howard K. Reinert, *Department of Biology, Lehigh University, Bethlehem, PA 18015.*

Vulnerable

GREEN SALAMANDER
Aneides aeneus (Cope and Packard)
Family Plethodontidae
Order Caudata

DESCRIPTION: This lungless salamander has a back pattern of yellowish-green lichen-like patches set on a black background. Adults reach a total length of about 10.2 cm. Females are slightly longer than males and may be distinguished by eggs seen through the translucent belly skin. Adaptations include long legs and long toes with expanded tips, which allows this rock-crevice salamander to crawl upside down on a rough stone. *Aneides aeneus* is a completely terrestrial salamander with no aquatic larval stage. Hatchling young look like miniature adults.

RANGE: The green salamander is restricted to the southern Appalachian Mountains from northern Mississippi to extreme southwestern Pennsylvania.

Green Salamander (*Aneides aeneus*). Photograph by C. W. Bier, Western Pennsylvania Conservancy.

Aneides aeneus occurs in Pennsylvania in deep, cool, moist ravines on the western slope of Chestnut Ridge, Fayette County.

HABITAT: In Pennsylvania, *Aneides aeneus* is found on sandstone cliffs usually shaded by hemlocks and maples. *Aneides aeneus* is unique among Appala-chian salamanders, because it inhabits damp (but not wet) crevices in rock outcrops. These outcrops must be associated with mixed hardwood forests, but there is no specific tree species association.

LIFE HISTORY AND ECOLOGY: Mating usually occurs in May or early June, but has also been ob-

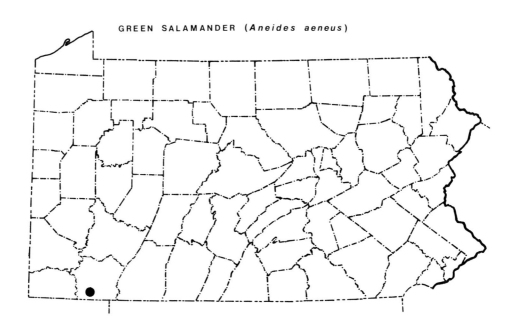

GREEN SALAMANDER (*Aneides aeneus*)

GREEN SALAMANDER (*Aneides aeneus*)

served in the autumn. In June the gravid female lies with the ventral surface pressed to the ceiling of a crevice, and over a 24 hr period deposits about 18 eggs that average 0.45 cm in diameter. The whitish-yellow yolk-filled eggs are held together by sticky mucus, and the egg mass is attached to the crevice ceiling by one or more short mucus cables. Hatching occurs in September. The female broods the eggs and may also guard the young a short time after hatching. The female lunges and bites at intruders, and does not actively feed during the 84 to 91 day incubation period. The home range is small; in one study whre 21 salamanders were marked only four moved more than 2.5 m. Except for brooding females, the salamanders do not defend territories. As many as 11 green salamanders may occupy a crevice. The major period of activity is at and after dusk.

SPECIALIZED OR UNIQUE CHARACTERISTICS: Aneides aeneus is of special ecological as well as evolutionary interest. Its sedentary nature and visibility (with the help of a flashlight) makes this salamander an excellent example for ecological studies. Unlike most of the salamanders in the Appalachian Mountains, the green salamander has a peculiar history. The ancestors of the genus originated in the Appalachian Mountains, then migrated

to the west coast as did many other types of salamanders. However, some of these western forms then migrated back to the east. As the Rocky Mountains, Sierra Nevadas, and Cascade Mountains uplifted, these populations became isolated, and as a result, the closest genetic relative of the green salamander is not found in the Appalachian Mountains but on the west coast.

RECOMMENDATIONS: The restricted habitat of *Aneides aeneus* makes them highly vulnerable to lumbering and land clearing. In Ohio, near Huntington, West Virginia, lumbering has forced the salamanders from their once shaded outcrops into caves. The green salamander should be protected, because it is known from only one area in Pennsylvania.

SELECTED REFERENCES:

BRUCE, R. C. 1968. The role of the Blue Ridge embayment in the zoogeography of the green salamander, *Aneides aeneus*. Herpetologica, 24:186–194.

GORDON, R. E. 1952. A contribution to the life history and ecology of the plethodontid salamander *Aneides aeneus* (Cope and Packard). Amer. Midland Nat., 74:666–701.

———. 1967. *Aneides aeneus*. Catalogue of American Amphibians and Reptiles, 30.1–30.2.

RICHMOND, N. D. 1952. First record of the green salamander in Pennsylvania, and other range extensions in Pennsylvania, Virginia and West Virginia. Ann. Carnegie Mus., 32:313–318.

PREPARED BY: Stephen R. Williams, *Department of Biology, The Pennsylvania State University, New Kensington Campus, 3550 Seventh Street Road, New Kensington, PA 15068* (present address: *Glendale Community College, 6000 West Olive Ave., Glendale, AZ 85301*).

Vulnerable

BROAD-HEADED SKINK
Eumeces laticeps (Schneider)
Family Scincidae
Order Squamata

OTHER NAMES: Scorpion.

DESCRIPTION: The broad-headed skink is a large (16.5–32 cm), lizard of the five-lined skink group. Juveniles have five bright yellow longitudinal stripes on a glossy black background, and a metallic blue tail. As they grow older and larger, the pattern becomes less contrasting, the stripes darken, background color becomes gray-brown, and the tail turns

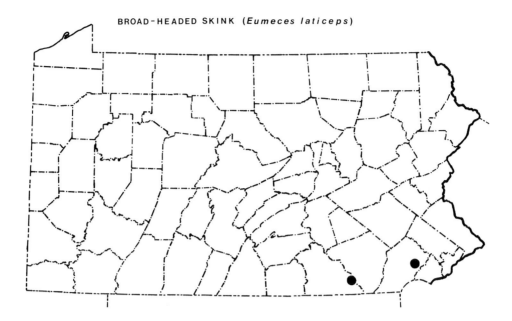

BROAD-HEADED SKINK (*Eumeces laticeps*)

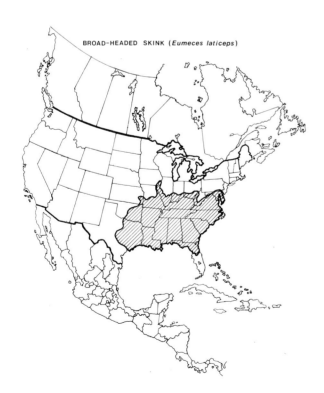

BROAD-HEADED SKINK (*Eumeces laticeps*)

gray. Adult females usually retain some traces of the striped pattern, but adult males become uniform gray-brown. In adult males the head becomes enlarged and broadened and turns bright orange-red.

The broad-headed skink is most similar to the five-lined skink, but can be distinguished by the absence of postlabial scales (present in five-lined skink) and by having five (four in the five-lined skink) upper lip scales between the subocular scale and the rostral scale on each side.

RANGE: The broad-headed skink has an extensive range in the eastern United States, from southern Pennsylvania and the Delmarva Peninsula southward to northern Florida, west into Kansas, Oklahoma, and Texas. In Pennsylvania, *Eumeces laticeps* has been found only in York (York Furnace) and Chester (West Chester) counties, but may also occur in Lancaster and Delaware counties.

LIFE HISTORY AND ECOLOGY: The broad-headed skink is found in wooded areas, and tends to be arboreal. Dead snags, fence posts, and trees, especially in woods openings, along roads, or field edges are preferred habitat. Mating occurs in late spring, and 6 to 10 eggs are laid in June. The female parent guards the eggs during incubation. The hatchlings measure 30 to 32 mm body length. Food includes a great variety of insects and other invertebrates, and small vertebrates (young lizards and mice).

SPECIALIZED OR UNIQUE CHARACTERISTICS: The broad-headed skink is the largest of the four species of lizards recorded from Pennsylvania. Old males, with their enlarged, bright-red heads, are impressive animals, and are generally regarded as dangerous (if not deadly) by uninformed observers.

BASIS OF STATUS CLASSIFICATION: Eumeces laticeps reaches the northern limit of its geographic range in southeastern Pennsylvania, and is certainly vulnerable to extirpation in the heavily urbanized environment of this part of the Commonwealth.

RECOMMENDATIONS: Further surveys should be conducted to determine if additional populations of the broad-headed skink exist in Pennsylvania. The species should be given legal protection, and the habitat of existing populations preserved.

SELECTED REFERENCES:

McCoy, C. J. 1982. Amphibians and reptiles in Pennsylvania. Spec. Publ. Carnegie Mus. Nat. Hist., 6:1–91.

Smith, H. M. 1946. Handbook of lizards. Comstock Publ. Co., Ithaca, New York, xxi + 557 pp.

Taylor, E. H. 1935. A taxonomic study of the cosmopolitan scincoid lizard genus *Eumeces* with an account of the distribution and relationship of its species. Univ. Kansas Sci. Bull., 23:1–643.

PREPARED BY: C. J. McCoy, *Section of Amphibians and Reptiles, Carnegie Museum of Natural History, Pittsburgh, PA 15213.*

Vulnerable

EASTERN KINGSNAKE
Lampropeltis getulus getulus (Linnaeus)
Family Colubridae
Order Squamata

OTHER NAMES: Chain snake, chain king snake, thunder snake, swamp wamper.

DESCRIPTION: A medium-sized (91.4—208.3 cm) black or brownish-black snake with 21 to 30 white, cream, or yellowish dorsal bands that are connected by lateral markings to form a chain-like pattern. The upper and lower labial scales and sides of the head are boldly marked with alternating bars of white and black. The young are identical in color and pattern to adults.

RANGE: The eastern kingsnake occurs from southern New Jersey southward into the northern part of Florida and the Florida Panhandle, west to the Appalachians and Mobile Bay. In Pennsylvania, this snake is known only from Lancaster County, but may occur in other areas in the vicinity of the Susquehanna Valley.

HABITAT: The eastern kingsnake is predominantly a lowland snake that occupies a wide variety of habitats, but may be found in upland areas along stream and river valleys. It prefers wet situations near the borders of swamps, streams, and rivers where adequate food is available.

LIFE HISTORY AND ECOLOGY: Although this is a common snake throughout much of its range, particularly in the south, very little is known concerning its life history and ecology. It is a terrestrial

Eastern Kingsnake (*Lampropeltis g. getulus*). Photograph supplied by Philadelphia Zoological Society.

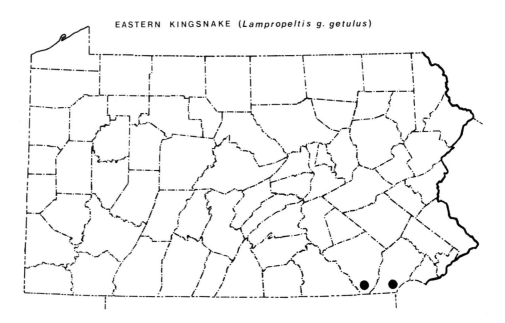

EASTERN KINGSNAKE (*Lampropeltis g. getulus*)

snake, and is most active during early to midmorning and again in the late afternoon and early evening. It eats a variety of prey species including small mammals, lizards, snakes (including venomous species), and amphibians. In some areas it has a preference for turtle eggs, which are normally abundant in its preferred habitat. Breeding occurs in late May to early June (earlier in the south). A clutch of

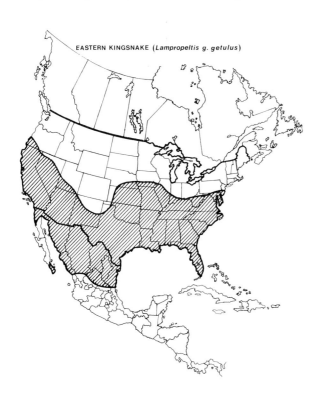

EASTERN KINGSNAKE (*Lampropeltis g. getulus*)

3–24 elongated eggs is laid from mid June to early August. Hatching occurs after an incubation period of 8 to 12 weeks, depending on the temperature. Natural enemies of this species include ophiophagic snakes (including other king snakes), predatory birds, and carnivorous mammals.

SPECIALIZED OR UNIQUE CHARACTERISTICS: Because of its behavior and feeding habits, this snake probably has economic value in the control of pest species, especially in agricultural areas where rodents are of particular concern. It may also control populations of the venomous copperhead (*Agkistrodon contortrix*).

BASIS OF STATUS CLASSIFICATION: In Pennsylvania, the eastern kingsnake has proven elusive, with only one documented specimen having been taken in the Commonwealth. This specimen was reportedly collected near Conestoga Creek, Lancaster County, in 1931 and was identified by the late Emmett Reid Dunn from a film. Other specimens have been reported from the vicinity of Conestoga Creek and the Susquehanna Valley in Lancaster County, and from Jennersville, Chester County (McCoy, 1982), but no specimens are available. McCoy (1982) listed the eastern kingsnake as a "probable" member of the Pennsylvania herpetofauna. Lack of adequate knowledge concerning the distribution and population levels within the Commonwealth warrants listing of this as a species of concern.

RECOMMENDATIONS: Field studies to establish distributional and ecological parameters for this species are urgently needed. Some protection has been afforded this species, and all other amphibians and reptiles in the Commonwealth, by prohibiting sale of this commercialized snake.

SELECTED REFERENCES:

McCOY, C. J. 1982. Amphibians and reptiles in Pennsylvania. Spec. Publ. Carnegie Mus. Nat. Hist., 6:1–91.

NETTING, M. G. 1936. The chain snake, *Lampropeltis getulus getulus* (L.) in West Virginia and Pennsylvania. Ann. Carnegie Mus., 25:77–82.

WRIGHT, A. H., and A. A. WRIGHT. 1957. Handbook of Snakes of the United States and Canada. Comstock Publ. Assoc., Ithaca, New York, 1:i–xviii + 1–564.

PREPARED BY: John D. Groves, *Reptile Department, Philadelphia Zoological Garden, Philadelphia, PA 19104.*

Vulnerable

ROUGH GREEN SNAKE
Opheodrys aestivus (Linnaeus)
Family Colubridae
Order Squamata

OTHER NAMES: Keeled green snake, grass snake, vine snake.

DESCRIPTION: The rough green snake is a medium-sized (56–81 cm), slender snake with keeled dorsal scales. The tail is attenuate and very long, averaging about 37 percent of the total length (Conant, 1951). The dorsal color is a uniform bright grass green. The underside and upper lip scales are white to yellow. Hatchlings are gray-green above and white below.

RANGE: The rough green snake has a large geographic range in the eastern United States, southward along the Gulf into Mexico. The range extends from southern New Jersey and southeastern Pennsylvania through Florida and the Keys, west to central Texas, Oklahoma, and eastern Kansas. Northern limits are reached in northern Missouri, southern Illinois, Indiana, and Ohio, and the southwestern corner of Pennsylvania. The species is absent from the northern Appalachians. In Pennsylvania, the rough green snake has been collected in Greene County in the southwest, and along the Maryland border in Chester County.

LIFE HISTORY AND ECOLOGY: Opheodrys aestivus is an arboreal species. Individuals are usually found climbing or resting in vegetation, from low bushes to small trees 6–9 m in height, frequently along the margins of streams, ponds, or lakes. The snakes pass virtually the entire activity season aloft, descending to the ground only to lay eggs and to hibernate. They sleep coiled on a twig fork, and feed on arboreal insects and spiders.

A clutch of 4–11 eggs is laid between mid-July and mid-August with hatching occurring from late

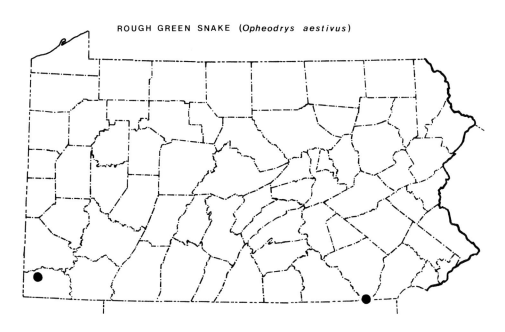

ROUGH GREEN SNAKE (*Opheodrys aestivus*)

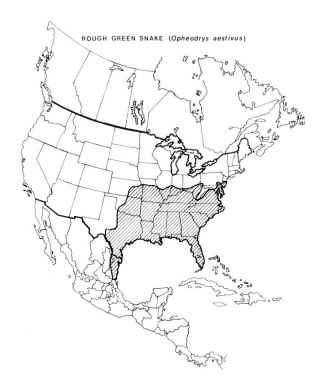

ROUGH GREEN SNAKE (*Opheodrys aestivus*)

August into September. Hatchlings average 18–20 cm in length.

SPECIALIZED OR UNIQUE CHARACTERISTICS: The rough green snake is one of several reptile species in Pennsylvania that enter the state on each side of the Appalachians, but are absent from the mountainous central section of the Commonwealth. This is of zoogeographic and systematic interest, as populations in the southwest and southeast corners of Pennsylvania are at the ends of a U-shaped distribution and may be significantly different both genetically and morphologically.

BASIS OF STATUS CLASSIFICATION: Sight records and other reports unsupported by collections suggest that the rough green snake may have an extensive range in the southern tier of Pennsylvania counties, northward to Westmoreland County in the west. Nevertheless, all Pennsylvania specimens are from two localities—Ninevah, Greene County, and Horseshoe Camp, Chester County (McCoy, 1982). Until additional localities are confirmed, the rough green snake is considered vulnerable in Pennsylvania because of this limited range.

RECOMMENDATIONS: The extent of the geographic range of this species in Pennsylvania should be determined by systematic collecting efforts in the preferred habitat, in counties along the southern border of the Commonwealth. The presence of viable populations at the two previously confirmed localities should also be verified.

SELECTED REFERENCES:

CONANT, R. 1951. The reptiles of Ohio. Univ. Notre Dame Press, South Bend, Indiana, second edition, 284 pp.

McCOY, C. J. 1982. Amphibians and reptiles in Pennsylvania. Spec. Publ. Carnegie Mus. Nat. Hist., 6:1–91.

PLUMMER, M. V. 1981. Habitat utilization, diet, and movements of a temperate arboreal snake (*Opheodrys aestivus*). J. Herpetol., 15:425–432.

WRIGHT, A. H., and A. A. WRIGHT. 1957. Handbook of snakes. Comstock Publ. Assoc., Ithaca, New York, 1:i–xviii + 1–564.

PREPARED BY: C. J. McCoy, *Section of Amphibians and Reptiles, Carnegie Museum of Natural History, 4400 Forbes Ave., Pittsburgh, PA 15213.*

Vulnerable

TIMBER RATTLESNAKE
Crotalus horridus Linnaeus
Family Viperidae
Order Squamata

OTHER NAMES: Banded rattlesnake.

DESCRIPTION: This is a snake of extremely variable coloration. Most commonly the pattern consists of dark brown or black crossbands on a ground color of sulfur yellow, brown, or gray. Often a faint brown mid-dorsal stripe is in evidence. The tail is black, both dorsally and ventrally. Completely black individuals are common and may predominate in certain populations. Coloration is independent of sex. Young are always crossbanded with dark markings on a gray ground color. Adults average 90–120 cm with Pennsylvania specimens rarely exceeding 152 cm.

The timber rattlesnake can be distinguished from the massasauga by its completely black tail and lack of white facial lines. In addition, the massasauga has nine large scales on the dorsal surface of the head, whereas the head of the timber rattlesnake is covered with numerous small scales.

RANGE: This species is widely distributed from New Hampshire southward through the Appalachian Mountains to northern Florida and westward

Timber Rattlesnake (*Crotalus horridus*). Photograph by H. K. Reinert.

along the Gulf Coast to eastern Texas, eastern Oklahoma and eastern Kansas. In the midwest, it is found as far north as southeastern Minnesota and western Wisconsin along the Mississippi River and its tributaries, and to southern Illinois, Indiana, and Ohio.

It is suspected that the timber rattlesnake occurred state-wide in precolonial days; however, in recent history it has not been recorded from the southeastern corner or western edge of Pennsylvania. The rattlesnake has largely been extirpated from populous areas, and its current distribution is confined to the mountainous regions of the Commonwealth.

HABITAT: The timber rattlesnake is indigenous to deciduous forests. Second growth stands with shrub ground cover are apparently preferred to mature forests. Forest openings dominated by blueberry (*Vaccinium* sp.) or laurel (*Kalmia* sp.) are occasionally frequented, as are rock outcrops. Hibernacula

TIMBER RATTLESNAKE (*Crotalus horridus*)

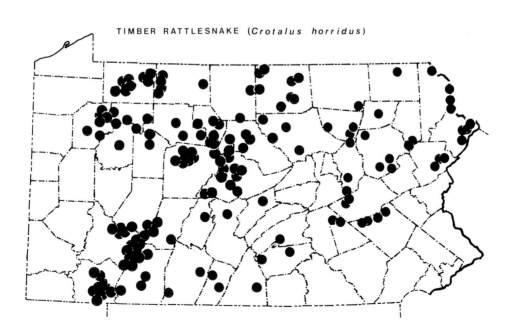

TIMBER RATTLESNAKE (*Crotalus horridus*)

are often situated on rocky, forested slopes with southern or southeastern exposure.

LIFE HISTORY AND ECOLOGY: Six to 11 offspring are produced between late August and early October. Available information indicates that timber rattlesnakes do not reproduce annually, but that a biennial or triennial cycle predominates. In all probability, most matings occur during the summer and autumn. Newborn snakes average 28 cm in total length. Approximately 5 years are required for females to reach a total length of 83 cm and apparent sexual maturity.

Rodents, shrews, chipmunks, and squirrels compose the bulk of the diet. Additional reported food items include birds, bird eggs, young rabbits, bats, and amphibians.

Rattlesnakes enter hibernation in mid to late October and emerge in late April or early May. The denning proclivity of this species is well documented, and communal hibernacula may contain large numbers of rattlesnakes in addition to copperheads, black rat snakes, and black racers. Reports of Pennsylvania dens containing over 100 snakes occur in the literature and in old newspaper accounts. Apparently aggregations of such size no longer occur, and a den of 20 rattlesnakes is now considered large.

Current research indicates that males disperse as far as 2–7 km during the summer months, while females remain much closer to the hibernation site. Gravid snakes in particular maintain very restricted activity ranges and are usually confined to basking sites within several hundred meters of the hibernaculum. Current data suggest that most individuals return to the same hibernation site over successive years.

SPECIALIZED OR UNIQUE CHARACTERISTICS: The timber rattlesnake is the largest of the three species of venomous snakes occurring in Pennsylvania. Despite its size, this snake has a generally mild disposition, and its bite is rarely fatal. The danger of rattlesnakes to campers, hikers, hunters, and fisherman is often greatly exaggerated. The probability of encountering and being bitten by a rattlesnake while participating in outdoor activities in Pennsylvania is exceedingly low.

Historically this species was the first rattlesnake encountered by the early colonists of North America and was the snake symbolically represented on the navy jack, Gadsden flag, and numerous colonial standards during the American Revolution.

BASIS OF STATUS CLASSIFICATION: The realization that rattlesnakes are an integral part of the deciduous forest ecosystem has not received widespread public acceptance. Consequently, most rattlesnakes are indiscriminantly killed even when encountered miles from populous areas or human habitations. In addition, collecting rattlesnakes for commercial and recreational purposes has gained in popularity, and Pennsylvania is plagued by numerous organized "snake hunts" which exploit rattlesnakes. A recent study indicated that many veteran snake collectors believe that rattlesnake populations have declined drastically in recent years, and most attributed this decline to over-collecting. Although the species is still relatively abundant throughout much of the mountainous portion of Pennsylvania, its slow growth to maturity and low reproductive potential make it exceedingly vulnerable to complete extirpation as a result of indiscriminate killing and collecting.

RECOMMENDATIONS: Research, particularly in the areas of reproduction, growth, habitat requirements, movements, and population densities, is required for adequate evaluation of the status of this species and for the design of effective management procedures.

A moratorium should be placed on organized "snake hunts" until research demonstrates that collecting, handling, and release into foreign environments produces no significant mortality and has no deleterious effect upon populations. In addition, season possession limits should be instituted to deter over-collecting by individuals. Commercial collecting is currently illegal, as Pennsylvania Fish Commission regulations prohibit the sale of native amphibians and reptiles.

Through mutual agreement between the Pennsylvania Fish Commission and the Department of Environmental Resources, all amphibians and reptiles are protected on approximately 25,000 acres of State Forest Natural Areas. This program should be expanded to include all state natural and wild areas including State Game Lands and State Forest Lands. Such a program would greatly aid the survival of rattlesnake populations in Pennsylvania.

Finally, educational programs designed to dispel prevalent myths concerning rattlesnakes and to foster an understanding of the importance of the rattlesnake in the ecosystem should be developed and made available to schools, sportsmen groups, park naturalists, and other outdoor-oriented organizations.

SELECTED REFERENCES:

GALLIGAN, H. J., and W. A. DUNSON. 1979. Biology and status of timber rattlesnake (*Crotalus horridus*) populations in Pennsylvania. Biol. Conserv., 15:13–58.
GLOYD, H. K. 1940. The rattlesnakes, genera *Sistrurus* and *Crotalus*. A study in zoogeography and evolution. Chicago Acad. Sci. Special Publ., 4: i–vii + 1–266.
KEENLYNE, K. D. 1978. Reproductive cycles in two species of rattlesnakes. Amer. Midland Nat., 100:368–375.
KLAUBER, L. M. 1972. Rattlesnakes. Vols I and II. Univ. California Press, Berkeley, 1,536 pp.
McCOY, C. J. 1975. Timber rattlesnake. Pennsylvania Forest Resources, 21:1–4.
REINERT, H. K. 1984. Habitat separation between sympatric snake populations. Ecology, 65:478–486.
WRIGHT, A. H., and A. A. WRIGHT. 1957. Handbook of snakes. Comstock Publ. Associates, Ithaca, New York, 2:565–1005.

PREPARED BY: Howard K. Reinert, *Department of Biology, Lehigh University, Bethelehem, PA 18015.*

Status Undetermined

NORTHERN COAL SKINK
Eumeces anthracinus anthracinus (Baird)
Family Scincidae
Order Squamata

DESCRIPTION: The northern coal skink is a medium-sized (13–17.8 cm), ground-dwelling lizard. The dorsal pattern consists of four light lines, two dorsolateral and two lateral, extending from the head onto the tail. The middorsal zone, between the dorsolateral lines, is bronze-colored. The lateral zones, between the light lines on each side, are black. The underside is white. Hatchlings are colored like adults, except that contrast between the longitudinal lines and interspaces is greater. The postmental scale (second scale behind the tip of the lower jaw) is undivided.

RANGE: The coal skink has a distribution of disjunct isolates, extending from western New York southward into Pennsylvania, through the northern Appalachians, Alabama, Mississippi, and Georgia, to the Gulf Coast. West of the Mississippi the range is continuous from southern Missouri and eastern Kansas to east Texas and western Louisiana. Populations in northern Georgia and Alabama are considered intergrades between the northern coal skink and the southern coal skink. In Pennsylvania, the northern coal skink occurs at scattered localities on the Allegheny Plateau and in the northcentral mountains, from Warren County in the west to Tioga County in the east, southward at least in Nittany Mountain, Centre and Union counties. The population at the type-locality ("North Mountain, near Carlisle," Cumberland ? County) may be disjunct.

LIFE HISTORY AND ECOLOGY: The northern coal skink is usually found under cover (rocks, logs, etc.) in heavily wooded hilly terrain. Courtship and mating occur in late May, and eight or nine eggs are laid in late June. The eggs are guarded by the female during the 4–5 week incubation period. Hatchlings range from 47 to 51 mm in total length. Food consists of insects, insect larvae, and other small terrestrial invertebrates. Practically nothing is known of growth, size, and age at maturity, population structure or other aspects of the life history of this species.

SPECIALIZED OR UNIQUE CHARACTERISTICS: The northern coal skink is one of only four lizard species recorded from Pennsylvania, and is the least-known of the four. Populations are scattered and extremely localized, and the secretive habits of the species makes it an elusive member of our fauna.

Northern Coal Skink (*Eumeces a. anthracinus*). Photograph by R. W. Van Devender.

BASIS OF STATUS CLASSIFICATION: Because of the localized nature of populations, they are particularly vulnerable to destruction by habitat modification. *Eumeces anthracinus* is apparently rare in Pennsylvania, but more information on distribution and abundance is needed to make a definitive assessment of status.

RECOMMENDATIONS: Two kinds of studies are needed to further assess the status of the northern

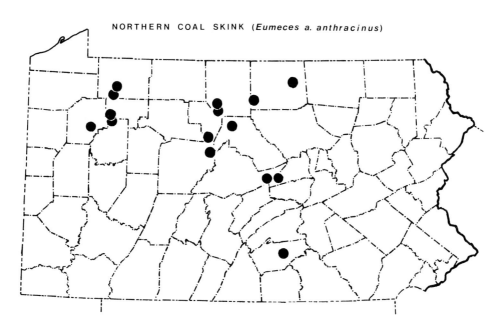

NORTHERN COAL SKINK (*Eumeces a. anthracinus*)

coal skink in Pennsylvania—surveys to define geographic range and abundance, and population studies to determine ecological requirements and life history characteristics.

SELECTED REFERENCES:

McCoy, C. J. 1982. Amphibians and reptiles in Pennsylvania. Spec. Publ. Carnegie Mus. Nat. Hist., 6: 1–91.

NORTHERN COAL SKINK
(*Eumeces a. anthracinus*)

Smith, H. M. 1946. Handbook of lizards. Comstock Publ. Co., Ithaca, New York, i–xxi + 1–557 pp.

PREPARED BY: C. J. McCoy, *Section of Amphibians and Reptiles, Carnegie Museum of Natural History, 4400 Forbes Ave., Pittsburgh, PA 15213.*

Status Undetermined

KIRTLAND'S SNAKE
Clonophis kirtlandii (Kennicott)
Family Colubridae
Order Squamata

OTHER NAMES: Kirtland's water snake.

DESCRIPTION: Kirtland's snake is a medium sized (36–46 cm) natricine with a small, narrow head. The dorsal pattern consists of four longitudinal rows of rounded dark brown to black spots on a ground color of light brown to orangish brown. The pattern may be darkened and the spots not discernible. The best recognition character is the bright red to red-orange belly, with a single longitudinal row of round black spots at each side. The dorsal scales are keeled.

RANGE: Kirtland's snake ranges from western Pennsylvania through most of Ohio and Indiana, westward into Illinois and Missouri. The northern range limit is in southern Michigan, and the southernmost localities are in extreme northern Kentucky, just across the Ohio River. In western Pennsylvania there is one recorded locality in Jefferson

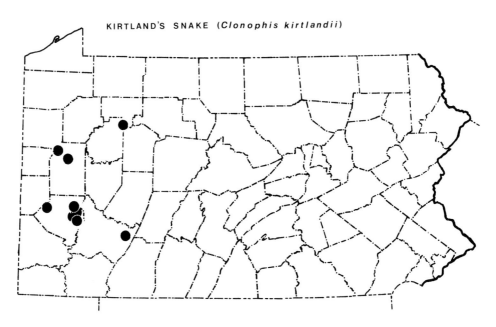

KIRTLAND'S SNAKE (*Clonophis kirtlandii*)

County (Cooksburg), and one in Westmoreland County (near Waterford). All other records are clustered either in northern Butler County or in Allegheny County, with the largest number in the eastern suburbs of Pittsburgh (Wilkinsburg, Forest Hills, Penn Hills). Two old records from the Delaware Valley, although supported by museum specimens (Conant, 1943), require verification. If Kirtland's snake is a prairie relict, as suggested by Conant

KIRTLAND'S SNAKE (*Clonophis kirtlandii*)

(1978), an extension of range to the east coast would be zoogeographically plausible.

LIFE HISTORY AND ECOLOGY: Kirtland's snake is the least aquatic of the North American "water" snakes. Preferred habitat is open wet meadows and swamp-forests. It has a decided predilection for newly-cleared land and vacant lots in suburban areas (Minton, 1972). Mating occurs in early spring (April, May) and the young are born in August or early September. There are four to 22 young, averaging 13–17 cm in length, in a brood. The principal food item is earthworms, although captive specimens will also take small slugs.

SPECIALIZED OR UNIQUE CHARACTERISTICS: The most unusual characteristic of Kirtland's snake in Pennsylvania is its seeming rarity. Nothing is known of the ecology or seasonality of local populations, and specimens are encountered so rarely that generalizations cannot be made about Pennsylvania populations of the species. Repeated searches, extending over several decades, have failed to produce specimens on a predictable basis from known localities of occurrence.

BASIS OF STATUS CLASSIFICATION: Populations of Kirtland's snake in the suburbs of Pittsburgh (five of the 10 known localities) are clearly in jeopardy. Minton (1972) has commented on the decline of Kirtland's snake with development of the suburban areas of Indianapolis, Indiana. Nevertheless, localities in Westmoreland and Jefferson counties indicate a potentially extensive geographic range in western Pennsylvania.

RECOMMENDATIONS: The highest priority should be given to distributional surveys to determine the geographic range and abundance of Kirtland's snake in western Pennsylvania. An attempt should be made to verify occurrence at reported localities, including those in the Delaware Valley. If possible, the ecological factors favoring survival of Kirtland's snake should be determined, and habitats that provide a proper combination of factors protected. Given the apparent rarity of the species, and the difficulty of locating populations, protection should be postponed until further data are available.

SELECTED REFERENCES:

CONANT, R. 1943. Studies on North American water snakes—1. *Natrix kirtlandi* (Kennicott). Amer. Midland Nat., 29: 313–341.
———. 1978. Distributional patterns of North American snakes: some examples of the effects of Pleistocene glaciation and subsequent climatic changes. Bull. Maryland Herp. Soc., 14: 241–259.
MINTON, S. A., JR. 1972. Amphibians and reptiles of Indiana. Indiana Acad. Sci., Indianapolis, v + 346 pp.
WRIGHT, A. H., and A. A. WRIGHT. 1957. Handbook of snakes. Comstock Publ. Co., Ithaca, New York, 1:i–xviii + 1–564.

PREPARED BY: C. J. McCoy, *Section of Amphibians and Reptiles, Carnegie Museum of Natural History, 4400 Forbes Ave., Pittsburgh, PA 15213.*

Status Undetermined
EASTERN HOGNOSE SNAKE
Heterodon platyrhinos Latreille
Family Colubridae
Order Squamata

OTHER NAMES: Spreading adder, blowing adder, and many others.

DESCRIPTION: The eastern hognose is a medium to large snake (51–84 cm) with a stocky body, thick neck, and short tail. The snout is pointed and upturned, and the rostral scale is keeled on the sides and above. The color pattern is variable. The usual pattern is alternating dorsal and lateral black spots on a ground color that ranges from cream to brown or orange. Entirely black individuals are common in some areas, and uniform gray, green, or reddish brown specimens occur more rarely. Observation of matings between uniform colored and spotted individuals may have led to folk tales of interspecies hybridization.

Eastern Hognose Snake (*Heterodon platyrhinos*). Photograph by C. J. McCoy.

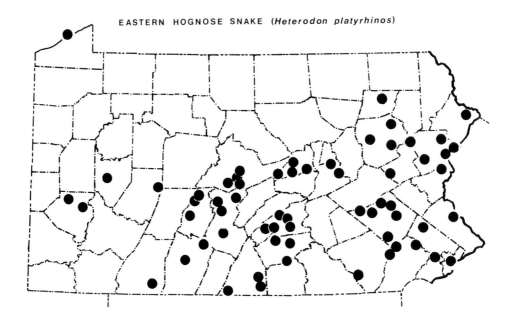

EASTERN HOGNOSE SNAKE *(Heterodon platyrhinos)*

RANGE: The eastern hognose snake occurs over most of the eastern United States, from Massachusetts to Florida, and from southern Ontario southward to east Texas. Western limits are reached in Minnesota, North Dakota, Nebraska, western Kansas, and western Oklahoma. In Pennsylvania, the eastern hognose snake occurs in three discrete distributional zones–along the border of Lake Erie and on Presque Isle; in the Ohio and Allegheny drainage of southwestern Pennsylvania; and in eastern Pennsylvania east of the Allegheny Front, south of Centre and Wyoming counties (McCoy and Bianculli, 1966).

LIFE HISTORY AND ECOLOGY: Heterodon platyrhinos is a burrowing snake that is limited to areas of sandy or extremely loose soil. Populations in Pennsylvania are found on the beaches of Lake Erie, in sandy river bottoms, and on sand ridges in the mountainous areas. The principal food item is toads (genus *Bufo*), but *Heterodon* also eats other amphibians and a variety of vertebrate and invertebrate prey. Mating occurs in March or April. A clutch of 4–61 (mean 22.5) soft-shelled eggs is laid in June or early July. The hatchlings, about 20 cm long, emerge after an incubation period of 40 to 60 days.

SPECIALIZED OR UNIQUE CHARACTERISTICS: This species has an amazing repertoire of defensive behaviors that are unique among North American snakes. When confronted with threatening situations, these snakes spread the jaws and neck "cobra fashion," hiss loudly, rise well off the ground, and strike with the mouth open. If these measures fail, the snake may roll over on its back and feign death, with mouth open and limp tongue protruding. Variations on these basic themes in individual snakes seem endless. Most of the dozens of vernacular names applied to *Heterodon platyrhinos* refer to some aspect of this defensive behavior.

EASTERN HOGNOSE SNAKE
(Heterodon platyrhinos)

BASIS OF STATUS CLASSIFICATION: Although *Heterodon platyrhinos* has a large geographic range in Pennsylvania, populations are localized in areas with suitable soil conditions. It is nowhere abundant, and observations indicate that numbers of hognose snakes have generally declined in recent years, particularly near the edges of the species range (Hudson, 1954; Platt, 1969). The reasons for this decline are not clear.

RECOMMENDATIONS: Studies should be initiated to determine the geographic distribution and population size of *Heterodon platyrhinos* in Pennsylvania, as a basis for future status classification decisions. Existing populations on state-owned lands should be protected from all molestation.

SELECTED REFERENCES:

HUDSON, R. G. 1954. An annotated list of the reptiles and amphibians of the Unami Valley, Pennsylvania. Herpetologica, 10:67–72.

McCoy, C. J., and A. V. BIANCULLI. 1966. The distribution and dispersal of *Heterodon platyrhinos* in Pennsylvania. J. Ohio Herp. Soc., 5:153–158.

PLATT, D. R. 1969. Natural history of the hognose snakes *Heterodon platyrhinos* and *Heterodon nasicus*. Univ. Kansas Publ., Mus. Nat. Hist., 18:253–420.

WRIGHT, A. H., and A. A. WRIGHT. 1957. Handbook of snakes. Comstock Publ. Assoc., Ithaca, New York, 1:i–xviii + 1–564.

PREPARED BY: C. J. McCoy, *Section of Amphibians and Reptiles, Carnegie Museum of Natural History, 4400 Forbes Ave., Pittsburgh, PA 15213.*

Extirpated

EASTERN TIGER SALAMANDER
Ambystoma tigrinum tigrinum (Green)
Family Ambystomatidae
Order Caudata

Ambystoma tigrinum is widely distributed over western Canada and most of the United States, south to the edge of the Mexican Plateau. *Ambystoma tigrinum tigrinum* is found from Long Island to northern Florida, Ohio to Minnesota and south to the Gulf. The subspecies is absent from the Appalachian Mountains and the Mississippi Delta. Intergradation with western subspecies occurs in a zone extending from western Minnesota southward to east Texas.

There are a few published localities for the eastern tiger salamander in Pennsylvania, but most are questionable. The only Pennsylvania locality which cannot be entirely discounted, although it too is suspect, is based on a recently transformed adult collected at Londongrove, Chester County, Pennsylvania. No specimen has been collected in Pennsylvania since 1859.

The eastern tiger salamander, at the northeastern limit of its range in Pennsylvania, has special habitat requirements. It is usually found in the vicinity of temporary or permanent field ponds, near or in mixed hardwood or coniferous forest. These secretive salamanders spend most of their lives in burrows below the ground except for the annual breeding migration to the pond. The areas of southeastern Pennsylvania where the species could be expected to occur are heavily populated, and natural habitats

Eastern Tiger Salamander (*Ambystoma t. tigrinum*). Photograph supplied by Philadelphia Zoological Society.

have been extensively modified, thus it is considered a recently extirpated species in Pennsylvania.

SELECTED REFERENCES:

DUNN, E. R. 1940. The races of *Ambystoma tigrinum.* Copeia, 1940: 154–162.
GEHLBACH, F. R. 1967. *Ambystoma tigrinum.* Catalogue of American Amphibians and Reptiles, 52.1–52.4
NETTING, M. G. 1938. The occurrence of the eastern tiger salamander, *Ambystoma t. tigrinum* (Green), in Pennsylvania and near-by states. Ann. Carnegie Mus., 27:159–166.
STINE, C. J., J. A. FOWLER, and R. S. SIMMONS. 1954. Occurrence of the eastern tiger salamander, *Ambystoma tigrinum* (Green) in Maryland with notes on its life history. Ann. Carnegie Mus., 33:145–148.

PREPARED BY: Stephen R. Williams, *Department of Biology, The Pennsylvania State University, New Kensington Campus, 3550 Seventh Street Road, New Kensington, PA 15068* (Present address: *Glendale Community College, 6000 West Olive Ave., Glendale, AZ 85301*).

Extirpated

EASTERN MUD SALAMANDER
Pseudotriton montanus montanus Baird
Family Plethodontidae
Order Caudata

In 1850, Spencer Fullerton Baird first identified *Pseudotriton montanus* from South Mountain, near Carlisle, Cumberland County, Pennsylvania. From the description of two adults, South Mountain became the type-locality for the species. In spite of numerous collecting attempts, this locality has never been confirmed. The subspecies ranges along the Atlantic Coastal Plain from southern New Jersey to northeastern Georgia. Other subspecies extend to central Florida, and eastern Louisiana, and occur west of the Appalachian Mountains in Tennessee, Kentucky, Ohio, West Virginia, and Virginia.

Pseudotriton m. montanus is a lowland salamander which lives in muddy springs, sluggish floodplain brooks, and swampy areas along streams. Adults are not generally found in water but usually are close to water beneath logs and stones, in decaying vegetation, and along stream banks in burrows which they may construct themselves. The preferred coastal plain habitat does not exist in Cumberland County, Pennsylvania. It is doubtful that *P. montanus* occurs now in the area, if indeed it ever did. Conant (1957) suggested it might be found in the lower Delaware Valley, as it occurs in adjacent Delaware and New Jersey, but natural habitats in the Delaware Valley have been largely destroyed by urbanization and industrial development.

SELECTED REFERENCES:

BAIRD, S. F. 1850. Revision of the North American tailed-batrachia, with descriptions of new genera and species. J. Acad. Nat. Sci. Philadelphia, 2(1):281–292.
CONANT, R. 1957. The eastern mud salamander, *Pseudotriton montanus montanus*: a new state record for New Jersey. Copeia, 1957:152–153.
MARTOF, B. S. 1975. *Pseudotriton montanus.* Catalogue of American Amphibians and Reptiles, 166.1–166.2.
MITTLEMAN, M. B., and H. T. GIER. 1948. American Caudata. III. The status of *Pseudotriton montanus* in Ohio. Amer. Midland Nat., 40:372–377.

PREPARED BY: Stephen R. Williams, *Department of Biology, The Pennsylvania State University, New Kensington Campus, New Kensington, Pennsylvania 15068* (present address: *Glendale Community College, 6000 West Olive Ave., Glendale, AZ 85301*).

Eastern Mud Salamander (*Pseudotriton m. montanus*). Photograph by Isabelle Hunt Conant.

Blanding's Turtle (*Emydoidea blandingii*). Photograph by R. W. Barbour.

Extirpated

BLANDING'S TURTLE
Emydoidea blandingii (Holbrook)
Family Emydidae
Order Testudines

Emydoidea blandingi generally occurs west and north of Pennsylvania. It ranges from southern Ontario southward through the Great Lakes region and westward to central Nebraska. Scattered colonies also occur in eastern New York, Connecticut, Massachusetts, New Hampshire, and Nova Scotia.

Pennsylvania specimens deposited in Carnegie Museum of Natural History were collected prior to 1906 at Conneaut Lake (CM 1388) and Linesville (CM 1389) in Crawford County. Netting (1932) thought Blanding's turtles may have reached Crawford County via the Beaver and Lake Erie Canal. Completed in 1844 but closed in 1871, and afterwards rapidly destroyed, this canal existed scarcely 30 years, yet these turtles may have migrated the 72 km of canal from Lake Erie to Conneaut Lake. The Linesville specimen is from a locality about four miles west of the old canal bed.

McCoy (1973) shows a locality at Presque Isle Bay, and there are several records of the species from the Erie area in the past 10 years. Whether these were released captives, waifs from across Lake Erie, or stragglers from farther west along the lakeshore is unknown. Netting (1932, 1939) also referred to Blanding's turtles in Lake Erie (presumably in Pennsylvania).

Netting (1932) also reported on specimens from Union and Northumberland counties near Lewisburg, but in 1939 discounted these as escaped animals.

The present distribution of Blanding's turtle in Pennsylvania is unknown, and if no colony occurs in the Erie area, it should be considered extirpated.

The reasons for the decline of *Emydoidea* in Pennsylvania are unknown. Perhaps it was never common. If the Beaver and Lake Erie Canal was the only pathway to Crawford County only a few individuals may have reached the Pymatuning area, and with the destruction of the canal, recruitment may have ceased. The Pymatuning Swamp at Linesville was radically altered by impoundment in 1934, and this may have created an unfavorable habitat for these turtles. Also, water quality in the area may have deteriorated because of increased human use. The species may still persist in the marshy Conneaut Outlet of Crawford County, which is protected as state game lands. Throughout its range, *Emydoidea* prefers shallow water bodies with soft bottoms and abundant aquatic vegetation; it is also found in lakes, ponds, creeks, and sloughs.

Should Blanding's turtle be found to occur in the state, its status should be changed to endangered and it and its critical habitat be given strict legal protection.

SELECTED REFERENCES:

GIBBONS, J. W. 1968. Observations on the ecology and population dynamics of the Blanding's turtle, *Emydoidea blandingi*. Canadian J. Zool., 46:288–290.
GRAHAM, T. E. 1979. Locomotor activity in the Blanding's turtle *Emydoidea blandingii* (Reptilia, Testudines, Emydidae): the phasing effect of temperature. J. Herpetol., 13:365–366.
GRAHAM, T. E., and T. S. DOYLE. 1977. Growth and population characteristics of Blanding's turtle, *Emydoidea blandingii*, in Massachusetts. Herpetologica, 33:410–414.
NETTING, M. G. 1932. Blanding's turtle, *Emys blandingii* (Holbrook), in Pennsylvania. Copeia, 1932:173–174.
———. 1939. Hand list of the amphibians and reptiles of Pennsylvania. Biennial Rept. Pennsylvania Fish Comm. for 1936–1938, pp. 109–132.
McCOY, C. J. 1973. *Emydoidea, Emydoidea blandingii*. Catalogue of American Amphibians and Reptiles, 136.1–136.4.

PREPARED BY: Carl H. Ernst, *Department of Biology, George Mason University, Fairfax, VA 22030.*

Extirpated

MIDLAND SMOOTH SOFTSHELL
Trionyx muticus muticus LeSueur
Family Trionychidae
Order Testudines

Trionyx muticus generally occurs west and south of Pennsylvania. It ranges from central Minnesota and the Missouri River in North and South Dakota southward to eastern New Mexico, southern Texas and the Florida panhandle. In Pennsylvania, it is known only from two specimens collected prior to 1900 in the Allegheny River at Neville Island, near Pittsburgh, Allegheny County, and at Foxburg, Clarion County. The Allegheny County specimen apparently has been lost, but that from Clarion County still exists in the Museum of Comparative Zoology, Harvard University (MCZ 1911). All softshelled turtles collected in the state more recently have been the spiny softshell, *Trionyx spiniferus*.

The present distribution of *Trionyx muticus* in Pennsylvania is unknown, but since it has not been found for over 80 years, it is considered extirpated. In other parts of its range, it inhabits large rivers and streams with moderate to fast currents, lakes, and impoundments, and less frequently shallow bogs. Waterways with sandy bottoms and few rocks or aquatic plants are preferred. If the turtle still exists in Pennsylvania, it probably is in habitats similar to these.

The factors involved in the decline of the smooth softshell in Pennsylvania are unknown. However, water quality in the Allegheny River during much of this century has been poor, due largely to acid drainage from coal mines and industrial pollution from steel mills and other factories. Also, softshells are highly palatable and commonly eaten, and overfishing may have contributed to their decline in the state.

SELECTED REFERENCES:

FITCH, H. S., and M. V. PLUMMER. 1975. A preliminary ecological study of the soft-shelled turtle, *Trionyx muticus*, in the Kansas River. Israel J. Zool., 24:1–15.
NETTING, M. G. 1944. The spineless soft-shelled turtle, *Amyda mutica* (LeSueur), in Pennsylvania. Ann. Carnegie Mus., 30:85–88.
PLUMMER, M. V. 1976. Some aspects of nesting success in the turtle, *Trionyx muticus*. Herpetologica, 32:353–359.
———. 1977. Notes on the courtship and mating behavior of the softshell turtle, *Trionyx muticus* (Reptilia, Testudines, Trionychidae). J. Herpetol., 11:90–92.
———. 1977. Activity, habitat and population structure in the turtle, *Trionyx muticus*. Copeia, 1977:431–440.
———. 1977. Reproduction and growth in the turtle, *Trionyx muticus*. Copeia, 1977:440–447.
PLUMMER, M. V., and H. W. SHIRER. 1975. Movement patterns in a river population of the softshell turtle, *Trionyx muticus*. Occas. Papers Mus. Nat. Hist., Univ. Kansas, 43:1–26.
WEBB, R. G. 1962. North American Recent soft-shelled turtles (Family Trionychidae). Univ. Kansas Publ., Mus. Nat. Hist., 13:429–611.
———. 1973. *Trionyx muticus*. Catalogue of American Amphibians and Reptiles, 139.1–139.2.

PREPARED BY: Carl H. Ernst, *Department of Biology, George Mason University, Fairfax, VA 22030.*

Midland Smooth Softshell (*Trionyx m. muticus*). Photograph by R. W. Barbour.

CHAPTER 5
BIRDS

Short-eared Owl (*Asio flammeus*). Photograph by J. P. Myers/VIREO.

CHAPTER 5—BIRDS

edited by

FRANK B. GILL

The Academy of Natural Sciences
Philadelphia, PA 19103

Table of Contents

INTRODUCTION

Major changes in the natural habitats of Pennsylvania have occurred since the days of pioneer settlement. Forests have been cut and are regenerating. Agricultural acreage first expanded and then declined. Exotic vegetation has replaced or mingled with indigenous plants. Marshes have been filled to provide a firm base for residential and industrial growth. These ecological changes have reduced some bird populations while being beneficial to others. Because future changes are likely to be as great or greater than those of the past, we must now take note of those that could lead to irreparable loss of our native birds. Only by being aware of the dangers can we take remedial actions.

This list of Pennsylvania birds deemed of special concern was compiled to heighten our awareness of possible danger points. To prepare this list, the committee reviewed the status of the approximately 200 species that breed in Pennsylvania. We did not include species that, although endangered elsewhere, do not or have not bred in Pennsylvania. Most of the species listed belong to three main categories—raptors, freshwater marsh dwellers, and birds of agricultural uplands. Raptors are often illegally killed, are vulnerable to pesticide poisoning, and often require special nesting sites. Freshwater marshes are localized in Pennsylvania and are easily threatened by development, recreational use, and pollution. Farmlands change in both quality and extent as agricultural practices evolve and as suburbia advances. Some of these changes are inevitable, some need not be. Some may pose short term problems, others reflect a more permanent inheritance from two centuries of human land use and abuse. All such considerations, however, emphasize that this list is not a final one immune from revision. Rather, some species will be added in the near future; some may be removed. To serve its intended function, therefore, this report must be considered a dynamic, not a static, working document, rather than a list of bird species doomed to local extirpation.

In preparing this document, we discovered how little we really know about the breeding distributions and status of most Pennsylvania birds. We are behind many states in this respect. Our ignorance is particularly acute for the north and south central counties of the Commonwealth. We hope, therefore, that one of the positive reactions to the summaries provided here will be an intensified effort to gather more information on Pennsylvania birds. We do a good job of reporting rarities each year. Hopefully, we can now begin to put equal effort into locating breeding populations of uncommon and endangered species. Again, we intend this document not as some sort of gospel, but rather as a catalyst for future field work in Pennsylvania.

We have included a brief description of each species of special concern for general purposes only.

Many of the species can only be identified by experienced observers. Study of one of the many excellent field guides now available will help inexperienced observers to identify birds on this list. To aid in the recognition of unfamiliar species we have included photographs from the collections of A. D. Cruickshank and the Academy of Natural Sciences of Philadelphia (VIREO). We are grateful to them for permission to use their photographs for this purpose.

For each species in this account, we have included two maps. One map represents the general breeding range of the species in North America. The species may be found in suitable habitat within this area in varying abundance. The other map represents known breeding locations in Pennsylvania during the past 20 years. The species may not necessarily be nesting at these locations at this time. Most of the existing species migrate through Pennsylvania and may therefore be seen in areas not shown on the maps, especially during the autumn, winter, and spring.

Assessment of the current status of the birds of Pennsylvania proved to be a surprisingly difficult task. No comprehensive, detailed work on Pennsylvania birds exists, although Todd's Birds of Western Pennsylvania provides some of the needed information. We required both a historical perspective and current knowledge. Therefore we organized a committee of regional experts on the birds of the state, many of them acknowledged "deans" with many years of experience with local ornithology. They, in turn, solicited advice from other observers in their regions. This work, therefore, reflects the efforts, knowledge and general consensus of many individuals. My personal role has been one of coordination and synthesis rather than of expertise on Pennsylvania birds.

I sincerely hope this document will aid wise management of the habitats and resources required by Pennsylvania birds. We enjoy them now, and must do what we can to insure that our successors will also have the opportunity to do so.

Frank B. Gill, *The Academy of Natural Sciences, Philadelphia, PA 19103.*

ACKNOWLEDGMENTS

The experts on the Committee on Pennsylvania Birds of Special Concern included Ralph Bell of Green County, Joseph Grom of Pittsburgh, Robert Leberman of Crawford and Westmoreland counties, Jean H. and James G. Stull of Erie County, David Pearson and Merrill Wood of the State College area, Phillip S. Street for the Poconos, Alexander Nagy of Hawk Mountain, and for southeastern Pennsylvania, Frank and Barbara Haas. John Ginaven contributed many hours to the synthesis of regional information into unified drafts that were then circulated back to the Committee and more broadly to field ornithologists throughout the Commonwealth for comment. We thank these individuals for their expertise and enthusiastic participation. Special acknowledgment is also due to many others who improved our files of relevant information, including Alan Brady, Ted J. Grisez, John C. Miller, Kenneth C. Parkes, Earl C. Shrive, Jr., Robert M. Schutsky, and Allen Schweinsberg.—Frank B. Gill, *Academy of Natural Sciences.*

SPECIES ACCOUNTS

prepared by

FRANK HAAS, BARBARA HAAS, AND JOHN A. GINAVEN

The Academy of Natural Sciences, Philadelphia, Pennsylvania 19103

Endangered

NORTHERN BALD EAGLE

Haliaeetus leucocephalus alascanus Townsend

Family Accipitridae

Order Falconiformes

DESCRIPTION: The Bald Eagle is a huge raptor with a 1.8–2.1 m wingspan. The adult with white head and tail is our national symbol and easily recognized. Immatures, however, are all dark and are often difficult to distinguish from the Golden Eagle.

RANGE: The range of the Northern Bald Eagle includes all of North America from Florida to California, from Nova Scotia to Alaska. In Pennsylvania, the Northern Bald Eagle formerly bred along the major rivers in the Commonwealth and some lakes. Now it only breeds in northwestern Pennsyl-

Bald Eagle (*Haliaeetus leucocephalus*). Photograph by A. D. Cruickshank/VIREO.

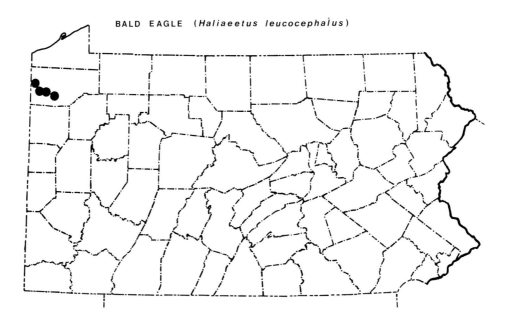

BALD EAGLE (*Haliaeetus leucocephalus*)

vania in the Pymatuning and Conneaut area. Only three or four breeding pairs are known at this time. Banding records have shown that Southern Bald Eagles will occasionally summer in Pennsylvania, returning south in the autumn to breed. Also, every spring and autumn there is a migration of Bald Eagles through the Commonwealth along the mountain ridges and river valleys. Several Bald Eagles

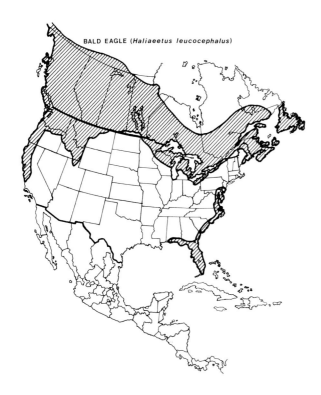

BALD EAGLE (*Haliaeetus leucocephalus*)

winter along the river valleys and along unfrozen lakes.

HABITAT: The habitat of the Northern Bald Eagle is riparian, near a river or lake. Nests usually are built close to a body of water.

LIFE HISTORY AND ECOLOGY: Bald Eagles nest in large trees, both coniferous and deciduous, as low as 9 m but usually higher. The nest consists of large sticks lined with grasses, twigs, weeds, or moss. The nest is built by both birds and is added to each year. It is used until it falls down or the birds perish. New nests are usually 1.5 m in diameter and 0.6 m in height and the size increases yearly.

Two eggs are normally laid (rarely three) a few days apart in April and are incubated by both parents for about 35 days. The young remain in the nest for 10 to 12 weeks. Once fully grown, the young birds may remain in the general area or migrate, returning in 4 to 5 years when they reach breeding age.

Bald Eagles eat both live prey and carrion, taking whatever is available. The bulk of their diet consists of fish, but birds and small mammals are also taken.

BASIS OF STATUS CLASSIFICATION: As of this writing, the only nesting Bald Eagles in Pennsylvania are in Crawford County. Only three or four pairs are known, and their nesting success has been sporadic at best over the past 20 years. Nesting Bald Eagles have been virtually extirpated from the rest of the Commonwealth. The causes of this probably include the use of persistent pesticides, human encroachment on nesting sites, and pollution of the waterways. Because of its small population located in a small area, a single major natural or man-made disaster could easily destroy the remaining pairs. The Bald Eagle is listed as endangered on the Federal List of Endangered Species.

RECOMMENDATIONS: The present nesting locations are protected from encroachment, but an aggressive policy aimed at limiting any human disturbance to the nesting areas must be established until the Bald Eagle population starts expanding. However, any prospective nesting locations should be monitored and given strict protection should any Bald Eagles be present during the nesting season. Continued enforcement of State and Federal laws protecting eagles is essential, and persistent pesticides must not be allowed to return to use.

SELECTED REFERENCES:

BENT, A. C. 1937. Life histories of North American birds of prey. Part 1. Bull. U.S. Nat. Mus., 167:1–409.

HICKEY, J. J., and D. W. ANDERSON. 1968. Chlorinated hydrocarbons and eggshell changes in raptorial and fish-eating birds. Science, 162:271–273.

PETERSON, R. T. 1980. A field guide to the birds. Houghton Mifflin Co., Boston, 384 pp.

POOLE, E. L. 1964. Pennsylvania birds. Livingston Publ. Co., Narberth, Pennsylvania, viii + 94 pp.

SNOW, C. 1973. Habitat management series for endangered species. Rept. 5: Southern Bald Eagle and Northern Bald Eagle. U.S. Dept. of the Interior, Bureau of Land Management, 58 pp.

STALMASTER, M. V., and J. R. NEWMAN. 1978. Behavioral responses of wintering Bald Eagles to human activity. J. Wildlife Mgmt., 42:506–513.

TODD, W. E. C. 1940. Birds of western Pennsylvania. Univ. Pittsburgh Press, Pittsburgh, xv + 710 pp.

WHITFIELD, D. W. A., J. M. GERRARD, D. W. DAVIS, and W. J. MAHER. 1974. Bald Eagle nesting habitat, density, and reproduction in central Saskatchewan and Manitoba. Canadian Field. Nat., 88:399–407.

Endangered
KING RAIL
Rallus elegans elegans Audubon
Family Rallidae
Order Gruiformes

DESCRIPTION: This large rail is a plump chicken-like bird that inhabits marshes. It has a long bill and is a bright rusty color. Rails are secretive terrestrial birds that fly weakly when flushed. They are most easily located by their loud calls, which in the case of this species is a resonant grunting bup-bup, bup-bup-bup.

RANGE: The King Rail occurs throughout much of the eastern United States. In Pennsylvania, it is a very rare and local breeder, with most records occurring from the southeastern and northwestern corners of the Commonwealth.

HABITAT: The preferred habitat of the King Rail is freshwater marshes.

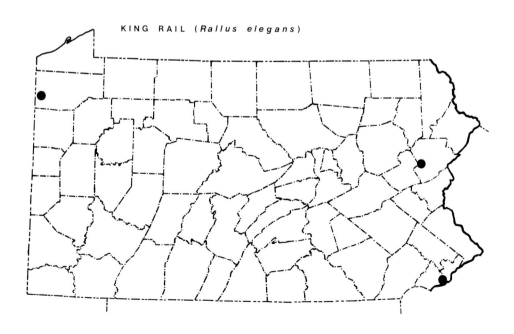

KING RAIL (*Rallus elegans*)

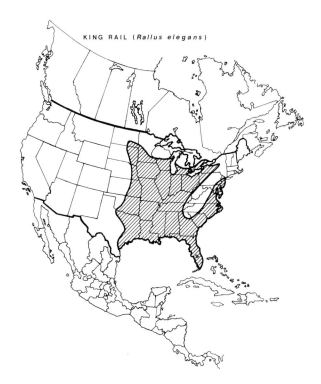

KING RAIL (*Rallus elegans*)

SELECTED REFERENCES:

BENT, A. C. 1926. Life histories of North American marsh birds. Bull. U.S. Nat. Mus., 135:1–490.
PETERSON, R. T. 1980. A field guide to the birds. Houghton Mifflin Co., Boston, 384 pp.
POOLE, E. L. 1964. Pennsylvania birds. Livingston Publ. Co., Narberth, Pennsylvania, viii + 94 pp.
RIPLEY, S. D. 1977. Rails of the world. Godine, Boston, xx + 406 pp.
TATE, J., and D. J. TATE. 1982. The Blue List for 1982. Amer. Birds, 36:126–135.
TODD, W. E. C. 1940. Birds of western Pennsylvania. Univ. Pittsburgh Press, Pittsburgh, xv + 710 pp.

Endangered

SHORT-EARED OWL
Asio flammeus flammeus (Pontoppidan)
Family Strigidae
Order Strigiformes

DESCRIPTION: A crow-sized, buffy brown owl with no "ear" tufts. Often flushed from the ground during the day, when it flies away like a large flopping moth.

LIFE HISTORY AND ECOLOGY: The nest of the King Rail is built in reeds or cattails a few centimeters to 45 cm above the water. The nest is made of grasses and reeds and is about 20 cm in diameter. From six to 15 eggs are laid in May and incubated for 21 to 23 days. The young leave the nest almost immediately after hatching, following the female. Living as it does in marshes, the King Rail is very difficult to observe, and confirmed nesting records rare. King Rails migrate in the autumn, wintering on the Atlantic and Gulf coasts. The diet of the King Rail consists of insects, slugs, tadpoles, crayfish, and seeds from aquatic plants.

BASIS OF STATUS CLASSIFICATION: Annual reports of King Rails in Pennsylvania are rare, and actual nest records are rarer. Historic records indicate that it was once more abundant (though never common) than it is today. The destruction of marshland in Pennsylvania obviously has affected this species, but there may also be some unknown factors contributing to its decline. Listed on National Audubon Society Blue List 1982.

RECOMMENDATIONS: Efforts should be made to determine if there are any viable King Rail populations in Pennsylvania at this time. Every effort should be made to preserve and expand wetland habitats in Pennsylvania.

RANGE: The range of the Short-eared Owl includes North America, Europe, and Asia. In Pennsylvania, it breeds very locally in extreme southeastern Pennsylvania. Formerly, it bred along the shores of Lake Erie and in Conneaut Marsh in Crawford County. Short-eared Owls winter throughout the Commonwealth in suitable habitat.

HABITAT: Marshes and meadows are the primary habitats of the Short-eared Owl.

LIFE HISTORY AND ECOLOGY: The Short-eared Owl nests on the ground, occasionally lining a depression with grasses, weeds, and feathers. Four to nine eggs are laid and incubated by the female for about 21 days. The young remain in the nest for another 4 to 5 weeks. The Short-eared Owl is migratory and winters in most of the United States. It is a common wintering bird in some agricultural areas of the Commonwealth. The food of the Short-eared Owl consists primarily of mice and rats with an occasional bird or other small mammal.

BASIS OF STATUS CLASSIFICATION: The Short-eared Owl in Pennsylvania only nests in areas that happen to be commercially valuable, that is, the marshes and meadows around the Philadelphia International Airport and formerly along the shores of Lake Erie. As such, the species is in great danger

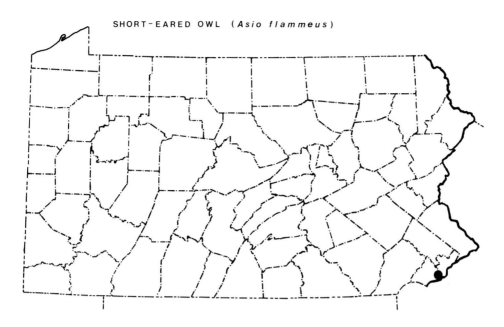

SHORT-EARED OWL (*Asio flammeus*)

of losing even more of its habitat. Listed on National Audubon Society Blue List 1982.

RECOMMENDATIONS: Efforts should be made to preserve and expand the remaining marshes in all sections of Pennsylvania.

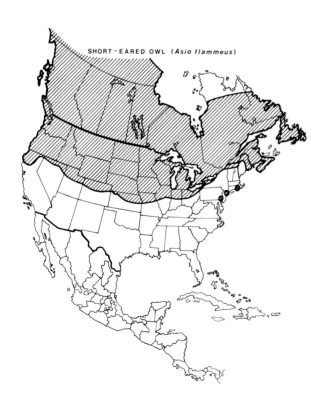

SHORT-EARED OWL (*Asio flammeus*)

SELECTED REFERENCES:

BENT, A. C. 1938. Life histories of North American birds of prey. Part 2. Bull. U.S. Nat. Mus., 170:1–482.

PETERSON, R. T. 1980. A field guide to the birds. Houghton Mifflin Co., Boston, 384 pp.

POOLE, E. L. 1964. Pennsylvania birds. Livingston Publ. Co., Narberth, Pennsylvania, viii + 94 pp.

TATE, J., and D. J. TATE. 1982. The Blue List for 1982. Amer. Birds, 36:126–135.

TODD, W. E. C. 1940. Birds of western Pennsylvania. Univ. Pittsburgh Press, Pittsburgh, xv + 710 pp.

Endangered

BEWICK'S WREN
Thryomanes bewickii altus Aldrich
Family Troglodytidae
Order Passeriformes

DESCRIPTION: Wrens are robust, active, small brown birds, which often cock their tails over their backs. This species is a fairly large wren with a long tail and a white line over the eye. The white corners on the tail are diagnostic but are difficult to see. Its loud song is quite like that of a Song Sparrow.

RANGE: The species occurs from the Northwest Pacific Coast to the central United States to southern Mexico. In Pennsylvania, it is a rare breeder in southwestern Pennsylvania, but it has also been recorded in north-central Pennsylvania.

HABITAT: Bewick's Wrens are most commonly

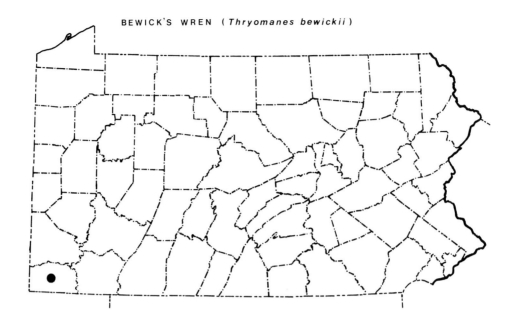

BEWICK'S WREN (*Thryomanes bewickii*)

found in open rural country around buildings and along ridge tops.

LIFE HISTORY AND ECOLOGY: Bewick's Wren nests in almost any type of cavity, from holes in trees to tin cans or discarded clothing hung in an outbuilding. From five to seven eggs are laid in May

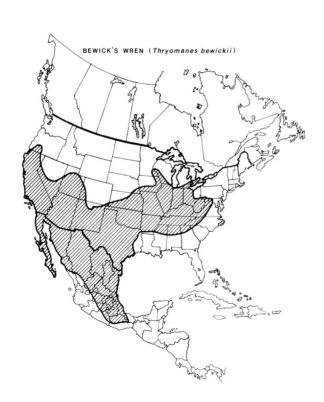

BEWICK'S WREN (*Thryomanes bewickii*)

and incubated for 2 weeks. The young stay in the nest for about 2 more weeks. Its habits and habitat are very similar to the House Wren, being found around human habitation. Bewick's Wren is insectivorous, with insects comprising 97 percent of its diet, with the remainder being some vegetable matter.

BASIS FOR STATUS CLASSIFICATION: Bewick's Wren was at one time a common nester in Greene County. However, in recent years there has been a drastic decline, with no pairs found in 1979 or 1980. The reasons for this decline are unclear. Competition with the House Wren may be a factor, as it is well documented that the two species are mutually exclusive when occurring in the same area. Listed on National Audubon Society Blue List 1982.

RECOMMENDATIONS: A thorough survey of southwestern Pennsylvania should be made to determine if any Bewick's Wrens remain. If so, they should be monitored to ascertain the factors affecting population levels.

SELECTED REFERENCES:

BENT, A. C. 1948. Life histories of North American nuthatches, wrens, thrashers, and their allies. Bull. U.S. Nat. Mus., 195: 1–475.
KROODSMA, D. E. 1973. Coexistence of Bewick's Wrens and House Wrens in Oregon. Auk, 90:341–352.

MILLER, E. V. 1941. Behavior of the Bewick Wren. Condor, 43:81–99.

NEWMAN, D. L. 1961. House Wrens and Bewick's Wrens in northern Ohio. Wilson Bull., 73:84–86.

POOLE, E. L. 1964. Pennsyvania birds. Livingston Publ. Co., Narberth, Pennsylvania, viii + 94 pp.

ROOT, R. B. 1969. Interspecific territoriality between Bewick's and House wrens. Auk, 86:125–127.

TATE, J., and D. J. TATE. 1982. The Blue List for 1982. Amer. Birds, 36:126–135.

TODD, W. E. C. 1940. Birds of western Pennsylvania. Univ. Pittsburgh Press, Pittsburgh, xv + 710 pp.

Threatened

LEAST BITTERN
Ixobrychus exilis exilis (Gmelin)
Family Ardeidae
Order Ciconiiformes

DESCRIPTION: A small black and tan heron with large buffy wing patches. It hides inconspicuously in marshes and may not be seen until flushed. Its small size and light colors distinguish it from the common Green Heron.

Least Bittern (*Ixobrychus exilis*). Photograph by A. D. Cruickshank/VIREO.

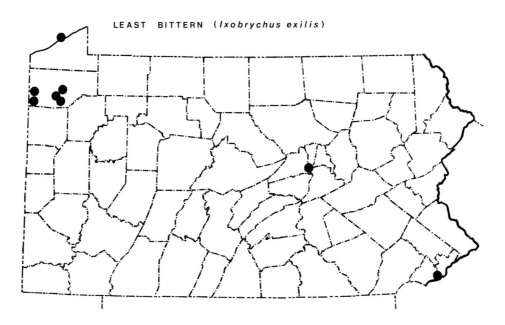

LEAST BITTERN (*Ixobrychus exilis*)

RANGE: The range of the Least Bittern includes eastern half of the United States and southern Canada and the Pacific Coast from Oregon to northern Mexico. In Pennsylvania, it breeds primarily in the marshes in the extreme southeastern and northwestern corners of the Commonwealth. There are a few reports of it breeding in other locations, but not regularly or in large numbers.

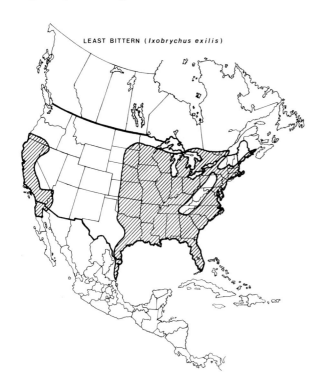

LEAST BITTERN (*Ixobrychus exilis*)

HABITAT: Marshes are the primary habitat of the Least Bittern.

LIFE HISTORY AND ECOLOGY: The nest of the Least Bittern is usually built, using reeds and grasses, above the water line in cattails or other suitable growth. The nest is about 15 cm in diameter. Four or five eggs are laid in mid- to late May and incubated for 16 to 17 days. The diet consists of small fish, amphibians, insects, and small mammals.

BASIS OF STATUS CLASSIFICATION: The Least Bittern in Pennsylvania nests in a highly vulnerable habitat—marshes. Because marshland continues to disappear in Pennsylvania, the Least Bittern is becoming even more restricted in its range. Continued destruction of marshes could result in its extirpation. Listed on National Audubon Society Blue List 1982.

RECOMMENDATIONS: Every effort should be made to preserve and expand marshes in Pennsylvania.

SELECTED REFERENCES:

BENT, A. C. 1926. Life histories of North American marsh birds. Bull. U.S. Nat. Mus., 135:1–490.

KUSHLAN, J. A. 1973. Least Bittern nesting colonially. Auk, 90: 685–686.

PETERSON, R. T. 1980. A field guide to the birds. Houghton Mifflin Co., Boston, 384 pp.

POOLE, E. L. 1964. Pennsylvania birds. Livingston Publ. Co., Narberth, Pennsylvania, viii + 94 pp.

TATE, J., and D. J. TATE. 1982. The Blue List for 1982. Amer. Birds, 36:126–135.

TODD, W. E. C. 1940. Birds of western Pennsylvania. Univ. Pittsburgh Press, Pittsburgh, xv + 710 pp.

WELLER, M. W. 1961. Breeding biology of the Least Bittern. Wilson Bull., 73:11–35.

Threatened

AMERICAN BITTERN
Botaurus lentiginosus (Rackett)
Family Ardeidae
Order Ciconiiformes

DESCRIPTION: A large, rich brown, short-necked heron, usually flushed from marshes. American Bitterns rarely feed in open water as other herons do. Blackish wing tips are conspicuous in flight. When frightened it points its bill skyward to blend in with reeds. This species resembles immature Night Herons which are grayer and more spotted.

RANGE: The geographic range of the American Bittern includes North America from Florida and southern California to the Arctic Circle. The species winters as far south as Panama. In Pennsylvania, it

American Bittern (*Botaurus lentiginosus*). Photograph by A. D. Cruickshank/VIREO.

AMERICAN BITTERN (*Botaurus lentiginosus*)

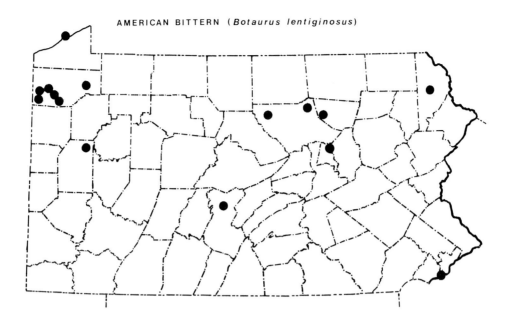

nests primarily in the extreme southeastern and northwestern corners of the Commonwealth. There are scattered breeding records throughout the Commonwealth. In winter, a few can occasionally be found in the Tinicum area.

HABITAT: As with the Least Bittern, the primary habitat of the American Bittern is marshes.

AMERICAN BITTERN (*Botaurus lentiginosus*)

LIFE HISTORY AND ECOLOGY: The American Bittern builds its nest about 30 cm above the water line in cattails or other reeds. The nest is made of reeds and grasses and is about 30 cm in diameter. Three to seven eggs are laid and incubated for 28 days. The young remain in the nest for about 2 weeks. Its food consists of fish, amphibians, reptiles, insects, and small mammals.

BASIS OF STATUS CLASSIFICATION: As with other marsh birds in Pennsylvania, the habitat of the American Bittern is declining. Although there are more locations where American Bitterns nest in Pennsylvania than there are for Least Bitterns, the habitat is still vulnerable to disturbance and destruction. Listed on National Audubon Society Blue List 1982.

RECOMMENDATIONS: Every effort should be made to preserve and expand marshes in Pennsylvania.

SELECTED REFERENCES:

BENT, A. C. 1926. Life histories of North American marsh birds. Bull. U.S. Nat. Mus., 135:1–490.
PALMER, R. S. 1962. Handbook of North American birds, vol. 1. Yale Univ. Press, New Haven, Connecticut, vii + 567 pp.
PETERSON, R. T. 1980. A field guide to the birds. Houghton Mifflin Co., Boston, 384 pp.
POOLE, E. L. 1964. Pennsylvania birds. Livingston Publ. Co., Narberth, Pennsylvania, viii + 94 pp.

TATE, J., and D. J. TATE. 1982. The Blue List for 1982. Amer. Birds, 36:126–135.

TODD, W. E. C. 1940. Birds of western Pennsylvania. Univ. Pittsburgh Press, Pittsburgh, xv + 710 pp.

Threatened

UPLAND SANDPIPER
Bartramia longicauda (Bechstein)
Family Scolopacidae
Order Charadriiformes

DESCRIPTION: A large light brown sandpiper occurring near airports and upland fields with short grass. The head appears too small for its large body. The bill is short and plover-like. Unlike most sandpipers, it often sits on wires and fence posts.

RANGE: The range of the Upland Sandpiper includes North and South America. In Pennsylvania, it is a very local breeder in suitable habitat in agricultural areas of the Commonwealth.

HABITAT: The habitats of the Upland Sandpiper include fallow fields, pastures, grassy areas at airports, wherever short grass occurs.

LIFE HISTORY AND ECOLOGY: The Upland Sandpiper builds its nest by scraping the ground between some tussocks of grass and occasionally lining it with some fine grasses. Three to five eggs are laid and incubated about 17 days. The young leave the nest almost immediately after hatching. The Upland Sandpiper arrives in Pennsylvania in late April to early May and winters in South America. The Upland Sandpiper is almost exclusively an insectivore, only occasionally eating some weed seeds.

BASIS OF STATUS CLASSIFICATION: The Upland Sandpiper has been declining in Pennsylvania for a long time. Prior to 1900 it was considered a common bird wherever suitable habitat occurred. Changing agricultural practices and pesticides have been factors in this decline. However, even where suitable habitat exists, similar declines have been noticed. Listed on National Audubon Society Blue List 1982.

RECOMMENDATIONS: A survey of the status of Upland Sandpipers should be conducted in Penn-

Upland Sandpiper (*Bartramia longicauda*). Photograph by A. D. Cruickshank/VIREO.

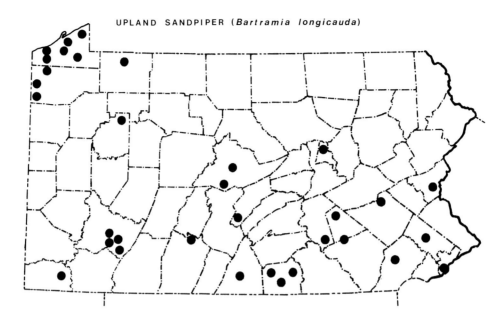

UPLAND SANDPIPER (*Bartramia longicauda*)

sylvania with a goal of determining the limiting factors on their populations. Then the necessary steps should be taken to reverse those factors.

SELECTED REFERENCES:

BENT, A. C. 1929. Life histories of North American shorebirds. Part 2. Bull. U.S. Nat. Mus., 146:1–412.

DORIO, J. C., and E. E. GRIEVE. 1979. Nesting and brood rearing habitat of the Upland Sandpiper. J. Minnesota Acad. Sci., 45:8–11.

JOHNSGARD, P. A. 1981. The plovers, sandpipers, and snipes of the world. Univ. Nebraska Press, Lincoln, xvi + 493 pp.

PETERSON, R. T. 1980. A field guide to the birds. Houghton Mifflin Co., Boston, 384 pp.

POOLE, E. L. 1964. Pennsylvania birds. Livingston Publ. Co., Narberth, Pennsylvania, viii + 94 pp.

TATE, J., and D. J. TATE. 1982. The Blue List for 1982. Amer. Birds, 36:126–135.

TODD, W. E. C. 1940. Birds of western Pennsylvania. Univ. Pittsburgh Press, Pittsburgh, xv + 710 pp.

UPLAND SANDPIPER (*Bartramia longicauda*)

Threatened

BLACK TERN
Chlidonias niger surinamensis (Gmelin)
Family Laridae
Order Charadriiformes

DESCRIPTION: Terns are small, long-winged, graceful, gull-like birds with slender, pointed bills. The Black Tern is easy to identify because it is all black. Winter plumages also include dark gray wings and back with dark head markings.

RANGE: The Black Tern breeds in interior North America from northwestern Pennsylvania to central California, north to Canada. In Pennsylvania, it migrates over the entire Commonwealth, but only nests in the northwestern corner of the Commonwealth, in Crawford and Erie counties.

HABITAT: Black Terns can be found around lakes and marshes.

Black Tern (*Chlidonias niger*). Photograph by A. D. Cruickshank/VIREO.

LIFE HISTORY AND ECOLOGY: The Black Tern builds a fragile nest consisting of reeds and grasses on top of matted reeds from the previous year. They usually lay three eggs and incubate them for 17 days. The young leave the nest after only a few days and are fed by the parents until they are able to fly. They are primarily insectivorous, occasionally taking small minnows and fry.

BASIS OF STATUS CLASSIFICATION: Black Terns nest in a relatively small area in Pennsylvania, and are therefore vulnerable to disturbances wheth-

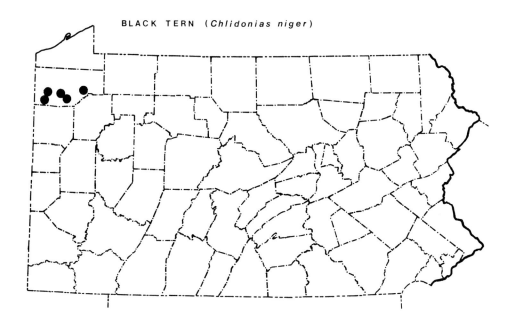

BLACK TERN (*Chlidonias niger*)

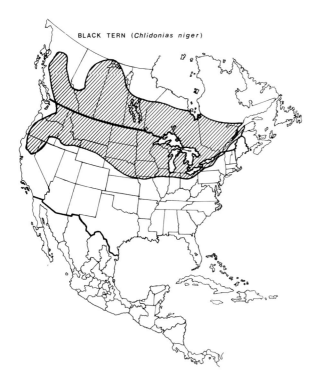

BLACK TERN (*Chlidonias niger*)

SELECTED REFERENCES:

BENT, A. C. 1921. Life histories of North American gulls and
    terns. Bull. U.S. Nat. Mus., 113:1–345.
PETERSON, R. T. 1980. A field guide to the birds. Houghton
    Mifflin Co., Boston, 384 pp.
POOLE, E. L. 1964. Pennsylvania birds. Livingston Publ. Co.,
    Narberth, Pennsylvania, viii + 94 pp.
TATE, J., and D. J. TATE. 1982. The Blue List for 1982. Amer.
    Birds, 36:126–135.
TODD, W. E. C. 1940. Birds of western Pennsylvania. Univ.
    Pittsburgh Press, Pittsburgh, xv + 710 pp.

Threatened

SEDGE WREN
Cistothorus platensis stellaris (Naumann)
Family Troglodytidae
Order Passeriformes

DESCRIPTION: A small, buff-colored wren with a streaked crown and black but *no white* eyeline. Its call is a dry chattering similar to clapping small stones together becoming quite rapid at the end.

RANGE: The range of the Sedge Wren is eastern North America and South America. In Pennsylvania, it formerly bred in scattered locations throughout the Commonwealth. Now almost non-existent as a breeder, with few reports of actual nesting in recent years.

HABITAT: The Sedge Wren inhabits wet meadows or fields.

LIFE HISTORY AND ECOLOGY: Sedge Wrens arrive on their breeding grounds anytime from May

er natural or man-made. One violent storm or loss of part of their breeding grounds could be disastrous for the Pennsylvania population. Local observers report a general decline in numbers in recent years. Listed on National Audubon Society Blue List 1982.

RECOMMENDATIONS: A survey should be conducted to identify all present nesting locations of Black Terns in Pennsylvania, and then steps should be taken to preserve and expand those areas.

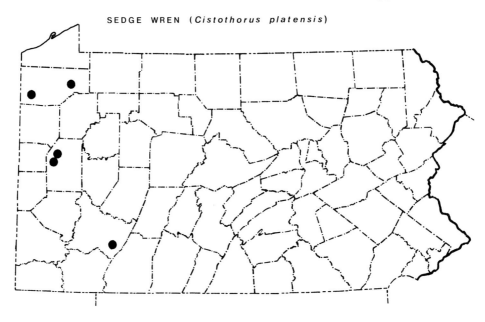

SEDGE WREN (*Cistothorus platensis*)

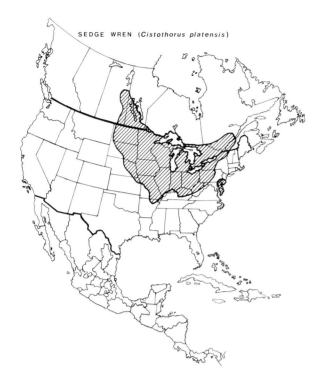

SEDGE WREN (*Cistothorus platensis*)

through August. They build a globular nest, suspended in weeds or grasses, 30 to 60 cm off of the ground. An average of seven eggs are laid and incubated for 2 weeks. The young leave the nest after another 2 weeks. The diet of the Sedge Wren consists of insects and spiders.

BASIS OF STATUS CLASSIFICATION: At one time (prior to 1950), the Sedge Wren could be found, although never abundantly, in many locations across the Commonwealth. Since that time, however, it has disappeared from most former locations and has declined or become sporadic in others. The reasons for its decline are unclear. The lack of undisturbed habitat with changing agricultural practices may be one factor. The others are unknown. Listed on National Audubon Society Species with Special Concerns 1982.

RECOMMENDATIONS: A survey should be made to determine the existence of any nesting Sedge Wrens in Pennsylvania. The population should then be monitored to determine the limiting factors and reasons for decline, and then steps should be taken to reverse those factors.

SELECTED REFERENCES:

BENT, A. C. 1948. Life histories of North American nuthatches, wrens, thrashers and their allies. Bull. U.S. Nat. Mus., 195: 1–475.

BURNS, T. J. 1982. Nests, territories, and reproduction of Sedge Wrens (*Cistothorus platensis*). Wilson Bull., 94:338–349.

CRAWFORD, R. D. 1977. Polygynous breeding of Short-billed Marsh Wrens. Auk, 94:359–362.

PETERSON, R. T. 1980. A field guide to the birds. Houghton Mifflin Co., Boston, 384 pp.

POOLE, E. L. 1964. Pennsylvania birds. Livingston Publ. Co., Narberth, Pennsylvania, viii + 94 pp.

TATE, J., and D. J. TATE. 1982. The Blue List for 1982. Amer. Birds, 36:126–135.

TODD, W. E. 1940. Birds of western Pennsylvania. Univ. Pittsburgh Press, Pittsburgh, xv + 710 pp.

WALKINSHAW, L. H. 1935. Studies of the Short-billed Marsh Wren (*Cistothorus stellaris*) in Michigan. Auk, 52:362–369.

Threatened

HENSLOW'S SPARROW
Ammodramus henslowii susorrans Brewster
Family Emberizidae
Order Passeriformes

DESCRIPTION: This is a small, short-tailed, secretive sparrow of weedy fields. The wings are rusty in color and the head is striped and olive in color. Its song, heard often at night, is an insect-like tslick.

RANGE: Henslow's Sparrows occur in the eastern United States. In Pennsylvania, it is found in localized areas in some western counties. There are occasional reports of nesting from other parts of the Commonwealth.

HABITAT: Henslow's Sparrow can be found in wet sedge fields as well as dry upland weedy fields.

LIFE HISTORY AND ECOLOGY: The nest is built on or near the ground at the base of a clump of vegetation. It is constructed of grasses and weeds and lined with finer grasses and hair. Three to five eggs are laid and incubated for about 11 days. The young stay in the nest for about 10 days. The diet of Henslow's Sparrow consists primarily of insects.

BASIS OF STATUS CLASSIFICATION: The Henslow's Sparrow once nested in scattered colonies throughout the Commonwealth. At the present time, however, the only known breeding areas are in the western portion and in the northeastern section. The reasons for this decline are unclear, but loss of habitat is probably a factor. Its habitat requirements seem to be very particular, and it abandons certain areas as the habitat changes even slightly. A "colonial nester," several pairs can be found in a small

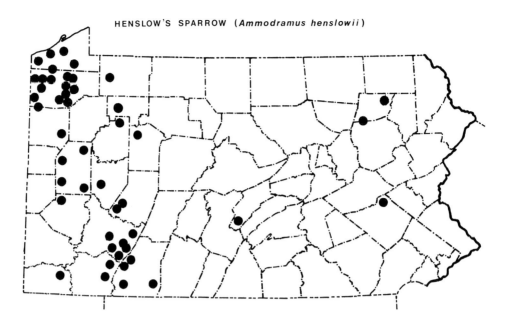

HENSLOW'S SPARROW (*Ammodramus henslowii*)

area, which makes them appear more common than they really are. Listed on National Audubon Society Species with Special Concerns 1982.

RECOMMENDATIONS: A survey should be taken to determine the limiting factors on Henslow's Sparrow populations and then steps should be taken to reverse those factors.

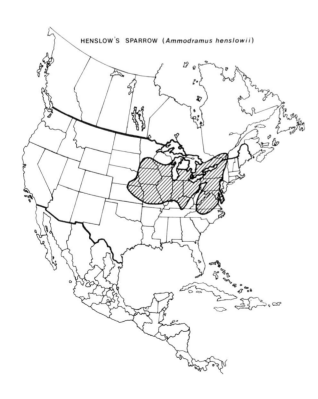

HENSLOW'S SPARROW (*Ammodramus henslowii*)

SELECTED REFERENCES:

BENT, A. C. 1968. Life histories of North American cardinals, grosbeaks, buntings, towhees, finches, sparrows and allies. Part 2. Bull. U.S. Nat. Mus., 237:603–1248.

PETERSON, R. T. 1980. A field guide to the birds. Houghton Mifflin Co., Boston, 384 pp.

POOLE, E. L. 1964. Pennsylvania birds. Livingston Publ. Co., Narberth, Pennsylvania, viii + 94 pp.

ROBINS, J. D. 1971. A study of the Henslow's sparrow in Michigan. Wilson Bull., 83:39–48.

TATE, J., and D. J. TATE. 1982. The Blue List for 1982. Amer. Birds, 36:126–135.

TODD, W. E. C. 1940. Birds of western Pennsylvania. Univ. Pittsburgh Press, Pittsburgh, xv + 710 pp.

Vulnerable

GREAT BLUE HERON
Ardea herodias herodias Linnaeus
Family Ardeidae
Order Ciconiiformes

DESCRIPTION: This is an easily recognizable, large, dark heron with a height of about 1.2 m. It has a long neck which it folds back in flight. Its dark blue gray color, lighter head and large size readily identify it.

RANGE: The Great Blue Heron occurs throughout the United States, southern Canada, and Mexico. In Pennsylvania, it breeds primarily along the northern tier of the Commonwealth and around the lower Susquehanna River, although it has been reported

Great Blue Heron (*Ardea herodias*). Photograph by A. D. Cruickshank/VIREO.

from all parts of the Commonwealth during migration and post-breeding wandering. Great Blue Herons will spend the winter in Pennsylvania near marshes, lakes, or streams as long as there is some open water nearby.

HABITAT: Great Blue Herons are riparian, living near rivers, lakes, or marshes. Nests usually are built in trees near water.

LIFE HISTORY AND ECOLOGY: Great Blue

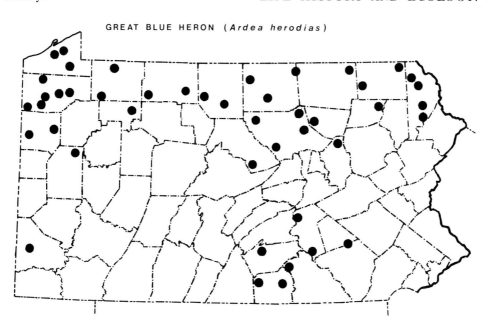

GREAT BLUE HERON (*Ardea herodias*)

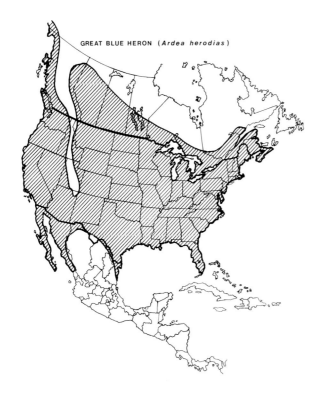

GREAT BLUE HERON (*Ardea herodias*)

Herons are colonial nesters. Rookeries of 30 to 40 nests are not uncommon in suitable habitat. The nest is usually built high in a tree in March or April. It is a large bulky affair made of sticks and twigs and averages about a meter in diameter. Three to five eggs are laid and incubated for about 28 days. The young stay in the nest several weeks. Young herons frequently leave the nest before they can fly and die from the fall or neglect. Herons have a habit of wandering in any direction after breeding and can occur anywhere at that time. Since they breed very early in the spring, herons seen in late June and after do not necessarily signify breeding locations. Non-breeding birds have also been known to show up in non-breeding areas during the nesting season. They regularly winter in many areas throughout the Commonwealth. Their food consists of fish, reptiles, amphibians, small mammals, and birds.

BASIS OF STATUS CLASSIFICATION: Where it nests in forests, the rookeries are subject to destruction and disturbance from logging operations. Where it nests near marshes, the habitat is disappearing. This species seems to have great population fluctuations, sometimes abandoning rookeries for several years before returning. Its colonial habits and habitat requirements make it quite vulnerable to

many man-made factors. Listed on National Audubon Society Species with Special Concerns 1982.

RECOMMENDATIONS: A survey should be made to determine the location and size of Great Blue Heron rookeries in Pennsylvania. Steps should then be taken to protect these sites from disturbance or destruction.

SELECTED REFERENCES:

BENT, A. C. 1926. Life histories of North American marsh birds. Bull. U.S. Nat. Mus., 135:1–490.
PALMER, R. S. 1962. Handbook of North American birds, vol. 1. Yale Univ. Press, New Haven, Connecticut, vii + 567 pp.
PETERSON, R. T. 1980. A field guide to the birds. Houghton Mifflin Co., Boston, 384 pp.
POOLE, E. L. 1964. Pennsylvania birds. Livingston Publ. Co., Narberth, Pennsylvania, viii + 94 pp.
PRATT, H. M. 1970. Breeding biology of Great Blue Herons and Common Egrets in central California. Condor, 72:407–416.
TATE, J., and D. J. TATE. 1982. The Blue List for 1982. Amer. Birds, 36:126–135.
TODD, W. E. C. 1940. Birds of western Pennsylvania. Univ. Pittsburgh Press, Pittsburgh, xv + 710 pp.

Vulnerable

COOPER'S HAWK
Accipiter cooperii (Bonaparte)
Family Accipitridae
Order Falconiformes

DESCRIPTION: This crow-sized hawk has short rounded wings and a long rounded tail. It has a slate blue back and reddish breast. However, immatures have a brownish back and streaked breast. When it flies it gives a few rapid wing beats and then a short glide. Cooper's Hawk can be confused with the smaller Sharp-shinned Hawk.

RANGE: The geographic range of Cooper's Hawk includes North and Central America. In Pennsylvania, it is an uncommon breeder over most of the Commonwealth, but rare in the southeastern section. It is an uncommon winter resident throughout the Commonwealth.

HABITAT: The primary habitat of Cooper's Hawk includes both deciduous or mixed coniferous forests.

LIFE HISTORY AND ECOLOGY: Cooper's Hawks build their nests from 6 to 18 m up in trees. The nest is made of sticks and twigs lined with the

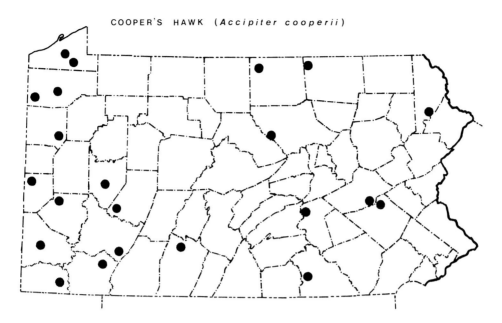

COOPER'S HAWK (*Accipiter cooperii*)

outer bark of oak or pine trees. It is built by both sexes and a new nest is usually constructed each year. The nest is usually about 60 cm wide and 20 cm high. Four or five eggs are laid and incubated by both sexes for approximately 4 weeks. The young remain in the nest for another 4 weeks. The food of the Cooper's Hawk is primarily birds, although some small mammals and reptiles are also eaten. Cooper's

Hawks migrate every spring and autumn, but the breeding range and wintering range overlap in Pennsylvania, so they may be seen here anytime of year.

BASIS OF STATUS CLASSIFICATION: As a predator, especially feeding on insectivorous birds, the Cooper's Hawk is particularly vulnerable to persistent pesticides in the food chain. The habitat required for nesting (extensive stands of forest) is also disappearing in many areas of the Commonwealth due to development for housing and industrial purposes. This is most evident in southeastern Pennsylvania, where it is no longer a breeding bird. Continued encroachment and destruction of habitat will lead to a diminishing Cooper's Hawk population which could become critical if left unchecked. Listed on National Audubon Society Species with Special Concerns 1982.

RECOMMENDATIONS: Because it nests in forests, the exact abundance and distribution of Cooper's Hawks in Pennsylvania is not known. A study should be made to assess the population and its trends throughout the Commonwealth. Continued enforcement of state and federal protection laws is also necessary.

SELECTED REFERENCES:

BENT, A. C. 1937. Life histories of North American birds of prey. Part 1. Bull. U.S. Natl. Mus., 167:1–409.
BROWN, L., and D. AMADON. 1968. Eagles, hawks and falcons

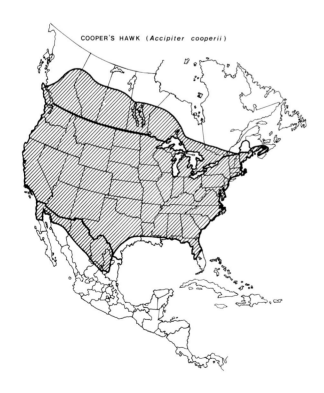

COOPER'S HAWK (*Accipiter cooperii*)

of the world. Hamlyn Publ. Group Limited, Middlesex, Great Britain, 2:445–945.

MENG, H. 1959. Food habits of nesting Cooper's Hawks and Goshawks in New York and Pennsylvania. Wilson Bull., 71: 169–174.

PETERSON, R. T. 1980. A field guide to the birds. Houghton Mifflin Co., Boston, 384 pp.

POOLE, E. L. 1964. Pennsylvania birds. Livingston Publ. Co., Narberth, Pennsylvania, viii + 94 pp.

STORER, R. W. 1966. Sexual dimorphism and food habits in three North American Accipiters. Auk, 83:423–436.

TATE, J., and D. J. TATE. 1982. The Blue List for 1982. Amer. Birds, 36:126–135.

TODD, W. E. C. 1940. Birds of western Pennsylvania. Univ. Pittsburgh Press, Pittsburgh, xv + 710 pp.

Vulnerable

RED-SHOULDERED HAWK
Buteo lineatus lineatus (Gmelin)
Family Accipitridae
Order Falconiformes

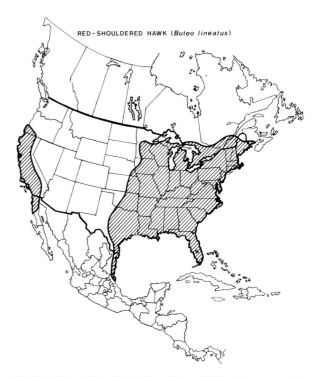

RED-SHOULDERED HAWK (*Buteo lineatus*)

DESCRIPTION: The Red-shouldered Hawk is a large, bulky hawk with wide wings and a wide, rounded tail. Adults are mostly brown with reddish shoulder patches and an orange breast. The tail is marked with narrow black and white bands, easily seen when it soars overhead.

RANGE: The Red-shouldered Hawk occurs in North America, exclusive of the Rocky Mountain region. In Pennsylvania, it is a rare to common nester throughout the Commonwealth. It is an uncommon migrant throughout Pennsylvania and is a rare to uncommon winter resident throughout the Commonwealth.

HABITAT: The Red-shouldered Hawk primarily inhabits forested areas.

LIFE HISTORY AND ECOLOGY: The Red-shouldered Hawk builds its nest about 6 to 18 m above the ground, with no preference shown for any particular species of tree. The nest is about 60 cm wide, 30 cm high and is built of sticks and twigs, lined with inner bark, sprigs of evergreen, feathers, and down. They will occasionally re-use the same

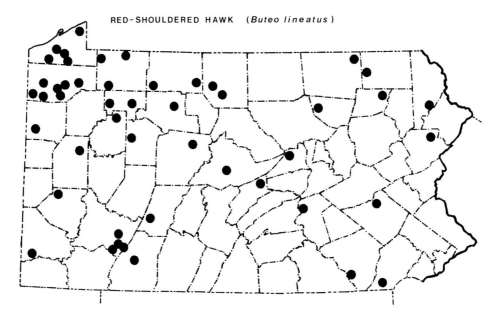

RED-SHOULDERED HAWK (*Buteo lineatus*)

nest, but often build a new one each year. They are very loyal in returning to the same territory year after year. Three eggs are usually laid in April or May and incubated by both sexes for 28 days. Young remain in the nest for another 6 weeks. The food of Red-shouldered Hawks consists of reptiles, amphibians, birds, and small mammals.

BASIS OF STATUS CLASSIFICATION: The principal threat to the Red-shouldered Hawk is loss of habitat. Where its habitat exists, the species is holding its own. However, many forested areas of Pennsylvania are either being destroyed or fragmented, making them unsuitable for this species. This hawk could see a downward trend in its population should this process continue. Listed on National Audubon Society Blue List 1982.

RECOMMENDATIONS: Studies should be made to determine the size and nature of the habitat requirements of this species and then steps taken to preserve areas that meet these criteria.

SELECTED REFERENCES:

BEDNARZ, J. C., and J. J. DINSMORE. 1982. Nest sites and habitat of Red-shouldered and Red-tailed hawks in Iowa. Wilson Bull., 94:31–45.

BENT, A. C. 1937. Life histories of North American birds of prey. Part 1. Bull. U.S. Nat. Mus., 167:1–409.

BROWN, L., and D. AMADON. 1968. Eagles, hawks, and falcons of the world. Hamlyn Publ. Group Limited, Middlesex, Great Britain, 2:445–945.

PETERSON, R. T. 1980. A field guide to the birds. Houghton Mifflin Co., Boston, 384 pp.

POOLE, E. L. 1964. Pennsylvania birds. Livingston Publ. Co., Narberth, Pennsylvania, viii + 94 pp.

PORTNOY, J. W., and W. E. DODGE. 1979. Red-shouldered Hawk nesting ecology and behavior. Wilson Bull., 91:104–117.

TATE, J., and D. J. TATE. 1982. The Blue List for 1982. Amer. Birds, 36:126–135.

TODD, W. E. C. 1940. Birds of western Pennsylvania. Univ. Pittsburgh Press, Pittsburgh, xv + 710 pp.

Vulnerable

NORTHERN HARRIER
Circus cyaneus hudsonius (Linnaeus)
Family Accipitridae
Order Falconiformes

DESCRIPTION: This is a slim hawk with long, rounded wings and a long tail having a very conspicuous white rump patch. The male is light with black wing tips, the female brown. This species is often seen flying low over marshes or fields with the wings held up at an angle.

Northern Harrier (*Circus cyaneus*). Photograph by A. D. Cruickshank/VIREO.

NORTHERN HARRIER (*Circus cyaneus*)

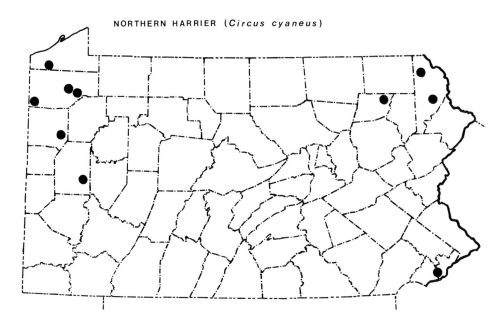

RANGE: The Northern Harrier may be found in North and Central America. In Pennsylvania, it is an uncommon nester in northwestern and southeastern sections of the Commonwealth, but is rare as a nester elsewhere. The Northern Harrier migrates and winters, in suitable habitat, throughout the Commonwealth.

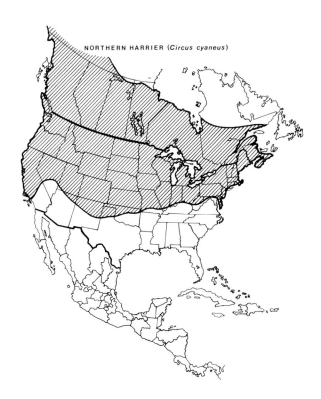

NORTHERN HARRIER (*Circus cyaneus*)

HABITAT: Marshes and agricultural areas are the habitats commonly used by the Northern Harrier.

LIFE HISTORY AND ECOLOGY: The Northern Harrier nests on or near the ground in a structure made of sticks, straws, and grasses. The nest varies from flimsy to well made. It is about 38 to 75 cm wide and varies greatly in height. The female does most of the building, although the male will gather materials. An average clutch of five eggs is laid and incubated almost exclusively by the female for about 24 days. Young spend an additional month in the nest before leaving. The food of the Northern Harrier is composed mostly of mice and rats, with some birds, fish, and insects making up the balance.

BASIS OF STATUS CLASSIFICATION: Although content with dry agricultural areas in winter time, the Northern Harrier prefers marshes for nesting. This habitat is rapidly disappearing in Pennsylvania, which is why the Northern Harrier is presently limited to small sections of the Commonwealth. The vulnerability of this habitat reflects directly on this species. Listed on National Audubon Society Blue List 1982.

RECOMMENDATIONS: Every effort should be made to preserve and expand marshes in Pennsylvania.

SELECTED REFERENCES:

BENT, A. C. 1937. Life histories of North American birds of prey. Part 1. Bull. U.S. Nat. Mus., 167:1–409.

HAMMERSTROM, F. 1969. A harrier population study. Pp 367–383, *in* Peregrine Falcon populations: their biology and decline (J. J. Hickey, ed.), Univ. Wisconsin Press, Madison, xxii + 596 pp.

HECHT, W. R. 1951. Nesting of the Marsh Hawk at Delta, Manitoba. Wilson Bull., 63:167–176.

PETERSON, R. T. 1980. A field guide to the birds. Houghton Mifflin Co., Boston, 384 pp.

POOLE, E. L. 1964. Pennsylvania birds. Livingston Publ. Co., Narberth, Pennsylvania, viii + 94 pp.

TODD, W. E. C. 1940. Birds of western Pennsylvania. Univ. Pittsburgh Press, Pittsburgh, xv + 710 pp.

Vulnerable

BOBWHITE
Colinus virginianus virginianus (Linnaeus)
Family Phasianidae
Order Galliformes

DESCRIPTION: The Bobwhite is a small, brown, chicken-like bird, best known for its clear call of its own name—Bobwhite. The male has distinct black and white stripes on its head. The female has duller buffy stripes.

RANGE: The Bobwhite occurs in eastern United States and Mexico, northwestern United States, and northwestern Mexico. In Pennsylvania, it is found primarily in the southern counties, but has been found as far north as Potter County.

HABITAT: Habitats where the Bobwhite occurs include farmland, hedgerows, abandoned fields, and woodland margins.

LIFE HISTORY AND ECOLOGY: The Bobwhite builds its nest on the ground under brush or in tall grasses. A depression is lined with fine grasses and an arch is woven over the nest in an ovenlike fashion. From 12 to 20 eggs are laid and incubated for 23 days. Young leave the nest almost immediately after hatching. The Bobwhite is omnivorous, eating seeds, fruit, leaves, buds, tubers, insects, spiders, myriapods, crustaceans, mollusks, and batrachians.

BASIS OF STATUS CLASSIFICATION: The Bobwhite reaches the northern limits of its range in Pennsylvania, and as such is vulnerable to severe winters. When there is a lot of snow, especially with a hard crust, the Bobwhite is unable to get enough food, and many perish. The Pennsylvania Game Commission no longer stocks Bobwhite, although some private breeders and sportsmans clubs do release some birds in a few locations. The birds that

Bobwhite (*Colinus virginianus*). Photograph by A. D. Cruickshank/VIREO.

BOBWHITE (*Colinus virginianus*)

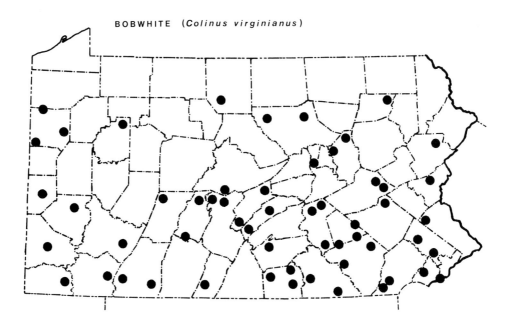

have been introduced in the past were from southern stock which may not have been capable of surviving harsh winters. These birds may have interbred with the northern birds, thereby reducing the native birds' hardiness. In addition, changes in agricultural practices along with expanded urbanization, which have reduced Bobwhite habitat, have been factors in the decline in Bobwhite populations in Pennsylvania in recent years. Listed on National Audubon Society Species with Special Concerns 1982.

RECOMMENDATIONS: The primary threat to the Bobwhite is weather, over which we have no control, but loss of habitat is also a factor in the decline of this species. The population should be monitored, and hunting prohibited or reduced along with habitat restoration in areas that show declining populations.

SELECTED REFERENCES:

BENT, A. C. 1932. Life histories of North American gallinaceous birds. Bull. U.S. Nat. Mus., 162:1–490.

JOHNSGAARD, P. A. 1973. Grouse and quails of North America. Univ. Nebraska Press, Lincoln, xx + 553 pp.

PETERSON, R. T. 1980. A field guide to the birds. Houghton Mifflin Co., Boston, 384 pp.

POOLE, E. L. 1964. Pennsylvania birds. Livingston Publ. Co., Narberth, Pennsylvania, viii + 94 pp.

ROSENE, W. 1969. The Bobwhite Quail: its life and management. Rutgers Univ. Press, New Brunswick, New Jersey, xxv + 418 pp.

TATE, J., and D. J. TATE. 1982. The Blue List for 1982. Amer. Birds, 36:126–135.

TODD, W. E. C. 1940. Birds of western Pennsylvania. Univ. Pittsburgh Press, Pittsburgh, xv + 710 pp.

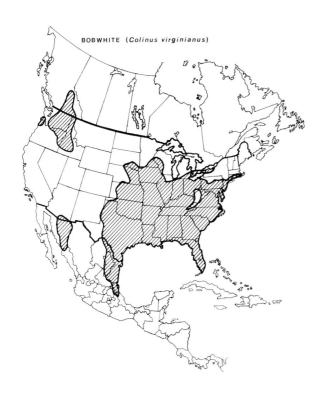

BOBWHITE (*Colinus virginianus*)

Vulnerable

BARN OWL
Tyto alba pratincola (Bonaparte)
Family Tytonidae
Order Strigiformes

DESCRIPTION: The Barn Owl is a crow-sized owl

Barn Owl (*Tyto alba*). Photograph by A. D. Cruickshank/VIREO.

with a heart-shaped white face, buffy wings and back, and white underparts. It is usually seen at night flying moth-like over farm fields.

RANGE: The Barn Owl occurs in southern Canada, United States, and Mexico, but is absent from many montane areas. In Pennsylvania, it is primarily found in the southeastern third of the Commonwealth and the western counties. Occasionally, it is found in the valleys between the mountains in central Pennsylvania.

HABITAT: The Barn Owl prefers open agricultural areas.

LIFE HISTORY AND ECOLOGY: The Barn Owl nests in hollow trees, barns, abandoned houses, and similar places. No nest is built. From three to 11

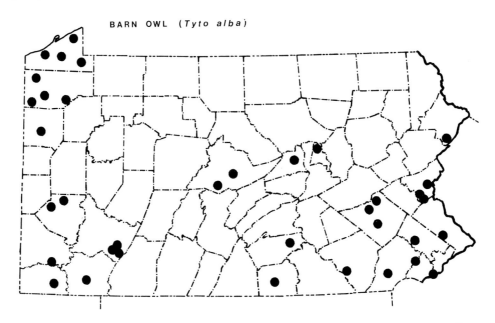

BARN OWL (*Tyto alba*)

eggs are laid, generally in the spring, but nesting will occur anytime of the year if the food supply is adequate. They are incubated by the female for 21 to 34 days. The young stay at the nesting location for 8 to 10 weeks. The food of the Barn Owl is primarily rats and mice.

BASIS FOR STATUS CLASSIFICATION: The Barn Owl is near the northern limits of its range in Pennsylvania, and is therefore affected by severe winters. This creates a great fluctuation in the population which makes it difficult to assess its long term trends in this Commonwealth. Loss of farmland in some areas has reduced the population, and construction of pigeon-proof barns has also had an adverse impact on this species. The feeling among most observers is that there has been a decline in the Commonwealth, but this needs more study. Listed on National Audubon Society Species with Special Concerns 1982.

RECOMMENDATIONS: A study should be undertaken to assess the recent past and present status of Barn Owls in Pennsylvania. Farmers should be encouraged to erect nesting boxes for owls. Preservation of farmland should be encouraged.

BARN OWL (*Tyto alba*)

SELECTED REFERENCES:

BENT, A. C. 1938. Life histories of North American birds of prey. Part 2. Bull. U.S. Nat. Mus., 170:1–482.

EARHART, C. M., and N. K. JOHNSON. 1970. Size dimorphism and food habits of North American owls. Condor, 72:251–264.

PETERSON, R. T. 1980. A field guide to the birds. Houghton Mifflin Co., Boston, 384 pp.

POOLE, E. L. 1964. Pennsylvania birds. Livingston Publ. Co., Narberth, Pennsylvania, viii + 94 pp.

TODD, W. E. C. 1940. Birds of western Pennsylvania. Univ. Pittsburgh Press, Pittsburgh, xv + 710 pp.

WALKER, L. W. 1974. Barn Owls. Pp. 3–20, *in* The book of owls, Alfred A. Knopf, New York, xiii + 255 pp.

Red-headed Woodpecker (*Melanerpes erythrocephalus*). Photograph by A. D. Cruickshank/VIREO.

Vulnerable

RED-HEADED WOODPECKER

Melanerpes erythrocephalus erythrocephalus

(Linnaeus)

Family Picidae

Order Piciformes

DESCRIPTION: This flashy woodpecker has a completely red head, black wings with conspicuous large, white wing patches, and a white breast. Adults are easily recognized by the complete red hood, while immatures have a brown head.

RANGE: The Red-headed Woodpecker is found in the United States, east of the Rocky Mountains. In Pennsylvania, it nests locally throughout the Commonwealth. Some individuals overwinter, whereas others migrate.

HABITAT: The Red-headed Woodpecker occurs in deciduous forest, preferably near water, and swampy woods.

LIFE HISTORY AND ECOLOGY: The Red-headed Woodpecker digs cavities for its nest in dead tree trunks or branches, or in poles. Four to seven eggs are laid and incubated for 2 weeks. The young remain in the nest for 3 to 4 weeks. The diet of this woodpecker is split between insects and vegetable matter such as nuts, seeds, and berries.

BASIS OF STATUS CLASSIFICATION: The population of Red-headed Woodpeckers has been on the decline for many years. Once a common bird throughout the Commonwealth, it is now found very locally in small numbers. It is speculated that competition from Starlings for nesting holes is the prime reason for this decline, but there may be other reasons as well. The recent demand for firewood is denuding many of the woodlots in the state of dead snags suitable for cavity nesters. Listed on National Audubon Society Species with Special Concerns 1982.

RECOMMENDATIONS: A survey should be made to determine the status of the Red-headed Woodpecker in Pennsylvania and factors affecting its population levels. Landowners should be encouraged not to cut down all dead trees.

RED-HEADED WOODPECKER (*Melanerpes erythrocephalus*)

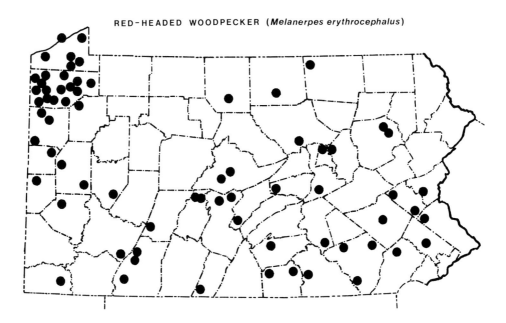

SELECTED REFERENCES:

BENT, A. C. 1939. Life histories of North American wood-peckers. Bull. U.S. Nat. Mus., 174:1–334.

KILHAM, L. 1977. Early breeding season behavior of Red-headed Woodpeckers. Auk, 94:231–239.

PETERSON, R. T. 1980. A field guide to the birds. Houghton Mifflin Co., Boston, 384 pp.

POOLE, E. L. 1964. Pennsylvania birds. Livingston Publ. Co., Narberth, Pennsylvania, viii + 94 pp.

RELLER, A. W. 1972. Aspects of behavioral ecology of Red-headed and Red-bellied woodpeckers. Amer. Midland Nat., 88:270–290.

TATE, J., and D. J. TATE. 1982. The Blue List for 1982. Amer. Birds, 36:126–135.

TODD, W. E. C. 1940. Birds of western Pennsylvania. Univ. Pittsburgh Press, Pittsburgh, xv + 710 pp.

Vulnerable

PURPLE MARTIN
Progne subis subis (Linnaeus)
Family Hirundinidae
Order Passeriformes

DESCRIPTION: Swallows are medium-sized birds with thin pointed wings and notched tails. This largest swallow is entirely dark purple in the male, whereas a grayish breast is present in the female.

RANGE: The geographic range of the Purple Martin includes much of North and South America. It nests throughout Pennsylvania except on some of the higher plateaus.

HABITAT: The Purple Martin can be found around farms, and suburban and rural areas where nest boxes have been erected.

LIFE HISTORY AND ECOLOGY: The Purple Martin now nests almost exclusively in man-made nest boxes. Once a colony is established, the birds will return year after year unless some disaster befalls them. They eat flying insects, and in many communities people enjoy observing and protecting the

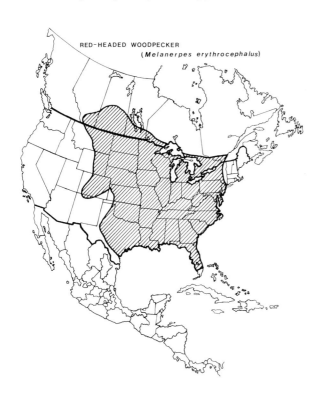

RED-HEADED WOODPECKER
(*Melanerpes erythrocephalus*)

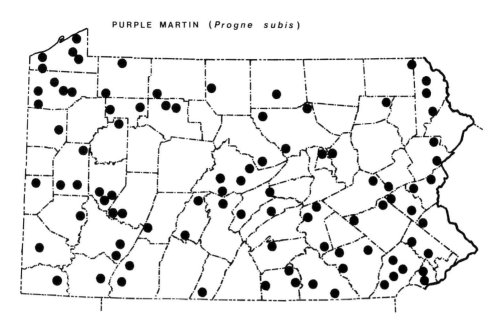

PURPLE MARTIN (*Progne subis*)

colonies. The first martins return in March and lay three to eight eggs. These are incubated for about 2 weeks. The young leave the nest after 3 to 4 weeks, but may return to the nest for several days.

BASIS OF STATUS CLASSIFICATION: In 1972, Hurricane Agnes had a devastating effect on the

Purple Martin population in Pennsylvania. Feeding exclusively on flying insects makes them very vulnerable to extended periods of rain which prevent feeding. The population has yet to recover, and many colonies remain in low numbers or have been abandoned. Prior to 1972, however, the number of colonies was on a decline because landowners were neglecting the birdhouses. Listed on National Audubon Society Species with Special Concerns 1982.

RECOMMENDATIONS: A campaign to erect Purple Martin houses should be instituted in order to encourage the establishment of more colonies.

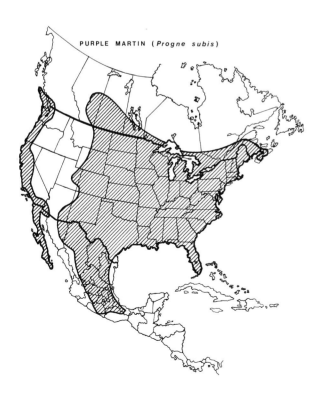

PURPLE MARTIN (*Progne subis*)

SELECTED REFERENCES:

ALLEN, R. W., and M. M. NICE. 1973. A study of the breeding biology of the Purple Martin (*Progue subis*). Amer. Midland Nat., 47:606–665.

BENT, A. C. 1942. Life histories of North American flycatchers, larks, swallows and their allies. Bull. U.S. Nat. Mus., 179: 1–555.

JOHNSTON, R. F., and J. W. HARDY. 1962. Behavior of the Purple Martin. Wilson Bull., 74:243–252.

MAYFIELD, H. F. 1969. Purple Martin population changes over fifteen years. Auk, 86:522–528.

PETERSON, R. T. 1981. A field guide to the birds. Houghton Mifflin Co., Boston, 384 pp.

POOLE, E. L. 1964. Pennsylvania birds. Livingston Publ. Co., Narberth, Pennsylvania, viii + 94 pp.

TATE, J., and D. J. TATE. 1982. The Blue List for 1982. Amer. Birds, 36:126–135.

TODD, W. E. C. 1940. Birds of western Pennsylvania. Univ. Pittsburgh Press, Pittsburgh, xv + 710 pp.

Marsh Wren (*Telmatodytes palustris*). Photograph by A. D. Cruickshank/VIREO.

Vulnerable

MARSH WREN
Cistothorus palustris palustris (Wilson) and
Cistothorus palustris dissaeptus (Bangs)
Family Troglodytidae
Order Passeriformes

DESCRIPTION: The Marsh Wren is a small brown wren with a conspicuous white eye-stripe and black and white back stripes. Its reedy song, often heard at night, reminds some people of a sewing machine.

RANGE: The range of the Marsh Wren includes

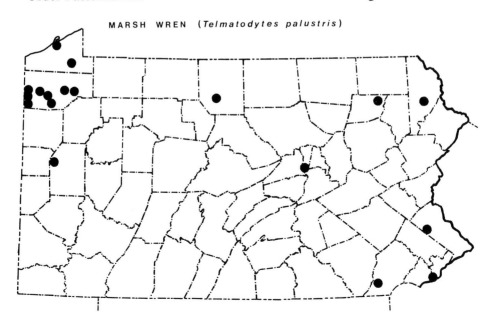

MARSH WREN (*Telmatodytes palustris*)

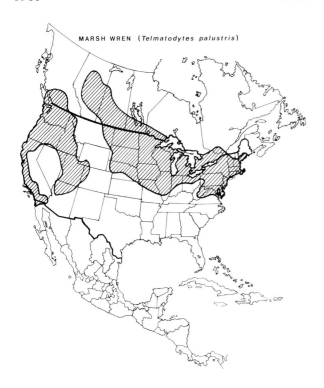

MARSH WREN (*Telmatodytes palustris*)

United States and southern Canada. In Pennsylvania, the *palustris* race is a common breeder in the tidal marshes around Philadelphia, whereas the *dissaeptus* race is uncommon in scattered marshes around the remainder of the Commonwealth.

HABITAT: The Marsh Wren is found primarily in association with freshwater and tidal marshes.

LIFE HISTORY AND ECOLOGY: The Marsh Wren returns to its breeding areas in May. It has a nesting behavior, which includes building several dummy nests in addition to the one used for rearing young. The nest is built 30 cm or more above the ground in reeds, grasses or bushes. Three to five eggs are laid and incubated for 13 days. The young remain in the nest for about 2 weeks. The food of the Marsh Wren consists primarily of insects.

BASIS OF STATUS CLASSIFICATION: The Marsh Wren inhabits a vanishing habitat in Pennsylvania—marshland. As the marshes disappear, so too do the birds that require that habitat. Because of this, the Marsh Wren is very much of concern as a breeding species in Pennsylvania.

RECOMMENDATIONS: Every effort should be made to preserve and expand freshwater and tidal

marshes in Pennsylvania. Dr. K. C. Parkes has pointed out, "The type locality of the species is the 'borders of the Schuylkill and Delaware (rivers, Philadelphia).' This is the only area in the state where the nominate race breeds, the inland populations, what few of them there are, being referable to *Cistothorus palustris dissaeptus.* As representing the topotypical population, whatever remnant populations breed around Philadelphia should receive special attention."

SELECTED REFERENCES:

BENT, A. C. 1948. Life histories of North American nuthatches, wrens, thrashers and their allies. Bull. U.S. Nat. Mus., 195: 1–475.
PETERSON, R. T. 1980. A field guide to the birds. Houghton Mifflin Co., Boston, 384 pp.
POOLE, E. L. 1964. Pennsylvania birds. Livingston Publ. Co., Narberth, Pennsylvania, viii + 94 pp.
TODD, W. E. C. 1940. Birds of western Pennsylvania. Univ. Pittsburgh Press, Pittsburgh, xv + 710 pp.
VERNER, J. 1964. Evolution of polygamy in the Long-billed Marsh Wren during the breeding season. Evolution, 18:252–261.
VERNER, J., and G. H. ENGELSEN. 1970. Territories, multiple-nest building and polygyny in the Long-billed Marsh Wren. Auk, 87:557–567.
WELTER, W. A. 1935. The natural history of the Long-billed Marsh Wren. Wilson Bull., 47:3–34.

Vulnerable

EASTERN BLUEBIRD
Sialia sialis sialis (Linnaeus)
Family Muscicapidae
Order Passeriformes

DESCRIPTION: Slightly larger than a sparrow, this bird is unmistakable with its bright blue back and wings and its reddish breast. The female is duller than the male.

RANGE: The Eastern Bluebird occurs in the southern portion of eastern Canada and the eastern half of the United States. In Pennsylvania, it is found throughout the Commonwealth where suitable habitat and nest sites occur. It migrates throughout the Commonwealth and many small flocks winter here.

HABITAT: The Eastern Bluebird occupies such habitats as open rural country, edges of forests, and open swampy woods.

LIFE HISTORY AND ECOLOGY: The Eastern

Eastern Bluebird (*Sialia sialis*). Photograph by A. D. Cruickshank/VIREO.

Bluebird requires a cavity for nesting. They do not dig their own cavity, but must find an old woodpecker hole, a cavity in an old tree branch, or manmade nest boxes. A nest of grasses is placed in the cavity, and three to seven eggs are laid. The incubation period lasts about 12 days, and the young leave the nest after about 2 weeks. The diet of the Bluebird consists of insects with smaller amounts of vegetable matter.

BASIS OF STATUS CLASSIFICATION: Eastern Bluebirds have suffered from competition for nest-ing sites with Starlings and House Sparrows. In recent years, however, the erection of Bluebird houses in many portions of the Commonwealth has had a dramatic effect on the Bluebird populations in those areas. Because of its current dependence on manmade structures for nesting sites, the Eastern Bluebird population in Pennsylvania could suffer drastic declines if birdhouses are not maintained. The Eastern Bluebird, being an early migrant (beginning of March), is also subject to late winter storms which can kill many of them. Listed on National Audubon Society Blue List 1982.

EASTERN BLUEBIRD (*Sialia sialis*)

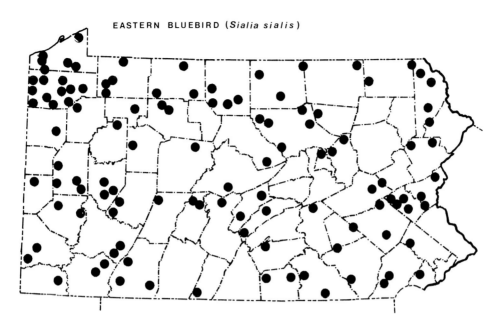

RECOMMENDATIONS: The erection of Bluebird houses should be encouraged throughout the Commonwealth to help maintain adequate nesting sites for the species.

SELECTED REFERENCES:

BENT, A. C. 1949. Life histories of North American thrushes, kinglets and their allies. Bull. U.S. Nat. Mus., 196:1–454.

KRIEG, D. C. 1971. The behavioral patterns of the Eastern Bluebird (*Sialia sialis*). New York State Mus. Sci. Serv. Bull., 415:1–139.

LASKEY, A. R. 1939. A study of nesting Eastern Bluebirds. Bird-banding, 10:23–32.

PEAKALL, D. B. 1979. The Eastern Bluebird: its breeding season, clutch size and nesting success. Living Bird, 9:239–256.

POOLE, E. L. 1964. Pennsylvania birds. Livingston Publ. Co., Narberth, Pennsylvania, viii + 94 pp.

TATE, J., and D. J. TATE. 1982. The Blue List for 1982. Amer. Birds, 36:126–135.

TODD, W. E. C. 1940. Birds of western Pennsylvania. Univ. Pittsburgh Press, Pittsburgh, xv + 710 pp.

Vulnerable

GRASSHOPPER SPARROW
Ammodramus savannarum pratensis (Vieillot)
Family Emberizidae
Order Passeriformes

DESCRIPTION: The Grasshopper Sparrow is a small sparrow with a short tail, a striped crown, and a buffy breast. It is most easily identified by its insect-like, buzzy song.

RANGE: The Grasshopper Sparrow occurs in the United States, Mexico, Cuba, and the Bahamas. In Pennsylvania, it breeds throughout the Commonwealth, but is very localized and is absent in some sections. It is more abundant in the southern counties than in the northern countries.

HABITAT: The primary habitat of the Grasshopper Sparrow is grassy or weedy fields.

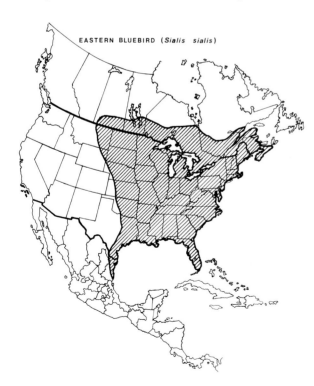

EASTERN BLUEBIRD (*Sialis sialis*)

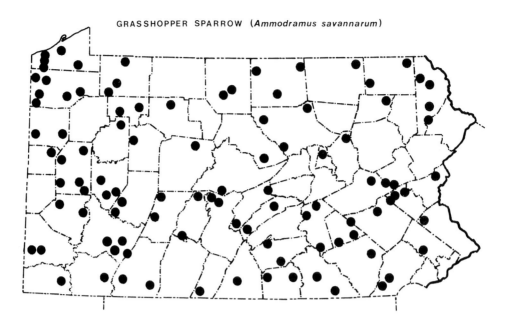

GRASSHOPPER SPARROW (*Ammodramus savannarum*)

LIFE HISTORY AND ECOLOGY: The Grasshopper Sparrow returns to Pennsylvania in April. Its nest is built in a slight depression in the ground at the base of a clump of grass and is composed of stems and blades of grass and lined with finer grass and rootlets. Four or five eggs are laid and incubated for about 12 days. The young leave the nest after about 9 days. The diet of this species consists largely of grasshoppers along with other insects and weed and grain seeds.

BASIS OF STATUS CLASSIFICATION: Although this species can still be found throughout most of its former range in Pennsylvania, it has disappeared from the extreme southeastern portion and has declined elsewhere. Changing agricultural practices (that is, early harvesting and fewer fallow fields) has reduced the habitat available to the Grasshopper Sparrow. In addition, much farmland in Pennsylvania is being developed for housing or being abandoned to forest. If these trends continue, this and several other sparrows could become threatened. Listed on National Audubon Society Blue List 1982.

RECOMMENDATIONS: The population of Grasshopper Sparrows in Pennsylvania should be monitored. Suitable habitat should be identified and management techniques developed to maintain such habitat.

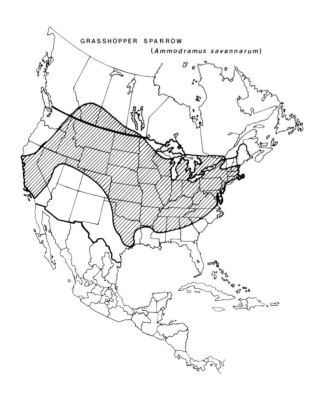

GRASSHOPPER SPARROW (*Ammodramus savannarum*)

SELECTED REFERENCES:

BENT, A. C. 1968. Life histories of North American cardinals, grosbeaks, buntings, towhees, finches, sparrows and allies. Part 2. Bull. U.S. Nat. Mus., 237:603–1248.
PETERSON, R. T. 1980. A field guide to the birds. Houghton Mifflin Co., Boston, 384 pp.
POOLE, E. L. 1964. Pennsylvania birds. Livingston Publ. Co., Narberth, Pennsylvania, viii + 94 pp.
TATE, J., and D. J. TATE. 1982. The Blue List for 1982. Amer. Birds, 36:126–135.

TODD, W. E. C. 1940. Birds of western Pennsylvania. Univ. Pittsburgh Press, Pittsburgh, xv + 710 pp.

WHITEMORE, R. C. 1979. Short-term change in vegetation structure and its affect on Grasshopper Sparrows in West Virginia. Auk, 96:621–625.

Vulnerable

VESPER SPARROW
Pooecetes gramineus gramineus (Gmelin)
Family Emberizidae
Order Passeriformes

DESCRIPTION: This medium-sized brown sparrow can be identified by its white outer tail feathers when it flushes from the grass. It also has a light eye-ring and a reddish shoulder patch seen at close range.

RANGE: The Vesper Sparrow may be found in North America into Mexico. In Pennsylvania, it breeds throughout most of the Commonwealth in suitable habitat.

HABITAT: Dry weedy fields are the primary habitat of the Vesper Sparrow.

LIFE HISTORY AND ECOLOGY: The Vesper Sparrow returns to Pennsylvania in April, although some overwinter here. A nest of grasses and weeds is built on the ground, well hidden by nearby vegetation. Three to five eggs are laid and incubated for about 12 days. The young leave the nest after about 9 days. The diet consists of insects and seeds.

BASIS OF STATUS CLASSIFICATION: Although the Vesper Sparrow can still be found throughout most of its former range in Pennsylvania, there is a consensus among observers that it is declining. The primary reason seems to be habitat loss and changing agricultural practices.

RECOMMENDATIONS: The population of Vesper Sparrows should be monitored to determine its current population trend and the limiting factors on its abundance. Steps should then be taken to reverse those factors.

SELECTED REFERENCES:

BENT, A. C. 1968. Life histories of North American cardinals, grosbeaks, buntings, towhees, finches, sparrows and allies. Part 2. Bull. U.S. Nat. Mus., 237:603–1248.

Vesper Sparrow (*Pooecetes gramineus*). Photograph by A. D. Cruickshank/VIREO.

VESPER SPARROW (*Pooecetes gramineus*)

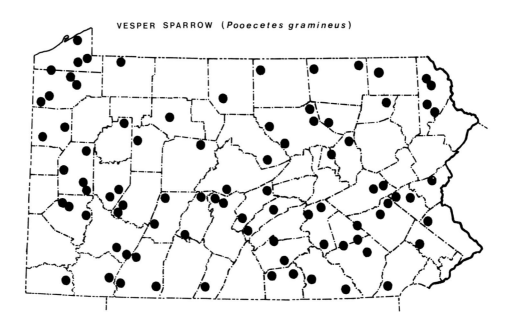

PETERSON, R. T. 1980. A field guide to the birds. Houghton Mifflin Co., Boston, 384 pp.

POOLE, E. L. 1964. Pennsylvania birds. Livingston Publ. Co., Narberth, Pennsylvania, viii + 94 pp.

TATE, J., and D. J. TATE. 1982. The Blue List for 1982. Amer. Birds, 36:126–135.

TODD, W. E. C. 1940. Birds of western Pennsylvania. Univ. Pittsburgh Press, Pittsburgh, xv + 710 pp.

VESPER SPARROW (*Pooecetes gramineus*)

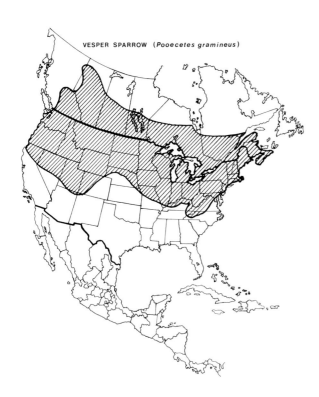

Status Undetermined

NORTHERN GOSHAWK
Accipiter gentilis atricapillus (Wilson)
Family Accipitridae
Order Falconiformes

DESCRIPTION: Larger than a crow, this hawk has wide rounded wings and a long tail. The adult has a gray back and wings, with a very light breast, and a conspicuous white stripe over the eye. The immature is brown with a streaked breast.

RANGE: The range of the Northern Goshawk is North America. In Pennsylvania, it is a rare to uncommon breeder in northern tier counties and on higher mountains through central Pennsylvania. Northern Goshawks winter throughout the Commonwealth.

HABITAT: The habitat of the Northern Goshawk is the forested areas of the Commonwealth.

LIFE HISTORY AND ECOLOGY: The Northern Goshawk builds its nest from 9 to 23 m up in either deciduous or coniferous trees. The nest is built of sticks and twigs lined with bark, evergreen branches, feathers, and down. It frequently uses the same nest and occasionally uses other abandoned nests. Three or four eggs are laid in April or May and incubated mostly by the female for 4 to 5 weeks. The young leave the nest in about 4 to 5 weeks. The Northern Goshawk preys on birds and small mammals.

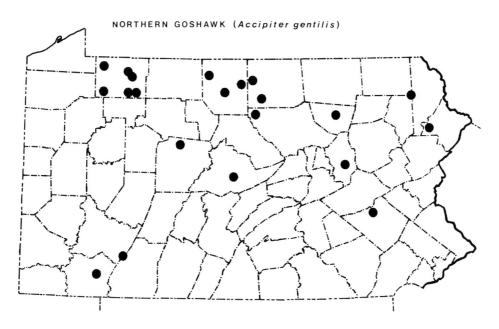

NORTHERN GOSHAWK (*Accipiter gentilis*)

BASIS OF STATUS CLASSIFICATION: Because of its preference for deep woods, little is known about the breeding status of Northern Goshawks in Pennsylvania. The Northern Goshawk appears to be on the increase during the past few years, especially since the winter invasion of 1972–1973. Its exact status, however, is unknown.

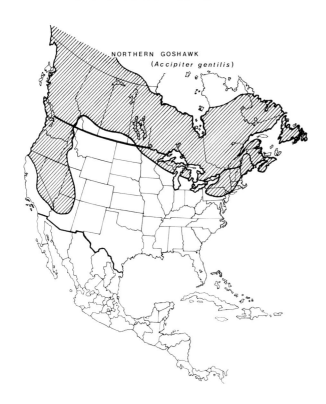

NORTHERN GOSHAWK
(*Accipiter gentilis*)

RECOMMENDATIONS: A study should be undertaken to determine the current status of Northern Goshawks in Pennsylvania and to determine the factors affecting their population.

SELECTED REFERENCES:

BENT, A. C. 1937. Life histories of North American birds of prey. Part 1. Bull. U.S. Nat. Mus., 167:1–409.

BROWN, L., and D. AMADON. 1960. Eagles, hawks and falcons of the world. Hamlyn Publ. Group Limited, Middlesex, Great Britain, 2:445–945.

MENG, H. 1959. Food habits of nesting Cooper's Hawks and Goshawks in New York and Pennsylvania. Wilson Bull., 71:169–174.

PETERSON, R. T. 1980. A field guide to the birds. Houghton Mifflin Co., Boston, 384 pp.

POOLE, E. L. 1964. Pennsylvania birds. Livingston Publ. Co., Narberth, Pennsylvania, viii + 94 pp.

STORER, R. W. 1966. Sexual dimorphism and food habits in three North American Accipiters. Auk, 83:423–436.

TATE, J., and D. J. TATE. 1982. The Blue List for 1982. Amer. Birds, 36:126–135.

TODD, W. E. C. 1940. Birds of western Pennsylvania. Univ. Pittsburgh Press, Pittsburgh, xv + 710 pp.

Status Undetermined

SHARP-SHINNED HAWK
Accipiter striatus velox (Wilson)
Family Accipitridae
Order Falconiformes

DESCRIPTION: This is a small hawk with short rounded wings and a large square tail. The adult has a slate blue back and a reddish breast. Immatures

SHARP-SHINNED HAWK (*Accipiter striatus*)

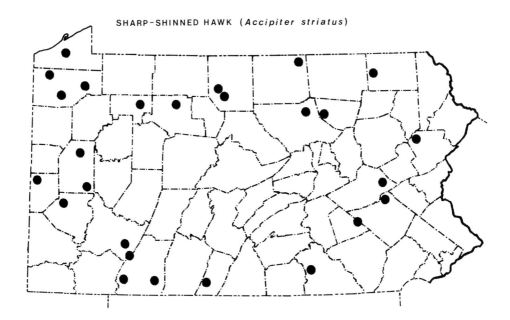

are brown with streaked breasts. In flight, it gives a few rapid wing beats and then a short glide.

RANGE: The Sharp-shinned Hawk occurs in North and Central America. In Pennsylvania, it is an uncommon to rare breeder throughout most of the Commonwealth. There are no recent breeding records for southeastern Pennsylvania. The Sharp-

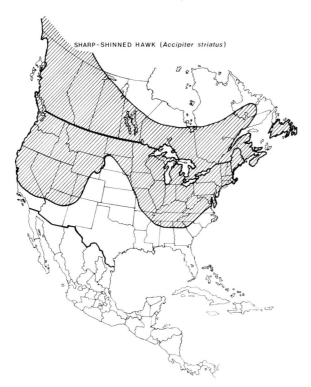

SHARP-SHINNED HAWK (*Accipiter striatus*)

shinned Hawk migrates and winters throughout the Commonwealth.

HABITAT: Forests are the primary habitat of the Sharp-shinned Hawk, where they prefer nesting in mature conifers.

LIFE HISTORY AND ECOLOGY: Sharp-shinned Hawks build their nests almost exclusively in conifers at a height of 6 to 18 m above the ground. A new nest is built each year of sticks and twigs, occasionally it is lined with pine bark. The nest is about 60 cm wide and 16 cm high. Four to five eggs are laid in April or May and incubated by both sexes for about 3 weeks. The young stay in the nest for another 3 to 4 weeks. The primary food of the Sharp-shinned Hawk is small birds, but small mammals are also taken.

BASIS OF STATUS CLASSIFICATION: Observers from around the Commonwealth have indicated a recent decline in the population of Sharp-shinned Hawks, but are uncertain as to its cause. Its population is certainly below its former abundance due to the loss of much of the coniferous woods in Pennsylvania. It also probably has been affected by the use of persistent pesticides. Listed on National Audubon Society Blue List 1982.

RECOMMENDATIONS: A study needs to be undertaken to assess the current status of the Sharp-shinned Hawk in Pennsylvania.

SELECTED REFERENCES:

BENT, A. C. 1937. Life histories of North American birds of prey. Part 1. Bull. U.S. Nat. Mus., 167:1–409.

BROWN, L., AND D. AMADON. 1968. Eagles, hawks and falcons of the world. Hamlyn Publ. Group Limited, Middlesex, Great Britain, 2:445–945.

MUELLER, H. C., and O. D. BERGER. 1970. Prey preferences in the Sharp-shinned Hawk: the role of sex, experience and motivation. Auk, 87:452–457.

PETERSON, R. T. 1980. A field guide to the birds. Houghton Mifflin Co., Boston, 384 pp.

POOLE, E. L. 1964. Pennsylvania birds. Livingston Publ. Co., Narberth, Pennsylvania, viii + 94 pp.

STORER, R. W. 1966. Sexual dimorphism and food habits in three North American Accipiters. Auk, 83:423–436.

TATE, J., and D. J. TATE. 1982. The Blue List for 1982. Amer. Birds, 36:126–135.

TODD, W. E. C. 1940. Birds of western Pennsylvania. Univ. Pittsburgh Press, Pittsburgh, xv + 710 pp.

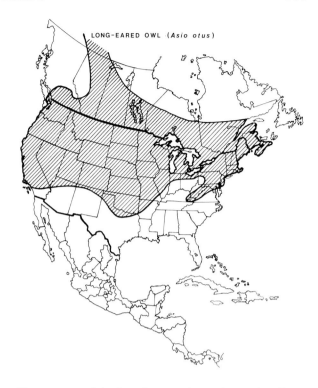

LONG-EARED OWL (*Asio otus*)

Status Undetermined

LONG-EARED OWL
Asio otus wilsonianus (Lesson)
Family Strigidae
Order Strigiformes

DESCRIPTION: A crow-sized, gray owl with prominent "ear" tufts and a streaked breast. This owl often sits close to the trunk in a conifer making it difficult to observe.

RANGE: The Long-eared Owl may be found in the temperate zones of North America. In Pennsylvania it is a very rare breeder at few locations across the Commonwealth. It migrates throughout the Commonwealth and winters in many areas throughout the Commonwealth.

HABITAT: The preferred habitat of the Long-eared Owl is thick stands of conifers.

LIFE HISTORY AND ECOLOGY: The Long-eared

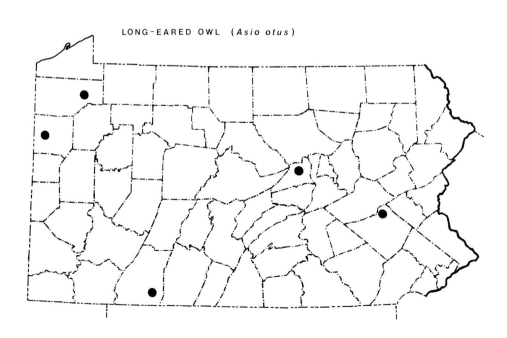

LONG-EARED OWL (*Asio otus*)

Owl usually uses old nests of crows, hawks or squirrels, and occasionally nests in tree cavities. From three to eight eggs are laid and incubated by the female for 3 weeks. The young remain in the nest for another 4 to 5 weeks. The Long-eared Owl feeds almost exclusively on rats and mice.

BASIS OF STATUS CLASSIFICATION: Because of its shyness, nocturnal habits and infrequent calling, the Long-eared Owl is easily missed and may be more common than realized. The general feeling among observers is that it has suffered a decline in recent years, but this needs to be verified.

RECOMMENDATIONS: A study should be undertaken to determine the current status of Long-eared Owls in Pennsylvania.

SELECTED REFERENCES:

ARMSTRONG, W. H. 1958. Nesting and food habits of the Long-eared Owl in Michigan. Publ. Michigan St. Univ., Biol. Ser., 1:61–96.

BENT, A. C. 1938. Life histories of North American birds of prey. Part 2. Bull. U.S. Nat. Mus., 170:1–482.

PETERSON, R. T. 1980. A field guide to the birds. Houghton Mifflin Co., Boston, 384 pp.

POOLE, E. L. 1964. Pennsylvania birds. Livingston Publ. Co., Narberth, Pennsylvania, viii + 94 pp.

TODD, W. E. C. 1940. Birds of western Pennsylvania. Univ. Pittsburgh Press, Pittsburgh, xv + 710 pp.

Status Undetermined

WHIP-POOR-WILL
Caprimulgus vociferus vociferus Wilson
Family Caprimulgidae
Order Caprimulgiformes

DESCRIPTION: This robin-sized brown bird is so well camouflaged that it is only seen when flushed from leaves on the ground. In flight the male shows prominent white tail patches. Its whip-poor-will song is heard continuously through the night.

RANGE: The Whip-poor-will occurs in the eastern United States, southwestern United States, and western Mexico. It winters on the Gulf Coast and in Mexico. In Pennsylvania, it is found throughout the Commonwealth in suitable habitat.

Whip-poor-will (*Caprimulgus vociferus*). Photograph by A. D. Cruickshank/VIREO.

WHIP-POOR-WILL (*Caprimulgus vociferus*)

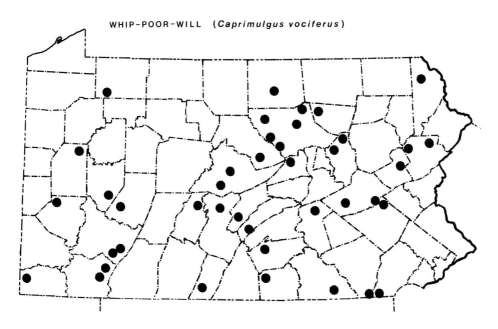

HABITAT: The preferred habitats of the Whip-poor-will are second growth forests and scrub barrens.

LIFE HISTORY AND ECOLOGY: The Whip-poor-will does not build a nest. Instead, two eggs are laid on the ground where they are incubated for 2 to 3 weeks. The young stay near the nest site until they are ready to fly. Their diet consists exclusively of insects.

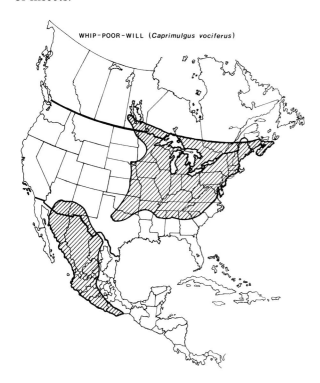

WHIP-POOR-WILL (*Caprimulgus vociferus*)

BASIS OF STATUS CLASSIFICATION: The general consensus of observers throughout the Commonwealth is that Whip-poor-wills are declining in numbers. This seems to be a result of changes in habitat, but this is not certain. Listed on National Audubon Society Species with Special Concerns 1982.

RECOMMENDATIONS: A survey should be made to determine the status of Whip-poor-wills in Pennsylvania.

SELECTED REFERENCES:

BENT, A. C. 1940. Life histories of North American cuckoos, goatsuckers, hummingbirds and their allies. Bull. U.S. Nat. Mus., 176:1–506.
PETERSON, R. T. 1980. A field guide to the birds. Houghton Mifflin Co., Boston, 384 pp.

Status Undetermined

YELLOW-BELLIED SAPSUCKER
Sphyrapicus varius varius (Linnaeus)
Family Picidae
Order Piciformes

DESCRIPTION: The pale yellow belly of this medium-sized woodpecker can only be seen at close range. The best distinguishing characteristics of this species are the long white patches on the black wings and the red forehead. The male also has a red throat. Immatures are mostly brown with the white wing patches.

Yellow-bellied Sapsucker (*Sphyrapicus varius*). Photograph by A. D. Cruickshank/VIREO.

RANGE: The range of the Yellow-bellied Sapsucker includes most of North America. In Pennsylvania, it breeds in the northern tier counties and on the high ridges in southwestern Pennsylvania. It migrates throughout the Commonwealth and winters in some locations.

HABITAT: The Yellow-bellied Sapsucker is most often seen in deciduous forests and orchards.

LIFE HISTORY AND ECOLOGY: Although a few

Yellow-bellied Sapsuckers spend the winter in Pennsylvania, most of them migrate and return in April and May to the mountains of the northern and southwestern parts of the Commonwealth. Upon arrival at their breeding grounds, they dig a cavity or use an old one in a dead branch or trunk of a tree for their nest. Deciduous trees are preferred, with a variety of species being used. From 4 to 7 eggs are laid and incubated for 2 weeks. The young remain in the nest for several weeks, emerging in juvenile plumage. The diet of the Yellow-bellied

YELLOW-BELLIED SAPSUCKER (*Sphyrapicus varius*)

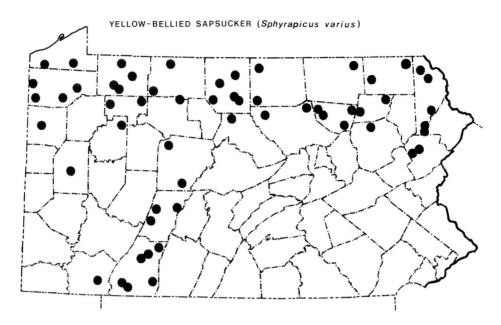

Sapsucker consists of insects, tree sap, and some berries and nuts. The Yellow-bellied Sapsucker obtains much of its food by drilling numerous holes in the bark of trees and drinking the sap. In the nesting area, this causes great damage to the afflicted trees, but the trees are seldom valuable commercial species. Yellow-bellied Sapsuckers have also been known to catch insects on the wing in a manner similar to flycatchers.

BASIS OF STATUS CLASSIFICATION: Although the Yellow-bellied Sapsucker can still be found in the mountains of Pennsylvania, there is a general feeling among observers that there has been a decline in recent years. This seems most evident during migration. However, no studies have been made to determine their abundance or population trends.

RECOMMENDATIONS: A survey should be undertaken to determine the present status of Yellow-bellied Sapsuckers in Pennsylvania, and the population should then be monitored to determine any trends.

SELECTED REFERENCES:

BENT, A. C. 1939. Life histories of North American Woodpeckers. Bull. U.S. Nat. Mus., 174:1–334.

HOWELL, T. R. 1952. Natural history and differentiation in the Yellow-bellied Sapsucker. Condor, 54:237–282.

KILHAM, L. 1962. Breeding behavior of Yellow-bellied Sapsuckers. Auk, 79:31–43.

————. 1964. The relations of breeding Yellow-bellied Sapsuckers to wounded birches and other trees. Auk, 81:520–527.

POOLE, E. L. 1964. Pennsylvania birds. Livingston Publ. Co., Narberth, Pennsylvania, viii + 94 pp.

TODD, W. E. C. 1940. Birds of western Pennsylvania. Univ. Pittsburgh Press, Pittsburgh, xv + 710 pp.

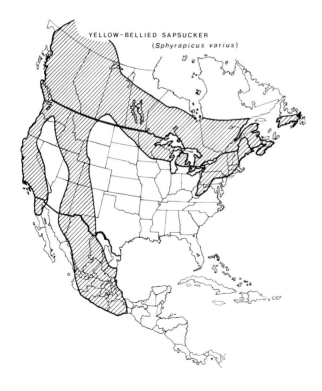

YELLOW-BELLIED SAPSUCKER
(*Sphyrapicus varius*)

Status Undetermined

LEAST FLYCATCHER
Empidonax minimus (Baird and Baird)
Family Tyrannidae
Order Passeriformes

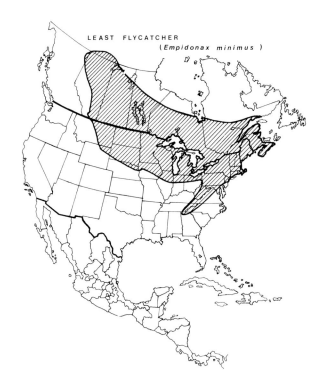

DESCRIPTION: Flycatchers are small birds, which usually sit quietly on branches, occasionally darting out to catch flying insects. This species, the smallest in the area, is gray on top and light underneath with two white wing bars and eye-ring. However, it is only safely identified by its sharp continuous chebek call.

RANGE: The range of the Least Flycatcher includes North America, east of the Rocky Mountains, and Central America. It is found throughout Pennsylvania, although it has been absent from many areas in recent years.

HABITAT: Prime habitat for for the Least Flycatcher includes open woodlands, edges of woods, and orchards.

LIFE HISTORY AND ECOLOGY: The Least Flycatcher arrives in Pennsylvania in late April and May. A deeply cupped nest is built on a branch of a tree seldom higher than 4.5 m above the ground. It lays three to six eggs and incubates them for about 12 days. The young remain in the nest for about 11 days. The Least Flycatcher is almost exclusively insectivorous.

BASIS OF STATUS CLASSIFICATION: Most observers feel that the number of Least Flycatchers has been declining in recent years. The reasons are unknown. Although it is still widespread throughout the Commonwealth, it seems to be becoming scarce or absent in some areas. Listed on Audubon Society Species with Special Concerns 1982.

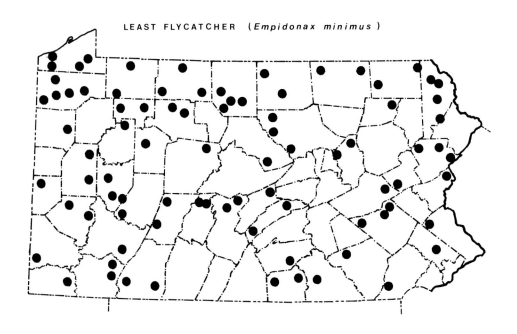

LEAST FLYCATCHER (*Empidonax minimus*)

RECOMMENDATIONS: The status of Least Flycatchers in Pennsylvania should be monitored to determine present population trends.

SELECTED REFERENCES:

BENT, A. C. 1942. Life histories of North American flycatchers, larks, swallows, and their allies. Bull. U.S. Nat. Mus., 179: 1–555.

PETERSON, R. T. 1980. A field guide to the birds. Houghton Mifflin Co., Boston, 384 pp.

TATE, J., and D. J. TATE. 1982. The Blue List for 1982. Amer. Birds, 36:126–135.

TODD, W. E. C. 1940. Birds of western Pennsylvania. Univ. Pittsburgh Press, Pittsburgh, xv + 710 pp.

WALKINSHAW, L. H. 1966. Summer observations of the Least Flycatcher in Michigan. Jack-pine Warbler, 44:151–168.

Status Undetermined

BOBOLINK
Dolichonyx oryzivorus (Linnaeus)
Family Icteridae
Order Passeriformes

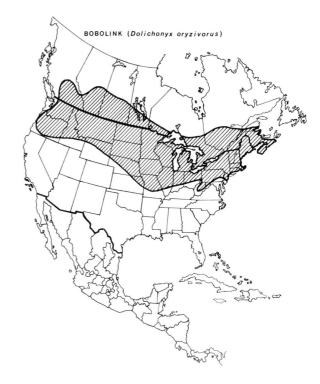

BOBOLINK (*Dolichonyx oryzivorus*)

DESCRIPTION: Slightly larger than a sparrow, this bird is black underneath with a buffy patch on the back of its head, prominent white wing patches, and a white rump patch. The female and the winter male are rather drab yellowish birds with brown streaks on the upperparts.

RANGE: Bobolinks occur in the northern United States and southern Canada. In Pennsylvania, it breeds mostly in the northern half of the Commonwealth with a few colonies in the southern half. It migrates over most of the Commonwealth.

HABITAT: Large fields with tall grasses are the primary habitat of the Bobolink.

LIFE HISTORY AND ECOLOGY: The Bobolink builds its nest on the ground by simply lining a small

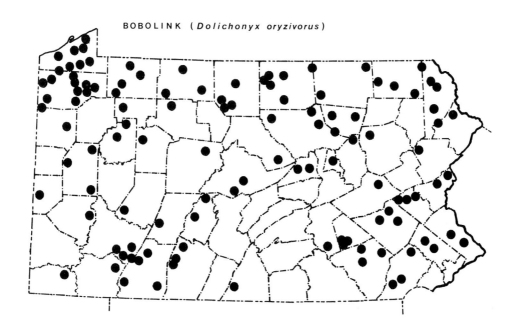

BOBOLINK (*Dolichonyx oryzivorus*)

depression with coarse grasses and weed stems. From four to seven eggs are laid and incubated for 10 to 13 days. Young leave the nest after about 2 weeks. On its breeding grounds, the Bobolink eats a mixture of insects and weed seeds. However, during migration, they have been known to devastate rice fields in the southern states.

BASIS OF STATUS CLASSIFICATION: The Bobolink, once an abundant bird in Pennsylvania, has suffered from being shot in the southern states and from changing agricultural practices in the northern states. The early harvesting of hay fields before the Bobolink has completed its nesting cycle has eliminated the species from many areas. Although it can still be found nesting in many areas of the Commonwealth, the present population trends are unclear and need to be studied.

RECOMMENDATIONS: The Bobolink populations in Pennsylvania should be monitored to determine their present status, trends, and limiting factors.

SELECTED REFERENCES:

BENT, A. C. 1958. Life histories of North American blackbirds, orioles, tanagers, and allies. Bull. U.S. Nat. Mus., 211:1–549.
MARTIN, S. C. 1971. Polygyny in the Bobolink: habitat quality and the adaptive complex. Unpublished Ph.D. dissertation, Oregon State Univ., Corvallis.
PETERSON, R. T. 1980. A field guide to the birds. Houghton Mifflin Co., Boston, 384 pp.
POOLE, E. L. 1964. Pennsylvania birds. Livingston Publ. Co., Narberth, Pennsylvania, viii + 94 pp.
TODD, W. E. C. 1940. Birds of western Pennsylvania. Univ. Pittsburgh Press, Pittsburgh, xv + 710 pp.
WITTENBERGER, J. F. 1976. Habitat selection and the evolution of polygyny in Bobolinks (*Dolichonyx oryzivorus*). Unpublished Ph.D. dissertation, Univ. California, Davis.

Extirpated

OSPREY
Pandion haliaetus carolinensis (Gmelin)
Family Pandionidae
Order Falconiformes

The Osprey is found worldwide, and until the early 1900's nested in Pennsylvania along the major rivers and lakes. It still migrates through Pennsylvania in spring and autumn, and occasional nonbreeding birds have been observed during the summer. The Osprey in recent years (since World War II) has been strongly affected by the use of persistent pesticides and populations have drastically declined throughout the east coast. However, the Osprey had already vanished from Pennsylvania before these pesticides were developed. Therefore, it is unclear as to what caused the Ospreys to abandon the Commonwealth. A re-introduction program is currently underway to re-establish the species in Pennsylvania. If successful, the program should be encouraged and expanded. Listed on National Audubon Society Species with Special Concerns 1982.

SELECTED REFERENCES:

BENT, A. C. 1937. Life histories of North American birds of prey. Part 1. Bull. U.S. Nat. Mus., 167:1–409.
HICKEY, J. J., and D. W. ANDERSON. 1968. Chlorinated hydrocarbons and egg-shell changes in raptorial and fish-eating birds. Science, 162:271–273.
PETERSON, R. T. 1980. A field guide to the birds. Houghton Mifflin Co., Boston, 384 pp.
POOLE, E. L. 1964. Pennsylvania birds. Livingston Publ. Co., Narberth, Pennsylvania, viii + 94 pp.
REESE, J. G. 1977. Reproductive success of Ospreys in central Chesapeake Bay. Auk, 94:202–221.
TATE, J., and D. J. TATE. 1982. The Blue List for 1982. Amer. Birds, 36:126–135.
TODD, W. E. C. 1940. Birds of western Pennsylvania. Univ. Pittsburgh Press, Pittsburgh, xv + 710 pp.

Extirpated

PEREGRINE FALCON
Falco peregrinus anatum Bonaparte
Family Falconidae
Order Falconiformes

The Peregrine Falcon was once widespread throughout the eastern United States. However, in the last 30 years there has been a drastic decline in the entire area. There have been no confirmed reports of Peregrine Falcons nesting in Pennsylvania since the 1950's. Persistent pesticides were a major factor in the decline of this species. A re-introduction program is currently underway in Pennsylvania, but has had only limited success. This program should be continued and encouraged.

SELECTED REFERENCES:

BENT, A. C. 1938. Life histories of North American birds of prey. Part 2. Bull. U.S. Nat. Mus., 170:1–482.
CADE, T. J., and R. FYFE. 1970. The North American peregrine survey, 1970. Canadian-Field Nat., 84:231–245.
ENDERSON, J. H. 1965. A breeding and migration survey of the Peregrine Falcon. Wilson Bull., 77:327–339.
HICKEY, J. J. (ed.). 1969. Peregrine Falcon populations: their biology and decline. Univ. Wisconsin Press, Madison, xxii + 596 pp.

Osprey (*Pandion haliaetus*). Photograph by A. D. Cruickshank/VIREO.

PETERSON, R. T. 1980. A field guide to the birds. Houghton Mifflin Co., Boston, 384 pp.

POOLE, E. L. 1964. Pennsylvania birds. Livingston Publ. Co., Narberth, Pennsylvania, viii + 94 pp.

RICE, J. N. 1969. The decline of the Peregrine population in Pennsylvania. Pp. 155–163, *in* Peregrine Falcon populations: their biology and decline (J. J. Hickey, ed.), Univ. Wisconsin Press, Madison, xxii + 596 pp.

TODD, W. E. C. 1940. Birds of western Pennsylvania. Univ. Pittsburgh Press, Pittsburgh, xv + 710 pp.

Extirpated

GREATER PRAIRIE CHICKEN
Tympanuchus cupido cupido (Linnaeus)
Family Phasianidae
Order Galliformes

The Greater Prairie Chicken formerly was locally distributed in barren or burnt-over lands on the Pocono Plateau in eastern Pennsylvania. It appears to have been extirpated from the Commonwealth by the early nineteenth century. This race of the Greater Prairie Chicken, known as the Heath Hen, became extinct in 1932.

SELECTED REFERENCES:

BENT, A. C. 1932. Life histories of North American gallinaceous birds. Bull. U.S. Nat. Mus., 162:1–490.

POOLE, E. L. 1964. Pennsylvania birds. Livingston Publ. Co., Narberth, Pennsylvania, viii + 94 pp.

TODD, W. E. C. 1940. Birds of western Pennsylvania. Univ. Pittsburgh Press, Pittsburgh, xv + 710 pp.

Piping Plover (*Charadrius melodus*). Photograph by A. D. Cruickshank/VIREO.

Extirpated

PIPING PLOVER
Charadrius melodus circumcinctus (Ridgway)
Family Charadriidae
Order Charadriiformes

The Piping Plover nested at Presque Isle until the late 1940's or 1950's. The lack of protection of the nesting sites and the subsequent use of the nesting habitats by recreationists resulted in extirpation of this species from the Commonwealth. This species still nests in limited numbers on the Canadian shore of Lake Erie. If the former nesting area at Presque Isle were strictly protected, the Piping Plovers might return. Listed on National Audubon Society Blue List 1982.

SELECTED REFERENCES:

JOHNSGARD, P. A. 1981. The plovers, sandpipers and snipes of the world. Univ. Nebraska Press, Lincoln, xvi + 493 pp.

PETERSON, R. T. 1980. A field guide to the birds. Houghton Mifflin Co., Boston, 384 pp.
POOLE, E. L. 1964. Pennsylvania birds. Livingston Publ. Co., Narberth, Pennsylvania, viii + 94 pp.
TATE, J., and D. J. TATE. 1982. The Blue List for 1982. Amer. Birds, 36:126–135.
TODD, W. E. C. 1940. Birds of western Pennsylvania. Univ. Pittsburgh Press, Pittsburgh, xv + 710 pp.

Extirpated

COMMON TERN
Sterna hirundo hirundo Linnaeus
Family Laridae
Order Charadriiformes

The Common Tern formerly nested at Presque Isle State Park, but it has not been reported as nesting in the area since 1962. The birds were driven out by excessive disturbance from recreationists because of the lack of protection by the Commonwealth of Pennsylvania. If the former nesting area were strictly protected, the Common Tern may return as a nesting species. Listed on National Audubon Society Species with Special Concerns 1982.

Common Tern (*Sterna hirundo*). Photograph by A. D. Cruickshank/VIREO.

SELECTED REFERENCES:

BENT, A. C. 1921. Life histories of North American gulls and terns. Bull. U.S. Nat. Mus., 113:1–345.

PALMER, R. S. 1941. A behavior study of the Common Tern (*Sterna hirundo hirundo* L.). Proc. Boston Soc. Nat. Hist., 42:1–119.

PETERSON, R. T. 1980. A field guide to the birds. Houghton Mifflin Co., Boston, 384 pp.

PINKOWSKI, B. C. 1980. Adaptations of Common Terns nesting on an island reservoir. Prairie Naturalist, 12:111–112.

POOLE, E. L. 1964. Pennsylvania birds. Livingston Publ. Co., Narberth, Pennsylvania, viii + 94 pp.

TATE, J., and D. J. TATE. 1982. The Blue List for 1982. Amer. Birds, 36:126–135.

TODD, W. E. C. 1940. Birds of western Pennsylvania. Univ. Pittsburgh Press, Pittsburgh, xv + 710 pp.

Extirpated

LOGGERHEAD SHRIKE

Lanius ludovicianus migrans Palmer
Family Laniidae
Order Passeriformes

The Loggerhead Shrike is reported to have nested in the northwestern counties of Pennsylvania until 1934. There have been no confirmed nesting reports since then. The species still migrates as well as over-winters in the Commonwealth. It is recommended that a survey be conducted to determine if the species still nests in Pennsylvania. If so, the species should be monitored to determine the limiting factors on its population. Listed on National Audubon Society Blue List 1982.

SELECTED REFERENCES:

BENT, A. C. 1950. Life histories of North American wagtails, shrikes, vireos, and their allies. Bull. U.S. Nat. Mus., 197: 1–411.

BUSBEE, E. L. 1977. The effects of dieldrin on the behavior of young Loggerhead Shrikes. Auk, 94:28–35.

PETERSON, R. T. 1980. A field guide to the birds. Houghton Mifflin Co., Boston, 384 pp.

POOLE, E. L. 1964. Pennsylvania birds. Livingston Publ. Co., Narberth, Pennsylvania, viii + 94 pp.

SMITH, S. M. 1973. An aggressive display and related behavior in the Loggerhead Shrike. Auk, 90:287–298.

TATE, J., and D. J. TATE. 1982. The Blue List for 1982. Amer. Birds, 36:126–135.

TODD, W. E. C. 1940. Birds of western Pennsylvania. Univ. Pittsburgh Press, Pittsburgh, xv + 710 pp.

Lark Sparrow (*Chondestes grammacus*). Photograph by A. D. Cruickshank/VIREO.

Extirpated

DICKCISSEL

Spiza americana (Gmelin)
Family Emberizidae
Order Passeriformes

Prior to 1880, the Dickcissel was a locally common breeder in the Delaware and Susquehanna river valleys and western Pennsylvania. Although a few nests have been reported since then, it currently is unknown* as a breeding bird in Pennsylvania. There are many records of migrants and wintering Dickcissels throughout the Commonwealth. Listed on National Audubon Society Blue List 1982.

SELECTED REFERENCES:

BENT, A. C. 1968. Life histories of North American cardinals, grosbeaks, buntings, towhees, finches, sparrows and allies. Part 1. Bull. U.S. Nat. Mus., 237:1–602.

HARMESON, J. P. 1974. Breeding ecology of the Dickcissel. Auk, 91:348–359.

LONG, C. A., C. F. LONG, J. KNOPS, and D. H. MATULIONIS. 1965. Reproduction in the Dickcissel. Wilson Bull., 77:251–256.

---

* *Note added in proof:* A pair of Dickcissels nested in Clarion County in 1983.

PETERSON, R. T. 1980. A field guide to the birds. Houghton Mifflin Co., Boston, 384 pp.

POOLE, E. L. 1964. Pennsylvania birds. Livingston Publ. Co., Narberth, Pennsylvania, viii + 94 pp.

TATE, J., and D. J. TATE. 1982. The Blue List for 1982. Amer. Birds, 36:126–135.

TODD, W. E. C. 1940. Birds of western Pennsylvania. Univ. Pittsburgh Press, Pittsburgh, xv + 710 pp.

ZIMMERMAN, J. T. 1982. Nesting success of Dickcissels (*Spiza americana*) in preferred and less preferred habitats. Auk, 99: 292–298.

Extirpated

BACHMAN'S SPARROW

Aimophila aestivalis bachmani (Audubon)
Family Emberizidae
Order Passeriformes

The Bachman's Sparrow was once a rare breeder in southwestern Pennsylvania, but no nests have been recorded since 1937. This sparrow is a southern species whose normal range extends to just south of western Pennsylvania. The nesting records from 1909 to 1937 may have been a temporary northward expansion of its range, or it was overlooked prior to 1909 and was withdrawing from Pennsylvania during the ensuing years. Listed on National Audubon Society Blue List 1982.

SELECTED REFERENCES:

BENT, A. C. 1968. Life histories of North American cardinals, grosbeaks, buntings, towhees, finches, sparrows and allies. Part 2. Bull. U.S. Nat. Mus., 237:603–1248.

BROOKS, M. 1938. Bachman's Sparrow in the north-central portion of its range. Wilson Bull., 50:86–109.

PETERSON, R. T. 1980. A field guide to the birds. Houghton Mifflin Co., Boston, 384 pp.

POOLE, E. L. 1964. Pennsylvania birds. Livingston Publ. Co., Narberth, Pennsylvania, viii + 94 pp.

TATE, J., and D. J. TATE. 1982. The Blue List for 1982. Amer. Birds, 36:126–135.

TODD, W. E. C. 1940. Birds of western Pennsylvania. Univ. Pittsburgh Press, Pittsburgh, xv + 710 pp.

Extirpated

LARK SPARROW

Chondestes grammacus grammacus (Say)
Family Emberizidae
Order Passeriformes

The Lark Sparrow was a former rare breeder in southwestern Pennsylvania. There are also recent records from other parts of the Commonwealth–Bedford County and Huntingdon County. Individual sight records are scattered throughout the Commonwealth. The most recent nesting occurred in 1931. Although this species has been seen in Pennsylvania since that time, it is generally recorded during migration, and no new nests have been found.

SELECTED REFERENCES:

BENT, A. C. 1968. Life histories of North American cardinals, grosbeaks, buntings, finches, sparrows, and allies. Part 2. Bull. U.S. Nat. Mus., 237:603–1248.

PETERSON, R. T. 1980. A field guide to the birds. Houghton Mifflin Co., Boston, 384 pp.

POOLE, E. L. 1964. Pennsylvania birds. Livingston Publ. Co., Narberth, Pennsylvania, viii + 94 pp.

TODD, W. E. C. 1940. Birds of western Pennsylvania. Univ. Pittsburgh Press, Pittsburgh, xv + 710 pp.

Extinct

PASSENGER PIGEON

Ectopistes migratorius (Linnaeus)
Family Columbidae
Order Columbiformes

The Passenger Pigeon was formerly an abundant transient and nesting species throughout much of the Commonwealth. The last reports of Passenger Pigeons in Pennsylvania were in 1906. The last living Passenger Pigeon died on September 1, 1914.

SELECTED REFERENCES:

SCHORGER, A. W. 1955. The Passenger Pigeon: its natural history and extinction. Univ. Wisconsin Press, Madison, xiii + 424 pp.

POOLE, E. L. 1964. Pennsylvania birds. Livingston Publ. Co., Narberth, Pennsylvania, viii + 94 pp.

TODD, W. E. C. 1940. Birds of western Pennsylvania. Univ. Pittsburgh Press, Pittsburgh, xv + 710 pp.

CHAPTER 6
MAMMALS

Indiana Bat (*Myotis sodalis*). Photograph by R. W. Barbour.

CHAPTER 6—MAMMALS

edited by

Hugh H. Genoways

Section of Mammals
Carnegie Museum of Natural History
4400 Forbes Ave.
Pittsburgh, PA 15213

Table of Contents

INTRODUCTION

The mammals in Pennsylvania have long been under the management authority of the Pennsylvania Game Commission, but it was not until 1978 that an effort was made to deal with threatened and endangered mammals in the Commonwealth. At this time, Michael J. Puglisi was appointed as Coordinator for the Threatened and Endangered Species Program within the Game Commission. In late February 1979, Mr. Puglisi asked Hugh H. Genoways to chair an informal study group on endangered mammals in Pennsylvania. The immediate concern of this group was to be the development of a list of threatened and endangered species. The current list and the following chapter are outgrowths of the work of this informal study group.

The mammal committee of what eventually would be called the Pennsylvania Biological Survey first met on 25 and 26 May 1979 at the Powdermill Nature Reserve of Carnegie Museum of Natural History. The committee was composed of 11 members from universities, colleges, and museums throughout the Commonwealth. At the first meeting classification categories were discussed and agreed upon, and a preliminary list of endangered, threatened, vulnerable, and status undetermined mammals was drawn up. This list was revised and refined through subsequent correspondence. The preliminary list was presented at a public meeting at the Carnegie Museum of Natural History in March 1981, and to the Game Commission in Harrisburg at a meeting held in May 1981. With consideration of input from both the public and the Game Commission, the final list, presented here, was agreed upon by the committee.

The original list included the black bear (*Ursus americanus*) as vulnerable, but this species is not included in the final list. We believe that both of these decisions are correct. Between our original committee meeting in 1979 and now, a number of actions have been taken by the Game Commission that we believe insures the status of this species in the Commonwealth. The Commission has pursued a vigorous program of research and management for black bears. The hunting of black bears has been restricted to those counties in the Commonwealth having high populations of bears and has been closed in the counties with low densities of bears. Hunters must now obtain a special license to hunt black bears so that the number of hunters can be regulated. All of these were very positive steps in preserving black bear populations in Pennsylvania.

This example helps illustrate an extremely important point concerning this list of species and others in this book. These are not static lists that will be good for years to come but rather these are dynamic lists that must be reviewed and updated on at least a yearly basis. We expect that new species will be added to the list, and some species already on the list will be moved into more and more restrictive categories as we learn more about their biology, and their status within the Commonwealth continues to deteriorate. On the other hand, we expect some species to eventually be removed from the list as we learn more about their biology and management techniques are introduced that reverse current trends.

Three species of marine mammals—harbor seal (*Phoca vitulina*), hooded seal (*Cystophora cristata*), and harbor porpoise, (*Phocoena phocoena*)—have occasionally been sighted in the Delaware River near Philadelphia. However, these species are not in-

cluded in the current list because these are only wandering individuals that do not breed or form permanent populations in the Commonwealth. Although they are not included on a list for Pennsylvania, it must be remembered that these species are completely protected wherever they occur by provisions of the Federal Marine Mammal Act of 1972 and Federal Endangered Species Act of 1973. Three other species, which are included on this list—Indiana bat (*Myotis sodalis*), eastern wolf (*Canis lupus lycaon*), and eastern cougar (*Felis concolor couguar*)—are considered to be endangered under provisions of the Federal Endangered Species Act of 1973. These species would be fully protected when, or if, they occur in Pennsylvania.

I believe there are some groupings of species on this list of mammals that can be recognized. Undoubtedly, the largest group is the large carnivores and artiodactyls. The large carnivores were seen as direct competitors of man, threatening his game and livestock as well as man himself. These species were systematically eliminated as the human population of the Commonwealth expanded. The wapiti, moose, and bison were undoubtedly eliminated from Pennsylvania by over-exploitation by European settlers. It must be pointed out, however, that most of the depletion of species in this group occurred before 1900 and the implementation of game management.

There are six species of bats on the list. We lack summertime data for these species, which would add significantly to our understanding of the status of these species. There is definitely a need for a vigorous program of netting bats during the warm months throughout the Commonwealth. Five taxa of shrews are considered to be Status Undetermined in Pennsylvania. A program of pitfall trapping would add significantly to our understanding of these taxa.

Several of the species are directly tied to aquatic habitats in the Commonwealth and several others occur primarily in moist habitats directly associated with wetlands. Clearly this habitat may be one of the most threatened in Pennsylvania. The major problem faced by all mammalian species in Pennsylvania is habitat degradation and loss. Any future management plan must include acquisition of land that provides a variety of habitats so that we do not lose the diversity of our mammalian fauna.

Hugh H. Genoways, *Section of Mammals, Carnegie Museum of Natural History, 4400 Forbes Ave., Pittsburgh, PA 15213.*

ACKNOWLEDGMENTS

I would like to acknowledge first the involvement of Michael J. Puglisi in the formation of the mammal committee and for his constant work with us as we have completed this project. Frank Dunstan, National Audubon Society, and Clark Shiffer, Fish Commission, along with Mike Puglisi, were instrumental in the formation of the Pennsylvania Biological Survey, which coordinated this overall project.

My job as chairman of this committee would have been impossible without the hard work and dedication of the following scientists who composed the mammal committee: Kenneth Andersen, Gannon University; Harry N. Cunningham, Behrend Campus of Penn State University; Peter L. Dalby, Clarion University; John E. Enders, Keystone Junior College; John S. Hall, Albright College; Gordon L. Kirkland, Jr., Shippensburg University; Joseph F. Merritt, Powdermill Nature Reserve of Car-

negie Museum of Natural History; Duane A. Schlitter, Carnegie Museum of Natural History; Alan Woolf, Southern Illinois University; David A. Zegers, Millersville University. It should be noted that all of these people served on this committee on a completely voluntary basis, giving both their time and money. Thanks are also due to some of the home institutions of the committee members for providing release time so that they could attend meetings.

I would personally like to thank Craig C. Black, formerly Director of the Carnegie Museum of Natural History, for supporting my participation in this work. Much of the distributional data used in this chapter was gathered under a grant from the Landfall Foundation to H. H. Genoways and D. A. Schlitter to study the mammals of Pennsylvania.—Hugh H. Genoways, *Carnegie Museum of Natural History.*

SPECIES ACCOUNTS

Endangered

INDIANA BAT
Myotis sodalis (Miller and G. M. Allen)
Family Vespertilionidae
Order Chiroptera

OTHER NAMES: Social bat, Indiana myotis, pink bat.

DESCRIPTION: The Indiana bat is a medium-sized, dark-colored *Myotis.* The color of the base of the hairs is dark black for over two-thirds of its length, followed by a narrow grayish band, not sharply delimited from the black band of the base. The tips of the hairs may be either dark gray to black or dark brown to light brown. The tips of the hairs are never glossy or burnished. When the fur is viewed in yellow light the hairs may give an illusion of being tinted dark purple. The foot is somewhat small and the foot hairs are present but inconspicuous. The calcar, which is the cartilage support to the edge of the interfemoral membrane, is strongly keeled. The keel is best seen on a fresh specimen by shining a strong light through the stretched out membrane between the foot and the tail. Measurements for the Indiana bat are: total length 91–144 mm and tail 23–44 mm.

Myotis sodalis is most easily confused with *Myotis lucifugus,* the little brown bat. It is distinguished from *M. lucifugus* by its dark, non-glossy fur, which in *M. lucifugus* is much darker and more sharply delimited from the color of the tip. *Myotis lucifugus* has a larger foot, with long, conspicuous hairs, and

no keel on the calcar. Males and females are the same size.

RANGE: Since its description in 1928, the range of the Indiana bat has been recorded in the midwest and eastern United States from the western edge of the Ozark region in Oklahoma to central Vermont, to southern Wisconsin, and as far south as northern Florida. Distribution seems to be associated with major cavernous limestone areas and areas just north of cave regions (Hall, 1962).

Information on the distribution and abundance of the Indiana bat in Pennsylvania is found in several papers by Charles E. Mohr (1932*a,* 1932*b,* 1933, 1939, and 1945) and in Hall (1962, 1979*a*). These studies report the species at 13 localities in nine counties as follows: Westmoreland, Mifflin, Centre, Franklin, Fayette, Huntingdon, Bedford, Fulton, and Blair. All of these localities are represented by specimens in museum collections except the Blair County and Fulton County sites (Hall, 1979*a*). All records for the Indiana bat in Pennsylvania are from caves or abandoned mine tunnels.

Mohr (1932*b*) recorded the estimated colony sizes of *Myotis sodalis* in various caves. The largest group was 2,000 in a cave in Centre County. Other colonies numbered 500 or less. In 1965 Hall (1979*a*) estimated 1,000 Indiana bats in a mine in Blair County. Thus, an estimate of the total known past populations of *Myotis sodalis* in Pennsylvania would be about 5,000 individuals.

During the winters of 1978–1979 and 1979–1980,

INDIANA BAT (*Myotis sodalis*)

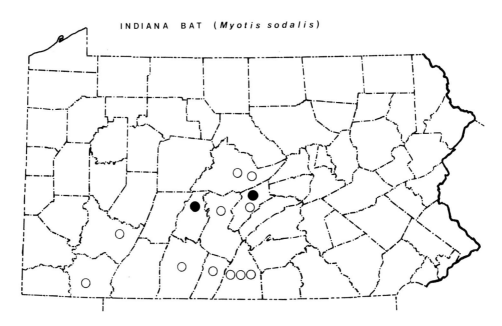

John S. Hall, Albright College, conducted a survey of the Indiana bat in Pennsylvania (Hall, 1979*a*, 1979*b*). All localities known for the species were investigated as well as other likely caves and mine tunnels. That survey resulted in finding only one remaining winter colony of 150 individuals in the mine tunnel in Blair County and the sighting of one individual in a cave in Mifflin County (closed circles

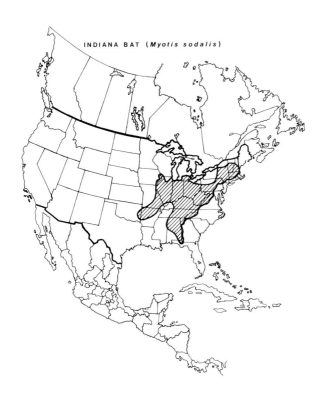

INDIANA BAT (*Myotis sodalis*)

on accompanying map; other localities where the species has been recorded in the past but were not seen in this recent survey are represented by open circles). The species had disappeared from all other known past localities and was not found in any other seemingly favorable hibernating site.

The Indiana bat has been greatly reduced in numbers in Pennsylvania from the 1930's to the 1970's and is nearly extinct in the Commonwealth. In 1980, gates were placed over the entrances to the mine in Blair County to prevent further disturbance to this last remaining colony. This mine and the bats are now under the protection of the Department of Environmental Resources and the Pennsylvania Game Commission.

HABITAT: The Indiana bat hibernates in caves and abandoned mine tunnels during the late autumn, winter, and early spring. During the summer the bats are dispersed away from the caves, presumably roosting in trees (Humphrey et al., 1977). This species has not been found during the summer months in Pennsylvania. The only records in the Commonwealth are for winter hibernating colonies. The type of hibernaculum appears to be medium to large caves and mine tunnels. Very small caves are not suitable for the Indiana bat.

Within the cave the most critical factor involved in the selection of the hibernation site is temperature. The temperature zone in a cave selected by the Indiana bat is between 4° and 6°C in mid-winter. This cold zone has to be fairly close to an entrance or in a cave where there are multiple entrances creating a strong, cold draft of air through the cave (Hall, 1962).

In Pennsylvania the limestone with the larger caves extends from the southwest corner through the central and southern portions of the Commonwealth. The distribution of the species coincides with this area of limestone.

The summer habitat of the species is poorly known throughout its total range. Most findings of the Indiana bat in the summer in the midwest have been associated with a riverine habitat (Hall, 1962; Mumford and Cope, 1958). Easterla and Watkins (1969) reported finding a small nursery colony in Missouri by mist-netting over a small pond and along a stream in a mature woodland.

LIFE HISTORY AND ECOLOGY: The Indiana bat is an insect eater as are all bats in Pennsylvania. The bat enters caves and mine tunnels to hibernate starting in mid-September. All the bats seem to be in hibernation by the first of November. During hibernation the Indiana bat forms dense clusters comprising about 250 bats per square foot. The clustering behavior is distinctive for the species. The cluster seems to form as a radiating group on rough ceilings or sidewalls. The type of clustering is the best way to distinguish the species from the little brown bat (*Myotis lucifugus*), which forms semidense clusters in rows along projecting ledges on sidewalls or cracks in the ceiling. The little brown bat cannot cluster on the smooth ceiling surfaces, but must have its claws hooked over a definite projection (Hall, 1962).

The Indiana bat begins to leave hibernation in mid-March and all individuals are out around the first of May. The summer habitat and behavior is unknown in Pennsylvania.

BASIS OF STATUS CLASSIFICATION: The habit of dense aggregation has been carried to a high degree in *Myotis sodalis*. The species is found in only a few caves but in high population numbers. This behavior makes the species vulnerable to serious decline if only a few colonies are disturbed (Hall, 1962). Because of this aggregation and disturbance to the critical hibernating caves by spelunkers and commercialization, *Myotis sodalis* is listed as endangered by the U.S. Fish and Wildlife Service.

Serious decline of the species has taken place throughout its entire range between the 1930's and 1970's. Humphrey (1978) estimated a 28% reduc-

tion in known populations of the species from 1960 to 1975. Only one colony of 150 individuals is known to remain in Pennsylvania as mentioned previously. *Myotis sodalis* is very sensitive to disturbance while in hibernation. The bats will arouse from torpidity when disturbed by light, noise or temperature changes.

RECOMMENDATIONS: The only way to protect a colony of Indiana bats is to prohibit all human traffic into the winter caves and mines. The mine in Blair County has been gated and should be maintained in good condition. A survey trip every two years is recommended to monitor the colony.

Further searching for the Indiana bat in Pennsylvania is recommended. The most likely new finds would be in abandoned mine tunnels. Also, mist-netting along streams and at cave entrances might result in finding additional sites for the species.

SELECTED REFERENCES:

EASTERLA, D. A., and L. C. WATKINS. 1969. Pregnant *Myotis sodalis* in northwestern Missouri. J. Mamm., 50:372–373.
HALL, E. R. 1981. The mammals of North America. John Wiley & Sons, New York, 1:xv + 1–600 + 90.
HALL, J. S. 1962. A life history and taxonomic study of the Indiana bat, *Myotis sodalis.* Reading Public Museum and Art Gallery, 12:1–68.
———. 1979a. Status of the endangered Indiana bat, *Myotis sodalis,* in Pennsylvania. Unpublished report to the Pennsylvania Game Commission.
———. 1979b. Status of the endangered Indiana bat, *Myotis sodalis,* in Pennsylvania. Report #2. Unpublished report to the Pennsylvania Game Commission.
HUMPHREY, S. R. 1978. Status, winter habitat, and management of the endangered Indiana bat, *Myotis sodalis.* Florida Sci., 41:65–76.
HUMPHREY, S. R., A. R. RICHTER, and J. B. COPE. 1977. Summer habitat and ecology of the endangered Indiana bat, *Myotis sodalis.* J. Mamm., 58:334–346.
MOHR, C. E. 1932a. *Myotis subulatus leibii* and *Myotis sodalis* in Pennsylvania. J. Mamm., 13:160–161.
———. 1932b. The seasonal distribution of bats in Pennsylvania. Proc. Pennsylvania Acad. Sci., 6:1–6.
———. 1933. Pennsylvania bats of the genus *Myotis.* Proc. Pennsylvania Acad. Sci., 7:39–43.
———. 1939. Bat tagging in Pennsylvania. Proc. Pennsylvania Acad. Sci., 13:43–45.
———. 1945. Sex ratios of bats in Pennsylvania. Proc. Pennsylvania Acad. Sci., 19:65–69.
MUMFORD, R. E., and J. B. COPE. 1958. Summer records of *Myotis sodalis* in Indiana. J. Mamm., 39:586–587.
THOMSON, C. E. 1982. *Myotis sodalis.* Mammalian Species, 163:1–5.

PREPARED BY: John S. Hall, *Department of Biology, Albright College, Reading, PA 19604.*

Small-footed Myotis (*Myotis leibii*). Photograph by R. W. Barbour.

Threatened

SMALL-FOOTED BAT
Myotis leibii (Audubon and Bachman)
Family Vespertilionidae
Order Chiroptera

OTHER NAMES: Small-footed myotis, least brown bat.

DESCRIPTION: Myotis leibii is a small bat with a tiny foot which measures less than 8 mm. The forearm is shorter than those of other *Myotis*, 30–36 mm. The ears and face are black, giving a definite black facial mask appearance. The hair has a black basal band, followed by a glossy brown tip. The small size, black face, small foot, and short forearms distinguish this species from the other three species of *Myotis* in Pennsylvania.

RANGE: Three subspecies of *Myotis leibii* are recognized. Two forms are found throughout the western half of the United States from Saskatchewan, Alberta, and British Columbia in Canada south to Chihuahua in Mexico. In the East the subspecies *M. leibii leibii* ranges from New England southward to Georgia. In the eastern United States the small-footed bat has always been a rare mammal. Most records are for hibernating individuals, with only an occasional summer record (Barbour and Davis, 1969).

Published information on the distribution and abundance of *M. leibii* in Pennsylvania is found in several papers by Charles E. Mohr (1932a, 1932b, 1933, 1939, 1942, 1945). Mohr found the species in seven caves in four counties (open circles on accompanying map). Mohr banded and released over 170 individual *M. leibii*. Most of them were found in four caves in Centre and Mifflin counties. Mohr (1945) reported that he had examined 363 *M. leibii* over a 14 year period in Pennsylvania. Of this number, 151 were found in Stover Cave, Centre County. The numbers of *M. leibii* found by Mohr in central Pennsylvania is the largest seen anywhere in the eastern United States. Records of *M. leibii* during summer months are rare. One specimen was taken

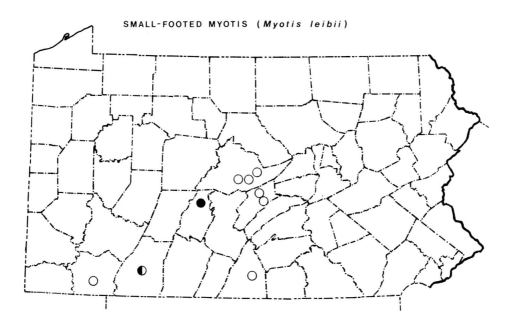

SMALL-FOOTED MYOTIS (*Myotis leibii*)

on Laurel Ridge, Westmoreland County, on 1 July 1959 (Doutt et al., 1967; half-closed circle on accompanying map).

Recent investigations indicate that *M. leibii* has nearly disappeared from previously known localities. Hall (1968) found two individuals hibernating in Aitkin Cave, Mifflin County, during the winter of 1964–1965.

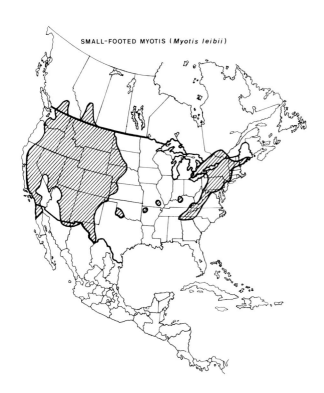

SMALL-FOOTED MYOTIS (*Myotis leibii*)

Hall (1979*a*, 1979*b*) reports that during a survey of hibernating bat populations in 1978 and 1979, *M. leibii* was not seen in any of the caves where Mohr had found them between 1932 and 1944. The only *M. leibii* seen in the survey by Hall were 10 individuals mist-netted at the entrance of a mine tunnel in Blair County (closed circle on accompanying map) on 27 April 1979.

The species may be more abundant than suspected from observation of hibernating individuals. Barbour and Davis (1969) reported many individuals were mist-netted at the entrance of a Kentucky Cave during the summer of 1963. The best way to study the species is by mist-netting at cave entrances during the warm months of the year. Mist-netting could be productive between April and October.

HABITAT: Myotis leibii hibernates in caves and mine tunnels in Pennsylvania. The species is usually found close to entrances where the temperature is just above freezing. Mohr (1932) reported that the caves where he found most individuals were located in heavy hemlock forests in the foothills of mountains which rise to 2,000 feet. The species has been found hibernating under rocks in the cave floor (Barbour and Davis, 1969).

LIFE HISTORY AND ECOLOGY: Little is known of the ecology of the small-footed bat. This species appears to enter hibernation later than other bats and may move around during the winter months. This bat is solitary, never forming clusters, but several individuals may be in close proximity in the same cave. The largest cave colonies of 100–120 individuals were seen by Mohr in two caves in Mifflin County in the 1930's.

The summer habits of *M. leibii* in Pennsylvania are unknown. In the western United States small colonies have been seen in buildings (Barbour and Davis, 1969). This species has often been captured during mist-netting at cave entrances during late summer and early autumn (Barbour and Davis, 1969). Hall (1979*b*) mist-netted 10 individuals at a mine tunnel entrance in Blair County, Pennsylvania, on 27 April 1979.

BASIS OF STATUS CLASSIFICATION: Myotis leibii has always been a rare bat in Pennsylvania. However, there has been a severe reduction in numbers of individuals seen in caves from the survey by Mohr in the 1930's and the survey by Hall in 1978 and 1979 as mentioned previously. This reduction in hibernating individuals is serious enough to consider the species as threatened.

RECOMMENDATIONS: Hall (1979*a*, 1979*b*) found *Myotis leibii* only at the mine tunnel in Blair County. This mine also contains the only known colony of the endangered Indiana bat. The mine has been gated and closed to human traffic, and the gates should be maintained in good condition.

Further study of the species in Pennsylvania should be conducted by continuing to search additional caves and mine tunnels for hibernating colonies, and by mist-netting caves and mine entrances during the late summer and autumn.

SELECTED REFERENCES:

BARBOUR, R. W., and W. H. DAVIS. 1969. Bats of America. Univ. Press Kentucky, Lexington, 286 pp.

DOUTT, J. K., C. A. HEPPENSTALL, and J. E. GUILDAY. 1967. Mammals of Pennsylvania. Pennsylvania Game Comm., Harrisburg, 281 pp.

HALL, J. S., and F. J. BRENNER. 1968. Summer netting of bats at a cave in Pennsylvania. J. Mamm., 49:779–781.

———. 1979*a*. Status of the endangered Indiana bat, *Myotis sodalis,* in Pennsylvania. Unpublished report to the Pennsylvania Game Commission.

———. 1979*b*. Status of the endangered Indiana bat, *Myotis sodalis,* in Pennsylvania. Report #2. Unpublished report to the Pennsylvania Game Commission.

MOHR, C. E. 1932*a*. *Myotis subulatus leibii* and *Myotis sodalis* in Pennsylvania. J. Mamm., 13:160–161.

———. 1932*b*. The seasonal distribution of bats in Pennsylvania. Proc. Pennsylvania Acad. Sci., 6:1–6.

———. 1933. Pennsylvania bats of the genus *Myotis.* Proc. Pennsylvania Acad. Sci., 7:39–43.

———. 1939. Bat tagging in Pennsylvania. Proc. Pennsylvania Acad. Sci., 13:43–45.

———. 1942. Bat tagging in Pennsylvania turnpike tunnels. J. Mamm., 23:375–379.

———. 1945. Sex ratios of bats in Pennsylvania. Proc. Pennsylvania Acad. Sci., 19:65–69.

PREPARED BY: John S. Hall, *Department of Biology, Albright College, Reading, PA 19604.*

Threatened

EASTERN WOODRAT
Neotoma floridana (Ord)
Family Cricetidae
Order Rodentia

OTHER NAMES: Allegheny woodrat, cave rat, cliff rat, woodrat, trade rat.

DESCRIPTION: The Allegheny woodrat is a rather large woodrat, head and body averaging about 220 mm and tail averaging about 180 mm. The pelage is a buffy gray above, but slightly darker in the middle of the back. The sides are buffy and the underparts and paws are white. The head is gray with long whiskers. The tail is furry and slightly bicolored. The ears are large and somewhat naked.

The only other species that the woodrat might be confused with in Pennsylvania is the Norway rat, which is browner in color and has a naked tail.

RANGE: Neotoma floridana magister is distributed along the Appalachian Mountains from northern Alabama through central Tennessee, Kentucky, southern Ohio, West Virginia, western Virginia, Pennsylvania and into southern New York, northern New Jersey and western Connecticut.

The population of woodrats in the northeastern area from Tennessee north along the Appalachian Mountain system into Connecticut was considered a separate species until Schwartz and Odum (1957) relegated *Neotoma magister* to subspecific status under *N. floridana,* the eastern woodrat.

During the mammal survey of Pennsylvania under the Pittman-Robertson Project, the Allegheny woodrat was found abundantly along the Appalachian Mountains, both north and south of the Great Valley (Grimm and Whitebread, 1952; Roslund, 1951; Richmond and Roslund, 1949; Grimm and Roberts, 1950; Gifford and Whitebread, 1951; Roberts and Early, 1952).

The distribution of the woodrat in Pennsylvania

Eastern Woodrat (*Neotoma floridana*). Photograph by J. S. Hall.

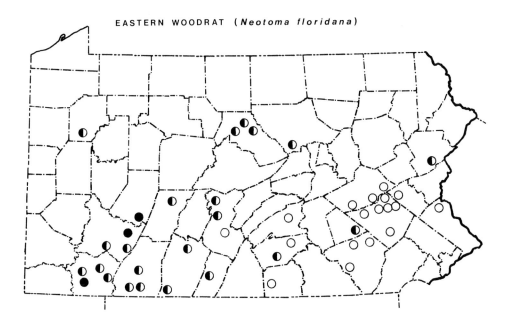

EASTERN WOODRAT (*Neotoma floridana*)

appears to be concentrated in the southeast in Berks, Schuylkill, Lehigh, and Lancaster counties and in the southwest in Fayette and Westmoreland counties. Other scattered sites are found between these two major areas. The population of woodrats in Pennsylvania appeared to be healthy during the 1940's and early 1950's according to the mammal survey of the Pittman-Robertson Project (Fig. 2).

During 1978 and 1979, John S. Hall, Albright College, conducted a survey of bat populations in caves throughout the Commonwealth for the Pennsylvania Game Commission. During that survey, Hall (personal communication) noted a general absence of woodrat signs in caves in the central and southeastern part of the Commonwealth. Definite presence of the woodrat could only be found in the southwest in Fayette, Westmoreland, and Indiana counties (closed circles on accompanying map). The woodrat was definitely gone from known localities in Berks, Schuylkill, Lehigh, Huntingdon, and Lancaster counties in 1978–1979 according to Hall (on the accompanying map open circles represent sites where the species was recorded in the past but was not found in 1978–1979; the half-closed circles represent known localities of occurrence that were not visited in the recent survey).

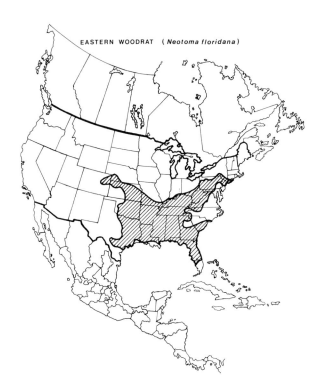

EASTERN WOODRAT (*Neotoma floridana*)

HABITAT: The Allegheny woodrat typically lives in limestone caves or broken rock habitat such as cliff faces, boulder piles, or coarse talus (Poole, 1940; Doutt et al., 1967). Such habitat is found throughout the limestone areas of the Commonwealth, cliff faces along the Appalachian Mountains, and specifically at water gaps where cliff faces and boulder piles are usually abundant.

LIFE HISTORY AND ECOLOGY: The nest of the

Allegheny woodrat is usually found near an entrance on a dry cave floor, on narrow ledges along cave passages, or in inaccessible crevices of large rocks. The nest is of the shredded bast fibers of several types of trees, with an outside diameter of about 460 mm and a cavity about 120 mm in diameter (Poole, 1940).

A large variety of plants are used as food by this species. Food material is gathered outside the cave at night and is stored in piles near the nest. The rats may be active during the daytime inside the cave but are strictly nocturnal outside the cave.

Near the nest the rats also make piles of debris gathered during foraging. This debris includes most anything the rat encounters, including human trash, sticks, stones, and other natural debris. The function of this behavior is unknown.

Details of the reproductive cycle are poorly known. Poole (1940) states that two or three litters of two to four young are raised each year. The young appear to be born between mid-March and September. This woodrat adjusts well to captivity.

BASIS OF STATUS CLASSIFICATION: According to field observations made by John S. Hall during 1978 and 1979, the Allegheny woodrat seems to be absent from localities in eastern Pennsylvania, where it was abundant in the 1930's to 1940's. Hall could find no woodrats in all known past localities in Berks, Schuylkill, Lancaster, Bucks, Lehigh, Cumberland, Adams, Perry, and Huntingdon counties. This area includes the entire past known range of the species in eastern Pennsylvania (Fig. 2).

Definite signs of woodrat habitation were found in Hall's survey in 1978–1979 only in Fayette, Westmoreland, and Indiana counties. Other localities in western and north-central areas of the state were not investigated by Hall.

RECOMMENDATION: Populations of the woodrat seem to be decreasing drastically in Pennsylvania, especially in the eastern part of the Commonwealth. Extensive studies need to be done concerning the present status and distribution of woodrat populations in Pennsylvania. Information concerning ecological requirements, especially species of plants required for food and nest building, needs to be obtained for the species.

With the identification of the status of present populations and ecological requirements, perhaps some measures could be undertaken to prevent further declines in certain areas of the Commonwealth.

SELECTED REFERENCES:

Doutt, J. K., C. A. Heppenstall, and J. E. Guilday. 1967. Mammals of Pennsylvania. Pennsylvania Game Comm., Harrisburg, 281 pp.

Gifford, C. L., and R. Whitebread. 1951. Mammal survey of south central Pennsylvania. Final Report Pittman-Robertson Project 38-R. Pennsylvania Game Comm., Harrisburg, 75 pp.

Grimm, W. C., and H. A. Roberts. 1950. Mammal survey of southwestern Pennsylvania. Final Report Pittman-Robertson Project 24-R. Pennsylvania Game Comm., Harrisburg, 99 pp.

Grimm, W. C., and R. Whitebread. 1952. Mammal survey of northeastern Pennsylvania. Final Report Pittman-Robertson Project 42-R. Pennsylvania Game Comm., Harrisburg, 82 pp.

Poole, E. L. 1940. A life history sketch of the Allegheny woodrat. J. Mamm., 21:249–270.

Richmond, N. D., and H. R. Roslund. 1949. Mammal survey of northwestern Pennsylvania. Final Report Pittman-Robertson Project 20-R. Pennsylvania Game Comm., Harrisburg, 67 pp.

Roberts, H. A., and R. C. Early. 1952. Mammal survey of southeastern Pennsylvania. Final Report Pittman-Robertson Project 43-R. Pennsylvania Game Comm., Harrisburg, 70 pp.

Roslund, H. R. 1951. Mammal survey of north central Pennsylvania. Final Report Pittman-Robertson Project 37-R. Pennsylvania Game Comm., Harrisburg, 55 pp.

Schwartz, A., and E. P. Odum. 1957. The woodrats of the eastern United States. J. Mamm., 38:197–205.

PREPARED BY: John S. Hall, *Department of Biology, Albright College, Reading, PA 19604.*

Vulnerable

KEEN'S LITTLE BROWN BAT
Myotis keenii (Merriam)
Family Vespertilionidae
Order Chiroptera

OTHER NAMES: Say's bat, Trouessart's bat, eastern long-eared bat, Acadian bat.

DESCRIPTION: Keen's little brown bat is a medium-sized *Myotis* with long ears (17–19 mm) and a narrow pointed tragus. This species is most easily confused with *M. lucifugus* and *M. sodalis,* which have shorter ears (14–16 mm). Keen's little brown bat is never found in large groups or clusters as these other two species of *Myotis.*

RANGE: Myotis keenii is distributed over most of the eastern United States from Manitoba across southern Canada and Newfoundland south to Florida and west to Wyoming. In the West and North-

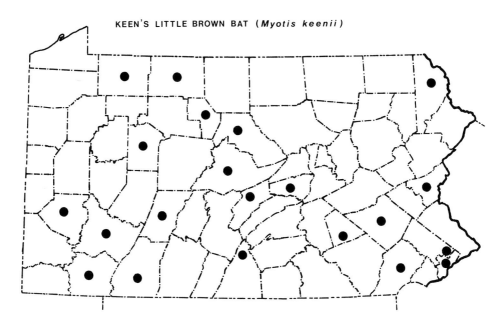

KEEN'S LITTLE BROWN BAT (*Myotis keenii*)

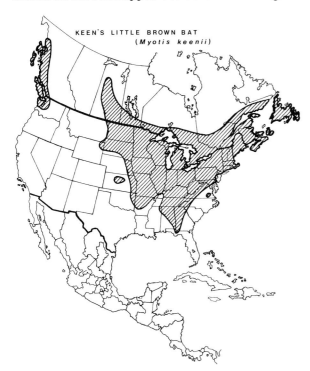

KEEN'S LITTLE BROWN BAT
(*Myotis keenii*)

west the species is found from Alaska south along the coast to Puget Sound, Washington.

Keen's little brown bat is most likely found throughout the Commonwealth of Pennsylvania. Counties with localities for which specimens of the species have been examined or reported in the literature are indicated on the accompanying map. This species has never been found in large numbers and its distribution appears to be local and irregular.

HABITAT: Myotis keenii is widely distributed throughout the eastern United States but is mainly a northern species. Keen's bat is most often encountered in mines or caves while hibernating, in eastern Canada and northeastern United States, from Nebraska to Vermont (Barbour and Davis, 1969).

Maternity groups have been encountered occasionally during the summer in trees and buildings, and number less than 30 individuals in a colony (Mumford and Cope, 1964; Brandon, 1961; Barbour and Davis, 1969; Doutt et al., 1967). Keen's little brown bat has often been captured in larger numbers during mist-netting of cave entrances during the summer and early autumn (Poole, 1932; Hall and Brenner, 1968), even though only a few individuals can be found roosting in the caves in summer or in hibernation during the winter.

During a study of bat populations in Pennsylvania in the 1930's, Mohr (1932, 1945) found *M. keenii* hibernating in only 10 caves, with no more than a half dozen individuals in each cave. However, Mohr reported that Keen's little brown bat was very common during the summer months, when he took 141 specimens in nets at a cave entrance in Berks County, during August and September.

Hall and Brenner (1968) mist-netted a cave in Mifflin County on 17 nights during the summers of 1964 and 1965. Of 1,233 bats netted, 173 were *M. keenii,* and the others were *Myotis lucifugus,* the common little brown bat. Hall (1979) reported that during a search of 16 caves and mines during the winter of 1978–1979, Keen's little brown bat was found in only two of the caves with only three individuals observed. There appears to be a reduction in the distribution and numbers found during hibernation from Mohr's studies in the 1930's to Hall's survey in 1978–1979.

LIFE HISTORY AND ECOLOGY: The life history of Keen's little brown bat is similar to the other cave bats in Pennsylvania. They are insect feeders, hibernate in caves and mine tunnels from October to March or April, have young during early summer in trees or buildings, and return to caves in the autumn.

During hibernation this species is solitary and often crawls into small cracks, deep holes, or behind rocks, making them difficult to find. Thus the species may be more abundant than we realize from visible individuals.

BASIS OF STATUS CLASSIFICATION: As mentioned above, Hall found only three individual *M. keenii* in caves during a survey of winter bat populations throughout the Commonwealth. These data seem to warrant a vulnerable classification. However, the species seems to be abundant during the summer and early autumn as indicated from mist-netting studies as stated above.

RECOMMENDATIONS: Further study needs to be done on the abundance of Keen's little brown bat in Pennsylvania. Mist-netting studies seem to be a productive method of obtaining data on distribution and abundance. Continued studies of the species may indicate that a classification is not warranted.

SELECTED REFERENCES:

BARBOUR, R. W., and W. H. DAVIS. 1969. Bats of America. Univ. Press Kentucky, Lexington, 286 pp.
BRANDON, R. A. 1961. Observations of young Keen's bats. J. Mamm., 42:400–401.
DOUTT, J. K., C. A. HEPPENSTALL, and J. E. GUILDAY. 1967. Mammals of Pennsylvania. Pennsylvania Game Comm., Harrisburg, 281 pp.
FITCH, J. H., and K. A. SHUMP, JR. 1979. *Myotis keenii.* Mammalian Species, 121:1–3.
HALL, E. R. 1981. The mammals of North America. John Wiley & Sons, New York, 1:xv + 1–600 + 90.
HALL, J. S., and F. J. BRENNER. 1968. Summer netting of bats at a cave in Pennsylvania. J. Mamm., 49:779–781.
———. 1979. Status of the endangered Indiana bat, *Myotis sodalis,* in Pennsylvania. Unpublished report to the Pennsylvania Game Commission.
MOHR, C. E. 1932. The seasonal distribution of bats in Pennsylvania. Proc. Pennsylvania Acad. Sci., 6:1–6.
———. 1945. Sex ratios of bats in Pennsylvania. Proc. Pennsylvania Acad. Sci., 19:65–69.
MUMFORD, R. E., and J. B. COPE. 1974. Distribution and status of the Chiroptera of Indiana. Amer. Midland Nat., 72:473–489.
POOLE, E. L. 1932. A survey of mammals of Berks County, Pennsylvania. Reading Public Mus. and Art Gallery Bull., 13:1–74.

PREPARED BY: John S. Hall, *Department of Biology, Albright College, Reading, PA 19604.*

Vulnerable

SNOWSHOE HARE
Lepus americanus Erxleben
Family Leporidae
Order Lagomorpha

OTHER NAMES: Snowshoe rabbit, varying hare, gray rabbit, white rabbit, big brown rabbit, brown jackrabbit, bush rabbit, swamp jackrabbit (Godin, 1977).

DESCRIPTION: This is the only species of hare native to Pennsylvania. The females are slightly larger than males (Godin, 1977). Measurements, in mm, are 473–520, total length; 40–61, tail; 130–147, hind foot; 68–78, ear; 1.5–1.6 kg in weight (Doutt et al., 1966). The fine-haired pelage is dense and soft. From November to March the snowshoe hare is white except for the terminal outer third of the ear which is black; the legs and occasionally the head retain some brown in Pennsylvania specimens (Doutt et al., 1966). This color change is due to the white-tipped guard hairs which, when parted, reveal their darker bases. As spring approaches, these hairs are replaced with others that are tipped with an ochraceous or yellowish-brown washed with black, darkest along the back and rump. The chin, throat, and abdomen usually are bright buffy to roan in color. The large hind feet, with long digits that can be widely separated, are particularly well furred in the winter, thus aiding in insulation and forming the snowshoe-like footprints characteristic of this species. The skull differs from the cottontails (*Sylvilagus floridanus* and *S. transitionalis*) by its larger size and the presence of flared-out postorbital processes which are not fused at their posterior tips to the frontals (Burt, 1957). Furthermore, in *Lepus* the interparietal is fused with the parietals whereas there is no fusion evidenced on this portion of the skull in *Sylvilagus* (Hall, 1981).

RANGE: This species occurs in woodlands extend-

Snowshoe Hare (*Lepus americanus*). Photograph by R. W. Barbour.

ing from Alaska to Newfoundland, ranging southward to the northern border of the United States, and extending south in the Rocky Mountains to New Mexico, the Sierra Nevada Mountains of California, and in the east, the Appalachian Mountains to eastern Tennessee and western North Carolina (Hall, 1981). Before Pennsylvania was logged, the snowshoe hare was found from Pymatuning in the west, across the northern half of the Commonwealth to the Pocono Mountain counties of Wayne and Pike. The hares extended south along the mountains in lessening numbers to Centre and Mifflin counties (Doutt et al., 1966). The present range of the hare is quite restricted, as indicated by the findings of the Pennsylania Mammal Survey, published in six separate reports from 1946–1956.

In an effort to slow or stop its retreat in the Commonwealth, the Pennsylvania Game Commission from time to time has imported hares from New Brunswick, releasing them in areas where they once occurred. During the winters of 1975–1976 to 1979–1980, for example, 4,677 hares were released in various counties with suitable habitat. The Game Commission has not acquired additional hares up to the date of publication. A number of sportsmen's organizations also purchase and release hares, although no effort was made to determine the numbers involved. Restocking during the 1920's of hares

(from Maine) by the Game Commission is reported in several of the Pennsylvania Mammal Survey reports. Interestingly, the native snowshoe hare is assigned to the subspecies *L. americanus virginianus* Harlan, whereas the imported New Brunswick hares are most likely *L. a. americanus* Erxleben (Hall, 1981).

HABITAT: The favored habitat in Pennsylvania, according to Doutt et al. (1966), is cool, shrubby bogs, swamplands, and other areas heavily thickened with rhododendron, spruce, hemlock, willow, alders, or other brushy cover. During the summer, the snowshoe hare subsists on a variety of grasses and forbs. In the winter, it browses on the buds, twigs, and bark of many dormant woody plants. The leaves of rhododendron and laurel are consumed, as well as are the needles of hemlock and spruce when other browse is scarce. Unfortunately for the hares, white-tailed deer have increased in numbers, and undoubtedly compete for some of the same food resources (Bookhout, 1965), stripping away protective cover at the same time.

LIFE HISTORY AND ECOLOGY: For an animal so widely distributed, there are few home range studies. Adams (1959), in his Montana study, determined the home range of males and females to be 10 ha and 7.6 ha, respectively. O'Farrell (1965)

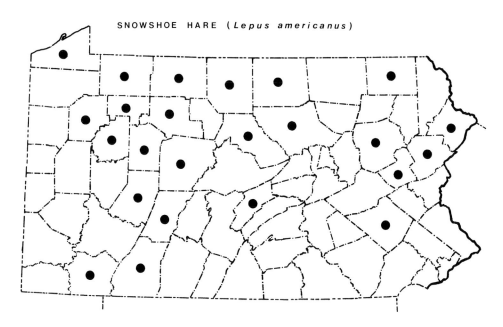

SNOWSHOE HARE (*Lepus americanus*)

calculated a home range of about 5.6 ha for both sexes in an Alaskan study, and Rongstad and Tester (1971) determined a range of 7.2–12.8 ha for two females in Minnesota. They usually make definite beaten runways, most notably in swamps during the winter. Snowshoe hares do not normally dig or use abandoned dens or holes as do cottontails. A simple form in a protected spot is used regularly throughout

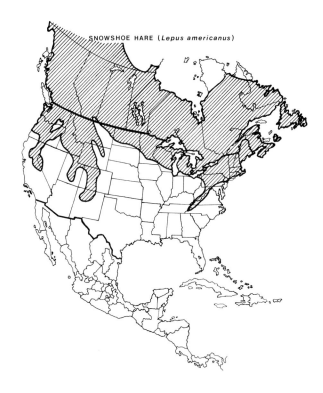

SNOWSHOE HARE (*Lepus americanus*)

the year. They are most active from dusk to dawn (Burt, 1957; Godin, 1977).

This species is known to fluctuate tremendously in numbers over a 10–11 year period. They may increase from one per square mile to several hundred, at which time there is likely to be a dramatic decline in numbers (Keith, 1963). Such fluctuations are unknown in Pennsylvania, perhaps because extensive tracts of prime habitat have rarely existed here. While only a guess, a peak density of several dozen snowshoe hares per square mile of prime habitat might be expected in Pennsylvania.

While rather social much of the year, during the breeding season, the males and pregnant females display some antagonism towards each other. It is likely that territoriality is displayed at such times (Burt, 1957; Doutt et al., 1966; Godin, 1977).

Breeding in this promiscuous species begins in early spring (March, April) and continues throughout the summer, resulting in the production of 2–3 litters. There is a postpartum estrus, and the gestation period averages 36–37 days (Severaid, 1942, 1945). The first litter of the year tends to be the smallest, with 3–4 young normal for a summer litter (Bookhout, 1965; Rowan and Keith, 1956; Severaid, 1942, 1945). The precocial young are able to walk and hop when one day old (Rongstad and Tester, 1971). The young stay hidden and apart during the day, and are not visited by the mother, who stays some distance away. During the early evening, the doe and young meet, whereupon she nurses the young for the single 5–10 minute period she spends with them each day. The young are weaned at approximately 4 weeks of age (Severaid, 1942). The hares do not become sexually mature until the following year (Keith and Meslow, 1967).

BASIS OF STATUS CLASSIFICATION: The snowshoe hare is known from approximately one-third of Pennsylvania's counties, based upon data compiled by the Carnegie Museum of Natural History. Realistically, the species' distribution today probably includes fewer counties. More importantly, the populations of snowshoe hares are generally small and widely dispersed. The maturation of the woodlands and the relatively high numbers of white-tailed deer have reduced both the dense cover and browse that the hares require. The effect on native populations of numerous snowshoe hare introductions, particularly those including other subspecies, is unknown. The hunting season for snowshoe hares, while short and allowing for only four individuals per season, may need to be reexamined to reflect regional differences in hare densities and management practices.

RECOMMENDATIONS: The concerns mentioned above can be substantially alleviated if the following suggestions receive appropriate attention.

1. An updated county by county census of the species is needed to determine those counties which have viable populations.
2. Future introductions of snowshoe hares should be discouraged because:
   a. They are possibly destroying the biological integrity (genome) of the native populations, particularly because most introductions represent another subspecies. Biosystematic and ecological studies on the animals would do much to clarify the matter.
   b. There is the potential danger of introducing diseases and/or parasites to native hares.
   c. Introductions are often marked for failure unless there is a concomitant effort to improve habitat and to undertake an active research program into the dynamics of introductions with the species involved.
3. Develop and implement a habitat improvement plan for snowshoe hares. It may be designed to sustain stable populations in some counties, while improving numbers in counties where hares are few or have been eliminated altogether.
4. The hunting season may need to be changed to

reflect snowshoe hare populations in various regions of the Commonwealth.

The assistance of the Pennsylvania Game Commission is gratefully acknowledged for making readily available their past records of snowshoe hare introductions.

SELECTED REFERENCES:

ADAMS, L. 1959. An analysis of a population of snowshoe hares in northwestern Montana. Ecol. Monogr., 29:141–170.
BOOKHOUT, T. A. 1965. Feeding coactions between snowshoe hares and white-tailed deer in northern Michigan. Trans. N. American Wildlife and National Resources Conf., 30:321–335.
BURT, W. H. 1957. Mammals of the Great Lakes Region. Univ. Michigan Press, Ann Arbor, 246 pp.
DOUTT, J. K., C. A. HEPPENSTALL, and J. E. GUILDAY. 1966. Mammals of Pennsylvania. Pennsylvania Game Comm., Harrisburg, 288 pp.
GODIN, A. J. 1977. Wild mammals of New England. Johns Hopkins Univ. Press, Baltimore, 304 pp.
HALL, E. R. 1981. The mammals of North America. John Wiley & Sons, New York, 1:xv + 1–600 + 90.
KEITH, L. B. 1963. Wildlife's ten-year cycle. Univ. Wisconsin Press, Madison, Wisconsin, 201 pp.
KEITH, L. B., and E. C. MESLOW. 1967. Juvenile breeding in the snowshoe hare. J. Mamm., 48:327.
O'FARRELL, T. P. 1965. Home range and ecology of snowshoe hares in interior Alaska. J. Mamm., 46:406–418.
RONGSTAD, O. J., and J. R. TESTER. 1971. Behavior and maternal relations of young snowshoe hares. J. Wildlife Mgmt., 35:338–346.
ROWAN, W. M., and L. B. KEITH. 1956. The reproductive potential and sex ratios of snowshoe hares in Alberta. Canadian J. Zool., 34:273–281.
SEVERAID, J. H. 1942. The snowshoe hare: Its life history and artificial propagation. Maine Dept. Inland Fisheries and Game, 95 pp.
———. 1945. Breeding potential and artificial propagation of the snowshoe hare. J. Wildlife Mgmt., 9:290–295.

PREPARED BY: Peter L. Dalby, *Biology Department, Clarion University, Clarion, PA 16214.*

Vulnerable

ROCK VOLE
Microtus chrotorrhinus (Miller)
Family Cricetidae
Order Rodentia

OTHER NAMES: Yellow-nosed vole.

DESCRIPTION: In size and external morphology, the rock vole resembles the common meadow vole (*Microtus pennsylvanicus*). Total and tail lengths of adult rock voles are 140–185 mm and 42–64 mm,

Rock Vole (*Microtus chrotorrhinus*). Photograph by R. W. Barbour.

respectively (Kirkland and Jannett, 1982). The eyes are small and the ears protrude slightly beyond the body fur. The dorsal pelage of the rock vole is a glossy bister (yellowish-brown) contrasting with the chestnut brown of the meadow vole. The rock vole is distinguished by its ochraceous/saffron-colored snout. In many specimens, this color extends back on the head as far as the ears (Kirkland and Jannett, 1982).

RANGE: The geographic range of the rock vole extends broadly across eastern Canada from Labrador and the Maritime Provinces westward to northeastern Minnesota; however, it constricts sharply southward into a narrow peninsula extending through the Appalachians to North Carolina and Tennessee (Kirkland and Jannett, 1982). Within Pennsylvania, the rock vole is known in recent times only from four counties in the northeastern portion of the Commonwealth (Luzerne, Sullivan, Wayne, and Wyoming). This species was more widespread in Pennsylvania during the late Pleistocene, as evidenced by the remains of rock voles from cave deposits in southern Pennsylvania (Guilday et al., 1964 (indicated on the accompanying map by a triangle)).

HABITAT: The common name rock vole aptly describes the habitat of *M. chrotorrhinus.* Rocks or talus are usually a conspicuous habitat component throughout its range. Water, either in the form of surface or subsurface streams, is another important habitat component (Martin, 1971; Kirkland and Knipe, 1979). Although a few specimens have been collected in open talus or "balds," rock voles are principally forest dwellers. They tend to prefer cool, moist forests having a lush herbaceous understory, frequently dominated by ferns (Kirkland and Jannett, 1982).

LIFE HISTORY AND ECOLOGY: Like most other members of the genus *Microtus,* the rock vole is a grazer, feeding primarily on green vegetation. Bunchberry (*Cornus canadensis*) is a preferred food item. Rock voles frequently harvest forbs and cache the cut portions in subsurface cavities beneath rocks (Whitaker and Martin, 1977).

Rock voles exhibit a typical microtine pattern of reproduction with each adult female potentially capable of producing a succession of litters throughout the reproductive season as a result of postpartum estrus (Martin, 1971). However, the fecundity of *M. chrotorrhinus* appears to be lower than that of the meadow vole. Although litter size in *M. chrotorrhinus* averages approximately 3.7 embryos for the species as a whole, there is a pronounced cline of increasing litter size with latitude (Martin, 1971).

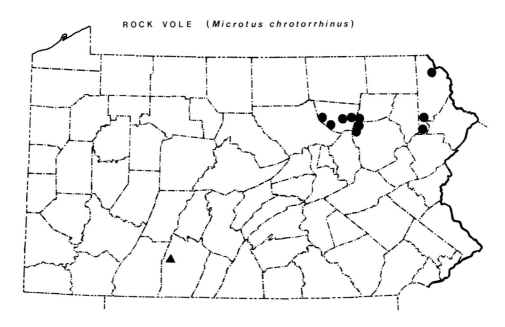

ROCK VOLE   (*Microtus chrotorrhinus*)

The only litter size data from Pennsylvania specimens are two placental scar counts of 3 and 5 (CM specimens).

BASIS OF STATUS CLASSIFICATION: The rock vole is classified as Vulnerable in Pennsylvania because it apparently exists in small isolated populations which occupy a restricted range of habitats within a limited geographic region. Only about 15 Pennsylvania specimens have been collected, all from a few scattered localities in the northeastern quadrant of the Commonwealth. The Pennsylvania populations may also be genetically isolated. Whereas only about 45 km separates the Wayne Co., Pennsylvania, population from the nearest New York population in Sullivan Co., there is an approximately 390 km hiatus in the known distribution of *M. chrotorrhinus* between localities in Sullivan and Luzerne counties, Pennsylvania, and the nearest known locality to the south in Tucker Co., West Virginia (Kirkland, 1977). Within this range disjunction encompassing nearly all of Pennsylvania, there are many sites with apparently suitable rock vole habitat; the absence of *M. chrotorrhinus* from this region, except for fossil remains, is an enigma.

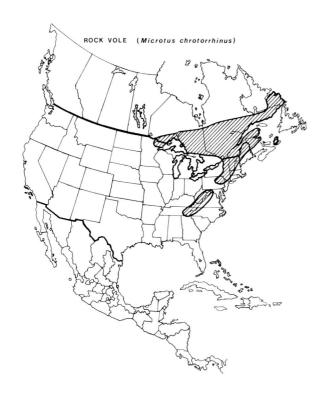

ROCK VOLE   (*Microtus chrotorrhinus*)

RECOMMENDATIONS: A major effort must be made to determine if the rock vole is presently as restricted in numbers and distribution in Pennsylvania as previous sampling indicates. Because the habitat preferences of the Rock Vole have been well-documented, steps should be taken to preserve suitable habitats within its known area of occurrence or, at least, to protect these habitats from destructive development. This is particularly critical since the mountainous region of northeastern Pennsylvania is under increasing pressure from commercial and recreational development interests.

SELECTED REFERENCES:

GUILDAY, J. E., P. S. MARTIN, and A. D. MCCRADY. 1964. New Paris No. 4: A late Pleistocene Cave Deposit in Bedford County, Pennsylvania. Bull. Nat. Speliological Soc., 26:121–194.

KIRKLAND, G. L., JR. 1977. The rock vole, *Microtus chrotorrhinus* (Miller) (Mammalia: Rodentia), in West Virginia. Ann. Carnegie Mus., 46:45–53.

KIRKLAND, G. L., JR. and F. J. JANNETT, JR. 1982. *Microtus chrotorrhinus*. Mammalian Species, 180:1–5.

KIRKLAND, G. L., JR., and C. M. KNIPE. 1979. The rock vole (*Microtus chrotorrhinus*) as a Transition Zone species. Canadian Field-Nat., 93:319–321.

MARTIN, R. L. 1971. The natural history and taxonomy of the rock vole, *Microtus chrotorrhinus*. Unpublished Ph.D. dissert., Univ. Connecticut, Storrs, 123 pp.

WHITAKER, J. O., JR., and R. L. MARTIN. 1977. Food habits of *Microtus chrotorrhinus* from New Hampshire, New York and Quebec. J. Mamm. 58:99–100.

PREPARED BY: Gordon L. Kirkland, Jr., *The Vertebrate Museum, Shippensburg University, Shippensburg, PA 17257.*

Vulnerable

SPOTTED SKUNK
Spilogale putorius (Linnaeus)
Family Mustelidae
Order Carnivora

OTHER NAMES: Polecat, civet cat, civet, hydrophobia skunk.

DESCRIPTION: As is typical of the New World skunks (Mephitinae), the spotted skunk is black with distinct white markings. In contrast to the larger striped skunk (*Mephitis mephitis*) which generally has two uninterrupted stripes extending from the head towards the tail, the spotted skunk has four white stripes. Beginning on the head, the stripes are continuous on the anterior portion of the body; posteriorly they break up into a series of dashes and spots, the pattern varying among individuals. There is a white blaze on the forehead, and the tail is tipped with white hairs. Spotted skunks are smaller and more slender than striped skunks. Total length generally ranges from 400–525 mm with a tail length of 180–225 mm (Doutt et al., 1973). Males are slightly larger than females (Van Gelder, 1959).

RANGE: The range of the spotted skunk encompasses a large portion of the United States, Mexico, and Central America as far south as Costa Rica (Hall, 1981). It extends northward into Canada only in western British Columbia. In the United States, it is excluded from the northern Great Plains, portions of the Mississippi Valley, the Great Lakes region, New England and most of the Atlantic Coastal Plain. The range of this species barely reaches into Pennsylvania (Gifford and Whitebread, 1951; Latham and Studholme, 1947). It has been recorded from only three south-central counties—Bedford, Franklin and Fulton. These localities represent the northeastern-most limits of the distribution of the spotted skunk.

HABITAT: In Pennsylvania, as well as in the adjacent states of Maryland and West Virginia, the spotted skunk is most abundant in rocky habitats, either ridge tops or ravines, and has been collected at elevations ranging from 700–3,100 ft (Bookhout, 1964; Larson, 1968). Throughout other portions of eastern North America, the spotted skunk normally inhabits agricultural lands; it has been reported from the vicinity of farmyards and farm buildings in Pennsylvania and western Maryland (Latham and Studholme, 1947; Larson, 1968). Evidence of habitat segregation between spotted and striped skunks is lacking, and both species may occupy similar habitats throughout their zone of sympatry.

LIFE HISTORY AND ECOLOGY: The majority of spotted skunks from Pennsylvania have been collected by commercial trappers rather than trained biologists. As a result, much of the information on the ecology and life history of the spotted skunk in Pennsylvania is anecdotal in nature. Evidence from other regions of eastern North America indicate that spotted skunks are nocturnal (Davis, 1974). In contrast to the exclusively terrestrial striped skunk, spotted skunks are adept climbers and may occasionally nest in trees (Golley, 1962). Spotted skunks are omnivorous, feeding on insects, small mammals, birds and eggs, fruit, nuts, reptiles, and assorted invertebrates (Doutt et al., 1973; Davis, 1974).

Breeding takes place in March/April and parturition occurs in late May or June after a 50 to 65 day gestation period (Mead, 1968). The presence and/or duration of delayed implantation is in question. Litter size averages 5.5 young with a range of 4–9 (Mead, 1968). Whereas two litters per year may be produced in the south, it is likely that only one litter per year is produced in the northern portions of its range (Doutt et al., 1973).

BASIS OF STATUS CLASSIFICATION: The spotted skunk is a peripheral species in Pennsyl-

Spotted Skunk (*Spilogale putorius*). Photograph by R. A. Mead.

vania, and as such, it may be expected to occur in small, isolated populations which are restricted to appropriate habitat. Such a species is by definition vulnerable to extirpation either by habitat destruction or overharvesting. The preferred rocky habitats of the spotted skunk may provide it with a certain amount of protection because they usually are not easily accessible to humans and are not considered to be prime sites for either development or timber harvesting. Each year up to a half dozen or more spotted skunks from Pennsylvania are purchased by fur dealers in Bedford and Fulton counties. It is impossible to determine what percentage of the annual catch or what percentage of the total population

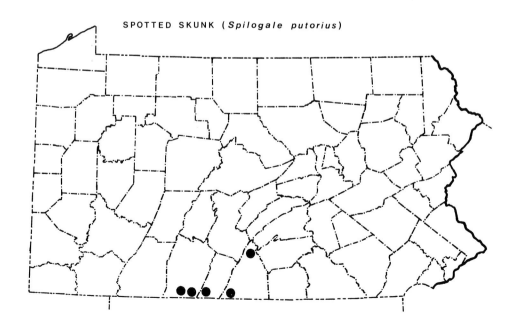

SPOTTED SKUNK (*Spilogale putorius*)

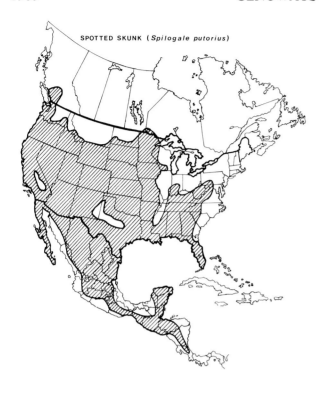

SPOTTED SKUNK (*Spilogale putorius*)

these sales represent. The traditionally low prices paid for spotted skunks coupled with the objectionable aspects of handling them prompt many trappers to discard *Spilogale* carcasses, as well as those of *Mephitis*. Regardless of how conservative these fur dealer records may be, they serve to document the presence of a permanent population of spotted skunks in the southern tier counties of central Pennsylvania. Although apparently viable, this population is potentially vulnerable to overexploitation since specimens are most frequently captured in traps set for other more commercially valuable furbearers.

RECOMMENDATIONS: At present, the spotted skunk population in Pennsylvania appears to be surviving well in spite of some mortality during the trapping season. Because most spotted skunks are taken accidentally, laws to prohibit harvesting them would be largely ineffective in diminishing mortality. There is, however, a need for more detailed information on the ecology and life history of the spotted skunk in the Commonwealth. This could be partially met if the carcasses of accidentally trapped or killed specimens could be brought to appropriate scientific institutions or state agencies for study and preservation.

ACKNOWLEDGEMENTS: Information on recent sightings, captures, or purchases of Pennsylvania Spotted Skunks was provided by Jesse C. Asper (Newburg), Richard M. Crawford, Sr. (Everett), Ralph S. Gipe (Newburg), and Edwin M. Hawbaker (Ft. Loudon).

SELECTED REFERENCES:

BOOKHOUT, T. A. 1964. The Allegheny spotted skunk in Maryland. Chesapeake Sci., 5:213–215.

DAVIS, W. B. 1974. The mammals of Texas. Bull. Texas Parks and Wildlife Dept, Austin, 41:1–294.

DOUTT, J. K., C. A. HEPPENSTALL, and J. E. GUILDAY. 1973. Mammals of Pennsylvania. Pennsylvania Game Comm., Harrisburg, 3rd edition, 283 pp.

GIFFORD, C. L., and R. WHITEBREAD. 1951. Mammal survey of south central Pennsylvania. Final Report Pittman-Robertson Project 38-R. Pennsylvania Game Comm., Harrisburg, 75 pp.

GOLLEY, F. B. 1962. Mammals of Georgia. Univ. Georgia Press, Athens, 218 pp.

HALL, E. R. 1981. The mammals of North America. John Wiley & Sons, New York, 2:vi + 601–1181 + 90.

LARSON, J. S. 1968. Notes on the spotted skunk in Maryland. Chesapeake Sci., 9:204–206.

LATHAM, R. M., and C. R. STUDHOLME. 1947. Spotted skunk in Pennsylvania. J. Mamm., 28:409.

MEAD, R. A. 1968. Reproduction in eastern forms of the spotted skunk (genus *Spilogale*). J. Zool. (London), 156:119–136.

VAN GELDER, R. G. 1959. A taxonomic revision of the spotted skunks (genus *Spilogale*). Bull. Amer. Mus. Nat. Hist., 117:229–392.

PREPARED BY: Gordon L. Kirkland, Jr., *The Vertebrate Museum, Shippensburg University, Shippensburg, PA 17257.*

Vulnerable

RIVER OTTER
Lutra canadensis (Schreber)
Family Mustelidae
Order Carnivora

OTHER NAMES: Land otter, otter.

DESCRIPTION: The river otter has a streamlined, cylindrical appearance; the neck is nearly as wide as the short, flattened skull. Adults are more than 1 m long and weigh about 5–11 kg. Males are somewhat larger than females. The upper parts are brown to nearly black when wet; under parts paler; and lower jaw and throat whitish (Hall, 1981). The 30–50 cm long oval tail is thick at the base and tapers to a blunt end. Otters are well equipped for an aquatic existence; the small ears can be closed under water;

River Otter (*Lutra canadensis*). Photograph by A. Woolf.

the eyes are near the top of the head permitting sight while swimming; and the short legs possess five webbed toes on each foot. No other species resembles the river otter in Pennsylvania.

RANGE: Otters formerly ranged throughout North America except for the extreme southwest, and portions of the west (Hall, 1981). Doutt et al. (1966) reported their range in Pennsylvania as throughout the Commonwealth except the southeastern corner; however, they considered otters rare, with a few surviving in the Pocono Mountains, but extirpated in the remainder of the Commonwealth. Eveland (1978) estimated from 285 to 465 otters in the state based on a survey of District Game Protectors. Distribution was primarily limited to seven counties within the Pocono Plateau region of northeastern Pennsylvania, but some were reported in four other counties. The existence of viable breeding populations anywhere other than the Pocono region has not been demonstrated. Current population trends have not been determined, but Eveland (unpublished report) has suggested a decline since 1978.

HABITAT: Extensive water is a principal component of otter habitat (Mowbray et al., 1976). Lakes, marshes, streams, and rivers all provide otter habitat; but, in Pennsylvania rivers and their tributaries

are the major aquatic habitat available for river otters. The carnivorous otter is dependent upon aquatic organisms, especially fish, to meet nutrient and energy needs. Thus, habitat orientation is toward aquatic areas and associated riparian zones with abundant aquatic and semi-aquatic food resources. Although the river otter population in Pennsylvania is mainly restricted to the northeast, it appears that suitable aquatic habitat does exist in the northcentral region of the Commonwealth.

LIFE HISTORY AND ECOLOGY: Little is known about the life history and ecology of the species in Pennsylvania. River otters are known to travel more than 1.6 km in a matter of minutes and have been found far from water in Maryland (Mowbray et al., 1976). These data suggest that the otter has the ability to disperse into unoccupied habitat, but this does not appear to be happening in Pennsylvania. Fergus (N.D.) speculated that the urbanized Scranton/Wilkes-Barre area may be a barrier preventing expansion from the northeast to the northcentral region.

Melquist and Hornocker (1979) reported about one otter per 2–3 km waterway (straightline distance) in Idaho. There was one family group (adult female plus 2–3 pups) per 15 km waterway; and one breeding male per 20–30 km. These data are from

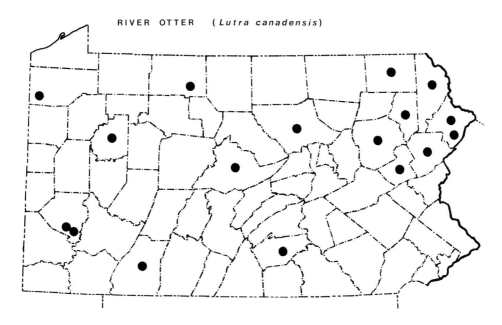

RIVER OTTER (*Lutra canadensis*)

excellent habitats in the Rocky Mountain west and may not reflect densities that can be expected in Pennsylvania.

Studies of river otter reproduction in Maryland were reported in Mowbray et al. (1976); corpora lutea of pregnancy averaged 2.74 and litter sizes (implanted embryos) 2.73. The implanted litter size is comparable to the 2.75 found in Oregon (Tabor

and Wight 1977). Otters may or may not breed every year. Mowbray et al. (1976) did not believe that all adults bred every year in Maryland, but Tabor and Wight (1977) reported that otters bred annually.

BASIS OF STATUS CLASSIFICATION: The river otter has been classified as vulnerable in Pennsylvania because it exists only in one or a few restricted geographic areas or habitats within the Commonwealth.

RECOMMENDATIONS: Completely protected in the Commonwealth since 1954, no evidence is available to indicate that the population status of the river otter has improved, nor is the population status known. Suitable aquatic habitat is a requirement to maintain otter populations. Otters cannot exist in areas where water pollution has eliminated or reduced aquatic life needed to sustain them. Any steps taken to improve the quality of aquatic habitats are beneficial to otters and could result in population increases.

A research program should be initiated to define the status of the otter in Pennsylvania and to find ways to assure the welfare of remnant populations and possibly increase their distribution and abundance. The following specific goals are recommended:

1. Delineate the present distribution and population status.
2. Identify critical aquatic habitats and define steps

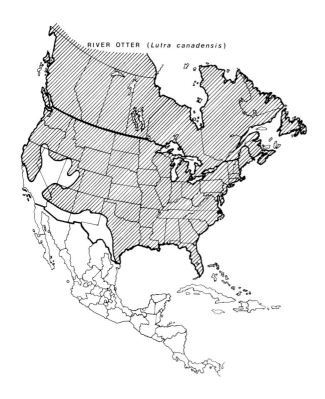

RIVER OTTER (*Lutra canadensis*)

that may be taken for habitat protection and preservation or enhancement of water quality.

3. Determine if barriers exist that prevent the northeast population from expanding into apparently suitable habitats in the northcentral portion of the Commonwealth.

4. Identify potential, but unoccupied, otter habitat throughout the Commonwealth and determine the feasibility of a trap and transplant program to stock those sites.

SELECTED REFERENCES:

DOUTT, J. K., C. A. HEPPENSTALL, and J. E. GUILDAY. 1966. Mammals of Pennsylvania. Pennsylvania Game Comm., Harrisburg, 265 pp.

EVELAND, T. E. 1978. The status, distribution and identification of suitable habitat of river otters in Pennsylvania. Unpublished M.S. thesis, East Stroudsburg State College, Pennsylvania, 54 pp.

FERGUS, C. N. D. Otter. Pennsylvania Game Commission Wildlife Notes 175-11, Harrisburg, 2 pp.

FIELD, R. J. 1970. Winter habits of the river otter (*Lutra canadensis*) in Michigan. Michigan Acad., 3(1):49–58.

HALL, E. R. 1981. Mammals of North America. John Wiley & Sons, New York, 2:vi + 601–1181 + 90.

HAMILTON, W. J., JR. 1961. Late fall, winter and early spring foods of 141 otters from New York. New York Fish Game J., 8:106–109.

HAMILTON, W. J., JR., and W. R. EADIE. 1964. Reproduction in the otter, *Lutra canadensis*. J. Mamm., 45:242–252.

KNUDSEN, K. F., and J. B. HALE. 1968. Food habits of otters in the Great Lakes region. J. Wildlife Mgmt., 32:89–93.

LIERS, E. E. 1951. Notes on the river otter (*Lutra canadensis*). J. Mamm., 35:1–9.

MELQUIST, W. E., and M. G. HORNOCKER. 1979. Methods and techniques for studying and censusing river otter populations. Univ. Idaho For. Wildlife Range Expt. Sta. Tech. Rept. 8:1–17.

MOWBRAY, E. E., J. A. CHAPMAN, and J. R. GOLDSBERRY. 1976. Preliminary observations on otter distribution and habitat preferences in Maryland with descriptions of otter field sign. Proc. Northeast Fish and Wildlife Conf., 33:125–131.

TABOR, J. E., and H. M. WIGHT. 1977. Population status of the river otter in western Oregon. J. Wildlife Mgmt., 41:692–699.

PREPARED BY: Alan Woolf, *Cooperative Wildlife Research Laboratory, Southern Illinois University–Carbondale, Carbondale, IL 62901.*

Vulnerable

BOBCAT
Lynx rufus (Schreber)
Family Felidae
Order Carnivora

OTHER NAMES: Bay lynx, wild cat, barred bobcat, pallid bobcat.

DESCRIPTION: Bobcats are medium-sized cats with short tails; large, tufted ears, and broad short heads. Males range in weight from 7.2 to 31 kg and the smaller females from 5.7 to 24 kg (Hall, 1981). The higher weight ranges are not common; the average adult is about 7 to 9 kg (Doutt et al., 1966). Coloration varies among individuals and localities, ranging from grayish to buffy to reddish upper parts, usually with black spots. The bobcat can be distinguished from the lynx (*Lynx canadensis*) by a tail that is more than half the length of the hind foot and tipped with black only above; the lynx has a shorter tail that is completely tipped with black (Hall, 1981).

RANGE: Hall (1981) reported a distribution of 12 subspecies in parts of Canada, Mexico, and throughout the United States. Young (1958) showed a similar distribution, but with two fewer subspecies. *Lynx rufus rufus,* the subspecies in Pennsylvania, was reported to range throughout the state by Doutt et al. (1966). Fergus (N.D.) noted the general range as a broad band through the mountainous regions of the state with some populations also in northwestern and southcentral Pennsylvania. A 1979 Game Commission survey of District Game Protectors disclosed known or suspected presence of bobcats in all but 21 counties. Counties with the largest suspected populations were Clinton, Fayette, Lycoming, and Sullivan. The entire statewide estimate was 612 to 797 bobcats (Michael Puglisi, Pennsylvania Game Commission Biologist, personal communication). Although these data are very subjective, they are the only indication of current distribution and population status.

HABITAT: The bobcat inhabits mainly the mountainous, wooded terrain of Pennsylvania. Forest habitat in early and mid-successional stages is preferred, but the brushy second growth forest that characterized Pennsylvania in the early 1900's is now mature with a closed canopy. Optimum habitat provides an interspersion of the woodlands with thick, brushy areas; open fields; swamps; weed grown areas; and terrain broken with rocky ledges and outcrops. Preferred habitats provide a diversity essential to support an abundance of small mammals as prey species. In large, continuous blocks of mature forest, bobcats do not thrive. The most extensive areas of favorable habitat prevail in the northcentral portion of the Commonwealth, but even there, the forest is mature and cannot be considered optimum

Bobcat (*Lynx rufus*). Photograph by A. Woolf.

habitat. Any activities or environmental events that retard succession, create forest openings, or otherwise promote thick herbaceous and understory vegetation will increase prey abundance and thus improve habitat for bobcats.

LIFE HISTORY AND ECOLOGY: Prey species are mainly small mammals and birds with rabbits and hares perhaps the most important prey. Young (1958) reported that rabbits were a major source of food in every section of the United States and that the "bobcat goes with the rabbit." The close dependence of the bobcat on prey abundance dictates habitat requirements, distribution, and population status.

Bobcats are territorial and home range size varies mainly with food supply. Hamilton (1979) estimated home ranges for three adult males in Missouri between about 47 and 67 square km. Home range sizes in Pennsylvania are unknown.

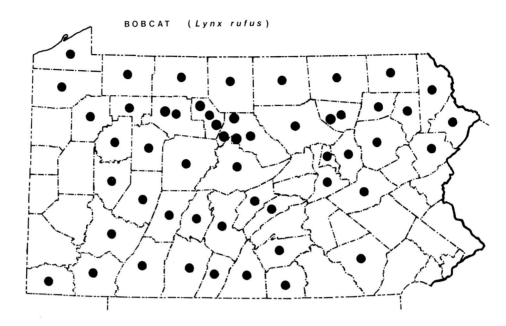

BOBCAT (*Lynx rufus*)

Breeding usually occurs in late winter and 1 to 4 young are born after a 50 to 60 day gestation period (Hall and Kelson, 1959). Young (1958) said there are indications that birth may occur during any month and that a bobcat may litter twice a year; this is not known to occur in Pennsylvania. A recent review by McCord and Young (1982) provides current information on the life history economics and

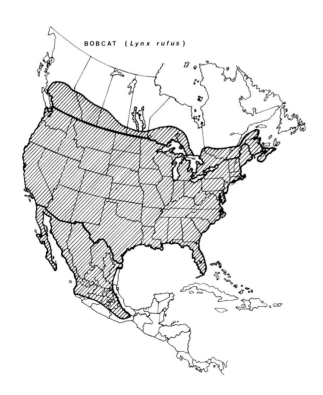

BOBCAT (*Lynx rufus*)

management of the bobcat and lynx in North America.

BASIS OF STATUS CLASSIFICATION: Bounties paid since the 1800's were removed in 1938 when low population densities became apparent. Complete protection under the Game Laws was afforded in 1970. Doutt et al. (1966) thought that there might be less than 100 in the Commonwealth. A survey of District Game Protectors in 1970 yielded an estimate of 391 to 652 bobcats. Although both the 1970 and 1979 surveys are imprecise, they do reflect low numbers statewide, and little, if any, population increase in spite of full protection for about 9 years.

The bobcat is classified as vulnerable because it is apparently rare (low population density) over a relatively broad range in the state. Development of remote areas, disturbances from recreation and recreational vehicles, and habitat changes were cited by Fergus (N.D.) as the main reasons for the decline of this species. These factors are likely to continue, in addition to current high values of bobcat pelts which may further jeopardize the status of this species in Pennsylvania in spite of complete protection. The main potential for improvement of status lies in increased utilization of the state's timber resources. If the now mature forests are returned to early successional stages by timber harvest, bobcat habitat will be enhanced and populations in more remote areas may thrive.

RECOMMENDATIONS: Because of the nocturnal

habits and secretive behavior of the bobcat, its status in Pennsylvania remains subject to question; virtually no research has been conducted in the Commonwealth. Areas of high quality habitat should be determined and intensive efforts made to study the population status of bobcats in selected regions. A well publicized effort should be made to obtain and verify information on sightings, tracks, signs, etc. to better delineate distribution and areas of possible relative abundance. Complete protection should be continued and the status re-evaluated by Game Commission staff on an annual basis. In the near future, this species may warrant consideration for "threatened" status in the Commonwealth.

SELECTED REFERENCES:

BAILEY, T. N. 1974. Social organization in a bobcat population. J. Wildlife Mgmt., 38:435–446.

BAILEY, T. N. 1981. Factors of bobcat social organization and some management implications. Pp. 984–1000, in Worldwide Furbearer Conference Proceedings (J. A. Chapman and D. Pursley, eds.), Frostburg, Maryland, 2:viii + 653–1551.

CREED, W. A., and J. E. ASHBRENNER. 1976. Status report on Wisconsin bobcats, 1975. Dept. Nat. Res. Research Rept. 87, Madison, Wisconsin, 9 pp. (mimeo).

CROWE, D. M. 1975. A model for exploited bobcat populations in Wyoming. J. Wildlife Mgmt., 39:408–415.

DOUTT, J. K., C. A. HEPPENSTALL, and J. E. GUILDAY. 1966. Mammals of Pennsylvania. Pennsylvania Game Comm., Harrisburg, 265 pp.

FERGUS, C. N. D. Bobcat. Pennsylvania Game Commission Wildlife Notes 175-3, Harrisburg, 2 pp.

HALL, E. R. 1981. Mammals of North America. John Wiley & Sons, New York, 2:vi + 601–1181 + 90.

HAMILTON, D. A. 1979. Bobcat studies in Missouri. Performance Report, Endangered Species Project SE-1, Study 3, 6 pp. (mimeo).

MARSHALL, S. D., and J. H. JENKINS. 1966. Movements and home ranges of bobcats as determined by radio-tracking in the upper coastal plain of west-central South Carolina. Proc. Southeast Assoc. Game Fish Comm., 20:206–214.

McCORD, C. M., and J. E. CARDOZA. 1982. Bobcat and Lynx. Pp. 728–766, in Wild mammals of North America: biology, management, and economics (J. A. Chapman and G. A. Feldhamer, eds.), John Hopkins Press, Baltimore, xiii + 1147 pp.

YOUNG, S. P. 1958. The bobcat of North America. Stackpole, Harrisburg, Pennsylvania, 193 pp.

PREPARED BY: Alan Woolf, *Cooperative Wildlife Research Laboratory, Southern Illinois University–Carbondale, Carbondale, IL 62901.*

Status Undetermined

MARYLAND SHREW
Sorex fontinalis Hollister
Family Soricidae
Order Insectivora

DESCRIPTION: The Maryland shrew is one of the smallest mammals native to Pennsylvania. In coloration and external morphology, it resembles the slightly larger masked shrew (*Sorex cinereus*). Average total and tail lengths for Pennsylvania *S. fontinalis* are only 86 mm and 33 mm, respectively (Kirkland, 1977). In contrast, *S. cinereus* from east-

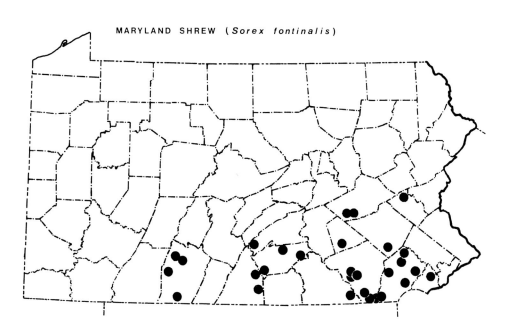

MARYLAND SHREW (*Sorex fontinalis*)

MARYLAND SHREW (*Sorex fontinalis*)

it appears to be a lowland species, seldom being captured on ridge tops or above 300 m altitude. Specimens have been collected in both forested and non-forested habitats (Roberts and Early, 1952). Moister sites such as wet meadows may be preferred, as well as hedgerows or other sites where Japanese honeysuckle (*Lonicera japonica*) is present.

LIFE HISTORY AND ECOLOGY: Although little is known about the life history and ecology of the Maryland shrew, it is believed to be similar in many respects to the masked shrew.

BASIS OF STATUS CLASSIFICATION: The Maryland shrew has been classified as Status Undetermined partly because of questions regarding its taxonomic status. Originally recognized as a distinct Austral species (Hollister, 1911), the Maryland shrew was relegated to subspecific status on the basis of a non-statistical analysis in which a zone of intergradation between *S. fontinalis* and *S. cinereus* was presumably detected in Berks and Chester counties, Pennsylvania (Poole, 1937). A recent re-evaluation of the taxonomic status of the Maryland shrew based on statistical analyses of specimens from both the regions of sympatry and allopatry of the Maryland and masked shrews confirmed the morphological distinctiveness of the Maryland shrew and failed to detect a zone of intergradation between these two shrews (Kirkland, 1977). These results suggest that the Maryland shrew is a distinct species and warrants recognition as such (Junge and Hoffmann, 1981). This taxonomic question aside, relatively little is known about the abundance, ecological distribution, and general life history of the Maryland shrew in Pennsylvania, and as a consequence, it is classified as Status Undetermined.

ern Pennsylvania average 94 mm for total length and 36 mm for tail length (Kirkland, 1977). Dorsal pelage in the Maryland shrew is dark sepia with the rump being the darkest region (Hollister, 1911). Pigment intensity gradually decreases towards the belly so that the venter is brownish gray. In eastern Pennsylvania, pigmentation in masked shrews tends to be lighter than that of the Maryland shrew. The skull of the Maryland shrew is distinguished by its conspicuously constricted rostral region bearing the unicuspid tooth row. The rostral region is also shorter, giving the unicuspid row a more crowded appearance than that of the masked shrew.

RANGE: The Maryland shrew is limited in distribution to eastern Pennsylvania, eastern West Virginia, Maryland and the Delmarva Peninsula (Delaware/Maryland/Virginia east of the Chesapeake Bay). Within the Commonwealth, it is generally found south and east of the major mountains of central and northern Pennsylvania. Specimens have been collected in Bedford, Berks, Chester, Cumberland, Delaware, Franklin, Lancaster, Lehigh, Perry, Schuylkill, and York counties.

HABITAT: The habitat preferences of the Maryland shrew are not fully understood. Throughout its range,

RECOMMENDATIONS: The Maryland Shrew apparently does not have critical habitat requirements, and its small size dictates that viable populations may be able to survive in small undeveloped sites throughout its range. The relatively small number of specimens in museum collections and the lack of good habitat and life history data for this shrew are important reasons to recommend additional research to gain a fuller knowledge of the distribution and ecology of this species in Pennsylvania. Of particular interest would be the careful documentation of localities and microhabitats of *S. fontinalis* and *S. cinereus* to determine if these two shrews are truly syntopic.

SELECTED REFERENCES:

HOLLISTER, N. 1911. Remarks on the long-tailed shrews of the eastern United States, with description of a new species. Proc. U.S. Nat. Mus., 40:377–381.

JUNGE, J. A., and R. S. HOFFMANN. 1981. An annotated key to the long-tailed shrews (genus *Sorex*) of the United States and Canada, with notes on middle American *Sorex*. Occas. Papers Mus. Nat. Hist., Univ. Kansas, 94:1–48.

KIRKLAND, G. L., JR. 1977. A re-examination of the subspecific status of the Maryland shrew, *Sorex cinereus fontinalis* Hollister. Proc. Pennsylvania Acad. Sci., 51:43–46.

POOLE, E. L. 1937. Pennsylvania records of *Sorex cinereus fontinalis*. J. Mamm., 18:96.

ROBERTS. H. A., and R. C. EARLY. 1952. Mammal survey of southeastern Pennsylvania. Final Report Pittman-Robertson Project 43-R. Pennsylvania Game Comm., Harrisburg, 70 pp.

PREPARED BY: Gordon L. Kirkland, Jr., *The Vertebrate Museum, Shippensburg University, Shippensburg, PA 17257.*

Status Undetermined

WATER SHREW
Sorex palustris punctulatus (Hooper)
Family: Soricidae
Order: Insectivora

OTHER NAMES: West Virginia water shrew.

DESCRIPTION: The West Virginia water shrew is similar in size and appearance to the white-lipped shrew, another water shrew subspecies found in the Pennsylvania region. Members of this semi-aquatic species weigh about 10 to 16 g and are about 150 mm long including a 75 mm tail. Male and female water shrews are about the same size and have a dark blackish upper body and tail with light grayish underparts. The large hind toes have fringes of stiff hairs (Burt and Grossenheider, 1964). This unique characteristic, as well as the dark upper body and relatively large size, serve to separate this species from all other shrew species in Pennsylvania. Only expert mammalogists can distinguish *Sorex palustris punctulatus* from the white-lipped shrew (*Sorex palustris albibarbus*).

RANGE: The known distribution of the West Virginia water shrew is limited to the Allegheny-Appalachian mountain chain from the Georgia-Tennessee-North Carolina border north to West Virginia into Pennsylvania. A single specimen was collected in the Commonwealth at Tumbling Cove Run in the Negro Mountains, Somerset Co. (Hall, 1981).

HABITAT: Little information concerning the habitat requirements of this subspecies is available. In

Water Shrew (*Sorex palustris*). Photograph by R. W. Barbour.

WATER SHREW (*Sorex palustris punctulatus*)

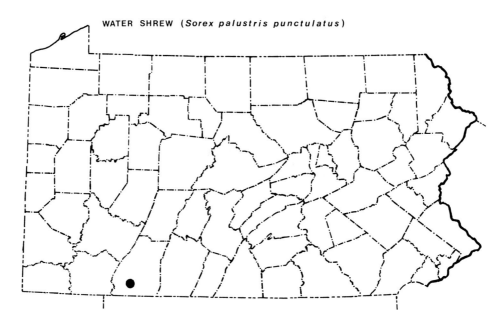

the Great Smoky Mountains National Park of Tennessee, Linzey and Linzey (1971) found this shrew living near the margins of a mountain stream beneath overhanging banks and in rock crevices from 1,120 to 1,420 m elevation. In this region, the West Virginia water shrew was taken from mountain areas with generally scant vegetative cover where the dominant plants appeared to be hemlock, red spruce,

yellow birch, and rhododendron (Conway and Pfitzer, 1952).

LIFE HISTORY AND ECOLOGY: Information is lacking on the life history and ecology of *Sorex palustris punctulatus* in Pennsylvania or other regions. Local populations are probably small and scattered. The species apparently has a long breeding season. *Sorex palustris punctulatus,* and all other water shrew subspecies, apparently dive year-round in water to procure food. The physiological responses to diving exhibited by such a small mammal are of special scientific interest.

BASIS OF CLASSIFICATION: This subspecies has been assigned to the status undetermined category because absolutely nothing is known about the status and ecology of populations within the Commonwealth. *Sorex palustris punctulatus* has never been studied in Pennsylvania. Indeed, the only existing specimen for the Commonwealth was initially identified as *Sorex palustris albibarbus.*

RECOMMENDATIONS: A field research program should be conducted to locate populations and study the local distribution, life history, and ecology of the *Sorex palustris punctulatus* in Pennsylvania. Collection efforts should be concentrated along the banks of forested mountain streams in the southeastern and central regions of the Commonwealth. The taxon probably will be removed from the species of special concern list as it becomes better known

WATER SHREW (*Sorex palustris punctulatus*)

because preferred habitat of *Sorex palustris punctulatus* appears to be restricted to remote mountain areas which are seldom exposed to substantial disturbance due to human activity.

SELECTED REFERENCES:

BURT, W. H., and R. P. GROSSENHEIDER. 1964. A field guide to the mammals. Houghton Mifflin Co., Boston, second edition, 284 pp.

CONWAY, C. H., and D. W. PFITZER. 1952. *Sorex palustris* and *Sorex dispar* from the Great Smoky Mountains National Park. J. Mamm., 33:106–108.

HALL, E. R. 1981. The mammals of North America. John Wiley & Sons, New York, 1:xv + 1–600 + 90.

LINZEY, A. V., and D. W. LINZEY. 1971. Mammals of Great Smoky Mountains National Park. Univ. Tennessee Press, Knoxville, 144 pp.

PREPARED BY: John E. Enders, *Sartorius Filters, 304 Second Street, P.O. Box 185, Dalton, PA 18414.*

Status Undetermined

WATER SHREW

Sorex palustris albibarbus (Cope)
Family Soricidae
Order Insectivora

OTHER NAMES: White-lipped shrew, eastern marsh shrew.

DESCRIPTION: The water shrew weighs about 10 to 16 g, but nevertheless it is still the second largest shrew in Pennsylvania (Doutt et al., 1977). The elongated tail of this semi-aquatic species is about as long as its 75 mm body. The hind toes are partially webbed with unique fringes of short, stiff hairs for swimming. The eyes and external ears are quite small, and the fur has a velvety appearance. The sexes are similar in size and color; the upper parts of the body and tail are a dark gray-black to brownish color and the underparts are a lighter grayish-white to brown (Godin, 1977). The chin and throat of the water shrew are noticeably lighter than the remainder of its underparts (Doutt *et al.,* 1977). The relatively long tail distinguishes the water shrew from the short-tailed shrew *Blarina brevicauda.* The water shrew is markedly larger and darker than all other shrews in the Commonwealth.

RANGE: The water shrew is known to occur from southeastern Canada and Maine, south to Rhode Island, Connecticut, New York, and central, north-central, and northeastern Pennsylvania (Hall, 1981; Godin, 1977). In Pennsylvania, specimens have been taken from Mifflin, Centre, Potter, Bradford, Sullivan, Wyoming, Luzerne, Monroe, and Pike counties. Many of the existing Pennsylvania specimens were collected by Grimm and Whitebread (1952) during a 2-year field trapping survey of northeastern Pennsylvania. These workers suggested the subspecies is more widely distributed in the Commonwealth than their results indicated.

HABITAT: The subspecies appears to have restrict-

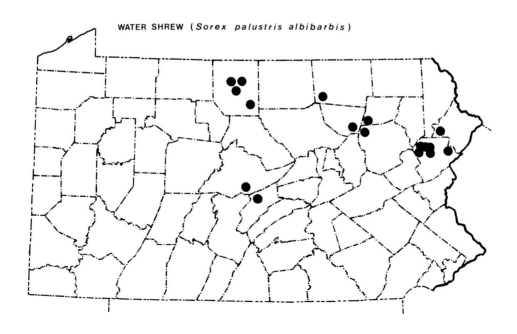

WATER SHREW (*Sorex palustris albibarbis*)

WATER SHREW (*Sorex palustris albibarbis*)

ed habitat requirements. Most of the 16 water shrews reported by Grimm and Whitebread (1952) were collected from montane areas near high gradient, rock-bedded creeks and streams in traps placed in crevices formed by rocks and tree roots. The surrounding northern forest vegetation consisted of heavy strands of hemlock, spruce, and rhododendron. A few specimens were taken along mountain streams in areas of scant vegetation, but none were taken along the shores of lakes or ponds. Favorable habitat conditions are located in areas of high elevation in the central, northcentral, and northeastern portions of the Commonwealth.

LIFE HISTORY AND ECOLOGY: Specific information on the life history, home range size, dispersal tendencies, reproduction, population dynamics, and predator-prey relationships of this subspecies in Pennsylvania is not available, and very little data are available from other regions. Local populations in the Commonwealth appear to be small and scattered (Grimm and Whitebread, 1952). The animal mainly eats a variety of aquatic and terrestrial invertebrates (Doutt et al., 1977). The species apparently has a long breeding season.

All water shrew subspecies are unique in that they apparently dive year-round in water to procure food. The physiological responses to diving exhibited by

this very small mammal is of specific scientific interest (Calder, 1969).

BASIS OF STATUS CLASSIFICATION: This subspecies has been assigned to the status undetermined category because virtually nothing is known about the status and ecology of populations within the Commonwealth. The water shrew has not been studied in Pennsylvania and, due to the patchy nature of its distribution coupled with the remoteness of its preferred habitat, the animal is only rarely collected during research on other small mammals.

RECOMMENDATIONS: A field research program should be conducted to locate populations and study the local distribution, life history and ecology of the water shrew in Pennsylvania. Collection efforts should be concentrated along the banks of forested mountain streams. While the water shrew does have rather narrow habitat requirements, the taxon will probably be removed from the species of special concern list as a better understanding of its status is obtained. It is typically found in remote mountainous areas that are seldom subjected to heavy amounts of disturbance due to human activity. It is doubtful that this trend of minimal habitat disturbance will change in the near future.

SELECTED REFERENCES:

CALDER, W. A. 1969. Temperature relations and underwater endurance of the smallest homeothermic diver, the water shrew. Comp. Biochem. Physical., 30:1075–1082.
DOUTT, J. K., C. A. HEPPENSTALL, and J. E. GUILDAY. 1977. Mammals of Pennsylvania. Pennsylvania Game Comm., Harrisburg, fourth edition, 283 pp.
GODIN, A. J. 1977. Wild mammals of New England. Johns Hopkins Univ. Press, Baltimore, 304 pp.
GRIMM, W. C., and R. WHITEBREAD. 1952. Mammal survey of northeastern Pennsylvania. Final Report Pittman-Robertson Project 42-R. Pennsylvania Game Comm., Harrisburg, 82 pp.
HALL, E. R. 1981. The mammals of North America. John Wiley & Sons, New York, 1:xv + 1–600 + 90.

PREPARED BY: John E. Enders, *Sartorius Filters, 304 Second Street, P.O. Box 185, Dalton, PA 18414.*

Status Undetermined

PYGMY SHREW
Microsorex hoyi
Family Soricidae
Order Insectivora

DESCRIPTION: The pygmy shrew is the smallest member of the mammalian fauna of Pennsylvania. It most closely resembles the masked shrew (*Sorex cinereus*); however, the pygmy shrew is somewhat smaller with a slightly shorter tail than the masked shrew. The two species can only be definitely distinguished by examination of the unicuspid teeth at the front of the toothrow. In the pygmy shrew, the third unicuspid has been compressed anteroposteriorly and the fifth unicuspid is minute; therefore, only three unicuspids are easily seen when viewed from the lateral side. In the masked shrew by contrast, five unicuspids are easily seen in lateral view.

The eyes and external ears are small and the fur is short and velvety. The upper parts of the body are dark brown with lighter colored sides. The underparts are gray with tints of white or rusty brown. Individuals weigh 2.5 to 4.0 g. Average external measurements of pygmy shrews are as follows: total length, 85 mm; length of tail, 29.5 mm; length of hind foot, 9.5 mm.

Long (1972a) recognized two species in this genus; however, the most recent reviser of this group (Diersing, 1980) only recognized a single species, *M. hoyi*. Diersing (1980) placed the genus *Microsorex* as a subgenus of *Sorex* but this arrangement is not followed.

RANGE: The pygmy shrew occurs throughout most of central and southern Canada, Alaska, and the north-central and northeastern United States. The species also has populations extending along the Rocky Mountains and Appalachian Mountains. Although the species reaches as far south as northern Georgia, Pennsylvania is a major gap in the distribution along the Allegheny-Appalachian mountains. The species is known from localities in adjacent areas of Ohio, New York, and Maryland, but documented specimens are not available from Pennsylvania (Hall, 1981).

HABITAT: The pygmy shrew seems to prefer boreal habitats where wet and dry soils are available. Pygmy shrews have been captured in swamps and marshes, but others have been taken in dry upland situations. Most individuals have been captured within 100 meters of water. Pygmy shrews are commonly found in areas undergoing succession where such plants as birch, aspen, jack pine, blackberry, and raspberry are found. Specimens of pygmy shrew are commonly captured in association with red-backed voles, *Clethrionomys gapperi*.

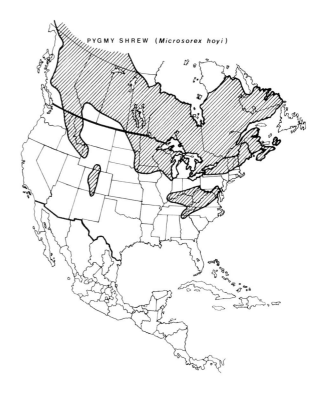

PYGMY SHREW (*Microsorex hoyi*)

LIFE HISTORY AND ECOLOGY: No data are available for the pygmy shrew in Pennsylvania. Few records of reproduction are available concerning this shrew from throughout its geographic range but the evidence that is available indicates that five to eight young are produced in each litter and these are borne during the summer months. Population density was estimated to 0.52 individual/hectare in upper Michigan.

The food of the pygmy shrew is primarily larval and adult insects. Insect groups reportedly taken include lepidopterans, coleopterans, and dipterans.

BASIS OF CLASSIFICATION: Only one specimen of this species has previously been reported from Pennsylvania (Roslund, 1951; Doutt et al., 1967). This specimen was recovered from the stomach of a red fox trapped in Potter Co. Re-examination of this specimen has revealed, however, that it is a masked shrew and not a pygmy shrew (Diersing, 1980). Pygmy shrews are known from New York, Maryland, and West Virginia and have been reported from two late Pleistocene cave faunas (Guilday et al., 1964, 1966) in the Commonwealth. Of seven species of shrews in the cave fauna from Bedford County, pygmy shrews were the third most abundant species. There seems to be no obvious reasons why the pygmy shrew should not be part of the modern mammalian fauna of Pennsylvania.

RECOMMENDATIONS: An intensive program of pitfall trapping in the montane habitats of the Allegheny Mountains should be undertaken to search for the presence of pygmy shrews in the Commonwealth. This study should be designed to provide information on the distribution, life history, and habitat preferences of this shrew as well as other species of shrews that would also be taken.

SELECTED REFERENCES:

BROWN, L. N. 1967. Ecological distribution of six species of shrews and comparison of sampling methods in the central Rocky Mountains. J. Mamm., 48:617–623.

DIERSING, V. E. 1980. Systematics and evolution of the pygmy shrews (subgenus *Microsorex*) of North America. J. Mamm., 61:76–101.

DOUTT, J. K., C. A. HEPPENSTALL, and J. E. GUILDAY. 1967. Mammals of Pennsylvania. Pennsylvania Game Comm., Harrisburg, 281 pp.

GUILDAY, J. E., H. W. HAMILTON, and A. D. McCRADY. 1966. The bone breccia of Bootlegger Sink, York County, Pa. Ann. Carnegie Mus., 38:145–163.

GUILDAY, J. E., P. S. MARTIN, and A. D. McCRADY. 1964. New Paris No. 4: A Pleistocene cave deposit in Bedford County, Pennsylvania. Bull. Nat. Speleo. Soc., 26:121–194.

HALL, E. R. 1981. The mammals of North America. John Wiley & Sons, New York, 1:xv + 1–600 + 90.

HAMILTON, W. J., JR. and J. O. WHITAKER, JR. 1979. Mammals of the eastern United States. Cornell Univ. Press, Ithaca, New York, 2nd ed., 346 pp.

LONG, C. A. 1972a. Taxonomic revision of the mammalian genus *Microsorex* Coues. Trans. Kansas Acad. Sci., 74:181–196.

———. 1972b. Notes on habitat preference and reproduction in pygmy shrews. Canadian Field-Nat., 86:155–160.

———. 1974. *Microsorex hoyi* and *Microsorex thompsoni.* Mammalian Species, 33:1–4.

ROSLUND, H. R. 1951. Mammal survey of northcentral Pennsylvania. Final Report Pittman-Robertson Project 37-R. Pennsylvania Game Comm., Harrisburg, 55 pp.

SPENCER, A. W., and D. PETTUS. 1966. Habitat preferences of five sympatric species of long-tailed shrews. Ecology, 47:677–683.

PREPARED BY: Hugh H. Genoways, *Carnegie Museum of Natural History, 4400 Forbes Avenue, Pittsburgh, PA 15213.*

Status Undetermined

LEAST SHREW
Cryptotis parva (Say)
Family Soricidae
Order Insectivora

OTHER NAMES: Little short-tailed shrew, little shrew, field shrew, and small blarina (Godin, 1977).

DESCRIPTION: This is one of the smallest (4.0–6.0 g) shrews. The sexes are equal in size and measure, in mm, 75–89, total length; 13–20, tail length; 9–11, hind foot (Doutt et al., 1966). Like other shrews, *C. parva* has a long and pointed snout, black eyes, and the ears are nearly concealed in the fur. The short, slender bicolored tail, less than half the length of the head and body, along with its small size, allow this species to be easily identified.

The sexes are similarly colored, and seasonal color variation does exist. The fine, velvety pelt is dark

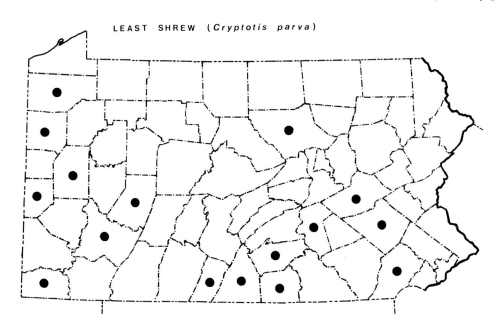

LEAST SHREW (*Cryptotis parva*)

LEAST SHREW (*Cryptotis parva*)

brown above and ashy gray below in winter, and somewhat paler in the summer.

Whitaker (1974) mentioned that the skull is small, but broader and higher than in species of *Sorex*. The rostrum is short and the zygomatic arches are incomplete. As in most other North American shrews, the teeth have chestnut-colored cusps. This is the only genus of shrew in Pennsylvania with a total of 30 teeth. On the upper jaw, there are four unicuspid teeth, but the fourth is tiny and hidden from lateral view, because it lies somewhat medial to the much larger third unicuspid and the adjoining tricuspid.

RANGE: The least shrew is found throughout the eastern half of the United States (Hall, 1981; Whitaker, 1974) but ranges no further north than lower South Dakota, Minnesota, Wisconsin, Michigan, Ontario, New York, and Connecticut. The species extends westward to extreme western South Dakota, Nebraska, Kansas, Oklahoma, and much of the eastern half of Texas, where it continues southward, extending throughout much of Central America. Doutt et al. (1966) believed *C. parva* is probably found throughout Pennsylvania, although specimens are not known from large portions of the northern, central, and southwestern parts of the Commonwealth. According to Hall (1981), the subspecies found throughout Pennsylvania is *C. parva parva* (Say).

HABITAT: In Pennsylvania, the least shrew is found in grasslands, inhabiting meadows, old fields, dry, stony, abandoned pasturelands, coastal swamps, and hay fields (Doutt et al., 1966). However, their populations are apparently widely scattered. This fact, coupled with their small size, results in a paucity of information about their actual numbers and distributional patterns in the state.

LIFE HISTORY AND ECOLOGY: Because the species is so difficult to capture using conventional live-trapping techniques, little is known of its population dynamics. Densities of several animals per ha and home ranges of several thousand m² were estimated by Howell (1954). They appear to be somewhat social; Whitaker (1974) lists a number of authors who have found several individuals to over two dozens in a leaf or grass nest at one time. Their runways, about the diameter of a pencil, radiate from their nest sites. Rodent runways are also utilized. Consuming nearly their weight in food each day, they prey predominately on insects (adults and larvae) and earthworms (Hamilton, 1944; Whitaker and Mumford, 1972).

The breeding season for this species in Pennsylvania and other states in the northern part of its range probably extends from March to November (Hamilton, 1944). An average litter size of 4 to 5 is given by numerous authors (Whitaker, 1974). Gestation lasts approximately three weeks (Conaway, 1958). Weaning occurs early in the fourth week after birth (Hamilton, 1943; Conaway, 1958; Gould, 1969).

BASIS OF STATUS CLASSIFICATION: Cryptotis parva has been documented from numerous counties, particularly those in the southern half of the Commonwealth. The habitat in which it is found is in no danger of disappearing. However, whether it is because *C. parva* is near the periphery of its range, or for some other reason, the species is not as commonly observed in Pennsylvania as it is in many other states. Biologists involved with small mammal trapping normally do not use the correct trapping methods for capturing such small animals. Their capture, therefore, is usually incidental to the main reason for trapping. Until more is known about the distribution and population dynamics of this shrew in Pennsylvania, its "status undetermined" classification is appropriate.

RECOMMENDATIONS: Pitfall traps are recognized by mammalogists as the most effective trap type for capturing shrews and some species of rodents. Extensive trapping at locations where the least shrew has been captured in the past should be undertaken. Likewise, extensive trapping in other areas of the Commonwealth is recommended. Pitfall trapping techniques allow for live or dead capture. Such a trapping effort will provide the appropriate distribution and population dynamics data necessary for a future reevaluation of its status.

SELECTED REFERENCES:

CONAWAY, C. H. 1958. Maintenance, reproduction, and growth of the least shrew in captivity. J. Mamm., 39:507–512.

DOUTT, J. K., C. A. HEPPENSTALL, and J. E. GUILDAY. 1966. Mammals of Pennsylvania. Pennsylvania Game Comm., Harrisburg, 288 pp.

GODIN, A. J. 1977. Wild mammals of New England. Johns Hopkins University Press, Baltimore, 304 pp.

GOULD, E. 1969. Communication in three genera of shrews (Soricidae): *Suncus, Blarina,* and *Cryptotis.* Comm. Behav. Biol., Part A, 3:11–31.

HAMILTON, W. J., JR. 1943. The mammals of eastern United States. Comstock, Ithaca, New York, 432 pp.

———. 1944. The biology of the little short-tailed shrews, *Cryptotis parva.* J. Mamm., 25:1–7.

HALL, E. R. 1981. The mammals of North America. John Wiley & Sons, New York, 1:xv + 1–600 + *90.*

HOWELL, J. C. 1954. Populations and home ranges of small mammals on an overgrown field. J. Mamm., 35:177–186.

WHITAKER, J. O., JR. 1974. *Cryptotis parva.* Mammalian Species, 43:1–8.

WHITAKER, J. O., JR., and R. E. MUMFORD. 1972. Food and ectoparasites of Indiana shrews. J. Mamm., 53:329–335.

PREPARED BY: Peter L. Dalby, *Biology Department, Clarion University, Clarion, PA 16214.*

Status Undetermined

SEMINOLE BAT
Lasiurus seminolus (Rhoads)
Family Vespertilionidae
Order Chiroptera

OTHER NAMES: Mahogany bat.

DESCRIPTION: The Seminole bat is a medium-sized bat with long, pointed wings and short rounded ears. The tail membrane is heavily furred on the dorsal surface. The dorsal fur is a deep mahogany color, sometimes tipped with silver. The forearm of this species measures 35–45 mm in length. The sexes are similar in external appearance.

The Seminole bat appears identical to the red bat (*Lasiurus borealis*) except for color of fur. In the former the color is a deep mahogany, whereas the latter is red or yellowish in color. From the other brightly colored tree bats the Seminole bat can be distinguished by size and color as well. It is smaller than the gray hoary bat and although nearly the same size as the silver-haired bat, the latter is black with white-tipped dorsal hairs. All the other potentially confusing species in the state are brown bats with little if any fur on the tail membranes.

RANGE: The Seminole bat is confined to the southeastern United States from southeastern Virginia through to southeastern Oklahoma and thence through eastern Texas and Mexico as far south as Veracruz. Three localities as far north as New York

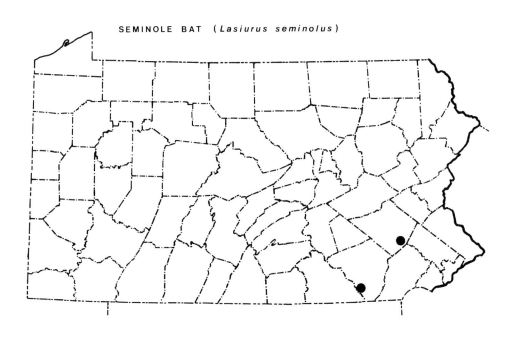

SEMINOLE BAT (*Lasiurus seminolus*)

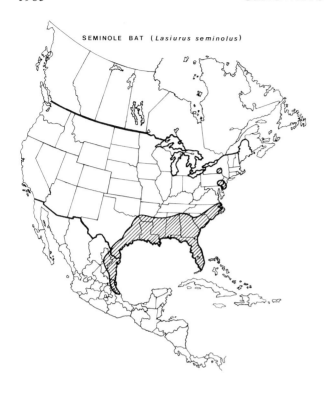

SEMINOLE BAT (*Lasiurus seminolus*)

have been reported for this species. Autumn specimens have been reported for Ithaca, New York, and Hopewell, Berks County, and the shore of the Susquehanna River near the mouth of Fishing Creek, Lancaster County, Pennsylvania.

HABITAT: The Seminole bat is a tree-roosting species found commonly in clumps of Spanish moss in the south. Although this moss does not occur in Pennsylvania, this species should be looked for roosting in trees or hawking insects in the forest or along the forest edge and clearings, and over streams or other openings over water.

LIFE HISTORY AND ECOLOGY: Over much of its range in the south, this species is the most abundant bat seen flying in the evenings. It is active at all seasons, even on warm evenings during the winter. It rarely flies when temperatures fall below 18°C. Usually three or four young are born during late May and June.

A definite shift of individuals southward occurs in the autumn in the southern United States. The Seminole bat, like several other species, wanders extensively after the young are weaned. The wandering accounts for numerous records of the species outside of the normal breeding range.

BASIS OF STATUS CLASSIFICATION: Until data are available to indicate that the Seminole bat breeds in the state, the available records from this area must be interpreted as wandering vagrants. Both Pennsylvania records were captured well into September at a time when such wandering is known to occur for this species. For now, it is best to classify this species as status undetermined.

RECOMMENDATIONS: More data are needed on the biology of this species to indicate whether or not it breeds in the Commonwealth. Most work on bats in the Commonwealth has involved searching caves in winter, netting cave entrances, or shooting in the summer. Although easily collected by shooting, *Lasiurus seminolus* is difficult to mist net with traditional ground-level netting. These bats feed in the forest canopy and seldom fly at ground level. A survey involving sky-netting must be implemented in suitable forested areas to determine if this species is a summer resident before its status can be clarified.

SELECTED REFERENCES:

BARBOUR, R. W., and W. H. DAVIS. 1969. Bats of America. Univ. Press Kentucky, Lexington, 286 pp.

DOUTT, J. K., C. A. HEPPENSTALL, and J. E. GUILDAY. 1966. Mammals of Pennsylvania. Pennsylvania Game Comm., Harrisburg, 288 pp.

LAYNE, J. N. 1955. Seminole bat, *Lasiurus seminolus*, in central New York. J. Mamm., 36:453.

POOLE, E. L. 1949. A second Pennsylvania specimen of *Lasiurus seminolus* (Rhoads). J. Mamm., 30:80.

PREPARED BY: Duane A. Schlitter, *Section of Mammals, Carnegie Museum of Natural History, 4400 Forbes Ave., Pittsburgh, PA 15213.*

Status Undetermined

SILVER-HAIRED BAT
Lasionycteris noctivagans (Le Conte)
Family Vespertilionidae
Order Chiroptera

OTHER NAMES: Silvery bat.

DESCRIPTION: The silver-haired bat is a medium-sized bat with black dorsal fur that is silver-tipped. The membranes are black, with the tail membrane covered with fur dorsally. The black ears are short, naked, and rounded. The forearm length

Silver-haired Bat (*Lasionycteris noctivagans*). Photograph by R. W. Barbour.

measures from 37 to 44 mm. Sexes are similar in external features.

Because of its dark color, the silver-haired bat will not be confused with other bats in Pennsylvania with the exception of the hoary bat. From the hoary bat, the silver-haired bat can be distinguished by overall smaller size, naked ears, and less heavily-furred tail membrane. In the silver-haired bat the black tail membrane is visible through the hairs, whereas in the hoary bat the tail membrane is heavily furred.

RANGE: Silver-haired bats occur south of a line across southern Canada roughly even with the south tip of James Bay, thence southward nearly to the southern border of the United States. Within this geographic area, these bats are sometimes relatively abundant. Records of occurrence within Pennsylvania and adjacent states indicate that this species occurs throughout the Commonwealth.

HABITAT: The silver-haired bat is a species of the northern forests. The young are raised in the area

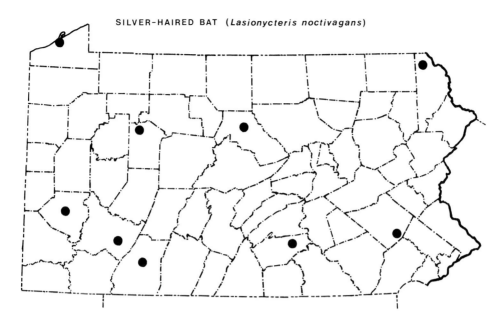

SILVER-HAIRED BAT (*Lasionycteris noctivagans*)

from the northern states northward into Canada nearly to the treeless zone.

Locally these bats occur in all forested areas, particularly along streams and about forest ponds. Individuals roost under tree bark, in woodpecker holes, and in bird nests. During migrations, they may be found resting in numerous other shelters such as open sheds, garages, outbuildings, and in piles of slabs, lumber, railroad ties, or fenceposts. They hibernate in trees, buildings, rock crevices, and other similarly protected places. The normal hibernating sites are probably trees but such data are scarce on the species. They never seem to enter limestone caves.

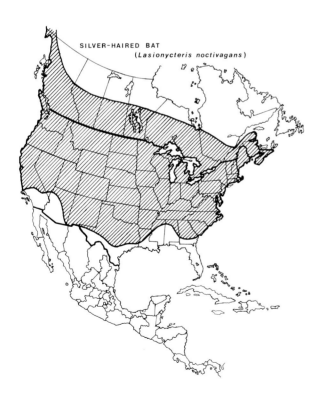

SILVER-HAIRED BAT
(*Lasionycteris noctivagans*)

LIFE HISTORY AND ECOLOGY: Two young are born in late June or July. Females seem to segregate from males, at least during the summer months. During the summer months, nearly all adult individuals checked in the northern states and Canada have been females. In Pennsylvania, 11 of 16 specimens taken in the summer months were females.

Circumstantial evidence strongly suggests that silver-haired bats migrate. In many areas where they are unknown in summer, they are fairly common in spring and autumn. In these areas they are regular and dependable visitors. Bird banders regularly capture this species in mist nets set along bird migration routes, especially in September. At these times more than a single individual are commonly captured, suggesting that the bats travel in groups. Individuals have been sighted on barren islands, miles from the mainland, and have been captured on ships where weary bats have descended to rest.

There are many reports of colonial behavior in this species. However, these reports are mostly from the previous century and none are backed by voucher specimens. There are no valid reports during the last 70 years and such behavior should not be accepted until further data are available on the subject.

Summer day roosts must be located and studied before any definitive conclusions can be drawn.

BASIS OF STATUS CLASSIFICATION: Little is known about the biology of the silver-haired bat in Pennsylvania. Although potentially occurring throughout the Commonwealth, this bat is seldom seen or taken since it does not frequent caves or mines, except in winter, and little summer mist-netting has been done in the Commonwealth. Until more recent data on its biology in the Commonwealth are available, it is best to leave it as status undetermined.

RECOMMENDATIONS: A program of summer mist-netting should be implemented to determine how widespread and common this species is in the Commonwealth. At the same time, careful attention should be paid to the sex ratio, age, and reproductive status of all bats taken in order to determine if the silver-haired bat is a breeding summer resident or whether the population consists of males only with the females merely passing through on their way north. With data of this type, it is reasonable to suspect this species can be removed entirely from this list.

SELECTED REFERENCES:

BARBOUR, R. W., and W. H. DAVIS. 1969. Bats of America. Univ. Press Kentucky, Lexington, 286 pp.

DOUTT, J. K., C. A. HEPPENSTALL, and J. E. GUILDAY. 1966. Mammals of Pennsylvania. Pennsylvania Game Comm., Harrisburg, 288 pp.

FRUM, W. G. 1953. Silver-haired bat, *Lasionycteris noctivagans,* in West Virginia. J. Mamm., 34:499–500.

HAMILTON, W. J., JR. 1943. The mammals of eastern United States. Comstock Publ. Assoc., Ithaca, New York, 432 pp.

KUNZ, T. H. 1982. *Lasionycteris noctivagans.* Mammalian Species, 172:1–5.

PREPARED BY: Duane A. Schlitter, *Section of Mammals, Carnegie Museum of Natural History, 4400 Forbes Ave., Pittsburgh, PA 15213.*

Status Undetermined

EVENING BAT
Nycticeius humeralis humeralis (Rafinesque)
Family Vespertilionidae
Order Chiroptera

OTHER NAMES: Twilight bat.

DESCRIPTION: The evening bat is a rather small to medium-sized brown bat, resembling the com-

Evening Bat (*Nycticeius humeralis*). Photograph by R. W. Barbour.

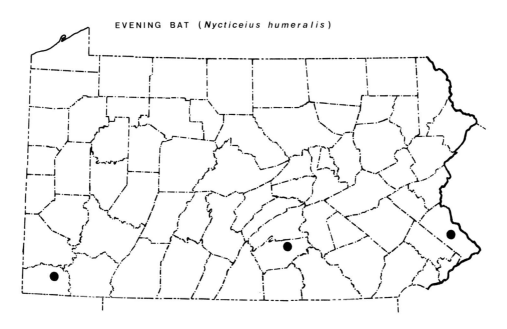

EVENING BAT (*Nycticeius humeralis*)

mon big brown bat (*Eptescicus fuscus*) in external features. The fur is a medium brown and the ears and all membranes are dark, chocolate brown in color. The evening bat differs from *Eptesicus fuscus* in its smaller size and possession of only two upper incisors as opposed to four upper incisors. The short curved, rounded tragus readily separates it from any species of *Myotis*.

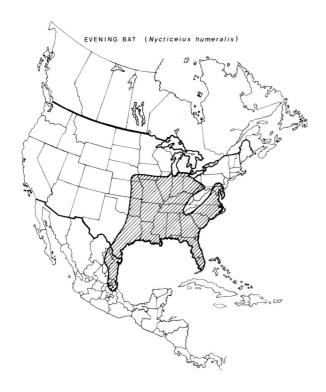

EVENING BAT (*Nycticeius humeralis*)

Females are slightly larger than males in the evening bat. Forearms of this species vary from 33–39 mm in length. The calcar in this species is not keeled.

RANGE: The evening bat occurs over most of the southeastern United States reaching the northern limits of its range in southern Pennsylvania. Westward it occurs from central Ohio, southern Michigan, and Ontario, central Iowa, to southeastern Nebraska, thence south through eastern Mexico as far as Veracruz.

Within Pennsylvania, the evening bat has been found in only three places, all along the southern border. An early record, part of the Baird collection at the Smithsonian Institution, was obtained from Carlisle, Cumberland County, in the 1850's. A second record of occurrence was a breeding colony found on the Waynesburg College campus at Waynesburg, Greene County. A single female specimen collected by Clay Gifford on 8 September 1936 on the north side of Hannah Hill, Waynesburg, is deposited at Carnegie Museum of Natural History. Finally, Doutt et al. (1966) reported a specimen collected by H. A. Surface from Buckingham, Bucks County, around the turn of the century.

HABITAT: *Nycticeius humeralis* is found roosting most commonly in buildings, especially attics, and cavities of trees. They do not commonly frequent caves. Maternity colonies are found in houses. The winter habitat is completely unknown. Individuals accumulate large reserves of fat in autumn, amounts sufficient for either hibernation or a long migration.

LIFE HISTORY AND ECOLOGY: Evening bats congregate by the hundreds in maternity colonies. These colonies are usually found in attics of houses where only the single species seems to occur.

The absence of this species in the northern part of its range during winter seems to strongly indicate migration. Roosts are vacated by mid-October and banded individuals have been recaptured over 400 miles south of their banding site. However, there is still no information where summer inhabitants of northern roosts spend the winter months.

In Missouri, individuals studied lived an average of two years with a few individuals reaching five years.

Sexes segregate during the period when the young are born. Young are born during June in the north. Typically twins are born but a high percentage of triplets occur. By approximately 20 days the juveniles are airborne.

BASIS OF STATUS CLASSIFICATION: Both the distribution and biology of the evening bat are poorly studied in Pennsylvania as in most parts of the northern portions of its range. Because it seldom enters caves, this species is not often seen or taken by biologists. The last known record of occurrence was in 1939 in the southwestern part of Pennsylvania.

Little summer mist-netting of bats has been done in Pennsylvania so few data are available from the period when this bat is most active in the Commonwealth. Until more recent data are available, little can be said about the status of this species. It must be considered as status undetermined for the present.

RECOMMENDATIONS: Field studies in other states, particularly in the northwestern parts of its range, indicate that although formerly considered rare it was in fact quite common during the summer. An extensive program of summer mist-netting as well as searching for roosts must be undertaken. Based on other studies, it seems reasonable to expect that suitable populations of evening bats will be found in the Commonwealth as a result of such research. However, if such should be the case, property owners where maternity colonies may occur should be encouraged to protect these colonies. Since large numbers of females may collect in these col-

onies, destruction of these colonies will have a profound effect on the overall population structure in the Commonwealth.

SELECTED REFERENCES:

BARBOUR, R. W., and W. H. DAVIS. 1969. Bats of America. Univ. Press Kentucky, Lexington, 286 pp.
DOUTT, J. K., C. A. HEPPENSTALL, and J. E. GUILDAY. 1966. Mammals of Pennsylvania. Pennsylvania Game Comm., Harrisburg, 281 pp.
GRIMM, W. C., and H. A. ROBERTS. 1950. Mammal Survey of Southwestern Pennsylvania. Final Report of Pittman-Robertson Project 24-R. Pennsylvania Game Comm., Harrisburg, 99 pp.
ROBERTS, H. A., and R. C. EARLY. 1952. Mammal Survey of Southeastern Pennsylvania. Final Report of Pittman-Robertson Project 43-R. Pennsylvania Game Comm., Harrisburg, 70 pp.
WATKINS, L. C. 1972. *Nycticeius humeralis.* Mammalian Species, 23:1–4.

PREPARED BY: Duane A. Schlitter, *Section of Mammals, Carnegie Museum of Natural History, 4400 Forbes Ave., Pittsburgh, PA 15213.*

Status Undetermined

NEW ENGLAND COTTONTAIL
Sylvilagus transitionalis (Bangs)
Family Leporidae
Order Lagomorpha

OTHER NAMES: Wood rabbit, mountain cottontail.

DESCRIPTION: The New England cottontail resembles the eastern cottontail (*Sylvilagus floridanus*) in pelage and external morphology. The dorsum is pinkish buff to ochraceous buff and has a pronounced black wash. There is usually a black spot between the ears and never a white spot or blaze on the forehead (Chapman, 1975). In contrast, the eastern cottontail frequently possesses a white blaze on the forehead and usually lacks the black spot between the ears. In *S. transitionalis,* the ears appear short and rounded; the inside is heavily furred with the anterior outer border black and the posterior inner border ochraceous to buffy. The ears in *S. floridanus* appear longer and more pointed; the inside is sparsely furred with the anterior outer border brown and the posterior inner border pale buffy to white (Fay and Chandler, 1955). Although some eastern cottontails may possess many of the pelage and color characteristics of New England cottontails, in general, they appear lighter in color because

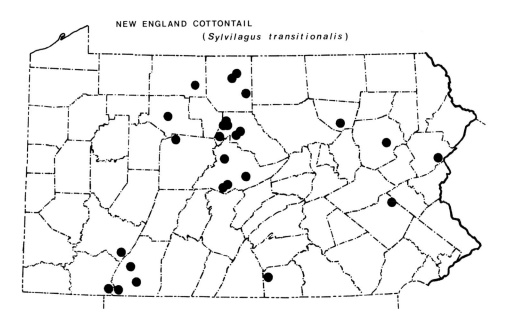

NEW ENGLAND COTTONTAIL
(*Sylvilagus transitionalis*)

of the less pronounced black wash. Cranially, these two rabbits are more distinctive. Diagnostic characteristics for the New England cottontail include the jagged and irregular posterior margins of the nasals, the slender, tapering postorbital processes (usually not touching the cranium posteriorally), and the vestigial or short supraorbital processes. Also, the skull of *S. transitionalis* is more delicate and the auditory bullae are smaller than in any of the subspecies of *S. floridanus* (Chapman, 1975). In the eastern cottontail, the posterior margins of the nasals are smooth, the postorbital processes are broad and not tapering (usually attached to the cranium posteriorally), and the supraorbital processes are well developed. The New England cottontail is smaller than the eastern cottontail in nearly all external and cranial characters (Chapman and Morgan, 1973). In addition, the two rabbits are karyotypically distinct, with *S. transitionalis* having 2N = 52 and *S. floridanus* having a 2N = 42 (Chapman and Morgan, 1973).

RANGE: The original range of the New England cottontail extended from New England southward through the Middle Atlantic states and along the Appalachian Mountains as far south as Alabama and Georgia (Chapman, 1975). Having been extirpated from portions of its original range, the New England cottontail presently occupies a more restricted geographic area and may currently exist as a series of isolated refugial populations scattered throughout most of its former range (Chapman and Stauffer, 1982). In Pennsylvania, the New England cottontail is limited in distribution to the mountainous portions of the northeastern and central regions of the state. During the Pennsylvania Mammal Survey (1948–1952), *S. transitionalis* were collected in 10 counties: Adams, Bradford, Centre, Clinton, Luzerne, McKean, Mifflin, Pike, Potter, and Union.

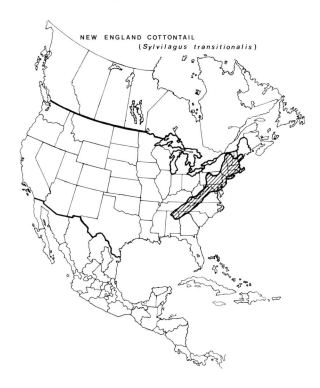

NEW ENGLAND COTTONTAIL
(*Sylvilagus transitionalis*)

HABITAT: In Pennsylvania, the New England Cottontail is primarily a species of the forested uplands and mountains. It tends to favor forests with dense understories of shrubby vegetation. In northeastern Pennsylvania and throughout the mid- and southern Appalachians, *S. transitionalis* is often common in the brushy habitat characteristic of 5–10 year old clearcuts (Chapman and Stauffer, 1982). Much of the research on habitat preference in the New England cottontail has been conducted in southern New England where *S. transitionalis* inhabits a variety of forest types (Eabry, 1968); however, it is apparently being displaced by *S. floridanus* in the more open austral forests (Fay and Chandler, 1955). One basic habitat difference between *S. transitionalis* and *S. floridanus* is that in heavily forested regions, the eastern cottontail requires at least some relatively open land, whereas the New England cottontail does not (Fay and Chandler, 1955).

LIFE HISTORY AND ECOLOGY: In comparison with the substantial pool of information on distribution, habitat preferences, and abundance of the eastern cottontail, relatively little is known about the general life history and ecology of the New England cottontail; however, in many respects, it resembles the eastern cottontail in its general life history. Food habit studies have indicated that the New England cottontail has a narrower dietary potential than the eastern cottontail (Nottage, 1972). The gestation period in *S. transitionalis* is approximately 28 days, and during each breeding season, females may produce two or three litters of from three to eight young per litter (Chapman, 1975). Of critical significance is the fact that interbreeding occurs with unknown frequency between *S. transitionalis* and *S. floridanus* (Chapman, 1975). Cross-breeding has been successful in the laboratory, and a wild-caught individual from West Virginia has been identified as a hybrid (Chapman and Morgan, 1973). Certainly, any dilution of New England cottontail's gene pool resulting from interbreeding with eastern cottontails would adversely affect prospects for the survival of certain local populations.

BASIS OF STATUS CLASSIFICATION: The New England cottontail is classed as Status Undetermined because of inadequate data on its current distribution and abundance in Pennsylvania. In other regions, the New England cottontail has been experiencing a long-term decline in numbers, coincident with its displacement by the eastern cottontail (Johnston, 1972). In pre-settlement times, the forest-dwelling *S. transitionalis* apparently was ecologically segregated from *S. floridanus* which inhabited the river bottoms and glades. The clearing of forests, development of agricultural lands, and construction of transportation corridors (highways, railroads) greatly expanded the open and edge habitats preferred by the eastern cottontail, presumably to the detriment of the New England cottontail. The eastern cottontail not only expanded its distribution within the original pre-settlement zone of sympatry of the two species, but it extended its range northward into New England where it had not previously occurred (Johnston, 1972). The encroachment of *S. floridanus* into the range and habitats of *S. transitionalis* was fostered by the introduction of large numbers of cottontails into areas formerly inhabited exclusively by the New England cottontail. The competitive position of the eastern cottontail may have been enhanced by the infusion of diverse genetic material from various species and subspecies of *Sylvilagus* in what has been termed the "Niche Width-Introduction Hypothesis" (Chapman and Stauffer, 1982).

RECOMMENDATIONS: In as much as the decline in the numbers and consequent reduction in the geographic distribution of the New England cottontail have been attributed to the impact of habitat alterations and the massive introductions of various species and subspecies of *Sylvilagus,* any management program for this species in Pennsylvania should address these two problems. Thus, within regions of the Commonwealth where the New England cottontail is known or presumed to occur, state-owned land should be managed to maintain habitat suitable for the New England cottontail, as well as to minimize the adverse impact of any habitat alterations. In addition, private landowners should be encouraged to manage their lands to benefit this species. In order to minimize the problem of gene pool swamping, laws should be established to strictly regulate the importation, release, or transplantation of all members of the genus *Sylvilagus* (cottontails) within the Commonwealth of Pennsylvania. Because the New England and eastern cottontails are so similar externally, it would be difficult to promulgate laws to control the shooting of New England cottontails; however, restrictions on the hunting of any cottontails within certain forested habitats might prove effective in decreasing mortality in the New England cottontail.

ACKNOWLEDGEMENTS: Information on the status and distribution of the New England cottontail was provided by Dr. Joseph A. Chapman, University of Maryland, Center for Environmental and Estuarine Studies, Appalachian Environmental Laboratory, Frostburg State College Campus, Frostburg, Maryland 21532.

SELECTED REFERENCES:

CHAPMAN, J. A. 1975. *Sylvilagus transitionalis.* Mammalian Species, 55:1–4.

CHAPMAN, J. A., and R. P. MORGAN II. 1973. Systematic status of the cottontail complex in western Maryland and nearby West Virginia. Wildlife Monogr., 36:1–54.

CHAPMAN, J. A., and J. R. STAUFFER, JR. 1982. The status and distribution of the New England cottontail. Pp. 973–983, *in* Proc. World Lagomorph Conf., (K. Myers and C. D. MacInnes, eds.), Univ. Guelph, Guelph, Canada, xix + 983 pp.

EABRY, H. S. 1968. An ecological study of *Sylvilagus transitionalis* and *S. floridanus* of northeastern Connecticut. Agri. Exp. Sta., Univ. Connecticut, 27 pp.

FAY, F. H., and E. H. CHANDLER. 1955. The geographic and ecological distribution of cottontail rabbits in Massachusetts. J. Mamm., 36:415–424.

HOLDERMANN, D. A. 1978. The distribution and abundance of eastern cottontail (*Sylvilagus floridanus*) and New England cottontail (*S. transitionalis*) populations on a grouse management area in central Pennsylvania. Unpublished Master's thesis, Pennsylvania State Univ., University Park, xi + 82 pp.

JOHNSTON, J. E. 1972. Identification and distribution of cottontail rabbits in southern New England. Agr. Exp. Sta., Univ. Connecticut, 70 pp.

NOTTAGE, E. J. 1972. Comparative feeding trials of *Sylvilagus floridanus* and *Sylvilagus transitionalis.* Agric. Exp. Sta., Univ. Connecticut, 39 pp.

PREPARED BY: Gordon L. Kirkland, Jr., *The Vertebrate Museum, Shippensburg University, Shippensburg, PA 17257.*

Status Undetermined

EASTERN FOX SQUIRREL
Sciurus niger vulpinus Gmelin
Family Sciuridae
Order Rodentia

DESCRIPTION: The fox squirrel is a tree squirrel, larger than the more common gray squirrel (*Sciurus carolinensis*). *S. n. vulpinus* measures 510–592 mm total length, 218–280 mm tail length, 69–79 mm hind foot, and 879–1,017 g total weight. They are tawny-brown, grizzled with considerable gray above and white to pale rufous or yellowish-brown below. Tail is tawny rufous mixed with black. The under-

side of the tail is tawny-red (Doutt et al., 1967). This subspecies is generally grayer on the back and sides than other subspecies, except of course *S. n. cinereus.*

RANGE: This subspecies is known from central West Virginia to the Chesapeake Bay and from central Virginia through the southeastern portion of Pennsylvania. Marginal records are: Pennsylvania—Carlisle; Maryland—Calvert County; West Virginia—White Sulfur Springs and Lewisburg (Hall, 1981). Range in Pennsylvania extends west to the Blue Mountains (Doutt et al., 1967). The marginal record in western Pennsylvania ("Rothruck") reported by Hall (1981) is probably incorrect. The specimen, in the Museum of Comparative Zoology, Harvard University, was collected by Rothruck somewhere in Pennsylvania (Schlitter, personal communications). Other specimens collected from western Pennsylvania appear to be more like *S. n. rufiventer* from the Midwest than like *S. n. vulpinus* from West Virginia and Maryland. Therefore, the only "good" specimens of *S. n. vulpinus* appear to be from east of the Blue Mountains.

Taylor (1976) considers those specimens collected east of the Susquehanna River to have been *S. n. cinereus,* the Delmarva fox squirrel. This difference of opinion highlights the uncertain taxonomic status of *S. n. vulpinus* (see "Basis of Status Classification").

HABITAT: Preferred habitats include open hardwood forest (Hall and Kelson, 1959) and woodlots containing a few scattered mature trees (preferably oaks) and often in close proximity to pastures (Doutt et al., 1967). Anecdotal information indicates that good habitat for fox squirrels should include: 1) old, hollow oaks for nesting, 2) pasture nearby, and 3) a supply of nuts and seeds including hickory, oak, walnut, black cherry, beech, elm, basswood, maple, ash, chestnut, or conifer (Doutt et al., 1967). One universal characteristic of good fox squirrel habitat is an open understory within small woodlots and forest edges or park-like conditions (Flyger and Lustig, 1976).

LIFE HISTORY AND ECOLOGY: *S. n. vulpinus* has not been extensively studied. However, observations of other subspecies indicate that fox squirrels are rather asocial (Cahalane, 1947). Other studies indicate fox squirrels organize into social hierarchies (Bernard, 1972). Adults come together

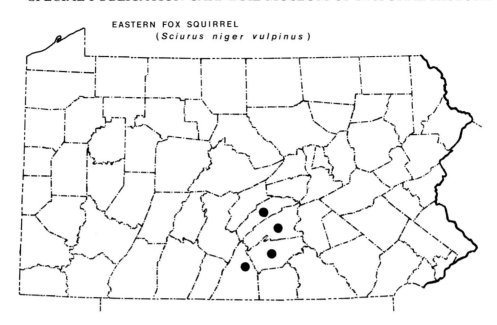

EASTERN FOX SQUIRREL
(*Sciurus niger vulpinus*)

to mate in mid-winter and often mate again in the spring. Gestation lasts 45 days; litters vary from one to six young. Normal life span is from 4 to 6 years (Hall and Kelson, 1959). They use both winter and summer leaf nests and also den in hollow trees (Cahalane, 1947; Hall and Kelson, 1959).

Although arboreal, fox squirrels forage on the ground more and are less agile when climbing than

EASTERN FOX SQUIRREL
(*Sciurus niger vulpinus*)

gray squirrels (Bangs, 1896; Burt, 1957; and Hall and Kelson, 1959). Food items include nuts and seeds of hickory, oak, walnut, blackberry, beech, holly, elm, basswood, maple, ash, chestnut, and/or conifers. Corn is often a preferred food (Cahalane, 1947; Doutt et al., 1967). In the spring the sap of trees (especially maples) is heavily utilized by fox squirrels, often causing severe tree damage. These squirrels are also known to rob birds' nests (Hall and Kelson, 1959).

Several authors have suggested competition between gray and fox squirrels. Poole (1944) and Lustig and Flyger (1976) report declines in *S. n. cinereus* associated with increases in abundance of gray squirrels. These density changes are likely due to changes in the structure of the habitat, making it more favorable to *S. carolinensis.*

Predators of fox squirrels include foxes, large hawks and owls, and humans (Burt, 1957). No recent data are available on survival, abundance, or natality of *S. n. vulpinus. S. n. cinereus* apparently was common in Lancaster County before 1830 (Poole, 1944), but since then *S. carolinensis* has become the common diurnal squirrel. The past abundance of *S. n. vulpinus* in the state is unknown. However, this subspecies is probably not as abundant as it once was (Flyger and Lustig, 1976; Doutt et al., 1967).

BASIS OF STATUS CLASSIFICATION: "Status undetermined" is recommended. The difficulty of assessing the status of this squirrel is compounded by taxonomic problems. These problems are three-fold: 1) *S. n. vulpinus* as a distinct entity is based upon a few, older museum specimens. More recently collected specimens from the historical range of *S. n. vulpinus* show considerable overlap in color patterns with that of *S. n. rufiventer,* the western sub-species. (Within *S. niger* designation of subspecies is based upon color patterns primarily.) Thus whether *S. n. vulpinus* should be considered a distinct subspecies is open to question. 2) Other subspecies are known to be highly variable in color pattern (Dr. Peter Weigl, Wake Forest University, personal communication). Therefore, these individuals designated as either *S. n. rufiventer* and *S. n. vulpinus* may represent color morphs of one subspecies. 3) Past introductions of *S. n. rufiventer* into the range of *S. n. vulpinus* may have swamped the gene pool such that *S. n. vulpinus,* if it did exist in the past, no longer exists as a separate entity.

Regardless of the taxonomic category of these squirrels "status undetermined" is recommended because 1) no recent research is available concerning the abundance of fox squirrels, 2) they are probably rare (Flyger and Lustig, 1976), if not extirpated from Pennsylvania, and 3) their abundance is probably less than in the past. A recent survey of Game Protectors in the southeastern portion of the Commonwealth revealed few small populations and no large populations of fox squirrels.

RECOMMENDATIONS: Because of the taxonomic problems outlined previously and because the species has not been reviewed systematically since Bangs (1896), taxonomic review of *S. niger* is certainly needed.

Research into the ecological status of *S. n. vulpinus* is certainly recommended. Studies of the present geographic distribution and abundance of fox squirrels in Pennsylvania are needed. In addition because of the paucity of information on food habits, social organization, behavior, and habitat preferences, more intensive field studies are also desirable. Further knowledge of the nature and extent of competition between *S. n. vulpinus* and *S. carolinensis* is also required before any management approach for fox squirrels can be successful. Flyger and Lustig (1976) present recommendations for the reestablishment of fox squirrels in the east. Habitat requirements of fox squirrels indicate that these creatures should do well on golf courses, cemeteries, college campuses, hospital grounds, parks, suburban communities, and pastured woodlots. Flyger and

Lustig (1976) also give criteria and procedures for reintroduction. Reestablishment of the eastern fox squirrel into suitable habitat in Pennsylvania should be worth the effort. Recently the Pennsylvania Game Commission has attempted to introduce fox squirrels 1) on Haldeman Island in the Susquehanna River, 2) to Middle Creek Wildlife Refuge and 3) to Pinchot State Park. Unfortunately, these animals are *S. n. rufiventer.* If those individuals native to southeastern Pennsylvania do in fact deserve separate subspecific status as *S. n. vulpinus,* establishment of other subspecies in the historical range of *S. n. vulpinus* is undesirable because these new individuals may flood whatever gene pool is left for *S. n. vulpinus,* thus eliminating *S. n. vulpinus* as a distinct subspecies from Commonwealth. A halt to introductions other than those involving *S. n. vulpinus* is recommended until 1) taxonomic review of the species is completed and 2) the status of remaining population of the eastern subspecies is determined. If *S. n. vulpinus* remains a separate and viable subspecies, then reintroduction of specimens from West Virginia or Maryland is preferable to introduction of *S. n. rufiventer.*

ACKNOWLEDGMENTS: Drs. G. Kirkland, H. Genoways, and D. Schlitter provided access to the mammal collections at Shippensburg State College and the Carnegie Museum of Natural History. Genoways and Schlitter inspected the specimen at the Museum of Comparative Zoology, Harvard. Mike Steele helped gather much of the data in this report. Dale Scheffer, Chief Game Management Division, Pennsylvania Game Commission, and 37 game protectors provided information on fox squirrels populations. Gary J. Taylor and Drs. V. Flyger and P. Weigl provided useful information.

SELECTED REFERENCES:

BANKS, O. 1896. A review of the squirrels of eastern North America. Proc. Biol. Soc. Washington, 10:145–167.

BERNARD, R. J. 1972. Social organization of the fox squirrel. Unpublished M. S. thesis, Michigan State Univ., East Lansing.

BURT, W. H. 1957. Mammals of the Great Lakes region. Univ. Michigan Press, Ann Arbor, 246 pp.

CAHALANE, V. H. 1947. Mammals of North America. The MacMillan Company, New York, 682 pp.

DOUTT, J. K., C. A. HEPPENSTALL, and J. E. GUILDAY. 1967. Mammals of Pennsylvania. Pennsylvania Game Comm., Harrisburg, 283 pp.

FLYGER, V., and L. W. LUSTIG. 1976. The potential for reestablishing fox squirrels in portions of their former range in the northeastern states. Trans. Northeast Fish Wildlife Conf., 33:13–17.

HALL, E. R. 1981. The mammals of North America. John Wiley & Sons, New York, 1:xv + 1–600 + *90*.

HALL, E. R., and K. R. KELSON. 1959. The mammals of North America. The Ronald Press, New York, 1:xxx + 1–546 + *79*.

LUSTIG, L. W., and V. FLYGER. 1976. Observations and suggested management practices for the endangered Delmarva fox squirrel, Proc. Ann. Conf. Southeast Assoc. Game Fish Comm., 29:433–440.

POOLE, E. L. 1944. The technical names of the northeastern fox squirrels. J. Mamm., 25:315–317.

TAYLOR, G. J. 1976. Range determination and habitat description of the Delmarva fox squirrel in Maryland. Unpublished M.S. thesis, Univ. Maryland, College Park.

PREPARED BY: David A. Zegers, *Department of Biology, Millersville University, Millersville, PA 17551.*

Status Undetermined

MARSH RICE RAT
Oryzomys palustris
Family Cricetidae
Order Rodentia

OTHER NAMES: Rice rat, swamp rice rat, northern rice rat.

DESCRIPTION: A medium-sized rat that would be most easily confused with smaller individuals of the introduced Norway rat (*Rattus norvegicus*). The fur of the marsh rice rat is not as harsh as that of the Norway rat, its tail is more slender, and it has two rows of cusps on the molar teeth rather than three. The fur of the upper parts of the marsh rice rat is brown with a wash of gray mixed with some black hairs. The belly is much paler than the back being whitish gray or silver gray. The tail is long and slender, scaly, and very sparsely haired; it is brown or blackish brown but is never bicolored. The hind feet are relatively large and are white above. Range of external measurements of adult specimens from New Jersey and Delaware are as follows: total length, 217–260 mm; length of tail, 103–119 mm; length of hind foot, 28–31 mm; length of ear, 7–15 mm. These individuals weighed between 49.4 and 66.9 g.

RANGE: The geographic range of the marsh rice rat is primarily in the Gulf and Atlantic coastal lowlands from southern Texas to New Jersey. The species also occurs in the lowlands of the Mississippi

MARSH RICE RAT (*Oryzomys palustris*)

River Valley and in the areas surrounding its principal tributaries (Hall, 1981).

HABITAT: The marsh rice rat is a semi-aquatic species that is found in greatest abundance in the marshes and swamps and other wetlands of the Gulf and Atlantic coastal lowlands. In New Jersey and Delaware, all specimens were captured in salt marshes surrounding Delaware Bay. The majority of the specimens was taken in salt marshes that were regularly flooded on high tide (Arndt et al., 1978). In the northern part of its range, the meadow vole, *Microtus pennsylvanicus,* is a common associate of the marsh rice rat.

LIFE HISTORY AND ECOLOGY: There is no information on the life history or ecology of this species in Pennsylvania. In Maryland, marsh rice rats were found to be polyestrous with breeding occurring from March to November. The gestation period is 25 days with a postpartum estrus. Litter sizes range from one to six young. Estimates of average home range are from 0.23 ha to 0.37 ha. Population density estimates range from 0.1 individual per hectare in coastal Louisiana to 50 individuals per hectare in the Florida everglades. In New Jersey and Delaware, the apparent rarity of the marsh rice rats may result from secretive habits, difficulty to trap, and relatively inaccessible habitat. Arndt et al. (1978) found the species to be at least locally abundant in the salt marshes around Delaware Bay.

There is broad variation reported for the diet of this species. This is probably influenced at least in part by season and local habitat. Sharp (1967) working in a salt marsh in Georgia reported marsh rice rats to be primarily carnivorous. Many other authors have found the food of this species to be mainly seeds and succulent plant parts.

BASIS OF CLASSIFICATION: There are no confirmed records of the marsh rice rat from Pennsylvania although the species is locally abundant in adjacent areas of New Jersey and Delaware (Arndt et al., 1978). There are, however, several reports which lead us to believe that the species may have once occurred in Pennsylvania. Ulmer (1951) reported an incident where five marsh rats were frightened out of a nest in the Tinicum marshes, Delaware Co., in 1916. None of the individuals were captured to confirm the sight identification. Roberts and Early (1952) reported that Dr. Robert K. Enders of Swarthmore College had noted the presence of *Oryzomys* skulls in owl pellets found 8 miles north of the Delaware River. Unfortunately, the source of the marsh rice rats could not be located. Marsh rice rat remains are known from several archeological sites in southwestern Pennsylvania (Gilmore, 1946; Guilday and Mayer-Oakes, 1952; Guilday, 1955, 1961). It was estimated that these were no more than 500 years old.

Formerly there apparently was an area of the preferred habitat of the marsh rice rat in southeastern Pennsylvania along the Delaware River. There is enough evidence to suppose that the species may have once occurred in these salt marsh habitats in the Commonwealth. However, most of these areas adjacent to the river in the vicinity of Philadelphia and Chester have been drained and reclaimed for industrial sites. Because of our total lack of information on the marsh rice rat in Pennsylvania and because of major alterations in its preferred habitat, its status is undetermined.

RECOMMENDATIONS: An intensive survey should be undertaken to locate undisturbed salt marshes and other swamps and marshes in Delaware and Philadelphia counties. Such areas as the Tinicum Wildlife Preserve and the Philadelphia International Airport may have appropriate habitats. If appropriate areas are located, a program of trap-

ping and research should be instituted to determine if the marsh rice rat is a member of the mammalian fauna of Pennsylvania and, if it is, to gather data on its life history and population levels and cycles.

SELECTED REFERENCES:

ARNDT, R. G., F. C. RHODE, and J. A. BOSWORTH. 1978. Additional records of the rice rat, *Oryzomys palustris* (Harlan) from New Jersey and Delaware. Bull. New Jersey Acad. Sci., 23:65–72.
GILMORE, R. M. 1946. Mammals in archaeological collections from southwestern Pennsylvania. J. Mamm., 27:227–234.
GUILDAY, J. E. 1955. Animal remains from an Indian village site, Indiana County, Pennsylvania. Pennsylvania Arch., 25: 142–147.
———. 1961. Vertebrate remains from the Varner site. Pennsylvania Arch., 31:119–124.
GUILDAY, J. E., and W. J. MAYER-OAKES. 1952. An occurrence of the rice rat (*Oryzomys*) in West Virginia. J. Mamm., 33: 253–255.
HALL, E. R. 1981. The mammals of North America. John Wiley & Sons, New York, 2:vi + 601–1181 + 90.
HAMILTON, W. J., JR. 1946. Habits of the swamp rice rat, *Oryzomys palustris palustris* (Harlan). Amer. Midland Nat., 36: 730–736.
HAMILTON, W. J., JR., and J. O. WHITAKER, JR. 1979. Mammals of the eastern United States. Cornell Univ. Press, Ithaca, New York, 2nd ed., 346 pp.
PARADISO, J. L. 1969. Mammals of Maryland. N. Amer. Fauna, 66:iv + 1–193.
RHOADS, S. N. 1903. The mammals of Pennsylvania and New Jersey. Privately published, Philadelphia, 266 pp.
ROBERTS, H. A., and R. C. EARLY. 1952. Mammal survey of southeastern Pennsylvania. Final Report Pittman-Robertson Project 43-R. Pennsylvania Game Comm., Harrisburg, 70 pp.
SHARP, H. F., JR. 1967. Food ecology of the rice rat, *Oryzomys palustris* (Harlan), in a Georgia salt marsh. J. Mamm., 48: 557–563.
SVIHLA, A. 1931. Life history of the Texas rice rat (*Oryzomys palustris texensis*). J. Mamm., 12:238–242.
ULMER, F. A., JR. 1951. Notes on the rice rat in New Jersey and Pennsylvania. J. Mamm., 32:121–122.
WOLFE, J. L. 1982. *Oryzomys palustris.* Mammalian Species, 176:1–5.

PREPARED BY: Hugh H. Genoways, *Carnegie Museum of Natural History, 4400 Forbes Avenue, Pittsburgh, PA 15213.*

Status Undetermined

GAPPER'S RED-BACKED VOLE
Clethrionomys gapperi rupicola. E. L. Poole
Family Cricetidae
Order Rodentia

OTHER NAMES: Red-backed mouse, red-backed vole, boreal redback vole.

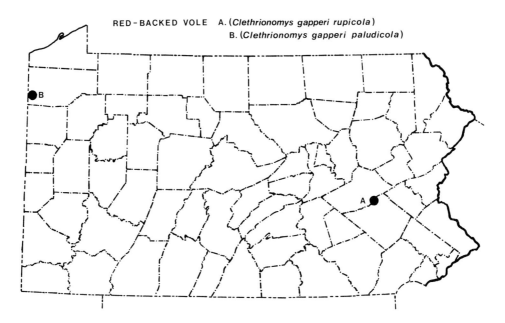

RED-BACKED VOLE   A.(*Clethrionomys gapperi rupicola*)
                  B.(*Clethrionomys gapperi paludicola*)

RED-BACKED VOLE (*Clethrionomys gapperi*)

DESCRIPTION: The red-backed vole can be distinguished from other voles inhabiting Pennsylvania by its short tail and reddish dorsum. It resembles the pine vole (*Microtus pinetorum*) in these characters, but in *C. gapperi* the reddish color is restricted to the dorsum. In addition, *C. gapperi* possesses larger ears and tail and longer and coarser

pelage than the pine vole. Total length of *C. gapperi* from Pennsylvania ranges from 120 to 158 mm; length of tail, 30 to 50 mm; hind foot, 17 to 21 mm; ear from notch, 12 to 16 mm; weight ranges from 16 to 38 g (Bailey, 1897; Hall, 1981; Doutt et al., 1977). Male and female *C. gapperi* are similar in size and color. The dorsum is characterized by a broad reddish band progressing from the forehead to rump. The nose and sides of head and body are grayish washed with pale buff. The hair of the venter has a silvery appearance sometimes washed with pale buff. The tail of *C. gapperi* is bicolored (dark brown to black above, whitish below).

The subspecies *C. g. rupicola* is restricted to Kittatinny Ridge and vicinity of Berks and Schuylkill counties, Pennsylvania. It differs from *C. gapperi gapperi* of Pennsylvania by being of grayer coloration and larger size. The skull is also longer and larger than other subspecies of red-backed voles in Pennsylvania (Poole, 1949).

RANGE: Twenty-nine subspecies of *C. gapperi* are currently recognized (Hall, 1981). The species is distributed across Canada, then south along the Appalachian Mountains to northern Georgia. It occurs in northern Michigan, most of Wisconsin, Minnesota, North Dakota and the northern tip of Iowa. In the west, it occurs in the Rocky Mountains south to southwestern New Mexico and Arizona. The Columbia River marks the southern limit for northwestern subspecies of the red-backed vole which then progresses northward into British Columbia.

HABITAT: Clethrionomys gapperi rupicola is confined to the crest of the Kittatinny Ridge and mountains immediately to the north, Lebanon, Schuylkill, Northampton, Lehigh, and Berks counties, Pennsylvania (Roberts and Early, 1952). Its range is allopatric with the more widely distributed *C. g. gapperi*, but there is little difference in the habitat requirements of these two subspecies. Both are found in rocky habitats characterized by a dense forest cover. Suitable habitat includes mesic communities of black birch, yellow birch, and hemlock in this region of Pennsylvania. *Clethrionomys gapperi rupicola* also occurs along stream margins and marshy areas in these mountains, although, these ecological associations are suboptimal for this race (Poole, 1949).

LIFE HISTORY AND ECOLOGY: Little information is available to document life history and ecology of the two restricted subspecies reported in this account and that to follow. Gapper's red-backed vole shows demographic trends generally similar to other forest-dwelling herbivorous small mammals. In the eastern United States, numbers range from about two to 65 voles per hectare. For a given year, density tends to increase during summer, reaching peak numbers in late summer and early autumn with a gradual decline in abundance through winter, resulting in low density in spring. Red-backed voles are polyestrous and exhibit a post-partum estrous. Gestation period ranges from 17 to 19 days. The breeding season begins during late March or early April and continues into November. Litter size ranges from 2 to 6 (mean, 5). Mean home range of Gapper's red-backed vole ranges from 0.01 to 0.50 ha. This great variation in size of home range is due to many factors including habitat sampled and density of a population. Red-backed voles are omnivorous, opportunistic feeders which show dietary shifts in response to the character and condition of the habitat, season and availability of food. Foods eaten by *C. gapperi* include vegetative portions of plants, nuts, seeds, berries, mosses, lichens, ferns, fungi, and arthropods.

BASIS OF CLASSIFICATION: C. g. rupicola is represented in Pennsylvania by an isoalted population located along the Kittatinny Ridge. Because of this restricted distribution a status of "undetermined" is warranted. Little published information is available detailing ecological requirements of this race.

RECOMMENDATIONS: An examination should be undertaken of specimens of *C. g. rupicola* from localities noted above. Morphological characters should be compared with those of *C. g. gapperi* in order to establish discernible differences in these subspecies. Following examination of museum specimens, field work is necessary to elucidate local habitat requirements of this isolated race in Pennsylvania. Lastly, in order to accurately determine the proper status of *C. g. rupicola*, the location of habitats must be evaluated in light of potential for industrial and/or recreational development.

SELECTED REFERENCES:

BAILEY, V. 1897. Revision of the American voles of the genus *Evotomys*. Proc. Biol. Soc. Washington, 11:113–138.
DOUTT, J. K. 1941. New *Clethrionomys* from Utah and Pennsylvania. Proc. Biol. Soc. Washington, 54:161–164.
DOUTT, J. K., C. A. HEPPENSTALL, and J. E. GUILDAY. 1977. Mammals of Pennsylvania. Pennsylvania Game Comm., Harrisburg, 4th ed., 283 pp.
HALL, E. R. 1981. The mammals of North America. John Wiley & Sons, New York, 2:vi + 601–1181 + 90.
MERRITT, J. F. 1981. *Clethrionomys gapperi*. Mammalian Species, 146:1–9.
POOLE, E. L. 1949. A new race of the red-backed mouse (*Clethrionomys*) from Pennsylvania. Not. Naturae, Acad. Nat. Sci. Philadelphia, 212:1–3.
ROBERTS, H. A., and R. C. EARLY. 1952. Mammal survey of southeastern Pennsylvania. Final Report Pittman-Robertson Project 43-R. Pennsylvania Game Comm., Harrisburg, 70 pp.

PREPARED BY: Joseph F. Merritt, *Powdermill Nature Reserve, Carnegie Museum of Natural History, Star Route South, Rector, PA 15677.*

Status Undetermined
GAPPER'S RED-BACKED VOLE
Clethrionomys gapperi paludicola Doutt
Family Cricetidae
Order Rodentia

OTHER NAMES: Red-backed mouse, red-backed vole, boreal redback vole.

DESCRIPTION: C. gapperi paludicola resembles other red-backed voles (*C. gapperi*) in size and appearance (See description of *C. g. rupicola* above).

RANGE: Twenty nine subspecies of *C. gapperi* are currently recognized (Hall, 1981). Within Pennsylvania, *C. g. paludicola* is reported only from the vicinity of Pymatuning Reservoir, Crawford County, Pennsylvania.

HABITAT: C. g. paludicola occupies boggy situations in the vicinity of the Pymatuning Reservoir. Gapper's red-backed vole is a mesic-adapted species occurring principally in forests characterized by moss-covered boulders, ferns, and an abundant litter of stumps, rotting logs and exposed roots. Microhabitat features which maintain a moist environment for foraging and nesting seem to be important to the life history of this small mammal.

LIFE HISTORY AND ECOLOGY: Ecological requirements and life history information are summarized in the account of *C. g. rupicola* earlier and are applicable for *C. g. paludicola.*

BASIS OF STATUS CLASSIFICATION: As was the case with *C. g. rupicola,* the subspecies *C. g. paludicola* shows an isolated and localized distribution in northwestern Pennsylvania. Because of this restricted distribution, a status of "undetermined" is warranted. No published information is available detailing ecological relationships of this subspecies in Pennsylvania.

RECOMMENDATIONS: The same recommendations are suggested for *C. g. paludicola* as those recommended for *C. g. rupicola* earlier. Specimens from Crawford County (Pymatuning Swamp area) should be examined with respect to comparative morphology with the parapatric *C. g. gapperi,* in order to establish discernible differences in form. Also, intensive field work is recommended in order to elucidate local habitat requirements of this disjunct race. Habitat utilization and requirements must be evaluated in light of potential for industrial and/or recreational development.

SELECTED REFERENCES:

DOUTT, J. K., C. A. HEPPENSTALL, and J. E. GUILDAY. 1977. Mammals of Pennsylvania. Pennsylvania Game Comm., Harrisburg, 4th ed., 283 pp.

HALL, E. R. 1981. The mammals of North America. John Wiley & Sons, New York, 2:vi + 601–1181 + 90.

MERRITT, J. F. 1981. *Clethrionomys gapperi.* Mammalian Species, 146:1–9.

POOLE, E. L. 1949. A new race of the red-backed mouse (*Clethrionomys*) from Pennsylvania. Not. Naturae, Acad. Nat. Sci. Philadelphia, 212:1–3.

RICHMOND, N. D., and H. R. ROSLAND. 1949. Mammal survey of northwestern Pennsylvania. Final Report Pittman-Robertson Project 20-R. Pennsylvania Game Comm., Harrisburg, 67 pp.

PREPARED BY: Joseph F. Merritt, *Powdermill Nature Reserve, Carnegie Museum of Natural History, Star Route South, Rector, PA 15677.*

Status Undetermined

COYOTE
Canis latrans (Say)
Family Canidae
Order Carnivora

OTHER NAMES: Brush wolf, prairie wolf.

DESCRIPTION: Canis latrans is a slender, doglike animal similar in size to a small collie. Key physical characteristics are its long, narrow, pointed muzzle, yellow eyes, relatively long and slender legs, erect, pointed ears, long, dense fur, and bushy drooping tail. The fur of both sexes may range from a gray to yellow-gray color with considerable variation among individuals (Godin, 1977). Adult males are usually larger than females (Andrew and Boggess, 1978). The pointed ears, dense underfur, and bushy tail of the coyote can be used to distinguish it from domestic dogs. The red fox (*Vulpes vulpes*) and the gray fox (*Urocyon cinereoargenteus*) are noticeably smaller than *Canis latrans.* The eastern coyote is usually larger than the western subspecies of coyote (Hilton, 1978). Coydogs, offspring of coyote-domestic dog crosses, typically have darker fur compared to coyotes (McGinnis, 1979). Detailed analyses of several skull measurements are required in order to be reasonably certain of the identity of the last three animals.

RANGE: Canis latrans has a large distribution ranging from El Salvador and Costa Rica north to north-central Alaska and east through western and south-central Northwest Territory, central Saskatchewan, Manitoba, and Ontario, southern Quebec and western New Brunswick (Hall, 1981). The species almost certainly occurs in all of the contiguous states (Gipson, 1978). Specimens have been collected from more than one-half of the counties in Pennsylvania. The species probably occurs throughout the state, but coyotes appear to be more common in the northern regions of the Commonwealth (McGinnis, 1979).

HABITAT: As its distribution throughout the Commonwealth would indicate, the coyote has rather general habitat requirements. It is most frequently found in areas near second growth woodlands and fields interspersed with thickets and marshlands, but it may also live in wilderness parks, along streams and rivers, and even suburban areas (Godin, 1977).

LIFE HISTORY AND ECOLOGY: Coyotes sleep

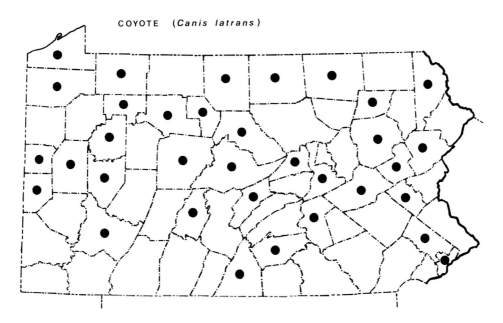

COYOTE (*Canis latrans*)

on the ground in dense cover, but use self-dug dens or the burrows of other animals when litters of 5–7 pups are born in April or early May. The gestation period is about 60–65 days, and pups leave the den at about 3 weeks of age. Weaning takes place at about 9 weeks. Pups and the adult pair stay together into the autumn. The species is known to feed on a wide variety of items including deer, rodents, rabbits, garbage and carrion (Gier, 1975; Bekoff, 1977; Ozoga and Harger, 1966; Richens and Hugie, 1974; McGinnis, 1979). While coyotes may kill deer, most are probably scavenged (McGinnis, 1979). *Canis latrans* lives in close association with humans in some areas of the country and is harvested as a fur bearer.

BASIS OF STATUS CLASSIFICATION: Canis latrans has been assigned to the status undetermined list because information on its status in Pennsylvania is limited. One reason for the paucity of data is that, even though individuals escaped from captivity as early as the 1880's, the species appears to have only recently invaded Pennsylvania from New York and possibly Ohio, and researchers have had insufficient time to critically examine the animal in detail. Secondly, an inherent difficulty in conducting research on the coyote is that it is a secretive animal present in relatively low population numbers. Finally, the specimens that are collected usually are taken by hunters and trappers and rarely receive the attention of the scientific community.

RECOMMENDATIONS: An extensive telephone or mail survey of game protectors, trapping and hunting club organizations, and nature study groups should be used to gather general information about possible locations of *Canis latrans* in the Commonwealth. A trapping program combined with a radiotelemetry and possibly snow tracking study should then be undertaken to locate populations and research the ecology of the animal. Special attention

COYOTE (*Canis latrans*)

should be given to coyote food habitats to ascertain the impact of predation on game populations; special attention should be given also to the systematics of these populations to firmly establish the differences among coyote, coydogs, and the eastern coyote. It is suspected that *Canis latrans* will be removed from the species of special concern list as more data on the animal are gathered.

SELECTED REFERENCES:

ANDREWS, R. D., and E. K. BOGGESS. 1978. Ecology of coyotes in Iowa. Pp. 249–264, *in* Coyotes: biology, behavior, and management (M. Bekoff, ed.), Academic Press, New York, 384 pp.

BEKOFF, M. 1977. *Canis latrans.* Mammalian Species, 79:1–9.

GIER, H. T. 1975. Ecology and social behavior. Pp. 247–262, *in* The wild canids: their systematics, behavioral ecology and evolution (M. W. Fox, ed.), Van Nostrand Reinhold Co., New York, 508 pp.

GIPSON, P. S. 1978. Coyotes and related *Canis* in the southeastern United States with a comment on Mexican and Central American *Canis.* Pp. 191–208, *in* Coyotes: biology, behavior, and management (M. Bekoff, ed.), Academic Press, New York, 384 pp.

GODIN, A. J. 1977. Wild mammals of New England. Johns Hopkins Univ. Press, Baltimore, 304 pp.

HALL, E. R. 1981. The mammals of North America. John Wiley & Sons, New York, 2:vi + 601–1181 + 90.

HILTON, H. 1978. Systematics and ecology of the eastern coyotes. Pp. 209–228, *in* Coyotes: biology, behavior, and management (M. Bekoff, ed.), Academic Press, New York, 384 pp.

MCGINNIS, H. J. 1979. Pennsylvania coyotes and their relationship to other wild *Canis* populations in the great lakes region and the northeastern United States. Unpublished M.S. thesis, Pennsylvania State Univ., University Park, 227 pp.

OZOGA, J. J., and E. M. HARGER. 1966. Winter activities and feeding habits of northern Michigan coyotes. J. Wildlife Mgmt., 30:809–818.

RICHENS, V. B., and R. D. HUGIE. 1974. Distribution, taxonomic status, and characteristics of coyotes in Maine. J. Wildlife Mgmt., 38:447–457.

PREPARED BY: John E. Enders, *Sartorius Filters, 304 Second Street, P.O. Box 185, Dalton, PA 18414.*

Status Undetermined

BADGER

Taxidea taxus

Family Mustelidae

Order Carnivora

OTHER NAME: North American badger.

DESCRIPTION: Taxidea taxus is a short-legged, stout-bodied member of the weasel family. It should

BADGER (*Taxidea taxus*)

not be confused with any other species of mammals in Pennsylvania because of its general body form, coloration, and large claws on the forefeet. This is a terrestrial species which is highly adapted for digging. The middle claw of the forefoot may be over an inch long. The nose, crown of the head, and neck are dark brown or black. The sides of the head are white as is a slender stripe from the nose over top of the head to the shoulders. The remainder of the upper parts have a grizzled appearance because of mixing of hairs which have yellowish white, pale brown to black, and white segments. The tail is short.

Total length of adult badgers is from 600 to 730 mm, length of tail 105 to 135 mm, and length of hind foot 95 to 128 mm. Adult badgers will weigh 6.8–11.4 kg, with males larger than females.

RANGE: This is a species primarily of the open grasslands and deserts of central and western United States, south-central Canada, and northern Mexico. The easternmost undisputed records are from central Ohio and southeastern Ontario (Snyder, 1935; Leedy, 1947; Long, 1972; Hall, 1981).

HABITAT: This species occurs primarily in prairie and desert habitats but it is known from Alpine tundra to the lower austral life zone. The altitudinal range of the species is from below sea level in Death Valley to over 3,100 m. There is evidence that the species is extending its range eastward possibly as the result of habitat alteration and introductions by humans (Leedy, 1947; Nugent and Choate, 1970).

LIFE HISTORY AND ECOLOGY: There is no information on the life history or ecology of this species in Pennsylvania. Badgers breed in summer and early autumn but implantation is delayed until sometime between December and February. Young are born in March and early April. The young are furred and blind; nursing occurs through June. The litters usually contain three young. There are few reliable density estimates for badgers but one badger per 2.5 square km seems reasonable. Individuals are solitary except during breeding season.

Badgers have been recorded as taking a wide range of animal matter but their primary food is small rodents such as thirteen-lined ground squirrels and pocket gophers. The badger is highly fossorial and will burrow to catch prey as well as to construct dens.

BASIS OF CLASSIFICATION: There are two recorded occurrences of the badger in Pennsylvania. Game Protector Bruce W. Catherman recorded "A badger was killed in Indiana County by Russell Olsen, Blairsville," in the Pennsylvania Game News (17(2):21) in May 1946. The second specimen is deposited in the collections of Carnegie Museum of Natural History (CM 61342). The specimen, which was taken in Uniontown, Fayette Co., was brought to the Museum by Game Protector T. W. Meehan. The Museum's records indicate that this female specimen was taken on 22 September 1950 but no other circumstances of its capture were recorded.

Nugent and Choate (1970) in discussing other records to the east of Ohio in New York and Connecticut concluded that the situation may be more complex than simply the eastward dispersal of badgers in response to cutting of the eastern forests. They found that badgers were commercially raised in New York and that individuals escaped from these farms and many others were probably released when the price of fur dropped. They believed that some of these individuals became established in the agricultural areas of New York and have dispersed from there into New England.

It is possible that these early records of badgers in Pennsylvania resulted from similar commercial operations. However, more recent records in western Pennsylvania may be expected as a result of a natural eastward dispersal of the badger. Opening of the right-of-ways along interstate highways has provided optimum habitat for the badger leading directly from Ohio into western Pennsylvania. The badger can be expected to disperse eastward along these narrow ribbons of grassland as one of its preferred food items, the thirteen-lined ground squirrel, follows the same routes. Until we know more about the current status of the badger in Pennsylvania, it can only be considered status undetermined.

RECOMMENDATIONS: No organized research effort on this species would be feasible. However, Game Protectors and the general public should be made aware that we need data on this species. If badgers are inadvertently killed such as on highways or while trapping for other species, these specimens should be salvaged so that they may be deposited in appropriate institutions in the Commonwealth. If living individuals are sighted, these should be reported to the appropriate authorities so that they can be protected and studied. Our top priority for this species should be the gathering of as much scientifically accurate information as possible so that we may determine its status in Pennsylvania.

SELECTED REFERENCES:

HALL, E. R. 1981. The mammals of North America. John Wiley & Sons, New York, 2:vi + 601–1181 + 90.
HAMILTON, W. J., JR., and J. O. WHITAKER, JR. 1979. Mammals of the eastern United States. Cornell Univ. Press, Ithaca, New York, 2nd ed., 346 pp.
LEEDY, D. L. 1947. Spermophiles and badgers move eastward in Ohio. J. Mamm., 28:290–292.
LONG, C. A. 1972. Taxonomic revision of the North American badger, *Taxidea taxus.* J. Mamm., 53:725–759.
———. 1973. *Taxidea taxus.* Mammalian Species, 26:1–4.
NUGENT, R. F., and J. R. CHOATE. 1970. Eastward dispersal of the badger, *Taxidea taxus,* into the northeastern United States. J. Mamm., 51:626–627.
SARGEANT, A. B., and D. W. WARNER. 1972. Movements and denning habits of a badger. J. Mamm., 53:207–210.
SNYDER, L. L. 1935. A badger specimen from Port Dover, Norfolk County, Ontario. Canadian Field-Nat., 49:136–137.
WRIGHT, P. L. 1966. Observations on the reproductive cycles of the American badger (*Taxidea taxus*). Symp. Zool. Soc. London, 15:27–45.

PREPARED BY: Hugh H. Genoways, *Section of Mammals, Carnegie Museum of Natural History, 4400 Forbes Avenue, Pittsburgh, PA 15213.*

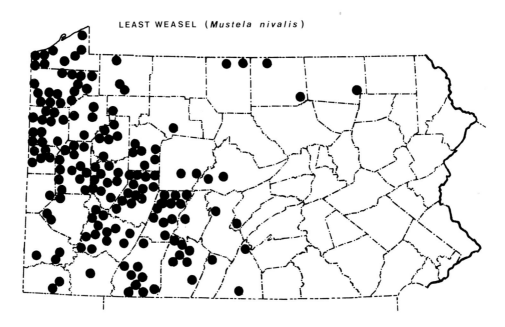

LEAST WEASEL (*Mustela nivalis*)

Status Undetermined

LEAST WEASEL
Mustela nivalis
Family Mustelidae
Order Carnivora

OTHER NAMES: Mouse weasel.

DESCRIPTION: The species *Mustela nivalis* is weasel-like in appearance, with a long, slender body (about the thickness of a man's thumb), short legs and stubby tail. The least weasel is the smallest member of the Order Carnivora. Coloration is dark brown throughout, except white on the chin, throat, chest and lower belly. The tail is entirely brown. In the north, least weasels are entirely white in winter, and some least weasels from Pennsylvania are white or partially white in winter. Measurements for *M. n. allegheniensis* reported from Pennsylvania are as follows: total length, 181 to 206 mm; length of tail, 31 to 44 mm; hind foot, 20 to 25 mm; ear from notch, 10 to 14 mm; weight, 38 to 59 g (Doutt et al., 1977). Females of the species tend to be smaller than males. The least weasel is distinguished from the long-tailed weasel (*Mustela frenata*) and the ermine (*Mustela erminea*) by its smaller size, shorter tail and the lack of a black tip on the tail.

RANGE: The species *M. nivalis* is Holarctic, occurring across North America and in Eurasia from Siberia to the British Isles. The race *M. n. allegheniensis* occurs in the Appalachian Mountains from

Pennsylvania to North Carolina and Tennessee. It ranges westward south of the Great Lakes to Illinois and Wisconsin. The type locality for *M. n. allegheniensis* is near Beallsville, Washington County, Pennsylvania (Rhoads, 1901). In Pennsylvania, the least weasel is found in the western and central parts of the Commonwealth, but is absent from the north-

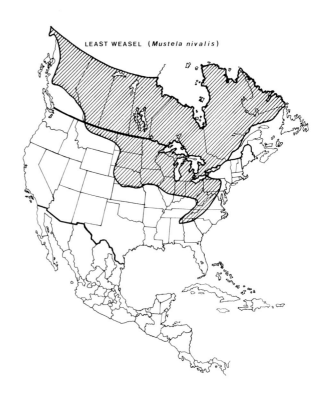

LEAST WEASEL (*Mustela nivalis*)

eastern and eastern sections. The distribution of the least weasel shown in accompanying map is based on examination of 315 skins submitted for bounty from 1948 to 1951 (Richmond and McDowell, 1952). Skins examined were from 187 townships in 31 counties of Pennsylvania.

HABITAT: Little information is available concerning the habitat requirements of the least weasel. Optimal habitat is probably brushy areas, open woodlands, old fields and pastureland which support high numbers of prey specics of small mammals (principally meadow voles and white-footed mice). The least weasel is also reported to occur in forests of oak, hickory and hemlock.

LIFE HISTORY AND ECOLOGY: Unlike other weasels in Pennsylvania, least weasels may bc reproductively active year-round and produce two to three litters per year of four to six young per litter. The gestation period is about 35 days, and, unlike other weasels in the state, does not show an arrested phase (Hamilton, 1943; Doutt et al., 1977). The home range of the least weasel reported from northeastern Iowa, is approximately 0.8 ha (Polderoer, 1942). This weasel feeds primarily on mice, although it also eats small birds and arthropods. Nests have been located both beneath the ground and in trees. The least weasel is preyed upon by house cats, barn owls and occasionally snakes (Hamilton, 1943; Burt, 1946; Handley, 1949; Doutt et al., 1977).

BASIS OF STATUS CLASSIFICATION: The least weasel could be called "rare" throughout its range at least from the standpoint of it rarely being observed in nature because of its nocturnal and secretive behavior. However, although published information is sparse, it indicates that the least weasel may actually be fairly common throughout its range. Published reports show that the least weasel demonstrates a good deal of flexibility in habitat selection—ranging from pastureland to forests. Although, superficially it appears to be represented by adequate numbers within Pennsylvania, the lack of information warrants a closer look and assignment of the status of "undetermined."

RECOMMENDATION: An effort should be undertaken to determine the present status of the least weasel in Pennsylvania. Over 30 years have passed since the status of this weasel was evaluated by Richmond and McDowell (1952). Since their report, a large portion of the range of this species has been subjected to disturbance in the form of mining operations, agricultural practices, industrial complexes and recreational facilities. It is believed that a re-evaluation of the status of the least weasel in Pennsylvania is required.

REMARKS: Authors adopting the name *Mustela nivalis* consider it to be Holarctic, and conspecific with the Old World form. Others employ the name *Mustela rixosa* designating a distinct New World species.

SELECTED REFERENCES:

BURT, W. H. 1946. The mammals of Michigan. Univ. Michigan Press, Ann Arbor, xv + 288 pp.

DOUTT, J. K., C. A. HEPPENSTALL, and J. E. GUILDAY. 1977. Mammals of Pennsylvania. Pennsylvania Game Comm., Harrisburg, 4th ed., 283 pp.

HALL, E. R. 1981. The mammals of North America. John Wiley & Sons, New York, 2:vi + 601–1181 + 90.

HAMILTON, W. J., JR. 1943. The mammals of eastern United States. Comstock Publishing Co., Inc., Ithaca, New York, 10 + 432 pp.

HANDLEY, C. O., JR. 1949. Least weasel, prey of barn owl. J. Mamm., 30:431.

POLDEROER, E. B. 1942. Habits of the least weasel (*Mustela rixosa*) in northeastern Iowa. J. Mamm., 23:145–147.

RHOADS, S. N. 1901. *Putorius allegheniensis* Rhoads. Proc. Acad. Nat. Sci., Philadelphia, 52:751.

———. 1903. The mammals of Pennsylvania and New Jersey. Privately published, Philadelphia, 266 pp.

RICHMOND, N. D., and R. D. MCDOWELL. 1952. The least weasel (*Mustela rixosa*) in Pennsylvania. J. Mamm., 33:251–253.

PREPARED BY: Joseph F. Merritt, *Powdermill Nature Reserve, Star Route South, Rector, PA 15677.*

Status Undetermined

MARTEN
Martes americana americana (Turton)
Family Mustelidae
Order Carnivora

OTHER NAMES: American marten, pine marten, American sable, Hudson's Bay sable.

DESCRIPTION: The marten is about the size of a mink. Its bushy tail is about half the length of the body; its broad head tapers to a sharp nose; and it has relatively large ears, giving it a rather fox-like appearance. Its pelage is soft and lustrous and quite variable in color, although, in general, it can be said

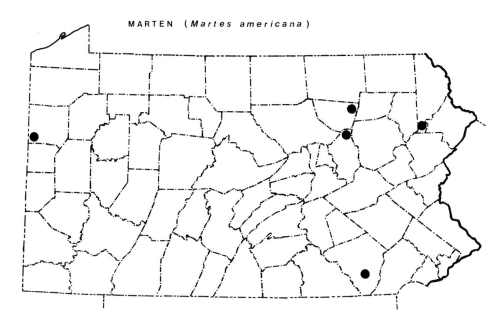

MARTEN (*Martes americana*)

its dorsal surface is dark brown with the tail and legs being almost black, and the head grayish. Males are roughly 15 percent larger than females. Average total lengths and tail lengths of males and females, respectively, are: 600 mm, 175 mm and 540 mm, 160 mm. Males weigh an average 995 g to females 661 g.

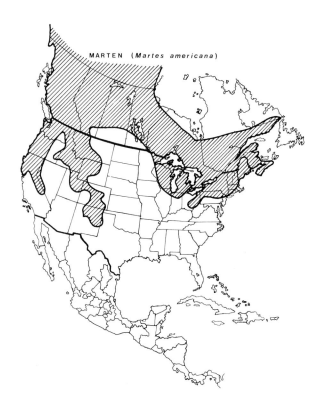

MARTEN (*Martes americana*)

RANGE: The distribution of the marten extends from extreme northwestern Alaska, across Canada south of Hudson's Bay to the Maritime Provinces. It follows the western mountain ranges south into central California and northern New Mexico. In the eastern half of the continent it occupies the Great Lakes region and dips into southern Ohio and the northern tip of West Virginia. It progresses eastward through the northern half of Pennsylvania, New York, and New England.

HABITAT: The marten's distribution is linked to the coniferous forest habitat typical of Canadian, Hudsonian, and Upper Transitional life zones. Hamilton (1958) showed the preferred habitat in New York State to be forests of white and red spruce and balsam fir found mostly in the Catskills and Adirondacks. While he reported they may move into rock maple, hemlock and yellow birch zones, they seem to favor areas with deep cold swamps and steep mountain slopes above an elevation of 610 m.

LIFE HISTORY AND ECOLOGY: The marten is arboreal but it spends considerable time on the ground where it preys upon mice, particularly red-backed voles (*Clethrionomys* sp.) and other microtines, red squirrels (*Tamiasciurus* sp.), flying squirrels (*Glaucomys* sp.), and other small mammals. In some parts of its range, birds such as grouse make up an important supplement to mammalian prey. Insects, carrion, and fruit in season constitute the remainder of its diet. Activity is principally nocturnal throughout the year, although marten may also be active on cloudy, overcast days within an average home range of 2.38 km² for males and 0.70 km² for females.

Mating occurs in July and August. After delayed implantation and arrested development in the blastocyst stage, the young are born after a gestation period of about 250 days. The average number of young per litter is 2.6. Most do not reach sexual maturity until two years of age, although some (about 20%) can mate when 15 months old. Population densities in optimum habitat range from 0.58 to 1.70 animals per km².

BASIS OF STATUS CLASSIFICATION: According to mammalogists at the Carnegie Museum of Natural History there are occasional reports of sightings of marten in Pennsylvania. However, the most recent specimen they have on record is one collected from Mercer County in 1970. In 1963 a specimen was collected from Wayne County. Since that county abuts the Catskills of New York State, it is possible that this was an animal which had strayed from the Adirondack region where the species is known to be relatively plentiful. Prior to this, it was thought that the marten no longer existed in northeastern Pennsylvania. The last marten to be recorded from northcentral Pennsylvania was from Sullivan County in 1900. The southern limits of marten in Pennsylvania seemed to have been Crawford, Forest, Elk, Cameron, Tioga, Sullivan, Columbia, Wyoming, and Wayne counties, although the most southerly record within the Commonwealth was reported from Lancaster County early in this century. While marten were considered to be abundant in the northern tier mountain counties, they are thought to have been extirpated from that region by 1900.

Because this mammal has been prized as a valuable furbearer much of its decline from other parts of its range has been attributed to overtrapping as well as lumbering. In the northeastern region of Pennsylvania, the elimination of virgin forest of white pine, hemlock, red spruce, and some hardwoods may account for the disappearance of the marten from the Commonwealth.

RECOMMENDATIONS: With the fairly recent specimens from Mercer and Wayne counties and "word of mouth" reports of sightings that continue to be received, there is reason to suggest that some marten are moving northward from West Virginia and southward from New York State. A systematic program to monitor the borders of Pennsylvania where preferred marten habitat extends from neighboring states should be encouraged, while more intensive field work within the interior of the Commonwealth must also be undertaken in order to gain a truer estimate of the status of this species.

SELECTED REFERENCES:

BANFIELD, A. W. F. 1974. The mammals of Canada. Univ. Toronto Press, Toronto, 438 pp.

DOUTT, J. K., C. A. HEPPENSTALL, and J. E. GUILDAY. 1967. Mammals of Pennsylvania. Pennsylvania Game Comm., Harrisburg, 281 pp.

GODIN, A. J. 1977. Wild mammals of New England. Johns Hopkins Univ. Press, Baltimore, 304 pp.

GRIMM, W. C., and R. WHITEBREAD. 1952. Mammal survey of northeastern Pennsylvania. Final Report Pittman-Robertson Project 42-R. Pennsylvania Game Comm., Harrisburg, 82 pp.

HAGMEIER, E. M. 1956. Distribution of marten and fisher in North America. Canadian Field-Nat., 70:101–148.

HALL, E. R. 1981. The mammals of North America. John Wiley & Sons, New York, 2:vi + 601–1181 + 90.

HAMILTON, W. J., JR. 1958. Past and present distribution of marten in New York. J. Mamm., 39:589–591.

MECH, L. D., and L. L. ROGERS. 1977. Status, distribution, and movements of martens in northeastern Minnesota. U.S.D.A. Forest Service Res. Pap. NC-143, 7 pp.

ROSLUND, H. R. 1951. Mammal survey of northcentral Pennsylvania. Final Report Pittman-Robertson Project 37-R. Pennsylvania Game Comm., Harrisburg, 55 pp.

PREPARED BY: Harry N. Cunningham, Jr., *Division of Science, Engineering, and Technology, Behrend College of The Pennsylvania State University, Erie, PA 16563.*

Status Undetermined
FISHER
Martes pennanti pennanti (Erxleben)
Family Mustelidae
Order Carnivora

OTHER NAMES: Pekan, Pekan cat, Pennant's marten, fisher marten, fisher cat, fisher weasel, black cat, black fox.

DESCRIPTION: The fisher is one of the larger members of the weasel family. It is usually brown on the upper back, shoulders, and head. While sometimes mistaken for a large black cat, its limbs are much shorter, body much narrower, and its long bushy tail tapers toward its tip. Its head is broad, but narrows at the snout, and has short rounded ears and small eyes. Males are much larger than females and have a coarser pelt. Average total lengths

Fisher (*Martes pennanti*). Photograph by L. L. Master.

and tail lengths of males and females, respectively, are 940 mm, 350 mm and 810 mm, 310 mm. Males average 3.7 kg in weight, whereas females average 2.1 kg.

RANGE: The distribution extends from extreme northwestern Canada southward via the Rocky Mountains into Montana, Idaho, and Oregon, and via the Sierras into California. In the east, the geographic range includes all of Canada south of Hudson's Bay; the upper midwestern, middle Atlantic, and New England states. Records indicate fisher once occurred as far south as West Virginia, Tennessee, and western North Carolina. Its distribution is similar to that of the marten but does not extend as far northward.

HABITAT: It is generally agreed that the fisher requires a habitat with a continuous closed canopy such as in spruce-fir forests and other conifer association. However, they are more likely than martens to be found in hardwoods, especially beech woods and dense second growth forests. They tend to avoid open areas or sparsely covered forests.

LIFE HISTORY AND ECOLOGY: The fisher is arboreal, although less so than the closely related marten, *Martes americana.* It thus includes in its diet some prey which are also arboreal, such as red squirrels (*Tamiasciurus* sp.), flying squirrels (*Glaucomys* sp.), and porcupines (*Erithizon dorsatum*). Snowshoe hares (*Lepus americanus*), voles, mice, and other small mammals, carrion, birds, and fruit round out the diet. Mammals are thought to comprise about 80% of its food. Fishers are particularly well adapted for killing porcupines and may exercise some control over their population.

The home range is approximately 26 km² in which they travel in regular hunting circuits. The males' home range is more extensive than that of females. Fishers are active both day and night.

Fishers have delayed implantation and thus, they have an unusually long gestation period (average 352 days). Breeding occurs in March and April. Average litter size is 2.7. The young are born helpless and may not reach sexual maturity until 2 years of age.

Estimates of fisher population densities are highly variable and have been reported to range one animal per 0.65 km² to one per 285 km². More recent estimates are based on a combination of radiotelemetry, live-trapping, and systematic analysis of questionnaires sent to trappers and game officials. This information suggests that fishers achieve maximum densities of no more than one per 13 km².

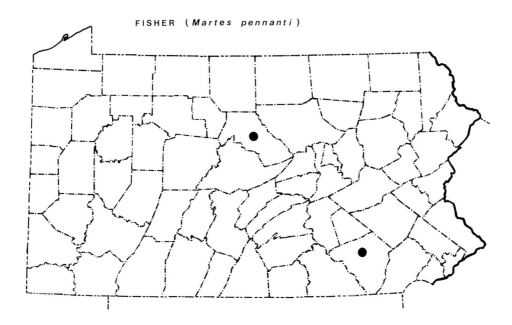

FISHER (*Martes pennanti*)

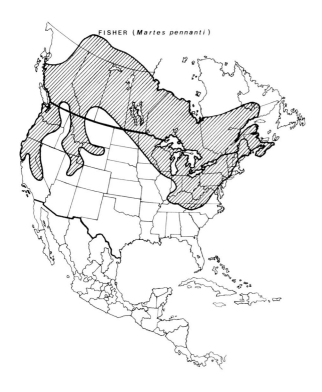

FISHER (*Martes pennanti*)

BASIS OF STATUS CLASSIFICATION: There seems to be indirect evidence that fisher do still exist or have been reintroduced to Pennsylvania. There are no *verifiable* records, however, upon which to establish status other than "Undetermined."

A letter was sent to a representative game protector from each of the 67 counties of the Commonwealth. There were 26 responses of which three provided positive information on fishers. From Lehigh County, it was reported that a fisher had been killed by dogs in a fencerow between two fields. The animal had ear tags identifying it as a native of New York State and had been released by the New York Conservation Department in a trap and transfer program. Fulton County reported "rumors" of a fisher being killed just south of the county, in West Virginia. A game protector of Clinton County could give no verified records of fisher, but felt that reports of "black panther" sightings might well be fishers. He had also sent a picture of a carcass of a possible fisher to Dr. John George at The Pennsylvania State University, University Park (personal communication) for verification. George said the carcass was rather badly decomposed and could not determine if it was a fisher—although "it could very well have been." Dr. George is convinced that fishers do exist in Pennsylvania and he cited the six or seven instances of reports of "black panthers" being seen, particularly from Wayne, Pike and Clinton counties. He also saw the tracks of a large mustelid in Elk County in 1967. In 1981 he received a call from a woman in Centre County complaining of "a large black animal" which had been harassing her cat and which was capable of "climbing trees and catching squirrels."

Fishers were reported to be rare or non-existent in Michigan and Wisconsin by the late 1920's, and a similar decline in their population was seen throughout most of their range in eastern North America. Fishers at one time occurred throughout all of the northeastern half of Pennsylvania, extending as far south as Forest, Elk, Clearfield, Centre, Cumberland and Lancaster counties but the last one was reported in 1921 from Holtwood in Lancaster County. The last record of a fisher in north-central Pennsylvania was from Clinton County in 1901, while the species had vanished from northwestern Pennsylvania by 1900.

Logging and burning of forests as well as the high prices formerly paid for their furs are the usual reasons set for the decline of fisher populations throughout its range. Curtailing trapping seasons for several years and restocking programs have led to the successful reestablishment of fishers in several areas of their range. Noteworthy among these are Montana, Michigan, Wisconsin, Nova Scotia, and New York. Indeed, if the "black panther" reported and other previously mentioned sightings from Pennsylvania prove to be fisher, it may well be that it is a result of the overspill from the New York reestablishment of the species in the Adirondacks.

RECOMMENDATIONS: It appears obvious that if a more accurate appraisal of the status of the fisher in the Commonwealth is to be attained, a rigorous research effort should be launched in the areas where the most frequent "black panther" sightings have been recorded. Extended observation periods coupled with live-trapping attempts are strongly suggested as the means to this end.

SELECTED REFERENCES:

BANFIELD, A. W. F. 1974. The mammals of Canada. Univ. Toronto Press, Toronto, 438 pp.

DODDS, D. G., and A. M. MARTELL. 1971. The recent status of the fisher, *Martes pennanti pennanti* (Erxleben), in Nova Scotia. Canadian Field-Nat., 85:63–65.

GODIN, A. J. 1977. Wild mammals of New England. Johns Hopkins Univ. Press, Baltimore, 304 pp.

GRIMM, W. C., and R. WHITEBREAD. 1952. Mammal survey of northeastern Pennsylvania. Final Report Pittman-Robertson Project 42-R. Pennsylvania Game Comm., Harrisburg, 82 pp.

HAGMEIER, E. M. 1956. Distribution of marten and fisher in North America. Canadian Field-Nat., 70:149–168.

HALL, E. R. 1981. The mammals of North America. John Wiley & Sons, New York, 2:vi + 601–1181 + 90.

HAMILTON, W. J., JR., and A. H. COOK. 1955. The biology and management of fisher in New York. New York Fish and Game J., 2:13–35.

IRVINE, G. W., L. T. MAGNUS, and B. J. BRADLE. 1964. The restocking of fisher in lake states forests. Trans. North American Wildlife Nat. Res. Conf., 29:307–315.

PETERSON, R. L. 1966. The mammals of eastern Canada. Oxford Univ. Press, Toronto, 465 pp.

POWELL, R. A. 1981. *Martes pennanti.* Mammalian Species, 156:1–6.

———. 1982. The Fisher: life history, ecology and behavior. Univ. Minnesota Press, Minneapolis, 217 pp.

RAND, A. L. 1944. The status of the fisher, *Martes pennanti* (Erxleben) in Canada. Canadian Field-Nat., 58:77–81.

ROSLUND, H. R. 1951. Mammal survey of northcentral Pennsylvania. Final Report Pittman-Robertson Project 37-R. Pennsylvania Game Comm., Harrisburg, 55 pp.

WECKWERTH, R. P., and P. L. WRIGHT. 1968. Results of transplanting fishers in Montana. J. Wildlife Mgmt., 32:977–980.

PREPARED BY: Harry N. Cunningham, Jr., *Division of Science, Engineering, and Technology, Behrend College of The Pennsylvania State University, Erie, PA 16563.*

Status Undetermined

MOUNTAIN LION
Felis concolor couguar Kerr
Family Felidae
Order Carnivora

OTHER NAMES: Puma, panther, cougar, catamount, long-tailed cat.

DESCRIPTION: The cougar is a large, slender cat with small, rounded ears. Upper parts are grizzled gray or dark brown to shades of buff, cinnamon, tawny, cinnamon-rufous or ferruginous. Ventral side is dull whitish with buff across the abdomen. Sides of the muzzle are black with white on chin and throat. External surfaces of ears are black. Young cougars have black spots on a buffy back. Adult males weigh from 67–103 kg, females weigh from 36–60 kg (Hall, 1981).

RANGE: This subspecies formerly ranged from South Carolina and Tennessee to New Brunswick, southern Quebec, and eastern Ontario and from the east coast to Lake Michigan and the Indiana-Illinois border (Hall, 1981). Its range included all of Pennsylvania.

HABITAT: Panthers are highly adaptable animals that can live in a wide variety of habitats from the swamps of Florida to the boreal forest. In western North America they live in brushlands and rugged terrain. In those areas the most consistent feature of their habitat is the presence of mule deer (Russell, 1978). So few confirmed sightings of panthers have been made in the east that little is known of habitat requirements here.

LIFE HISTORY AND ECOLOGY: Young and

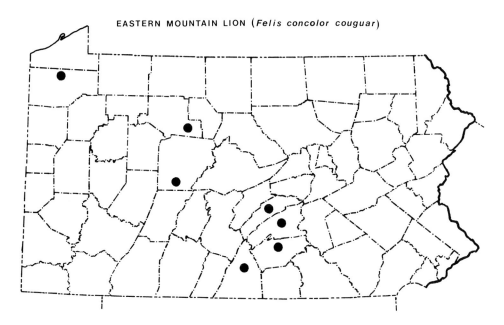

EASTERN MOUNTAIN LION (*Felis concolor couguar*)

Goldman (1946) and Russell (1978) summarize the known ecology and natural history of this species. Nearly all of this information comes from studies of western subspecies (for example, Christensen and Fischer, 1976; Phillips and Jonkel, 1977).

Home ranges for established, resident females are about 39 to 80 square km, and 65–90 square km for males (Russell, 1978). Density and causes of mortality have been studied by Hornocker (1970), Seidensticker, et al. (1973), and Sitton and Wallen (1976). Territoriality appears to be a significant factor regulating density of mountain lions in the Idaho Primitive Area (Hornocker, 1969). Although disease and parasites are common among panthers, they probably do not limit the size of populations because 1) dens are used only for short periods of time, 2) no bedding is used in dens, 3) panthers do not eat spoiled meat, 4) they are solitary, 5) they move continuously, and 6) densities are naturally low (Russell, 1978).

Other aspects of behavior have been studied by Hornocker (1970), Robinette (1959), Sitton and Wallen (1976), and others. Panthers are solitary creatures. They are social only 1) for courtship, 2) when males resolve territorial disputes, 3) when females have dependent cubs, or 4) when siblings travel together for several months after separating from their mother (Russell, 1978).

Mountain lions will eat almost any animal material as well as some grasses and berries. In western North America, panthers do kill and consume cattle or sheep frequently in areas where stock remains on the open range and calves are dropped throughout the year (Russell, 1978).

BASIS OF STATUS CLASSIFICATION: The last cougar documented to have been killed in Pennsylvania (Doutt et al., 1967) was probably a former captive (Puglisi, personal communication and McGinnis, 1982). Although undocumented reports

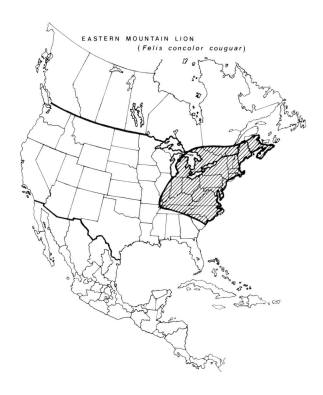

EASTERN MOUNTAIN LION
(*Felis concolor couguar*)

of sightings remain, assessing the validity of these reports is difficult without specimens (undesirable for an endangered species), good unambiguous photographs, or unmistakable sign or tracks. The problem is confounded by individuals that have caught cubs in the western part of the continent and transported them to the east for pets or display where the animals are often intentionally or unintentionally released. Shy and retiring, cougars can live in close proximity to humans without detection (Wright, 1967). Therefore, it is possible that some cougars are present in the Commonwealth. However, one should not be optimistic that cougars remain in Pennsylvania for two reasons. 1) Cougars are large predators with a rather solitary habit such that each individual requires large areas of habitat. Viable populations, therefore, require extensive tracts of relatively uninterrupted habitat. 2) Humans appear unable to coexist with other large predators. Since North America was first colonized, humans have systematically destroyed cougar populations by trapping and hunting for fur and for the purpose of predator control.

RECOMMENDATIONS: Some habitat suitable for cougars remains in Pennsylvania. Other eastern states are working to determine the status of cougars in those states. We recommend efforts to assess the status of cougars in Pennsylvania and to insure the preservation of any that might still exist.

ACKNOWLEDGMENTS: Dr. Harry Cunningham made useful comments concerning this manuscript. Helen J. McGinnis and Michael Puglisi provided much useful information.

SELECTED REFERENCES:

CHRISTENSEN, G. C., and R. J. FISCHER (eds.). 1976. Transactions of the mountain lion workshop, Jan. 13–14, 1976, Sparks, Nevada. U.S. Fish and Wildlife Serv., Portland, Oregon, 213 pp.
DOUTT, J. K., C. A. HEPPENSTALL, and J. E. GUILDAY. 1967. Mammals of Pennsylvania. Pennsylvania Game Comm., Harrisburg, 283 pp.
HALL, E. R. 1981. The mammals of North America. John Wiley & Sons, New York, 2:vi + 601–1181 + 90.
HORNOCKER, M. G. 1969. Winter territoriality in mountain lions. J. Wildlife Mgmt., 33:457–464.
———. 1970. An analysis of mountain lion predation upon mule deer and elk in the Idaho Primitive Area. Wildlife Monogr., 21:1–39.
MCGINNIS, H. 1982. On the trail of the Pennsylvania cougar. Pennsylvania Game News, 53(2):2–8.
PHILLIPS, R. L., and C. JONKEL (eds.). 1977. Proceedings of the 1975 Predator Symposium. For. Conserv. Exp. Sta., Univ. Montana, Missoula.
ROBINETTE, W. L., and O. W. MORRIS. 1959. Food habits of the cougar in Utah and Nevada. J. Wildlife Mgmt., 23:261–273.
RUSSELL, K. R. 1978. Mountain lion. Pp. 207–225, in Big game of North America: ecology and management (J. L. Schmidt and D. L. Gilbert, eds.), Wildlife Management Institute, Stackpole Books, Harrisburg, 494 pp.
SEIDENSTICKER, J. C., IV, M. G. HORNOCKER, W. V. WILES, and J. P. MESSICK. 1973. Mountain lion social organization in the Idaho Primitive Area. Wildlife Monogr., 35:1–60.
SITTON, L. W., and S. WALLEN. 1976. California mountain lion study. California Dept. Fish and Game, Sacramento, 40 pp.
WRIGHT, B. S. 1967. The status of the cougar in the northeast. Trans. Fed.-Prov. Wildlife-Conf., 31:76–82.
YOUNG, S. P., and E. A. GOLDMAN. 1946. The puma, mysterious American cat. The Stackpole Co., Harrisburg, Pennsylvania, 358 pp.

PREPARED BY: David A. Zegers, *Department of Biology, Millersville University, Millersville, PA 17551.*

Status Undetermined
LYNX
Lynx canadensis (Kerr)
Family Felidae
Order Carnivora

OTHER NAMES: Canada lynx, lynx cat, and gray wild cat (Godin, 1977). The terms "Lynx" or "Wildcat" are used for the Bobcat (*Lynx rufus*), so one must use care when reading articles or conversing with others who might be referring to one or both species of felids.

DESCRIPTION: This species, if seen in the field, or if a complete pelt is not studied, could be confused with a bobcat. Both species are approximately the same size, but the lynx has longer legs, larger spreading feet, long, black ear tufts, and generally a shorter tail with its tip entirely black. Measurements, in cm, are: 83–100, total length; 10–13, tail; 22–25, hind foot. Weight is 6.8–11.4 kg, with large animals up to or exceeding 16 kg. Males are somewhat larger than females (Godin, 1977; Hall, 1981). There are 28 teeth in the skull of *Lynx* and 30 in *Felis*; as a result, three cheek teeth are present on each side of the upper jaw for the former, but four for the latter. Lynx and bobcat skulls overlap in size. However, they may be distinguished because the lynx has the length of the upper carnassial more than 16.6 mm, and the lower carnassial more than 13.5 mm. In addition, the anterior condyloid foramen is separate

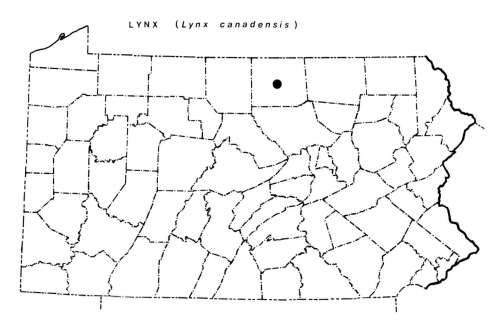

LYNX (*Lynx canadensis*)

LYNX (*Lynx canadensis*)

from the foramen lacerum posteriorus, and the presphenoid is more than 5 mm at its greatest width (Burt, 1957).

In pelage characteristics, the young and immatures are spotted, with some streaking, on a light fawn-colored base. The summer coloration for adults is yellowish gray, with scattered, black-tipped guard hairs down the back. The legs are yellowish, and indistinctly spotted (Burt, 1957). The lighter winter pelt is long, thick, silky, and loose, giving the animal a fluffy appearance. The crown of the head is brownish, but heavily sprinkled with white-tipped hairs, and the nose and cheeks are grayish. The ears have a central gray spot on the black posterior surface, with brownish black on the tips of the ear tufts and along the margins. The well-developed cheek ruff, chin, and throat are grayish white or light brown, particularly on the insides of the legs. The broad feet are heavily furred above and below, thus providing a well-insulated, snowshoe-type pad for deep snow (Godin, 1977).

RANGE: The lynx is recorded from Alaska, across all of Canada and the southern tip of Baffin Island, and southward into the United States to a line roughly extending from Pennsylvania to Kansas, then dipping southwards into Colorado and Utah before swinging northward to southern Idaho and Oregon (Hall, 1981). For Pennsylvania, the lynx may have been extirpated in the late 1800's and early 1900's. The Pennsylvania Game Commission has on file a series of newspaper accounts and early scientific reports that discuss sightings, trappings, and shootings of lynx in the Commonwealth. Rhoads (1903) was largely responsible for investigating many of these, but no actual animals, skins, or skulls were observed by him or other reliable scientists. Most of these unsubstantiated reports are from the northern and mountainous one-third of Pennsylvania, but questionable records also exist for the southern counties of Somerset and Lancaster. The only documented case of the species in Pennsylvania consists of the pelt of a male, collected on 10 November 1923, near Antrim, Tioga Co., and maintained in the Reading Public Museum and Art Gallery.

HABITAT: The lynx inhabits the unbroken, mature, boreal forests and rarely ventures into open lands (Seton, 1929; Godin, 1977).

LIFE HISTORY AND ECOLOGY: Most of the following, unless noted otherwise, is from Godin (1977). Lynxes are usually solitary but apparently do hunt at times with others; they are also seen together during the breeding season, and when the female is followed by her kittens. Hunting activity occurs mainly during the evening. They are agile animals, traveling easily over fallen timber and rough terrain. Bounds of several meters are commonplace in such instances or when chasing prey. For all their agility, lynxes are not fast. Discovered in open situations, dogs and even men have caught them after a pursuit of a mile or so (Seton, 1929). Apparently having an inquisitive nature, they might follow a person for hours, but are not known to attack.

Prey throughout most of their range consists primarily of snowshoe hares, and in fact, high lynx densities are generally correlated with high numbers of this leporid (Elton and Nicholson, 1942). Other prey include rabbits, squirrels, chipmunks, mice, porcupines, skunks, waterfowl and game birds, including their eggs, and occasionally fish and carrion (Saunders, 1963a; Nellis and Keith, 1968; Brand et al., 1976). Fawns and even adult deer are infrequently taken, as well as caribou (Seton, 1929; Bergerud, 1971).

The home ranges were found by Saunders (1963b) to range from about 15 to 21 square km in his Newfoundland study. Brand et al. (1976) calculated that the individuals in their Alberta study had home ranges of approximately 11 to 50 square km, with an average of 28 square km. Both studies were conducted in the winter, and sexes were unknown except for several females with kittens. Such family groups tended to have a smaller home range than solitary adults. Some overlap with adjacent lynx home ranges does occur. The distance traveled while foraging was reported by the same researchers and Nellis and Keith (1968) to be roughly 3 to 9 km, the greater distances at periods when hunting success was low.

The reproductive biology of the lynx is poorly known. The breeding season presumably occurs in late winter, and birth occurs after a gestation period of 2 months. The birth place is some secluded, protected place, such as in hollow logs, under fallen timber, or within some rocky cavity. Litter size averages about four, with something closer to three during periods of food scarcity and five at times of bountiful food supplies (Brand et al., 1976; Brand and Keith, 1979). The female has four mammae. While Seton (1929) reported a case where a kitten was born with its eyes open, Walker et al. (1975) stated eye opening occurred at 1–10 days. The young are weaned at 2 months of age, but remain with the female until the following spring. At approximately the same time, the spotting and striping pattern of the kittens disappears. It has been reported that over half of the yearling females have litters. Postpartum mortality of kittens is extremely high during years of low food availability (Brand et al. 1976).

BASIS OF STATUS CLASSIFICATION: The only documented specimen of the lynx in Pennsylvania was taken approximately 60 years ago. Considering that many unsubstantiated reports of the species were made during the late 1800's and very early 1900's, there is little reason to doubt that it once inhabited a number of counties in the Commonwealth.

Maine appears to have viable Lynx populations, and some are also found in the White Mountains of New Hampshire (Godin, 1977). Vagrants are infrequently taken in New York and may be looked for near the New York-Pennsylvania line.

RECOMMENDATIONS: Perhaps another decade or two of public awareness and changing land use patterns, coincident with increasingly older timber tracts, might result in the lynx expanding southward from its northeastern refugia in New England. If indeed such a scenario does occur, wildlife biologists at that time can make appropriate recommendations.

The assistance of the New York Bureau of Wildlife and the Pennsylvania Game Commission is gratefully acknowledged.

SELECTED REFERENCES:

BERGERUD, A. T. 1971. The population dynamics of Newfoundland caribou. Wildlife Monogr, 25:1–55.

BRAND, C. J., and L. B. KEITH. 1979. Lynx demography during a snowshoe hare decline in Alberta. J. Wildlife Mgmt., 43: 827–849.

BRAND, C. J., L. B. KEITH, and C. A. FISCHER. 1976. Lynx responses to changing snowshoe hare densities in central Alberta. J. Wildlife Mgmt., 40:416–428.

BURT, W. H. 1957. Mammals of the Great Lakes Region. Univ. Michigan Press, Ann Arbor, 246 pp.

ELTON, C., and M. NICHOLSON. 1942. The ten year cycle in numbers of the lynx in Canada. J. Animal Ecol., 11:215–244.

GODIN, A. J. 1977. Wild mammals of New England. Johns Hopkins Univ. Press, Baltimore, 304 pp.

HALL, E. R. 1981. The mammals of North America. John Wiley & Sons, New York, 2:vi + 601–1181 + 90.

NELLIS, C. H., and L. B. KEITH. 1968. Hunting activities and success of lynxes in Alberta. J. Wildlife Mgmt., 32:718–722.

RHOADS, S. N. 1903. The mammals of Pennsylvania and New Jersey. Privately printed by the author, Philadelphia, 266 pp.

SAUNDERS, J. K., JR. 1963a. Food habits of the lynx in Newfoundland. J. Wildlife Mgmt., 27:384–390.

———. 1963b. Movements and activities of the lynx in Newfoundland. J. Wildlife Mgmt., 27:390–400.

SETON, E. T. 1929. Lives of game animals. Doubleday, Doran and Co., Garden City, New York, 1 (part 1):xxxix + 1–337.

WALKER, E. P., ET AL. 1975. Mammals of the world. Johns Hopkins Press, Baltimore, 3rd ed., 2:viii + 645–1500.

PREPARED BY: Peter L. Dalby, *Biology Department, Clarion University, Clarion, PA 16214.*

Extirpated

EASTERN TIMBER WOLF
Canis lupus lycaon Schreber
Family Canidae
Order Carnivora

OTHER NAMES: Gray wolf, eastern wolf.

This subspecies of timber wolf once ranged from Quebec to northern Florida and from the east coast to the Mississippi River and was found throughout Pennsylvania (Hall, 1981). However, it has now been extirpated from most of its range. The decline of the wolf in Pennsylvania as elsewhere is due to persecution and exploitation by humans (Mech, 1970). Wolves have been hunted and trapped in efforts to reduce predation on livestock and game herds and for their fur. Another problem for the wolf is the red-ridinghood syndrome. Many people still fear wolves and have a strong urge to eradicate them. Although there are no documented cases of wolves attacking humans (except for cases of rabid wolves, Mech, 1970) which make these fears unfounded, nevertheless our persecution of the wolf has been successful. Wolves are probably extirpated from Pennsylvania. One should not be optimistic that any

remain for two reasons. First, the social and hunting behavior and territoriality of wolf packs required large, relatively undisturbed tracts of land to support viable populations. The second, and perhaps as important, reason is the inability of most people to live with other large predators without exploiting and persecuting them. Several excellent reviews of wolf biology and the relationship between wolf and man include: Murie (1944), Young and Goldman (1944), Mech (1970), Van Ballenberghe (1974), and Van Ballenberghe et al. (1975).

ACKNOWLEDGMENTS: Dr. Harry Cunningham made helpful comments concerning this manuscript. Helen J. McGinnis provided useful information.

SELECTED REFERENCES:

HALL, E. R. 1981. The mammals of North America. John Wiley & Sons, New York, 2:vi + 601–1181 + 90.

MECH, L. D. 1970. The wolf: the ecology and behavior of an endangered species. Natural History Press, Garden City, New Jersey, 384 pp.

MURIE, A. 1944. The wolves of Mount McKinley. U.S. Nat. Park Serv. Fauna Ser., 5:1–238.

VAN BALLENBERGHE, V. 1974. Wolf management in Minnesota: an endangered species case history. Trans. N. Amer. Wildlife Nat. Res. Conf. 39:313–320.

VAN BALLENBERGHE, V., A. W. ERICKSON, and D. BYMAN. 1975. Ecology of the timber wolf in northeastern Minnesota. Wildlife Monogr., 43:1–43.

YOUNG, S. P., and E. A. GOLDMAN. 1944. The wolves of North America. Amer. Wildlife Instit., Washington, D.C., 636 pp.

PREPARED BY: David A. Zegers, *Department of Biology, Millersville University, Millersville, PA 17551.*

Extirpated

WOLVERINE
Gulo gulo Pallas
Family Mustelidae
Order Carnivora

OTHER NAMES: Glutton.

The wolverine is an inhabitant of boreal forests (Burt, 1957). Traps, poisons, and habitat loss have almost extirpated the wolverine in the United States, and its present range does not include any of the northeastern states (Hornocker et al., 1979). In Pennsylvania, it was considered to have been rare during the nineteenth century, and the only documented record of this species is a specimen trapped near Great Salt Lick, Portage Twp., Potter County, sometime around 1858 (Rhodes, 1903).

SELECTED REFERENCES:

BURT, W. H. 1957. Mammals of the Great Lakes Region. Univ. Michigan Press, Ann Arbor, 246 pp.

HORNOCKER, M., C. JONKEL, and L. D. MECH. 1979. Meat eaters. Pp. 209–281, *in* Wild animals of North America, (T. B. Allen, ed.), National Geographic Society, Washington, D.C., 406 pp..

RHODES, S. N. 1903. The mammals of Pennsylvania and New Jersey. Privately published, Philadelphia, 266 pp.

PREPARED BY: Kenneth W. Andersen, *Biology Department, Gannon University, Erie, PA 16541.*

Extirpated

WAPITI

Cervus elaphus canadensis Erxleben
Family Cervidae
Order Artiodactyla

OTHER NAMES: Eastern elk.

Prior to the civilization of eastern United States the wapiti occurred throughout the forests of the region (Hall, 1981). In Pennsylvania, the Pocono region appears to have been an area of greatest concentration (Doutt et al., 1977). According to Seton (1929) it was first extirpated by hunters in southern Pennsylvania by 1830, and by 1845 it was absent in the Pocono region. The last recorded killing of a wapiti in Pennsylvania was in November 1867 in the region of Clarion (Seton, 1929). A review of the demise of wapiti in Pennsylvania and reintroductions from herds of western United States during the early part of the twentieth century are given by Gerstell (1936).

SELECTED REFERENCES:

DOUTT, J. K., C. A. HEPPENSTALL, and J. E. GUILDAY. 1977. Mammals of Pennsylvania. Pennsylvania Game Comm., Harrisburg, 280 pp.

GERSTELL, R. 1936. The elk in Pennsylvania: its extermination and reintroduction. Pennsylvania Game News, 7:6–7, 26.

HALL, E. R. 1981. The mammals of North America. John Wiley & Sons, New York, 2:vi + 601–1181 + 90.

SETON, E. T. 1929. Lives of game animals. Doubleday and Co., Inc., Garden City, New York, 3:15–17.

PREPARED BY: Kenneth W. Andersen, *Biology Department, Gannon University, Erie, PA 16541.*

Extirpated

MOOSE

Alces alces (Linnaeus)
Family Cervidae
Order Artiodactyla

The moose formerly ranged over much of the boreal forests in New England and as far south as the northern woodlands of Pennsylvania (Hamilton, 1963). They were reported to be numerous in the eighteenth century in the Allegheny Mountains (Goodwin, 1936). Neither the time of the final extirpation of moose in the Commonwealth nor the cause is certain; however it was probably extirpated from Pennsylvania in 1790 or 1791 (Cahalane, 1942). Some early records of its occurrence are given by Merrill (1920).

SELECTED REFERENCES:

CAHALANE, V. H. 1942. Wildlife vistas of the eastern Highlands. Audubon Mag., 44:101–111.

FRANZMANN, A. W. 1981. *Alces alces.* Mammalian Species, 154:1–7.

GOODWIN, G. G. 1936. Big game animals in the northeastern United States. J. Mamm., 17:48–50.

HAMILTON, W. J., JR. 1963. The mammals of eastern United States. Hafner Publ. Co., New York, 432 pp.

MERRILL, S. 1920. The moose book. E.P. Dutton and Co., New York, 2nd ed., 366 pp.

PREPARED BY: Kenneth W. Andersen, *Biology Department, Gannon University, Erie, PA 16541.*

Extirpated

BISON

Bison bison (Linnaeus)
Family Bovidae
Order Artiodactyla

OTHER NAMES: American buffalo.

Bison once ranged over much of eastern and central United States (Hall, 1981), and it was common in Pennsylvania woods as late as 1750 (Seton, 1929). It was especially common in the valleys and mountain glades of the Ohio, Monogahela, and Allegheny rivers (Rhodes, 1903). The last bison in Pennsylvania were killed by hunters around 1801 (Allen, 1942) or 1810 (Seton, 1929:657–658). It was extirpated from all of eastern United States by 1825 (Matthiessen, 1959).

SELECTED REFERENCES:

ALLEN, G. M. 1942. Extinct and vanishing mammals of the Western Hemisphere. Spec. Publ., American Committee for International Wildlife Protection, New York, 11:xv + 620.

HALL, E. R. 1981. The mammals of North America. John Wiley & Sons, New York, 2:vi + 601–1181 + 90.

MATTHIESSEN, P. 1959. Wildlife in America. The Viking Press, New York, 304 pp.

RHODES, S. N. 1903. The mammals of Pennsylvania and New Jersey. Privately published, Philadelphia, 266 pp.

SETON, E. T. 1929. Lives of game animals. Doubleday and Co., Inc., Garden City, New York, 3:1–780.

PREPARED BY: Kenneth W. Andersen, *Biology Department, Gannon University, Erie, PA 16541.*

INDEX TO SCIENTIFIC NAMES

INDEX TO COMMON NAMES